The Managerial Decision-Making Process

FIFTH EDITION

E. Frank Harrison, Ph.D.

San Francisco State University

HOUGHTON MIFFLIN COMPANY   Boston   New York

To my wife, Monique

Sponsoring Editor: Kathleen L. Hunter
Senior Associate Editor: Susan M. Kahn
Project Editor: Tamela C. Ambush
Editorial Assistant: Ryan P. Jones
Senior Production / Design Coordinator: Carol Merrigan
Senior Manufacturing Coordinator: Priscilla Abreu
Marketing Manager: Juli Bliss

Cover Design: Minko Dimov

Printed in the U.S.A.

Library of Congress Catalog Card Number: 98-72037

ISBN: 0-395-90821-3

23456789–DOH–02 01 00 99

Brief Contents

Preface   xi

PART ONE   FOUNDATIONS OF MANAGERIAL DECISION MAKING   1

Chapter 1   An Overview of Decision Making   3
Chapter 2   The Decision-Making Process   37
Chapter 3   Rational Decision Making   74
Chapter 4   Values for Decision Making   110

PART TWO   INTERDISCIPLINARY ASPECTS OF MANAGERIAL DECISION MAKING   145

Chapter 5   Eclectic Approaches to Decision Making   147
Chapter 6   The Psychology of Decision Making   176
Chapter 7   The Sociology of Decision Making   213
Chapter 8   The Social Psychology of Decision Making   249
Chapter 9   Political Aspects of Decision Making   281

PART THREE   FOUNDATIONS OF STRATEGIC DECISION MAKING   317

Chapter 10   Strategic Decision Perspectives   319
Chapter 11   Strategic Decision Success   344

PART FOUR   IMPLEMENTING STRATEGIC DECISIONS   371

Chapter 12   **Case Set No. 1:** The Cuban Missile Crisis and the Iranian Hostage Crisis   373
Chapter 13   **Case Set No. 2:** The Chrysler Bailout Decision and the *Challenger* Disaster   408
Chapter 14   **Case Set No. 3:** General Motors and Philip Morris   442
Chapter 15   **Case Set No. 4:** The Walt Disney Company   469

Glossary   495
Bibliography   503
Index   537

Contents

NOTE: Each chapter contains a Summary, Review and Discussion Questions, Notes, and Supplemental References.

Preface   xi

PART ONE   FOUNDATIONS OF MANAGERIAL DECISION MAKING   1

1 An Overview of Decision Making   3

Profile of a Decision   4
Decision Making and Problem Solving   5
The Significance of Decision Making   6
Decision Making: A Generic Process   8
Decision Theory   9
The Scope of Decision Making   10
A Typology of Decisions   18
The Locus of Choice   22
Managerial Aspects of Decision Making   24
Perspectives on Managerial Decision Making   25
The Practice of Decision Making   28

2 The Decision-Making Process   37

Nature of the Process   37
Setting Managerial Objectives   42
Searching for Alternatives   45
Comparing and Evaluating Alternatives   50
The Act of Choice   55
Implementing Decisions   60
Follow-up and Control   64

3 Rational Decision Making   74

Rational Versus Nonrational Behavior   74
The Concept of Maximizing Behavior   79
The Case for Maximizing Behavior   81
The Case Against Maximizing Behavior   84
The Concept of Satisficing Behavior   89
The Case for Satisficing Behavior   93
The Case Against Satisficing Behavior   99

4 Values for Decision Making   110

The Concept of Values   110
The Hierarchy of Values   114
Classification of Values   117
Managerial Values   119
Ethical Behavior   127
Value Conflicts   131
Value Judgments   133

PART TWO   INTERDISCIPLINARY ASPECTS OF MANAGERIAL DECISION MAKING   145

5 Eclectic Approaches to Decision Making   147

Decision-Making Models   148
Behavioral Disciplines for Decision Making   159
Quantitative Disciplines for Decision Making   165
The Fusion of Behavioral and Quantitative Disciplines for
    Decision Making   169

6 The Psychology of Decision Making   176

Personality in Decision Making   176
Willingness to Accept Risk in Choice Behavior   186
Perception in Decision Making   192
Subconscious Influences on Decision Making   201

7 The Sociology of Decision Making   213

Profile of a Group   214
Theories of Group Behavior   215

Group Norms and Conformity   218
Group Structure   220
Group Communication   224
Characteristics of Effective Groups   227
Groupthink   229
Group Decision-Making Perspectives   231
Group Decision-Making Profiles   236

8   *The Social Psychology of Decision Making*   249

Individual Versus Group Decision Making   250
Conflict in Decision Making   258
Participation in Decision Making   262
Gender Differences and Similarities in Decision Making   268

9   *Political Aspects of Decision Making*   281

A Profile of Power   282
The Managerial Decision-Making Class   284
Conceptual Foundations of Political Power   291
Profiles of Political Power in Decision Making   297
Dimensions of Managerial Decision-Making Power   300
Constraints on Managerial Decision-Making Power   304

PART THREE   FOUNDATIONS OF STRATEGIC DECISION MAKING   317

10   *Strategic Decision Perspectives*   319

The Nature of Strategic Decisions   320
The Environment of Strategic Decision Making   322
Uncertainty in Strategic Decision Making   327
The Concept of Strategic Gap   330
The Variations of Strategic Gap   334
The Strategic Decision-Making Process   336

11   *Strategic Decision Success*   344

A Profile of Decision Success   345
Determinants of Strategic Decision Success   347
A Model for Strategic Decision Success   354
A Composite Approach to the Evaluation of Strategic Decision Success   362

PART FOUR   IMPLEMENTING STRATEGIC DECISIONS   **371**

12   Case Set No. 1: The Cuban Missile Crisis and the Iranian Hostage Crisis   373

The Cuban Missile Crisis: A Perspective   374
The Decision-Making Process in the Cuban Missile Crisis   378
Special Evaluation of the Cuban Missile Crisis   383
The Iranian Hostage Crisis: A Perspective   385
The Decision-Making Process in the Iranian Hostage Crisis   388
Comparative Case Determinants of Strategic Decision Success   397
Comparative Case Classifications of Strategic Decision Success   402

13   Case Set No. 2: The Chrysler Bailout Decision and the Challenger Disaster   408

The Chrysler Bailout Decision: A Perspective   410
The Strategic Gap at Chrysler   412
The Decision-Making Process in the Chrysler Bailout Decision   416
The Challenger Disaster: A Perspective   424
The Decision-Making Process in the Challenger Disaster   425
Comparative Case Determinants of Strategic Decision Success   430
Comparative Case Classifications of Strategic Decision Success   433

14   Case Set No. 3: General Motors and Philip Morris   442

General Motors: A Perspective   443
The Strategic Gap at General Motors in 1978   446
The Decision-Making Process at General Motors   450
Philip Morris: A Perspective   453
The Strategic Gap at Philip Morris in 1984   455
The Decision-Making Process at Philip Morris   457
Comparative Case Determinants of Strategic Decision Success   460
Comparative Case Classifications of Strategic Decision Success   464

15   Case Set No. 4: The Walt Disney Company   469

The Walt Disney Company: A Perspective   470
The Strategic Gap at Disney in 1990   471
The Decision-Making Process for Eurodisney   474
The Strategic Gap at Disney in 1995   479

The Decision-Making Process for Capital Cities/ABC   481
Comparative Case Determinants of Strategic Decision Success   484
Comparative Case Classifications of Strategic Decision Success   488

Glossary   495

Bibliography   503

Index   537

Preface

Decision making is an evolving area of study and one of considerable importance to practicing managers, as well as to professors and students of management. Regrettably, the subject of decision making is usually seen as merely one of several activities that differentiate managers from other employees in an organization; but decision making is a complex process that must be understood completely before it can be practiced effectively. Moreover, it is a process of definable and impressive proportions—one that deserves all the time and attention that can be devoted to it. In judging the performance of an individual manager or the organizational record of multiple managers, the evaluation invariably is reduced to one question: how many successful decisions have been made by the entity being judged? In the real world of organizational decision making there is an expectation of managerial success. Managers are invariably rewarded for effective decision making and criticized or censured for failure in decision making. The sine qua non of good management is a track record of decision success. It is the most meaningful measure of managerial merit. It is the most significant contribution that management can make in any kind of formal organization.

Given its obvious and cogent aura of organizational significance, it is surprising to note that decision making has not been pursued extensively as a subject in its own right. It is often slighted in books and articles on management, and many books on quantitative methods entangle decision making in a maze of matrices, diagrams, and formulas. The analysis accorded the subject of decision making in scholarly journals usually focuses only on the decision itself, rather than on the process of arriving at an outcome that meets an objective. Finally, most books on organization theory and administrative behavior discuss decision making as an ancillary activity connected with setting objectives, formulating plans, and accomplishing the leadership function.

The Managerial Decision-Making Process, Fifth Edition, aims to provide a new perspective for making decisions and teaching the subject of decision making. This perspective is of an integrated and interdisciplinary decision-making process in which rational decision makers pursue strategic choices that will provide successful outcomes within discernible bour daries. One of this book's principal contributions is that it focuses on deci   at the top of the organization in a multidisciplinary context— other books and articles on the subject have conspicuously

In this edition, the primary focus is on strategic decis rationale here is that strategic choices made at the top of invariably trigger dozens or even hundreds of other decisions of lesser magnitude at descending levels of management. Strategic decisions, therefore, set the tone and tempo of managerial decision making for every individual and unit throughout the entire organization. Consequently, the study of decisions should begin with those strategic choices made by the senior executives that commit the organization to the attainment of long-range strategic objectives. If the decision making at the top of the organization is ineffective, then the choices made at lower levels of management will be the same. Similarly, if top management's strategic choices tend to be successful, that success reflects favorably on the numerous lesser decisions made in the process of implementing such choices.

This book is divided into four parts. Part I, "Foundations of Managerial Decision Making," contains four chapters centered on a managerial decision-making process that features rational choices made by effective decision makers. Part II, "Interdisciplinary Aspects of Managerial Decision Making," consists of five highly eclectic chapters. These five chapters introduce the reader to an interdisciplinary approach to decision making intended for use by managers and administrators in organizations of all types. In Part III, "Foundations of Strategic Decision Making," the emphasis broadens from managerial decision making to strategic choice. The two chapters in this section imbue the reader with a full understanding of the complexity and significance of the strategic decisions made by top management along with some of the determinants for successful strategic choices. The individual chapters have been reviewed, revised, and updated to reflect the latest thinking in their subject areas. With the assimilation of the theories, concepts, and frameworks presented in Parts I–III, the reader has more than enough knowledge to evaluate real-world strategic decision cases from both the public sector and private enterprise.

Part IV, "Implementing Strategic Decisions," contains four chapters with two case studies in each chapter. These cases illustrate the consequences of the effective use or the virtual disregard of the concepts and frameworks advanced in this book. Two of the eight cases are entirely new; three have been selectively updated; and the remaining three have been reevaluated using the new concepts and frameworks introduced in the previous chapters of this book.

Chapter 12 presents "The Cuban Missile Crisis" and "The Iranian Hostage Crisis," both established cases revisited with new techniques for evaluation. Chapter 13 contains "The Chrysler Bailout Decision" and "The *Challenger* Disaster." The Chrysler bailout case has been updated, and the *Challenger* case has been reevaluated using the latest methods set forth in this book. Chapter 14 presents two cases from private enterprise, "General Motors" and "Philip Morris." The financial information in both of these cases has been updated. Chapter 15 is entirely new to this edition. It explores two strategic decisions made by top management in the Walt Disney Company. The first case deals with the Eurodisney theme park in France; the second case presents and evaluates Disney's acquisition of Capital Cities/ABC in 1995. All of the cases in these four chapters are evaluated individually and comparatively within a given chapter. They are intended to illustrate the applicability of the ideas presented in this book.

The Managerial Decision-Making Process, Fifth Edition, will be useful to a wide audience. In the field of higher education, it applies to courses in business administration, public administration, educational administration, and hospital administration, as well as to executive development courses, managerial seminars, and supervisory workshops conducted in colleges and universities. Managers also can use the theories and concepts herein when making strategic choices at the top of the organization as well as countless lesser decisions necessary to implement a given choice successfully. These theories and concepts apply with equal validity to both public sector institutions and private enterprise organizations. Decisions are more likely to be successful if managers and administrators understand the rationale for the structure of choices made in pursuit of organizational objectives. This book can assist greatly in attaining that end.

The multiple dimensions of arriving at a choice contribute significantly to the complexity of the managerial decision-making process. Much additional research is necessary before decision making can be revealed in all its diversity. In the interim, managers, professors, and students should try to adopt a broader perspective toward decision making, one that places decision making squarely at the center of the manager's functions. It should focus on the many variables and antecedent conditions leading up to the moment of choice and should acknowledge the many related considerations that must be taken into account when the choice is put into effect. Finally, this perspective should reflect the need to control events in a manner consistent with the original objective of the decision. It is hoped that this book will provide the reader with such a perspective.

This book was evaluated in great depth by several reviewers who have used it as a text in their courses. Their comments were comprehensive and incisive and included many recommendations for additions, deletions, and other modifications. Each suggestion was carefully evaluated in light of the book's intended purpose and audience. No suggestion went unnoticed. The aggregate of the adopted changes has contributed greatly to the content, coverage, and clarity of the book.

The reviewers' suggestions that were implemented fall into two main categories. The first category includes the "hot button" items that are currently popular in the management literature:

- *Values.* Chapter 4 on values for decision making was completely reviewed and updated.
- *Intuition.* The section in Chapter 6 dealing with the psychology of decision making was reviewed and selectively updated.
- *Teamwork.* Chapter 7 on group decision making thoroughly covers the issue of teamwork.

- *Technology.* This topic is included in Chapter 10 as part of the discussion on the strategic gap.
- *Finance.* Considerable financial information is included in the cases dealing with private enterprise in Part IV.

The second category of reviewers' improvements focuses on features and supplements intended to make the book more meaningful and useful for both students and instructors:

- *Updated cases.* All of the six cases in Part IV that were carried forward from the last edition have been selectively updated.
- *New cases.* The two cases in Chapter 15 dealing with strategic decisions made by the Walt Disney Company are entirely new.
- *Instructor's Resource Manual.* The instructor's guide has been reviewed and expanded to include questions for the new Chapter 15.
- *Additional graphic figures.* New illustrations enhance the text in selected chapters.
- *Visual aids.* The fifth edition includes a supplemental PowerPoint slide presentation of selected graphic figures and applicable concepts from each chapter.

The contributions of all the reviewers of this and previous editions are greatly appreciated. I especially thank the following people:

Vikas Anand	Joseph G. Giacofci	Gwyn Myers
Arizona State University	*Marywood College*	*Woodbury University*
Bill Brant	Barbara Goodman	Gerald E. Parker
American College	*Wayne State University*	*St. Louis University*
Dan Braunstein	Cecil G. Howard	Roberta Snow
Oakland University	*Howard University*	*West Chester University*
Henry Coleman	Gretchen Munroe	
St. Mary's College	*St. Leo College*	

In concluding these prefatory remarks, a special note of appreciation is due Professor Monique A. Pelletier, Ph.D., San Francisco State University, for her unstinting professional efforts in the completion of this fifth edition. Indeed, her invaluable assistance in the production of the final manuscript and its countless ancillary items contributed greatly to the high quality and professional excellence of the final product.

E. F. H.

PART ONE

Foundations of Managerial Decision Making

CHAPTER ONE

An Overview of Decision Making

*T*his chapter introduces the subject of decision making by managers in organizations of all types. There are numerous scenarios and situations of all kinds in which decision making can and does take place. But the primary focus of this book is on managerial decision making at the organizational level. This is the most important thing that managers do in carrying out their myriad and complex organizational responsibilities. Additionally, these managerial decisions constitute a critical factor in the competitiveness and growth of our entire economic system, the stability and well-being of our total society, and the continuing survival of our sovereign nation-state. Given the overarching significance of managerial decision making, the purpose of this beginning chapter is to provide the reader with a meaningful overview of the complex process of decision making by managers, executives, and administrators in all types of organizations. The topics selected for presentation in this chapter deal with some of the most significant aspects of managerial decisions. Subsequent chapters provide comprehensive in-depth presentations of other significant aspects that should be considered and assimilated by practicing and potential managerial decision makers. Having absorbed the content of this chapter, the reader will have a new and expanded perspective on managerial decision making. This perspective will facilitate the assimilation of the theories, concepts, frameworks, and cases that constitute the remainder of this book. In essence, Chapter 1 is the starting point for a journey intended to extend and enrich the competencies of those who aspire to or are engaged in the making of managerial decisions.

Decision making is an integral part of the management of any kind of organization. More than anything else, competence in this activity differentiates the manager from the nonmanager and, more important, the effective manager from the ineffective manager. It would be difficult to find many managers who do not consider themselves good decision makers. Any suggestion that a given manager might improve his or her decision-making techniques probably would elicit a highly defensive reaction. For example, who among the readers of this book would admit to not being a good decision maker?

Managers' opinions about their own decision-making abilities are heavily influenced by what they feel a good decision is. For some it is a choice arrived at by the consensus of one or more groups in the organization. For others it is any decision that does not elicit unfavorable reactions from those affected by it. Or it may simply be the choice among available alternatives that offers the highest possible payoff. Or perhaps it is a decision that is reached only after a careful search for alternatives within clear boundaries and that is implemented smoothly with obvious benefits for those it affects.

This diversity of viewpoints about the goals and techniques of decision making renders it difficult to evaluate a manager's abilities and performance in this area. There is no universal agreement on what constitutes a really good decision, and there is no generally accepted approach to good decision making. Much is assumed, but considerably less is known about this more important managerial activity. It is hoped that this book, through the presentation of relevant theory and viable conceptual frameworks, will help managers in organizations of all types become more effective decision makers.

PROFILE OF A DECISION

In discussing decision making, it is customary to focus on one or more of three things: (1) the decision-making process, (2) the decision maker, and (3) the decision itself. Focusing for the moment on the decision itself, we may note a variety of definitions for the term *decision*. To illustrate, Ofstad states alternative definitions in the following passage:

> To say that a person has made a decision may mean (1) that he has started a series of behavioral reactions in favor of something, or it may mean (2) that he has made up his mind to do a certain action, which he has no doubts that he ought to do. But perhaps the most common use of the term is this: "to make a decision" means (3) to make a judgment regarding what one ought to do in a certain situation after having deliberated on some alternative courses of action.[1]

In their book on the organizational aspects of choice, Shull and his associates define the decision-making process as

> a conscious and human process, involving both individual and social phenomena, based upon factual and value premises, which includes a choice of one behavioral activity from among one or more alternatives with the intention of moving toward some desired state of affairs.[2]

Herbert A. Simon, in his classic work on the science of management decision making, treats it as a process synonymous with the whole process of management.[3] In Simon's words,

> Decision making comprises three principal phases: finding occasions for making a decision; finding possible courses of action; and choosing among courses of action.[4]

Emory and Niland view a decision as only one step in an intellectual process of differentiating among relevant alternatives. It is the point of selection and commitment. . . . The decision maker chooses the preferred purpose, the most reasonable task statement, or the best course of action.[5]

Eilon accurately observes that most of the definitions of a decision indicate that "the decision maker has several alternatives and that his choice involves a comparison between these alternatives and an evaluation of their outcome."[6]

In this book a **decision** is defined as a moment, in an ongoing process of evaluating alternatives for meeting an objective, at which expectations about a particular course of action impel the decision maker to select that course of action most likely to result in attaining the objective.

The process within which this moment of choice occurs is treated extensively in Chapter 2. In fact, this book's primary concern is with decisions that are made as part of an interdisciplinary process by decision makers who are, for the most part, trying to accomplish stated objectives.

DECISION MAKING AND PROBLEM SOLVING

There is a tendency in the literature and in the real world to view decision making and problem solving as identical activities.[7] They are not the same thing, however. Decisions can be and are often made and implemented successfully in the absence of problems. Moreover, problems can be and often are identified and solved in the absence of decisions. "The presumption of effectiveness in decision making and the concept of a problem . . . make the notions of decision making and problem solving closely allied. Yet in their fullest meaning the terms are not synonymous."[8]

Even though they are not interchangeable, decision making and problem solving are often closely related. In this regard, Braverman notes:

> Problem solving and decision making are not synonymous. However, decision making [often] involves problem solving and . . . problem solving [often] leads to some decision. The process of selecting a particular course of action from a set of alternatives [may constitute] a problem, and [possibly] a difficult one . . . decisions [may be] the end result of a problem-solving process. . . . Problems [may] result from attempts to achieve the [objectives] of the organization. . . . But solutions by themselves do not achieve [objectives]. It is the decisions resulting from these solutions that achieve [objectives]. . . . Without a decision a problem solution [may be] worthless. Consequently, problem solving and decision making go hand in hand.[9]

Costello and Zalkind observe that the terms **decision making** and **problem solving** are often used interchangeably. They differentiate the two by stating that problem solving involves the process of thoughtfully and deliberately striving to overcome obstacles in the path toward a goal. They confine the term *decision making* to the choice process, in which one among several possibilities is selected.[10] The interrelationship between decision making and problem solving is obviously the source of the confusion between the terms. For example, Bass says, "a problem exists requiring decision making if there is a barrier between a current and a desired state of affairs. . . . Again, a problem arises if the organization cannot automatically move from a current steady state to a more preferred one. A problem will be sensed if the current state is judged undesirable even if no goal or desired state can be discerned."[11]

Even in those instances in which decision making is oriented toward the solution of one or more problems, however, it is discernibly different from problem solving as such. Bass continues, "Decisions are action oriented. They are judgments which directly affect a course of action. The decision process involves both thought and action culminating in an act of choice."[12] Decision-making situations involving the solution of a problem contain at least two dilemmas that must be reconciled simultaneously. The first is the problem itself, which may require one or more decisions to solve. The second dilemma stems from the action that must be taken to implement the choice in pursuit of an outcome that will solve the problem that necessitated the decision in the first place. Now the distinction between decision making and problem solving seems to be clear. Problem solving may or may not require action. Problems can be solved indefinitely in the abstract, but this is not so with decisions. "A decision is therefore first of all an act, but an *act* requiring judgment," says Cornell. "A *judgment* requires a choice to become a decision. For if there is no choice, the decision has already been made."[13] Once the choice has been made the decision must be implemented. It is when actions are taken to implement the choice that problem solving clearly diverges from decision making. Problem solving has no commitment to action. It is concerned with developing a solution to overcome an obstacle leading toward a desired state. Decision making encompasses both the solution and the requirement to transform it into an implemented choice through a series of actions involving both change and commitment.

On balance, then, decision making is a more comprehensive process than problem solving. To the extent that it is involved at all, problem solving is only part of decision making. Particular kinds of decisions may necessitate problem solving; but the presence of problem solving is not sufficient to justify a claim of decision making. The terms, then, are interrelated but not interchangeable.

THE SIGNIFICANCE OF DECISION MAKING

"Decisions are the core transactions of organizations. Successful [organizations] 'outdecide' their competitors in at least three ways: They make better decisions; they make decisions faster; and they implement decisions more."[14] Without a doubt decision making is the most significant activity engaged in by managers in all types of organizations and at any level. It is the one activity that most nearly characterizes the behavior of managers, and the one that clearly differentiates managers from other occupations in the society. "Decision making is at the heart of what administrators and managers do."[15] Drucker notes, for example:

> Decision making is only one of the tasks of an executive. It usually takes a small fraction of his time. But to make the important decision is the *specific* executive task. Only an executive makes such decisions. An *effective* executive makes these decisions as a systematic process with clearly defined elements and in a distinct sequence of steps. Indeed to be expected . . . to make decisions that have significance and positive impact on the entire organization, its performance, and its results characterize the effective executive.[16]

"Of all the managerial functions which executives perform, whether at top, middle, lower, or even worker levels," Cornell says, "the act of making a decision is without equal in importance — that is to say the act of making the *right* decision about the *right* problem or opportunity."[17] This philosophy "is not meant to downgrade the ever-needed and classical functions of planning, organizing, staffing, operating, controlling, appraising, and numerous others which must be carried on. . . . [It] is also not meant to downgrade the necessity of management having to deal on a daily basis with technical skills, human skills, conceptual skills, and even imagination and risk. It does mean that . . . decision making is inherent in every interrelationship of men, machines, material, and technology."[18]

Managerial decision making constitutes a school of thought that believes that the central focus of management is on decision making.[19] According to this school, management thought is evolving in a context of managerial decision making. Managerial values and behavior are oriented toward making managerial choices between and among alternatives that will attain managerial objectives and fulfill organizational purposes. All managerial actions lead toward and stem from managerial decisions, and managerial performance is best evaluated according to the success of managerial decisions.

But whether or not one regards decision making as constituting a school of management thought, it is difficult to gainsay the significance and centrality of this activity. To be sure managers and executives do many things besides make decisions. Nonetheless the current and lasting impact of managerial performance is centered in the efficacy of management choices. Decision making invariably involves a commitment of resources, and given a finite quantity of resources, choices to commit and consume them must be taken seriously. Decision making also tends to result in some kind of organizational change, which invariably affects current relationships and future prospects. As such, change adds to the significance of managerial decision making.

As will be noted later in this chapter, decisions have varying degrees of significance. Those decisions made by top management are often vital to the long-term strategy of the organization, so that clearly such choices are highly significant. Decisions made by middle managers are usually concentrated in the major administrative responsibility centers of the organization. The success of these choices undergirds the strategic decisions made by top management. And last, but certainly not least, the day-to-day commitments of resources made by operating management in the technical areas of the organization provide a foundation for the commitments and changes initiated by decisions made at the higher levels of management. Although it may be somewhat one dimensional to explain managerial behavior in a context of decision making, such explanations do encompass the principal thrust of significant managerial actions in formal organizations.

DECISION MAKING: A GENERIC PROCESS

Like management itself, decision making is a generic process that is applicable to all forms of organized activity. Indeed the generic qualities of decision making compose the central underpinning of this book. It is all too common to associate decision making with business or business-related organizations and thus, by implication, with profit-oriented enterprise. The fact that decision making of a managerial nature has been employed for centuries by the military, governments, and religious orders is usually overlooked by those who take this perspective. In fact, it was not until the Industrial Revolution in England that managerial decision making came to be applied to industrial operations. And it was only as recently as the turn of the twentieth century that managerial decision making began to be applied in any systematic way to business enterprise in the United States.[20]

It is also fairly common in schools and colleges of business to teach managerial decision making as though it applied primarily to large corporations. This traditional association of decision making with private enterprise has given rise to a host of decision-making techniques, mainly quantitative, that are meant to be used by the profit-conscious sector of the society. In point of fact, however, any type of organization or activity that needs to be managed requires managerial decision making.[21] Since all types of organizations require some degree of management, it follows that both management and managerial decision making are generic. Koontz states the case for management as a generic discipline (and, by association, managerial decision making as a generic process) even more precisely.

> It does not really matter what is being managed, whether business, government, charitable or religious organizations, or even universities, the task of every manager at every level is to [decide] so as to accomplish group purposes with the least expenditure of material or human resources.[22]

The vehicle of managerial decision making as a generic process is the universality of management itself. As Albers points out, "The management process is present in all kinds of organizations — business, governmental, military, labor, educational, and religious."[23] Where there are managers there are decisions. Therefore if management is universal, managerial decision making is generic to management's universe.

The need for and incidence of decision making exists in all types of organizations. In industrial concerns, marketing and production decisions permit the firm to provide goods and services to consumers. In universities the administrators of colleges and departments regularly have to make decisions about allocating scarce fiscal, physical, and human resources.[24] Hospitals, military organizations, and government agencies likewise employ administrators who must continually choose among alternative courses of action in fulfilling their managerial responsibilities.[25] Most management theorists agree that management characterizes all types of organizations.[26] If, as Simon suggests,[27] decision making is synonymous with management, then both must be generic in all forms of organized activity.

Our case for decision making as a generic process has thus far focused only on organizations in the United States. The case becomes global in scope if we expand our outlook to include multinational organizations headquartered in the United States, those headquartered in other countries, and uninational organizations in other countries. There is, however, considerable evidence that the managerial decision-making process has been applied with great success by American multinational companies in Europe[28] and by multinational companies throughout the world.[29]

> The [managerial decision-making process] represents the common fabric of managers. . . . It is universally found wherever people work together to achieve common objectives. It is, for example, used successfully by the executive in the United States, the business leader in Japan, the government official in Turkey, and the military officer in France. . . . However, the important observation is that what a manager does . . . is basic and consists of the same type of activities no matter what is managed.[30]

Given the generic nature of the decision-making process, it follows that managerial decision makers should be able to shift from one type of organization to another. This is exactly what happens in the real world. Managers move between companies and industries; military leaders move into government and industry; government officials move into industry; and business executives move into and out of government.

Such shifts as these do not mean that the specific details of the organization are unimportant, but rather that general decision-making skills and principles are at work, enabling the manager to master specific applications and problems in order to accommodate a different organizational setting.[31]

DECISION THEORY

Decision theory as an academic discipline is relatively young. It is only since World War II that operations research, statistical analysis, and computer programming have given the process of choice a scientific aura, and only within the last twenty-five or thirty years have the behavioral sciences — sociology, psychology, and social psychology — begun to contribute to the body of knowledge making up decision theory.

Even today the literature in the field has a strongly quantitative orientation. That is, the decision maker is assumed to have: (1) a fixed objective, (2) almost unlimited time and money to spend in search and evaluation activities, (3) virtually perfect information regarding the probability of alternative outcomes, and (4) inexhaustible cognitive powers for comprehending, assimilating, and retaining an infinite number of variables. (Although such assumptions may be necessary to quantify a decision-making situation, they do limit the applicability of quantitative methods in decision making and dictate extreme caution in interpreting and using quantified results.)

Some writers concede that although decision making is accomplished through a process, this process must be highly procedural if not actually quantified.[32] Other authors treat decision making as a complex exercise in mathematics or statistics.[33] Several books present decision making primarily through a series of cases,[34] whereas others give some attention to the behavioral aspects of decision making, but usually by compiling articles from scholarly journals.[35] In fact, few, if any, books focus on decision making as an integrated process accomplished within an interdisciplinary framework.[36] And the articles in the behavioral sciences and management journals are usually concerned with the moment of choice in the decision-making process.[37]

Clearly there is a need to expand and improve the study of decision making if only because of the obvious pervasiveness and significance of choice-oriented behavior. In this context, there are three observations of decision-making behavior that are particularly relevant to the purposes of this book. First, managers are often unaware of how they make decisions and why they prefer one alternative to others. Second, managers appear to show little concern for the quality of their own decisions, although many of them are quick to point out apparent deficiencies in the choice behavior of others. Finally, it seems evident that the study of decision making has not received the emphasis it clearly deserves by virtue of its significance in society.[38] The relative newness of decision theory as an academic discipline doubtless accounts for the diversity of approaches to the subject. Still, there exists a need for a unified, interdisciplinary approach that combines the behavioral and quantitative aspects of the field into a cohesive process useful to academicians, consultants, and managers in all forms of organizations. This is an ambitious undertaking, and one that will require much energy and time. But the effort is worth making, and it is hoped that this book will help.

THE SCOPE OF DECISION MAKING

Decision making occurs at several levels. The first and perhaps the most basic level is that of the individual acting to satisfy his or her psychological needs. Beyond that are levels of group, organizational, and metaorganizational decision making. Figure 1.1, on page 11, conceptualizes the scope of decision making as it is presented in this chapter. In its most basic sense, decision making begins at the level of the individual. Individuals come

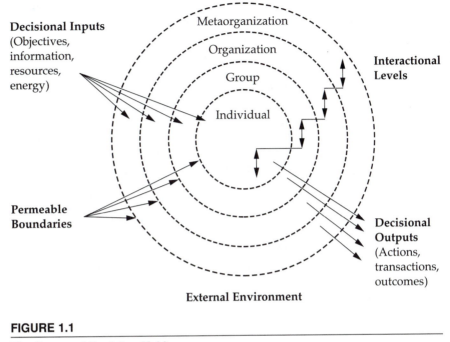

FIGURE 1.1

The Scope of Decision Making

together to form decision-making groups, and both individuals and groups constitute decision making by managers at the organization level. This level is the primary focus of this book. For their part organizations are subsets of larger aggregates designated metaorganizations. These aggregates represent the broadest scope of decision making and include systems of enterprise, societies, and nation-states. The entire scope of decision making is delimited by permeable boundaries through which decisional inputs are transmitted from the external environment and across which decisional outputs are transmitted into the external environment. These inputs and outputs traverse a hierarchy of interactional levels reflecting the interconnectedness of the principal aggregates of the scope of decision making.[39] For its part, the external environment consists of the principal stakeholder groups of a given organization or metaorganization. "Stakeholders are defined as any person, group, or organization that can place a claim on an organization's [or metaorganization's] attention, resources, or output, or is affected by that output."[40] The remainder of this section focuses in greater detail on the principal aggregates that constitute the scope of decision making.

Individual Decision Making

According to Maslow, human beings are motivated by a hierarchy of needs, the highest being the need for self-actualization, or the need to become all that one is capable of becoming.[41] However, self-actualization can take many forms and be pursued with varying degrees of intensity.[42] The satisfaction of a lower-level need for one individual may, for example, represent a kind of ultimate fulfillment for another. Still the concept of a hierarchy of human needs provides a useful framework for analyzing individual decisions.

Decision making by individuals reflects certain common characteristics.[43] Clearly there are differences in decision-making skills among people. It also appears that individuals tend to want too much rather than too little information and may take too long to arrive at decisions. Individuals seem unable to make full use of information, especially when it is multidimensional. Similarly, individual decision makers are often reluctant to revise their opinions on the basis of new information. Individuals, in other words, tend to give too much weight to preliminary information and don't like to change early erroneous commitments in light of new evidence. There is also evidence that individual decision makers may develop and consider too few courses of action when making a choice.[44]

Individual decision makers tend to make choices in ways that are markedly at variance with normative decision theory. For example, studies of individual choice have shown that:

1. Human subjects tend to overestimate low probabilities and underestimate high probabilities.

2. Individuals appear to be insensitive to the sample size of their observations.

3. Individuals adjust their first approximations to an estimate on the basis of additional evidence.

4. Individuals tend to be overconfident of their ability to estimate the probability of an uncertain event.[45]

5. Individuals tend to overestimate the probability of events that actually occur, as well as the extent to which they or others would have been able to predict past events.

6. Human subjects reveal a tendency to compare pairs of alternatives rather than a whole list.

7. Individuals tend to minimize reliance on explicit trade-offs or other numerical computations.

8. Individuals exhibit choices that are sometimes inconsistent and intransitive.

9. On balance, human subjects often behave in ways that dispel the notion that they are proper decision theorists with well-disciplined objective functions.[46]

In making choices, individuals tend to go through a simplified sequential elimination process somewhat as follows:

1. Alternatives tend to be viewed as a set of aspects.

2. At each stage in the process of choice, one aspect is selected with the order being determined probabilistically: more important aspects have a higher probability of being considered early.

3. Any alternative that fails to meet an aspiration level with respect to the considered aspect is eliminated.

4. The process continues until all alternatives but one are eliminated.[47]

Much of an individual's decision making is done to solve problems — personal, employment, or social. The following is a general statement of the decision-making or problem-solving approach of individuals:

1. Problem solving by individuals entails the use of strategies (plans or patterns) of searching for relevant alternatives, especially when the slightest degree of complexity prevails. The greater the cognitive strain imposed by the problem constraints such as time, information availability, and recall capability, the simpler the rules of search. The individual usually tries to minimize cognitive strain in part by his or her choice of problem-solving techniques.

2. Problem-solving behavior is adaptive. Individuals start with a tentative solution, search for information, modify the initial solution, and continue until there is some balance between expected and realized results.

3. Even in the most restricted problem-solving situation, the individual's personality and aversion to or preference for risk enter into his or her choice of strategies, use of information, and ultimate solution.[48]

In summary, individuals tend to employ rather simple strategies, even in the presence of complex problems, to obtain desirable solutions. Further, individual decision making is constrained by imperfect information, time and cost factors, frequently severe cognitive limitations, and diverse psychological forces.

Group Decision Making

In our complex society individuals usually find need satisfaction as members of groups that have particular purposes.

> The decisions that affect the future of our civilization and of the human race are, increasingly, made in a *group* context. . . . The study of individual decision making has limited utility in understanding how these groups make decisions. Group processes are not simply extensions and elaborations of the processes that characterize individuals; when people convene in groups, a new entity is created, with its own dynamics and complexity, and "its" decisions cannot be predicted even from a thorough knowledge of its constituent members.[49]

Often individuals must compromise their personal desires if the group is to arrive at a consensus. This, of course, is the reason group decisions represent more than just a collection of desires of the individual members.[50] Presumably such a synthesis is more workable than a decision made unilaterally by an individual. But it is not necessarily a better decision in terms of satisfying individual needs or attaining organizational goals.[51] It simply represents an expansion of the scope of choice, from a single to a multiple decision maker.

It is also true that a group normally provides a broader range of knowledge that may yield a more penetrating analysis of a given set of alternatives. Still the need to obtain a consensus of the members is often time-consuming and frustrating to the individual who prefers the relative freedom of unilateral choice. Other individuals, of course, prefer to make decisions as members of a group because the risk of personal criticism is less and the responsibility for unfavorable results is shared.[52]

Groups have both strengths and weaknesses as decision-making entities. The strong points for groups permit them to:

1. Discuss problems or situations and discover causes, complexities, and consequences
2. Edit and react to documents, drafts, or suggestions
3. Narrow the field of decision alternatives by their reactions
4. Act as an extension of the responsible manager in actions intended to implement decisions successfully
5. Create a climate of involvement, symbolically involving the entire community
6. Represent the constituencies or stakeholders affected by the decision at least to some extent
7. Come to understand the nature of the managerial objectives or problems that occasion the need for decisions
8. Reach conclusions that benefit the total community or organization rather than special interests or particular individuals[53]

Some of the more obvious weaknesses of groups include:

1. A pronounced difficulty in drafting policies, procedures, and papers of any sort. Groups edit or comment; they usually don't write.
2. A tendency to decide at a deliberate pace that is anything but quick. Usually the group structure requires that members hear one another out before making a decision.
3. A disinclination or inability to take the initiative. Groups tend to react and respond rather than proact and initiate.[54]

But the scope of decision making does not stop at the level of the group. After all, a group is simply an entity within a larger aggregate called an organization.[55] The organization constitutes the total enterprise or institution. Within it, numerous groups function to accomplish the objectives. A decision made by a particular group may commit the entire organization to a certain course of action. But more likely, such a decision will be made by several groups, be reviewed at several levels in the formal structure, and eventually be ratified by the chief executive or top administrator.[56] A decision at the organizational level is therefore much more complex than a choice made at the group level because a group is only a subset of an organization.

Organizational Decision Making

According to Alexis and Wilson, decision making in organizations displays many of the properties that are functionally similar to individual decision making.[57] Decision-making frameworks of organizations are adaptive, in the sense that search strategies and decision rules are modified constantly as a result of the organization's decision-making experiences. Like individuals, organizations give priority to simple search rules in seeking to reduce the strain of having to deal with complex ones.[58]

Organizational decision making, or decision making by managers in formal organizations, is the central focus of this book. Managers, as individuals enacting special decision-making roles in formal organizations, carry with them the characteristics of individual decision makers. These are modified in varying degrees, however, by the demands of the managerial role in a context of varying organizational complexity. Consequently, organizational decision making is much more involved than decision making at the individual or group level.[59] Many writers in management believe that organizational decision making is ill structured and ambiguous.[60] "Organizational decision making is an important, if not the most important, aspect of organizational life," says Bass. "But it is a messy rather than an orderly process, particularly if the problems for which decisions are needed are ill-structured rather than well-structured."[61]

Following is a list of some of the basic characteristics of decision making at the level of the organization:

1. Organizations make extensive use of programmed decisions that involve reasonably well-structured patterns of search. Naturally the more complex and significant the decision, the more extensive the search process will be.

2. Organizations often use rather simple rules of thumb to make decisions as well as the complex analytical frameworks that are often attributed to organizational decision making.[62]

3. Again, the complexity, uniqueness, and significance of the decision are determining factors. Obviously some decisions don't permit rule-of-thumb treatment.

4. Organizations make decisions that are bound and biased by the local rationality of the decision unit. That is, given the constraints in the situation and the uncertainties of the moment, organizations are likely to make decisions that are optimal in their spheres but suboptimal when reviewed in the larger totality.[63]

5. Organizations engage in a directed search for relevant alternatives. The choice of decision rules and strategies is constrained by the desire to minimize the uncertainties.

6. Organizations learn. To the extent that they are part of open systems, there is little doubt that they learn from and adapt to their environment.[64]

Recent research in decision making at the level of the organization has revealed numerous patterns and characteristics reflective of the degree of complexity inherent in the choices made by individuals enacting managerial roles. For example, managers often tend to gather information, but not use it — they ask for more information and then ignore it. They make decisions first and look for the relevant information afterward.[65] In fact, managers seem to gather a great deal of information that has little or no decision relevance.[66] Moreover, decision makers at the level of the organization often fail to accept recommendations for change and exhibit a reluctance to make innovations. In many cases, there is a pronounced unwillingness on the part of organizations and their managers even to acknowledge the need for change.

In addition, organizations frequently exhibit a kind of ordered disorder in decision making. Actions in one part of the organization seem only loosely coupled to events in some other part. Solutions appear to have only a tangential connection to problems. There is, in short, a kind of disorderliness that leads some people to doubt the orderliness of organizational decision making.[67] Moreover, the preferences of organizations often manifest considerable imprecision, which detracts from a conception of orderly decision making. Even if preferences are precise, they are often inconsistent, and preferences that are expressed frequently are not followed. There appears in many instances to be a fundamental mismatch between notions of rational choice and the behavior of managers in complex organizations. Decision making seems to represent an arena for symbolic actions directed toward purposes other than rational outcomes.[68]

The alleged disorder and imprecision of decision making at the level of the organization needs much additional study for confirmation, however, for there appears to be more reason to believe that organizational decision making is both rational and systematic. Moreover, managers who are effective decision makers seem to behave within discernible and defensible boundaries of choice in committing their organizations to various courses of action.[69] It is the thesis of this book that decision making at the organizational level takes place primarily through the basic functions of the manager, which include (1) planning, (2) organizing, (3) staffing, (4) directing, and (5) controlling.[70] For example, management forms objectives only after making decisions about the organization's basic purposes. To accomplish the objectives within some selected period of time, plans are formulated in the light of decisions made for resource requirements. In pursuit of the objectives set forth in the plans, management sets up a division of labor and establishes functional specialties and reporting relationships. Candidates are identified and selected according to the requirements reflected in the established positions, which compose the formal structure. The organization progresses toward fulfillment of the objectives contained in the plan via countless daily decisions required to make a product or dispense a service. Choices to take or withhold corrective action when comparing actual against standard performance affect control of operations. As Simon has stated, "Decision making is synonymous with managing."[71] It is the dynamic element that activates and sustains the managerial process.

Metaorganizational Decision Making

The scope of decision making extends beyond the managerial process at the level of the organization. The totality of organizations makes up the system of enterprise, which in the United States is capitalism.[72] Decisions made at the level of the system of enterprise tend to be oriented toward (1) consumer welfare, (2) allocation of resources, and (3) production and distribution of goods and services.[73] Although the primary focus is on macroeconomics at this level, the decision-making process is analogous to that employed at the individual, group, and organizational levels.

Decisions are also made at the level of the total society. Here the primary objective is social welfare with significant stress on (1) the good life, (2) culture, (3) civilization, (4) order, and (5) justice. The principal orientation is not of an economic nature, as at the level of the system of enterprise. Bernthal cites the basis for decisions at this level rather well in the following excerpt:

> It is necessary to see the importance to a culture and civilization of developing not only vigor in economic activity, but also of devoting man's energies to the civilizing process, once economic survival is assured. A surplus of goods . . . make[s] it possible for man to devote more energy and attention to the creation of works of literature, architecture, sculpture, music . . . [and] to the establishment of orderly societies . . . and just rules.[74]

Because organizations exist within the society's economic system, managers need to be responsive to the total society's decisions and the reasons for them.

Nations reflecting particular ideologies make up the world. For example, mainland China's ideology is communism, which calls for a totalitarian state within which the dictates of the political system subordinate individual freedom. On the other hand, the United States is a democracy whose laws are made by the people and administered with a maximum emphasis on personal freedom and the right to individual self-expression. Frequently, such ideological differences lead to tension, strain, and outright hostility between nations. Even when national ideologies are compatible, nations interact mainly to attain pragmatic objectives, such as trade concessions and geopolitical advantages. Still, with some modifications, decisions made at this level follow essentially the same process as those at subordinate levels.[75] It is well known, for example, that "presidents and premiers do sit down with their advisers and weigh alternatives, consider possible outcomes, and try to assess the probabilities that various outcomes will follow a given action."[76]

The scope of decision making is indeed broad. It begins at the level of the individual and extends to the deliberations of the groups that form the organization. Organizations, in turn, make up the overall system of enterprise, which forms part of the total society; and societies make up nations that espouse ideologies. The sum of these metaorganizations is the whole world.

A TYPOLOGY OF DECISIONS

In an organizational context, it is particularly important to differentiate the decisions made by management. Some decisions, for example, are very significant and highly consequential in their outcomes. There are few of these decisions, but their high level of importance offsets their small number. Conversely, there are other decisions, usually of an administrative nature, that affect the allocation of resources in various parts of the organization. Ineffective action in making decisions of this type may be costly, but it is seldom threatening to the long-term health of the total organization. Finally, the large number of decisions made by the vast majority of managers and supervisors at the operating level is usually not crucial to any particular aspect of the organization's well-being. It is imperative for management to know which kind of decision it is making. If a given decision is potentially significant, it should not be made as though it is routine and inconsequential. To act in this manner is to underestimate the complexity of the choice and to understate the value of its outcome, thereby contributing to a failed result. Alternatively, a given decision that is commonplace and of minimal consequence should not be made as though it is essential to the continued good fortune of the organization. To act in this manner is to overestimate the complexity of the choice and to overstate the value of its outcome, thereby incurring unjustified opportunity cost along with an indefensible waste of scarce resources. In essence, management needs to know the kind of decision at hand in order to make and implement it to the best advantage of the total organization.

We will now set forth a typology of decisions for use in describing the decision-making process and its interdisciplinary framework in the chapters to follow.

Various experts in the field of decision theory have advanced ways of classifying decisions. Perhaps the best known of these classifications is

Simon's distinction between programmed and nonprogrammed decisions. According to him:

> Decisions are programmed to the extent that they are repetitive and routine, to the extent that a definite procedure has been worked out for handling them. . . . If a particular problem recurs often enough, a routine procedure will usually be worked out for solving it. . . . Decisions are nonprogrammed to the extent that they are novel, unstructured, and consequential. There is no cut-and-dried method for handling the problem because it hasn't arisen before, or because its precise nature and structure are elusive or complex, or because it is so important that it deserves a custom-tailored treatment.[77]

Drucker made essentially the same distinction, but he labeled programmed decisions "generic" and nonprogrammed decisions "unique."[78]

Delbecq went slightly beyond Simon and Drucker with his three-point classification of decisions:

1. **Routine decisions.** The organization or group agrees upon the desired goal, and technologies exist to achieve the goal.
2. **Creative decisions.** There is a lack of an agreed-upon method of dealing with the problem. This lack of certitude may relate to incomplete knowledge of causation or to the absence of an appropriate solution strategy.
3. **Negotiated decisions.** Because of differences in norms, values, or vested interests, opposing factions confront each other concerning either ends or means, or both.[79]

Gore also proposed a three-point classification, composed of routine, adaptive, and innovative decisions. The distinctions in this classification are that adaptive decisions deal with problems rather than with the recurring tasks of routine decisions, and innovative decisions deal with major changes in activities and operations that lead to changes in goals, purposes, or policies.[80] Even within this scheme, however, there is a lot of interdependence among the decisions. In Gore's words:

> Routine decisions activate, channel, and terminate hundreds of units of behavior in such a way that broad goals are implemented through the same activities that meet immediate objects. Since both the conditions under which the goals can be realized and the goals themselves are constantly changing, routinized activities must continually be adapted to maintain a satisfactory rate of goal achievement. But since on a broader field, the objects embodied in goals are changed from time to time, the innovative decision exists. The essential rhythm of organizational adjustment is from routine to adaptive to routine; or from routine to adaptive to innovative and back to adaptive and eventually to routine again.[81]

Stufflebeam and his colleagues classified decisions along two dimensions: (1) whether the decision pertains to means or ends, and (2) whether the decision is relevant to the mission of the organization.[82] His classification was subsequently modified by Sharples to delineate planning and operational decisions.[83] Mintzberg identified three decision-making modes that encompass choices made in most kinds of organized activity.[84] His typology includes:

1. **Entrepreneurial decisions.** The preferred decision-making environment is characterized by high levels of certainty. The choices are motivated by proactive considerations and are oriented toward growth over the long term.

2. **Adaptive decisions.** The preferred decision-making environment in this case is also characterized by high levels of certainty, but the choices are motivated by reactive considerations with an indeterminant orientation for the short term.

3. **Planning decisions.** The preferred decision-making environment is fraught with risk. The choices are motivated by both proactive and reactive considerations and are oriented toward growth and efficiency over the long term.[85]

Thompson imparted a dynamic quality to the foregoing classifications with his two-dimensional scheme for decision-making strategies.[86] Thompson's classification is set forth in Figure 1.2 below. He describes four basic strategies:

1. **Computational strategy.** There is considerable certainty of cause/effect relationships, and there are strong preferences for possible outcomes.[87]

2. **Judgmental strategy.** Preferences for possible outcomes are strong, but cause/effect relationships are highly uncertain.[88]

3. **Compromise strategy.** There is a good deal of certainty regarding cause/effect relationships, but preferences for possible outcomes are not strong.[89]

Knowledge Regarding the Outcome	Preference for the Outcome	
	Strong Preference	Weak Preference
High Level of Knowledge	Computational Decision-Making Strategy	Compromise Decision-Making Strategy
Low Level of Knowledge	Judgmental Decision-Making Strategy	Inspirational Decision-Making Strategy

FIGURE 1.2

The Concept of Decision-Making Strategies

4. **Inspirational strategy.** Preferences for possible outcomes are not strong, and there is considerable uncertainty for cause/effect relationships.[90]

(Thompson's classification scheme, especially the differences between a computational strategy and a judgmental strategy, is adopted as a primary evaluative concept in this book.)

It is fairly easy to see how much these several classification schemes have in common. Essentially, each can be reduced to two basic categories: (1) routine, recurring, and certain, and (2) nonroutine, nonrecurring, and uncertain. Although there are other variables, these form a single thread through the several classifications. Table 1.1 shows all the classes divided into the two categories according to their structures and strategies. Category I includes the routine, recurring decisions that are handled with a high degree of certainty. Category II includes the nonroutine, nonrecurring decisions characterized by uncertainty as to the outcome.

The significance of differentiating between these two categories becomes apparent when one realizes that "the management of most companies' daily operations abounds with highly programmed decisions: consider merely the highly routinized rules that normally guide the everyday management of

TABLE 1.1   A Categorization of Decision Characteristics

	Category I Decisions	*Category II Decisions*
Classifications	Programmable; routine; generic; computational; negotiated; compromise	Nonprogrammable; unique; judgmental; creative; adaptive; innovative; inspirational
Structure	Procedural; predictable; certainty regarding cause/effect relationships; recurring; within existing technologies; well-defined information channels; definite decision criteria; outcome preferences may be certain or uncertain	Novel, unstructured, consequential, elusive, and complex; uncertain cause/effect relationships; nonrecurring; information channels undefined; incomplete information; decision criteria may be unknown; outcome preferences may be certain or uncertain
Strategy	Reliance upon rules and principles; habitual reactions; prefabricated response; uniform processing; computational techniques; accepted methods for handling	Reliance on judgment, intuition, and creativity; individual processing; heuristic problem-solving techniques; rules of thumb; general problem-solving processes

inventories, production schedules, machine and manpower allocations, cost estimation, mark-up pricing, etc."[91]

Management should not treat routine decisions as if they were non-routine. If a decision is indeed generic, valuable time and money should not be spent on it as if it were unique.[92] Moreover, management must not only differentiate the routine from the nonroutine decision, it must also try to understand better the structure and strategy of the nonroutine decision. This understanding will yield better ways to approach and make category II decisions.[93] The potential rewards from such improvements are set forth in the following statement:

> It is precisely this type of nonprogrammed decision making that forms the basis for allocating billions of dollars worth of resources in the economy every year. And, ironically, until we better understand the nature of such unprogrammed human decision processes, our sophisticated computer technology will be of slight aid for making this type of decision more effectively. . . . The potential payoff to management of scientific understanding of the economic, psychological, sociological, and political "laws" of nonprogrammed human judgment can be enormous.[94]

In addition to making better category II decisions, top management must differentiate such decisions from the category I type. In this way it will be able to concentrate most of its time and energy on strategic decision making. Table 1.1 reflects a categorization of decision characteristics attributable to category I and category II decisions. The primary focus in this book is on category II decisions. "This level of decision is the very essence of management. It occurs in all forms of organization: in private firms, in large public companies, . . . in local governments, in hospitals, in universities, in whatever the organization may be."[95] It is the level of decision that differentiates management from other callings and occupations in the total society.

THE LOCUS OF CHOICE

Many people feel that "ordinarily, decisions are made only by top executives. They may be correct for those decisions that rightfully belong 'at the top.' But the truth is that a great many decisions are made by middle and lower management and even lower operative groups and individuals."[96]

In terms of the organizational hierarchy, category I decisions are normally made at the level of operating management. This is where the technology of the organization is applied to transform raw inputs into finished outputs. Choices made at this level are usually routine and recurring, with a high degree of certainty associated with the outcome. Category I decisions may also be made at middle-management levels in the normal administrative processes of the organization. Again, the structure of the decision, in terms of its nature, frequency, and degree of certainty, will determine its strategy, which in turn will indicate the level of management at which the choice should be made.

In this context, it seems obvious that in organizations of any appreciable size, top management (that is, the vice-presidential or chief-executive level) should not make category I decisions. Managers at these levels are expected to conserve their time and energy for choices requiring judgment and creativity. They must bear in mind the need to adapt the organization to change and to the innovations of dynamic technology. Such managers should therefore concentrate primarily on category II decisions, which are nonroutine, nonrecurring, and uncertain of outcome. Organizations in which top managers are busy with category I choices usually don't delegate enough responsibility to lower levels of management, and, thus, motivation, efficiency, and effectiveness suffer. Further, if they concern themselves with category I decisions, top managers tend to neglect long-range objectives and strategies, which results in a kind of organizational myopia. There is a general disregard for long-range planning and an undue emphasis on short-range control.[97] The ultimate consequences for the organization can be only unfavorable. After all, in the absence of planning there is nothing to control; and operations tend to be conducted in a highly reactive atmosphere with problematical consequences resulting from unplanned choices.[98] Clearly, then, the proper concern of top management is category II choices, with category I decisions left to operating management. Middle management should, for the most part, also be concerned with category I choices, although in many situations this level will participate in category II decisions, also.[99]

With regard to decision making at the individual and group levels within a formal organization, the locus of choice seems evident. For example, individuals are more likely to make category I decisions. Such choices are routine and recurring and have a good deal of certainty associated with the outcome, so there is no need to convene a group to make these decisions. Yet it is interesting to note the number of organizations in which committees, task forces, and fact-finding groups spend countless hours making choices that have highly programmed outcomes. This is a classic example of treating generic decisions as if they were unique, in the name of participative management. Participation through group membership in a category I choice, where the outcome of the decision is highly certain, represents a tremendous waste of human resources. It also embodies a misconception regarding one of the basic purposes of group decision making — namely, to avoid unilateral choices that might work to the disadvantage of those affected by the choice. But this purpose bears principally on choices that involve the exercise of judgment, intuition, and creativity — in short, category II decisions. Such choices are the proper concern of group decision makers at the middle-management or, more appropriately, top-management level.

Individuals are less likely to make category II decisions than groups are. Because of their relative complexity, these decisions usually require more expertise than most individuals have. To be sure, an individual chief executive or top administrator may formally ratify a category II decision made by one or more groups in the organization. But it is becoming less common for these nonrecurring and consequential choices to be made unilaterally.[100]

In essence, then, and with reference to Table 1.1, category I decisions are most likely to be made by individual managers at the operating levels of the organization. Depending on the situation, though, such choices may also be made by middle managers, either individually or, with reduced effectiveness, in groups. For their part, top managers normally concentrate on category II decisions, which may be made in one or more groups that may include middle managers. The chief executive may formally ratify such decisions or, to a lesser extent, may make them unilaterally.

MANAGERIAL ASPECTS OF DECISION MAKING

Managerial decision making normally results in one or both of two states in a formal organization: (1) a change in organizational form or process, and / or (2) a commitment of fiscal, physical, or human resources. Management should be mindful of these two decision-making states prior to choosing among alternative courses of action.

To overlook or ignore the effects of organizational change is to invite possible adverse reaction to a choice, which may hamper progress toward the objective that gave rise to the decision. Management should remember that for every action there is a reaction. Change tends to create anxiety among those affected by it. Anxiety easily turns into hostility and resistance, which can effectively impede the successful implementation of the decision. Management can work to offset such dysfunctional effects by trying to anticipate adverse reaction to decisions that bring organizational change. This should begin early in the decision-making process and always before the time of implementation. The numerous techniques that facilitate organizational change invariably entail some form of participation in the making of the decision by those who are likely to be directly or indirectly affected by it. Suffice to say here that the need to anticipate effects of organizational change constitutes one of the two primary aspects of managerial decision making.[101]

The second primary aspect is the need to commit or recommit resources before and after the act of choice. The resources required to arrive at a choice are mainly the time and energy of the decision makers. These resources are discussed in the next chapter in the context of searching for alternatives. Our concern here is with the much larger aggregate of resources that usually must be committed following the act of choice.

Given the finite amount of resources available to most formal organizations, a managerial decision to commit resources for some group of very attractive purposes may preclude identical or similar commitments for some other group of purposes that is also very attractive. The concept at issue here is the **opportunity cost,** "which means that the cost of anything is the value of the best alternative, or the opportunity, that is sacrificed."[102] There are some standard statistical techniques for measuring the opportunity cost (or loss) associated with a choice from almost any set of quantified alternatives.[103] The point here is that, when they evaluate and compare alternatives, managers should be aware that the benefits expected from the choice of one alternative must be adjusted to reflect the benefits lost by not selecting some other alternative. Alternatives are seldom isolated from one another. At the very least there is a reciprocal relationship of opportunity cost. The need to anticipate the potential effects of organizational change resulting from a choice and the need to continually assess the opportunity cost associated with the same choice are the primary managerial aspects of decision making in formal organizations.

Since category II decisions are the primary focus of this book, it is appropriate to advance a set of properties that characterize all category II decisions made by managers in organizations of all types. In the absence of one or more of these characteristics, the decision at hand is not managerial and/or is not a category II decision.

1. There is an objective that stands to benefit the total organization over the long run.
2. The decision represents the best one from among a set of alternatives any one of which can conceivably attain the objective.
3. The outcome of the decision reflects an appreciable degree of uncertainty attributable to imperfect information, time and cost constraints, and the cognitive limitations of the managerial decision maker.
4. The decision usually involves some degree of change for the total organization or some major function or program.
5. The decision invariably requires a commitment of scarce resources with some opportunity cost.
6. The act of choice is a means to an end (the attainment of the objective), not an end in itself.
7. The decision maker often overestimates the likely success of the outcome of the decision.
8. The success of the decision is readily measurable in terms of the degree of objectives' attainment.

PERSPECTIVES ON MANAGERIAL DECISION MAKING

This section presents four perspectives that are a substantial departure from the traditional view of decision making in a number of segmented activities, each with a particular emphasis conditioned by the education, interests, and perception of the decision maker.

The Integrative Perspective

Decision making is a process that pervades all of the managerial functions. From the formulation of a plan, which provides a framework for making choices to accomplish objectives, to the development and activation of controls, which ensure the relation of actual to intended performance, managers are constantly selecting from among alternatives. Much of the decision-making behavior is second nature to professional managers. They do it without consciously proceeding from one step to another. Their actions are objectives oriented, their thought processes are purposeful and rational. Still, as they proceed toward making and eventually implementing a choice, they go through an integrated series of actions defined in Chapter 2 as the decision-making process. From the setting of objectives through the search and into the comparison and evaluation of alternatives preparatory to the choice, which is subsequently implemented and monitored to ensure an outcome in keeping with the original objective, decision making is an integrated process. To be sure, the emphasis given to different parts of the process will vary with the choice at hand, but a successful outcome invariably results from the performance of each step in the overall process. This is the principle of **integrative decision making** — a principle advanced in this book and one that is followed by most effective managerial decision makers.

The Interdisciplinary Perspective

Decision making draws liberally on the behavioral sciences and the quantitative disciplines. The integration of these sciences and disciplines occurs throughout the several stages in the decision-making process. Although it is difficult to assign a weight to the relative significance of each body of knowledge, the behavioral sciences are more widely applicable throughout the decision-making process. Consequently, they constitute the primary focus of this book. For example, quantitative techniques, explicated in a vast array of other books, apply mainly to the comparison and evaluation of alternatives. But the psychological factors, such as (1) personality, (2) propensity for accepting or avoiding risk, (3) perception, and (4) the subconscious mind, influence the behavior of the decision maker from the setting of the objective to the attainment of the final outcome. Moreover, a shift from individual to group decision making confronts the decision maker with a new set of variables. Now he or she must contend with the sociological factors inherent in arriving at a consensual choice. In a group, the decision maker usually must accommodate his or her preferences, adjust his or her aspirations, and frequently modify his or her behavior to gain acceptance by the group and to ensure that the collective decision contains at least some part of his or her original objective. For a highly motivated and aggressive individual, the adjustment to a group decision-making situation may be painful or even impossible. For a more passive individual, one who may be desirous of avoiding risk or criticism, the diffused personal responsibility for a group-oriented consensual choice may appear particularly inviting.

The blending of multiple disciplines within the decision-making process is the particular focus of Chapter 5. This fusion of the behavioral sciences and the quantitative disciplines is the foundation for the principle on **interdisciplinary decision making** — a principle that embodies the eclectic nature of effective managerial decision making.

The Interlocking Perspective

The term *interlock* means to unite or engage in a way that motion in any one part of the system will be constrained by some other part of the system. As such, this term describes perfectly the concept of *bounded rationality* which is introduced in Chapter 3. In bounded rationality the decision maker is constrained from obtaining maximized results by the boundaries of imperfect information, time and cost constraints, and human cognitive limitations. He or she is further constrained by the expectation that the decisions made will result in the attainment of the organization's objectives. The decision maker is also constrained by the expectation that decisions will not work to the perceived disadvantage of the numerous stakeholder groups that constitute the external environment within which the organization functions. Motion or change in any part of this total system will be constrained by some other part of the system because all of the constraints and expectations in bounded rationality are interlocked. Every action produces a reaction, and the decision maker must be sensitive and responsive to numerous forces and variables as he or she proceeds toward a choice. In this way the outcome of the decision is far more likely to meet the original objective which is the underlying rationale for the principle on **interlocking decision making.**

The Interrelational Perspective

At the level of the organization, decision making is synonymous with the process of management. From the setting of objectives to the incorporation of those objectives into a plan concurrent with the establishment of the position requirements in the organization structure through the staffing and directing of the organization toward its objectives within the limits of established controls, the manager is continually involved in making decisions. Decision making occurs regularly in all of the functions performed by managers. However, the interrelationship of the total process of management with the decision-making process is most apparent in planning and control within the total organization.

By virtue of its orientation toward the future, a plan tends to reduce uncertainty for the decision maker. The objectives that guide the plan are also the point of departure leading toward the choice and implementation of favored alternatives. Therefore, a plan provides a framework for making decisions that will serve the organization's long-term purposes.[104] Decision making is also interrelated with the organization's control system as control, in turn, is connected to the plan. For example, the objectives used for planning and decision making are also reflected in the standards of the control system against which the actual results of planned and implemented choices are measured. Moreover, much of the information used to develop the plan and to search for alternatives leading toward a decision also provides the means within the control system for signaling departures from choices made with planned outcomes. This linkage of decision making with planning and control at the level of the organization forms the basis for the principle of **interrelational decision making** — a principle that epitomizes the interrelatedness of decision making with the primary functions of management.

THE PRACTICE OF DECISION MAKING

The theories, concepts, and principles presented in this book are not necessarily innovative in themselves. What is new and different is the integration and synthesis of individual ideas and paradigms into meaningful and useful constructs. For example, parts of the decision-making process have been discussed, in one fashion or another, in many places in the management literature. But the entire process has never been presented in the context of an integrated and interdisciplinary framework that unites the traditional quantitative disciplines and the newer behavioral disciplines into a composite theory of managerial decision making. Further, the notion of rational decision making has been treated extensively by statisticians, economists, and mathematicians as an exercise in optimization or maximization. Now for the first time there is a plausible and practical definition of rationality that is applicable to decisions made at any level in any type of organization.

Management practices are not easy to change. The natural tendency is to stick with methods that have been successful and are familiar. Often it is necessary to demonstrate beyond a reasonable doubt that a new approach will have substantial benefits before any change will be accepted. Nevertheless, if organizations of all types are to survive, they must remain open and amenable to new ideas and fresh approaches. The theories, concepts, and principles presented and demonstrated in this book can be of inestimable benefit to managerial decision makers everywhere. Of course, the final choice lies with management. Perhaps the only real constraint is traditional resistance to change. We hope this resistance can be overcome.

SUMMARY

This chapter has presented a comprehensive definition of the term *decision*. It is simply a moment in an ongoing process of evaluating alternatives for meeting an objective. It is the moment when a decision maker selects the course of action that appears most likely to result in the attainment of the objective. This chapter also differentiated decision making and problem solving, principally because of the common tendency to regard the two activities as synonymous and interchangeable. It was noted that decision making is a more comprehensive process than problem solving. To the extent that it is involved at all, problem solving is only part of decision making. Particular kinds of decisions may necessitate problem solving; but the presence of problem solving is not sufficient to justify a claim of decision making.

The significance of decision making stems from the fact that it affects all the functions of managers in formal organizations. The current and lasting impact of managerial performance is inextricably centered in the efficacy of managerial choices. Most of managerial behavior can be explained in a context of decision making. Making decisions of all types at all levels is the principal thrust of significant managerial actions. The true measure of management is reflected in the success of its decisions over time.

The decision-making process is generic, since the making of choices is endemic to all levels of management in all types of organized activity throughout the world. It was noted in this chapter that decision theory is still a relatively new field. Most current orientations have a strong quantitative emphasis that focuses on the decision itself rather than on the process within which the choice takes place. It is significant that a decision is simply a means to an end, not, as is frequently assumed, an end in itself. The end is, of course, the outcome that will result from the choice — an outcome, it is hoped, that will attain the objective(s) that gave rise to the integrated process of decision making.

This chapter also discussed the scope of decision making on four levels: individual, group, organizational, and metaorganizational. The scope of decision making is conceptualized in Figure 1.1. In making decisions, individuals tend to go through a simplified sequential elimination process. For their part, groups have both strengths and weaknesses as decision-making entities. According to some writers, decision making at the level of the organization is accomplished in disorder and with imprecision. But in my opinion these allegations require more study before they may be accepted as valid. With all its imperfections, organizational decision making appears to be both rational and systematic. Making choices within the organization is accomplished through the basic functions of the manager. I agree with Simon that good management and effective decision making are synonymous. Metaorganizational decision making extends the process of choice to the national level. But even at this exalted level, decision making follows essentially the same process as at subordinate levels.

The focus of this book is on decision making at the level of the organization. This chapter reviewed different ways of classifying decisions and then advanced a typology comprising two categories: category I — the routine, recurring decisions that are handled with a high degree of certainty — and category II — the nonroutine, nonrecurring decisions characterized by considerable uncertainty as to the outcome. A special variety of category II choices is that of strategic decisions, which are vital to the long-term health of the organization and which are discussed more completely in Chapter 10. The nomenclature of category I and category II decisions is set forth in Table 1.1.

Of particular importance in this chapter is the typology of decision-making strategies advanced by Thompson. This typology is set forth in Figure 1.2. According to Thompson, a *computational strategy* is one with a considerable certainty of cause/effect relationship and strong preferences for possible outcomes. This type of strategy is most appropriate for category I choices. Thompson further notes that a *judgmental strategy* is one with strong preferences for possible outcomes but where cause/effect relationships are highly uncertain. This is the appropriate strategy for category II choices. These two classifications of computational strategy and judgmental strategy will figure prominently in concepts and models of managerial and strategic decision making presented in this book. Thompson's classification of *compromise strategy* is most applicable in the political aspects of corporate decision making or in the making of political decisions in the public sector. His final classification of *inspirational strategy* relates to the intuitive or creative aspects of decision making.

Decisions are made at all levels of management in formal organizations. Nonetheless, the locus of choice indicates that category I decisions should be made by operating management, whereas category II choices are the clear responsibility of top management. Middle management supervises the making of category I decisions and assists in the making of category II decisions. The locus of choice also indicates that strategic decisions, as a special metalevel of category II choices, must be accomplished by top management. This chapter also sets forth two principal considerations that constitute the primary managerial aspects of decision making. Managers should bear these considerations in mind both before and after a decision is made. They are (1) the potentially adverse consequences of organizational change stemming from a decision and (2) the ever-present opportunity cost of selecting a given alternative from a set of related alternatives. This chapter advanced a set of properties that characterize all category II decisions made by managers in organizations of all types.

This chapter also advanced perspectives on managerial decision making embodying four basic principles that guide and influence decision makers in organizations of all types. The *integrative* principle reflects the pervasive qualities of decision making in all of the basic functions of the manager. The assimilation and adoption of this perspective seems certain to enhance decision outcomes at all levels in all types of organizations. The *interdisciplinary* principle unites the quantitative disciplines and the behavioral sciences in all of the stages of the managerial decision-making process. This principle embodies the eclectic nature of effective managerial decision making. The *interlocking* principle is centered in the concept of bounded rationality to be presented in Chapter 3. This principle indicates that the decision maker is precluded from obtaining a maximized result by the pervasive constraints of imperfect information, time and cost, and cognitive limitations as well as the organization's objectives and the expectations of its multiplicity of stakeholders. Assimilation and acceptance of this principle will increase the likelihood of decision outcomes compatible with the original objective of the managerial decision maker. The *interrelational* principle is focused on the specific relationship between the decision-making process and particular functions of management with a particular emphasis on the functions of planning and control. The practice of all of the principles set forth in this chapter will improve management's prospects for decision success. All that remains to partake of these benefits is the perennial need to overcome traditional resistance to change.

REVIEW AND DISCUSSION QUESTIONS

1. Why is it important that management differentiate category I from category II decisions? Discuss.
2. What are the four principles that are derived from the perspectives on decision making set forth in this chapter? Discuss their comparative importance.
3. Discuss this statement: decision making is synonymous with management.
4. In what way is decision making at the level of the individual analogous to that at the organizational level? In what way, if any, is it different?
5. In what way is decision making at the organizational level an integral part of the managerial process?
6. Do you agree that managerial decision making is a generic process? Why or why not?
7. Discuss this statement: to say that decision making is synonymous with problem solving is to understate the complexity of the former and to overstate the pervasiveness of the latter.
8. Is it appropriate for category I decisions to be made by a committee? Why or why not?
9. In your opinion, does management do a good job of preparing organizations for internal change resulting from decisions? Discuss.
10. Why is a computational decision-making strategy ill-suited for a category II decision? Discuss.

NOTES

1. H. Ofstad, *An Inquiry into the Freedom of Decision* (Oslo: Norwegian Universities Press, 1961), p. 5.
2. Fremont A. Shull, Jr., Andre L. Delbecq, and L. L. Cummings, *Organizational Decision Making* (New York: McGraw-Hill, 1970), p. 31.
3. Herbert A. Simon, *The New Science of Management Decision* (New York: Harper & Row, 1960), p. 1.
4. Ibid.
5. C. William Emory and Powell Niland, *Making Management Decisions* (Boston: Houghton Mifflin, 1968), p. 12.
6. Samuel Eilon, "What Is a Decision?" *Management Science* (December 1969), B-172.
7. See Oswald Huber, "Decision Making as a Problem Solving Process," in *New Directions in Research on Decision Making*, ed. B. Brehmer et al. (New York: Elsevier Publishing Co., 1986), pp. 108–138.
8. Shull, Delbecq, and Cummings, *Organizational Decision Making*, p. 56.
9. Jerome D. Braverman, *Management Decision Making* (New York: AMACOM, 1980), pp. 19–20.
10. Timothy W. Costello and Sheldon S. Zalkind, eds., *Psychology in Administration: A Research Orientation* (Englewood Cliffs, N.J.: Prentice-Hall, 1963), p. 334.
11. Bernard M. Bass, *Organizational Decision Making* (Homewood, Ill.: Richard D. Irwin, 1983), p. 3.
12. Ibid.
13. Alexander H. Cornell, *The Decision Maker's Handbook* (Englewood Cliffs, N.J.: Prentice-Hall, 1980), p. 9.
14. David J. McLaughlin, "Strengthening Executive Decision Making," *Human Resource Management*, 34, No. 3 (Fall 1995), 443.
15. David J. Hickson et al., "Decision and Organization — Processes of Strategic Decision Making and Their Explanation," in *Managerial Decision Making*, ed. D. J. Hickson (England: Dartmouth, 1995), p. 77.
16. Peter F. Drucker, "The Effective Decision," *Harvard Business Review* (January–February 1967), 98.
17. Cornell, *Decision Maker's Handbook*, p. 13.
18. Ibid.
19. See Harold Koontz, "The Management Theory Jungle Revisited," *Academy of Management Review* (April 1980), 175–187.
20. See Claude S. George, Jr., *The History of Management Thought*, 2nd ed. (Englewood Cliffs, N.J.: Prentice-Hall, 1972), and Daniel A. Wren, *The Evolution of Management Thought* (New York: Ronald Press, 1972).
21. Gregory Streib, "Applying Strategic Decision Making in Local Government," *Public Productivity and Management Review*, 15, No. 3 (Spring 1992), 341–353.
22. Harold Koontz, "A Model for Analyzing the Universality and Transferability of Management," *Academy of Management Journal* (December 1969), 416.
23. Henry H. Albers, *Principles of Management: A Modern Approach*, 4th ed. (New York: Wiley, 1974), p. 4.
24. See, for example, B. D. Owens, "Decision Theory in Academic Administration," *Academy of Management Journal* (June 1968), 221–232.
25. See, for example, Thomas D. Clark, Jr., and William A. Schrode, "Public-Sector Decision Structures: An Empirically-Based Description," *Public Administration Review* (July–August 1979), 343–354.
26. Robert Albanese, *Managing: Toward Accountability for Performance*, 3rd ed. (Homewood, Ill.: Richard D. Irwin, 1981), p. 8.
27. Simon, *New Science of Management Decision*, p. 1.
28. J. J. Servan-Schreiber, *The American Challenge* (New York: Atheneum, 1968).
29. Richard J. Barnet and Ronald E. Muller, *Global Reach: The Power of Multinational Corporations* (New York: Simon & Schuster, 1974).
30. George R. Terry and Stephen G. Franklin, *Principles of Management*, 8th ed. (Homewood, Ill.: Richard D. Irwin, 1982), p. 36.
31. Dalton E. McFarland, *Management: Formulations and Practices*, 5th ed. (New York: Macmillan, 1979).
32. See Emory and Niland, *Making Management Decisions*, pp. 1–22.
33. See John Aitchison, *Choice Against Chance: An Introduction to Statistical Decision Theory* (Reading, Mass.: Addison-Wesley, 1970); D. V. Lindley, *Making Decisions* (New York: Wiley-Interscience, 1971); and Albert N. Halter and Gerald W. Dean, *Decisions Under Uncertainty with Research Applications* (Cincinnati: South-Western, 1971).
34. See Rossall J. Johnson, *Executive Decisions*, 2nd ed. (Cincinnati: South-Western, 1970); Francis J.

Bridges, Kenneth W. Olm, and J. Allison Barn-hill, *Management Decisions and Organizational Policy*, 2nd ed. (Boston: Allyn and Bacon, 1977); and Alvar O. Elbing, *Behavioral Decisions in Organizations*, 2nd ed. (Glenview, Ill.: Scott, Foresman, 1978).

35. See Costello and Zalkind, *Psychology in Administration*, and Marcus Alexis and Charles Z. Wilson, eds., *Organizational Decision Making* (Englewood Cliffs, N.J.: Prentice-Hall, 1967).

36. One possible exception is the book by Shull, Delbecq, and Cummings, *Organizational Decision Making*, in which the authors focus mainly on the behavioral sciences, but not within a decision-making process. A second possible exception is the excellent book by Ronald J. Ebert and Terence R. Mitchell, *Organizational Decision Processes* (New York: Crane, Russak, 1975), in which the authors treat nearly every aspect of decision making, but still not within any sort of integrated process.

37. For example, see A. J. Eccles and D. Wood, "How Do Managers Decide?" *The Journal of Management Studies*, 9 (October 1972), 291–302; John H. Harvey, "Determinants of the Perception of Choice," *Journal of Experimental Social Psychology* (March 1973), 164–179; and Ronald J. Taylor, "Perceptions of Problem Constraints," *Management Science*, 22 (September 1975), 22–29.

38. Robin M. Hogarth, *Judgement and Choice* (New York: Wiley, 1980), p. ix.

39. Mark P. Kriger and Louis B. Barnes, "Organizational Decision-Making as Hierarchical Levels of Drama," *Journal of Management Studies*, 29, No. 4 (July 1992), 439–457.

40. Streib, "Applying Strategic Decision Making in Local Government," p. 349.

41. See A. H. Maslow, "A Theory of Human Motivation," *Psychological Review*, 50, (1943), 370–396.

42. For a comprehensive delineation of Maslow's concept of self-actualization, see Francis Heylighen, "A Cognitive-Systematic Reconstruction of Maslow's Theory of Self-Actualization," *Behavioral Science* (January 1992), 39–58.

43. See, for example, D. E. Broadbent, "Aspects of Human Decision Making," *Advancement of Science*, 24 (September 1967), 53–64.

44. For a more complete exposition of the characteristics of individual decision makers, see

L. P. Schrenk, "Aiding the Decision Maker — A Decision Process Model," *Ergonomics*, 12 (July 1969), 543–557.

45. J. Edward Russo and Paul J. H. Shoemaker, "Managing Overconfidence," *Sloan Management Review* (Winter 1992), 7–17.

46. This listing was excerpted with appropriate modifications from Gerardo R. Ungson and Daniel N. Braunstein, *Decision Making: An Interdisciplinary Inquiry* (Boston: Kent, 1982), pp. 95–96.

47. A. Tversky, "Elimination by Aspects: A Theory of Choice," *Psychological Review*, 79 (1972), 281–299.

48. Alexis and Wilson, *Organizational Decision Making*, pp. 73–74.

49. Walter C. Swap and Associates, eds., *Group Decision Making* (Beverly Hills, Calif.: Sage, 1984), p. 9.

50. See B. Aubrey Fisher, "Decision Emergence: Phases in Group Decision Making," *Speech Monographs*, 38 (March 1970), 53–66.

51. See Charles R. Holloman and Hal W. Hendrick, "Adequacy of Group Decisions as a Function of the Decision-Making Process," *Academy of Management Journal* (June 1972), 175–184.

52. Hugh J. Haley and Brendon G. Rule, "Group Composition Effects on Risk Taking," *Journal of Personality*, 39 (March 1971), 150–161.

53. John A. Dunn, Jr., "Organizational Decision Making," in *Group Decision Making*, ed. Walter C. Swap and Associates (Beverly Hills, Calif.: Sage, 1984), p. 307.

54. Ibid., pp. 307–308.

55. See Maneck S. Wadia, "Management and the Behavioral Sciences: A Conceptual Scheme," *California Management Review* (Fall 1965), 65–72, for a discussion of the relationships among individuals, groups, and organizations.

56. See, for example, E. Eugene Carter, "The Behavioral Theory of the Firm and Top-Level Corporate Decisions," *Administrative Science Quarterly*, 16 (December 1971), 413–428.

57. Alexis and Wilson, *Organizational Decision Making*.

58. Ibid., p. 76.

59. See Gordon A. Kingsley and Pamela N. Reed, "Decision Process Models and Organizational Context: Level and Sector Make a Difference," *Public Productivity & Management Review* (Summer 1991), 397–413; and Patricia Doyle Corner et al., "Integrating Organizational and Individual Information Processing Perspectives on

Choice," *Organization Science*, 5, No. 3 (August 1994), 294–308.

60. See, for example, James G. March and Johan P. Olsen, *Ambiguity and Choice in Organizations*, 2nd ed. (Bergen, Norway: Universitetsforlaget, 1979).

61. Bass, *Organizational Decision Making*, p. 19.

62. See, for example, William J. Baumol and Richard E. Quandt, "Rules of Thumb and Optimally Imperfect Decisions," *American Economic Review*, 54 (March 1964), 23–46.

63. See John W. Sutherland, *Administrative Decision-Making: Extending the Bounds of Rationality* (New York: Van Nostrand Reinhold, 1977), especially Chapter 1, "Sources of Suboptimality," pp. 1–50.

64. Alexis and Wilson, *Organizational Decision Making*, pp. 76–78.

65. Charles A. O'Reilly, III, "The Use of Information in Organizational Decision Making: A Model and Some Propositions," in *Research in Organizational Behavior*, vol. 5, ed. L. L. Cummings and B. M. Staw (Greenwich, Conn.: JAI Press, Inc., 1983), pp. 103–139.

66. Amitai Etzioni, "Humble Decision Making," *Harvard Business Review* (July–August 1989), 122–126.

67. See James G. March, "Decision Making Perspective," in *Perspectives on Organization Design and Behavior*, ed. A. H. Van de Ven and W. F. Joyce (New York: Wiley-Interscience, 1981), pp. 205–248; and James G. March and Johan P. Olsen, eds., *Ambiguity and Choice in Organizations*, 2nd ed. (Bergen, Norway: Universitetsforlaget, 1979).

68. See Ungson and Braunstein, *Decision Making: An Interdisciplinary Inquiry*, pp. 96–107, for a more complete discussion of these points and references.

69. Streib, "Applying Strategic Decision Making in Local Government," p. 348.

70. See Harold Koontz and Heinz Weihrich, *Essentials of Management*, 5th ed. (New York: McGraw-Hill, 1990), for a description of the basic functions of the manager.

71. Simon, *New Science of Management Decision*, p. 1.

72. See Wadia, "Management and the Behavioral Sciences," pp. 66–67.

73. See Wilmar F. Bernthal, "Value Perspectives in Management Decisions," *Journal of the Academy of Management* (December 1962), 193, 196, for a discussion of objectives at the level of the system of enterprise.

74. Ibid., p. 194.

75. See George J. Church, "How Reagan Decides," *Time* (December 13, 1982), 12ff.

76. Martin Patchen, "Decision Theory in the Study of National Action: Problems and a Proposal," *Journal of Conflict Resolution* (June 1965), 165–176.

77. Simon, *New Science of Management Decision*, pp. 5–6.

78. Peter Drucker, *The Effective Executive* (New York: Harper & Row, 1967), pp. 122–125.

79. Andre L. Delbecq, "The Management of Decision-Making Within the Firm: Three Strategies for Three Types of Decision-Making," *Academy of Management Journal* (December 1967), 329–339.

80. William J. Gore, "Decision-Making Research: Some Prospects and Limitations," in *Concepts and Issues in Administrative Behavior*, ed. Sidney Mailick and Edward H. Van Ness (Englewood Cliffs, N.J.: Prentice-Hall, 1962), pp. 49–65.

81. Ibid., p. 58.

82. Daniel Stufflebeam et al. *Educational Evaluation and Decision-Making* (Itasca, Ill.: Peacock Publishers, 1971).

83. Brian Sharples, "Rational Decision-Making in Education: Some Concerns," *Educational Administration Quarterly*, 11 (Spring 1975), 55–65.

84. Henry Mintzberg, "Strategy-Making in Three Modes," *California Management Review* (Winter 1973), 44–53.

85. Ibid., p. 49.

86. See James D. Thompson, *Organizations in Action* (New York: McGraw-Hill, 1967), pp. 134–135; Christopher Rowe, "Analyzing Management Decision-Making: Further Thoughts After the Bradford Studies," *Journal of Management Studies* (January 1989), 29–46; and Richard Butler, *Designing Organizations: A Decision-Making Perspective* (New York and London: Routledge, 1991), 59–61.

87. See Ulysses S. Knotts, Jr., and Ernest W. Swift, *Management Science for Management Decisions* (Boston: Allyn and Bacon, 1978), for examples of techniques that compose a computational strategy.

88. See Peer Soelberg, "Unprogrammed Decision Making," in *Studies in Managerial Process and Organizational Behavior*, ed. John H. Turner, Allan C.

Filley, and Robert H. House (Glenview, Ill.: Scott, Foresman, 1972), pp. 135–144, for a discussion of the use of a judgmental strategy.

89. See Charles E. Lindblom, "The Science of 'Muddling Through.'" *Public Administration Review*, 19 (1959), 79–88, for a discussion of the rationale underlying the use of a compromise strategy.

90. See Irvin Summers and Major David E. White, "Creativity Techniques: Toward Improvement of the Decision Process." *Academy of Management Review*, 1 (April 1976), 99–107, for a presentation of the use of an inspirational strategy.

91. Soelberg, "Unprogrammed Decision Making," p. 135.

92. See Drucker, *The Effective Executive*, for further development of this point.

93. For a proposed composite approach to the making of category II decisions, see Harvey J. Brightman, "Differences in Ill-Structured Problem Solving Along the Organizational Hierarchy," *Decision Sciences*, 9 (January 1978), 1–18.

94. Soelberg, "Unprogrammed Decision Making," p. 136.

95. David J. Hickson, ed., *Managerial Decision Making* (England: Dartmouth, 1995), p. xi.

96. Cornell, *The Decision Maker's Handbook*, p. 10.

97. McLaughlin, Strengthening Executive Decision Making."

98. For a comprehensive discussion of the relationship between planning and control, see E. Frank Harrison, *Management and Organizations* (Boston: Houghton Mifflin, 1978), pp. 196–199.

99. For a conceptual approach to the making of different types of decisions at different levels of management, see Thomas A. Petit, "A Behavioral Theory of Management," *Journal of the Academy of Management* (December 1967), 341–350.

100. Ibid., p. 446.

101. For more detailed analyses of providing for the effects of organizational change resulting from managerial decision making, see Frank A. Heller, *Managerial Decision Making* (London: Tavistock, 1971); and Victor H. Vroom and Phillip W. Yetton, *Leadership and Decision Making* (Pittsburgh: University of Pittsburgh Press, 1973).

102. Donald S. Watson, *Price Theory and Its Uses*, 2nd ed. (Boston: Houghton Mifflin, 1968), p. 148.

103. See, for example, Leonard J. Kazmier, *Statistical Analysis for Business and Economics*, 3rd ed. (New York: McGraw-Hill, 1978), pp. 342–343, 384–387.

104. See J. Scott Armstrong, "The Value of Formal Planning for Strategic Decisions: Review of Empirical Research," *Strategic Management Journal*, 3 (1982), 197–211; and Deepak K. Sinka, "The Contribution of Formal Planning to Decisions," *Strategic Management Journal*, 11 (1990), 479–492.

SUPPLEMENTAL REFERENCES

Amey, Lloyd R., ed. *Readings in Management Decision*. London: Longman, 1973.

Axelrod, Robert, ed. *Structure of Decision*. Princeton, N.J.: Princeton University Press, 1976.

Bass, Bernard M., *Organizational Decision Making*. Homewood, Ill.: Irwin, 1983.

Beach, Lee Roy. *Making the Right Decision*. Englewood Cliffs, N.J.: Prentice-Hall, 1993.

Braybrooke, David, and Charles E. Lindblom. *A Strategy of Decision*. New York: Free Press, 1963.

Bross, Irwin D. J. *Design of Decision*. New York: Free Press, 1953.

Chia, Robert. "The Concept of Decision: A Deconstructive Analysis." *Journal of Management Studies*, 31, No. 6 (November 1994), 781–806.

Dawson, Roger. *The Confident Decision Maker*. New York: Morrow, 1993.

Donaldson, Gordon, and Jay W. Lorsch. *Decision Making at the Top*. New York: Basic Books, 1983.

Duncan, W. Jack. *Decision Making and Social Issues*. Hinsdale, Ill.: Dryden Press, 1973.

Fisk, George, ed. *The Psychology of Management Decision*. Lund, Sweden: CWK Gleerup, 1967.

Hill, Percy H., et al. *Making Decisions: A Multidisciplinary Introduction*. Reading, Mass.: Addison-Wesley, 1978.

Hogarth, Robin M. *Judgment and Choice*. New York: Wiley, 1980.

Jennings, David, and Stuart Wattam. *Decision Making: An Integrated Approach*. London: Pitman, 1994.

Jones, Manley Howe. *Executive Decision Making*. Homewood, Ill.: Richard D. Irwin, 1962.

Lamb, Robert Boyden, ed. *Competitive Strategic Management*. Englewood Cliffs, N.J.: Prentice-Hall, 1984.

Linstone, Harold A. *Multiple Perspectives for Decision Making*. New York: North-Holland, 1984.

March, James G., and Herbert A. Simon. *Organizations*. New York: Wiley, 1958.

Miller, David W., and Martin K. Starr. *The Structure of Human Decisions*. Englewood Cliffs, N.J.: Prentice-Hall, 1967.

Mockler, Robert J. *Management Decision Making and Action in Behavioral Situations*. Austin, Texas: Austin Press, 1973.

Nutt, Paul C. *Making Tough Decisions*. San Francisco: Jossey-Bass, 1989.

Pennings, Johannes M., and Associates. *Organizational Strategy and Change*. San Francisco: Jossey-Bass, 1985.

Saaty, Thomas L. *Decision Making for Leaders*. Belmont, Calif.: Wadsworth, 1982.

Shapira, Zur, ed. *Organizational Decision Making*. New York: Cambridge University Press, 1997.

Simon, Herbert A. *Administrative Behavior*. 4th ed. New York: Free Press, 1997.

_____. *Models of Man*. New York: Wiley, 1957.

Sjoberg, Lennart, Tadeusz Tyszka, and James A. Wise, eds. *Human Decision Making*. Bodafors, Sweden: Bokforlaget Doxa, 1983.

Tuite, Matthew, Roger Chisholm, and Michael Radnor, eds. *Interorganizational Decision Making*. Chicago: Aldine, 1972.

Weber, C. Edward, and Gerald Peters. *Management Action: Models of Administrative Decisions*. Scranton, Pa.: International Textbook, 1969.

Young, Stanley. *Management: A Decision-Making Approach*. Belmont, Calif.: Dickenson, 1968.

CHAPTER TWO

The Decision-Making Process

*O*ne of the major themes of this book is that decision making in formal organizations should take place as an interrelated and dynamic process. Since the making of decisions in the real world is often unstructured,[1] a process-oriented approach may seem different from traditional ways of arriving at a choice. Nonetheless, the benefits of this approach are considerable, and its use seems certain to improve managerial decision making in organizations of all types. Moreover, business executives, government administrators, military officers, and managers in any type of formal organization all perform the several functions that make up the decision-making process. In effect, then, the process approach provides a comprehensive framework for students intent on learning about management, as well as a means for practicing managers to evaluate and improve their own performance as decision makers.

The definition of decision making as a process consisting of several functions is advantageous for several reasons: (1) it indicates the dynamic nature of decision making; (2) it depicts decision-making activities as occurring over varying spans of time; (3) it implies that the decision-making process is continuous and, thus, that it is an ever-present reality of organizational life; and (4) it suggests that, at least to some extent, managerial decision making can direct and control the nature, degree, and pace of change within the organization.

NATURE OF THE PROCESS

There are various views on the process of decision making. Simon assigns three major elements to the process: (1) finding occasions for making a decision, (2) finding possible courses of action, and (3) choosing among courses of action.[2] Witte advances the notion of decision making as a total process involving discernible and separate activities: (1) information gathering, (2) development of alternatives, (3) evaluation of alternatives, and (4) choices.[3] The process espoused by Schrenk focuses on three elements: (1) problem recognition, (2) problem diagnosis, and (3) action selection.[4] Janis envisions a decision-making process with five stages: (1) recognition of a challenge, (2) acceptance of the challenge, (3) meeting the challenge through a choice, (4) committing oneself to the choice, and (5) adherence to the choice.[5] Eilon advances a comprehensive process composed of eight stages, which begins with information input and culminates in a choice.[6] Mintzberg and his associates offer an incredibly complex formal structure derived from twenty-five "unstructured" decision-making processes that are then organized into a general model of interrelated strategic decision processes.[7] Fredrikson proposes a method for organizing noneconomic criteria in a decision-making process that includes four stages: (1) developing a criteria set, (2) posing criteria questions, (3) scaling the responses, and (4) choosing among alternatives.[8] Nutt advances a decision-making process made up of: (1) exploring possibilities, (2) assessing options, (3) testing assumptions, and (4) learning.[9] Kickert and van Gigch propose a process leading to the decisions about the organization of the decision-making process."[10] And, finally, Holsapple and Moskowitz set forth several principal constraints that limit the use of whatever decision-making process is being used.[11]

There is no doubt that the process-oriented approach to managerial decision making is on the rise.[12] In this book we will consider the decision-making process from a three-dimensional perspective. We base this perspective on the premise that decision making is synonymous with management, and, therefore, the process of decision making should have as its central focus the management of formal organizations. The first dimension of decision making is the individual functions of the process, each with certain inherent properties. The second dimension is the total process, characterized by a host of interrelationships among its functions and by certain properties of its own. The third dimension is the dynamism of the total process, which is a product of the properties and relationships of the individual functions and the total process.

The Functions of Decision Making

The components of the decision-making process are the functions of decision making. This definition is in keeping with the standard definition of a **function** as "one of a group of related actions contributing to a larger action."[13] In a social science context, the concept of function

> involves the notion of a structure consisting of a set of relations among unit entities, the continuity of the structure being maintained by a life-process made up of the activities of the constituent units. . . . "Function" is the contribution which a partial activity makes to the total activity of which it is a part.[14]

The functions of decision making are:

1. **Setting managerial objectives.** The decision-making process starts with the setting of objectives, and a given cycle within the process culminates upon reaching the objectives that gave rise to it. The next complete cycle begins with the setting of new objectives.

2. **Searching for alternatives.** In the decision-making process, search involves scanning the internal and external environments of the organization

for information. Relevant information is formulated into alternatives that seem likely to fulfill the objectives.

3. **Comparing and evaluating alternatives.** Alternatives represent various courses of action that singly or in combination may help attain the objectives. By formal and informal means alternatives are compared based on the certainty or uncertainty of cause-and-effect relationships and the preferences of the decision maker for various probabilistic outcomes.

4. **The act of choice.** Choice is a moment in the ongoing process of decision making when the decision maker chooses a given course of action from among a set of alternatives.

5. **Implementing the decision.** Implementation causes the chosen course of action to be carried out within the organization. It is that moment in the total decision-making process when the choice is transformed from an abstraction into an operational reality.

6. **Follow-up and control.** This function is intended to ensure that the implemented decision results in an outcome that is in keeping with the objectives that gave rise to the total cycle of functions within the decision-making process.

Decision Making: An Interrelated Process

The functions of decision making are highly interrelated within the decision-making process. Bass notes the interrelatedness of the process as follows:

> Decision making is an orderly process beginning with the discovery by the decision maker of a discrepancy between the perceived state of affairs and the desired state. This desired state is usually between an ideal and a realistically attainable state. Alternative actions . . . are selected or invented. One of these alternatives emerges as the action of choice followed by justification for it. Then comes its authorization and implementation. The process cycle is completed with feedback about whether the action resulted in movement toward the desired state of affairs. If the perceived and desired state of affairs have not narrowed sufficiently, a new cycle is likely to commence.[15]

Figure 2.1 illustrates the interrelationships among the functions of decision making set forth in this book. The process begins with the setting of objectives the attainment of which requires a search for information. The analysis of the information derived from the search compares the alternatives discovered in light of (1) attaining the objectives, (2) the opportunity costs of alternatives not selected, and (3) likely internal effects on the organization following a choice. The comparison considers the trade-off values among these features and a choice is made based on the **trade-off values.***

Trade-off value means that some amount of one kind of performance may be substituted for another kind of performance — for example, an increase in the probability of attaining objectives may be worth an adverse internal effect on the organization.

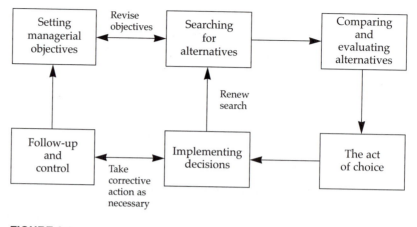

FIGURE 2.1

The Decision-Making Process

The chosen alternative is normally implemented through established organizational structures and processes. At this point the decision is implemented. For follow-up and control of the implemented decision, established information systems quickly reveal to management the actual outcome of the decision. Thus, management can determine how implementation affects the intended outcome inherent in the managerial objectives.

The success of the decision-making process is highly dependent on the functions that are the components of the process. **Success** in this context means the attainment of the objectives that started the process. "You cannot have a partial . . . decision-making process; you either have the whole, unified process or you have nothing."[16] The process is normally sequential, rather than hit-or-miss. For example, if managerial objectives are absent, there is no basis for a search. Without the information obtained through a search, there are no alternatives to compare. Without a comparison of alternatives, the choice of a particular course of action is unlikely to yield desired results. Without effective implementation of a choice, the actual outcome of the decision is unlikely to be the attainment of the managerial objectives. And, finally, in the absence of follow-up and control, the successful implementation of a decision is difficult. Thus the functions constituting the decision-making process must be organized if the process is to accomplish its purposes effectively. We can easily demonstrate the interrelatedness of the process by starting with any one of the functions of decision making and working forward or backward through the process. There is a definite need for a framework that organizes the functions of decision making, if only to improve the making of managerial decisions in formal organizations. The framework illustrated in Figure 2.1 shows both the interrelatedness of the functions and their sequential organization.

Decision Making: A Dynamic Process

"Decision making is a dynamic process: complex, redolent with feedback and sideways, full of search detours, information gathering, and information ignoring, fueled by fluctuating uncertainty, fuzziness, and conflict; it is an organic unity of both predecision and postdecision stages."[17]

The dynamics of the decision-making process are centered in the interrelationships between and among the functions of decision making.

> A [decision-making] function is thus not a separate entity but an integral part of a larger entity made up of various functions that are related to one another as well as to the larger entity. Hence . . . the total is different from the sum of its parts. Only . . . [when] viewed in this light does the [decision-making] process emerge as truly dynamic.[18]

This passage suggests that the dynamics of the decision-making process result from the effects of the decision-making functions on one another in combination, and that, isolated from the process, the decision-making functions might not be performed in the best way. **Synergy*** in the decision-making process results from effective interaction among the functions that make up the process. Synergy contributes to the process a positive element that is not obtainable from the simple, independent performance of a series of discrete actions. Synergy, then, is one of the principal benefits of the dynamics of the decision-making process.

The dynamics of the decision-making process will now be described in terms of the principal subprocesses among the functions of decision making depicted in Figure 2.1.

The first subprocess begins when it becomes apparent to management through the function of follow-up and control that corrective action is necessary to ensure that the implemented decision results in the attainment of the managerial objectives. Such corrective action may involve (1) reordering operations, (2) rescheduling work flow, (3) reassigning personnel, or (4) doing some combination of these three measures. The second subprocess begins when management realizes that the corrective action necessary to effectively implement the original decision is not working or is too costly to continue. At this point, the search may be renewed to identify new, more practical alternatives or to reconsider alternatives that were judged to be second or third best in the initial cycle of decision making. The third subprocess is a last resort to be taken when corrective action at the point of implementation has failed and a renewed search has not produced another viable choice. This subprocess involves a revision of managerial objectives. It may be, for example,

---

*In this book *synergy* is defined as "the optimal integration of what was formerly differentiated." This definition is borrowed from Charles Hampden-Turner, "Synergy as the Optimization of Differentiation and Integration by the Human Personality," in *Studies in Organizational Design,* eds. Jay W. Lorsch and Paul R. Laurence (Homewood, Ill.: Irwin and Dorsey Press, 1970), p. 187.

that the objectives are too ambitious and therefore unattainable without extraordinary effort and expense. If so, a scaling down to a level within the capabilities of the organization may be mandatory. If, on the other hand, the point of implementation reveals that objectives are too easy to attain, they should be escalated through a renewed search to match the capabilities of the organization.

The decision-making process as depicted in Figure 2.1 is especially applicable to the category II decisions described in Chapter 1. These are the basically nonroutine and nonrecurring choices with a good deal of uncertainty of outcome. As such, they require the full decision-making process. On the other hand, category I decisions, which by definition are routine, recurring, and less uncertain, do not require all the steps set forth in Figure 2.1. If, for example, a particular type of decision tended to recur often, there would be no need to repeatedly search for alternatives. Most likely, a policy or a procedure would be established to handle such decisions. But at the beginning, before it becomes evident that a decision belongs in category I, the full decision-making process is applicable. The subprocesses of identifying new alternatives and taking corrective action in the presence of implementation difficulties may also render the process applicable to category I choices.

Nonrecurring choices of a rather routine nature also do not require the full sequence of decision making, especially where the outcome is fairly certain. In summary, then, the total decision-making process of Figure 2.1 is most applicable to category II decisions.

It is apparent that the decision-making process is both highly interrelated and dynamic. Each individual decision-making function is a kind of microcosm in that it has certain inherent properties of its own. Still it is the macrocosm — the total decision-making process, in which all of the decision-making functions interact in concert to produce the synergistic effects necessary to attain the managerial objectives — that is of primary concern to students and managers alike. The dynamics of the decision-making process are inherent in the interrelatedness of the decision-making functions. Such functions are accomplished in a sequential and interrelated fashion in the first instance and, as necessary modifications and revisions are made, through the several subprocesses in succeeding instances.

Having discussed the dynamics of the total decision-making process, we will now turn to a more detailed description of each of the functions of the process with a view toward clarifying each function's significance for effective management.

SETTING MANAGERIAL OBJECTIVES

The foundation of the decision-making process lies in the objectives that give it purpose, direction, and continuity.[19] The setting of managerial objectives is the first function of decision making, and attainment of the objectives represents the culmination of a given cycle within the decision-making process.

Objectives, which underlie the effective management of any type of formal organization, are not abstractions. They are the commitments to action through which the mission of the organization is carried out, and they are the standards against which the performance of management is measured. "If objectives are only good intentions they are worthless. They must degenerate into work. And work is always specific, always has — or should have — unambiguous, measurable results, a deadline and a specific assignment of responsibility."[20] The importance of objectives as a foundation for the managerial decision-making process is expressed in the following statement of the principle of the objective: "Before initiating any course of action, the objectives in view must be clearly determined, understood, and stated."[21] *Thus an objective may be defined as the end point toward which management directs its decision making.*

It is particularly useful to differentiate between the terms **objective** and **goal.** "An objective is a specific category of purpose that includes the attainment by an organization of certain states or conditions; a goal may be viewed as a subset of an objective, expressed in terms of one or more specific dimensions."[22]

Advantages of Managerial Objectives

Objectives are required for all activities that contribute to the basic purposes of the organization. Objectives enable management to plan and organize such activities. With objectives, management explains the whole range of organizational phenomena in a small number of general statements that can be tested in practice. Objectives enable managers to appraise the soundness of their decisions while they are being made; and objectives offer a framework for predicting and analyzing managerial performance in pursuing successful outcomes of decisions.[23]

Objectives serve as yardsticks for measuring, comparing, and evaluating the success of decisions in accomplishing organizational purposes. Indeed objectives serve as the basis for rational decision making by managers in formal organizations. Objectives can also be good motivators because they make it easier for individuals to relate the reaching of personal goals to the work of the organization. They know what is expected of them and are, thus, more certain of how to carry out their duties and responsibilities. In turn, they are able to serve themselves and the organization more efficiently. Managerial objectives, then, provide a means to fuse the fulfillment of human needs and the accomplishment of the organizational mission.

The Hierarchy of Managerial Objectives

Managerial objectives tend to create a kind of hierarchy that can be related to the formal structure of managerial responsibilities and authority.

In complex organizations objectives are structured in a hierarchy in which the objectives of each unit contribute to the objectives of the next higher unit. And a broad objective . . . states the purpose of the entire organization. This is true of all organizations — military, educational, government, and business.[24]

In effect, there are "objectives within objectives within objectives."[25] A useful technique for analyzing the hierarchy of objectives in a formal organization is to view it as a means-end chain.[26] As Simon explains, "The fact that [objectives] may be dependent for their force on other more distant ends leads to the arrangement of these [objectives] in a hierarchy — each level to be considered as an end relative to the levels below it and a means relative to the levels above it."[27]

Managerial objectives, then, serve as a primary function of decision making that initiates and completes a given cycle within the decision-making process *and* they also link together the total organization by fostering common purpose and unified action. The sum of all the objectives below the level of top management serves as a means to attain the objectives of the total organization. This in turn permits the organization to accomplish its basic purposes. In one sense, therefore, all objectives are means, although, at various times and depending on its level in the hierarchy, a given objective will also serve as an end.

Characteristics of Managerial Objectives

One approach to ensuring that managerial objectives possess the characteristics essential for successful decision making is to make them satisfy relevant criteria. Such criteria may be applied by asking a series of questions:

1. *Relevance.* Are the objectives related to and supportive of the basic purposes of the organization?
2. *Practicality.* Do the objectives recognize obvious constraints?
3. *Challenge.* Do the objectives provide a challenge for managers at all levels in the organization?
4. *Measurability.* Can the objectives be quantified, if only in an order-of-importance ranking?
5. *Scheduling ability.* Can the objectives be scheduled and monitored at interim points to ensure progress toward their attainment?
6. *Balance.* Do the objectives provide for a proportional emphasis on all activities and keep the strengths and weaknesses of the organization in proper balance?
7. *Flexibility.* Are the objectives sufficiently flexible or is the organization likely to find itself locked into a particular course of action?
8. *Timeliness.* Given the environment within which the organization operates, is this the proper time to adopt these objectives?
9. *State of the art.* Do the objectives fall within the boundaries of current technological development?

10. *Growth.* Do the objectives point toward the growth of the organization, rather than toward mere survival?

11. *Cost effectiveness.* Are the objectives cost effective in that the anticipated benefits clearly exceed the expected costs?

12. *Accountability.* Are the assignments for the attainment of the objectives made in a way that permits the assessment of performance on the part of individual managers throughout the organization?

If a given set of managerial objectives meets most of these criteria, it possesses the characteristics essential to effective decision making at all levels of management. Such objectives will provide adequate guidance for managerial decision making and are unlikely to be displaced by nonpurposive behavior. The displacement of objectives occurs when the means to an end becomes an end in itself, and the attainment of managerial objectives is highest where displacement is minimal.[28]

SEARCHING FOR ALTERNATIVES

Once the managerial objectives are set, the next function in the decision-making process is the search for information from which to fashion alternatives. For purposes of explanation, this function of decision making will be simply designated as **search** or **search activity.** Like the other functions of decision making, it is accomplished by individuals enacting managerial roles as decision makers at the level of the organization. Managers are susceptible to the myriad limitations of most human decision makers. "Much evidence indicates that superficial information search and processing biases cause gross errors in human decision making."[29] It is appropriate to repeat here that human decision makers at the level of the organization manifest at least the following imperfections and flaws in searching for alternatives from which to arrive at a choice:

1. They gather information and then don't use it.
2. They ask for more information and tend to ignore it.
3. They often make decisions first and look for the relevant information afterward.
4. They tend to gather a great deal of information that has little or no relevance to the decision-making situation at hand.[30]

The focus in this book is on the way that search activity *should* be accomplished as an integral part of the decision-making process. The seemingly limitless imperfections in managers' search activity do not reduce the need to improve this part of the decision-making process. In this context, the assumptions underlying search at the level of the organization set forth by Cyert and March are particularly relevant.[31]

1. *Search is motivated.* The motivation for search from this book's viewpoint is to develop a set of alternatives from which to make a choice the implementation of which is likely to result in the attainment of a managerial objective.

2. *Search is simplistic.* Management has an abiding desire to simplify its models of search for economic reasons and to accommodate its own cognitive limitations.

3. *Search is biased.* Managers are individuals and human decision makers first and foremost. Their role as agents of the organization does not divest them of the human frailty for bias.[32]

Perspectives on Search Activity

In some ways search is like prospecting. One assumes that the objects of search are passive elements distributed in some manner throughout the environment. Alternatives and information about them are obtained as a result of deliberate search. However, information does not always come to decision makers in this way. In fact, it may be more realistic to think of search as a mating process. That is, not only are decision makers looking for alternatives but alternatives are looking for decision makers.[33]

Contrary to some opinions, the search for alternatives is parallel rather than sequential. The decision maker considers several potentially acceptable alternatives at the same time. The evaluation of each is a multistage affair; at each step new information is collected and evaluated about some of the attributes of a given alternative.

During the search activity, the decision maker seldom views his or her evaluation of alternatives as final. The ones that do not possess important attributes of the objective are rejected immediately, but acceptable alternatives are kept in the decision maker's active file until he or she is ready to make a choice. In fact, the decision maker may well continue the search for better alternatives even though a perfectly acceptable one in terms of the objective has been found.[34]

In their discussion of the "open model" for decision making, Wilson and Alexis describe two primary levels of search activity. The first is the search for a limited number of alternatives, in which the decision maker employs various methods of scanning to find a few selected alternatives relevant to the objective. The second is the search for a satisfactory solution, which takes the form of a close comparison and evaluation of the alternatives discovered at the first level.[35] If the decision maker perceives the world as providing many good alternatives, only a few will be examined. Of course, the decision maker's subconscious screening mechanism further limits the search activity by rejecting obviously unsuitable alternatives.[36]

Search is obviously motivated by a felt need to obtain information from which to develop a set of alternatives relevant to the managerial objectives at hand. It is not a continuous activity in its own right but, rather, a function of the current cycle in the decision-making process. The search activity will persist as long as acceptable alternatives are not obtained. It will subside within a given cycle of the decision-making process once the decision makers perceive that a sufficient number of acceptable alternatives from which to make a choice have been developed.[37] In a somewhat broader context, however, search is a continuous activity to the extent that decision making is a continuous process.

Search is also an activity that is biased by several factors.

> The desirabilities of alternatives, the interpretations of [objectives], and hence the search for additional alternatives are mediated by human perceptions. Organizations establish rules which limit the range of decision alternatives that will be considered, and these rules are based on past experience. Furthermore, the rules and degree of acceptability (or the criteria for acceptability) will change with the success and failure experiences of the organization.[38]

Managerial values, human perceptions, and the psychological acceptance or avoidance of risk all act together in varying degrees to bias the search for alternatives.

The Structure of Search

There are several ways to describe the structure of the search activity. A somewhat static approach is the four-part classification advanced by Aguilar.

1. **Undirected viewing.** General exposure to information where the viewer has no specific purpose in mind with the possible exception of exploration. Although undirected, this mode of viewing involves a definite orientation by virtue of the selection of particular sources and the general experience and interest of the viewer.

2. **Conditioned viewing.** Directed exposure, not involving active search, to a more or less clearly identified area or type of information. This mode of viewing differs from undirected viewing in that the viewer is sensitive to particular kinds of data and is ready to assess their significance as they are encountered.

3. **Informal search.** A relatively limited and unstructured effort to obtain specific information for a specific purpose. It differs from conditioned viewing in that the information wanted is actively sought. Informal search can take many forms, ranging from soliciting information to increasing the emphasis on relevant sources or acting in a way that will improve the possibility of encountering the desired information.

4. **Formal search.** A deliberate effort — usually following a preestablished plan, procedure, or methodology — to secure specific information relating to a specific issue. It differs from informal search principally in that it is programmed or quasi-programmed in nature.[39]

This book assumes that most of the search activity that acts as a function of the managerial decision-making process is either the third or fourth type. The first and second types seem oriented more toward decision making outside of formal organizations.

Lest one mistakenly assume that the search activity by individuals enacting roles as managerial decision makers at the level of the organization is highly structured, it is useful to recall that

> looked at in the large, organizations exist to suppress data. Some data are screened in but most are screened out. The very structure of organizations — the units, the levels, the hierarchy — is designed to reduce data to manageable and manipulatable proportions. . . . at each level there is not only compression of data but absorption of uncertainty. It is not the things in themselves but data-reduction summaries that are passed up until, at the end, executives are left with mere chains of inferences. Whichever way they go, error is endemic: If they seek original sources, they are easily overwhelmed; if they rely on what they get, they are easily misled.[40]

Managers engaged in search are not only hampered by the structure and processes of their organizations; they are also constrained by their own flaws as human decision makers. For example, managers continually seek a balance in their search activity among (1) the cost of additional information, (2) the amount of the perceived payoffs, and (3) their own levels of aspiration.[41] Moreover, there is still a substantial gap between the quantity of information available and the right kind of information for use in decision making.[42] Even when they have concrete statistical information, managers tend toward situational sources.[43]

In spite of these obvious imperfections, Ebert and Mitchell set forth a fairly dynamic structure of search for use in managerial decision making.[44] The elements of this structure include (1) initiation of search, (2) object(s) of search, and (3) media of search. As noted previously, search is presumed to arise from a felt need for information from which to fashion alternatives that are relevant to managerial objectives. Thus, the object of search, for our purposes, is simply to develop a set of alternatives likely to attain the managerial objectives that initiate a given cycle in the decision-making process.

Ebert and Mitchell delineated the principal media of search as: (1) physical, (2) perceptual, or (3) cognitive.[45] The physical and perceptual media require interaction between the decision maker and his or her environment; whereas the cognitive medium resides in the mind of the decision maker. Obviously these media are all encompassing.

Ference conceptualized a more practical approach to the structure of search.[46] His structure includes (1) contact with other individuals by appropriate means to obtain information, (2) concessions that may be necessary to obtain the information, and (3) recognition of the time required to obtain the information. Ference noted that information received from a given source should be compared for its credibility and its value to similar information received from other sources. Cravens observed that there is still much to learn about the relationship between information processed as a part of the search activity and its use in the decision-making process.[47]

Regardless of how one perceives the structure of the search activity, it seems fairly obvious that the time and effort required to obtain additional information should be considered in relation to the information's value.

The Cost of Additional Information

The search for alternatives is normally conducted with limited time and money. In other words, there is only so much effort that can be devoted to the search activity. Further, no matter how much time and money are spent in pursuit of additional information that can be formulated into alternatives, the search seldom obtains all the information related to a particular objective.[48] Consequently whatever information is gathered during the search activity is always incomplete or imperfect, and the number of alternatives is limited accordingly.[49] And what is more important, the cost of continually trying to perfect information rises exponentially, and the value of additional units of information declines precipitously at some point. This relationship is illustrated in Figure 2.2.

The vertical axis in Figure 2.2 measures the value and cost of additional units of information. Cost should be readily obtainable from the accounting records of an organization, and some value, generally of a monetary nature,

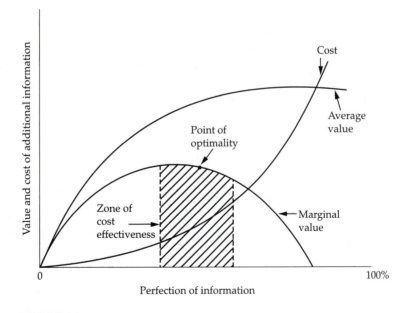

FIGURE 2.2

The Cost of Additional Information

can usually be credited to additional information.[50] The horizontal axis measures the increasing perfection of information from 0 to 100 percent. The area in the plane of Figure 2.2, therefore, reflects the effect on cost and value of additional units of information leading toward perfection.

The cost curve rises rather slowly, because the initial units of information often require relatively little effort. However, as more and more information is sought, it becomes increasingly difficult to obtain, and the cost curve climbs exponentially. The average-value curve in the figure moves in a direction opposite to that of the cost curve. The early units of information increase in value as alternatives resulting from their use begin to take shape at relatively low cost. However, as additional information is sought, the average-value curve declines because the information is worth less than the cost of obtaining it. The average-value curve normally takes some time to turn down, because the cumulative value of the early units of information offsets the sharply rising cost of the later units. There comes a point, however, when the cumulative cost outweighs the cumulative value, and at this point the average-value curve begins to decline.

The marginal-value curve in Figure 2.2 is an even more sensitive indicator of the cost of additional information. It reflects the value of the next unit of information rather than the average cumulative value of all units. The marginal-value curve declines much sooner and more steeply than the average-value curve. The **point of optimality** is the most desirable point on the marginal-value curve, where the next unit of information will decline in marginal value and one less unit will result in a loss in marginal value. It is the point where the marginal value of the last unit is as high as it can be and, thus, where the pursuit of additional information should stop. As a practical matter, however, determining a precise point of optimality is difficult, and, therefore, a **zone of cost effectiveness** around the point of optimality, as shown in Figure 2.2, is much more useful.[51] A zone of cost effectiveness allows the searcher to obtain enough information to formulate alternatives within reasonable time and cost constraints, and it minimizes the possibility of overlooking valuable data. But it also stops the searcher from proceeding with the search to the point where the marginal-value curve becomes negative. (In Figure 2.2, this is the point where the cost curve begins to rise faster than the average-value curve.) The zone of cost effectiveness is, therefore, the best governor for most kinds of search.

COMPARING AND EVALUATING ALTERNATIVES

Once the search yields a sufficient amount of information to fashion a set of alternatives, the next function in the decision-making process is to compare and evaluate these alternatives. This function epitomizes the interrelatedness of the decision-making process. For example, in using the available information to compare and evaluate alternatives, the decision maker must focus on anticipated outcomes that will probably meet the objectives only through follow-up and control after a choice is made and implemented.

The overriding purpose in the decision-making process is to attain the objectives that serve as a foundation for the process. There will be, for any objective, many ways of seeking attainment. Each alternative will produce a different degree of attainment of a given objective and hence a different value of the measure of effectiveness. "The number of alternatives depends on how much effort the decision maker puts into a search for them. Thus, there are possible alternatives which the decision maker is completely unaware of, just as there are alternatives which the decision maker will disregard without consideration."[52] The alternatives are not given but must be sought out by an expenditure of resources.[53] From the known set of alternatives deemed worthy of additional consideration, the decision maker must determine which one is most likely to meet the objective at hand. Thus the decision maker is confronted with the need to make an estimate of effectiveness for each alternative. To accomplish these estimates, the decision maker must have some idea of the relationships between alternatives and outcomes in relation to the objectives.[54]

Comparing and evaluating alternatives

> can be haphazard or orderly. It appears more profitable to be orderly. Yet, more often than not, decision makers make a choice from among alternatives on a fairly haphazard basis. . . . If we consider what should be done, criteria upon which evaluation will be based need to be established. Weights may be attached to each of these criteria. Risk preferences need to be explicated. Outcomes yielding as much gain as possible with the least risk of loss are sought. The consequences of implementing each alternative are estimated as well as the potential new problems generated by each alternative.[55]

The key to making the best decision is to determine what results are wanted, then evaluate the various alternatives toward achieving that objective. The task here is to examine each alternative to determine which will most likely attain the objective with minimum difficulty and risk.[56]

Multidimensional Perspectives

Comparing and evaluating alternatives is typically a multistage, repetitive function involving progressively deeper investigation of various courses of action. Two multistage patterns seem most common in this decision-making function. The first pattern reduces a large number of ready-made alternatives to a few feasible ones, which are then compared and evaluated preparatory to choice and implementation. The second pattern involves a more extensive and multidimensional evaluation of a single alternative that may have emerged from the search activity or evolved from the first pattern.[57]

Janis and Mann graphically describe this decision-making function as follows:

> The decision maker dismisses or eliminates from further consideration any alternative that appears to be ineffectual or too costly. . . . The decision maker

now proceeds to a more thorough [comparison] and evaluation, focusing on the pros and cons of each of the surviving alternatives in an effort to select the best available course of action. . . . he deliberates about the advantages and disadvantages of each alternative until he feels reasonably confident about selecting the one that will best meet his objectives. . . . Any alternative for which the anticipated losses emerge as prohibitive or as incommensurate with the anticipated gains is rejected and precluded from further consideration. . . . [At this stage] the decision maker becomes very careful in his appraisal. . . . he searches for more information to confirm the gains and losses to be expected from [his preferred alternative]. . . .

Sometimes after deliberating about each alternative in turn, the decision maker becomes dissatisfied with all of them. . . . At such times . . . he will . . . attempt to find a new course that might prove to be better than any of the ones he is currently contemplating. . . . Even when he reaches the point of feeling certain that he knows the best choice to make, he will usually be responsive to new information indicating that he may be overlooking an important consideration.[58]

Comparing and evaluating alternatives is usually accomplished in one or some combination of three modes: (1) judgment, (2) bargaining, and (3) analysis. In the judgmental mode, the decision maker arrives at a choice based on experience, values, perception, and intuition. Research has shown that, for the category II type of decisions identified in Chapter 1, judgment appears to be the favored mode of comparing and evaluating alternatives.[59] Possibly this is because it is the fastest, most convenient, and least stressful of the three modes. The bargaining mode is prevalent in decision-making situations where external forces dominate or the choice promises to be controversial. In such situations decision makers seek alternatives that permit the attainment of the managerial objectives as part of a compromise among concerned parties.[60]

Most of the literature in the field of decision theory emphasizes the analytic mode of comparing and evaluating alternatives. This mode "postulates that alternatives are carefully and objectively evaluated, their factual consequences explicitly determined . . . and then combined according to some predetermined utility function — a choice is finally made to maximize utility."[61] However, research also shows that, except for decisions of the category I type, managerial decision makers use the analytical mode very little.[62]

Virtually every student of [decision making] agrees that the selection of strategic alternatives requires consideration of a great number of factors, most of them "soft" or nonquantitative; as a result they find that [the function of comparing and evaluating alternatives] is in practice a crude one. . . . [This function] gets distorted, both by cognitive limitations, that is, by information overload, and by unintended as well as intended biases.[63]

The approach taken in this book is to meaningfully fuse the judgmental, bargaining, and analytic modes of comparing and evaluating alternatives. Here, of course, we refer primarily to category II decisions. The judgmental mode must dominate category II decisions. Still, managerial decision makers may find it quite advantageous to make selective use of the analytic mode. And in decision-making situations where the choice promises to be controversial, selective use of the bargaining mode, in combination with analysis and judgment, appears to favor a choice that will be acceptable to most affected parties after implementation.

A Typology of Alternatives

Decisions made without considering alternatives may have unfortunate consequences. Drucker makes this point succinctly in the following passage:

> Whenever one has to judge, one must have alternatives among which one can choose. A judgment in which one can only say "yes" or "no" is no judgment at all. Only if there are alternatives can one hope to get insight into what is truly at stake. . . . A decision without an alternative is a desperate gambler's throw, no matter how carefully thought through it might be. . . . If one has thought through alternatives during the decision-making process, one has something to fall back on, something that has already been thought through, that has been studied, that is understood. Without such an alternative, one is likely to flounder dismally when reality proves a decision to be inoperative.[64]

March and Simon have developed a useful typology for differentiating alternatives on the basis of expected outcomes.

1. A **good alternative** is one that, if accepted, is likely to result in a positively valued state of affairs for the decision maker.

2. A **bland alternative** is one that, if chosen, is unlikely to produce either a positively or a negatively valued state of affairs for the decision maker.

3. A **mixed alternative** is one that, if undertaken, is likely to result in both a positively and a negatively valued outcome for the decision maker.

4. A **poor alternative** is one that, if chosen, is likely to result in a negatively valued outcome for the decision maker.[65]

In this context it is well to recall that "one alternative is always the alternative of doing nothing."[66]

Even though an obvious need for a decision exists, managerial decision makers should not select poor alternatives where the negatively valued outcome is worse than no decision at all. In such cases, the search activity may be renewed to discover new alternatives or the objectives may be scaled down to a level where attractive alternatives are more readily forthcoming.[67]

In the formulation of alternatives, the decision maker can be guided by his or her previous steps — that is, the objectives of the organization that have been stated, the problems identified and defined, the hypothetical solutions considered, the information gathered and analyzed, and the assumptions made.[68]

The Anticipation of Outcomes

The objective in making a decision, whether at the level of the individual or at the level of the organization, is to choose from among the most promising alternatives the one (or ones) that will produce the largest number of desirable consequences and the smallest number of unwanted consequences. One way to determine which alternative is most desirable is to test each one by imagining that it has already been put into effect. It is then possible to try to trace the most probable desirable and undesirable consequences of adopting that particular alternative.[69]

Within the judgmental mode, analysis may be used to estimate the desirability of the expected consequences of several alternatives. This is done by ordering preferences based on the utility function of the decision maker. Individuals normally exercise a preference for some things over other things. *Utility* literally means want-satisfying power.[70] Utility lies in the mind of the decision maker. It is subjective, not objective. The theory of utility is based on a set of axioms; for example:

1. **Closure axiom.** A person always prefers one of two outcomes or is indifferent.

2. **Transitivity axiom.** If A is preferred to B, and B is preferred to C, then A is preferred to C.

Without the transitivity axiom, for instance, it would be difficult to link the many subpreference systems of the decision maker. Still, utility functions are difficult to establish for decision makers with any degree of precision:

> Each outcome must have an assigned, interval-scaled-value. Structuring utility functions with such properties is not always feasible. Except where money or some easily measurable commodity can be taken as equivalent to measures of utility or at least related in an ascertainable manner, the determination of utilities, or even proof of their existence, is a most difficult matter.[71]

The outcome predictability of alternatives is based on three possible states of nature:

1. **Certainty.** It is assumed that there is complete and accurate knowledge of the consequences of each alternative.

2. **Uncertainty.** The consequences of each alternative cannot be defined even within a probabilistic framework.

3. **Risk.** It is assumed that accurate knowledge exists about the probability distribution of the consequences of each alternative.[72]

Certainty implies a state of awareness on the part of the decision maker that seldom exists, and genuine uncertainty is almost as uncommon. Usually the decision maker is able to assign subjective probabilities to expected outcomes. The more common state of nature is incomplete or imperfect information, which means that the expected outcome contains an element of risk for the decision maker. There are many statistical techniques by which the decision maker can obtain usable estimates of the risk inherent in a particular set of alternatives.

In summary, there are at least five principal components in the decision-making function of comparing and evaluating alternatives.

1. Make an evaluation of the anticipated benefits and costs for each alternative. (Benefits and costs are estimated for all alternatives before closure on any single one.)

2. Develop an estimate of the risks and uncertainties related to the likelihood that a given alternative will result in an outcome that will fully or partially attain the managerial objectives.

3. Make closure on some one alternative or, possibly, some combination of available alternatives. (Closure initiates the process of authorization described in detail by Mintzberg, Raisinghani, and Theoret.)[73]

4. Justify the choice of a given alternative by concentrating further on its attributes for attaining the objectives.

5. Ascertain and evaluate the outcome likely to result from implementing the chosen alternative.[74]

The alternative finally selected must, of course, be the one that seems most likely to meet the managerial objectives. This selection is the act of choice in the overall decision-making process. It is presented in this book as a decision-making function in its own right.

THE ACT OF CHOICE

The act of choice is, in one sense, the high point of the decision-making process. "The *decision* itself is the culmination of the process. Regardless of the problem, the alternatives, the decision aids, or the consequences to follow, once a decision is made, things begin to happen. Decisions trigger action, movement, and change."[75] However, the act of choice is still only a part of the process, not, as is so often assumed, the entire process in itself. In this regard, Simon noted:

> All of these images have a significant point in common. In them, the decision maker is a man at the moment of choice, ready to plant his foot on one or another of the routes that lead from the crossroads. All of the images falsify decision by focusing on its final moment. All of them ignore the whole lengthy, complex process of alerting, exploring, and analyzing that precede that final moment.[76]

Simon's point is well taken. To focus solely on the act of choice is to disregard or minimize all the actions necessary to create the conditions of choice, not to mention the succession of postdecision actions essential to transform the choice into acceptable results.[77] To be sure, if the act of choice "is given exclusive attention, many antecedent and associated phenomena are excluded from analysis."[78]

By now we are familiar with the antecedent phenomena referred to: (1) setting managerial objectives, (2) searching for alternatives, and (3) comparing and evaluating alternatives. And we know that the decision-making process does not stop with the act of choice. It continues on through implementation and follow-up and control, with new alternatives being identified and existing objectives reset or updated to reflect changing conditions and emerging knowledge. Indeed, decision making directed toward the attainment of managerial objectives is a dynamic, interrelated process and not a simple series of discrete actions.

Multidimensional Perspectives

Examining the dynamics of reaching a decision yields further insight into the act of choice:

> The criteria that the decision maker uses for identifying his favorite alternative are very few. . . . The decision maker's comparison among alternatives quickly reduces to a pro-con argument between two, and only two alternatives . . . the objective being for the decision maker to bring his perception of the facts and his evaluation of goal attributes into line with his predisposition that the preferred choice candidate dominates his second-best alternative. . . . The decision maker finally makes his decision when he has constructed himself a satisfactory decision rule — a goal weighting function . . . which enables him to explain the . . . dominance of his choice candidate. (Unless, of course, the decision maker is forced by some deadline to make his decision by that time. If so, however, the decision maker will still choose his choice candidate, but with much more felt uncertainty about the "rightness" of his decision.)[79]

The principal focus in the act of choice is on category II decisions, the nonroutine, nonrecurring, highly uncertain choices. Category II decisions require the use of a judgmental decision-making strategy simply because the decision maker has imperfect knowledge of cause-and-effect relationships. The use of quantitative techniques in comparing and evaluating alternatives can reduce the uncertainty confronting the decision maker. But uncertainty is always present to some degree simply because the decision maker has only incomplete or imperfect information.

The decision maker always considers the alternatives in light of the managerial objectives. Some alternatives will permit the objectives to be attained in part. Very few alternatives will achieve the objectives completely. If the antecedent functions in the decision-making process have been carried out effectively, the choices available to the decision maker will be few in number and of varying complexity. The tendency in the act of choice is to discard the marginally acceptable alternatives. The decision maker concentrates on those choices that are less complex in terms of attaining the managerial objectives.

The cognitive limitations of decision makers weigh against a detailed consideration of many alternatives that are too complex. Ideally the courses of action derived from comparing and evaluating alternatives will be few in number and as noncomplex as possible.

The act of choice confronts the decision maker with discernible constraints in the form of (1) cognitive limitations, (2) incomplete or imperfect information, and (3) time and cost restrictions. Clearly these constraints, in varying intensity and degree, are formidable obstacles to the act of choice.

The act of choice is further impeded by selected psychological forces affecting the decision maker. These forces will be presented more fully in Chapter 6. A brief overview will suffice at this point. In making choices, human decision makers often find themselves harassed by time pressures, distractions, and the use that is made of evidence.[80] Research has also shown that the time taken by decision makers to arrive at a choice is a function of task complexity.[81] More complex choices necessitate more time to reduce errors, which in turn increases cost. Beyond some point both complexity and cost become unacceptable, and the decision maker chooses a course of action that holds additional promise of error. In other cases, decision makers require less justification than they should for choices with apparently desirable outcomes,[82] and spend more time than they should making a choice from a small number of alternatives.[83] Moreover, decision makers tend to credit themselves with a high level of involvement when a choice has favorable consequences and a low level of involvement when the outcome is unfavorable.[84] The act of choice, then, is affected by the decision maker's ego enhancement and ego defense. There is also abundant research to show that decision makers will frequently elect to continue with an existing course of action rather than cope with the uncertainty of a probabilistic outcome ensuing from a difficult or costly choice.[85]

Finally, an abundant literature focuses on the tendency of human decision makers to experience regret and dissonance once a choice is made and the consequences become starkly apparent.[86] There can be little doubt that human frailty pervades the act of choice and renders the entire decision-making process amenable to scrutiny and question at virtually every point.

Models of Choice Making

The decision maker will usually find that the best alternative is not always readily apparent. Even the best decisions will normally be compromises among competing alternatives.[87] The best alternative for the decision maker may be quite distasteful to the people or organizations affected. Ideally, the decision maker should select an alternative that will further as m   ·different objectives as possible. The alternative finally chosen may very that is not the best for a particular objective, but it may further th/ in some degree, of several objectives, without jeopardizing the/ any single one.[88]

A decision is relatively easy to make when one alternative clearly provides more wanted and fewer unwanted results than any other alternative. However, this blissful state is unusual. In fact, decision makers normally encounter several difficulties in choosing among various alternatives:

1. One difficulty arises when two or more alternatives seem equally attractive. If both (or all) will serve equally well, the choice is a matter of indifference and can be made be tossing a coin.

2. Another difficulty arises when it becomes apparent to the decision maker that no *single* alternative will serve the purpose of the choice. In such cases, it may be advisable to employ the best two or three alternatives simultaneously.

3. A further difficulty occurs when the unwanted results or undesirable consequences appear so overwhelming that they immobilize the decision maker. In this case, the search process may be expanded to encompass other alternatives or the objectives may require modification or revision if this is possible.

4. The decision maker may find himself confused by an overabundance of alternatives. In that event, organizing the alternatives into homogeneous groups and intensifying the comparison and evaluation of each group may reveal new attributes or unwanted results that will help simplify the act of choice.

5. Occasionally, it will become evident to the decision maker that none of the alternatives will accomplish the objectives. This difficulty may be resolved by intensifying the search to find new alternatives or by modifying the objectives to accommodate the available alternatives.[89]

The literature on decision making contains numerous approaches to the act of choice. A given approach should be derived from all the principal variables in the decision-making situation at hand. It is entirely possible for a decision maker to make the right choice using the wrong approach. It is much more likely, however, for the best choice to ensue from the right approach. In documenting the models of (or approaches to) choice for this book, we draw heavily on the work of Robin Hogarth.[90]

The principal models of choice are as follows:

1. **Linear model.** This is a measurable compensatory model. Each dimension or variable in this model is quantified and is given a weight reflecting its relative importance. The evaluation of each alternative is then the sum of the weighted values on its dimensions. The alternative with the greatest sum for all dimensions is the obvious choice. A simplistic formula for the linear model shows that:

Value of alternative = sum (relative weight scale value) of all dimensions.

The principal weakness of the linear model is its heavy reliance on numeric values. It assumes, for example, that all outcomes are compensatory and that all the dimensions of a given alternative can be measured. As will be noted in Chapter 3, this is an untenable assumption.

2. **Conjunctive model.** This is a noncompensatory model. It is one in which "the decision maker sets certain cut-off points on the dimensions such that any alternative that falls below a cut-off is eliminated."[91] The conjunctive rule states: "any [decision] not meeting a minimum cut-off level on any characteristic is eliminated. The Federal Drug Administration uses a conjunctive [model] in issuing standards . . . that all ethical drugs must meet."[92]

3. **Disjunctive model.** This approach to choice seeks the best attribute or characteristic that is presumed to denote the best alternative. In this model "a decision maker will permit a low score on a dimension provided there is a very high score on one of the other dimensions. In other words, in the disjunctive model, the [alternatives] would be evaluated according to [their] best attribute regardless of the levels on the other attributes."[93] Alternatives are essentially compared on their best characteristic. "The [alternative] with the highest rating in its best characteristic is chosen."[94]

4. **Lexicographic model.** This model "first ranks the [attributes or] characteristics in order of importance and then selects the alternative rated best on the most important characteristic. If two or more [alternatives] rate equally, the next most important characteristic is used as a tie breaker."[95]

5. **Elimination-by-aspects model.** This model was developed by Tversky.[96] A sequential type, it assumes that alternatives consist of a set of aspects or characteristics. "At each stage of the process, an aspect, i.e., dimension, is selected according to a probabilistic scheme . . . and alternatives that do not include the aspect are eliminated. The process continues until only one alternative remains."[97] The empirical evidence suggests that elimination-by-aspects is a commonly used decision rule.[98]

It is also interesting to note that these models tend to focus mainly on the outcome likely to result from the choice. Often there is little if any consideration of the cost of using one or more models.[99] Some authors believe that decision makers follow a "principle of minimum effort" in arriving at choice.[100] Decision makers also appear to minimize the importance of accuracy in selecting and using models of choice. Perhaps this phenomenon accounts for the lesser emphasis accorded the cost of making a choice and the inclination to adopt an approach that minimizes effort.

Characteristics of Choice

Regardless of which model is used by the decision maker in selecting a best alternative, some characteristics of the decision task itself as well as those of the decision maker influence the act of choice. These characteristics constitute the essence of a contingency model of choice developed by Beach and

Mitchell.[101] They are presented here because they apply generically to almost any model of choice.

With regard to the decision task in the act of choice, the following characteristics are pertinent:

1. *Unfamiliarity.* The degree to which the decision task is foreign to the decision maker
2. *Ambiguity.* The degree to which the decision task is unclear to the decision maker
3. *Complexity.* The number of different components of the decision task — that is, the number of alternatives to be considered, the amount of relevant information to be considered, and the number of criteria on which the decision will be judged[102]
4. *Instability.* The degree to which the criteria, objectives, and constraints of the decision task change during and after the act of choice
5. *Reversibility.* The degree to which the choice can be reversed if things go poorly
6. *Significance.* The importance of the choice to the organization and the decision maker
7. *Accountability.* The degree to which the decision maker is accountable for the results of the choice
8. *Time and/or money constraints.* The limitations on time and money in the process of decision making and the act of choice.

In addition to the decision task itself, the act of choice is influenced by at least three significant characteristics of the decision maker. These are:

1. *Knowledge.* The amount of knowledge relevant to the act of choice that is possessed by the decision maker
2. *Ability.* The degree of intelligence and competence possessed by the decision maker
3. *Motivation.* The desire of the decision maker to excel and succeed

Obviously numerous combinations of these characteristics related to the decision task and the decision maker will influence the selection and use of a particular model of choice. However, a choice made without implementation is merely an interesting abstraction. Implementation turns the choice from intellectual fodder into a commitment of time, energy, and resources.

IMPLEMENTING DECISIONS

Much of the literature on decision making at the level of the organization doesn't go beyond the act of choice. This emphasis makes the decision an end in itself rather than a means to accomplish managerial objectives within an interrelated and dynamic process. In point of fact, the real value of a decision becomes apparent only after it is implemented. "It is not enough to select the best alternative. If the decision is not adequately implemented the favorable outcome will not be achieved. Effective decision makers devise plans to carry out their decisions. They anticipate the likely setbacks and are ready with countermeasures."[103] "Once a decision has been made, appropriate action must be taken to ensure that the decision will be carried out as planned. . . . All too often even the best decisions fail to be implemented due to lack of resources, such as necessary funds, space, or staff, or some other failure, such as inadequate supervision of subordinates and employees."[104] Cornell captures the complexity of implementing decisions in the following passage:

> Constraints surface in the Implementation Phase, constraints of a physical, administrative, distributional fairness and political nature, in addition to the ever-present financial and other resource constraints. . . . The "adversary process" is triggered and if care is not taken, a good [decision] can be negated by those who attack it. . . . This can be an agonizing period for one who may have devoted his or her very best to the [decision], but it is the real world.
>
> Then too, it is during the phases of implementation . . . that other unforeseen effects appear. Things that were believed measurable may prove not to be so; unknowns and uncertainties appear which require adjustments. . . — all of which are designed to *reduce* the amount of uncertainty and to make known the unknown; to treat side effects and spillovers which may not have been foreseen, especially the important external ones.[105]

"A decision brilliantly conceived can prove worthless without effective implementation."[106] "Converting the decision into action is [a] major element in the decision process. While thinking through the boundary conditions is the most difficult step in decision making, converting the decision into effective action is usually the most time-consuming one. Yet a decision will not become effective unless the action commitments have been built into it from the start. Until then it is only a good intention."[107]

The small number of articles related to implementing decisions have usually taken a somewhat one-dimensional approach to the subject. For example, Phillips took note of organizational structure as a principal determinant in successfully implementing decisions.[108] Kolaja et al. studied the period of time over which decisions are implemented.[109] Staw and Fox noted the tendency of managers to commit additional resources to some implemented decisions that appear to be headed for failure.[110] Shumway et al. concluded that there is a diffusion rather than a concentration of formal authority in implementing decisions in formal organizations.[111] Doktor and Hamilton studied the influence of cognitive style on implementing decisions.[112] Finally, Floyd and Wooldridge examined the effect of understanding on consensus and commitment in implementing managerial decisions.[113]

In a somewhat more comprehensive effort, Stagner did a study of 217 vice presidents in different business firms in which he noted the following significant findings:

1. Profit maximization is not the only objective in implementing business decisions.

2. There are appreciable differences in the style of decision making.

3. A manager's power within the organization tends to affect his or her part in the decision making process.

4. Profitability is related to variations in the manner of making and implementing decisions.

5. Personality variables are significant in the decision-making process.[114]

Few articles and studies have concentrated on what it takes for a decision to be successful. Successful decisions are more than good decisions. Once made, the choice must be implemented so that its effect satisfies the managerial objectives. A good decision's quality may be offset by poor acceptance that hinders operations. Measures of successful decisions are subjective at best. One example is the three-part basis for examining the "goodness" of a decision that was advanced by Shull, Delbecq, and Cummings.[115] According to them, a decision is successful if it: (1) remains viable following implementation, (2) manifests an acceptable degree of congruency between the actual outcome and the expected outcome, and (3) elicits enthusiasm and skill from those who must carry it out.[116]

Samuel Trull developed one of the most comprehensive models for appraising the success of a given decision. Trull's model came as a result of a study of the decision-making process in one hundred complex organizations of all types. It is summarized in Figure 2.3. According to Trull, the success of a decision is a function of its quality and its implementation. A decision's quality, in turn, is judged by (1) its compatibility with existing operating constraints, (2) its timeliness, (3) its incorporation of the optimum amount of information, and (4) the decision maker's influence on it. And successful decision implementation is a product of (1) avoidance of conflict of interest, (2) a positive risk-reward factor, and (3) how well the decision is understood by those who must carry it out.[117]

The findings of Trull's study are of special interest to managers responsible for implementing as well as making decisions. On balance, most of the decisions reviewed in the study were made within well-defined operating constraints, such as policies, procedures, and the established way of doing business. Regrettably, decision makers displayed no conscious effort to determine the optimum time for making a choice.[118] More often than not, a decision was made after the most desirable time.

Trull's study also found that managers spent little systematic effort on weighing the kind of decision being made against the cost of the information required. In terms of Figure 2.2, there was little regard for the marginal value of additional information. The increasing cost of attempting to perfect the information added little to the information's value. Interestingly, Trull also found that the greater the perceived authority of the decision maker, the

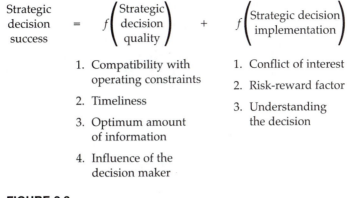

FIGURE 2.3

Evaluation of Strategic Decision Success

greater the effort by the organization to ensure the decision's success. However, this finding should not be unexpected, since decisions made at the top of an organization will usually carry the most weight with managers at subordinate levels.

Trull's findings about conflict of interest resulting from decision implementation were inconclusive. He did find that the managers were quite willing to accept more uncertainty in the outcome of their decisions without demanding commensurate rewards. Presumably these managers either felt that they *had* to accept more risk or were unaware that they were assuming additional uncertainty and therefore did not demand offsetting benefits. It is difficult to imagine that rational managers would otherwise knowingly expose themselves to a greater chance of failure.

Finally, how the decisions were understood by those required to carry them out depended on the openness of communication and the participation of such individuals in the decision-making process. *Perceived involvement* in the process of choice, rather than *actual involvement*, was important to the decision's success. Communicating with the organization and affected groups or individuals and getting personal commitments increased the chances of acceptance and successful implementation.[119]

March and Olsen observe that there are many obstacles to the successful implementation of almost any decision.[120] Chief among these obstacles are (1) the reduced importance of a decision once it has been made and implemented, (2) the control of the outcome of a decision by those who were not involved in its making, and (3) the development of new situations and problems to command the attention of the decision makers once the choice has been implemented. "Any one of these factors alone will produce some kinds of disparities between decision and implementation."[121]

One way to ensure effective implementation is to adopt a policy of preventive decision making. Problems prevented are problems solved. The technical problems of operating constraints, timing, cost effectiveness of information, and risk-reward factors need to be considered as thoroughly as possible. The human problems of conflict of interest, understanding, and the perceived authority of the decision maker require careful scrutiny before implementation. Together these technical and human variables hold the key to successful decisions.

The ultimate test of decisions involving human beings is how they change people's behavior when they are implemented. There are few decisions so technically precise that they cannot be undermined by an unmotivated employee's response. The following passage states the importance of the human being in the implementation phase:

> Man, as the vehicle through which the decisions are implemented, reacts not only to the quality of the decision but to the total socio-technical environment associated with the decision. He cannot be manipulated in the same sense that other resources can be. Therefore, the manager's job is not limited to the exercise of knowledge and skill in choosing desirable solutions: it also includes the knowledge and skill required to transform those solutions into the dynamics of behavior in a particular organizational social system.[122]

In summary, research findings, as well as observations made regularly in the world of formal organizations suggest that managers need to substantially improve the implementation of decisions, especially in the areas of timing, cost, and the acceptance of risk.[123] Such improvements will be forthcoming if implementation is considered early in the decision-making process rather than, as is so often the case, after the choice.

FOLLOW-UP AND CONTROL

Once the decision is implemented, the manager cannot simply assume that its outcome will further the managerial objectives. As Drucker so accurately notes:

> Information monitoring and reporting have to be built into the decision to provide continuous testing, against actual results, of the expectations that underlie the decisions. Decisions are made by men. Men are fallible; at best, their works do not last long. Even the best decision has a high probability of being wrong. Even the most effective one eventually becomes obsolete.[124]

A system of follow-up and control is essential to ensure that the results agree with those expected at the time the decision was made. According to Koontz and Weihrich, a system of control involves three steps: (1) establishing standards, (2) measuring performance against the standards, and (3) correcting deviations from the standards.[125]

The standards are usually expressed in measurable terms, but do not have to be. Standards should be flexible rather than rigid. That is, there should be some tolerance within which performance may vary without drawing an extreme reaction from management. Further, the standards should reflect the managerial objectives. This is not to suggest, however, that the original objectives should be inflexible. The progress of the implemented decision may indicate a need to revise or update the objectives, in which case the entire decision-making process will be reactivated.

Performance is measured by observing the results of the implemented decision.[126] Results may be observed manually by human viewers or mechanically by automated scanning devices. In any event, the measurements should be continuous lest the results of the decision depart substantially from the standards reflecting the managerial objectives. With continuous measurements, timely corrective action can keep results within an acceptable range so that the outcome of the implemented decision will be more likely to meet the managerial objectives.

Standards that reflect the managerial objectives and measurements of results that are continuous will facilitate the correction of deviations from the expected results. Corrective action may involve any one of a number of things, such as (1) reordering operations, (2) redirecting personnel, or (3) resetting the managerial objectives. Again, proper timing and action appropriate to the situation are an integral part of any control system. Overreaction by management to deviations from the standards can be both costly and dysfunctional to the organization.

SUMMARY

This chapter described the decision-making process as made up of six functions. These functions are (1) setting managerial objectives, (2) searching for alternatives, (3) comparing and evaluating alternatives, (4) the act of choice, (5) implementing decisions, and (6) follow-up and control. Figure 2.1 diagrammed the decision-making process and revealed the interrelatedness of its six functions. The dynamic qualities of the decision-making process were discussed in the context of its three subprocesses. These subprocesses include (1) corrective action as necessary to ensure successful implementation of the choice, (2) renewing the search to discover new alternatives or to reconsider other existing alternatives, and (3) revising the managerial objectives to match available alternatives and the ease or difficulty of implementation. The decision-making process is most applicable to category II decisions.

Managerial objectives were described as the foundation of the decision-making process; reaching a set of managerial objectives culminates a given cycle within the whole process. Within most formal organizations, several cycles go on at the same time within the decision-making process, as potential or actual choices tend to be in varying stages of progression. Managerial objectives have some rather obvious advantages, take the form of a hierarchy in formal organizations, and reflect certain discernible criteria of effectiveness.

The search activity is motivated by a felt need to obtain information from which to fashion a set of alternatives relevant to the managerial objectives. Search is an activity that is flawed by the imperfections of human decision makers. It is also biased by the values, perceptions, and experiences of managers engaged in the decision-making process. The structure of search can be classified into (1) indirect viewing, (2) conditioned viewing, (3) informal search, and (4) formal search. Managers continually seek a balance in their search activity among (1) the cost of additional information, (2) the amount of the perceived payoffs, and (3) their own levels of aspiration. The cost of additional information should be related to the marginal value of such information. Figure 2.2 diagrammed this critical relationship.

Comparing and evaluating alternatives is typically a multistage, repetitive function involving progressively deeper investigation of various courses of action. The first pattern reduces a large number of ready-made alternatives to a few feasible ones, which are then compared and evaluated preparatory to choice and implementation. The second pattern involves a more extensive and multidimensional evaluation of a single alternative that may have emerged from the search activity or evolved from the first pattern. This function is usually accomplished in one or some combination of three modes: (1) judgment, (2) bargaining, and (3) analysis. This book advocates fusing these three modes into a composite mode with proportions appropriate to the decision-making situation. For category II decisions, particularly those of a strategic nature, the emphasis should be on judgment.

The act of choice is, in a sense, the high point in the decision-making process. It is, however, still only a part of the process, not, as is so often assumed, the entire process. To focus solely on the act of choice is to disregard or minimize all the antecedent actions necessary for choice, not to mention the succession of postdecision actions essential to transform the choice into acceptable results. The decision maker obviously wants to select that alternative or combination of alternatives that appears most likely to attain the managerial objectives. Because of constraints, which include cognitive limitations, imperfect information, and time and cost restrictions, decision makers must use a judgmental strategy in making category II choices. The use of judgment, in combination with bargaining and analysis, need not detract from the success of decisions that are effectively implemented.

It is entirely possible for a given decision maker to make the right choice using the wrong approach. It is much more likely, however, for the best choice to ensue from the right approach. This chapter presented five models for (or approaches to) the act of choice: (1) the linear model, a compensatory model that assumes that the choice should be determined by the highest total value of a given alternative, which is the sum of its relative weight and the relative scale value of all its dimensions; (2) the conjunctive model, a noncompensatory model in which the decision maker eliminates from further consideration any alternative whose dimensions in total or in part do not reach a predetermined cut-off level; (3) the disjunctive model, a

noncompensatory model in which the alt
its best attribute or characteristic is pres
regardless of the levels of its other attribut
noncompensatory model in which the att
alternatives are rank ordered and that altern
the highest rank-ordered attribute is the choi
aspects model, a noncompensatory model i
alternatives that do not include desired aspects
alternative remains. The value of the outcome i
one of these models should be reduced to refle
model to the act of choice. This chapter also delii
that are generic to almost any model of choice.

The real value of a decision becomes apparent only after it is implemented. A decision brilliantly conceived can prove worthless without effective implementation. Until a decision is consummated by the commitments
that are characteristic of implementation, it is only a good intention. There
are few comprehensive studies of implementing decisions and fewer still of
the measures of successfully implemented decisions. Trull's study stands as
a notable exception in this regard. Of considerable importance, his study
highlighted areas in which managers tend to fall short in implementing decisions. These areas include: (1) timing, (2) cost, and (3) acceptance of risk.
Successfully implemented decisions also require follow-up and control,
in which managerial decision makers receive continuous information that
shows how the actual outcomes of an executed decision compare with the
outcomes inherent in the managerial objectives.

REVIEW AND DISCUSSION QUESTIONS

1. Should decision makers pursue additional information beyond the point
   of optimality? Discuss.

2. In what specific ways do the three subprocesses epitomize the dynamics
   of the decision-making process?

3. What would you recommend to practicing managers to help them improve the implementation of their decisions? Base your answer on the
   findings of Trull's study.

4. What are some of the specific advantages of managerial objectives in the
   decision-making process?

5. What is meant if one says that managerial decision makers should focus
   primarily on outcomes? Discuss.

6. What are some of the forces that act to require an integrated progression
   of activities within a given cycle in the decision-making process?

7. What are some of the human and organizational factors that act to bias the search activity?

8. What is the principal weakness of the linear model of choice?

9. Differentiate the disjunctive model and the lexicographic model of choice in terms of their principal dissimilarity.

10. In terms of the six functions of decision making set forth in this chapter, what is management's area of greatest weakness and what action do you recommend to improve it?

NOTES

1. See, for example, James G. March and Johan P. Olsen, *Ambiguity and Choice in Organizations*, 2nd ed. (Norway: Universitetsforlaget, 1979).

2. Herbert A. Simon, *The New Science of Management Decision* (New York: Harper & Row, 1960), p. 1.

3. Eberhard Witte, "Field Research on Complex Decision-Making Processes — The Phase Theorem," *International Studies of Management and Organization* (Summer 1972), 156–182.

4. L. P. Schrenk, "Aiding the Decision Maker — A Decision Process Model," *Ergonomics*, 12 (July 1969), 543–557.

5. Irving L. Janis, "Stages in the Decision-Making Process," in *Theories of Cognitive Consistency: A Sourcebook*, ed. Robert P. Abelson et al. (Chicago: Rand McNally, 1968), pp. 577–588.

6. Samuel Eilon, *Management Control*, 2nd ed. (New York: Pergamon, 1979), pp. 135–162.

7. Henry Mintzberg, Duru Raisinghani, and André Theoret, "The Structure of 'Unstructured' Decision Processes," *Administrative Science Quarterly*, 21 (June 1976), 246–275.

8. E. Bruce Fredrikson "Noneconomic Criteria and the Decision Process." *Decision Sciences*, 2 (January 1971), 25–52.

9. Paul C. Nutt, *Making Tough Decisions* (San Francisco: Jossey-Bass, 1989), p. 36.

10. Walter J. M. Kickert and John P. van Gigch, "A Metasystem Approach to Organizational Decision-Making," *Management Science*, 25, No. 12 (December 1979), 1217–1231.

11. Clyde W. Holsapple and Herbert Moskowitz, "A Conceptual Framework for Studying Complex Decision Processes," *Policy Sciences*, 13 (1980), 83–104.

12. See, for example, Paul C. Nutt, "Preventing Decision Debacles," *Technological Forecasting and Social Change*, 38 (September 1990), 159–174; and Ola Svenson, "Some Propositions for the Classification of Decision Situations," in *Contemporary Issues in Decision Making*, ed. K. Borcherding, O. I. Larichev, and D. M. Messick (New York: Elsevier Publishing Co., 1990), pp. 149–157.

13. *Webster's New Collegiate Dictionary* (Springfield, Mass.: G. & C. Merriam; 1977), p. 465.

14. A. R. Radcliffe-Brown, "Concept of Function in Social Sciences," *American Anthropologist*, 37 (July–September 1935), 19.

15. Bernard M. Bass, *Organizational Decision Making* (Homewood, Ill.: Richard D. Irwin, 1983), p. 4.

16. Gregory Streib, "Applying Strategic Decision Making in Local Government," *Public Productivity and Management Review*, 15, No. 3 (Spring 1992), 342.

17. Milan Zeleny, "Descriptive Decision Making and Its Applications," in *Applications of Management Science*, ed. Randall L. Schultz (Greenwich, Conn.: JAI Press, 1981), I, 333.

18. Maneck S. Wadia, *The Nature and Scope of Management* (Chicago: Scott, Foresman, 1966), p. 67.

19. See, for example, E. Frank Harrison, *Management and Organizations* (Boston: Houghton Mifflin Co., 1978), pp. 81–91; Paul C. Nutt, "The Influence of Direction Setting Tactics on Success in Organizational Decision Making," *European Journal of Operational Research*, 60 (1992) 19–30; Paul C. Nutt, "Formulation Tactics and the Success of Organizational Decision Making," *Decision Sciences* 23 (May/June 1992), 519–540; and Jurgen Huaschildt, "Goals and Problem-Solving in

Innovative Decisions," in *Empirical Research on Organizational Decision-Making*, ed. E. Witte and H.-J. Zimmerman (New York: Elsevier Publishing Co., 1986), pp. 3–19.

20. Peter F. Drucker, *Management: Tasks — Responsibilities — Practices* (New York: Harper & Row, 1973), p. 101.

21. John F. Mee, "Objectives in a Management Philosophy," in *Management in Perspective*, ed. William E. Schlender, William G. Scott, and Alan C. Filley (Boston: Houghton Mifflin, 1965), p. 61.

22. Dalton E. McFarland, *Management: Principles and Practices*, 4th ed. (New York: Macmillan, 1974), p. 7.

23. Drucker, *Management*, p. 101.

24. Herbert G. Hicks, *The Management of Organizations: A Systems and Human Resources Approach*, 2nd ed. (New York: McGraw-Hill, 1972), p. 62.

25. Charles H. Granger, "The Hierarchy of Objectives," *Harvard Business Review* (May–June 1964), 63.

26. Hicks, *Management of Organizations*, p. 62.

27. Herbert A. Simon, *Administrative Behavior*, 2nd ed. (New York: Free Press, 1957), p. 63.

28. See W. Keith Warner and A. Eugene Haas, "Goal Displacement and the Intangibility of Organizational Goals," *Administrative Science Quarterly* (March 1968), 539–555; and Peter M. Blau and W. Richard Scott, *Formal Organizations: A Comparative Approach* (San Francisco: Chandler, 1962), pp. 228–239.

29. For a fairly complete listing of the major sources of bias organized by the stages of information processing, see Robin M. Hogarth and Spyros Makridakis, "Forecasting and Planning: An Evaluation," *Management Science* (February 1981), 115–137.

30. Gerardo R. Ungson and Daniel N. Braunstein, eds., *Decision Making: An Interdisciplinary Inquiry* (Boston: Kent, 1982), p. 97.

31. Richard M. Cyert and James G. March, *A Behavioral Theory of the Firm* (Englewood Cliffs, N.J.: Prentice-Hall, 1963).

32. Ibid., p. 121.

33. R. M. Cyert, W. R. Dill, and J. G. March, "The Role of Expectations in Business Decision Making," *Administrative Science Quarterly* (December 1958), 337.

34. Peer Soelberg, "Unprogrammed Decision Making," in *Studies in Management Process and Organizational Behavior*, ed. John H. Turner, Alan C. Filley, and Robert J. House (Glenview, Ill.: Scott, Foresman, 1972), p. 141.

35. Charles Z. Wilson and Marcus Alexis, "Basic Frameworks for Decision," *Journal of the Academy of Management* (August 1962), 163.

36. James G. March and Herbert A. Simon, *Organizations* (New York: Wiley, 1958), p. 115.

37. For further development of this point, see Cyert and March, *A Behavioral Theory of the Firm*, p. 121.

38. Ronald J. Ebert and Terence R. Mitchell, *Organizational Decision Processes* (New York: Crane, Russak, 1975), p. 71.

39. Francis Joseph Aguilar, *Scanning the Business Environment* (New York: Macmillan, 1967), pp. 19–21.

40. Aaron Wildavsky, "Information as an Organizational Problem," *Journal of Management Studies* (January 1983), 29.

41. John T. Lanzetta and Vera F. Kanareff, "Information Cost, Amount of Payoff, and Level of Aspiration as Determinants of Information Seeking in Decision Making," *Behavioral Science*, 7 (October 1962), 459–473.

42. See D. Ronald Daniel, "Management Information Crisis," *Harvard Business Review* (September–October 1961), 111–121; and Gary J. Gaeth and James Shanteau, "Reducing the Influence of Irrelevant Information on Experienced Decision Makers," *Organizational Behavior and Human Performance*, 33 (1984), 263–282.

43. Eugene Borgida and Richard E. Nisbett, "The Differential Impact of Abstract vs. Concrete Information on Decisions," *Journal of Applied Social Psychology*, 7, No. 3 (1977), 258–271.

44. Ebert and Mitchell, *Organizational Decision Processes*, pp. 72–74.

45. Ibid., p. 74.

46. Thomas P. Ference, "Organizational Communication Systems and the Decision Process," *Management Science*, 17 (October 1970), B-83 to B-96.

47. David W. Cravens, "An Exploratory Analysis of Individual Information Processing," *Management Science* (June 1970), B-656 to B-669.

48. Charles A. Reilly, III, "The Use of Inform Organizational Decision Mak Some Propositions," in *Researc Behavior*, vol. 5, ed. L. L. Cum

M. Staw (Greenwich, Conn.: JAI Press, Inc. 1983), pp. 103–139.

49. Etzioni, Amitai, "Humble Decision Making," *Harvard Business Review* (July–August 1989), 122–126.

50. See Richard M. Greene, Jr., ed., *Business Intelligence and Espionage* (Homewood, Ill.: Dow Jones-Irwin, 1966), pp. 44–46, for one technique of computing the value of additional information.

51. See Klaus Brockhoff, "Decision Quality and Information," in *Empirical Research on Organizational Decision Making*, ed. E. Witte and H.-J. Zimmerman (New York: Elsevier Science Publishers, 1986), pp. 249–265 for organizational research on some optimal level for processing relevant information.

52. Howard E. Thompson, "Management Decisions in Perspective," in *Management in Perspective*, ed. William E. Schlender, William G. Scott, and Alan C. Filley (Boston: Houghton Mifflin, 1965), p. 137.

53. Ernest R. Alexander, "The Design of Alternatives in Organizational Contexts," *Administrative Science Quarterly*, 24 (September 1979), 382–404.

54. Thompson, "Management Decisions in Perspective," p. 137.

55. Bass, *Organizational Decision Making*, pp. 69–70.

56. Arthur Sondak, "How to Answer the Question, 'What Should I Do?'" *Supervisory Management* (December 1992), 4–5.

57. Mintzberg, Raisinghani, and Theoret, "The Structure of 'Unstructured' Decision Processes," p. 257.

58. Irving L. Janis and Leon Mann, *Decision Making: A Psychological Analysis of Conflict, Choice, and Commitment* (New York: Free Press, 1977), pp. 174–175.

59. Mintzberg, Raisinghani, and Theoret, "The Structure of 'Unstructured' Decision Processes," p. 258. Also see Soelberg, "Unprogrammed Decision Making."

60. See Charles E. Lindblom, "The Science of 'Muddling Through,'" *Public Administration Review*, 19 (1959), 79–88, for a description of the bargaining mode of comparing and evaluating alternatives.

61. Mintzberg, Raisinghani, and Theoret, "The Structure of 'Unstructured' Decision Processes," p. 258.

62. Ibid. See also Soelberg, "Unprogrammed Decision Making," and E. Eugene Carter, "The Behavioral Theory of the Firm and Top-Level Corporate Decisions," *Administrative Science Quarterly*, 16 (December 1971), 413–428.

63. Mintzberg, Raisinghani, and Theoret, "The Structure of 'Unstructured' Decision Processes," p. 259.

64. Peter F. Drucker, *The Effective Executive* (New York: Harper & Row, 1967), pp. 147, 150.

65. James G. March and Herbert A. Simon, *Organizations* (New York: Wiley, 1958), p. 114.

66. Drucker, *Management*, p. 475.

67. Hans G. Gemunden and Jurgen Hauschildt, "Number of Alternatives and Efficiency in Different Types of Top-Management Decisions," *European Journal of Operational Research*, 22 (1985), 178–190.

68. Francis J. Bridges, Kenneth W. Olm, and J. Allison Barnhill, *Management Decisions and Organizational Policy* (Boston: Allyn and Bacon, 1971), p. 20.

69. Manley Howe Jones, *Executive Decision Making* (Homewood, Ill.: Richard D. Irwin, 1962), p. 57.

70. Donald Stevenson Watson, *Price Theory and Its Uses*, 2nd ed. (Boston: Houghton Mifflin, 1968), p. 58.

71. Wilson and Alexis, "Basic Frameworks for Decisions," p. 157.

72. Ibid., p. 154.

73. Mintzberg, Raisinghani, and Theoret, "The Structure of 'Unstructured' Decision Processes," pp. 259–260.

74. Bass, *Organizational Decision Making*, p. 70.

75. Percy H. Hill et al., *Making Decisions: A Multidisciplinary Introduction* (Reading Mass.: Addison-Wesley, 1978). p. 24.

76. Simon, *New Science of Management Decision*, p. 1.

77. Timothy D. Wilson, et al., "Introspecting About Reasons Can Reduce Post-Choice Satisfaction," *Personality and Social Psychology Bulletin*, 19, No. 3 (June 1993), 331–339.

78. Fremont A. Shull, Jr., André L. Delbecq, and L. L. Cummings, *Organizational Decision Making* (New York: McGraw-Hill, 1970), p. 30.

79. Soelberg, "Unprogrammed Decision Making," pp. 141–142.

80. Peter Wright, "The Harassed Decision Maker: Time Pressures, Distractions, and the Use of Evidence," *Journal of Applied Psychology*, 59, No. 5 (1974), 555–561.

81. Robin M. Hogarth, "Decision Time as a Function of Task Complexity," in *Utility, Probability and*

Human Decision Making, ed. D. Wendt and C. Vlek (Dordrecht, Holland: D. Reidel, 1975), pp. 321–338.

82. Henry Morlock, "The Effect of Outcome Desirability on Information Required for Decisions," *Behavioral Science* (July 1967), 296–300.

83. Charles A. Kiesler, "Conflict and the Number of Choice Alternatives," *Psychological Reports*, 18 (February 1966), 603–610.

84. Ben Harris and John H. Harvey, "Self-Attributed Choice as a Function of the Consequence of a Decision," *Journal of Personality and Social Psychology* (June 1975), 1013–1019.

85. William Samuelson and Richard Zelkhauser, "Status Quo Bias in Decision Making," *Journal of Risk and Uncertainty*, 1 (1988), 7–59; and William S. Silver and Terence R. Mitchell, "The Status Quo Tendency in Decision Making," *Organizational Dynamics* (Spring 1990), 34–46.

86. See, for example, "Bad Decisions and Dissonance: Nobody's Perfect," in *Theories of Cognitive Consistency: A Sourcebook*, eds. Robert P. Abelson et al. (Chicago: Rand McNally, 1968), pp. 485–490.

87. See Bass, *Organizational Decision Making*, pp. 94–95.

88. Jones, *Executive Decision Making*, p. 89.

89. Ibid., pp. 90–92.

90. In particular, see Robert M. Hogarth, *Judgement and Choice* (New York: Wiley, 1980), pp. 53–74.

91. Ibid., p. 57.

92. Steven M. Shugan, "The Cost of Thinking," *Journal of Consumer Research* (September 1980), 100.

93. Hogarth, *Judgement and Choice*, p. 57.

94. Shugan, "The Cost of Thinking," p. 100.

95. Ibid.

96. A. Tversky, "Elimination by Aspects: A Theory of Choice," *Psychological Review*, 79 (1972), 281–299.

97. Hogarth, *Judgement and Choice*, pp. 57–58.

98. Eric J. Johnson, *Deciding How to Decide: The Effort of Making a Decision* (Chicago: Center for Decision Research, University of Chicago, 1979), p. 8.

99. Shugan, "The Cost of Thinking," p. 100.

100. Johnson, *Deciding How to Decide*, p. 3.

101. Lee Roy Beach and Terence R. Mitchell, "A Contingency Model for the Selection of Decision Strategies," *Academy of Management Review* (July 1978), 439–449.

102. For a discussion of complexity in decision making, see Kenneth T. McCrimmon and Ronald N. Taylor, "Decision Making and Problem Solving,"

in *Handbook of Industrial and Organizational Psychology*, ed. Marvin D. Dunnette (Chicago: Rand McNally, 1976), pp. 1397–1454.

103. Daniel D. Wheeler and Irving L. Janis, *A Practical Guide for Making Decisions* (New York: Free Press, 1980), p. 9.

104. Hill et al., *Making Decisions*, p. 25.

105. Alexander H. Cornell, *The Decision Maker's Handbook* (Englewood Cliffs, N.J.: Prentice-Hall, 1980), pp. 125–126.

106. Shull, Delbecq, and Cummings, *Organizational Decision Making*, p. 15.

107. Peter F. Drucker, "The Effective Decision," *Harvard Business Review*, 45 (January–February 1967), p. 96.

108. Lawrence D. Phillips, "Organizational Structure and Decision Technology," *Acta Psychologica*, 45 (1980), 247–264.

109. Jiri Kolaja et al. "An Organization Seen as a Structure of Decision Making," *Human Relations*, 16, No. 4 (1963), 351–357.

110. Barry M. Staw and Frederick V. Fox, "Escalation: The Determinants of Commitment to a Chosen Course of Action," *Human Relations*, 30, No. 5 (1977), 431–450.

111. C. R. Shumway et al., "Diffuse Decision-Making in Hierarchical Organizations: An Empirical Examination," *Management Science*, 21, No. 6 (1975), 697–707.

112. Robert H. Doktor and William F. Hamilton, "Cognitive Style and the Acceptance of Management Science Recommendations," *Management Science* (April 1973), 884–894.

113. Steven W. Floyd and Bill Wooldridge, "Managing Strategic Consensus: The Foundation of Effective Implementation," *Executive*, 6, No. 4 (November 1992), 27–39.

114. Ross Stagner, "Corporate Decision Making: An Empirical Study," *Journal of Applied Psychology* (February 1969), 1–13.

115. Shull, Delbecq, and Cummings, *Organizational Decision Making*.

116. Ibid., p. 15.

117. Samuel G. Trull, "Some Factors Involved in Determining Total Decision Success," *Management Science* (February 1966), B-270–B-280.

118. See Allen C. Bluedorn and Robert B. Denhardt, "Time and Organizations," *Journal of Management*, 14 (1988), 229–320.

119. See Floyd and Wooldridge, "Managing Strategic Consensus: The Foundation of Effective Implementation."

120. March and Olsen, *Ambiguity and Choice in Organizations.*

121. Ibid., pp. 378–379.

122. Alvar O. Elbing, *Behavioral Decisions in Organizations* (Glenview, Ill.: Scott, Foresman, 1970), p. 322.

123. Another pertinent study may be found in A. J. Eccles and D. Wood, "How Do Managers Decide?" *Journal of Management Studies*, 9 (October 1972), 291–302.

124. Peter F. Drucker, "The Effective Decision."

125. Harold Koontz and Heinz Weihrich, *Essentials of Management*, 5th ed. (New York: McGraw-Hill, 1990), pp. 394–395.

126. See John L. Brown and Neil M. Agnew, "Feedback Bias from Ignoring the Outcome of Rejected Alternatives," *Behavioral Science* (January 1987), 34–41; and Elizabeth Creyer, James R. Bettman, and John W. Payne, "The Impact of Accuracy and Effort Feedback and Goals on Adaptive Decision Behavior," *Journal of Behavioral Decision Making*, 3 (1990), 1–16.

SUPPLEMENTAL REFERENCES

Alexis, Marcus, and Charles Z. Wilson, eds. *Organizational Decision Making*. Reading, Mass.: Addison-Wesley, 1970.

Amey, Lloyd R., ed. *Readings in Management Decision*. London: Longman, 1973.

Axelrod, Robert, ed. *Structure of Decision*. Princeton, N.J.: Princeton University Press, 1976.

Braverman, Jerome D. *Management Decision Making*. New York: AMACOM, 1980.

Browne, Mairead. *Organizational Decision Making and Information*. Norwood, N.J.: Ablex, 1993.

Butler, Richard. *Designing Organizations: A Decision-Making Perspective*. London and New York: Routledge, 1991.

Donaldson, Gordon and Jay W. Lorsch. *Decision Making at the Top*. New York: Basic Books, 1983.

Gore, William J. *Administrative Decision Making: A Heuristic Model*. New York: Wiley, 1964.

Harrison, J. Richard, and James G. March, "Decision Making and Postdecision Surprises: The Politically Competent Manager." *Administrative Science Quarterly* (March 1984), 26–42.

Heller, Frank A. *Managerial Decision Making*. London: Tavistock, 1971.

Howard, John A., James Hulbert, and John U. Farley. "Organizational Analysis and Information-Systems Design: A Decision-Process Perspective." *Journal of Business Research* (April 1975), 133–148.

Jennings, David, and Stuart Wattam. *Decision Making: An Integrated Approach*. London: Pitman, 1994.

Keen, Peter G. W., and Michael S. Scott Morton. *Decision Support Systems*. Reading, Mass.: Addison-Wesley, 1978.

Linstone, Harold A. *Multiple Perspectives for Decision Making*. New York: North-Holland, 1984.

March, James G. *Decisions and Organizations*. New York: Blackwell, 1988.

Nutt, Paul C. *Making Tough Decisions*. San Francisco: Jossey-Bass, 1989.

Nutt, Paul C. "Types of Organizational Decision Processes." *Administrative Science Quarterly* (September 1984), 414–450.

O'Reilly, Charles A., III. "The Use of Information in Organizational Decision Making: A Model and Some Propositions." In *Research in Organizational Behavior*. Ed., L. L. Cummings and B. M. Staw, Greenwich, Conn.: JAI Press, 1983, V, 103–139.

Quade, E. S. *Analysis for Public Decisions*. 2nd ed. New York: North-Holland, 1982.

Russo, J. Edward, and Paul J. H. Schoemaker. *Decision Traps*. New York: Simon & Schuster, 1989.

Saaty, Thomas L. *Decision Making for Leaders*. Belmont, Calif.: Wadsworth, 1982.

Snyder, Richard D. "A Decision-Making Approach to the Study of Political Phenomena." In *Approaches to the Study of Politics*. Ed. Roland Young. Evanston, Ill.: Northwestern University Press, 1958, pp. 3–38.

Springer, J. Fred. "Policy Analysis and Organizational Decisions." *Administration & Society* (February 1985), 475–508.

Steinbruner, John D. *The Cybernetic Theory of Decision.* Princeton, N.J.: Princeton University Press, 1974.

Sutherland, John W. *Administrative Decision-Making: Extending the Bounds of Rationality.* New York: Van Nostrand Reinhold, 1977.

Svenson, Ola. "Process Descriptions of Decision Making." *Organizational Behavior and Human Performance,* 23 (1979), 86–112.

Toda, Masanao. "The Decision Process: A Perspective." *International Journal of General Systems,* 3 (1976), 79–88.

Weber, C. Edward, and Gerald Peters. *Management Action: Models of Administrative Decisions.* Scranton, Pa.: International Textbook, 1969.

Young, Stanley, ed. *Management: A Decision-Making Approach.* Belmont, Calif.: Dickenson, 1968.

Zeleny, Milan. "Descriptive Decision Making and Its Applications." In *Applications of Management Science.* Ed. Randall L. Schultz. Greenwich, Conn.: JAI Press, 1981, I, 327–388.

Zey, Mary, ed. *Decision Making.* Newbury Park, Calif.: Sage Publications, 1992.

Zmud, Robert W. "An Empirical Investigation of the Dimensionality of the Concepts of Information." *Decision Sciences* (April 1978), 187–195.

CHAPTER THREE

Rational Decision Making

*T*he term *rational decision making* epitomizes the confusion and widely varying interpretations surrounding this most important activity of managers in formal organizations. On the one hand, the term is often applied solely to the choice itself; that is, the decision is rational or nonrational. On the other hand, it is frequently used to describe only the behavior of the manager as he or she proceeds toward the selection of a preferred alternative. Neither of these viewpoints provides a workable framework within which to improve decision making in the real world. What is needed is a meaningful definition of a rational decision combined with a profile of the behavior of a manager seeking to arrive at a choice that fits the definition. This chapter presents such a framework.

The chapter begins with a comparative analysis of rational and nonrational behavior. This is followed by a discussion of the traditional view of rational decision making, which involves maximizing behavior in the closed decision model. We then describe a more contemporary view of rational decision making, which deals with satisficing behavior in the open decision model. The chapter concludes with a presentation of decision making in the context of bounded rationality, which is cited as the most useful approach to decision making for managers in organizations of all types.

RATIONAL VERSUS NONRATIONAL BEHAVIOR

The term *rational* and the concept of rationality are subject to widely varying interpretations. Rational frequently refers to the overall process of making a decision or to some part of the behavioral pattern making up that process. An action is judged to be rational or nonrational according to the perspectives of the participants or observers. Occasionally, the decision itself as well as the process for making it is subjected to a similar judgment. The term rational also has certain medicolegal connotations that further distort its application.

The term has been variously defined by a number of authors. Hitt, for example, says, "Man is sometimes referred to as a rational animal. He is intelligent; he exercises reason; he uses logic; and he argues from a scientific standpoint. Indeed, man is considered by man to be the only rational animal."[1] Kakar, on the other hand, says that "rationality, which is closest to Aristotle's conception of *deliberate, intellectual* virtue, simply means a kind of purposive thinking in which various goals are weighed against each other and the selected course of action follows the drawing up of a balance sheet between goals and means, as well as between goals and other side effects arising as a consequence of reaching these goals."[2] Parsons specifies that "an act is rational insofar as (a) it is oriented to a clearly formulated unambiguous goal or set of values which are clearly formulated and logically consistent; (b) the means chosen are, according to the best available knowledge, adapted to the realization of the goal."[3] Other frequently used senses of the term *rational* as applied to actions include (1) "the widest sense of simply goal-directed action," (2) "the sense in which an action is said to be (maximally) rational if what is in fact the most efficient means is adopted to achieve a given end," (3) "the sense in which the means that is believed by the [individual] to be the most efficient is adopted to achieve the [individual's] end (whatever that may be)," (4) "the sense in which an action is in fact conducive to the [individual's] . . . 'long-term' ends," and (5) "the sense in which the [individual's] ends are the ends he ought to have."[4]

In a formal sense the term **rational** means "having or exercising the ability to reason; of sound mind; sane; manifesting or based on reason; logical."[5] In the context of a formal organization, however, rational behavior has a more specialized definition. According to Simon, "Rationality is concerned with the selection of preferred behavior alternatives in terms of some system of values whereby the consequences of behavior can be evaluated."[6] Simon also classifies behavior in the formal organization as objectively, subjectively, deliberately, organizationally, or personally rational, according to the values or goals of the individual.[7] Most individuals, in making a decision, believe that their objective is completely rational or logical at the moment. There is an objective, and there are several alternatives from which a choice is made (consciously or subconsciously) to achieve the objective.[8]

Rational behavior or rationality is a core concept of decision making.[9] "Rationality in the sense here intended is obviously a relative concept. Whether a given action — or the decision to perform it — is rational will depend on the objectives that the action is meant to achieve and on the relevant empirical information available at the time of the decision. Broadly speaking, an action will qualify as rational if, on the basis of the given information, it offers optimal prospects of achieving its objectives."[10] A classical formulation of rational decision making suggests that, faced with a need to make and implement a decision, a given individual will first clarify his or her goals, values, or objectives and then rank or otherwise organize them in his or her mind. This rational individual will then investigate all the important consequences attendant upon the selection of each of the alternatives at hand. It is then a relatively straightforward matter of comparing the consequences of each alternative with the goals, values, or objectives and selecting the alternative that promises the largest amount of favorable consequences.[11]

A kind of specious simplicity is associated with the notion of rational behavior in managerial decision making. Moreover, because one decision has been rational does not necessarily mean that the decision maker will *always* make rational decisions. A given manager may, for example, be patently rational in one decision-making situation and seemingly nonrational in another.[12] Although, presumably, the ideal rational decision maker would be rational for all choices at all times, it would be difficult and unprofitable to analyze a wide range of decisions made by a single person. Therefore, it would be difficult if not actually misleading to attempt to classify people rather than decisions as rational. "Even for a particular decision situation it would be more useful to classify people on a continuum of 'degree of rationality' rather than as 'rational' or not. After all, it seems rather extreme to call a person 'irrational' if he is not a perfect decision maker."[13]

Many writers, especially those in the disciplines of economics and statistics, believe that rational behavior means making a decision that, after a review of all the alternatives, promises to maximize the satisfaction or utility of the decision maker.[14] "The end of rational behavior, according to economic theory, is maximization of profits in the case of business firms and maximization of utility in the case of people in general."[15]

Simon makes the point that it is not feasible to attempt a search for every alternative. The human mind's limited capacity for comprehending all the alternatives for a given decision is implied by Simon's concept of bounded rationality. Moreover, Simon suggests that a more realistic rational choice is one that satisfices, or is simply good enough for, the intended purpose,[16] rather than a decision that maximizes utility or satisfaction.

Rational behavior in the decision-making process, then, simply involves the evaluation and the selection of some relevant alternative that offers a perceived advantage to the decision maker. The advantage that is intended to satisfice the objective may be material or psychological, and it may or may not be attained. All that is necessary is that it be perceived and sought by the decision maker. Moreover, the decision maker's choice need not be based on quantitative analysis, studied calculation, extended deliberation, or even deep reflection. *All that is necessary to make the choice a rational one is that an objective exist and that the decision maker perceive and select some alternative that promises to meet the objective.* This is not to say that the choice will not involve analysis or calculation, only that it does not have to. Further, the choice may be made under conditions of perfect information or complete uncertainty and still be perfectly rational. More likely, however, it will be made with incomplete or imperfect information and will therefore involve some amount of risk.

The foregoing definition of rational behavior seems broad enough to encompass choices based on emotional goals such as honor, prestige, or revenge, for contrary to the opinion of some management theorists, the definition of rationality as espoused in this book needs neither to preclude nor to inhibit normal human emotions.[17] In managerial decision making, rationality and emotionality are *not* the opposite ends of the spectrum.[18] Indeed it may be quite rational to satisfy an emotional objective, although if the emotion obscures a clear view of the consequences of an act, it may lead to nonrational behavior. Thus, it would be nonrational to satisfy a momentary passion if sober judgment revealed that the satisfaction in the long run would not be worth the cost.[19]

Similarly, nonrationality may take the form of failing to act in accordance with one's best estimate of costs, gains, and probabilities. Nonrationality may stem from such sources as (1) commitment to a dogma or theory that does not apply to the situation or shuts out relevant data, (2) education, training, and experience that prevents attainment of the whole view, and (3) limited or distorted perspectives resulting from bureaucratic narrow-mindedness.[20]

More often than not, nonrational behavior may be attributed to the decision maker's set of beliefs. "A belief may be characterized as a proposition accepted as true."[21] Beliefs may be regarded as nonrational if they are inadequate in some one or more of the following ways:

1. They are illogical, inconsistent, or self-contradictory, consisting of or relying on invalid influences.
2. They are partially or wholly false.
3. They are nonsensical.
4. They are situationally specific or ad hoc, that is, nonuniversal and bound to particular occasions.
5. They are deficient in some respect because of the manner in which they are held.[22]

In turn, beliefs tend to be deficient if they can be described as follows:

1. Based, partially or wholly, on irrelevant considerations
2. Based on insufficient evidence
3. Held uncritically, that is, not held open to refutation or modification by experience, regarded as "sacred" and protected by "secondary elaboration" against disconfirming evidence
4. Held unreflectively, without conscious consideration of their assumptions and implications and relations to other beliefs[23]

"One consequence of the above [enumeration] is that we must be careful in declaring beliefs [nonrational] — such a judgment can only be made on the basis of a knowledge of the information on which the person who formed a belief was operating. There is a good deal less [nonrationality] in the world than many of us want to believe; . . . many things that distress us result from perfectly rational behavior based on misinformation."[24] Moreover, decision makers occasionally need to protect themselves from seduction by a temporally nonrational side of their natures.[25] The resultant *imperfect rationality* will accommodate both reason and emotion. Imperfect rationality simply acknowledges the existence of nonrational behavior and seeks to mitigate its influence on the outcome of choices made within the uncertainty of the managerial decision-making process.

"The sources of [nonrational behavior] are not mathematical or psychodynamic, but rest more on the analysis of experience by phenomenologists and existentialists. [This form of behavior] can be compared to Sartre's assertions that the potential action of a person is always more than anything which is already determined. . . . It has a similar affinity to the concept of the leap of Kierkegaard and Camus, of making a decision with the realization that one can never know whether there was any basis for making it."[26]

Obviously nonrationality, as the term is used here, is slightly different from irrationality, which is frequently associated with various kinds of mental disorders. The concern here is only with what is rational or nonrational, and we assume that the decision maker is in full possession of his or her ability to reason. Decision-making behavior is nonrational only when decision makers do not use their faculties to accomplish some objective and pay attention to the consequences. Some writers believe that many decision makers are not clever enough to behave rationally.[27] According to this view, decision makers ought to be selected better and trained better. Other authors note that nonrationality derives from inherent characteristics of human beings.[28] "Consequently, not even experts can be fully rational and full rationality can only be reached by mathematical formulae or computer programs."[29] Finally, of course, there are certain practical restrictions on full rationality. "In realistic decision situations, values, alternatives and predictions interact; so decision makers have incomplete information, or they have more information than human beings can grasp."[30]

In the behavioral sciences it is fashionable to assume that humans are essentially nonrational beings.[31] For example, psychiatrists have pointed out the childhood emotional sources of value attitudes; psychologists have indicated that values are emotionally conditioned; sociologists have suggested that the values grow out of group norms and pressures; anthropologists have said that values and their rationale vary from culture to culture. To be sure, any assertion that proposes a completely rational person seems completely idealistic.[32]

But is seems self-evident that individuals are thinking and reasoning beings.[33] A given individual cannot, by definition alone, be labeled nonrational. Moreover, just as it is unwarranted to conclude that an individual's behavior is nonrational because it has emotional components, it is unwarranted to conclude that rational behavior is confined to the nonemotional areas.[34] In fact, much emotional energy continues to be channeled into rational as well as nonrational behavior.[35] Again the presence of some objective or purpose and the exercise of reasoning ability in some degree toward its attainment seem to be the most meaningful criteria to differentiate rational from nonrational behavior.[36]

THE CONCEPT OF MAXIMIZING BEHAVIOR

The concept of maximizing behavior has its roots in traditional economic theory, which postulates an "economic person."[37] This person is assumed to possess knowledge of the relevant aspects of his or her environment that is, if not absolutely complete, at least impressively clear and plentiful. The economic person is further assumed to have a well-ordered and stable set of preferences and a skill at computation. With this skill the economic person can calculate those alternative courses of action that will permit the attainment of the highest possible point on the scale of personal preferences.[38] In essence, this economic person is assumed to be primarily concerned with maximizing personal preferences or self-interest.[39] Economists refer to such preferences as **utility,** or want-satisfying power.[40] Utility resides in the mind of the individual. It is subjective, not objective. The economic person is presumed to have complete knowledge of the means to attain maximized utility and to know exactly what everyone else involved will do. Given this ideal state of affairs, the economic person has only to weigh the possibilities against one another rationally and to select that course of action offering maximum utility.[41]

Maximizing behavior assumes first and foremost that the decision maker is an economic person. Given this assumption, decision making is simply a process of maximizing expected utility. "It is assumed that there is a single homogeneous good, utility, that is present in all desired ends, and that an increased amount of any end brings with it an increased amount of utility. . . . Second, a set of well-defined and mutually exclusive alternatives is assumed, from which the decision maker is to choose one. Third, it is assumed that the decision maker is able to estimate the outcome and calculate the expected value of each alternative. Given these assumptions, the decision maker calculates the expected utility."[42] However, "maximizing [behavior] places considerable information processing demands on the decision maker. In the extreme sense, he is expected to generate the complete set of alternatives, to specify all possible outcomes, and then to process the alternatives and compare them to the criterion. By maximizing . . . he will be better off — by definition."[43]

The concept of an economic person originally sprang from the philosophy of hedonism, which held that individuals calculate the actions that will maximize their self-interest and behave accordingly. Adam Smith relied on this philosophy when he suggested that the pursuit of self-interest is sufficient to justify interaction between buyers and sellers in the marketplace.[44] "This economic [person] is the merchant pictured by Adam Smith; he is capable of seeing his own best economic interests and acting accordingly. Economic [person's] portrait is . . . clearly drawn in the classic summary of nineteenth century economic theory. . . . Economic [person] is pictured as basing his economic actions and associations not on habit or custom, but on a deliberate and knowledgeable reasoning about the possible results of his actions; his final choice is the course of action that can be expected to bring him maximum gain."[45] An individual is said to behave rationally if he attempts to obtain the maximum utility."[46] Maximizing behavior seeks a decision that is the optimal choice. The optimal choice or best possible decision is one that maximizes the value of a predetermined measure of utility.[47] "Men seem able to maximize expected utility rather well. . . . men consistently do what is best for them. . . . when a lot is at stake . . . men behave in such a way as to maximize expected utility."[48]

If it is assumed that managerial decision makers want to maximize their personal preferences, and that they perceive that this will happen through maximizing the organization's objectives, it may also be assumed that such managers will pursue the maximization of the organization's performance in meeting its objectives. To state the concept more plainly, if managers are rewarded on the basis of the organization's performance, and they are basically maximizers, they will try to maximize the outcome of their decisions for the organization so as to achieve the highest attainable amount of personal utility. To the extent that these managerial decision makers succeed and receive satisfactory rewards, their maximizing behavior will be reinforced and they will continue to try to make choices whose outcomes promise to maximize the performance of the organization.

Traditional economic theory treats the organization as a closed decision model.[49] In terms of the elements common to most decision situations, the closed model contains the following parts:

1. A fixed or relatively unchanging objective

2. A known set of relevant alternatives with corresponding outcomes

3. An established rule or set of relationships that produces a preference ordering of the alternatives

4. The maximization of some sought end such as profits, income, physical goods, or some form of utility[50]

5. General disregard of environmental constraints

Many of the widely accepted decision guides in economics and statistics are based on closed decision models. Such models are considered closed "because of the minimal weight given to the environment of the decision maker, and the complexity of the act of choice as such."[51]

Within the interlocking assumptions of utility maximization, complete rationality, perfect information, and the preferences of the decision maker and the organization, variables that won't fit are disregarded by assuming that all other things are equal. Within a given business organization, for example, it then becomes a simple matter to calculate by marginal analysis the profit-maximizing price-output relationship.[52]

Nearly everyone agrees that the closed decision model, with its emphasis on maximizing behavior, is not a good one for predicting the actual behavior of a given organization. As Machlup pointed out, the model is "not, as so many writers believe, designed to explain and predict the behavior of [business organizations]; instead it is designed to explain and predict changes in observed prices as effects of particular changes in conditions."[53] Still despite the obvious split between theory and reality, the closed decision model has some distinct advantages for understanding, predicting, and controlling organizations. To the extent that the model can be used as a planning device, it may inject some rationality into the other parts of the organization.[54]

THE CASE FOR MAXIMIZING BEHAVIOR

According to the precepts of classical economic theory, the majority of the proponents of maximizing behavior are managers in business organizations in which the primary objectives are profit, sales, and growth in resources. Indeed, such objectives provide the basic rationale for existence of private enterprise.[55] Managerial decision makers in the service organizations of the public sector are obviously not concerned with profit or sales. To be sure, even these decision makers may occasionally be trying to maximize resources in the form of operating budgets and capital assets. Nonetheless, the discussion in this and the next section focuses mainly on the business organization as the epitome of maximizing behavior by managerial decision makers.

For proponents of maximizing behavior the objective is profit. Consider, for example, the following statement by Milton Friedman, the well-known economist:

> Few trends could so thoroughly undermine the very foundations of our free society as the acceptance by corporate officials of a social responsibility other than to make as much money for their stockholders as possible. This is a fundamentally subversive doctrine.[56]

Friedman also stated that "unless the behavior of businessmen in some way or other approximated behavior consistent with the maximization of returns, it seems unlikely that they would remain in business for long. . . . The process of 'natural selection' thus helps to validate the (maximization of return) hypothesis — or rather, given natural selection, acceptance of the hypothesis can be based largely on the judgment that it summarizes approximately the conditions for survival."[57]

Phillips echoes Friedman's sentiment:

> Profit maximization must remain as the basic goal of business firms. In turn, the profit maximization approach can guide management in the area of social responsibility. Businessmen must be socially responsible insofar as social responsibility leads to higher profits.[58]

Rostow states the case for profit maximization when he notes that "if, as is widely thought, the essence of corporate statesmanship is to seek less than maximum profits, postwar experience is eloquent evidence that such statesmanship leads to serious malfunctioning of the economy as a whole."[59]

Many classical economists besides Friedman and Phillips accept the primacy of profit maximization in business organizations. Koplin is an excellent example, as the following passage attests:

> The application of the profit maximization assumption to the corporation is straightforward. The objective of the corporation is profit maximization. . . . The profits of the corporation will be maximized if it is so managed as to maximize the excess of revenues over costs, including in costs the supply prices of all factors, entrepreneurial and other.[60]

Machlup makes the point that "maximization of money profits is certainly the simplest objective function, but it works only in the case of firms exposed to vigorous competition." He further states that "when the management of a firm makes more than enough money, it need not go all out to maximize profits; it can afford to do a few other things that it likes, such as serving what by its own lights it regards as the national interest or indulging in other luxuries."[61]

In spite of his apparent flexibility, there is little doubt that Machlup considers the maximization of profit to be the overriding objective of business organizations. His perspective is in keeping with classical economic theory and the concept of maximizing behavior.

Other authors have made similar observations. "The economic theory of the firm does not merely postulate profits as the goal of the business concern. It states explicitly that the goal is maximum profits, and the entrepreneurs will try to move toward this objective in a rational manner."[62] According to this theory, "to deny profit maximization, of course, is to deny our ability to make determinant statements about anything."[63] "Maximization of residual profits becomes an instrumental goal toward achieving the more ultimate goals of survival and growth."[64] In a technical sense, profit is maximized when the cost of one more unit of production is exactly equal to the additional revenue from the sale of that unit or, in other words, when marginal cost is equal to marginal revenue.[65] However, the marginal analysis required to compute the precise point of profit maximization is defensible in theory but unattainable in practice.

Failure to maximize profit usually indicates some inefficiency on the part of a business organization. Indeed, this is perhaps the principal argument in favor of profit maximization. To maximize the excess of revenue over cost, the managerial decision maker will pursue programs designed to foster greater efficiency in the firm. But the pursuit of maximization does not ensure its attainment. And the attempt to maximize profit in the short run may subject the business organization to other costs that will, in the long run, work against its economic performance.

Some economists have suggested that business organizations ought to maximize economic objectives other than profit, or possibly some combination of profit and other economic objectives. For example, Baumol assigns profit a secondary role to sales. He asserts that sales have become an end in themselves, and that all that is required of the business firm is to record a minimally acceptable level of profit. So long as profits are high enough to keep stockholders satisfied and contribute adequately to financing company growth, management will try to increase sales revenues rather than to further increase profits.[66]

Galbraith essentially agrees with Baumol's hypothesis,[67] but Marris takes a slightly different approach to maximization. Arguing that "managers should choose the fastest growth policy they can get away with," Marris states that the primary economic objective is to maximize growth in size, defined as "the book value of fixed assets, plus inventory, plus net short-term assets, including cash reserves."[68] Herendeen essentially agrees with Marris's approach in that he advocates maximizing the growth rate in total assets.[69] Mabry notes that sales maximization and profit maximization are consistent goals that can be pursued simultaneously.[70] And Yeuing advocates the maximization of all primary objectives of the business organization.[71]

As was noted earlier, the case for maximizing behavior assumes that managerial decision makers will attempt to maximize outcomes as long as their efforts are reinforced in the form of tangible personal rewards. Unfortunately, there are no generally accepted techniques for determining precisely whether a given manager is a maximizer by nature. Monsen and Downs state that "managers act so as to maximize their own lifetime incomes."[72] Gordon, on the other hand, asserts that "the traditional reward of the business leader — the profits arising from business ownership — is not a primary incentive to the majority of top executives in our largest corporations."[73]

The available empirical evidence does not show conclusively that the managers of business organizations are motivated toward maximizing behavior. It does not even show a consistent correlation between maximized objectives and managers' financial compensation. For example, a study by McGuire, Chiu, and Elbing shows a positive correlation between executive income and sales, but not between executive income and profit.[74] This finding tends to support Baumol's hypothesis of sales maximization but not the more generally accepted theory of profit maximization. In a subsequent study, on the other hand, Lewellen and Huntsman conclude that reported profit and the market value of common stock are significant determinants of executive compensation and that sales are quite irrelevant for such purposes.[75] In another study Masson found that the managers of business organizations "are generally not motivated to be sales maximizers."[76] Masson notes that executive financial incentives are primarily related to growth in the market value of equity shares of ownership over the long run. Somewhat more typically, Prasad found that profit is a more significant determinant of executive compensation than sales, although sales seem to be discernibly important.[77] The model developed by Williamson shows a compatible and reinforcing relationship between the maximization of managerial utility and the maximization of profit.[78] Williamson notes that, given adequate opportunity, managers will tend to earn profit above a minimally acceptable level,

which will in turn provide them with both financial and nonfinancial satisfactions. However, Williamson does not say that managers must adopt maximizing behavior to achieve high levels of personal satisfaction. He merely
states that, given the opportunity, managers are likely to behave in this fashion. Williamson's model does appear to support the idea that maximization
of the primary objectives of business organizations can lead to maximization
of the personal goals of managers. But his model does not preclude the possibility that such personal goals can also be realized through nonmaximizing
behavior. In view of the mixed findings of the several studies cited above, it
is not clear whether maximization of profit, sales, or growth contributes the
most to managers' financial compensation. Nor is it clearly established that
high levels of financial compensation represent high levels of personal satisfaction for the managers of business organizations.[79] The personal goals of
power, status, and prestige may be stronger motivators than financial reward, and attainment of these goals is not empirically linked to maximization of the performance of business organizations. Thus the case for
maximization is less than conclusive.

THE CASE AGAINST MAXIMIZING BEHAVIOR

The case against maximizing behavior centers directly on the assumptions
underlying the closed decision model of traditional economic theory. In
summary, the closed model assumes (1) the ability to marshal most (if
not all) the information relevant to the objective at hand, (2) the ability to
quantify the information gathered, and (3) the desirability of disregarding
information that is not readily quantifiable. Environmental constraints are
seldom, if ever, considered in these calculations. It is a basic theme of this
book that these assumptions are faulty, and that maximizing behavior is
more theoretical than workable.

In Drucker's words:

> The first test of any business is not the maximization of profit but the
> achievement of sufficient profit to cover the risks of economic activity and
> thus to avoid loss. . . . the concept [of profit maximization] is worse than
> irrelevant: it does harm. It is a major cause for the misunderstanding of the
> nature of profit in our society and for the deep-seated hostility to profit. It is
> largely responsible for the worst mistakes of public policy. . . . And it is in large
> part responsible for the prevailing belief that there is an inherent contradiction
> between profit and a company's ability to make a social contribution.[80]

Remarking on business managers' perspectives on profit maximization,
McGuire states:

> I have never met a businessman (although there may be such men) who said
> that maximum profits was the objective of his enterprise. Most businessmen,
> to be sure, would like to make more profit than they are making now. . . .

however, most businessmen do not seem to know what maximum profits are; nor do they think they know the means for attaining this goal.[81]

Anthony criticizes profit maximization because in his view it is difficult, if not impossible, to attain and it is also immoral. According to Anthony, profit maximization is immoral because it favors the stockholders at the expense of the other constituencies of the organization. Anthony does not elaborate on the technical difficulties of maximization.[82]

Petit notes that maximization detracts from making socially responsible decisions:

> Effective decision making requires a clear understanding of ends. The profit maximizer has a single end, but the socially responsible manager must choose between alternative ends. . . . The manager who would be socially responsible must decide which . . . goals to emphasize in making decisions.[83]

McGuire, a business economist in his own right, takes strong exception to the idealistic aspects of profit maximization when he notes:

> Entrepreneurs [and, presumably, managers] desire greater profits than they are now making. As a generalized goal for enterprise there can be no quarrel with this statement. Unfortunately, however, as with all generalized goals, it [profit maximization] is simply non-operational. In fact, given the changes in social values that have occurred in recent years, this objective is analogous to the quest for academic excellence and educational quality touted so widely in institutions of higher education. . . . the prescriptive powers of profit maximization have been non-operational for the inhabitants of economic organizations.[84]

Hasan notes the illogic of relating profit maximization to the maximization of personal satisfaction for the manager.

> To replace profit maximization by utility maximization is to render the analysis meaningless and even misleading. We are in no position to assess the . . . mind of the entrepreneur or to know what the utility of money is to him. . . . [Indeed,] the maximization of profit cannot at all be viewed subjectively. . . . if a businessman cannot know precisely what will give him maximum satisfaction, an outsider, the economist, is all the more a poor judge in this matter.[85]

The notion of maximization is faulty for other, more specific reasons. First of all, there is a good deal of empirical evidence suggesting a conflict of interest between satisfaction of managers' utilities and the quest for profit. For example, Jensen and Meckling argue that managers may seek to maximize their own utility at the expense of the utility of the shareholders.[86] Also, there is no evidence that managers fail to derive satisfaction from attaining economic objectives at a less than maximum level. Nor is there evidence that, even if economic objectives could be maximized, doing so would necessarily enhance managers' satisfactions.

Another criticism of maximizing behavior has been advanced by Winter, who questions whether the objectives of a given business firm are so precisely ranked that the pursuit of the highest-ranked objectives automatically gives rise to maximization. And, even if objectives could be so systematically ordered, it is far from certain, according to Winter, that managers would pursue those with the highest rank to maximize the outcome. More typical behavior on the part of management in large, complex business organizations is to search for alternatives that will result in decisions that satisfy or just meet the objectives. This behavioral pattern is necessitated in these organizations by such variables as (1) the uncertainties about the situation at hand; (2) the necessity for group decision making in the face of different individual preferences; and (3) the many loyalties that may conflict and cause suboptimal decisions.[87]

Still another criticism of maximizing behavior points out that limits on the information available to management make it impossible to perform the precise marginal analysis necessary to maximize economic objectives. Because managers in the real world, like everyone else, must operate with incomplete information, they can know the economic implications of alternative courses of action only imperfectly. It is often possible for managers in business organizations to reduce uncertainty by gathering additional information. But an extended search takes time and costs money, and the value of the additional information may be considerably less than the incremental cost of acquiring it. In any event, no amount of extended search will yield perfect information, and the manager must always accept some risk, which by definition precludes maximization.

A slightly different criticism of maximizing involves the cognitive limitations of human beings. Since maximizing behavior presumes the ability to comprehend all the relevant variables in a given situation, natural human cognitive limitations tend to preclude maximization. As March and Simon point out, "An individual can attend to only a limited number of things at a time. The basic reason why the actor's definition of the situation differs greatly from the objective situation is that the latter is far too complex to be handled in all its detail."[88] In considering the limitations of human decision makers, it is well to recall that "the real decision maker is a very different man from his rational, economic, hypothetical counterpart. All the human characteristics of the [manager], particularly his psychological limitations, come into play in his decision making, affecting his ability to recognize problems, to ascertain alternatives, and to form a preference ordering."[89]

Katz and Kahn cite more specific limitations on the cognitive capacity of human decision makers that tend to militate against maximizing behavior.[90] According to them:

1. The decision maker's position in social space, the cultural norms operating in his environment, and the norms of the organization shape his values and his frame of reference for evaluating decision problems.

2. A decision maker's identification with outside reference groups and the reinforcements received from them leads to selective perception of incoming information.

3. The process of projection operates in decision situations, where one's own unrecognized feelings, faults, and inner conflicts are attributed to others. This encourages perceptions that others share the decision maker's own attitudes — a comfortable way to avoid collecting information.

4. Some decision makers have extremely simplified cognitive structures and undifferentiated thought processes that inhibit the capacity of making fine distinctions and encourage others to be perceived homogeneously.

5. Dichotomized thinking is a special case of the latter, where people and pieces of information relevant to decision making are placed in simple opposing categories.

6. The condition of cognitive nearsightedness operates so that decision makers respond first to immediate and visible information and alternatives, rejecting more remote, complex, or long-range solutions.

7. Finally, there is a tendency for decision makers to adopt over-simplified notions of causation: close and interesting factors are seen as causes in the analysis of problems and in the determination of alternative consequences.[91]

In the context of maximizing behavior, the term *maximum profit* must be qualified further. Does profit maximization mean striving toward the highest known and attainable profit? The answer to this question appears to be negative. Methods to increase profits may be known but shunned by the managers of business organizations. Certain ways of making profit are considered unethical. Thus maximization must take into account the firm's goodwill or the reputation of its brand name. Moreover, an unusually high rate of profit may, in the opinion of some business executives, lead to the introduction of new taxes or government regulation. High levels of profit may also lead to demands for wage increases by employees or the entry of new businesses in the field. Therefore, management may seek something less than what appears to be the highest attainable level of profit.[92]

Once the myth of profit maximization is dispelled, the necessary level of profit becomes readily apparent. Katona alludes to this level of profit when he asks, "If business[es] strive for profits, but not for maximum profits, what is their clear aim? It may be that they seek to attain 'satisfactory' profits."[93] Anthony is somewhat more precise when he suggests that the objective be considered as earning a satisfactory return on capital employed (a "satisfactory" return being equitable compensation paid for the use of capital).[94] For purposes of this book, it is suggested that *a necessary and acceptable level of profit is equal to the cost of long-term capital invested in the business*. This level of profit should be sufficient to cover the after-tax cost of long-term debt, the fixed and variable charges associated with preferred stock, and a residual return to the common stockholders in the form of dividends and reinvested earnings that will induce them to retain their ownership in the business. This is a defensible level of profit for which management should not be faulted. It is a level as far from maximization as that concept is from reality.[95]

There can be little doubt that subjective constraints on maximizing behavior temper the actions of managers in business organizations. In fact, the maximization of any economic objective may be ruled out by what the managers believe to exist or choose to recognize. For example, a firm might refuse to bribe judges, civil servants, and employees of other firms even though it would help maximize profit. Furthermore, it may be defensible to observe ethical constraints, provided the rewards of the nonobservance are not too great and the moral force of the constraints is generally recognized.[96] Moreover, when a certain degree of market control has been attained, slavishly continuing to pursue maximum profit might lead to immediate financial gains, but it would doubtless hurt the corporation's relations with the general public, organized labor, government regulatory agencies, and legislative or executive authority.

In summary, the assumptions underlying maximizing behavior are faulty. Objectives are not fixed. The known set of alternatives is always incomplete because it is impossible to obtain perfect information. And human beings' cognitive limitations preclude serious consideration of a large number of alternatives.[97] Many of the variables that must be considered in any attempt at maximization are not easily quantified. Therefore, a precise preference ranking of the firm's objectives or its alternatives that will maximize outcome is most unlikely.

Perhaps most important of all, maximization tends to disregard environmental effects. As illustrated in the following passage, such disregard can only work against the long-term well-being of the organization:

> In most developed countries of the world — and certainly in the United States — public opinion and political pressures no longer tolerate the results flowing from pursuit of the purely economic and competitive processes to their logical end. The community more often than not prefers continuous employment and stability to the minor price advantage tossed out by competition. Political action will be invoked against unduly low wages, against undersupply of an essential product, against unemployment, perhaps even against oppressive price fluctuations. In truth, the state, energized by democratic processes, is always a factor, actual or potential.[98]

Wilson and Alexis have summarized some of the major shortcomings of maximizing behavior in the closed decision model: goals are not defined in as clear-cut a manner as closed decision models hypothesize. Goal-striving behavior occurs within a range of structure of goals. The selection of a particular goal or goal structure is itself a decision. Moreover, information is generally inadequate to identify all alternatives, and relevant alternatives are not necessarily stable; they change with successive decisions. There is serious doubt as to the ability of the closed decision model to stimulate complex choice behavior, although it may do very well for simple choices.[99]

Additional limitations on maximizing behavior become apparent in considering the human predicament of decision making. This predicament is articulated by Shackle:

> If choice is originative, it can be effective, it can give a thrust to the course of things intended to secure its ends. In order to secure its ends, choice must apply a knowledge of what will be the consequence of what. But the sequel of an action chosen by one man will be shaped by circumstance, and its circumstances will include the actions chosen now and actions to be chosen in time to come by other men. If, therefore, choice is effective, it is unpredictable and thus defeats, in some degree, the power of choice itself to secure exact ends. This is the human predicament. . . . Decision is not, in its ultimate nature, calculation, but origination.[100]

If, as correctly noted by Shackle, decision making is not founded on calculation, the assumptions underlying maximizing behavior are rendered completely untenable. Moreover, the origination of choice, as noted by Shackle, is founded on the objectives that underlie the decision-making process. For these reasons, the rational model of decision making espoused by most traditional economic theorists is totally inappropriate for managerial decision making in the real world.[101] Conversely, the process model of choice founded on an objectives-oriented outcome (or one that bespeaks origination as espoused by Shackle) is clearly preferable for managerial decision making.

Given all these limitations on maximizing behavior, decision makers in formal organizations must temper their expectations and settle for somewhat less than the greatest quantity or value attainable. In fact, only the most programmable decisions of the category I type could conceivably qualify for the closed decision model; and even these choices are subject, at the very least, to environmental constraints.

Therefore, the point can be made that maximizing behavior in the closed model is not suitable for most of the decisions made in formal organizations. This restriction certainly applies to all category II decisions and doubtless also applies to a majority of category I choices. Organizational decision makers are thus restricted to choices that satisfice rather than those that maximize outcomes.

THE CONCEPT OF SATISFICING BEHAVIOR

Satisficing means finding a satisfactory, rather than an optimum, course of action.[102] The satisficing decision maker differs from the maximizing decision maker in that constraints, both internal and external, limit the global rationality, and consequently the behavior and processes of choice, for the latter.[103] The nature of satisficing behavior depends upon certain attributes of the decision maker — for instance, his or her desire to achieve, or **level of aspiration**, and his or her persistence and perceptions.

The central proposition of the satisficing concept is that in choosing among alternatives, decision makers seek satisfactory outcomes. In the words of March and Simon:

> Most human decision making, whether individual or organizational, is concerned with the discovery and selection of satisfactory alternatives; only in exceptional cases is it concerned with the discovery and selection of optimal alternatives.[104]

March and Simon make a key distinction between optimal and satisfactory alternatives as follows:

> An alternative is **optimal** if (1) there exists a set of criteria that permits all alternatives to be compared, and (2) the alternative in question is preferred, by these criteria, to all other alternatives.
>
>   An alternative is **satisfactory** if (1) there exists a set of criteria that describes minimally satisfactory alternatives, and (2) the alternative in question meets or exceeds all these criteria.[105]

The basic difference, of course, is that in the optimal situation the decision maker is assumed to have all the alternatives against which to apply the criteria, whereas in the satisfactory situation the decision maker merely applies the criteria to any minimally satisfactory alternative that is good enough to meet the objective.[106]

George notes the impracticality attendant upon maximizing behavior in a futile quest for a supposedly optimal choice as follows:

> Because the search for a course of action that will yield the highest possible payoff is often impractical, most people settle for a course of action that is "good enough," one that offers a sufficient rather than a maximum payoff. Not only does the use of "satisficing" as a decision rule fit the severe limitations of man's capacity to process information. . . . it is also an appropriate way of adjusting to the fact that to apply an "optimizing" decision rule requires enormous quantities of information and analytical resources such as are often simply available or could be obtained only at great cost.[107]

The foundation of satisficing behavior lies in the open decision model. Wilson and Alexis describe the structure of the open model as follows:

1. The decision maker starts out with an idealized goal structure. He defines one or more action goals as a "first approximation" of the "ideal goal" in the structure. The action goal(s) may be considered as representative of the decision maker's *aspiration level*.

2. The decision maker engages in search activity and defines a limited number of outcomes and alternatives. His analysis proceeds from loosely defined rules of approximation. The limited alternatives defined establish a starting point for further search toward a solution.

3. Search among the limited alternatives is undertaken to find a "satisfactory" as contrasted with an "optimal" solution. "Satisfactory" is defined in terms of the aspiration level or action goals.[108]

In satisficing behavior, perceived utility strongly influences the search for information about the decision maker's objective. The important thing is the perceived utility of the information and alternatives at hand since, in general, the decision maker has difficulty estimating the utility of alternatives not yet available.[109] The decision maker's level of aspiration is instrumental in determining whether a satisficing alternative exists among those already available. If one or more satisficing alternatives exist, no search begins (or ongoing search stops); if no satisficing alternative exists, search for additional alternatives begins (or is continued). The concept of satisficing behavior means that the search for alternatives considers only two facets of the decision-making situation, namely the expected utility of the best of the alternatives at hand, and the expected cost of the search activity; the expected utility of the alternatives to be had only after the search activity is not considered.[110] Conversely, in maximizing behavior, the decision maker tends to assume that the search activity is justified or that all of the alternatives are in hand.

According to Simon, managerial decision makers must "satisfice because they do not have the wits to maximize."[111] Satisficing behavior involves a search for alternatives through search strategies that vary in complexity.[112] The initial phases of the search activity use simplistic search strategies. The decision maker scans past experience for similar situations. Immediate alternatives tend to take precedence over long-run courses of action. Until the decision maker is driven to an expanded search activity, the search for alternatives is conducted as close to the familiar aspects of the managerial objectives as possible. Failure to find an acceptable alternative leads to an intensified reexamination of the alternatives under consideration, along with a possible reevaluation of the managerial objectives. Subsequent failure leads to a lowering of the decision maker's level of aspiration, which takes the form of a scaling down of the managerial objectives. The motivation for search increases as time pressure grows.[113] Legal restrictions, organizational structure, and the locus of responsibility for the search activity form additional limitations on decision making within the concept of satisficing behavior.[114]

In essence, satisficing behavior occurs when the managerial decision maker sets up a feasible level of aspiration and then searches for alternatives until finding one that achieves the level. As soon as a satisficing alternative is found, the search stops and the decision maker proceeds toward implementation of the satisficing course of action.[115] In Simon's words: "the decision maker has formed some *aspiration* as to how good an alternative he should find. As soon as he [discovers] an alternative for choice meeting his level of aspiration, he [terminates] the search and [chooses] that alternative."[116]

It should be emphasized that a satisficing decision is not necessarily a second- or third-best choice by definition. Without further search, at least to some point of optimality, there is no way of ascertaining a best choice or a second-best choice. Therefore, all that can be said is that a satisficing choice is, by definition, one that meets the objectives. Given a challenging objective, a realistic level of aspiration, and an appreciation of the cost of additional information, the decision maker's acceptance of a satisficing alternative is eminently rational, as we have defined that term in this chapter.[117]

It is appropriate at this point to provide a precise definition of some key terms to be used throughout this book. The *closed decision model* with emphasis on *maximizing behavior* is considered to be analogous to the so-called *rational model* of decision making advocated by traditional economic theorists in previous sections of this chapter. (Note: This model is presented in greater detail in Chapter 5 as part of Table 5.1.) This book assumes that the term *rational* as applied in this classical approach to decision making is a misnomer stemming from traditional use in the quantitative disciplines of economics, mathematics, and statistics. Conversely, the *open decision model*, with its emphasis on *satisficing behavior*, is a lot like Simon's organizational model of decision making. (Note: This model is also presented in greater detail in Chapter 5 as part of Table 5.1.) But for purposes of this book the terms *open decision model* and *satisficing behavior* are considered synonymous with the process model of decision making set forth in Chapter 2 and displayed in Figure 2.1. Moreover, we assume that the process model presented in Chapter 2 (and later explicated in Table 5.1 in Chapter 5) is completely compatible with *rational decision making*, as the term *rational* is set forth in this chapter. It is also appropriate to note at this juncture that examples of maximizing behavior in the closed decision model and satisficing behavior in the open decision model are represented in the case sets that constitute Part IV of this book.

The significant differences between the structures of the open and closed decision models are as follows:

1. In the open model the fixed and predetermined objectives of the closed model are replaced by dynamic objectives and levels of aspiration.

2. In contrast to those of the closed model, alternatives and outcomes are not predetermined in the open model; neither are the relations between specific alternatives and outcomes assumed to be always defined.

3. In the open model the ordering of all alternatives is replaced by a search that considers fewer than all alternatives because of imperfect information, time and cost constraints, and cognitive limitations of the decision maker.

4. Maximizing behavior, which is a distinguishing characteristic of the closed model, is replaced in the open model by the search for an alternative or combination of alternatives that will satisfice an aspiration or the original objective.

5. The open model is characterized by openness to the environment, whereas the closed model disregards environmental forces or assumes that they are controlled or constant.[118]

The key element in the open decision model is the relationship between the expected outcome and the decision maker's level of aspiration. A given outcome is satisfactory only to the extent that it promises to meet the level of aspiration. If the expected outcome falls short of that level, the decision maker lowers the level and broadens the search to include other alternatives. If the expected outcome exceeds the level of aspiration, the decision maker raises that level and reduces the search activity to the smaller range of alternatives. If the alternatives indicate an outcome likely to meet the level of aspiration, the decision maker is satisfied and makes a choice from among these alternatives. It is not necessary that other alternatives be considered, only that the available alternatives promise an outcome at the level of aspiration. A decision made by this means in the open decision model is a satisficing decision.

Simon makes an interesting analysis of satisficing behavior in the following passage:

> Models of satisficing behavior are richer than models of maximizing behavior, because they treat not only of equilibrium but of the method of reaching it as well. Psychological studies of the formation and change of aspiration levels support propositions of the following kind: (a) When performance falls short of the level of aspiration, search behavior (particularly search for new alternatives of action) is induced. (b) At the same time, the level of aspiration begins to adjust itself downward until goals reach levels that are practically attainable. (c) If the two mechanisms just listed operate too slowly to adapt aspirations to performance, emotional behavior — apathy or aggression, for example — will replace rational adaptive behavior.[119]

The concept of satisficing behavior is not without its shortcomings, although they appear to be fewer than those of maximizing behavior. McGuire makes this point in the following excerpt:

> The emphasis on reality in theorizing and on the characteristics of the individual enhances the descriptive utility of the satisficing concept, but at the same time results in a more complex model for predicting behavior. . . . Certainly in terms of the number and nature of the variables that have to be known before it is possible to predict the behavior of the decision maker, the requirements of maximization are no less demanding than those of satisficing.[120]

On balance, it appears that viewing decision making in a satisficing framework within the open decision model is the more realistic attitude. Presumably, therefore, such a view promises choices that will be more successful at the time of implementation.

THE CASE FOR SATISFICING BEHAVIOR

Even though satisficing choices are made within the open decision model, it should not be assumed that the decision maker operates entirely free of constraints. To the contrary, the process of arriving at a satisficing choice is bounded by several limits within which the decision maker must operate.

This state of affairs has been labeled *bounded rationality* by Simon, and its explanation is the primary argument in the case for satisficing behavior.[121]

Simon has advanced a formal principle of bounded rationality as follows:

> The capacity of the human mind for formulating and solving complex problems is very small compared with the size of the problems whose solution is required for objectively rational behavior in the real world — or even for a reasonable approximation of such objective rationality.[122]

He then points out that these cognitive limitations require the decision maker to construct simplified models of real-world situations to deal adequately with them. The decision maker will then behave rationally with regard to the model, which is certainly not optimum in relation to the real world. Consequently, to predict behavior accurately, one would need to know all the variables that underlie the construction of the model, such as the values and psychological attributes of the decision maker.[123]

Lindblom agrees with Simon about the need to simplify the decision-making process in recognition of the choice maker's limited intellectual capacity for dealing with numerous and complex variables. In support of satisficing behavior, he offers the following pertinent comment:

> Ideally, rational-comprehensive analysis leaves out nothing important. But it is impossible to take everything important into consideration unless "important" is so narrowly defined that analysis is in fact quite limited. Limits on human intellectual capacities and on available information set definite limits to man's capacity to be comprehensive. In actual fact, therefore, no one can practice the rational-comprehensive method for really complex problems, and every administrator faced with a sufficiently complex problem must find ways to drastically simplify.[124]

Human decision makers do exhibit rationality, but only within their perception of a decision-making situation.[125] Such constraints or boundaries typically have been found to be quite narrow when compared to the complexity of category II decisions. Thus the capacity of the human mind tends to be overwhelmed by the information demands of these decisions. But decision makers attempt to make up for their limited abilities by constructing a simplified representation of the decision and behaving rationally within the constraints of this model. The concept of bounded rationality, therefore, is used prominently in theories of decision making to explain departures from the closed decision model with its emphasis on maximizing behavior.

Bounded rationality often stems from a psychological phenomenon that has been labeled **cognitive strain.** A decision maker's thought processes break down when he or she is subjected to an overload of information — that is, when the informational demands of the decision-making situation exceed the decision maker's ability to process information.[126]

Research studies in several different types of formal organizations have tended to confirm the presence of cognitive strain in complex decision-making situations.[127] There are some discernible psychological factors that contribute to the cognitive limitations of decision makers. A cross-section of these factors follows:

1. Human decision makers can retain only a few bits of information in short-term memory.[128]

2. The intelligence of the decision maker appears to be a limiting factor in processing and retaining information. More intelligent decision makers seem better able to cope with high loads of information processing.[129]

3. Dogmatic decision makers (that is, those with closed belief systems) tend to unduly restrict the amount of information they are willing to process, thereby limiting their cognitive processes.[130]

4. Decision makers who tend to think in concrete rather than abstract terms tend to be somewhat limited in their ability to process information.[131]

5. A decision maker's willingness to accept risk may limit the amount of information required to arrive at a choice. Risk takers may require less information than risk avoiders.[132]

6. A decision maker's level of aspiration influences the amount of information he or she needs to arrive at a choice. If the level is high, the decision maker may require more information; if the level is low, the decision maker may need less information. Consequently, the level of aspiration represents another special type of cognitive limitation.[133]

7. In general, older decision makers appear to have more cognitive limitations on handling information in a decision-making situation than younger decision makers.[134]

Given the cognitive limitations of the decision maker, there are other reasons a satisfactory solution in hand is more practical than a fruitless quest for an optimal solution:

> First, an optimal decision, made at one point in time, is generally suboptimum in terms of subsequent times. Since we are limited in our ability to foresee the future, it follows that it is useless to go to extreme lengths to search for the "most optimum" decision. It is complex enough to decide how far to go.
>
> Second, there are an enormous number of possible choices (strategies). Any attempt to obtain information about all of them would be self-defeating.
>
> Third, there are virtually innumerable factors outside the control of the decision maker. These states of nature affect the decision outcome. It would be impossible to list all of them let alone to determine the totality of their effects in order to determine the optimum action.[135] Often the necessary information just isn't available.[136]

Decision makers, then, seldom try to find the optimal solution to a decision problem. Rather, they define in a limited sense the ranges of outcomes within available strategies that would be good enough to meet their levels of aspiration or objectives. Then they select a strategy that is likely to achieve one of the satisfactory sets of outcomes and make a choice directed toward that end.[137]

Simon makes the point that administrative theory or the process of management itself is made necessary by the limits on the intellectual capacity of individuals:

> If there were no limits to human rationality, administrative theory would be barren. It would consist of the single precept: Always select that alternative, among those available, which will lead to the most complete achievement of your goals. The need for an administrative theory resides in the fact that there are practical limits to human rationality, and that these limits are not static, but depend upon the organizational environment in which the individual's decision takes place.[138]

Shull and his associates go beyond Simon's concept of bounded rationality to encompass what they call bounded discretion. According to them, decision makers operate within a discretionary area bounded by (1) social norms, (2) formal rules and policies, (3) moral and ethical norms, and (4) legal restrictions. Presumably the decision maker comes to accept these restrictions and perceives that "certain alternatives will be judged acceptable whereas other activities will be deemed illegitimate and inappropriate."[139]

Bounded rationality limits the rational decision maker in a host of ways. The main categories of limitations in terms of their sources are those that intrude into the decision-making process from outside the organization. These intrusions come from the external forces that make up the organization's environment. In addition to the externally imposed constraints and cognitive limitations that restrict the rational decision maker, there are many other factors that limit the decision maker to satisficing behavior:

1. *Information.* Rational decision makers may lack information or may act on inaccurate information; in either case, the range of alternatives may be affected.[140] It would appear to be a permanent liability of the decision-making process that relevant information is never completely adequate and testable.[141] The necessity to employ interpretive schemes and compensatory devices such as simplification of phenomena provide a related source of limitation.

2. *Time and cost constraints.* In formal organizations of all types, there are schedules to be met and budgets to be observed. As noted in Chapter 2, there is a zone of cost effectiveness beyond which the pursuit of additional information can lead only to information of high cost and low value. Moreover, time pressures may seriously restrict the number of possible courses of action that can be explored.[142]

3. *Communication failures.* Reasonably complete information may be present in the organization but not circulate to all the decision makers who need it to perform their roles satisfactorily. A given organization may be resistant to new information or the significance of new information may be lost because of the way messages are labeled and sorted.

4. *Precedent.* Previous actions and established policies may automatically narrow the deliberations of managerial decision makers. Previous action may prohibit consideration of a whole range of alternatives. Reversal of policies is difficult, especially in a large organization.

5. *Perception.* The selective discrimination of the setting may effectively limit decision making. What decision makers "see" is what they act upon. Through perception and judgment external and internal limitations gain their significance.[143]

Figure 3.1 illustrates the concept of bounded rationality. In the center of the figure is the decision maker who, within the broad context of managerial objectives, receives various kinds of information from the environment. This information includes (1) competitors' products, prices, and strategies, (2) knowledge about the technical state of the art in the main and associated product areas, (3) environmental factors such as productivity trends, price levels, and general consumer demand, and (4) managerial experience gained from similar or related decisions made in the past.

Three primary limitations, however, constrain the decision maker in acquiring and assimilating the information. The first of these, and the one

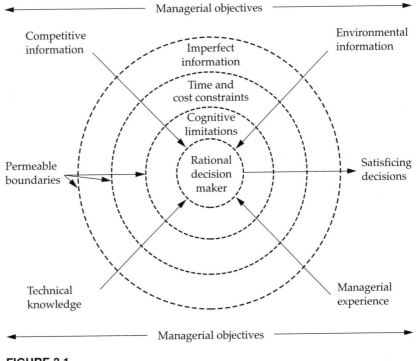

FIGURE 3.1

The Concept of Bounded Rationality

closest to the decision maker, is his or her intellectual ability to deal with only a few of the many complex variables bearing on the decision. The second is the practical constraint on the amounts of time and money that can be spent. And, of course, the third limitation is the impossibility of obtaining anything close to perfect information even if one had limitless time and money.

The boundaries in Figure 3.1 are decreasingly permeable, moving from the outer to the inner ring that houses the rational decision maker. The decision maker starts out with some amount of available information and then obtains additional information from the environmental sources. This additional information, when added to the information already in hand, makes up the total amount of information that will be used to formulate alternatives. It is not perfect information, however, because the decision maker is unable to obtain all the information about a particular set of alternatives. The information acquired, when added to the information in hand, makes the total amount of available information less imperfect than it was prior to the search activity. The degree of imperfection remaining after the search activity depends, of course, on (1) the nature of the decision itself, (2) the amount of information in hand at the outset of the search activity, (3) the availability of additional information, and (4) the time and cost constraints on the search activity.

As greater amounts of information are obtained, the permeable boundary of time and cost constraints is encountered and penetrated.[144] This penetration takes the form of increasing and then, beyond the point of optimality, decreasing marginal value for each additional unit of information (see Figure 2.2). How permeable the time-and-cost-constraints boundary is depends on the decision maker's awareness of and responsiveness to the marginal value of additional information. If, for example, the decision maker ignores the increasing cost and decreasing value of additional units of information, then the time-and-cost-constraints boundary will he highly permeable. On the other hand, if the decision maker is very sensitive to the marginal value of additional information, then the boundary will be less permeable and the information available after the search will be more imperfect. It is obvious, then, that imperfect information and time and cost constraints are intertwined. In general, given two decisions of somewhat equal complexity, where the amount of information in hand at the outset of the search and the availability of additional information are about equal, tighter time and cost constraints will tend to cause greater imperfection in the information from which to develop alternatives. This is not to suggest, however, that less information will necessarily result in a less satisfactory decision. To the contrary, in view of the cognitive limitations of the decision maker it may simplify the selection of alternatives and result in a better choice.

After the search is completed the boundary of cognitive limitations in Figure 3.1 is encountered and penetrated. The decision maker receives, interprets, and assimilates all the information available and then, according to his or her cognitive power, formulates a few relevant alternatives from which to make a satisficing choice. If the decision maker is intelligent and knowledgeable, the boundary will be more permeable than if his or her mental faculties are less developed.

Starting with a clearly defined set of managerial objectives, the rational decision maker receives information from several identifiable environmental sources. This information and the information in hand are used to form a set of relevant alternatives from which to make a satisficing choice. But the amount of information and consequently the number of alternatives are increasingly limited: first, by the unavailability of perfect information; second, by unavoidable time and cost constraints; and finally, by the cognitive limitations of the decision maker. The result of the dynamic process depicted in Figure 3.1 can be only a satisficing choice — one that will simply fulfill the objectives of the decision maker. Moreover, for a choice to be truly satisficing, it must also be compatible with the external forces that form the environment within which the organization exists. This is the concept of bounded rationality, another useful framework for better understanding, and thereby improving, the decision-making process in formal organizations.

THE CASE AGAINST SATISFICING BEHAVIOR

There are several alleged limitations that constitute the case against satisficing behavior. For one thing, in satisficing behavior, objectives tend to be limited by the rational decision maker's own levels of aspiration, which may or may not be in the best interests of the organization. Conversely, in the decision-making process delineated in Figure 2.1, the managerial objectives are intended to further the purposes of the organization rather than accommodate the decision maker's aspirations. Essentially, the process model is geared toward the organization whereas Simon's organizational model seems oriented toward the human frailties of the rational decision maker.

One possible shortcoming of satisficing behavior is the need to specify objectives in advance of decision making.[145] (This alleged limitation also applies to the process model of decision making depicted in Figure 2.1.) Suffice it to say that managers are expected to act in anticipation of attaining organizational objectives; and decision making in pursuit of such objectives is a justifiable confirmation of legitimate managerial behavior.

Another presumed shortcoming of satisficing behavior is   ﹍ highly complex variables that confront the rational decision mak   ﹍ly rule against a choice that furthers the purposes of the org﹍ be, for example, that constant awareness of cognitive lir﹍ impose an overwhelming cognitive strain on the ratic﹍ Without this awareness, the rational decision maker ma﹍

arrive at a choice that is more objectives-oriented, however one chooses to define that term.

Yet another potential disadvantage of satisficing behavior is that it appears to focus primarily on short-term results, possibly at the cost of long-term opportunities for the organization. The seemingly unending willingness to change from one alternative to another or to rescale objectives is strongly suggestive of a situational orientation with a short-term emphasis. The process model of decision making set forth in Figure 2.1 with its bent toward long-range planning should overcome this potential shortcoming of satisficing behavior.

Other criticisms of satisficing behavior relate to Simon's organizational model of decision making (see Table 5.1). For example, it is not uncommon to believe that a satisficing choice is a second-best decision simply because the decision maker is encouraged to accept the first alternative that promises to meet his or her aspiration level. This line of reasoning infers that the decision maker has a second-best aspiration level or one that has been scaled down to a level commensurate with mediocrity and the status quo. According to this view, "it is sufficient to look for 'good enough' solutions, satisficing some a priori determined goals or arbitrarily lowered aspiration levels. No creative generation of alternatives is involved, no search for excellence is encouraged."[146]

Such criticism reflects the bias and orientation of the critic rather then the values and preferences of the decision maker. Indeed criticism of this sort is usually simplistic and uninformed. It presumes a knowledge of the decision maker's situation and aspirations that is unattainable. Moreover, such criticism implies some idealized notion of "what should be" rather than acceptance of "what is" or "what has to be." Optimality is illusory at best and is usually a matter of the critic's perception. Satisficing is attainable at best and invariably is in the preference of the decision maker. It seems rather obvious, therefore, that a conceptualization of the best decision can be made only by the decision maker; and a satisficing choice is quite likely to meet this specification. In this context, Johnson notes:

> The best decision is the one the [responsible] executive says is ideal or the decision that is preferable. Also by definition the second best or acceptable decision is the decision he [or she] says he [or she] would make in the actual situation if the decision is different than the one he [or she] indicated as being best.[147]

Finally, satisficing behavior implicitly assumes that the behavioral aspects of decision making dominate in arriving at a choice that meets the objective of the rational decision maker. Ideally, of course, a balanced emphasis on both the quantitative and the behavioral aspects of decision making is most likely to result in an objectives-oriented outcome. It may be true, for example, that the behavioral disciplines predominate in managerial decision making. It is also true, however, that selective use of quantitative techniques in the integrated process of choice will help achieve outcomes that best serve the long-term interests of the organization (see Figure 2.1).

SUMMARY

This chapter focused on the concept of rational decision making. The term *rational* was defined broadly to mean decision making that is objectives-oriented. All that is necessary to make a given choice a rational one is the existence of an objective and selection of some alternative that, in the decision maker's view, promises to meet the objective. Rational behavior was contrasted with nonrational behavior, with the decision maker's orientation toward some objective being the principal difference between the two types of behavior. It is only when the decision maker does not use his or her ability to reason to accomplish some objective, while paying attention to the consequences of necessary interim actions, that his or her behavior is nonrational.

The concept of maximizing behavior postulates an "economic person" who seeks the highest possible level of personal preferences or utility. The notion of an economic person was originally derived from the philosophy of hedonism, which held that individuals calculate the actions that will maximize their self-interest and behave accordingly. Maximizing behavior treats the organization as a closed decision model. This concept also assumes that managers are basically maximizers who, if reinforcing rewards are forthcoming, will try to maximize the outcomes of their decision so as to achieve the highest possible amount of personal utility.

Maximizing behavior tends to be most common in business organizations with a particular emphasis on profit, sales, and growth in resources. It was also shown, by citing several empirical studies, that managerial satisfactions are not necessarily based on attainment of maximum outcomes in business organization. Moreover, there is little evidence to support the contention that managers tend to be maximizers by nature.

The case against maximizing behavior focused on the faulty assumptions of the closed decision model. In essence, objectives tend to be dynamic rather than fixed or unchanging. The known set of alternatives is always incomplete because of the impossibility of obtaining perfect information. And the cognitive limitations of human beings preclude serious consideration of a large number of alternatives. Many of the variables in a decision-making situation cannot be easily quantified. And it is virtually impossible to successfully implement any type of decision that has external effects without considering environmental forces.

The concept of satisficing behavior, which is based mainly on the open decision model, was presented. The case for this approach to decision making was also analyzed in detail, with special emphasis on the related concept of bounded rationality. Satisficing consists of ascertaining a course of action that is good enough in view of the intended objective or the current level of aspiration — that is, a satisfactory rather than an optimum course of action. Satisficing behavior differs from maximizing behavior in that constraints, both internal and external, limit the decision maker's assumed global rationality, which is essential to the concept of maximizing behavior.

The nature of satisficing behavior depends upon certain attributes of the decision maker such as level of aspiration, persistence, and perception. A satisficing choice is not necessarily a second- or third-best decision. Satisficing behavior simply means that the decision reached is one that is likely to achieve the decision maker's objective.

Satisficing decision makers operate in a condition called bounded rationality. Bounded rationality is a concept that takes into account the many constraints on rational decision makers in formal organizations. The principal constraints are those posed by external entities that intrude into the decision-making process and by the cognitive limitations of the decision maker, who must fashion an objectives-oriented choice from imperfect information within ever-present time and cost constraints. The net result of the decision-making process within bounded rationality is a satisficing choice that is likely to attain the managerial objectives and contribute to the basic purposes of the organization. In essence, managerial decision makers in formal organizations make satisficing choices that are quite rational within the external and internal boundaries of rationality. Such choices are best made within the process model of decision making.

Although satisficing behavior is not without its shortcomings, they appear to be fewer than the more serious limitations of maximizing behavior. Moreover, most of the actual or potential deficiencies in satisficing behavior can be overcome or offset by use of the decision-making process set forth in this book. It is not an exaggeration to assert that maximizing behavior in the closed decision model appears completely inappropriate for managerial decision making in formal organizations. In view of the boundaries within which a rational decision maker must operate, the assumptions underlying maximizing behavior are totally unrealistic. The concept of bounded rationality, within which a rational decision maker pursues satisficing choices in the open decision model, is a more meaningful and useful perspective on the integrated and dynamic process of managerial decision making.

REVIEW AND DISCUSSION QUESTIONS

1. Define and discuss rational decision making by managers in formal organizations as the term was used in this chapter.
2. Differentiate rational and nonrational behavior in a general sense and in a specific sense.
3. Discuss this statement: maximizing behavior is said to have its roots in traditional economic theory.
4. What are some arguments in favor of maximizing behavior at the level of the organization?
5. Is it reasonable to assume that most managerial decision makers are maximizers by nature? Why or why not?
6. What are the central ideas underlying the concept of satisficing behavior?

7. What are the principal shortcomings of satisficing behavior?

8. Identify the principal characteristics of the open decision model and contrast them with the closed decision model.

9. Is a given decision any less rational because it is satisficing rather than maximizing? Why or why not?

10. What are the principal boundary conditions within which rational decision makers pursue satisficing choices?

NOTES

1. William D. Hitt, "Two Models of Man," *American Psychologist*, 24 (July 1979), 654.

2. Sudhir Kakar, "Rationality and Irrationality in Business Leadership," *Journal of Business Policy*, 2 (Winter 1971–1972), 40.

3. Talcott Parsons, ed., *Max Weber: The Theory of Social and Economic Organization*, trans. A. M. Henderson and Talcott Parsons (New York: Free Press, 1974), p. 16.

4. Steven Lukes, "Some Problems About Rationality," *Archives Europeennes de Sociologie*, 8 (1967), 259–260.

5. *The American Heritage Dictionary of the English Language* (Boston: Houghton Mifflin, 1978), p. 1083.

6. Herbert A. Simon, *Administrative Behavior*, 2nd ed. (New York: Free Press, 1957), p. 75.

7. Ibid., pp. 76–77. See also Herbert A. Simon, "From Substantive to Procedural Rationality," in *Models of Bounded Rationality: Behavioral Economics and Business Organization*, Vol. 2, ed. Herbert A. Simon (Cambridge, Mass.: The MIT Press, 1982), pp. 424–443.

8. Manley Howe Jones, *Executive Decision Making* (Homewood, Ill.: Richard D. Irwin, 1962), p. 175.

9. George C. Winston, "Imperfectly Rational Choice," *Journal of Economic Behavior and Organization*, 12 (1989), 67–86.

10. Carl G. Hempel, "Rational Action," in *Proceedings and Addresses of the American Philosophical Association*, Vol. 35 (Yellow Springs, Ohio: Antioch Press, 1962), p. 5.

11. Michael J. White et al., *Managing Public Systems: Analytic Techniques for Public Administration* (North Scituate, Mass.: Duxbury Press, 1980), p. 126.

12. See Nils Brunsson, "Deciding for Responsibility and Legitimation: Alternative Interpretations of Organizational Decision Making," *Accounting, Organizations and Society*, 15 (1990), 47–59; and

John W. Meyer, "Sources and Effects of Decisions: A Comment on Brunsson," *Accounting, Organizations and Society*, 15 (1990), 61–65.

13. Wayne Lee, *Decision Theory and Human Behavior* (New York: Wiley, 1971), p. 10.

14. For example, see Richard M. Cyert, Herbert A. Simon, and Donald B Trow, "Observation of a Business Decision," in *Management: Readings Toward a General Theory*, ed. William B. Wolf (Belmont, Calif.: Wadsworth, 1964), p. 175.

15. George Katona, "Rational Behavior and Economic Behavior," *Psychological Review*, 60 (1953), 313; and Jack Feldman and Michael K. Lindell, "On Rationality," in *Organization and Decision Theory*, ed. Ira Horowitz (Norwell, Mass.: Kluwer Academic Publishers, 1990), pp. 83–164.

16. See Herbert A. Simon, *Models of Man* (New York: Wiley, 1957), p. 198. The concept of bounded rationality will be discussed in detail later in this chapter.

17. See, for example, Chris Argyris, "Some Limits of Rational Man Organization Theory," *Public Administration Review* (May–June 1973), 253–267. Also see Herbert A. Simon, "Organization Man: Rational or Self-Actualizing?" *Public Administration Review* (July–August 1973), 346–353, and Chris Argyris, "Organization Man: Rational and Self-Actualizing," *Public Administration Review* (July–August 1973), 354–357.

18. See, for example, Masanao Toda, "Emotion and Decision Making," *Acta Psychologica*, 45 (1980), 133–155.

19. Glenn H. Snyder, "Deterrence and Power," *Journal of Conflict Resolution* (June 1960), 174.

20. Ibid.

21. Lukes, "Some Problems About Rationality," p. 259.

22. Ibid.

23. Ibid.

24. Harold I. Brown, "On Being Rational," *American Philosophical Quarterly* (October 1978), 246.

25. Jon Elster, "Ulysses and the Sirens: A Theory of Imperfect Rationality," *Social Sciences Information*, 16, No. 5 (1977), 469–526.

26. Kurt W. Back, "Decisions Under Uncertainty: Rational, Irrational, and Non-Rational," *American Behavioral Scientist*, 4 (February 1961), 17.

27. See, for example, Nils Brunsson, "The Irrationality of Action and Action Rationality: Decisions, Ideologies, and Organizational Actions," *Journal of Management Studies* (January 1982), 29–44.

28. See, for example, L. R. Goldberg, "Simple Models or Simple Processes," *American Psychologist*, 28 (1968), 483–496.

29. Brunsson, "Irrationality of Action and Action Rationality," p. 31.

30. Ibid.

31. See, for example, Myles I. Friedman, *Rational Behavior* (Columbia: University of South Carolina Press, 1975); Hakan Wiberg, "Rational and Non-Rational Models of Man," in *The Context of Social Psychology: A Critical Assessment*, ed. Joachim Israel and Henri Tajfel (New York: Academic Press, 1972), pp. 297–369; and D. E. Broadbent, "Aspects of Human Decision Making," *Advancement of Science*, 24 (September 1967), 53–64.

32. Amitai Etzioni, "Rationality is Anti-Entropic," *Journal of Economic Psychology*, 7 (1986), 17–36; and Amitai Etzioni, "How Rational We?" *Sociological Forum*, 2 (1987), 1–20.

33. Amitai Etzioni, "Guidance Rules and Rational Decision Making," *Social Science Quarterly* (December 1985), 755–769; and Timothy M. Devinney, "Rationally Determined Irrationality: An Extension of the Thesis of Rationality as Anti-Entropic," *Journal of Economic Psychology*, 10 (1989), 303–319.

34. Charles L. Martin, "Feelings, Emotional Empathy and Decision Making: Listening to the Voices of the Heart," *Journal of Management Development*, 12, No. 5 (1993), 33–45.

35. Nigel Howard, "The Role of Emotions in Multi-Organizational Decision-Making, *Journal of the Operational Research Society*, 44, No. 6 (June 1993), 613–623.

36. Herbert A. Simon, "Rationality," in *Models of Bounded Rationality: Behavioral Economics and Business Organization*, Vol. 2, ed. Herbert A. Simon

(Cambridge, Mass.: The MIT Press, 1982), pp. 405–407.

37. Herbert A. Simon, "Economics and Psychology, in *Models of Bounded Rationality; Behavioral Economics and Business Organizations*, Vol. 2, ed. Herbert A. Simon (Cambridge, Mass.: The MIT Press, 1982), pp. 318–355.

38. Herbert A. Simon, "A Behavioral Model of Rational Choice," *Quarterly Journal of Economics*, 69 (February 1955), 99.

39. Timothy M. Devinney, "Rationally Determined Irrationality: An Extension of the Thesis of Rationality as Anti-Entropic," *Journal of Economic Psychology*, 10 (1989), 303–319.

40. George P. Huber, *Managerial Decision Making* (Glenview, Ill.: Scott, Foresman, 1980), p. 45.

41. George Katona, *Psychological Analysis of Economic Behavior* (New York: McGraw-Hill, 1963), p. 5.

42. Glenn H. Snyder and Paul Diesing, *Conflict Among Nations* (Princeton, N.J.: Princeton University Press, 1977), p. 340.

43. Kenneth R. MacCrimmon and Ronald N. Taylor, "Decision Making and Problem Solving," in *Handbook of Industrial and Organizational Psychology*, ed. Marvin D. Dunnette (Chicago: Rand McNally, 1976), p. 1442.

44. Edgar H. Schein, *Organizational Psychology* (Englewood Cliffs, N.J.: Prentice-Hall, 1965), p. 48.

45. Lee, *Decision Theory and Human Behavior*, p. 5.

46. Samuel Eilon, *Management Control*, 2nd ed. (New York: Pergamon, 1979), p. 147.

47. Samuel Eilon, "Goals and Constraints," *Journal of Management Studies*, 8 (October 1971), 292.

48. Ward Edwards, "Decision Making: Psychological Aspects," in *International Encyclopedia of the Social Sciences*, Vol. 4, ed. David Sills (New York: Macmillan and Free Press, 1968), p. 41.

49. Mark J. Machina, "Choice Under Uncertainty: Problems Solved and Unsolved," *Economic Perspectives*, 1 (Summer 1987), 121–154; and John Haltiwanger and Michael Waldman, "Rational Expectations and the Limits of Rationality: An Analysis of Heterogeneity," *American Economic Review*, 75 (June 1985), 326–340.

50. Marcus Alexis and Charles Z. Wilson, eds., *Organizational Decision Making* (Englewood Cliffs, N.J.: Prentice-Hall, 1967), pp. 73–74.

51. Charles Z. Wilson and Marcus Alexis, "Basic Frameworks for Decisions," *Academy of Management Journal* (August 1962), 152.

52. Kenneth J. Arrow, "Rationality of Self and Others in an Economic System," *Journal of Business*, 59 (1986), 385–399.

53. Fritz Machlup, "Theories of the Firm: Marginalist, Behavioral, Managerial," *American Economic Review* (March 1957), 9.

54. Thomas A. Petit, "A Behavioral Theory of Management," *Academy of Management Journal* (December 1967), 342.

55. Bruce E. Kaufman, "A New Theory of Satisficing," *The Journal of Behavioral Economics*, 19 (1990), 35–51.

56. Milton Friedman, *Capitalism and Freedom* (Chicago: University of Chicago Press, 1962), p. 133.

57. Milton Friedman, "The Methodology of Positive Economics," in *Essays in Positive Economics* (Chicago: University of Chicago Press, 1953), p. 35.

58. Charles F. Phillips, Jr., "What Is Wrong with Profit Maximization?" in *Management and the Behavioral Sciences*, ed. Maneck S. Wadia (Boston: Allyn and Bacon, 1968), p. 326.

59. Eugene V. Rostow, "To Whom and for What Ends Is Corporate Management Responsible?" in *The Corporation in Modern Society*, ed. Edward S. Mason (New York: Atheneum, 1967), p. 64.

60. H. T. Koplin, "The Profit Maximization Assumption," *Oxford Economic Papers*, 15, No. 2 (July 1963), 135.

61. Machlup, "Theories of the Firm," p. 22.

62. Joseph W. McGuire, *Theories of Business Behavior* (Englewood Cliffs, N.J.: Prentice-Hall, 1964), p. 56.

63. Joseph E. Haring and Gorman C. Smith, "Utility Theory, Decision Theory, and Profit Maximization," *American Economic Review* (September 1959), 582.

64. James D. Herendeen, "Alternative Models of the Corporate Enterprise: Growth Maximization and Value Maximization," *Quarterly Review of Economics and Business* (Winter 1974), 61.

65. McGuire, *Theories of Business Behavior*, pp. 56–57.

66. William J. Baumol, *Business Behavior, Value and Growth*, rev. ed. (New York: Harcourt, Brace & World, 1967). Also, see Duncan Bailey and Stanley E. Boyle, "Sales Revenue Maximization: An Empirical Vindication," *Industrial Organization Review*, 5, No. 1 (1977), 46–55.

67. John Kenneth Galbraith, *The New Industrial State* (Boston: Houghton Mifflin, 1967).

68. Robin Marris, "A Model of the 'Managerial' Enterprise," *Quarterly Journal of Economics* (May 1963), 188, 192.

69. Herendeen, "Alternative Models of the Corporate Enterprise."

70. Bevars Dupre Mabry, "Sales Maximization vs. Profit Maximization: Are They Consistent?" *Western Economic Journal* (March 1968), 154–160.

71. Patrick Yeuing, "Unifying Elements in the Theory of the Firm," *Quarterly Review of Economics and Business* (Winter 1969), 21–28.

72. R. Joseph Monsen, Jr., and Anthony Downs, "A Theory of Large Managerial Firms," *Journal of Political Economy* (June 1965), 225.

73. Robert Aaron Gordon, *Business Leadership in the Large Corporation* (Berkeley: University of California Press, 1961), pp. 312–313.

74. Joseph W. McGuire, John S. Y. Chiu, and Albar O. Elbing, "Executive Income, Sales, and Profits," *American Economic Review* (September 1962), 753–761.

75. Wilbur G. Lewellen and Blaine Huntsman, "Managerial Pay and Corporate Performance," *American Economic Review* (September 1970), 710–720.

76. Robert Tempest Masson, "Executive Motivations, Earnings, and Consequent Equity Performance," *Journal of Political Economy* (November–December 1971), 1278.

77. S. B. Prasad, "Top Management Compensation and Executive Performance," *Academy of Management Journal* (September 1974), 544–558.

78. Oliver E. Williamson, "Managerial Discretion and Human Behavior," *American Economic Review* (December 1963), 1032–1057.

79. See R. L. Opsahl and M. D. Dunnette, "The Role of Financial Compensation in Industry Motivation," in *Management and Motivation*, ed. V. H. Vroom and E. L. Deci (Baltimore: Penguin, 1970), pp. 127–159, for a discussion of contrasting views on the effect of financial incentives on managerial motivation in business organizations.

80. Peter F. Drucker, *Management: Tasks — Responsibilities — Practices* (New York: Harper & Row, 1973), p. 60.

81. Joseph W. McGuire, *Business and Society* (New York: McGraw-Hill, 1963), pp. 272–273.

82. Robert N. Anthony, "The Trouble with Profit Maximization," in *The Nature and Scope of Management*, ed. Maneck S. Wadia (Chicago: Scott, Foresman, 1966), pp. 47–55.

83. Thomas A. Petit, "Making Socially Responsible Decisions," *Academy of Management Journal* (December 1966), 308.

84. Joseph W. McGuire, "The Social Values of Economic Organizations," *Review of Social Economy* (April 1947), 62–63.

85. Zubair Hasan, "The Principle of Profit Maximization Reconsidered," *Indian Economic Journal* (September 1972), 62.

86. Michael C. Jensen and William H. Meckling, "Theory of the Firm: Managerial Behavior, Agency Costs and Ownership Structure," *Journal of Financial Economics*, 3, No. 4 (October 1976), 305–360.

87. Sidney G. Winter, Jr., "Economic 'Natural Selection' and the Theory of the Firm," *Yale Economic Essays*, 4, No. 1 (1964), 224–272.

88. James G. March and Herbert A. Simon, *Organizations* (New York: Wiley, 1958), p. 151.

89. L. Goslin and A. Rethans, *Basic Systems for Decision Making* (Dubuque, Iowa: Kendall/Hunt, 1980), p. 56.

90. Daniel Katz and Robert L. Kahn, *The Social Psychology of Organizations*, 2nd ed. (New York: Wiley, 1978).

91. Ibid., pp. 502–508. Quoted from Samuel A. Kirkpatrick, "Psychological Views of Decision-Making," in *Political Science Annual*, Vol. 6, ed. Cornelius P. Cotter (Indianapolis: Bobbs-Merrill, 1975), p. 68.

92. Katona, *Psychological Analysis of Economic Behavior*, p. 201.

93. Ibid.

94. Anthony, "The Trouble with Profit Maximization," p. 49.

95. E. Frank Harrison, *Management and Organizations* (Boston: Houghton Mifflin, 1978), pp. 467–468.

96. Winter, "Economic 'Natural Selection' and the Theory of the Firm," p. 267.

97. L. Jonathan Cohen, "Can Human Irrationality Be Experimentally Demonstrated?" *The Behavioral and Brain Sciences*, 4 (September 1981), 317–370.

98. Adolph A. Berle, "The Impact of the Corporation on Classical Economic Theory," in *Readings in Organization Theory: A Behavioral Approach*, ed. Walter A. Hill and Douglas M. Egan (Boston: Houghton Mifflin, 1966), p. 54.

99. Wilson and Alexis, "Basic Frameworks for Decisions," p. 160.

100. G. L. S. Shackle, "Decision: The Human Predicament," *Annals of the American Academy of Political and Social Science*, 412 (March 1974), 1.

101. See Harvey Leibenstein, "On Relaxing the Maximization Postulate," *The Journal of Business Economics*, 15 (Winter 1986), 3–16.

102. Kaufman, "A New Theory of Satisficing," p. 36.

103. Amitai Etzioni, "Normative-Affective Factors: Toward a New Decision-Making Model," *Journal of Economic Psychology*, 9 (1988), 125–150.

104. March and Simon, *Organizations*, pp. 140–141.

105. Ibid., p. 140.

106. Herbert A. Simon, "Theories of Decision-Making in Economics and Behavioral Science," in *Models of Bounded Rationality: Behavioral Economics and Business Organization*, Vol. 2, ed. Herbert A. Simon (Cambridge, Mass.: The MIT Press, 1982), pp. 287–317.

107. Alexander L. George, *Presidential Decisionmaking in Foreign Policy* (Boulder, Colo.: Westview, 1980), p. 40.

108. Wilson and Alexis, "Basic Frameworks for Decisions," p. 162.

109. Gary P. Latham and Glen Whyte, "The Futility of Utility Analysis," *Personnel Psychology*, 47 (1994), 31–46.

110. Folke Olander, "Search Behavior in Non-Simultaneous Choice Situations: Satisficing or Maximizing?" in *Utility, Probability, and Human Decision Making*, ed. Dirk Wendt and Charles Vlek (Boston: D. Riedel, 1975), pp. 297–320.

111. Herbert A. Simon, *Administrative Behavior*, 3rd ed. (New York: Free Press, 1976), p. xxvii.

112. Charles A. O'Reilly, III, "The Use of Information in Organizational Decision Making: A Model and Some Propositions," *Research in Organizational Behavior*, Vol. 5, ed. L. L. Cummings and Barry M. Staw (Greenwich, Conn.: JAI Press, 1983), pp. 103–139.

113. Anne Edland and Ola Svenson, "Judgment and Decision Making Under Time Pressure," in *Time Pressure and Stress in Human Judgment and Decision Making*, eds. A. John Maule and Ola Svenson (New York: Plenum, 1993), pp. 27–40.

114. Ronald J. Ebert and Terence R. Mitchell, *Organizational Decision Processes* (New York: Crane, Russak, 1975), pp. 93–94.

115. Donald N. Taylor, "Psychological Determinants of Bounded Rationality: Implications for Decision-Making Strategies," *Decision Sciences*, 6 (July 1975), 418.

116. Herbert A. Simon, "Rational Decision Making in Business Organizations," *American Economic Review* (September 1979), 503.

117. Herbert A. Simon, "Theories of Bounded Rationality," in *Models of Bounded Rationality: Behavioral Economics and Business Organization*, Vol. 2, ed. Herbert A. Simon (Cambridge, Mass.: The MIT Press, 1982), pp. 408–423.

118. Wilson and Alexis, "Basic Frameworks for Decisions," p. 162.

119. Herbert A. Simon, "Theories of Decision Making in Economics and Behavioral Science," in *Organizational Decision Making*, ed. Marcus Alexis and Charles Z. Wilson (Englewood Cliffs, N.J.: Prentice-Hall, 1967), p. 208.

120. McGuire, *Theories of Business Behavior*, p. 183.

121. See Simon, *Models of Man*, pp. 196–200.

122. Ibid., p. 198.

123. Ibid., p. 199.

124. Charles E. Lindblom, "The Science of 'Muddling Through,'" in *Studies in Managerial Process and Organizational Behavior*, ed. John H. Turner, Alan C. Filley, and Robert J. House (Glenview, Ill.: Scott, Foresman, 1972), p. 124.

125. Robert H. Frank, "Shrewdly Rational," *Sociological Forum*, 2 (Winter 1987), 21–41.

126. Taylor, "Psychological Determinants of Bounded Rationality," p. 409.

127. See, for example, Katona, *Psychological Analysis of Economic Behavior*; R. W. Kates, *Hazard and Choice Perception in Flood Plain Management* (Chicago: University of Chicago, Department of Geography, 1962); C. E. Lindblom, *The Intelligence of Democracy: Decision Making Through Mutual Adjustment* (New York: Free Press, 1965); and R. Wholstetter, *Pearl Harbor: Warning and Decision* (Stanford, Calif.: Stanford University Press, 1962).

128. See D. G. Elmes, "Short-Term Memory as a Function of Storage Load," *Journal of Experimental Psychology*, 81 (1969), 203–204; G. A. Miller, "The Magical Number Seven, Plus or Minus Two: Some Limits on Our Capacity for Processing Information," *Psychological Review*, 63 (1956), 81–97; and M. I. Posner, "Immediate Memory in Sequential Tasks," *Psychological Bulletin*, 60 (1963), 346–354.

129. See, for example, R. N. Taylor and M. D. Dunnette, "Influence of Dogmatism, Risk-Taking Propensity and Intelligence on Decision-Making Strategies for a Sample of Industrial Managers," *Journal of Applied Psychology*, 59, No. 4 (1974), 420–423.

130. See J. Block and P. Peterson, "Some Personality Correlates of Confidence, Caution, and Speed in a Decision Situation," *Journal of Abnormal Social Psychology*, 51 (1955), 34–41; and J. C. Brengelmann, "Abnormal and Personality Correlates of Certainty," *Journal of Mental Science*, 105 (1959), 142–162.

131. See, for example, H. M. Schroeder and P. Suedfeld, *Personality Theory and Information Processing* (New York: Ronald Press, 1971).

132. See, for example, J. S. Bruner, J. J. Goodnow, and G. A. Austin, *A Study of Thinking* (New York: Wiley, 1956); and Taylor and Dunnette, "Influence of Dogmatism, Risk-Taking Propensity and Intelligence on Decision-Making Strategies for a Sample of Industrial Managers."

133. See Sheldon Siegel, "Level of Aspiration and Decision Making," *Psychological Review*, 64 (1957), 253–262.

134. See, for example, W. K. Kirchner, "Age Differences in Short-Term Retention of Rapidly Changing Information," *Journal of Experimental Psychology*, 55 (1958), 352–358; M. W. Weir, "Developmental Changes in Problem-Solving Strategies," *Psychological Review*, 71 (1964), 473–490; and Mitzi M. S. Johnson, "Age Differences in Decision Making: A Process Methodology for Examining Strategic Information Processing," *Journal of Gerontology, PSYCHOLOGICAL SCIENCES*, 45 (March 1990), 75–78.

135. For a discussion of factors that affect decision making see Nathan Kogan and Michael A. Wallach, "Risk Taking as a Function of the Situation, the Person, and the Group," in *New Direction in Psychology*, III, ed. G. Mandler (New York: Holt, Rinehart and Winston, 1967), pp. 111–278.

136. David W. Miller and Martin K. Starr, *The Structure of Human Decisions*. (Englewood Cliffs, N.J.: Prentice-Hall. 1967), p. 50.

137. Farzad Moussavi et al., "Explaining Strategic Managers' Choice of Decision Tools: Cognitive Style-Representation Method Compatibility, *International Journal of Management*, 12, No. 3 (September 1995), 305–314.

138. Simon, *Administrative Behavior*, 2nd ed., pp. 240–241.

139. Fremont A. Shull, André L. Delbecq, and L. L. Cummings, *Organizational Decision Making* (New York: McGraw-Hill, 1970), pp. 18–19.

140. William F. Wright, "Cognitive Information Processing Biases: Implications for Producers and Users of Financial Information," *Decision Sciences*, 11 (April 1980), 284–298.

141. Rashi Glazer et al., "Locally Rational Decision Making: The Distracting Effect of Information on Managerial Performance," *Management Science*, 38, No. 2 (February 1992), 212–226.

142. See Dan Zakay and Stuart Wooler, "Time Pressure, Training and Decision Effectiveness," *Ergonomics* 27 (1984), 273–284; and Kathleen M. Eisenhardt, "Making Fast Strategic Decisions in High-Velocity Environments," *Academy of Management Journal*, 32 (1989), 543–576.

143. Richard C. Snyder, "A Decision-Making Approach to the Study of Political Phenomena," in *Approaches to the Study of Politics*, ed. Roland Young (Evanston, Ill.: Northwestern University Press, 1985), pp. 3–38.

144. Allen C. Bluedorn and Robert B. Denhardt, "Time and Organizations," *Journal of Management*, 14 (1988), 299–320.

145. James E. Martin, George B. Kleindorfer, and William R. Brashers, Jr., "The Theory of Bounded Rationality and Legitimation," *Journal for the Theory of Social Behaviour*, 17 (March 1987), 63–82.

146. Milan Zeleny, "Descriptive Decision Making and Its Applications," in *Applications of Management Science*, Vol. 1, ed. Randall L. Schultz (Greenwich, Conn.: JAI Press, 1981), p. 341.

147. Rossall J. Johnson, "Conflict Avoidance Through Acceptable Decisions," *Human Relations*, 27 (January 1974), 72.

SUPPLEMENTAL REFERENCES

Abelson, Robert P., and Ariel Levi. "Decision Making and Decision Theory." In *The Handbook of Social Psychology*. 3rd ed. Vol. 1. Ed. Gardner Lindzey and Elliot Aronson. New York: Random House, 1985, pp. 231–309.

Allison, Graham T. *Essence of Decision: Explaining the Cuban Missile Crisis*. Boston: Little, Brown, 1971.

Bass, Bernard M. *Organizational Decision Making*. Homewood, Ill.: Richard D. Irwin, 1983.

Benn, S. I., and G. W. Mortimore, eds. *Rationality and the Social Sciences*. London: Routledge & Kegan Paul, 1976.

Braverman, Jerome D. *Management Decision Making*. New York: AMACOM, 1980.

Brunsson, Nils. *The Irrational Organization*. New York: Wiley, 1985.

Collingridge, David. *Critical Decision Making*. New York: St. Martin's Press, 1982.

Cook, Karen Schweers, and Margaret Levi, eds. *The Limits of Rationality*. Chicago: University of Chicago Press, 1990.

Cornell, Alexander H. *The Decision-Maker's Handbook*. Englewood Cliffs, N.J.: Prentice-Hall, 1980.

Cyert, Richard M., and James G. March. *A Behavioral Theory of the Firm*. Englewood Cliffs, N. J.: Prentice-Hall, 1963.

Donaldson, Gordon, and Jay W. Lorsch. *Decision Making at the Top*. New York: Basic Books, 1983.

Eells, Ellery. *Rational Decision and Causality*. Cambridge: Cambridge University Press, 1982.

Einhorn, Hillel J., and Robin M. Hogarth. "Behavioral Decision Theory: Processes of Judgment and Choice." *Annual Review of Psychology*, 32 (1981), 53–88.

Erickson, Richard F. "Rationality and Executive Motivation." *Journal of the Academy of Management* (April 1962), 7–23.

Fisk, George, ed. *The Psychology of Management Decision*. Lund, Sweden: CWK Gleerup, 1967.

Hogarth, Robin M. *Judgement and Choice*. 2nd ed. New York: Wiley, 1987.

Kinder, Donald R., and Janet A. Weiss. "In Lieu of Rationality." *Journal of Conflict Resolution* (December 1978), 707–735.

Linstone, Harold A. *Multiple Perspectives for Decision Making*. New York: North-Holland, 1984.

Mack, Ruth P. *Planning on Uncertainty.* New York: Wiley-Interscience, 1971.

Mannheim, K. *Rational and Irrational Elements in Contemporary Society.* London: Oxford University Press, 1934.

March, James G. "Bounded Rationality, Ambiguity, and the Engineering of Choice," *Bell Journal of Economics* (Autumn 1978), 587–608.

March, James G., and Johan P. Olsen. *Ambiguity and Choice in Organizations.* Norway: Universitetsforlaget, 1976.

Moore, Peter G. *Risk in Business Decisions.* New York: Wiley, 1973.

Neisser, Ulric. "The Multiplicity of Thought." *British Journal of Psychology* (February 1963), 1–14.

Nelson, Richard R., and Sidney G. Winter. *An Evolutionary Theory of Economic Change.* Cambridge, Mass.: The Belknap Press of Harvard University Press, 1990.

Nisbett, Richard, and Lee Ross. *Human Inference: Strategies and Shortcomings of Social Judgment.* Englewood Cliffs, N.J.: Prentice-Hall, 1980.

Nozik, Robert. *The Nature of Rationality.* Princeton, N.J.: Princeton University Press, 1993.

Radner, Roy. "Satisficing." *Journal of Mathematical Economics,* 2 (1975), 253–262.

Saaty, Thomas L. *Decision Making for Leaders.* Belmont, Calif.: Wadsworth, 1982.

Simon, Herbert A. "Rationality as Process and as Product of Thought." *American Economic Review* (May 1978), 1–16.

Slovic, Paul. *From Shakespeare to Simon: Speculation — and Some Evidence — About Man's Ability to Process Information.* Monograph, Vol. 12. Eugene, Ore.: Oregon Research Institute, 1972.

Sjoberg, Lennart, Tadeusz Tyszka, and James A. Wise, eds. *Human Decision Making.* Bodafors, Sweden: Bokforlaget Doxa, 1983.

Steinbruner, John D. *The Cybernetic Theory of Decision.* Princeton, N.J.: Princeton University Press, 1974.

Sutherland, Stuart. *Irrationality: Why We Don't Think Straight.* New Brunswick, N.J.: Rutgers University Press, 1992.

Szaniawski, Klemens. "Philosophy of Decision Making." *Acta Psychologica,* 45 (1980), 327–341.

Weiss, Janet A. "Coping with Complexity: An Experimental Study of Public Policy Decision-Making." *Journal of Policy Analysis and Management,* 2 No. 1 (1982), 66–87.

Wright, Peter. "The Harassed Decision Maker: Time Pressures, Distractions, and the Use of Evidence." *Journal of Applied Psychology,* 59, No. 5 (1974), 555–561.

Zey, Mary, ed. *Decision Making: Alternatives to Rational Choice Models.* Newbury Park, Calif.: Sage Publications, 1992.

CHAPTER FOUR

Values for Decision Making

*T*he personal values of the decision maker and the values of the organization significantly influence the entire process of decision making. For example, the decision maker must consider the values of the organization in setting managerial objectives. The search activity will reflect the personal values of the decision maker attempting to shape the information obtained into alternatives that relate to the managerial objectives. Once the search activity is completed, the decision maker's personal values, conditioned by the organizational values reflected in the managerial objectives, influence the comparison and evaluation of alternatives. And, of course, at the moment of choice this same combination of values prevails. The making of the choice initiates the implementation function, in which the values of the organization usually supersede those of the decision maker. Finally, in the follow-up and control function of the decision-making process, the standards for measurement and corrective action to ensure outcomes in keeping with the managerial objectives reflect organizational values.

At any and all points in the integrated process of decision making, the personal values of the decision maker may conflict with the values of the organization. When this happens, the decision maker must often subordinate personal values to those of the organization. This is the case because a manager is assumed to personify the organization; and a manager's satisficing choice, made within the bounds of rationality, should further the basic purposes of the organization.

THE CONCEPT OF VALUES

The concept of values is an elusive one. Values mean different things to different people; therefore it is appropriate to begin the discussion of this concept with several definitions. Values may be regarded as "the normative standards by which human beings are influenced in their choice among the alternative courses of action they perceive."[1] Values may also be viewed as "conceptions of desirable states of affairs that are utilized in selective conduct as criteria for preference or choice or as justifications for proposed or actual behavior. . . . values are closely related, conceptually and empirically, to social norms."[2] "A value is an enduring belief that a specific mode of conduct or end-state of existence is personally or socially preferable to an opposite or converse mode of conduct or end-state of existence."[3] Values thus are abstract ideals, positive or negative, not tied to any specific object or situation, representing a person's beliefs about modes of conduct and ideal terminal states. Values are beliefs that transcendentally guide actions and judgments across specific objects and situations.[4]

A value may be viewed as a stated or implied conception of what an individual, group, or organization finds desirable. In terms of this conception the means and ends of action are selected from the available alternatives.[5]

Values are part of a person's life and thought, and the individual usually takes them for granted unless they are challenged. People acquire their values very early in life from parents, teachers, and other persons who are influential in their lives and who, in turn, acquired their values in a similar fashion. For example, child-rearing practices show the values of a family and of the social group to which the family belongs.[6]

Values are actually part of an individual's personality, especially if some values clearly dominate others. If we say, for example, that an individual decides among alternatives on the basis of whether the choice will benefit others, we are describing the decision maker's personality as well as values. In effect, values are a kind of guidance system used by an individual faced with a choice among alternatives.[7]

Like all beliefs, values involve knowledge or thought, emotion, and behavior. A value is a thought about the desirable rather than the undesirable. To say that a person has a value is to say that the person knows the correct way to behave or the correct result for which to strive. The individual can feel emotional about a value; he or she is emotionally for or against it, approves of those who follow it, and disapproves of those who do not follow it. A value has a behavioral component when it leads to action.[8]

Values tend to defy measurement and quantification except insofar as they can be ranked. People may disagree with the values of other individuals or particular groups and in that sense the values may be seen as inappropriate, but values cannot be proved or disproved.[9] Indeed, one of the principal shortcomings of maximizing behavior in the closed decision model is the inability to precisely measure values that influence the utility of alternatives. "Contemporary social science draws a sharp distinction between fact and value. Values cannot be empirically tested. Analysis can therefore neither verify any one person's values nor command agreement among persons on their values."[10]

Values serve as standards that guide the conduct of individuals in a variety of ways. Values permit individuals to do all of the following:

1. Take particular positions on social issues
2. Favor one particular political or religious ideology over another

3. Guide presentations of the self to others

4. Evaluate and judge, to give praise and fix blame on the self and others

5. Permit comparative assessment of self such as morality and competence in relation to others

6. Persuade and influence others

7. Permit rationalization of beliefs, attitudes, and actions to bolster personal feelings of morality and competence

8. Maintain and enhance self-esteem[11]

An individual's value system is a pattern of values ranked according to their relative importance.[12] In England's view "a personal value system is viewed as a relatively permanent perceptual framework which shapes and influences the general nature of an individual's behavior."[13] After a value is learned it becomes part of an organized system wherein each value is given a priority relative to other values. Such a relative ranking enables the individual to define change as a reordering of priorities and at the same time to see the total value system as relatively stable over time. "A value system is a learned organization of principles and rules to help one choose between alternatives, resolve conflicts, and make decisions."[14]

The personal value systems of managerial decision makers are of particular interest in this context. Such value systems have the following general qualities:

1. They affect the perception of situations and problems.

2. They affect the entire process of choice.

3. They affect interpersonal relationships.

4. They affect the perception of individual and organizational achievement and success.

5. They set the limits for ethical behavior.

6. They affect the acceptance of or resistance to organizational pressures and goals.[15]

Because of the differing interpretations of the concept of values, it becomes difficult for the individual to assess his or her own values, much less those of other individuals or the organization. Consequently, to understand the significance of values in the decision-making process, and in most other kinds of endeavor, the individual may find it useful to consider the following guidelines:

1. Many disagreements arise out of differing values.

2. Values, unless they are spelled out precisely, are not communicated automatically.

3. Personal values are arrived at subjectively and differ markedly between individuals.

4. Individuals tend to assume that their values are "normal" and that other individuals should accept or adopt these values.

5. Most individuals are largely unaware of their own value judgments, particularly as they relate to their own specialty.

6. An educated person is one who is aware of differing and frequently conflicting values, who recognizes his or her own system of values, and who then makes decisions with full awareness of their consequences.[16]

Personal and organizational values permeate all decisions. Value judgments arise out of the personal value system of the decision maker and are conditioned by organizational values. To be sure, one finds more value judgments in category II than in category I decisions. Still, values surround decisions made under all types of conditions and with all kinds of constraints. The values for decision making may be distinguished by the following general properties:

1. Values arise in response to the human need to exercise choice among mutually exclusive alternatives of action. Values have the property of selectivity — that is, the quality of ordering the options available in terms that those who have to make the choice will accept as decisive.

2. Values do not have the property of universality. That is, all individuals are not bounded by identical norms in making choices. Variability of values is evident from individual to individual, but most particularly among well-knit social groups and cultures.

3. Values have the property of substantial continuity from generation to generation, but this continuity comes mainly from social learning — a process of interpersonal communication, usually employing symbols to represent the values communicated. According to the best evidence available, social values are not inherited genetically. However, there are traits, certainly biological and presumably psychological as well, that may show up in a reasonably consistent and widespread fashion as social values.

4. Values can and do change, though they have a firm hold on human beings and constitute a relatively stable component of the personality.

5. To a very large extent, values are associated with the role that human beings fulfill or want to fulfill in society. In this regard, values have the property of imposing obligations, of defining what is expected of the person in a certain role. Conversely, role values define the rights that a person can expect to claim by virtue of fulfilling role obligations according to expectations.

6. Values have the property of spurring self-evaluation — that is, the capacity of a person to judge the propriety of his or her own conduct in reference to standards he or she has learned to apply to the self. These standards are often derived from the social groups of which the person

is a member; but sometimes they are viewed as dictates of superhuman authority or individual conscience. In any event, a value conveys to the person holding it a sense of personal imperative that makes the person feel subject to its direction.

7. Values have the property of self-inhibition; that is, they restrain action that is considered improper through a process of internalized control, rather than by external coercive sanctions. Often external sanctions reinforce the internal ones where societies seek to ensure uniform behavior. But it is the capacity to command a person's own mechanisms of control that is the property of the authentic value.[17]

Values provide a decision maker with a set of guidelines for steering through the entire decision-making process. Value judgments taken from personal values and overlaid by the values of the organization occur in the formulation of objectives, the search for alternatives, the evaluation of alternatives, the moment of choice, the point of implementation, and in follow-up and control. Naturally, the application of values and value judgments will vary with each decision; but each decision made will, in some degree, reflect both the decision maker's personal values and, more emphatically, the values of the decision maker's organization.

THE HIERARCHY OF VALUES

To apply a structure to the general concept, it is useful to specify a hierarchy of values. That is, values start at the level of the individual; the values of several individuals form the values of a group; several sets of group values make up organizational values; many sets of organizational values constitute the overall economic system, which in turn is part of the total society.

Bernthal has set forth a hierarchy of values that places human values at the top. He states the case for ultimate human values in the following passage:

Man's search for ultimate values is the story of life itself. Implied in every decision he makes is a judgment in terms of a priority of values, when goals come into conflict, and in terms of the ultimate decision criterion. In every business decision, the manager acts upon his own response to the basic philosophical question, "What is the nature of man?" Whether expressed or implied, the decision maker reveals his own philosophy of life in making these critical decisions.[18]

In keeping with the American tradition of democracy, all social, political, and economic arrangements are designed to assist the individual in achieving self-fulfillment.

The ultimate goals of the individual are generalized as freedom, opportunity, self-realization, and human dignity. These values assume a respect for the rights of others, a concern over justice and order under law, and a responsibility for maintaining and perpetuating systems that make this freedom possible.[19]

The values of individuals may also be viewed within a basic framework. Leys cites six independent values that guide the individual in various roles as decision maker, citizen, and human being:

1. *Happiness,* which is associated with desirable results and maximum satisfaction.
2. *Lawfulness,* which is related to precedents, customs, contracts, and authorizations.
3. *Harmony,* which is analogous with logical consistency, Platonic justice, order, plan, and the common good.
4. *Survival,* which is influenced by political power and friend-foe relationships.
5. *Integrity,* which is attained through self-respect, rationality of the individual, and peace of mind.
6. *Loyalty,* which is related to institutional trends and social causes.[20]

These independent values set forth by Leys parallel the ultimate values of Bernthal; that is, they are both guides to action at the individual level. In effect, such values make up the individual's total system of values, which in turn is a part of his or her personality. Further, as reflected in the following excerpt, the individual's value system permits him or her to cope with personal and social situations related to the fulfillment of basic needs:

> It should be emphasized that the integration of a personality as a concrete empirical action system can never be a simple "reflection" or "realization" of a value system. It must involve the adjustment of such a value system to the exigencies of the object situation and to the exigencies of organic needs.[21]

Individuals come together in groups and take on the values of the group to help achieve its basic purposes. Groups formed for decision making or other purposes must reach consensus. This results from continuing interaction among the members, which, of course, demands free and open communication.

Groups have norms or standards of conduct that the participants must observe as the price of continued membership. Homans has defined group norms as follows:

> A norm, then, is an idea in the minds of the members of a group, an idea that can be put in the form of a statement specifying what the members should do, ought to do, are expected to do, under given circumstances.[22]

Often it is necessary for the individual to compromise his or her personal values in the interest of maintaining group solidarity. However, such compromises may hurt less if the individual has internalized the values of the group. Elbing and Elbing stress this point in the following passage:

> Groups are recognized as forming, not only in relation to traditional economic functions, but also through social interaction around the work tasks. Such groups serve as personal reference points or "reference groups" for individuals. These "reference groups" in the firm [organization] serve as a source of norms, status, and values for those individuals identifying with them. Thus, groups are vital for their members . . . in their function of socializing individuals and of satisfying (or thwarting) in some degree individual social needs.[23]

Churchman views a group from two basic standpoints: (1) as an individual in its own right and (2) as a body made up of a set of individuals. In the first case, groups are alleged to have "minds of their own," and the values of the group are considered collectively, rather than related to the values of the individual members. More specifically, group values are related to the collective knowledge possessed by all the members as well as to the decisions made by the entire group. From the second standpoint, it is necessary to consider as primary the values of the individual members of the group and to develop a way to measure and combine them into a kind of composite value before it is possible to determine what is important for the group.[24]

Delbecq differentiates group values on the basis of the type of decision at hand.[25] His three-point typology of different kinds of decisions involves a change in group values from a simple sense of responsibility and commitment for routine decisions to an increasingly complex set of values for creative and negotiated decision making.

As individual values underlie the values of the group, so the values of the group give rise to the values of the total organization. Bernthal identifies the values at the level of the business organization as (1) profits, (2) survival, and (3) growth.[26] He places such values at the bottom of his hierarchy, below the values of the individual, society, and the economic system. In essence, his hierarchy suggests that

> responsible . . . management requires decisions and actions that contribute to the goals of the [organization] without violating higher goals or values . . . places human values above economic values . . . assumes that economic objectives can be achieved without denying the individual his basic right as a human being.[27]

For the purposes of this book, organizational values are synonymous with managerial values, and as such they will receive more extensive treatment in a subsequent section of this chapter.

The hierarchy of values does not stop at the level of the organization. It continues on to include the economic system and the total society. For example, the economic system's values cover the allocation of scarce resources and the production and distribution of goods and services; the values for the total society encompass the many facets of human needs and social welfare.

Many societal values are embedded within the social system and the political system. They are formidable environmental forces that managerial decision makers must assess thoroughly.

CLASSIFICATION OF VALUES

There are numerous ways to classify values. The importance of value classifications is that they permit the development of value profiles for individuals, groups, and organizations, which make it easier to predict behavior in decision-making situations. In this book, for example, the primary concern is with individuals as managerial decision makers in formal organizations. The subject of managerial values will be treated in the next section of this chapter. The discussion to follow in this section will present some basic classifications of personal values.

Spranger's original classification of aesthetic, theoretical, economic, political, social, and religious values was standardized by Allport. For years, Allport's scale was the only standardized instrument that claimed to measure personal values.[28] One of the best known and most useful classifications of personal values was advanced by Maslow.[29] Different subsets of values may independently fulfill Maslow's safety, security, love, self-esteem, and self-actualization needs. Maslow also speaks of B(being)-values and D(deficiency)-values. In essence, he proposed a hierarchy of needs in which certain values were more desirable for psychological fulfillment than others:

> For one thing, it looks as if there were a single ultimate value for mankind, a far goal toward which all men strive. This is called variously by different authors self-actualization, integration, psychological health, individuation, autonomy, creativity, productivity, but they all agree that this amounts to realizing the potentialities of the person, that is to say, becoming fully human, everything that the person can become.[30]

Maslow's concept of higher- and lower-order needs can be applied to decision makers to see if they are preoccupied with values that are adjustive, ego-defensive, or self-actualizing. Such a classification will make it easier to predict behavior in the integrated decision-making process.

England and his associates have suggested a two-dimensional classification of values. The first dimension relates to the *conceptual nature* of values and involves (1) a preferential approach based on likes, needs, desires, and interests, and (2) a normative approach focused on obligations and morals. The second dimension is centered on the *conceptual generality* of values and spans a continuum between very specific values and highly abstract or general values. According to England, the conceptual generality of an approach to values will be influenced by where the approach falls on the conceptual nature dimension.[31] For example, a preferential approach might deal with very specific values or a normative approach might relate to abstract or general values.

England's two-dimensional classification is of intellectual interest, but it requires much empirical testing before it can be called a general model of personal values.

Another approach to the classification of values is made by Bahm who makes a meaningful distinction between means and ends. In his classification a

> "means value" or "instrumental value" is any value which depends for its existence as a value upon its serving as a means to the bringing into existence or maintaining in existence an intrinsic value. An "end value" or "intrinsic value" is a value which is self-contained in the sense that it is not required to serve any other value in order for it to be a value.[32]

Bahm subdivides intrinsic values into (1) pleasant feelings, (2) satisfaction of desire, (3) enthusiasm, and (4) contentment.[33] Each of these ends values may be obtained by any one or some combination of instrumental values.

Rokeach developed a particularly useful classification of values. He differentiates **instrumental values** and **terminal values.** The latter term refers to desirable states of existence; the former designates desirable modes of conduct. Terminal values may be further subdivided into **personal values** and **social values.** Such end-states as salvation and peace of mind are personal values, while world peace and brotherhood are social values. Similarly, instrumental values may be differentiated into **moral values** and **competence values.** "Moral values refer to certain kinds of instrumental values which, when violated, arouse pangs of conscience or feelings of guilt for wrongdoing." Competence values relate to the self-actualization of the individual, and "their violation leads to feelings of shame about personal inadequacy rather than feelings of guilt about personal wrongdoing."[34]

Figure 4.1 illustrates Rokeach's classification of personal values. Cell I in Figure 4.1 represents a hypothetical individual who seeks self-enhancement as a terminal value and whose competence values will gear toward this end. As will be noted in the next section of this chapter, managerial decision makers, particularly those in business organizations, tend to fall into this category. Cell II represents a hypothetical individual who is committed to competence values in pursuit of social ends. Presumably, this cell would represent some managerial decision makers in public service organizations and possibly some in voluntary organizations. Cells III and IV doubtless reflect the value orientations of individuals who are not performing managerial roles in formal organizations. In this context, a recent study by Posner and Schmidt found that the values of business managers and federal government executives were more different than alike.[35] They noted that business managers placed greater emphasis on personal values enhanced through competence values, whereas government executives ascribed more importance to social values as desirable end states. These findings tend to substantiate the categorization in Figure 4.1 of business managers in cell I and government executives in cell II. There is little evidence to suggest that managerial decision makers are motivated by

Instrumental values	Terminal values	
	Personal values	Social values
Competence values	I	II
Moral values	III	IV

FIGURE 4.1

A Typology of Human Values

moral values in pursuing personal values or social values. Indeed, as will be illustrated in the next section of this chapter, the available evidence indicates that most managers worry little about social values and even less about moral values. In commenting on the nature of managerial moral standards, Bird and Waters note "the moral standards held by managers tend to be both imprecisely understood and only loosely and haphazardly followed."[36] Managerial decision makers seem, therefore, to fit rather well into cell I in Figure 4.1, although some may spill over into cell II, particularly in nonprofit organizations. Cells III and IV are presented simply to round out Rokeach's classification of personal values.

MANAGERIAL VALUES

Because the primary emphasis of this book is on managerial decision making at the level of the organization, it is appropriate to devote more intensive analysis to the subject of managerial values. Presumably, if managers and the principal stakeholders of the organization understand managerial values, the entire decision-making process will become more effective as a result. Elbing and Elbing state:

> A beginning point toward solving social value problems which are based on the assumptions and stereotypes of the values of [managers] is to make an empirical investigation to determine what in fact these values really are.[37]

Managerial values are a composite of the basic personal values already discussed and certain *acquired* values derived from the managerial role in formal organizations. In fact, one of the distinguishing characteristics of a manager is a strong sense of commitment to the organization; it is from this sense of commitment that a manager acquires those values peculiar to the discipline of management. Ewing states that "the most important feature of the managerial mind is its commitment to the life and growth of the organization." He

119

:o make a point that is central to this book — that the managerial
ıent is essentially the same regardless of the type of organization:

> ther the organization is an assembly room in a manufacturing plant, a
> ırnment bureau, a college, a military unit, or a large corporation with far-
> g divisions, the aim of the manager is to keep it operating and thriving. . . .
> nmitment to the organization is the lowest common denominator of their
> ›roaches; they differ in method, not principle.[38]

ıs commitment stems from the fact that the organization "offers per-
ɔpportunities for advancement, prestige, security, contact with people
ther satisfactions."[39] Managers in organizations of all types tend to act
primarily in their own self-interest.[40]

The evolution of management thought has been accompanied by changes
in managerial values.[41] In the United States, managerial values are associated
with the Calvinist ethic, which commands a person to be pious, thrifty, God-
fearing, hard-working, and concerned with individual salvation. According to
the doctrine of Adam Smith, published in 1776, the pursuit of self-interest
would bring about maximum social gain.[42] In conjunction with the Calvinist
ethic, Smith's doctrine of competitive economics molded the development
and evolution of managerial values in the United States from 1820 to 1930.[43]

Since the 1930s, then, management in the United States has experienced
a multitude of social and political pressures, as well as some significant
internal shifts. These pressures should have resulted in a modification of
prevailing managerial values. In fact the conventional wisdom still prevails;
management is still wedded to the doctrine of economic competition and the
Calvinist ethic. To be sure, there have been some changes in managerial
values, but they have stemmed more from a need to adapt to survive than
from an effort to improve the lot of all people. On balance the heralded transformation of managerial values in the twentieth century has been greatly
exaggerated.[44] This phenomenon is particularly true among managers in the
United States. But it is also true among managers in other countries. For
example, a recent study of American, Canadian, and Japanese managers by
Conner et al. revealed that, in terms of Rokeach's typology in Figure 4.1, all
three groups of managers fell into cell I with a strong orientation toward personal values implemented through competence values.[45]

Several studies have shed considerable light on the values of managers
in different kinds of organizations as well as at different levels and in different functions within the same organization.[46] The majority of these studies
have dealt with managers in business organizations.[47] Still there is some
evidence to justify a claim for generic managerial values in both private
enterprise and the public sector. For example, in their study of 387 highway
and transportation department executives, Boxx et al. noted that "executives desire employees who constantly strive to uphold the goals and values
of the organization."[48] Abbasi and Hollman, in their study of 198 city managers, found a managerial value profile "nearest to our stereotype of a 'businessman' and to what economists call the 'economic man'" with values

inclined "toward the useful, empirical, critical, and rational."[49] These recent findings from the public sector make it defensible to generalize the mainstream values of business executives and to apply them to most managerial decision makers.[50]

In the early 1960s Collins and Moore undertook a study of 110 business firms in Michigan to determine the psychological differences between entrepreneurs and professional managers. These firms were established between 1945 and 1958, and the founders (entrepreneurs) were still living and presumably successful. The research techniques for the study included in-depth interviews and the use of a personality projective device known as the Thematic Apperception Test. The findings about the personality differences and value orientations of the subjects may be summarized as follows:

1. Professional managers are more socially mobile than entrepreneurs.

2. Professional managers outstrip entrepreneurs in their ability to make decisions and resolve problems.

3. Entrepreneurs are less sure of themselves. Theirs is a world of never-ending relationships. Entrepreneurs operate in an environment of transactions. The "deal" is their stock in trade.

4. Professional managers channel their energies into their work. Entrepreneurs are less devoted to their work. They tend to be restless and want to move on.

5. Professional managers adapt easily to authority. Entrepreneurs tend to resist authority.

6. Professional managers adapt easily to interpersonal relations on the job. Entrepreneurs are at their best when dealing with people outside of the formal structure of the organization. Their strength is in transactions as opposed to hierarchical interpersonal relationships.[51]

These findings indicate that professional managers find it less difficult than entrepreneurs to compromise their personal values in favor of the values of the organization. Presumably, they would find it easy to internalize such values as profits, survival, and growth. On the other hand, entrepreneurs have a set of personal values that resist the structural context of a formal organization. Basically, they are rugged individualists who are happiest when their personal values can find unfettered expression in their business dealings.

George England's landmark study of the personal value systems of 1,072 American managers added greatly to the knowledge about this important subject. To gather his data, England used a personal-values questionnaire applying bipolar adjectives such as good-bad and active-passive. He divided values into *operating* values, or those that have the greatest influence on behavior, and *intended and adopted* values, or those that may be claimed but do not influence behavior to any great degree.[52] He then divided the values into five categories as shown in Table 4.1. The values marked by an asterisk in each of the five categories were rated as highly important by the managers in the survey. These are the operating values having the greatest influence on the managers' actions. The other values in the table influence the managers' behavior to a lesser degree. These are the intended or adopted values.

It is interesting to note the great importance that managers give to the goals of the organization. The rankings also show that managers have a strong group orientation. With the possible exception of creativity, the high ratings for the personal goals of the individual also have a definite organizational orientation, as do the ideas associated with people and the ideas about general topics.

The conclusions set forth by England as a result of his study are of interest:

> There is a general value pattern which is characteristic of American managers . . . as well as a great deal of variation in value systems from individual to individual. . . . Personal values operate at the level of corporate strategy and goals as well as the level of day-to-day decisions. . . . The personal value systems of individual managers influence the organization in both an indirect and direct manner at the same time that personal values are influenced by organizational life.[53]

As shown in Table 4.1, the managers' operating values centered on efficiency, productivity, profits, growth, leadership, and stability. Employee and social welfare were intended rather than operating values. The managers in the study also identified achievement, success, ability, ambition, skill, and competition as operating values, and gave less importance to values related to human or social needs. In 1972 Lusk and Oliver duplicated England's findings using a study design and questionnaire similar to that of the 1966 study. They found that "the differences between the value systems of the 1966 sample and the 1972 sample of managers' responses were very small."[54]

In Dent's study of 145 chief executives in five cities, the managers showed a strong interest in profit and a comparatively weak interest in employee and social welfare. Dent's study also revealed that entrepreneurs and professional managers are equally concerned about profit. This finding tends to refute the so-called enlightenment of the professional manager. Even more significant, however, is Dent's finding that business success is not furthered by interest in employee welfare or community betterment on the part of the managers.[55]

In a study of the value systems of 653 industrial managers, 178 research managers, and 157 scientists, Guth and Tagiuri used a questionnaire designed to separate values into the following categories: (1) theoretical, (2) economic, (3) aesthetic, (4) social, (5) political, and (6) religious. Definitions of these six categories were as follows:

1. **Theoretical** persons are interested mostly in the discovery of truth, in the systematic ordering of their knowledge.

2. **Economic** persons are mainly oriented toward what is useful.

3. **Aesthetic** persons find their chief interests in the artistic aspects of life, though they need not be artists.

TABLE 4.1 Ranking of Managerial Values by Category

Goals of Business Organizations	Personal Goals of Individuals	Groups of People	Ideas Associated with People	Ideas about General Topics
Organizational efficiency*	Achievement*	My company*	Ability*	Change*
High productivity*	Success*	Customers*	Ambition*	Competition*
Profit maximization*	Creativity*	Managers*	Skill*	Authority
Organizational growth*	Job satisfaction*	My boss*	Cooperation*	Caution
Industrial leadership*	Individuality	My subordinates*	Aggressiveness	Compromise
Organizational stability*	Money	Technical employees*	Loyalty	Conflict
Employee welfare	Influence	Employees*	Trust	Conservatism
Social welfare	Prestige	Me*	Honor	Emotions
	Autonomy	My coworkers*	Tolerance	Equality
	Dignity	Craftsmen*	Prejudice	Force
	Security	Owners*	Obedience	Liberalism
	Power	Stockholders*	Compassion	Property
	Leisure	White-collar employees*	Conformity	Rationality
		Blue-collar workers		Religion
		Government		Risk
		Laborers		
		Labor unions		

*Operating values of high importance

4. The essential value for **social** persons is the love of people — the altruistic or philanthropic aspect of love.

5. **Political** persons seek power, not necessarily in politics, but in whatever area they function.

6. **Religious** persons are those whose mental structures are permanently directed to the creation of the highest and most satisfying value experience.[56]

The industrial managers in the study ranked values for themselves in the following order of importance: (1) economic, (2) theoretical and political, (3) religious, (4) aesthetic, and (5) social. The managers felt their values would be ranked by other people as follows: (1) economic, (2) political, (3) theoretical, (4) aesthetic, (5) social, and (6) religious. By either self-ratings or ratings expected from others, the industrial managers in the study ranked the pragmatic economic and political values highest and gave somewhat equal importance to theoretical values. Essentially, this study agreed with the findings of England and those of Dent that managers have a strong organizational orientation and a high sense of practical values.

Many writers think that managers are more concerned with their personal aspirations than with the objectives of the organization. These writers allege that the managers' apparent concern with the well-being of the organization — its profits, efficiency, and growth — is only a front for the desire for personal gain and prestige. For example, Monsen, Saxberg, and Sutermeister state that when there is a conflict between personal values of the manager and the goals of the organization, "the manager will most frequently resolve the conflict by emphasizing his own personal goals." As they state the case:

> The basic desire of the professional manager is to maximize his self-interest or lifetime income in monetary and non-monetary terms. He may not even attempt to maximize the firm's profits, for such attempts might involve risks endangering his own interests — success in increasing profits may bring a bonus, but losses may mean loss of position and lifetime income.[57]

To perpetuate their own positions and to ensure steady growth in their monetary and nonmonetary lifetime incomes, managers shun risk and forgo the potential gains and losses that might result from taking a gamble. In effect, such pressures make managers seek satisficing rather than maximizing decisions. In this interpretation, "satisficers differ from maximizers only in capability, not in intention. They would like to maximize, but the limitations of their ignorance and their finite capacity cause them to adopt behavior different from that of a theoretical maximizer."[58]

Even though managers are expected to internalize the values of the organization, it still seems reasonable to assume that their own personal goals and values will guide their actions to some extent. Manley Howe Jones supports this position with the following statement:

> Whether we like it or not, people's personal goals play a dominant role in company decision making. When a man is making company decisions or deciding to accept and carry out company decisions proposed to him, he examines them in part with a view to whether they will further his own goals. . . . But in my opinion, it is neither improper nor unethical for a man to work in behalf of his personal goals, so long as he furthers the company goals and does not injure his fellow men.[59]

Several other studies of managerial values tend to support the organizational orientation of managerial decision makers. For example, one study using England's research model showed that managers relate more to the organization than do students enrolled in business administration.[60] Another study found that managers tend to evaluate their subordinates in terms of their subordinates' organizationally oriented systems of values.[61] Still another study found that managerial values in several other countries are similar to those found in the United States.[62] And, finally, it has been found that racial differences among American managers result in few significant differences in the organizational orientation of their values.[63]

A later survey of 6,000 executives and managers sponsored by the American Management Association (AMA) tends to confirm most of the foregoing rationale regarding managerial values.[64] Although the response rate for this survey was not high (24 percent), the 1,460 respondents constitute an appreciable population of managers. Like England's study, the profile of responses to the AMA survey revealed a strong organizational orientation in the values of the managers. Moreover, the responses also showed a discernible sense of self-interest on the part of the managers, which tends to confirm several earlier studies and much writing on the subject. In the words of Posner and Schmidt:

> The goal judged to be most important regardless of the manager's position in the hierarchy, age, gender, or educational level is organizational effectiveness. . . . A clustering of next most important goals include high productivity, organizational leadership, high morale, organizational reputation, and organizational efficiency. . . . The cluster of goals which were rated as third in importance includes profit maximization, organizational growth, and organizational stability. At the bottom of the list were value of the organization to the community and public service.[65]

The foregoing rankings were highly similar regardless of the level of management or the type of organization. Clearly, as noted by England and others, there is a pronounced organizational ethos in the values of American managers. Much additional research is required, however, to deepen our understanding of the impact of personal values on managerial decision making in organizational settings. Still it is apparent, as suggested by Connor and Becker, that "implications of values for organizational administration are best identified by considering the ways in which member values relate to specific managerial actions. It [seems] certain that decision making . . . is influenced by the values of those involved in the decision-making process."[66]

Two additional items are particularly significant in the AMA survey of managerial values. First, profit maximization was ranked low by all levels of management. "Executives ranked it seventh, middle managers ranked it ninth, and supervisory managers ranked it eleventh."[67] If these rankings reflect what executives and managers actually think about the primacy of profit, the arguments against profit maximization assume even greater cogency. Second, the high ranking accorded to "myself" as an organizational stakeholder by all three levels of management tends to confirm the assertions of many commentators that managers in general have a strong and possibly overriding self-interest in their decision making. In fact, the respondents in the AMA survey ranked themselves along with their customers, subordinates, and employees at the top of their list of organizational stakeholders. The general public and the stockholders are ranked close to the bottom as stakeholders in the organization. Such rankings tend to precipitate doubts regarding the commitment of business executives to the concepts of social responsibility[68] and people's capitalism.[69]

More recent surveys of managerial values reveal no decrease in the strong organization orientation of executive decision makers. In the case of social responsibility nearly all managers think it is important, but most — particularly top managers — see little hope for improvement.[70] There is always a hope on the part of social scientists and humanists that managerial values will have a more socially responsible emphasis. Such, however, is not the case. For example, a follow-up survey in 1991 of more than 1,000 managers by the

AMA revealed no significant change in the organizational orientation of the respondents since the original survey in 1981. As noted by the survey takers:

> What continues to be remarkable is the striking similarity in the relative ranking of organizational goals across the decade. Generally, the order or prioritization of these various goals remains the same, . . . there was considerable agreement about the importance of the [organizational] goals both across managers at different levels in the hierarchy and across hundreds of different types of organizations.[71]

The longitudinal survey by Lee of managerial values at different levels in selected companies spanning the period 1965 to 1986 revealed no change in the predominant organizational orientation of the values ranked by the respondent managerial decision makers.[72] The values of (1) decision making, (2) future planning, and (3) developing new methods occupied the top three positions through four surveys over a twenty-year period. And, finally, the survey of changes in executives' values from 1979 to 1989 by Korn/Ferry International revealed a consistent orientation toward organizational values.[73] It is also significant to note that in all of these surveys, the respondent managerial decision makers tend to rank social concerns near or at the bottom of their profile of values for decision making. Clearly the low priority accorded social responsibility tends to pervade the managerial values inputed to all parts of the decision-making process set forth in Figure 2.1.

In summary, managers' basic personal values are overlaid with values acquired from the managerial role. The bulk of the evidence suggests that in the event of a conflict of values, organizational values take precedence over personal values. It is more likely, however, that the manager would adapt his or her personal values to the basic purposes of the organization in such a way as to promote self-interest. The manager acquires personal values as part of the process of growing up. Organizational values are acquired from being a manager. Both sets of values are internalized, one set associated with the individual's life and the other with the managerial role. Ideally, the two sets of values complement and reinforce one another.

This relationship is conceptualized in Figure 4.2. In this figure, managerial values are depicted as a composite of individual values and organizational values. The intersection of these two sets of values as set forth in Figure 4.2 is about equal in the early years of a manager's affiliation with a given organization. As the manager progresses to higher levels of responsibility, the organizational values begin to increasingly overlap the individual values and the manager becomes a virtual extension of the corporation. At some point — in middle management or lower upper management — the manager's individual values become obscured or even totally eclipsed by the organizational values. By this time the manager is a personification of the corporation and a gatekeeper for successive generations of managers.

The notion that managers have abandoned the Calvinist ethic or outgrown the economic doctrine of Adam Smith does not square with reality. The evidence does suggest, however, that managers have modified their behavior

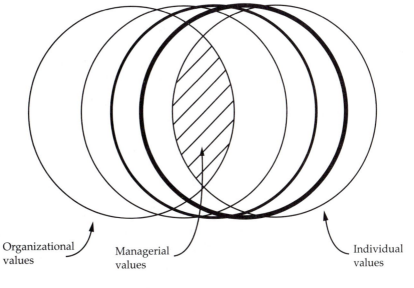

Organizational values   Managerial values   Individual values

FIGURE 4.2

Profile of Managerial Values

to accommodate external pressures caused by significant political and social changes. In terms of Rokeach's classification of terminal values, managers tend to hold personal values rather than social values as desirable end-states. With regard to Rokeach's classification of instrumental values, managers favor competence values over moral values as desirable modes of conduct. Given this value orientation, it is not hard to understand why managerial values form a significant boundary within which the rational managerial decision maker seeks a satisficing outcome in the open decision model.

ETHICAL BEHAVIOR

Ethics have been called the standards of decision making.[74] It has been stated that a decision is a process that has been affected with the ethical interest.[75] The role of ethics in the decision-making process is fairly straightforward:

1. In the development of a set of managerial objectives, it is necessary to consider the ethical interest in selecting among various opportunities and areas of potential improvement.

2. In the development of a range of relevant alternatives, it is impossible to avoid making value judgments among the possibilities emerging from the search activity.

3. In the evaluation of relevant alternatives in which the various possibilities are subjected to a value ordering, the ethical interest is clearly implied.

4. In the act of choice, the ethical interest is clearly interwoven into the selection of the best alternative.

5. Finally, in the implementation of a satisficing choice, the decision maker must consider the ethical interest in terms of potential consequences to those areas and individuals that will be affected by the decision.[76]

Philosophers have concerned themselves mainly with the question of what constitutes a "good" decision, a major concern of ethics. The system of values and code of ethics employed by the decision maker are no less important in evaluating the rationality of the process of choice than they are in philosophy. One can, for example, imagine some unethical behavior in the rational process of arriving at a rational decision. It is more difficult, however, to conceive of a rational approach to decision making without some system of values. Similarly, while ethical conduct may validate a claim of rational behavior in the decision-making process, the application of some values to a given choice is not in itself sufficient for this purpose.

A person makes an ethical decision . . . if and only if he decides what to do by essential reliance upon some ethical rule, principle, standard, or norm. By essential reliance is meant that had he not relied on the rule, he would not have decided to do what he did; or, if he had decided to do what he did then his *reason* for deciding would not have been the same; his reason would not have been an *ethical* principle, but some other sort of principle, perhaps one of business efficiency, class or national self-interest, or even personal advantage. . . . A rule, standard, or norm is ethical if and only if it takes into account the interests and situations of other persons affected by the [decision maker's] conduct and treats them impartially along with those of the [decision maker].[77]

Before discussing ethical behavior further, especially as it applies to the actions of managerial decision makers, we should set forth some working definitions:

1. **Ethical:** conforming to principles of human conduct; according to common usage, the following terms are more or less synonymous with *ethical: moral, good, right, just, honest.*

2. **Ethical standards:** principles or ideals of human conduct.

3. **Ethics:** the study of the morality of human actions; hence the standards for these actions.

4. **Morality:** the property of an action by means of which it conforms to a norm of human conduct.[78]

Lillie has stated:

There are several terms commonly used in judging human actions by ethical standards. We say that an action is "good" or "bad," "right" or "wrong," "moral" or "immoral." We say that we "ought" to do an action, that we "should" do it, or that it is our "duty" to do it; and of another kind of action we say that we "ought not" to do it, we "should not" do it, or it is our "duty" not to do it. . . . Ethics is primarily a quest for truth and the motive for studying it is the desire for knowledge. . . . We naturally want to know the truth about things, and ethics aims at finding out the truth about something that is both interesting and important — the rightness and wrongness of human conduct. There is no guarantee that the man who understands by means of ethical study the difference between right and wrong will necessarily follow the right.[79]

Moreover, even a person experienced in making moral judgments will often find it difficult to determine which action is right.

More specifically, ethics is the science of judging human ends and the relationship of means to those ends. It is also the art of controlling means so they will serve human ends. Viewed in this way, ethics involves the use of human knowledge to tell us something about the relationships among people or about the applicability of available instruments. Additionally, as an art, it employs techniques of judging and decision making as well as the tools of social control and personal development. Essentially, ethics really is or should be involved in all human activities.[80]

Business ethics, for example, studies mainly the relationship of business goals and techniques to human ends. It is concerned with the impact of acts on the good of the individual, the firm, the business community, and society as a whole.[81] Business ethics also treats the special obligations that a person accepts when he or she becomes a managerial decision maker:

> Obviously, then, business ethics appears to be concerned with what is good or bad managerial behavior. Businessmen are constantly faced with alternative courses of action, and choices must be made among competing situations. Because of the many complexities and variables within his enterprise, the business executive can seldom be sure that a particular choice or decision is absolutely right or absolutely wrong. He uses the best judgment possible, and he reasons as logically as he can in approaching his problems and reaching his conclusions.[82]

Several surveys have been conducted to ascertain the meaning of ethical behavior to organizational decision makers. For example, one survey[83] of 100 business managers revealed the following distribution of opinions regarding the meaning of the word ethical:

	First Choice	Second Choice
What my feelings tell me is right.	50	8
In accord with my religious belief.	25	14
Conforms to the Golden Rule.	18	15
What does the most good for the most people.	3	7
Customary behavior in our society.	3	6
Corresponds to my self-interest.	1	1
About the same as what is legal.	0	2
Contributes most to personal liberty.	0	1
What I want in that particular situation.	0	1

Exactly half of the business managers surveyed indicated that, as a first choice, ethical meant something internal or personal to them. Basically, this is a subjective response and therefore open to a variety of interpretations. The remaining half defined ethical in accordance with their religious beliefs or, what amounts to essentially the same thing, in terms of the Golden Rule: "Do unto others as you would have them do unto you." Interestingly enough, even as a second choice, there were few responses in which the business managers defined ethical in terms of some standard such as a legal doctrine, moral code, or social norm. Apparently ethical behavior for these managers depends on the way they feel rather than what someone expects from them.

Another study of 121 managers revealed that the respondents were greatly concerned with ethical behavior in general but felt little need to modify their personal behavior. The results of this study confirmed that ethics means different things to different people, and that there are no generally accepted standards of ethical behavior among managerial decision makers. This study also revealed that "managers have a propensity to capitalize on opportunities to be unethical, if those situations arise."[84] Still another study of 238 managers revealed that "managers experience pressure, real or perceived, to compromise their personal moral standards to satisfy organizational expectations."[85] For comparative purposes, this survey of 238 managers was coupled with a subsequent study of 343 managers from public service organizations. In this study, the managers in the public sector felt the managers in the private sector were less ethical than the latter felt themselves to be.[86] Such opinions matter little, however, simply because there is no yardstick for measuring ethical behavior. It appears, therefore, that managerial decision makers will continue to respond to organizational pressures within their own definitions of ethical behavior.

More recent studies of presumed ethical behavior by managerial decision makers do not alter the situational context in which ethics are considered, if they are considered at all. Karp and Abramms have reasserted the situational nature of ethics in business organizations.[87] Bird and Waters confirm that managers have few moral standards in which to anchor ethical behavior.[88] Another study documented the variability of ethical behavior from none to "more ethical" in the presence of concern and pressure from upper management.[89] Still another study noted that "the propensity toward ethical action is situationally specific."[90] Even the conceptual models of ethical behavior constructed by academicians have a predominant situational component.[91] Of even greater significance, however, the surveys of managerial values clearly assign a low rating to ethical concerns. In a recent study of managerial values, Posner and Schmidt report that from 1981 to 1991, "ethical codes and workshops remain a peripheral part of the corporate environment."[92] Lee's longitudinal study from 1965 to 1986 showed a continuous low ranking for ethical values.[93] And the Korn/Ferry International study of changes in business executives' values during the 1980s made no mention of ethical behavior.[94] It may be as stated by Peter Drucker that "there is no such thing as business ethics — a code distinct and unattached from all other ethics. There have always been a number of people who cheat, steal, lie or take bribes."[95] Still the call for systems of ethical behavior in all types of business organizations continues to rise.[96] There is ongoing reason to question the ethics of managers in business organizations. For example, one recent study involving a total of 800 firms over the decade of the 1980s showed that self-interest is a significant motivating factor in corporate managers' merger decisions.[97] Other studies allege that managers are concerned with their own advantage even at the expense of the shareholders.[98] Still other research studies raise doubts regarding the ethical interest of business organizations in environmental decisions, or even general organizational concerns for ethical conduct.[99]

These findings disagree somewhat with classical definitions and interpretations of ethical behavior. If ethics are indeed the standards of decision making, it appears that such standards may change to fit the mood of the decision maker and the variables in the situation at hand. Still, this possibility makes ethical behavior no less important in the decision-making process. Peers and those affected directly and indirectly by the choice of alternatives will judge the decision maker's ethics. It is not enough that the decision maker alone be convinced of the ethical quality of his or her actions. After all, managerial decisions of any complexity are not made in a vacuum. The decision maker is accountable to stockholders, the employees, the general public, and the many levels and agencies of government. A subjective standard for ethical behavior may be entirely acceptable for decisions that affect only the decision maker's personal life and well-being. But in the context of the organization, the decision maker had better adopt some objective standard that will withstand inevitable scrutiny and criticism.

Especially when implementing a satisficing choice in the open decision model, the decision maker must stay aware of the reaction of the several external forces in the environment. If these environmental forces find a given decision to be less than ethical, either in its formulation or execution, they will be less likely to accept it. On the other hand, if the decision maker's constituency thinks that a given decision will not work to its harm, the choice will doubtless be accepted on terms favorable to the organization. Clearly, then, the ethical interest can significantly affect the outcome of a satisficing choice.

VALUE CONFLICTS

Value conflicts occur at all levels in the decision-making process. Individuals frequently must compromise their personal values to retain membership in a group. In the event of disagreement, groups must in turn generally defer to the values of the organization. "The conflict between organizations and individuals is as old as society itself. The basis of the conflict is that while individuals by definition seek goals that will further their personal independence, organizations look for a commonality of individual efforts to achieve corporate goals."[100]

Organizations, as one of several types of entities in the total society, must get along with a host of environmental forces. As a special case, the manager, who presumably personifies the organization, will often find that personal values conflict with the goals and objectives of the organization. This conflict is presented forcefully in the following passage:

> The businessman is, first of all, a man. As a man, he shares the universal trait of wanting to be certain that his life has meaning and purpose. But the nature of his role as a businessman places him continuously in a position of conflict. It forces him constantly to choose between alternative courses of action reflecting differing priorities of values.
>
> In his analysis of these alternatives, and in consideration of the values they represent, the businessman inevitably finds himself in a state of inner conflict. He wants to do the right thing, but he does not always find it easy to know what the right thing is. Efforts to deny the existence of such conflict, however persistently pursued, offer only temporary and superficial relief. Like all men, the businessman inevitably returns to the question of ultimate values and to the question of whether his total life is serving those values in the way he would wish.[101]

For the manager and nonmanager alike, membership in a group, and especially a formal organization, places constraints on individual values.[102] The need to reach consensus at the group level and the need for unity of action and purpose at the organizational level require that the individual's values jibe with those of the collective entity. To be sure, the individual will preserve his or her own ultimate values to dictate choices that are not subject to compromise. Still, the individual must occasionally act less as an individual and more as a team or group member. As such, the individual may be required to compromise any one or more of the following personal values:

1. The value of "inner-directedness" as opposed to "other-directedness"

2. The value of uniqueness for itself alone

3. The value of freedom to pursue one's own goals and choices rather than imposed collective social goals

4. The value of aggressive self-assertion, initiative, entrepreneurship, and so-called rugged individualism[103]

Value conflicts between the organization and the total society usually occur in the context of social responsibility. The values of the organization have a strong economic orientation that often runs counter to prevailing social and political sentiments. In such cases, managerial decision makers must carefully weigh the effects of their choices on these powerful environmental forces. The value issue of business organizations is summarized in the following excerpt:

> We are interested not only in whether an intergroup relationship is efficient, productive, profitable, and equitable in economic terms but in such matters

as whether the relationship is socially exploitative or mutually serviceable, socially fulfilling or ego destructive, or characterized by hostility or cooperative good will. . . . We are interested in the fact that intergroup actions, far from consisting of merely economic transactions which work out economic values, are social transactions which work out social values in our business society.[104]

In the final analysis, whether an individual functions as a member of a group, a member of management, an employee of a formal organization, or simply a citizen of the total society, reality is whatever the individual's values allow him or her to recognize. And since each individual's values are unique, each individual's idea of the right thing to do will differ from others' ideas. As a general guide to action, individuals should remind themselves that

> many men assume that other persons of good intentions will see things the same way they do and brand those who disagree with them as unethical, immoral, or just plain stupid. By assuming that they can bring a set of absolute values to bear on any situation and thus reveal a course of action, they drastically over-simplify the situation, missing its impact on their interpretation of their values as well as the impact of their values on what they see before them. . . .
>
> What is needed is for each man to try to hold as criteria a very few ultimate values which for him represent essential truths and to cling to these criteria tenaciously and absolutely in every situation. He can then deal pragmatically with the inevitable conflicts of personal values inherent in any situation and work out the range of action uniquely appropriate to it, using his ultimate values as standards for judging the reality of the various courses of action.[105]

Value conflicts are inevitable in the process of decision making in formal organizations. However, the consequences of such conflicts are not necessarily unfavorable. For example, a conflict between personal and organizational values may cause a managerial decision maker to (1) rethink aspirations and objectives, (2) review and reject marginal alternatives, (3) revise relevant alternatives, (4) possibly reconsider impending choices, and (5) resist implementation practices that are likely to have an unfavorable impact on one or more areas. Therefore, value conflicts should be viewed as having both positive and negative aspects; and although it is desirable to minimize the negative side, it is equally desirable to capitalize on the positive side.[106] (Note: See the section entitled "Conflict in Decision Making" in Chapter 8.)

VALUE JUDGMENTS

In a basic sense the term **judgment** refers to "the capacity to make reasonable decisions."[107] "Judgment may be identified as the evaluation or categorizing of an object."[108] "Judgments may be accepted as direct inputs to the decision process, or they may be regarded as part of behavior useful in or essential to the process of reaching a decision."[109] "Judgment, it seems, is an ultimate category, which can only be approved or condemned by a further exercise of the same ability."[110] With respect to decision making, "judgment is an essential attribute in poorly structured situations. In this age of numbers and specialization, it is perhaps permissible to reassert the obvious: good judgment is a vital ingredient of [decision making]. Judgment addresses reality and value."[111] Decision making reflects both evaluative and predictive judgment; and the quality of a given decision depends upon the degree to which evaluative judgments reflect true preferences and predictive judgments are accurate.[112] Judgment about reality requires excellence in the capacity to imagine and to "assess the outcome of multiple, causal interactions, to apply appropriate time scales, to comprehend uncertainties, most of all perhaps to simplify without distorting by excluding the inessential."[113] Judgment about values is a less precise phenomenon.

The term *judgment* is not synonymous with the term *decision*.

> While judgment is generally an aid to choice, it is neither necessary nor sufficient for choice. That is, judgments serve to reduce the uncertainty and conflict in choice by processes of deliberative reasoning and evaluation of evidence. . . . The distinction between judgment and choice, which is blurred in the normative model, is exemplified in common language. For example, one can choose in spite of one's better judgment whereas the reverse makes little sense.[114]

Actually a judgment is a subset of a decision; and the several functions of the integrated decision-making process are interspersed with judgments made by the rational decision maker. *The principal difference between a judgment and a decision is that a decision requires a commitment to some form of action (or inaction), whereas a judgment does not require such a commitment.* For example, a judgment that alternative *A* is preferable to alternative *B* which in turn is preferable to alternative *C* does not require a commitment to implement alternative *A* or any other alternative. It is only when a commitment is made to select alternative *A* in preference to other known alternatives that a decision has materialized. Again the key phrase is *commitment to action (or inaction)*. It is theoretically possible (but not probable) to make endless judgments without making a decision. It is virtually impossible to make a decision, at least in the context of the integrated decision-making process, without making several judgments.

Judgment is part of the decision maker's cognitive process.[115] As such, judgment forms a process in its own right. The judgmental process has the following principal characteristics:

1. The substance of the judgmental process, that which is to be judged, is given and available; obtaining, discovering, or formulating inputs is not part of judgment.

2. The domain of the output — that is, the set of acceptable responses — is simple and well defined prior to the judgment. The response (judgment) itself is variously called a selection, evaluation, or classification, depending on the nature of the domain.

3. The judgmental process is not a simple transfer of information; judgment adds information to the substance of the process.

4. The judgmental process is not simply a calculation or the application of a given rule. .

5. The judgmental process finishes a more extended process — for example, thinking or decision making.

6. The judgmental process is rather immediate; it does not extend through time with phases, stages, subprocesses, and so on.

7. The judgmental process is different from searching, discovering, or creating, on the one hand, and from musing, browsing, or idly observing, on the other.[116]

Judgment is an essential part of making category II decisions, where the cause-and-effect relationships are uncertain and the decision situation is usually complex and nonrecurring. In such situations, with inadequate information from which to fashion factual judgments, the rational decision maker proceeds through the decision-making process on the basis of value judgments. A **value judgment,** then, is simply a special type of evaluation or categorization with which an individual addresses a decision-making situation. It is an evaluation or categorization based principally on values rather than on fact.

As a practical matter it is virtually impossible to separate an individual's value system from a judgment made by that individual. This is especially true in a poorly structured and complex decision-making situation. Judgments tend for the most part to combine both factual data and values. Therefore, a pure value judgment is most unlikely and the term itself is at least partly misleading. The principal significance of the term is simply that values are part of judgment. This relationship is fundamental to the decision-making process set forth in this book.

Value judgments are very important in comparing and evaluating alternatives preparatory to choice. Mack addresses this relationship as follows:

> Value judgments imply an appreciative system, a basis for distributing utility to outcomes. What is desirable must be defined in a fashion that makes it possible to say that this outcome is preferable to that outcome.[117]

In the process of attributing utility to outcomes, the decision maker orders alternatives according to how desirable they are within his or her system of values. The precise ordering of alternatives depends on value judgments made by the decision maker. Such judgments are conditioned by how much worth or utility the decision maker feels each alternative has. Presumably individual alternatives in a given set will have different utilities for the decision maker. Value judgments are made to rank the alternatives on the basis of perceived payoffs to the decision maker. Values and value systems are subjective, as are the resulting value judgments made to establish equally subjective utilities for alternative courses of action. So it is not hard to understand why maximizing behavior is an illusion. Clearly in complex and unstructured decision-making situations, the best the rational decision maker can hope to obtain is a satisficing outcome. The decision maker can quantify the utilities associated with given alternatives only partly on the basis of facts; and the facts may be of questionable reliability. Alternatives for category II decisions are ranked mainly on the basis of value judgments derived from biases, preconceptions, and stereotypes that tend to defy measurement. The utter futility of quantifying utilities in comparing and evaluating alternatives is well stated by Ebert and Mitchell:

> [The] striving for a theory of rational choice has resulted in an impressive array of mathematical developments, but a disappointing record of success in predicting and explaining choice behavior. Only in the simplest of situations have they [the mathematical developments] been shown to be a reasonable representation of choice behavior. . . . The problem of measurement as it relates to the multiple dimensions of human value systems results in inadequate representations of the relevant preference function in moderately and highly complex choice situations.[118]

With all their inherent subjectivity, value judgments remain the principal means for evaluating, classifying, and selecting from among numerous variables in each function of the integrated decision-making process.[119]

SUMMARY

This chapter has treated the subject of values for decision making. At the outset, it was stated that the personal values of the decision maker and the values of the organization significantly influence the entire process of decision making. Values mean different things to different people, and it was stated that values are the normative standards by which human beings are influenced in their choices among alternative courses of action. In effect, values provide a kind of guidance system used by an individual when confronted with decision-making situations.

An individual's value system is a set of values ranked according to their relative importance. A personal value system is a relatively permanent perceptual framework that shapes and influences the general nature of an individual's behavior. After a value is learned, it becomes part of an organized system wherein each value is given a priority relative to other values. In essence, a value system is a learned organization of principles and rules to help one choose between alternatives, resolve conflicts, and make decisions.

Values originate primarily at the level of the individual. It is also true, however, that groups have values, usually referred to as norms, and organizations have values implicit in their goals and objectives. Many sets of organizational values constitute the total economic system, which in turn is a subset of the larger society. In this regard, it is useful to conceive of a hierarchy of values, although the principal focus in this book is on values that are applied to decision making at the level of the organization.

This chapter presented several ways in which to classify values. Spranger's classification of aesthetic, theoretical, economic, political, social, and religious values was presented. It was noted that Maslow's hierarchy of human needs is one form of classifying values. England's two-dimensional classification of the conceptual nature and the conceptual generality of values was discussed. Bahm's classification of means values and ends values was mentioned briefly. Particular emphasis was given to Rokeach's classification of instrumental values and terminal values (see Figure 4.1). The subsets of the former are competence values and moral values; the subsets of the latter are personal values and social values. It was noted that managerial decision makers, particularly those in business organizations, tend to pursue the enhancement of personal values through competence values.

As a manager makes decisions to further the purposes of the organization, human values fuse with organizational values. Thus the managers' values necessarily reflect the organization's values (see Figure 4.2), even though, as is often the case, the latter values may conflict with some of the decision maker's personal values. In such cases, the manager will usually adjust personal values to the purposes of the organization so as to further his or her own aspirations, at least as much as possible.

This chapter also noted that several studies have revealed a long-term profile of managerial or organizational values with a strong economic orientation (see Table 4.1). Along with a visible tendency for managers to pursue their own aspirations as satisficing decision makers, the economic orientation of organizations requires the use of standards to ensure that choices made do not work to the disadvantage of any of the interest groups forming management's constituency. These standards for decision making are called ethics, and every part of the integrated process of arriving at a choice is affected with the ethical interest.

It was also noted, regretfully, that surveys of managers in large organizations reveal the absence of standards of ethical behavior that will stand up to scrutiny and criticism. In fact, ethical behavior is very subjective in the minds of most managerial decision makers; this apparently means they behave in a way that they, as individuals, believe is proper.

The lack of objective standards of ethics for decision making among managers suggests that they will behave responsibly only to avoid potentially unfavorable reactions in the environment to decisions made solely for the benefit of the organization. Again, however, this is simply another reason for emphasizing that satisficing choices made in the open decision model are most likely to further the purposes of the organization.

The term *value judgment* is at least partly misleading. It is virtually impossible to make a judgment in the absence of values. A judgment is an evaluation, classification, or selection from among a number of variables. A value judgment is a type of evaluation or categorization with which an individual addresses a decision-making situation. It is based on values rather than on fact. The principal significance of the term *value judgment* is that values are part of the total decision-making process.

A judgment is not synonymous with a decision. Decisions require judgments; but judgments do not require decisions. The principal difference between a judgment and a decision is that a decision requires a commitment to some form of action (or inaction), whereas a judgment requires no such commitment.

Judgments are essential for category II decisions that are, by definition, unstructured and complex. Few judgments of any consequence are required for category I decisions, which are routine, recurring, and fairly certain of outcome. Value judgments are most important in comparing and evaluating alternatives where decision makers assign priorities based on preferences for several alternatives. The identification of acceptable alternatives involves the decision maker's individual values and total system of values. The prioritization of these alternatives according to a subjective standard of utility involves value judgments by the decision maker. The decision maker's inability to get complete and perfectly reliable factual data, along with the unceasing application of the decision maker's biases, preconceptions, and stereotypes to the comparison and evaluation of alternatives, precludes maximizing behavior and calls for a satisficing choice in the open decision model. The need for value judgments throughout the decision-making process provides another boundary within which managerial decision makers seek rational outcomes.

REVIEW AND DISCUSSION QUESTIONS

1. What are the six general qualities of the personal value system of managerial decision makers?

2. The general properties of values for decision making render them distinguishable from other values. What are these general properties?

3. Is it completely accurate to characterize business ethics as specific to a given situation? Why or why not?

4. What were the findings of Collins and Moore with regard to the differences in values between entrepreneurs and professional managers?

5. What were the general conclusions resulting from the several studies of managerial values presented in this chapter? Do you agree? Why or why not?

6. Discuss this statement: A preoccupation with personal values and goals may act to make a given manager a satisficer rather than a maximizer.

7. Can a decision maker arrive at a rational choice based on unethical conduct? Discuss.

8. Why is it necessary for managerial decision makers to have some objective standards against which to measure the ethics of their actions?

9. Conflicts between the personal values of the individual and the goals and objectives of the organization seem inevitable. What can the individual do to resolve such conflicts?

10. Discuss this statement: Decisions always involve judgments, but judgments do not always result in decisions.

11. In what specific ways does the use of value judgments in decision making preclude maximizing behavior?

12. With regard to Rokeach's classification of values, do you believe that managers tend to pursue personal ends through the use of competence? Why or why not?

NOTES

1. Philip E. Jacob, James J. Flink, and Hedvah L. Schuchman, "Values and Their Function in Decision Making," *Supplement to the American Behavioral Scientist*, 5 (May 1962), 10.

2. R. M. Williams, Jr., "Individual and Group Values," *Annals of the American Academy of Political and Social Science* (May 1967), 23.

3. Milton Rokeach, *The Nature of Human Values* (New York: Free Press, 1973), p. 5.

4. Milton Rokeach, *Beliefs, Attitudes and Values* (San Francisco: Jossey-Bass, 1968; and H. B. Karp and Bob Abramms, "Doing the Right Things," *Training & Development* (August 1992), 37–41.

5. C. K. M. Kluckhohn, "Values and Value Orientations in the Theory of Action," in *Toward a General Theory of Action*, ed. T. Parsons and E. A. Shils (Cambridge, Mass.: Harvard University Press, 1951), pp. 388–433.

6. William D. Guth and Renato Tagiuri, "Personal Values and Corporate Strategy," *Harvard Business Review* (September–October 1965), 124–125.

7. Ibid., p. 125.

8. Rokeach, *The Nature of Human Values*, p. 7.

9. Ronald J. Ebert and Terence R. Mitchell, *Organizational Decision Processes* (New York: Crane, Russak, 1975), p. 54.

10. Charles E. Lindblom, *The Policy-Making Process* (Englewood Cliffs, N.J.: Prentice-Hall, 1968), p. 16.

11. Rokeach, *The Nature of Human Values*, p. 13.

12. Andrew F. Sikula, "Values and Value Systems: Importance and Relationship to Managerial and Organizational Behavior," *Journal of Psychology*, 78 (1971), p. 281.

13. George W. England, "Personal Value Systems of American Managers," *Academy of Management Journal* (March 1967), 54.

14. Rokeach, *The Nature of Human Values*, pp. 11, 14.

15. England, "Personal Value Systems of American Managers," p. 54.

16. Wilmar F. Bernthal, "Value Perspectives in Management Decisions," *Academy of Management Journal* (December 1962), 191.

17. Jacob, Flink, and Schuchman, "Values and Their Function in Decision Making," pp. 15–16.

18. Bernthal, "Value Perspectives in Management Decisions," p. 194.

19. Ibid., p. 195.

20. Wayne A. R. Leys, "The Value Framework of Decision Making," in *Concepts and Issues in Administrative Behavior*, ed. Sidney Mailick and Edward H. Van Ness (Englewood Cliffs, N.J.: Prentice-Hall, 1962), pp. 81–83.

21. Talcott Parsons and Edward A. Shils, eds., *Toward a General Theory of Action* (New York: Harper & Row, 1951), pp. 145–146.

22. George C. Homans, *The Human Group* (New York: Harcourt, Brace, 1950), p. 123.

23. Alvar O. Elbing, Jr., *Issue of Business* (N p. 112.

24. C. West Churchma *sion* (Englewood C pp. 300–302.

25. André L. Delbe Decision-Making egies for Three

41.
Org
proach

Academy of Management Journal (December 1967), 329–339.

26. Bernthal, "Value Perspectives in Management Decisions," p. 196.

27. Ibid., p. 195.

28. See E. Spranger, *Types of Men*, trans. P. J. W. Pigors (Halle: Niemeyer, 1928); P. E. Vernon and G. W. Allport, "A Test for Personal Values," *Journal of Abnormal and Social Psychology*, 26 (1931), 233–248; and G. W. Allport, P. E. Vernon, and G. Lindzey, *A Study of Values: A Scale for Measuring the Dominant Interests in Personality*, rev. ed. (Boston: Houghton Mifflin, 1951).

29. A. H. Maslow, *Motivation and Personality* (New York: Harper & Row, 1954).

30. A. H. Maslow, ed., *New Knowledge in Human Values* (New York: Harper & Row, 1959), p. 123.

31. G. W. England, K. Olsen, and N. Agarwal, *A Manual of Development and Research for the Personal Values Questionnaire* (Minneapolis: University of Minnesota, October 1971).

32. Archie J. Bahm, *Ethics as a Behavioral Science* (Springfield, Ill.: Charles C Thomas, 1974), p. 81.

33. Ibid., pp. 82–85.

34. Rokeach, *The Nature of Human Values*, pp. 7–8.

35. Barry Z. Posner and Warren H. Schmidt, "The Values of Business and General Government Executives: More Different than Alike," *Public Personnel Management*, 25, No. 3 (Fall 1996), 277–289.

36. Frederick Bird and James A. Waters. "The Nature of Managerial Moral Standards," *Journal of Business Ethics*, 6 (January 1987), 13; also see James Weber, "Managers' Moral Reasoning: Assessing Their Responses to Three Moral Dilemmas," *Human Relations*, 43 (1990), 687–702.

37. Elbing and Elbing, *The Value Issue of Business*, p. 202.

38. David W. Ewing, *The Managerial Mind* (New York: Free Press, 1964), p. 3.

39. Ibid.

40. See, for example, R. Joseph Monsen, Jr., and Anthony Downs, "A Theory of Large Managerial Firms," *Journal of Political Economy* (June 1964), 221–236.

41. See Fremont E. Kast and James E. Rosenzweig, *Organization and Management: A Systems Approach*, 2nd ed. (New York: McGraw-Hill, 1974),

pp. 25–49, for a comprehensive discussion of the evolution of managerial values.

42. See Adam Smith, *An Inquiry into the Nature and Causes of the Wealth of Nations*, ed. E. Cannan (New York: Modern Library, 1937).

43. Richard N. Farmer, "The Ethical Dilemma of American Capitalism," *California Management Review* (Summer 1964), 47–58.

44. S. K. Chakraporty, *Managerial Transformation by Values: A Corporate Pilgrimage* (Newbury Park, Calif.: Sage Publications, 1993).

45. Patrick E. Conner et al., "A Cross-National Comparative Study of Managerial Values: United States, Canada, and Japan," *Advances in International Comparative Management*, 8 (1993), 3–29; also see David A. Ralston et al., "The Impact of Managerial Values on Decision-Making Behaviour: A Comparison of the United States and Hong Kong," *Asia Pacific Journal of Management* (April 1993), 21–37.

46. See, for example, Barry Z. Posner, W. Alan Randolph, and Warren H. Schmidt, "Managerial Values Across Functions," *Group & Organization Studies*, 12 (1987), 373–385; and Sami M. Abbasi and Kenneth W. Hollman, "An Exploratory Study of the Personal Value Systems of City Managers," *Journal of Business Ethics*, 6 (1987), 45–53.

47. Examples of exceptions to this trend include Andrew F. Sikula, "The Values and Value Systems of Government Executives," *Public Personnel Management* (January–February 1973), 16–22; and W. Randy Boxx, Randall Y. Odom, and Mark G. Dunn, "Organizational Values and Value Congruency and Their Impact on Satisfaction, Commitment, and Cohesion: An Empirical Examination Within the Public Sector," *Public Personnel Management*, 20 (Spring 1991), 195–205; and Posner and Schmidt, "The Values of Business and Federal Government Executives: More Different than Alike."

48. Boxx, Odom, and Dunn, "Organizational Values," p. 204.

49. Abbasi and Hollman, "An Exploratory Study of the Personal Value Systems of City Managers," p. 51.

50. For an elaboration of the generic nature of management, see E. Frank Harrison, *Management and*

Organizations (Boston: Houghton Mifflin, 1978), particularly pp. 8–11.

51. Orvis F. Collins and David G. Moore, *The Enterprising Man* (East Lansing: Michigan State University, 1964), pp. 201–232.

52. England, "Personal Value Systems of American Managers," pp. 53–68.

53. Ibid., pp. 67–68.

54. Edward J. Lusk and Bruce L. Oliver, "American Managers' Personal Value Systems — Revisited," *Academy of Management Journal*, 17 (September 1974), 554.

55. James K. Dent, "Organizational Correlates of the Goals of Business Managements," in *Management in Perspective*, ed. William E. Schlender, William G. Scott, and Alan E. Filley (Boston: Houghton Mifflin, 1965), pp. 62–84.

56. Guth and Tagiuri, "Personal Values and Corporate Strategy," pp. 123–132. It should be noted that the classification of values used in this study was developed by Spranger and further delineated by Allport, Vernon, and Lindzey (see note 28).

57. R. J. Monsen, B. O. Saxberg, and R. A. Sutermeister, "The Modern Manager: What Makes Him Run?" *Business Horizons* (Fall 1966), 24.

58. R. Joseph Monsen, Jr., and Anthony Downs, "A Theory of Large Managerial Firms," in *Comparative Administrative Theory*, ed. Preston P. LeBreton (Seattle: University of Washington Press, 1968), p. 41.

59. Manley Howe Jones, *Executive Decision Making*, rev. ed. (Homewood, Ill.: Richard D. Irwin, 1962), pp. 114–115.

60. Donald N. De Salvia and Gary M. Gemmill, "An Exploratory Study of the Personal Value Systems of College Students and Managers," *Academy of Management Journal*, 14 (June 1971), 227–238.

61. John Senger, "Managers' Perceptions of Subordinates' Competence as a Function of Personal Value Orientations," *Academy of Management Journal*, 14 (December 1971), 415–423.

62. William Whitely and George W. England, "Managerial Values as a Reflection of Culture and the Process of Industrialization," *Academy of Management Journal*, 20 (September 1976), 439–453.

63. John G. Watson and Sam Barone, "The Self-Concept, Personal Values, and Motivational Orientation of Black and White Managers," *Academy of Management Journal*, 19 (March 1976), 36–48.

64. Barry Z. Posner and Warren H. Schmidt, "Values and the American Manager: An Update," *California Management Review* (Spring 1984), 202–216.

65. Ibid., pp. 204–205.

66. Patrick E. Connor and Boris W. Becker, "Values and the Organization: Suggestions for Research," in *Understanding Human Values*, ed. Milton Rokeach (New York: Free Press, 1979), p. 78.

67. Posner and Schmidt, "Values and the American Manager," p. 205.

68. See Keith Davis, "The Case for and Against Business Assumption of Social Responsibilities," *Academy of Management Journal* (June 1973), 313–317.

69. See Victor Perlo, "People's Capitalism and Stock-Ownership," *American Economic Review* (June 1958), 333–347.

70. John Humble et al., "The Strategic Power of Corporate Values," *Long-Range Planning*, 27, No. 6 (1994), 28–42.

71. Barry Z. Posner and Warren H. Schmidt, "Values and the American Manager: An Update Updated," *California Management Review*, 34 (Spring 1992), 84.

72. James A. Lee, "Changes in Managerial Values, 1965–1986," *Business Horizons*, 31 (July/August 1988), 29–37.

73. See *Korn/Ferry International's Executive Profile: A Decade of Change in Corporate Leadership* (New York: Korn/Ferry International, 1990).

74. Wayne A. R. Leys, *Ethics for Policy Decisions* (Englewood Cliffs, N.J.: Prentice-Hall, 1962), p. 4.

75. Kenneth Boulding, "The Ethics of Rational Decision," *Management Science*, 12 (February 1966), B-161.

76. Ibid., p. B-162.

77. Percy H. Hill et al., *Making Decisions: A Multidisciplinary Introduction* (Reading, Mass.: Addison-Wesley, 1978), pp. 36–37.

78. Raymond Baumhart, *Ethics in Business* (New York: Holt, Rinehart, Winston, 1968), p. 15.

79. William Lillie, *An Introduction to Ethics* (New York: Barnes & Noble, 1964), pp. 5, 18.

80. Thomas M. Garrett, *Business Ethics* (New York: Appleton-Century-Crofts, 1966), p. 4.

81. Ibid., p. 5.

82. Joseph W. Towle, ed., *Ethics and Standards in American Business* (Boston: Houghton Mifflin, 1964), p. 6.

83. Baumhart, *Ethics in Business*, p. 13, also see p. 5 for a discussion of surveys.

84. John W. Newstrom and William A. Ruch, "The Ethics of Management and the Management of Ethics," *MSU Business Topics*, 23 (Winter 1975), 29–37.

85. Archie B. Carroll, "Managerial Ethics: A Post-Watergate View," *Business Horizons*, 18 (April 1975), 79.

86. James S. Bowman, "Managerial Ethics in Business and Government," *Business Horizons*, 19 (October 1976), 48–54.

87. Karp and Abramms, "Doing the Right Thing."

88. Bird and Waters, "The Nature of Managerial Moral Standards," p. 13.

89. Gene R. Laczniak and Edward J. Inderrieden, "The Influence of Stated Organizational Concern upon Ethical Decision Making," *Journal of Business Ethics*, 6 (1987), 297–307.

90. John H. Barnett and Marvin J. Karson, "Personal Values and Business Decisions: An Exploratory Investigation," *Journal of Business Ethics* 6 (1987), 371–382.

91. F. Neil Brady, "Aesthetic Components of Management Ethics," *Academy of Management Review*, 11 (1986), 337–344; and Linda Klebe Trevino, "Ethical Decision Making in Organizations: A Person-Situation Interactionist Model," *Academy of Management Review*, 11 (1986), 601–617.

92. Posner and Schmidt, "Values and the American Manager: An Update Updated," p. 92.

93. Lee, "Changes in Managerial Values, 1965–1986."

94. *Korn/Ferry International's Executive Profile.*

95. Quoted in Jeffrey R. Holland, "The Value of Values: Shared Tasks for Business and Education in the 1980s," *Executive Speeches* (August–September 1994), 57.

96. Thomas H. Bivins, "A Systems Model for Ethical Decision Making in Public Relations," *Public Relations Review*, 18, No. 4 (1992), 365–383.

97. Francis K. Achampong and Wold Zemedkun, "An Empirical and Ethical Analysis of Factors Motivating Managers' Merger Decisions," *Journal of Business Ethics*, 14 (1995), 855–865.

98. Michael C. Jensen and William H. Meckling, "Theory of the Firm: Managerial Behavior, Agency Costs, and Ownership Structure," *Journal of Financial Economics*, 3 (1976), 305–360.

99. A. J. Grant, "Making Sense of Public Values: Environmental Controversies for Corporate Decision Makers," *Total Quality Environmental Management* (Summer 1995), 65–71; and Gene R. Lacniak and Edward J. Inerrieden, "The Influence of Stated Organization Concern upon Ethical Decision Making," *Journal of Business Ethics*, 6 (1987), 297–307.

100. William A. Evans, *Management Ethics* (Boston: Martinus Nijhoff, 1981), p. 130.

101. Edmund P. Learned, Arch R. Dooley, and Robert L. Katz, "Personal Values and Business Decisions," *Harvard Business Review* (March–April 1959), 112.

102. Barry Z. Posner and Warren H. Schmidt, "Value Congruence and Differences Between the Interplay of Personal and Organizational Value Systems," *Journal of Business Ethics*, 12 (1993), 341–347.

103. Elbing and Elbing, *The Value Issue of Business*, p. 103.

104. Ibid., p. 123.

105. Learned, Dooley, and Katz, "Personal Values and Business Decisions," p. 114.

106. See, for example, Jeanne M. Liedtka, "Value Congruence: The Interplay of Individual and Organizational Value Systems," *Journal of Business Ethics*, 8 (1989), 805–815; and Posner and Schmidt, "Value Congruence and Differences Between the Interplay of Personal and Organizational Value Systems, pp. 341–347.

107. *The American Heritage Dictionary of the English Language* (Boston: Houghton Mifflin, 1978), p. 709.

108. Allen Newell, "Judgment and Its Representation: An Introduction," in *Formal Representation of Human Judgment*, ed. Benjamin Kleinmuntz (New York: Wiley, 1968), p. 2.

109. "Judgments and the Language of Decisions," in *Human Judgments and Optimality*, ed. Maynard W. Shelly II, and Glenn L. Bryan (New York: Wiley, 1964), p. 10.

110. Sir Geoffrey Vickers, *The Art of Judgment, a Study of Policy Making* (London: Chapman & Hall, 1965), p. 13.

111. Ruth P. Mack, *Planning on Uncertainty* (New York: Wiley-Interscience, 1971), p. 195.

112. Robin M. Hogarth, *Judgement and Choice* (New York: Wiley, 1980), p. 3.

113. Vickers, *The Art of Judgment*, p. 73.

114. Hillel J. Einhorn and Robin M. Hogarth, "Behavioral Decision Theory: Processes of Judgment and Choice," in *Decision Making*, ed. Gerado R. Ungson and Daniel N. Braunstein (Boston: Kent, 1982), p. 32.

115. See George Mandler, "The Structure of Value: Accounting for Taste," in *Affect and Cognition*, The Seventeenth Annual Carnegie Symposium on Cognition, ed. Margaret Sydnor Clark and Susan

F. Fiske (Hillsdale, N.J.: Lawrence Erlbaum Associates, 1992), pp. 3–36.

116. Newell, "Judgment and Its Representation: An Introduction," pp. 5–6.

117. Mack, *Planning on Uncertainty*, p. 70.

118. Ebert and Mitchell, *Organizational Decision Processes*, p. 56.

119. For a comprehensive discussion of the use of value judgments in decision making, see William C. Waddell, "Values: A Challenge to a Science of Management," *University of Washington Business Review*, 29 (Winter 1970), 28–39.

SUPPLEMENTAL REFERENCES

Badr, H. A., E. R. Gray, and B. L. Kedia, "Personal Values and Managerial Decision Making: Evidence from Two Cultures." *Management International Review*, 22 (1982), 65–73.

Bazerman, Max H. *Judgment in Managerial Decision Making*, 3rd ed. New York: Wiley, 1994.

Bedau, Hugo, "Ethical Aspects of Group Decision Making." In *Group Decision Making*, ed. Walter C. Swap and Associates (Beverly Hills, Calif.: Sage, 1984), pp. 115–150.

Bell, Robert. "Professional Values and Organizational Decision Making." *Administration & Society* (May 1985), 21–60.

Brown, Martha A. "Values — A Necessary but Neglected Ingredient of Motivation on the Job." *Academy of Management Review*, 1 (October 1976), 15–23.

Cavanaugh, Gerald F. *American Business Values with International Perspectives*, 4th ed. Upper Saddle River, N.J.: Prentice-Hall, 1998.

Dressel, Paul L. "Values Cognitive and Affective." *Journal of Higher Education*, 15, No. 42 (1971), 400–405.

Ericson, Richard F. "The Impact of Cybernetic Information Technology on Management Value Systems." *Management Science* (October 1969), B-40–B-60.

Fritzsche, David J. "A Model of Decision-Making Incorporating Ethical Values." *Journal of Business Ethics*, 10 (1991), 841–852.

Gandz, Jeffrey, and Nadine Hayes, "Teaching Business Ethics." *Journal of Business Ethics*, 7 (1988), 657–669.

Graves, Clare W. "Levels of Existence: An Open System Theory of Values." *Journal of Humanistic Psychology*, 10 (Fall 1970), 131–155.

Hammond, Kenneth R., and Leonard Adelman. "Science, Values, and Human Judgment." *Science* (October 22, 1976), 389–395.

Heermance, Edgar L. *The Ethics of Business*. New York: Harper, 1926.

Hogarth, Robin. *Judgement and Choice*. 2nd ed. New York: Wiley, 1987.

Ladd, John. "Morality and the Ideal of Rationality in Formal Organizations." *Monist*, 54 (1970), 488–516.

McClelland, David C. "How Motives, Skills, and Values Determine What People Do," *American Psychologist*, 40, No. 7 (July 1985), 812–825.

McCoy, Bowen H. "Applying the Art of Action-Oriented Decision Making to the Knotty Issues of Everyday Business Life." *Management Review* (July 1983), 20–24.

McCoy, Charles S. *Management of Values*. Marshfield, Mass.: Pitman, 1985.

McKinney, John Paul. "The Development of Values: A Perceptual Interpretation." *Journal of Personality and Social Psychology* (May 1975), 801–807.

March, James G. *Decisions and Organizations*. New York: Blackwell, 1988.

Markin, Ron J. "A Philosophy of Management." *University of Washington Business Review* (April 1963), 67–78.

Mattersich, Richard. "The Incorporation and Reduction of Value Judgments in Systems." *Management Science*, 21 (September 1974), 1–9.

Messick, David M., and Max H. Bazerman, "Ethical Leadership and the Psychology of Decision Making," *Sloan Management Review* (Winter 1996), 9–22.

Miller, Samuel H. "The Tangle of Ethics." *Harvard Business Review* (January–February 1960), 59–62.

Nisbett, Richard, and Lee Ross. *Human Inference: Strategies and Shortcomings of Social Judgment.* Englewood Cliffs, N.J.: Prentice-Hall, 1980.

Parducci, Allen. "The Relativism of Absolute Judgments." *Scientific American* (December 1968), 84–90.

Pepitone, Albert. "The Role of Justice in Interdependent Decision Making." *Journal of Experimental Social Psychology*, 7 (January 1971), 144–156.

Pollak, Otto. "The Protestant Ethic and the Values of Middle Management." In *The Frontiers of Management Psychology*. Ed. George Fisk. New York: Harper & Row, 1964, pp. 29–37.

Rae, Douglas W. "Decision Rules and Individual Value in Constitutional Choice." *American Political Science Review*, 63, No. 1 (1969), 40–56.

Schein, Edgar H. "The Problem of Moral Education for the Business Manager." *Industrial Management Review*, 8 (1966), 3–14.

Schmidt, Warren H., and Barry Z. Posner. *Managerial Values in Perspective.* AMA Survey Report. New York: American Management Association, 1983.

Scott, William G., and David K. Hart. "The Moral Nature of Man in Organizations: A Comparative Analysis." *Academy of Management Journal* (June 1971) 241–255.

Selekman, Benjamin M., and Sylvia K. Selekman. *Power and Morality in a Business Society.* New York: McGraw-Hill, 1956.

Sherif, Muzafer, and Carl I. Hovland, eds. *Social Judgment.* New Haven: Yale University Press, 1961.

Sidgwick, Henry. *The Methods of Ethics.* 7th ed. Chicago: University of Chicago Press, 1962.

Sikula, Andrew F. "Values and Value Systems: Importance and Relationship to Managerial and Organizational Behavior." *Journal of Psychology*, 78 (July 1971), 277–286.

Swearinger, John E. "The Nature of the Executive Decision." *MSU Business Topics* (Spring 1965), 60–65.

Szaniawski, Klemens. "Philosophy of Decision Making." *Acta Psychologica*, 45 (1980), 327–341.

Walton, Clarence C. *Ethos and the Executive.* Englewood Cliffs, N.J.: Prentice-Hall, 1969.

Zhukov, Yu. M. "Values as Determinants in Decision Making. A Sociopsychological Approach to the Problem." *Soviet Psychology* (Fall 1980), 93–117.

PART TWO

Interdisciplinary Aspects of Managerial Decision Making

CHAPTER FIVE

Eclectic Approaches to Decision Making

We have indicated that managerial decision making is a dynamic process and that it is generic to all forms of organized activity. The generic qualities of the decision-making process make it synonymous with management. In addition to being generic, the process is eclectic. The word **eclectic** means "selecting what appears to be best in various doctrines, or styles" or, more simply, "composed of elements drawn from various sources."[1] Thus it describes precisely one of the intrinsic characteristics of the decision-making process. There is a growing awareness that managerial decision making is both a product of and an influence on the culture in which it exists. This awareness has resulted in a movement away from the traditional approaches to decision making that relied heavily if not exclusively on the disciplines of economics, mathematics, and statistics. Given the increasing complexity of modern culture and the attendant high rates of technological and social change, it is imperative that managerial decision making take into account relevant aspects of many disciplines.

"Decision making is a meeting ground for psychologists, economists, sociologists, organizational theorists, statisticians, philosophers, and others. It is an exciting field, endowed with a deep formal theory, a rich technology, numerous intriguing observations of individuals and organizations, and a growing body of experimental results."[2] "Decision theory . . . was developed first by mathematicians and economists. . . . Economists have been less concerned than psychologists with rationalizing human behavior and more concerned with choices that should be made to maximize profit or utility. Mathematicians, likewise, have usually been little concerned with explaining actual human choice. They have been more concerned with the mathematical theory of rational decision making, and more generally, with the development of the mathematics of extrema."[3] "The decision-making process is obviously complicated by the fact that different disciplines apply to different [decisions]. The students of . . . decision making must understand that there are no neat formulas to determine how much of each discipline will apply to a particular [decision] nor how much weight a decision maker should give the discipline."[4]

This chapter sets the stage for subsequent chapters in Part II. As such, it goes to the heart of the theme that underlies this book — managerial decision making is accomplished within an integrated process set forth in an interdisciplinary context. The eclectic aspects of managerial decision making are exemplified by the models of decision making set forth in the first major section of this chapter. The disciplines that permeate managerial decision making are subsequently divided into behavioral aspects and quantitative disciplines. Other books place a greater emphasis on a quantitative approach to managerial decision making. This approach is most appropriate for category I decisions made, for the most part, in the operational areas of the organization. This book emphasizes category II decisions which are more uncertain as to their outcome and which, because of their significance, tend to be made at upper levels of management. Consequently, we place considerably more emphasis on the behavioral aspects of managerial decision making with the quantitative disciplines in a corollary role.

DECISION-MAKING MODELS

The eclectic aspects of decision making are best illustrated within the framework of a set of models. Such models show graphically how much emphasis applicable disciplines receive in decision making.

Different interdisciplinary approaches to decision making may be viewed as decision-making models because they represent a particular segment of the real world at a given time and place under varying conditions. Because of the almost infinite number of variables in decision making, and because these variables have varying degrees of complexity, it is virtually impossible for the human mind to comprehend their full scope. Consequently, the decision maker must develop a model with a small number of causal variables that are both significant and understandable. If insufficient or incorrect variables are included, the model will not function as the real-world phenomenon does. If too many variables are included, even if they are the right ones, the model's complexity will work against understanding. Ideally, then, a decision-making model should include some optimum number of variables that will help explain the real-world phenomenon being modeled. Such a model should help the decision maker predict real-world phenomena with sufficient consistency and accuracy to be of considerable value.

Rice and Bishoprick have defined models in a way that is suitable for this discussion.

> Models can be mathematical, social, or philosophical. They can involve physical phenomena, emotional phenomena, or, in fact, anything capable of theoretical analysis. Because they are used in theoretical analyses, there have been many different models developed to explain the same or similar phenomena. Each theoretical discipline, in examining an occurrence, must develop its own model to explain it.[5]

Before presenting the decision-making models, several points should be noted:

1. The models presented are not mutually exclusive, in that different models will share some of the same components.

2. The models are simplified as much as possible. A scholar of any of the models will see that this simplification does not accommodate many of the qualifications, refinements, and nuances of a completely developed model.

3. There are many models of decision making that will not be presented. The literature of decision making is increasingly enriched by theoretical formulations and empirical investigations, and the possibilities for refinements of existing models and development of new models are virtually limitless. The models of decision making presented here, although not exhaustive, are representative of much of the current thinking with regard to decision making in formal organizations.[6]

The models presented here are intended to reflect assumptions and behavior relevant to decision making in various organizational settings.[7] They illustrate the eclectic aspects of decision making. This presentation should not be confused with the discussion later in this chapter dealing with the development and use of models as a technique for reducing uncertainty within the decision-making process.

The literature on decision making abounds with models that are relevant to this presentation. Allison, for example, discusses the Cuban missile crisis in the context of (1) a rational actor or "classical" model, (2) an organizational process model, and (3) a governmental (bureaucratic) politics model.[8] Steinbruner's book based on his doctoral dissertation at MIT advanced an analytic model, a cybernetic model, and a cognitive model.[9] And Anderson identified a rational model, an organizational model, and a cognitive model.[10] Linstone propounded models of decision making founded on a technical perspective, an organizational perspective, and a personal perspective.[11] The political aspects of decision making have been set forth on several occasions in a kind of political model by Lindblom.[12] Cohen, March, and Olsen advanced a so-called garbage-can model of decision making,[13] and for his contribution, Etzioni proposed a mixed-scanning model.[14] Finally, Nutt combined the principal elements of most of the above models into a typology of decision making models.[15]

Clearly there is virtually no limit to the number of models of decision making that can be developed to serve the purposes and advance the discipline of the model builder.[16] Models, founded on key assumptions and composed of key ingredients, help us better understand the complex nature of decision making. Because they reflect one dimensional and multidimensional perspectives on decision making, models constitute an ideal medium through which to illustrate the eclectic nature and the interdisciplinary character of managerial decision making. The models discussed in the sections to follow are most suitable for purposes of this book and most reflective of the current and emerging field of managerial decision making.[17]

The Rational Model

The rational model of decision making is essentially normative in that it is prescriptive rather than descriptive. It attempts to prescribe, on the basis of some rather precise assumptions, the conditions under which managers should make decisions in formal organizations. The rational model specifies those things that managers must do to be effective decision makers. Like most normative things, the rational model lacks a rationale or empirical defense explaining its particular assumptions and specified criteria. It is formally structured to the point of being mechanistic.

The rational model is the classical approach in the field of decision theory.[18] It provides the foundation for the quantitative disciplines of economics, mathematics, and statistics. Indeed the rational model is the main reason many people regard decision making as intrinsically quantitative.

> Classical "economic man" and the rational man of modern statistical decision theory and game theory make optimal choices in narrowly constrained, neatly defined situations. . . . the rational decision problem is reduced to a simple matter of selecting among a set of given alternatives, each of which has a given set of consequences, . . . the alternative whose consequences are preferred in terms of the [decision maker's] utility function which ranks each set of consequences in order of preference.[19]

The rational model explicitly presumes that if a given variable cannot be assigned a numeric value, it should be disregarded or assumed away as a constant or given value. It is a model that operates within a closed environment with a rather precise number of variables. Consequently the rational model is most applicable to category I decisions, although it is represented as being applicable to decisions of all types.

Somewhat simplistically the rational model assumes that "the decision maker is aware of all the options, i.e., available courses of action, and that the effects of all possible futures can be determined — at least in the short run."[20] One rather common variation of the rational model assumes that:

1. There is only one decision maker.
2. The decision maker has only one objective.
3. The objective can be written in quantitative terms.
4. The potential states of nature and courses of action are finite and have been identified.
5. The decision problem consists simply of choosing the best course of action.[21]

More comprehensively, the rational model translates the objectives of the decision maker into a preference function that represents in numerical terms the value or utility of a given set of alternatives. A set of the consequences of a particular choice is attached to each alternative. Variations are generated at this point by making different assumptions about the accuracy of the decision maker's knowledge of the consequences. A choice in the rational model consists of selecting the alternative whose consequences rank highest in the decision maker's payoff function — that is, the alternative with the highest positive utility for the decision maker.[22]

The rational model assumes that the decision maker must meet two principal requirements. First, given any two alternatives, A and B, the decision maker must always be able to tell whether A is preferred to B; B is preferred to A; or there is no particular preference for either A or B. This requirement is the so-called **closure axiom.** The second requirement is that all preferences must be transitive. For example, if A is preferred to B, and B is preferred to C, then A is preferred to C. This is the **transitivity axiom.**

However, the closure and transitivity axioms will not always hold for human choice.[23] Thus, they make up one of the many faulty assumptions of the rational model of decision making. Obviously, the closure axiom may not apply to decisions characterized by uncertainty, such as category II decisions. The transitivity axiom is concerned with logical consistency rather than the content of decisions. Therefore, it is of limited usefulness in dealing with the many dimensions of category II decisions. Transitivity obviously calls for an ability to quantify outcomes. However, the multifaceted nature of category II decisions tends to preclude anything approaching precise quantification. This renders intransitive the alternatives associated with such decisions.

The key ingredients and assumptions of the rational model, and other decision-making models to be discussed in this chapter, are reflected in Table 5.1.

At this point it is instructive to focus on the following principal shortcomings of the assumptions underlying the rational model:

1. Objectives are seldom fixed in any organizational setting. Managers must continually modify their objectives to reflect inevitable changes.

2. Managers seldom if ever have unlimited information about a given set of alternatives. For most category II decisions the available information is incomplete at best.

3. Managerial decision makers have cognitive limitations that restrict the amount of information and the number of alternatives they can consider.

4. It is unrealistic to assume that a decision-making situation in formal organizations will not bear time and cost constraints.

5. As noted above, the preference functions of decision makers tend to defy quantification, and alternatives of any complexity are seldom completely transitive.

A Typology of Decision-Making Models

	Primary Decision-Making Criterion	Key Ingredients	Key Assumptions
Rational (classical)	Maximized outcome	Objectives; specific states of nature; subjective probabilities; quantified utilities (payoffs); exhaustive alternatives; disregard of environment; computational decision-making strategy; short-term horizon; highly structured process	Fixed objectives; unlimited information; no cognitive limitations; no time and cost constraints; quantifiable and transitive alternatives; controlled variables; closed system; quantitatively limited outcomes
Organizational (neoclassical)	Satisficing outcome	Objectives; general states of nature; limited subjective probabilities; partially quantified utilities (payoffs); nonexhaustive alternatives; sensitive environment; judgmental decision-making strategy; short-term horizon; moderately structured process	Attainable objectives; limited information; cognitive limitations; time and cost constraints; partially quantifiable and intransitive alternatives; open system; qualitatively — and quantitatively — limited outcomes
Political (adaptive)	Acceptable outcome	Objectives; general states of nature; no probabilities; unquantifiable utilities (payoffs); nonexhaustive alternatives; dominant environment; compromise or bargaining decision-making strategy; restricted number of outcomes; short-term horizon; incremental steps; loosely structured process	Limited objectives; unlimited information; no cognitive limitations; no time and cost constraints; nonquantifiable and generally transitive alternatives; open system; environmentally limited outcomes; no "right" decision
Process (managerial)	Objectives-oriented outcome	Objectives; general states of nature; generally subjective probabilities; objectives-oriented utilities (payoffs); exhaustive alternatives; sensitive to environmental constraints; judgmental decision-making strategy with selective use of computation and compromise; long-term horizon; limited number of outcomes; highly structured process	Highly dynamic objectives; limited information; cognitive limitations; time and cost constraints; generally nonquantifiable and intransitive alternatives; open system; sequential decision-making functions; objectives-oriented outcomes

6. The variables in most decision-making situations cannot be completely controlled. Variables can be controlled completely only in some artificially contrived situations that presuppose a controlled environment with no externally induced changes and no need to consider relevant external constituencies.

7. At least for most category II decisions, the outcomes likely to result from the selection of a particular alternative tend to defy quantification, as do the utilities or preference functions of the decision makers.

8. The use of computational decision-making strategies seems most applicable to category I decisions.[24]

Given the obvious shortcomings of the rational model, why do economists, mathematicians, and statisticians seem so enamored of this classical approach to decision making?

> Probably because its use permits a rigorous intellectual reasoning process. If one [makes certain normative assumptions], a complete and completely consistent package of rules for [making decisions] can be devised, rules that can be expressed precisely in equations and illustrated by graphs, rules that provide correct answers to classroom problems and rules which, when they do not work in practice, can always be explained by "other things being equal."[25]

On the positive side, the rational model has some advantages if it is used selectively to support one of the other major decision-making models presented in Table 5.1. Particularly within the process model of decision making, the rational model may facilitate arriving at a choice by:

1. Combining estimates of outcome uncertainty, expressed as subjective probabilities, with measures of possible outcome consequences to obtain an overall measure of each alternative's desirability in terms of a specific decision-making criterion

2. Providing an explicit basis for guiding the search activity, particularly in evaluating the desirability of gathering additional information prior to making a decision

3. Providing a basis for reducing the number of relevant alternatives[26]

Several techniques that fall within the rational model are mentioned in later sections of this chapter. The process model we favor does not preclude using rational-model techniques that can be employed effectively in process-model decision making.

The Organizational Model

The rational model is the foundation for the quantitative disciplines in managerial decision making. Conversely, the organizational model combines the behavioral disciplines with quantitative analysis. Thus the decision maker's choice takes note of constraints caused by the external environment. In many ways the organizational model represents a neoclassical approach to decision making in formal organizations. That is, it foresakes the specific norms and prescriptions of the classical model and replaces them with a more open approach that provides for the many behavioral and environmental constraints imposed on managerial decision makers. Decision making in the organizational model is "a temporal process in which [decision makers] placed in an organized structure participate, with various objectives that are changing and contradictory, an imperfect knowledge of the possible alternatives and of their consequences, and a will to reach not a maximum of advantages but an acceptable level of satisfaction."[27]

The organizational model owes much of its currency to the research of Cyert and March. According to them, the organizational model is characterized by

1. Multiple, changing, acceptable-level goals
2. An approximate sequential consideration of alternatives. *The first satisfactory alternative evoked in the search activity is accepted*
3. The avoidance of uncertainty by following policy and procedures and reacting to feedback rather than attempting to predict consequences
4. Making and implementing choices within procedures and with the use of rules of thumb derived from experience[28]

Simon broadened the dimensions of the organizational model beyond the neoclassical approach advanced by Cyert and March. He notes five significant deviations from the rational model that reflect the behavioral aspects of managerial decision making in formal organizations.[29] These deviations are as follows:

1. *Factored problems.* Decision-making problems are so complex that only a limited number of aspects of each problem can be attended to at a time. Thus managerial decision makers divide (factor) problems into a number of roughly independent parts and deal with the parts one by one within the various units of the organization.
2. *Satisficing.* Maximizing of outcomes, which is characteristic of the rational model, is replaced by satisficing of outcomes in the organizational model. Managerial decision makers do not have all the alternatives related to a given choice. Therefore, they seek a course of action that is "good enough" to attain their objectives.
3. *Search.* Organizations generate alternatives by relatively stable, sequential search procedures. As in the neoclassical approach of Cyert and March, the discovery of an alternative that appears to meet the managerial objectives is sufficient to abort the search procedures.
4. *Uncertainty avoidance.* Also as in the neoclassical approach of Cyert and March, uncertainty tends to be avoided by making choices that emphasize short-run feedback to provide for timely changes in emerging outcomes that appear to diverge from the managerial objectives.

5. *Repertoires.* Organizations tend to have second and third alternatives that may be implemented if feedback indicates that the satisficing choice is not yielding a desirable outcome.[30]

As shown in Table 5.1 the organizational model represents a significant departure from the classical model. Fixed objectives are replaced by attainable objectives that may be scaled downward if the search does not reveal adequate alternatives. The organizational model acknowledges the constraints of (1) limited information, (2) cognitive limitations, and (3) time and cost limitations. As such, the organizational model introduces the disciplines of philosophy, psychology, and sociology into the decision-making situation. The prescriptive qualities of economics, mathematics, and statistics are softened in the organizational model.[31] This model is open to environmental influences and accepts outcomes on their qualitative as well as their quantitative merits. Whereas the classical model is best suited for category I decisions, the organizational model easily accommodates category II choices.

There are, however, some basic similarities between the classical and organizational models. Both models have a short-term horizon and are oriented toward immediate results. In the classical model the desire for a maximized outcome necessitates a short-range perspective. (As was noted in Chapter 3, maximizing behavior has an intrinsic orientation toward the short run.) The organizational model also seems concerned with rather immediate results. If, for example, feedback reveals that an implemented choice is not leading toward the intended outcome, management may substitute a second or even a third choice until the actual outcome appears to achieve the desired result. Such actions suggest that the organizational model is really aimed toward an optimum outcome that may work against long-term benefits. As a second similarity, both models operate within some discernible constraints. The rational model is constrained by the normative orientation of the quantitative disciplines. The organizational model is constrained by internal policies and procedures as well as the impetus toward a quick result.

The principal difference between the rational model and the organizational model is that the former seeks maximized outcomes, whereas the latter accepts satisficing outcomes. This crucial difference was the subject of Chapter 3. Many of the proponents of the classical model find ample grounds for criticism of the organizational model.[32] Suffice to say here, however, that the principal shortcoming of the organizational model is that it does not have a planning orientation directed toward long-range benefits for the organization.

The Political Model

The political model is based primarily on the disciplines of political science, philosophy, psychology, and sociology. This model is completely different from the classical model, which, as noted, is embedded firmly in the quantitative disciplines. Indeed, the political model's foundation is almost totally behavioral. With its orientation toward short-term results within a context of policy and procedure, the organizational model is similar to the political model. The principal difference between the two is that the political model employs a compromise or bargaining decision-making strategy and aims toward an outcome that is acceptable to many external constituencies. Conversely, the organizational model is, by definition, geared to outcomes that benefit the firm or the institution, at least in the short run.

A compromise strategy is the hallmark of political decision making. This model tends to disregard evaluative information because qualitative rather than quantitative input is emphasized: incremental decisions are made through a continuous series of adjustments as the views of partisans become known. There is a limited number of goals and objectives in the political model. There is also a good deal of manipulation in this model, as units within the organization vie for dominance and supremacy.

> The [political] model calls for the decision maker(s) to monitor a variety of power centers within the organization. . . . The emergence of sentiments and norms in these partisan [units] are tested against current priorities. . . . Thus decisions are not expected to correspond with any set of internally consistent logic. The decision maker merely adjusts to needs as they are expressed and perceived to be "significant." When partisans make their wishes clear and unequivocal, the decision maker attempts to incorporate them in the final decision.[33]

The political model of decision making is founded on the concept of incrementalism: "The central notion of incrementalism is that choice is marginal."[34] Decision makers should consider only small differences from the present condition or state of affairs. Presumably there is no justification for going beyond the current situation because we don't have the knowledge to predict outcomes and we would have too much difficulty in getting agreement on the relative priorities of the many values involved. Only alternatives that differ marginally from the status quo or from one another are seriously considered in the incremental approach, and only the small differences are subject to analysis. Moreover, there is no need in incrementalism to consider all the consequences likely to ensue from the choice of a given alternative. It is sufficient to consider only the obvious, interesting, high-profitability, near-term consequences. Incremental decision making is serial or continuous in nature. It is characterized by continuous attacks on a permanent but changing need within a particular unit at the level of the organization. Conditions are improved but problems are not solved through incremental decision making. This, of course, is the primary reason this approach is the sine qua non of the political model.[35]

> The decision maker focuses only on those policies that differ marginally from existing policies. Incrementalism allows for countless ends-means and means-ends adjustments. The [final choice] is not unique or even right; it develops with the continuous reformulation of the issues at hand. Consensus is not a prerequisite and often develops only after the decision has been made. Incremental decision making is . . . remedial, geared more to the alleviation of present, concrete imperfections than to the promotion of future goals.[36]

Whether reference is made to the disjointed incrementalism of Lind-blom[37] or the logical incrementalism of Quinn,[38] incremental decision making falls within the political model summarized in Table 5.1. For its part, the political model should be regarded as a primary paradigm of decision making in formal organizations of all types, although it seems most applicable to highly bureaucratized institutions in the public sector.

The primary requirements of the political model are as follows:

1. Rather than attempting a comprehensive survey and evaluation of all alternatives, managerial decision makers focus only on those policies that differ from existing policies.

2. Only a relatively small number of alternatives are considered.

3. For each alternative, only a restricted number of important consequences are evaluated.

4. The problem confronting the managerial decision makers is continually redefined. The incremental approach used in the political model allows for countless ends-means and means-ends adjustments that, in effect, make the decision more manageable.

5. Thus, there is no one decision or "right" choice but a never-ending series of attacks on the decision at hand through individual analysis and evaluation of each aspect of the decision.

6. As such, the political model, with its emphasis on incremental decision making, is geared more toward alleviating current problems than toward the development and implementation of choices promising long-range benefits.[39]

The principal differences between the classical and organizational models and the political model are listed below:

1. The setting of managerial objectives and the search for alternatives are accomplished concurrently rather than sequentially in the political model. These two functions of decision making are intermingled.

2. In the political model, ends and means are not distinct.

3. The test of a good decision in the political model is whether most of the decision makers agree on the likely outcome.

4. There is a minimal analysis of alternatives in the political model. Important outcomes, alternatives, and values are neglected in this model.

5. By proceeding incrementally and by comparing likely outcomes with established policies, the political model minimizes the uncertainty of decision making.[40]

Acceptance of the likely outcome by managerial decision makers and external constituencies is the primary criterion for successful decision making in the political model. Economic benefits, mathematical constructs, and statistical techniques play little part in the political model. Rather the behavioral aspects of decision making are predominant. As such, the political model is used in formal organizations that depend on external constituencies. Examples are government agencies and other types of public-service institutions. With its patent disregard for the economic aspects of decision making, it is unlikely that the political model will find wide acceptance in the private sector.[41] In a capitalistic system such as that in the United States, this model's inapplicability to business organizations must be seen as a major shortcoming. Still, it is difficult to dispute its selective applicability for category II decisions in public institutions.

The Process Model

The process model of decision making with its strong managerial emphasis and its objectives-oriented outcome is the model adopted in this book. This model was described in detail in Chapter 2. Consequently, the discussion in this chapter will center around Table 5.1 and the interdisciplinary aspects of the model. A close examination of Table 5.1 reveals that the process model is very similar to the organizational model. Both models draw selectively on the quantitative disciplines of economics, mathematics, and statistics. Both models recognize the behavioral disciplines of philosophy, psychology, and sociology. And both models are open to the external environment, which is subject to the disciplines of political science, anthropology, and the law. Indeed these two models of decision making are interdisciplinary in nearly every sense of the term.[42]

The differences between the process model and the organizational model are quite important. First, the process model is oriented toward long-term results. This model has a planning mode that is not apparent in the organizational model with its neoclassical approach to decision making.[43] The process model looks toward growth and the future. Conversely, the organizational model is geared toward quick changes in decisions when it becomes apparent that difficulties are being encountered at the point of implementation. The process model is strategic in its orientation; whereas the organizational model seems preoccupied with short-term tactical adjustments to meet attainable objectives.

Moreover, the organizational model seems somewhat constrained by policy and procedure or the established way of doing business. Conversely, the process model, with its long-term horizon, is designed to accommodate the innovative qualities that so often characterize category II decisions. In the organizational model policies and procedures seem to be more of an end than a means; whereas in the process model, with its managerial emphasis, policies and procedures are properly viewed as guides to action rather than ends in themselves.

Because of its eclectic nature, the process model derives part of its nomenclature from the other decision-making models. These eclectic qualities combine with the intrinsic characteristics of the process model to make it the epitome of interdisciplinary decision making.[44] For example, the process model employs some of the techniques of the rational model, which emphasizes the quantitative disciplines, to reduce uncertainty in comparing and evaluating alternatives. Additionally, the process model will from time to time use some of the bargaining techniques of the political model to make a proposed choice more acceptable to disagreeable constituencies. And as noted, the process model echoes the organizational model by emphasizing the human, institutional, and environmental constraints that confront managerial decision makers.

Let us combine and summarize the characteristics of the process model that have been presented here and in Chapter 2. The process model is governed by highly dynamic managerial objectives that, through a parallel and structured search for information, result in generally nonquantifiable and intransitive alternatives. Within the bounds of numerous constraints, a choice is made from these alternatives. The choice is then implemented with a reasonable assurance that, through follow-up and control procedures, the outcome will result in the attainment of the objectives.

BEHAVIORAL DISCIPLINES FOR DECISION MAKING

Several major disciplines, shown in Figure 5.1, influence the decision-making process. Unfortunately most views of decision making focus on only one or two of these disciplines. Such a limited perspective prevents a complete understanding of decision making as an eclectic and generic process and results in a view largely centered on the decision maker or the choice itself.

The purpose of this section and the next is to present an overview of the different disciplines that influence the decision-making process. Later chapters will discuss in much greater depth the several disciplines that bear on decision making. At this point they are presented in capsule form to demonstrate that decision making is an integrated, interdisciplinary process.

This section discusses the behavioral aspects of decision making, the next treats the quantitative aspects, and the final section explains the fusion of the behavioral and quantitative disciplines within the decision-making process.

It is appropriate to begin with a discussion of the behavioral aspects of decision making. As mentioned earlier, traditional decision theory tends to focus exclusively on the quantitative aspects of decision making. For example, economic theory postulates that decision makers proceed rather systematically to consider all possible alternatives and to make the one best choice from among different alternatives. As reflected in the following passage, this view of decision making is both incomplete and incorrect:

> Although facts are universal, the common interpretation of them is not. Interpretation is personal. It is dominated by concepts, beliefs, values, and ideas brought to the analysis. The filtering process of human perception can differ

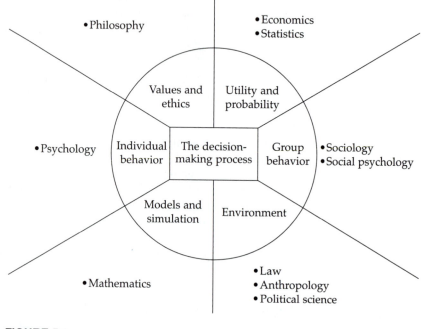

FIGURE 5.1

The Interdisciplinary Framework of Decision Making

from reality by including observations that are not real or by omitting them. . . . the real decision maker is a very different man from his rational, economic, hypothetical counterpart. All the human characteristics of the executive . . . come into play in his decision making.[45]

Following is a discussion of some of managers' behavioral characteristics that affect their decision making.

Philosophy

As noted in Chapter 4, values may be thought of as the guidance system a person uses when confronted with a choice among alternatives. A value can also be viewed as an explicit or implicit conception of what an individual or group, selecting from among available alternatives, regards as desirable ends and means to those ends. Viewed psychologically, values are an intrinsic part of a person's life and thought, and tend to be taken for granted unless they are questioned. People acquire values early in life and retain them throughout their existence.[46]

A good place to look for a person's value base is in his or her religious and moral philosophy, as well as in the person's philosophy for interacting with other individuals on a daily basis. Obviously, not all people adopt exactly the same religious philosophy or the same moral codes. Nor do all people adhere strictly to their codes. Real life requires many compromises and decisions may occasionally twinge the conscience. Sometimes an individual discovers a conflict between personal values and organizational values. This situation may confront the individual with a difficult choice.[47]

The term *ethics* can denote the application of values to the decision-making process. Ethics have been called "standards for decision making."[48] It has been stated that a decision results from a process that has been affected by the ethical interest.[49] The role of values and ethics in the decision-making process is fairly straightforward:

1. In the setting of objectives, it is necessary to make value judgments about selecting opportunities and making necessary improvements within time and resource constraints.

2. In developing a range of relevant alternatives, it is essential to make value judgments about the various possibilities that have emerged from the search activity.

3. At the time of the choice itself, the values of the decision maker, as well as the ethical considerations of the moment, are significant factors in the process.[50]

4. The timing and means for implementing the choice necessarily require value judgments, as well as an awareness of ethical interests.

5. Even in the follow-up and control stage of the decision-making process, value judgments are unavoidable in taking corrective action to ensure that the implemented choice has a result compatible with the original objective.

Clearly, then, values and ethics extend through the entire process of choice. Since they are part of the decision maker's life, they are reflected in the personal behavior of arriving at a choice and putting it into effect.

Psychology

It is difficult to refute the relevance of psychology to the behavior of the decision maker. Human behavior is for the most part learned, not inherited. Behavior is the outcome of conscious and subconscious selection processes and therefore must reflect both the limitations of human cognition and the complexity of man's total environment. In fact, human cognition acts as a kind of filtering system. Through imagery it separates the stimulus or cue from the resultant action. This imagery is constructed of relationships, experiences, values, and emotions. The image is the key element in cognitive behavior. It contains not only what is, but what might be. The individual not only knows, but realizes that he or she knows. A choice reflects the decision maker's personality and individual perceptions of people, roles, and organizations, as well as personal values and emotions.[51]

Some writers have been moved deeply by the assumed effect of the subconscious mind on the decision-making process. It has even been suggested that the subconscious is responsible for many erratic decisions, especially when these choices are said to be rationalized. By definition, a rationalized decision occurs when the decision maker succeeds in convincing himself or herself that the choice is in the best interests of the organization.[52] In most cases, however, such decisions do not help anyone, except possibly the decision maker. Presumably the process of rationalization can occur by design or subconsciously. In any event, it appears to be fairly common at all levels of decision making.

A broad range of psychological forces bears down on the decision maker throughout the process of choice. For example:

1. The decision maker's level of desire and need for achievement assume critical significance in the setting of objectives.[53]

2. The perceptual process of the decision maker is important in the search activity, and the filtering imagery of cognition exerts a marked influence on the comparison and evaluation of alternatives.

3. Whether the decision maker tends to accept or avoid uncertainty may influence his or her willingness to consider good alternatives that contain an element of risk. Especially cautious decision makers may wait for a sure thing that never materializes.

4. Conceivably, the decision maker's subconscious may combine with his or her conscious thoughts at the moment of choice, resulting in a decision that may be rationalized, once implementation and follow-up and control procedures reveal that it is falling short of the original objective.

5. Viewing only an outcome's favorable attributes, as a result of perceptual bias, may cause a decision maker to underestimate or overlook problems that will threaten the success of a potential choice.

6. An aggressive personality may overreact when, during the follow-up and control stage, it becomes apparent to the decision maker that his or her choice is going awry.

Decision makers cannot escape the diverse psychological forces that influence them. However, they should at least be aware that such forces exist and attempt to learn more about themselves so that they can make more enlightened choices.

Sociology and Social Psychology

A broad range of social values merges, consciously or subconsciously, with the decision maker's personal values.[54] Decision makers want to further their own goals and those of the organizations and groups to which they are loyal — their families, friends, and peers. If during the decision-making process a proposal is advanced that conflicts with the decision maker's own goals or those of one of the groups to which he or she is loyal, the decision maker will object to the proposal. Conversely, a decision maker who thinks a given proposal will advance his or her personal goals or the goals of those within his or her sphere of loyalty will probably support the proposal.[55]

Studies have shown that the collective behavior of a group is a direct consequence of individual decision procedures with the addition of a process for resolving conflict.[56] While some conflict may be constructive, it has been demonstrated that cooperative groups will, on the average, make better decisions than groups with extensive interpersonal conflict. Moreover, group members may react to interpersonal conflict by lowering their goals and shifting toward consensus.[57] Stated somewhat differently, individuals may be forced to compromise to arrive at a consensus. To the extent that the group's final choice meets the original objective of the decision-making process, the actions of the group may be considered effective.

To reduce conflict and dissent, groups frequently adopt decision rules for making a final choice. Majority opinion and unanimous agreement are two common decision rules. The former is more likely to speed up the decision-making process. It has been demonstrated that groups requiring complete unanimity find it harder to reach any decision at all. However, their decisions are likely to be superior to those of groups that require only a majority opinion.[58]

With regard to the decision-making process that was set forth in Figure 2.1 (see Chapter 2), the following observations on the disciplines of sociology and social psychology are especially significant:

1. Objectives, as established by groups, reflect the participants' personal and social goals, modified to reach consensus or to avoid conflict and dissent.[59]

2. When a group classifies (or ranks) objectives, the ranking reflects the participants' values and the stated criteria imposed by the interests represented in the group as they perceive the desired outcomes.

3. Developing alternatives is hard for groups formed to make decisions. This is true because the search for alternatives requires effective communication and the ability to evaluate alternatives. At this stage of the decision-making process the participants must have good information and they must know what to do with it if the best decisions are to come forth in the later stages.

4. Evaluating alternatives and choosing the one most likely to yield the original objective frequently involve conflict that can best be reduced by establishing decision rules early.

5. To the extent that the group formed to make a decision is also responsible for implementing the choice and following up to ensure control of the outcome, the decision-making process will be continuous and complete.

However, in the event that the decision is made by a group not responsible for its execution, the success of the outcome will depend upon successful communication and coordination between the decision makers and the decision implementers.

Group decision making follows the same integrated process of choice as decisions made by individuals. The individual who becomes a member of a group is subject to the same psychological forces that direct the making of a unilateral choice. In addition, the group member is also subject to sociological forces that constrain the search for a consensus. Effective groups are cohesive groups. To obtain cohesiveness it is necessary for the members of the group to follow a certain pattern of behavior with a minimum of conflict or dissent. Often individuals will find it difficult to compromise their desires and accept a group choice that falls short of their expectations. At other times, individuals may move rather easily into a group decision-making situation and experience little personal strain or frustration in what may be a drawn-out quest for consensus. There are as many reactions to changing from individual to group decision making as there are differences in the psychological makeup of individuals. The individual must accept sociological forces that, when added to his or her own psychological profile, result in a complex pattern of behavioral variables. This subject will appear again in later chapters, as part of a more detailed discussion of the sociology and social psychology of decision making.

Law, Anthropology, and Political Science

Organizations of all types operate in an environment containing forces that intrude on the decision-making process. Such forces include laws, political institutions, and the culture, traditions, and mores of the total society. Environmental forces become more complex in considering managerial decisions that are made by U.S. companies in foreign countries or those decisions made in the United States that indirectly affect overseas operations through a multinational corporate structure. Although the primary emphasis in this book is on managerial decisions made by U.S. executives, the international aspects and implications of such decisions are, depending on the scope of a given company's operations, considered as part of the external environment.

Decision makers must keep abreast of current and emerging legislation that can influence the process of choice. Important legislation governs the relationships between the employer and the employee; examples are the Clayton Act, the Wagner Act, and the Taft-Hartley Act. These laws were designed to protect workers from arbitrary acts of management affecting hours of work, overtime, working conditions, and wages.

Decision makers should also be mindful of legislation and government activities regulating business dealings with stockholders, consumers, and the general public. For example, to ensure that a business does not operate in a way that is harmful to the public, laws such as the Federal Food, Drug, and Cosmetic Act and the Securities Exchange Act have been enacted. In addition, the Sherman Act, the Clayton Act, and the Robinson-Patman Act maintain fair competition for large and small companies alike. These acts and many more form a set of constraints within which the decision maker must operate.

Anthropology influences the decision-making process in indirect ways. The customs, folkways, mores, and traditions of a total society influence the thought processes of the decision maker and operate externally to test and temper the outcome of the choice itself. Differences in religious beliefs and cultural backgrounds affect the reception accorded a particular decision and bear on its eventual success. To be sure, the United States is a relatively young country, with fairly new traditions. Still, within this country are many subcultures composed of a variety of ethnic groups. Even though their primary allegiance is to the United States, many of these groups retain the old beliefs and ways of doing things. Traditions and customs change slowly in such groups, and the institutions and folkways of America are not ingrained firmly enough to sever the bonds of past generations in different lands.

The political characteristic that most influences the process of choice in the United States is the pluralistic nature of the political system. Even though there are only two major political parties in America, the real power resides in various subgroups, such as unions, educators, professionals, the military, bureaucrats, and, of course, politicians themselves. Decision makers must be alert to changes in political sentiment that can thwart the successful outcome of choices, no matter how thoughtful. Landmarks in the general public's attitude, such as the perennial furor over pollution or the abiding concern about the safety features of new automobiles, must be considered by decision makers throughout the process of choice. In fact, the very pluralistic nature of our political system acts as a kind of check-and-balance mechanism serving to reduce decisions beneficial to special-interest groups and detrimental to the general welfare. The political aspects of decision making at the level of the organization are discussed in greater detail in Chapter 9.

The environment exerts a pervasive influence on the managerial decision-making process in formal organizations. It influences the selection of objectives, bounds the search, constrains the selection of alternatives, and directly affects the acceptance of an implemented choice. Thus, the environment of a given organization is a significant determinant of whether the organization's choices meet managerial objectives.

QUANTITATIVE DISCIPLINES FOR DECISION MAKING

The quantitative aspects of decision making are founded in the formal disciplines of economics, statistics, and mathematics. As we noted previously, these disciplines constitute the conceptual underpinning of decision theory as it is documented in its literature and presented in the classroom. It is a central theme of this book that decision making involves much more than the use of quantitative techniques to arrive at a presumably optimal choice. Decision making is accomplished through an interdisciplinary process. The quantitative disciplines, along with the behavioral disciplines, simply share in the functions that form this process.

The quantitative aspects of decision making are explained more fully in the numerous books that specialize in this area. The discussion to follow simply presents these disciplines in overview.

Economics and Statistics

Economics and statistics apply to the decision-making process mainly through their focus on the concept of utility.[60] This concept assumes the individual continuously seeks to maximize the satisfaction of his or her preferences, or utilities. For example, consider the following definition of rational behavior.

> When he behaves rationally, the consumer calculates deliberately, chooses consistently, and maximizes utility [defined as want-satisfying power]. . . . Consistent choice rules out vacillating and erratic behavior. . . . The maximization of utility means that the consumer makes those choices that will result in his having the greatest amount of utility.[61]

Thus the decision maker, desiring to maximize his or her utilities, selects from among available alternatives the one that will meet this continuous objective. Because the alternatives are not readily available, the decision maker must seek them out. This is the search activity that must be accomplished before the evaluation and choice phases are undertaken. The decision maker selects from among the available alternatives using the following rationale:

> Choices among . . . alternatives are explained in terms of maximization of utility: individuals are supposed to choose as they would if they attributed some common characteristic — designated utility — to various goods and then selected the combination of goods that yielded the largest total amount of this common characteristic.[62]

In the absence of perfect information, but with some limited knowledge of likely outcomes, the decision maker must assume some risk. Risk is made acceptable by the assignment of subjective probabilities to states of nature. This activity should reflect the various conditions that might prevail in the presence of the decision maker's choice. He or she then selects that alternative with the highest expected value for maximizing his or her utility.

The decision maker is in the worst position of all, however, when he or she has little or no information regarding the likely outcome of a choice. This situation is so uncertain that it may require an estimate or, at worst, a guess at the probabilities that should be assigned to the states of nature.

In a broad sense, then, uncertainty in decision making describes all shades of knowledge of the probability distribution of the states of nature.

This knowledge ranges from accurate estimates with nearly complete information, to a state of risk, to the extreme case in which no information is available.

In summary, then, economics and statistics bear on the decision-making process through their assumption that the decision maker continually seeks to maximize his or her utilities through the application of probability techniques. Probabilities are estimated according to the amount and type of information available.

In capsule form, as an overall approach to the decision-making process these quantitative disciplines make the following basic assumptions:

1. The decision maker has a fixed objective.
2. The decision maker is able to marshal most (if not all) of the alternatives that are relevant to the decision at hand.
3. These alternatives can all be quantified to some extent.
4. The decision maker disregards the variables that are not quantifiable.
5. The decision maker simply chooses the alternative that, as indicated numerically, promises to maximize his or her objective.

As a practical matter, however, these assumptions of maximizing behavior are wrong because they are based on the ability of the decision maker to identify and quantify all the alternatives related to a fixed objective. Objectives are rarely fixed, and decision makers are seldom able, even in the absence of normal time and cost constraints, to obtain perfect information with which to identify all alternatives. Consequently, the best that can be hoped for is a choice and an outcome that will satisfice a dynamic objective rather than maximize a fixed objective. (This subject is the principal topic of discussion in Chapter 3.)

In terms of the decision-making process depicted in Figure 2.1, the quantitative disciplines of economics and statistics are most applicable to the evaluation and comparison of alternatives. At this stage the use of quantitative techniques may help a decision maker arrive at a choice that will attain the original objective. To be sure, depending upon the orientation of the decision maker, quantitative methods may be used throughout the entire process of choice. Still, such methods or techniques are especially appropriate in the analysis and ranking of alternatives; but even then they serve as only one criterion of choice among many.

Mathematics

The discipline of mathematics appears in the decision-making process primarily through the development of models and their use to simulate real-life situations. "A model is any conceptual analogue, generally of a physical or mathematical nature, which is used to suggest empirical research."[63] A model is an attempt to represent some segment of reality and explain, in a simplified manner, the way that segment operates. In order to develop a mathematical model, all the variables, their weights and causal connections, must be measurable and expressed in quantitative form. A model replaces and represents a complex set of empirical relations.[64]

The construction of a model includes at least the following six steps:

1. Define the problem and determine the results expected from its solution. These results are the dependent variables and should be cast in numerical form.

2. Ascertain the causes of the problem, especially the ones that will influence the expected results. These causes are the independent variables and should also be quantified.

3. Determine and weight by some means the causal connections between the problem and the results expected from its solution.

4. Create a numerical equation that reliably expresses the relations between the independent variables (causes) and the dependent variables (expected results).

5. Test the reliability of the model (numerical equation) by substituting recent data from the real world for the independent variables and observing any discrepancies between the model's answers and the known recent effects on the dependent variables.

6. Revise the model as appropriate until the actual results are nearly equivalent to the expected results.

Once tested and validated, the model can be used to predict outcomes as well as solve problems by the process of simulation. **Simulation** refers to duplicating the essence of some part of the real world by means of a model, generally with the assistance of a computer.

> Computer simulation can be considered as an attempt to model . . .
> behavior . . . in order to study its reaction to specific changes. The simulation model is seldom . . . exact. . . . Rather, it is an approximation of continuous time dependent activity. If . . . properties and elements . . . are properly defined, then the tracing through by the computer of the simultaneous interaction of a large number of variables provides the basis for studying . . .
> behavior. A model . . . indicates relationships which are otherwise not obvious and has the capability of predicting . . . behavior.[65]

Simulation is primarily intended for the following purposes:

1. Experimenting, evaluating, and predicting the effects of changes in policies or operations without risk of a full-scale changeover

2. Demonstrating the possibility of success of new ideas or different courses of action with a minimum commitment of time and resources

3. Gaining a better understanding of existing operations, thus aiding management in deciding upon areas for improvement[66]

Two types of models are customarily used for simulation purposes:

1. The **deterministic model,** in which the same output values always result from any given set of input variables

2. The **probabilistic model,** in which the input variables are distributed around some average value and the output values take the form of a frequency distribution rather than, as in the case of the deterministic model, a set of single values[67]

Within the decision-making process, the following uses of models and simulation seem appropriate:

1. Models may help determine the feasibility and effectiveness of various objectives and goals prior to the spending of time and effort on search and evaluation.

2. Models may be used in formal search activities to uncover a comprehensive range of relevant alternatives with a minimum of effort.

3. Alternatives may be evaluated and compared by revising the model until the actual results appear to conform to the objective, thereby reducing the uncertainty of the outcome.

4. Once the decision is made and implemented, the model can still be used as a control device by monitoring the occurrence of the expected outcome within established time and cost constraints.

THE FUSION OF BEHAVIORAL AND QUANTITATIVE DISCIPLINES FOR DECISION MAKING

As noted in the discussion of decision-making models, the rational model with its classical emphasis on quantitative theory remains the traditional approach to the academic study of decision making. The addition of the behavioral disciplines in the formulation of the organizational model of decision making represented a significant departure from the traditional evolution of the field of decision theory.[68] For the first time the quantitative disciplines lost their traditional domination. Although the organizational model emphasizes the quantitative and the behavioral aspects of decision making fairly equally, it does not provide a workable framework for fusing these traditionally disparate disciplines.[69] It cannot truly achieve interdisciplinary outcomes that will attain dynamic managerial objectives. It remains for the process model of decision making to achieve this result.

The fusion of the behavioral and quantitative aspects of decision making is represented by the interrelated and dynamic decision-making process illustrated in Figure 2.1. Some type of quantitative technique can be applied to any or all of the six principal functions of decision making. And the values, personality, and perceptions of a single or group decision maker come to bear in each of the decision-making functions. Indeed one of the process model's principal benefits to managerial decision makers is that it allows the fusion of the human and the numerical in selecting among alternatives and analyzing variables, many of which are amenable to only limited quantification. Moreover, in the process model the managerial decision maker can proceed in sequential steps to obtain an outcome in keeping with established objectives. Decision makers should maintain a constant awareness of the effects of behavioral variables on each function of decision making. At the same time they should stay alert to the limitations of quantitative variables throughout the total decision-making process. This combined awareness seems most likely to yield outcomes that will attain managerial objectives.

Within the structure of the decision-making process, the managerial decision maker can perceive the likely effects of choices before they are made and predict the probable effects of outcomes on objectives. The decision-making process provides the managerial decision maker with an understandable and usable framework. Within this framework the decision maker can meaningfully blend behavioral and quantitative variables in pursuit of outcomes that will help fulfill organizational purposes.

Many variables that enter into making category II decisions are multi-dimensional. And such decisions most assuredly will continue to be made by fallible human decision makers managing in organizations that are trying to achieve some type of tangible result. So it is essential that the behavioral and quantitative aspects of decision making be fused in the most effective way.[70] For the time being, at least, the process model of decision making appears best suited to accomplish this end.

SUMMARY

This chapter focused on the theme that the decision-making process is eclectic in that it draws upon a wide variety of formal disciplines. The interdisciplinary aspects of decision making were described initially in the context of four decision-making models. The rational model has its foundation in the quantitative disciplines of economics, statistics, and mathematics. It is a normative model that represents the classical approach to decision making. The rational model is based on the assumption that all the significant variables in a given decision-making situation can be quantified to some degree. It is a model that operates within an artificially closed environment. Consequently, the rational model applies mainly to category I decisions.

The organizational model tends to be eclectic in that it combines the behavioral disciplines with quantitative analysis to arrive at a choice that fits the constraints caused by the external environment. As such, the organizational model represents a neoclassical approach to decision making. The principal shortcomings of the organizational model are that it has (1) a short-term horizon, (2) a low tolerance of uncertainty, and (3) an all-consuming emphasis on following the established way of doing business. In these shortcomings the organizational model is similar to the rational model.

The political model of decision making is characteristic of most organizations in the public sector. This model is almost totally behavioral in its orientation. The primary criterion for decision making in the political model is an outcome that is acceptable to many external constituencies. Consequently the political model employs a bargaining or compromise decision-making strategy. Given its deemphasis on objectives-oriented outcomes, the political model seems unlikely to be used widely in the private sector.

As noted previously, the process model of decision making with its strong managerial emphasis and its objectives-oriented outcomes is the model adopted in this book. The process model is forward-looking in that it has a planning mode not apparent in the other models of decision making. The process model is oriented toward innovation and organizational change with a particular emphasis on long-term results. The process model is well suited for category II decisions. It relies principally on a judgmental decision-making strategy but not to the complete exclusion of computational and compromise strategies for special decision-making situations. The process model epitomizes the eclectic nature and the interdisciplinary character of managerial decision making. It reinforces the role of management as decision maker in formal organizations of all types. The process model is both generic and interdisciplinary in nature, and its applicability to category II decisions seems obvious.

This chapter also presented an overview of the behavioral and quantitative aspects of decision making and related individual formal disciplines to the decision-making functions that make up the total decision-making process illustrated in Figure 2.1. It was stated that the effective fusion of the behavioral and quantitative disciplines is accomplished within the process model of decision making. The decision-making process provides a useful framework within which practicing managers can be aware of the human constraints on decision making as well as the inevitable limitations of quantitative techniques. The net result should be decisions more likely to attain managerial objectives and to fulfill organizational purposes.

REVIEW AND DISCUSSION QUESTIONS

1. What are the significant differences between the organizational model of decision making and the process model?
2. What are the significant similarities between the rational model of decision making and the organizational model?
3. In what specific ways is the process model different from the other models of decision making?
4. Why are decision-making models particularly useful to illustrate the interdisciplinary aspects of decision making?

5. Discuss the following statement: The philosophy of the decision maker pervades the process of choice.

6. What are the basic assumptions of economics and statistics with regard to the decision-making process?

7. What are some of the techniques employed by groups to minimize and avoid disabling conflict and dissent?

8. Discuss the following statement: The decision-making process provides a useful framework for the effective fusion of the behavioral and the quantitative aspects of decision making.

9. Discuss the following statement: The rational model of decision making is not well suited for category II decisions.

10. Why is it important for students and practicing managers to understand that decision making is eclectic in nature?

NOTES

1. *Webster's New Collegiate Dictionary* (Springfield, Mass.: G. & C. Merriam Co., 1977), p. 359.

2. Amos Tversky, "Remarks on the Study of Decision Making," in *Decision Making: An Interdisciplinary Inquiry*, ed. Gerardo R. Ungson and Daniel N. Braunstein (Boston: Kent, 1982), p. 321.

3. Wayne Lee, *Decision Theory and Human Behavior* (New York: Wiley, 1971), pp. 15, 17.

4. George A. Steiner, John B. Miner, and Edmund R. Gray, "Evaluating and Choosing Among Policy/Strategy Alternatives," in *Competitive Strategic Management*, ed. Robert Boyden Lamb (Englewood Cliffs, N.J.: Prentice-Hall, 1984), p. 175.

5. George H. Rice, Jr., and Dean W. Bishoprick, *Conceptual Models of Organization* (New York: Appleton-Century-Crofts, 1971), p. 3.

6. E. Frank Harrison, *Management and Organizations* (Boston: Houghton Mifflin, 1978), p. 204.

7. See E. Frank Harrison, "Interdisciplinary Models of Decision Making," *Management Decision*, 31 (1993), 27–33.

8. Graham T. Allison, *Essence of Decision: Explaining the Cuban Missile Crisis* (Boston: Little, Brown, 1971), pp. 29–30.

9. John D. Steinbruner, *The Cybernetic Theory of Decision* (Princeton, N.J.: Princeton University Press, 1974).

10. D. F. Anderson, "Mathematical Models and Decision Making in Bureaucracies: A Case Story Told from Three Points of View" (Ph.D. diss. MIT, 1977).

11. Harold A. Linstone, *Multiple Perspectives for Decision Making* (New York: North-Holland, 1984).

12. See David Braybrooke and Charles E. Lindblom, *A Strategy of Decision* (New York: Free Press, 1963); Charles E. Lindblom, "The Science of 'Muddling Through,'" *Public Administration Review*, 19 (Spring 1959), 79–88; and Charles E. Lindblom, "Still Muddling, Not Yet Through," *Public Administration Review* (November–December 1979), 517–536.

13. Michael D. Cohen, James G. March, and Johan P. Olsen, "A Garbage-Can Model of Organization Choice," *Administrative Science Quarterly*, 17 (March 1972), 1–25. Also see James G. March and Johan P. Olsen, *Ambiguity and Choice in Organizations* (Bergen, Norway: Universitetsforlaget, 1976).

14. Amitai Etzioni, "Mixed-Scanning: A 'Third' Approach to Decision Making," *Public Administration Review* (December 1967), 385–392.

15. Paul C. Nutt, "Models for Decision Making in Organizations and Some Contextual Variables Which Stipulate Optimal Use," *Academy of Management Review*, 1 (April 1976), 84–98; and Paul C. Nutt, "Influence of Decision Styles on the Use of Decision Models," *Technological Forecasting and Social Change*, 14 (1979), 77–93.

16. Paul J. H. Schoemaker and J. Edward Russo, "A Pyramid of Decision Approaches," *California Management Review* (Fall 1993), 9–31.

17. See, for example, Paul J. H. Schoemaker, "Strategic Decisions in Organizations: Rational and Behavioural Views," *Journal of Management Studies* (January 1993), 107–129; O. P. Kharbanda and E. A. Stallworthy, "Managerial Decision Making, Part I: Conventional Techniques," *Management Decision*, 28 (1990), 4–9; and O. P. Kharbanda and E. A. Stallworthy, "Managerial Decision Making, Part II: The New Techniques," *Management Decision*, 28 (1990), 29–35.

18. Michael B. Metzger and Charles R. Schwenk, "Decision Making Models, Devil's Advocacy, and the Control of Corporate Crime," *American Business Law Journal*, 28 (Fall 1990), 323–377; and Gerald F. Smith, "Towards a Theory of Managerial Problem Solving," *Decision Support Systems*, 8 (1992), 29–40.

19. Allison, *Essence of Decision*, p. 29.

20. Madhudar V. Joshi, *Management Science: A Survey of Quantitative Decision-Making Techniques* (Belmont, Calif.: Wadsworth, 1980), p. 70.

21. Ibid., p. 71.

22. Allison, *Essence of Decision*, pp. 29–30.

23. Ward Edwards, "The Theory of Decision Making," *Psychological Bulletin*, 54, No. 4 (1954), 381.

24. For additional shortcomings of the rational model of decision making see Catherine Gremion, "Toward a New Theory of Decision-Making?" *International Studies of Management and Organization* (Summer 1972), 125–141; Dennis J. Palumbo and Paula J. Wright, "Decision Making and Evaluation Research," *Policy Studies Journal*, 8 (1980), 1170–1177; and Renate Mayntz, "Conceptual Models of Organizational Decision-Making and Their Application to the Policy Process," in *European Contributions to Organization Theory*, ed. G. Hofstede and M. S. Kassem (Amsterdam: Van Gorcum, 1976), pp. 114–125.

25. Robert N. Anthony, "The Trouble with Profit Maximization," in *The Nature and Scope of Management*, ed. Maneck S. Wadia (Chicago: Scott, Foresman, 1966), p. 49.

26. Ronald J. Ebert and Terence R. Mitchell, *Organizational Decision Processes* (New York: Crane, Russak, 1975), p. 141.

27. Gremion, "Toward a New Theory of Decision-Making?" p. 130.

28. Richard M. Cyert and James G. March, *A Behavioral Theory of the Firm* (Englewood Cliffs, N.J.: Prentice-Hall, 1963), p. 113.

29. See Herbert A. Simon, *Models of Man* (New York: Wiley, 1957), pp. 196–206; Herbert A. Simon, *Administrative Behavior*, 2nd ed. (New York: Free Press, 1957); and Herbert A. Simon, "A Behavioral Model of Rational Choice," *Quarterly Journal of Economics*, 69 (February 1955), 99–118.

30. Cited in Allison, *Essence of Decision*, pp. 71–72.

31. Anna Grandori, "A Prescriptive Contingency View of Organizational Decision Making," *Administrative Science Quarterly*, 29 (1984), 192–209.

32. See, for example, Harvey J. Brightman, "Differences in Ill-Structured Problem Solving Along the Organizational Hierarchy," *Decision Sciences*, 9 (January 1978), 1–18; and Smith, "Towards a Theory of Managerial Problem Solving."

33. Paul C. Nutt, "Influence of Decision Styles on the Use of Decision Models," *Technological Forecasting and Social Change*, 14 (1979), 81.

34. Victor A. Thompson, *Bureaucracy and the Modern World* (Morristown, N.J.: General Learning Press, 1976), p. 66.

35. Ibid., pp. 66–67.

36. Jorge Stein, "Strategic Decision Methods," *Human Relations*, 34, No. 11 (1981), 922.

37. See Lindblom, "The Science of 'Muddling Through,'" pp. 79–88; and Lindblom, "Still Muddling, Not Yet Through," pp. 517–536.

38. See J. B. Quinn, "Logical Incrementalism," *Sloan Management Review* (Fall 1978), 7–21.

39. See Charles E. Lindblom, *The Intelligence of Democracy* (New York: Free Press, 1965), pp. 144–148; Etzioni, "Mixed-Scanning"; Braybrooke and Lindblom, *A Strategy of Decision*; and Lindblom, "The Science of 'Muddling Through.'"

40. Allison, *Essence of Decision*, p. 154.

41. See Gregory Streib, "Applying Strategic Decision Making in Local Government," *Public Productivity & Management Review*, 15, No. 3 (Spring 1992), 341–354.

42. See Orhan Kayaalp, "Towards A General Theory of Managerial Decisions: A Critical Appraisal," *SAM Advanced Management Journal* (Spring 1987), 36–42; and John R. Montanari, "Managerial Discretion: An Expanded Model of Organization Choice," *Academy of Management Review*, 3 (April 1978), 231–241.

43. See Henry Mintzberg, "Strategy-Making in Three Modes," *California Management Review* (Winter 1973), 47–49, for a description of the planning mode.

44. See, for example, E. Bruce Frederikson, "Non-economic Criteria and the Decision Process," *Decision Sciences*, 2 (January 1971), 25–52; Carlos L. Cifuentes, "Fundamentals of the Managerial Decision-Making Process," *International Studies of Management and Organization* (Summer 1972), 213–221; and Henry Mintzberg, Duru Raisinghani, and André Theoret, "The Structure of 'Unstructured' Decision Processes," *Administrative Science Quarterly*, 21 (June 1976), 246–275.
45. L. Goslin and A. Rethans, *Basic Systems for Decision Making* (Dubuque, Iowa: Kendall/Hunt, 1980), p. 56.
46. William D. Guth and Renato Tagiuri, "Personal Values and Corporate Strategies," *Harvard Business Review* (September–October 1965), 125.
47. Manley Howe Jones, *Executive Decision Making* (Homewood, Ill.: Richard D. Irwin, 1962), p. 125.
48. Wayne A. R. Leys, *Ethics for Policy Decisions* (Englewood Cliffs, N.J.: Prentice-Hall, 1962), p. 195.
49. Kenneth E. Boulding, "The Ethics of Rational Decision," *Management Science*, 12 (February 1966), B-161.
50. Ibid., B-162.
51. Charles Z. Wilson and Marcus Alexis, "Basic Frameworks for Decisions," *Journal of the Academy of Management* (August 1962), 150–164.
52. Robert C. Ferber, "The Role of the Subconscious in Executive Decision Making," *Management Science* (April 1967), B-519 to B-532.
53. See Wilson and Alexis, "Basic Frameworks for Decisions," pp. 162–164, for a discussion of this key relationship.
54. Ramon J. Aldag and Donald W. Jackson, Jr., "A Managerial Framework for Social Decision Making," *MSU Business Topics*, 23 (Spring 1975), 33–40.
55. Jones, *Executive Decision Making*, p. 122.
56. Geoffrey P. E. Clarkson and Francis D. Tuggle, "Toward a Theory of Group Decision Behavior," *Behavioral Science* (January 1966), 33–42.
57. Joseph L. Bower, "Group Decision Making: A Report of an Experimental Study," *Behavioral Science* (July 1965), 277–289.
58. Ibid.
59. Aldag and Jackson, "A Managerial Framework for Social Decision Making."
60. See George P. Huber, *Managerial Decision Making*. Glenview, Ill.: Scott, Foresman, 1980.
61. Donald Stevenson Watson, *Price Theory and Its Uses*, 2nd ed. (Boston: Houghton Mifflin, 1968), p. 9.
62. Milton Friedman and L. J. Savage, "The Utility Analysis of Choices Involving Risk," *Journal of Political Economy* (August 1948), 280.
63. Melvin H. Marx, "The General Nature of Theory Construction," in *Studies in Managerial Process and Organizational Behavior*, ed. John Turner, Alan C. Filley, and Robert J. House (Glenview, Ill.: Scott, Foresman, 1972), p. 35.
64. Jones, *Executive Decision Making*, pp. 98–99.
65. Alan J. Rowe, "Computer Simulation: A Solution Technique for Management Problems," in *Information for Decision Making: Quantitative and Behavioral Dimensions*, ed. Alfred Rappaport (Englewood Cliffs, N.J.: Prentice-Hall, 1970), p. 68.
66. Gordon B. Davis, Howard Ambill, and Herbert Whitecraft, "Simulation of Finance Company Operations for Decision Making," in *Decision Theory and Information Systems*, ed. William T. Greenwood (Cincinnati: South-Western, 1969), pp. 399–400.
67. Ibid., pp. 400–401.
68. Larry E. Pate, "Using Theories as 'Overlays' for Improved Managerial Decision Making," *Management Decision*, 26 (1988), 36–40.
69. Kayaalp, "Towards A General Theory of Managerial Decisions: A Critical Appraisal."
70. Schoemaker, "Strategic Decisions in Organizations: Rational and Behavioural Views."

SUPPLEMENTAL REFERENCES

Abelson, Robert P., and Ariel Levi. "Decision Making and Decision Theory." In *The Handbook of Social Psychology*, 3rd ed. Ed. Gardner Lindzey and Elliot Aronson. New York: Random House, 1985, I, 231–309.
Baumhart, Raymond, *Ethics in Business*. New York: Holt, Rinehart and Winston, 1968.
Carter, E. Eugene. "The Behavioral Theory of the Firm and Top-Level Corporate Decisions." *Administrative Science Quarterly*, 16 (December 1971), 413–428.
Chiattello, Marion L., and Robert J. Waller, "Relativism as a Cultural Influence on Twentieth Century Decision Making." *Decision Sciences*, 5 (April 1974), 209–224.

Clark, Thomas D., Jr. "Public-Sector Decision Structures: An Empirically-Based Description." *Public Administration Review* (July–August 1979), 343–354.

Collins, B. E., and H. Guetzkow. *A Social Psychology of Group Processes for Decision Making*. New York: Wiley, 1964.

Cornell, Alexander H. *The Decision Maker's Handbook*. Englewood Cliffs, N.J.: Prentice-Hall, 1980.

Costello, Timothy W., and Sheldon Zalkind, eds. *Psychology in Administration: A Research Orientation*. Englewood Cliffs, N.J.: Prentice-Hall, 1963.

Edwards, Ward. "Decision Making: Psychological Aspects." In *International Encyclopedia of the Social Sciences*. Ed. David Sills. New York: Macmillan and Free Press, 1968, pp. 34–42.

Fredrikson, E. Bruce. "Noneconomic Criteria and the Decision Process." *Decision Sciences*, 2 (January 1971), 25–52.

Gore, William J. *Administrative Decision Making: A Heuristic Model*. New York: Wiley, 1964.

Harrison, J. Richard, and James G. March. "Decision Making and Postdecision Surprises: The Politically Competent Manager." *Administrative Science Quarterly* (March 1984), 26–42.

Hill, Percy H., et al. *Making Decisions: A Multidisciplinary Introduction*. Reading, Mass.: Addison-Wesley, 1978.

Kaplan, John. "Decision Theory and the Factfinding Process." *Stanford Law Review* (June 1968), 1065–1092.

Linstone, Harold A., et al. "The Multiple Perspective Concept with Applications to Technology Assessment and Other Decision Areas." *Technological Forecasting and Social Change*, 20 (1981), 275–325.

Mohr, Lawrence B. "Organizations, Decisions, and Courts." *Law and Society* (Summer 1976), 621–641.

Moore, P. G. *The Business of Risk*. Cambridge, England: Cambridge University Press, 1983.

Nutt, Paul C. "Models for Decision Making in Organizations and Some Contextual Variables Which Stipulate Optimal Use." *Academy of Management Review*, 1 (April 1976), 84–98.

Park, Margaret K. "Decision-Making Processes for Information Managers." *Special Libraries* (October 1981), 307–318.

Pennington, Nancy, and Reid Hastie. "Juror Decision-Making Models: The Generalization Gap." *Psychological Bulletin*, 89, No. 2 (1981), 246–287.

Peterson, Cameron R., and Lee Roy Beach. "Man as an Intuitive Statistician." *Psychological Bulletin*, 68, No. 1 (1967), 29–46.

Quade, E. S. *Analysis for Public Decisions*. 2nd ed. New York: North-Holland, 1982.

Robinson, James A. "Decision Making: Political Aspects." In *International Encyclopedia of the Social Sciences*. Ed. David Sills. New York: Macmillan and Free Press, 1968, IV, 55–62.

Russo, J. Edward, and Paul J. H. Schoemaker. *Decision Traps: The Ten Barriers to Brilliant Decision Making and How to Overcome Them*. New York: Simon & Schuster, 1989.

Schoemaker, P. J. H. "Optimality Principles in Science: Some Epistemological Issues." In *The Quest for Optimality*. Ed. Jean H. P. Paelinck and Paulus H. Vossen. Sussex, England: Grower, 1984, pp. 4–31.

Shapira, Zir, ed. *Organizational Decision Making*. New York: Cambridge University Press, 1997.

Simon, Herbert A. "On How to Decide What to Do." *Bell Journal of Economics* (Autumn 1978), 494–507.

Snyder, Richard C. "A Decision-Making Approach to the Study of Political Phenomena." In *Approaches to the Study of Politics*. Ed. Roland Young. Evanston, Ill.: Northwestern University Press, 1958, pp. 3–38.

Thompson, James D. *Organizations in Action*. New York: McGraw-Hill, 1967.

Thompson, James D., and Arthur Tuden. "Strategies, Structures, and Processes of Organizational Decision." In *Comparative Studies in Administration*. Ed. James D. Thompson et al. Pittsburgh: University of Pittsburgh Press, 1959, pp. 195–216.

Tuite, Matthew, Roger Chisholm, and Michael Radnor, eds. *Interorganizational Decision Making*. Chicago: Aldine, 1972.

Ungson, Gerardo, and Daniel N. Braunstein, eds. *Decision Making: An Interdisciplinary Inquiry*. Boston: Kent, 1982.

Waddell, William C. "Values: A Challenge to a Science of Management." *University of Washington Business Review*, 29 (Winter 1970), 28–39.

Zeleny, Milan. "Descriptive Decision Making and Its Applications." In *Applications of Management Science*, Ed. Randall L. Schultz. Greenwich, Conn.: JAI Press, 1981, I, 327–388.

Zey, Mary, ed. *Decision Making*. Newbury Park, Calif.: Sage Publications, 1992.

The Psychology of Decision Making

*T*he decision-making process is accomplished by individuals acting singly or in groups to arrive at a satisficing choice among acceptable alternatives. A host of psychological forces governs the behavior of decision makers as they proceed toward rational decisions. These forces affect them individually at the conscious and subconscious levels. For example, the personality of a decision maker affects the way in which he or she reacts to frustration in the search for satisficing alternatives. The decision maker's perceptual process significantly conditions the view of a given alternative as satisficing. Moreover, when the decision maker compares, evaluates, and selects alternatives, his or her intellect comes into play, as do, perhaps to some immeasurable extent, forces imbedded deeply in his or her subconscious mind.

Indeed the psychological forces within decision makers affect their behavior throughout the entire integrated process of arriving at a choice. At the very best, their ability to control these forces is limited. The most that a decision maker can hope for is to gain greater understanding of self by acquiring deeper insight into his or her personality, perception, and willingness to accept risk in the process of choice. By this means, the psychological forces within the decision maker are more likely to work for, rather than against, an outcome that will meet the original objective.

There is a growing realization, supported by research, of the importance of a psychological dimension in the managerial decision-making process.[1] "Such a dimension reflects sensitivity to the feelings, emotions, and plight of employees, customers, suppliers, communities, and other constituencies affected by the implementation of managerial decisions. In short, decision makers are advised to listen to the 'voices of the heart,' so to speak, and avoid basing decisions solely on a cognitive, rationally analytical level of understanding."[2] This chapter is directed toward that end.

PERSONALITY IN DECISION MAKING

The basic psychological force affecting a decision maker is his or her personality.[3] There is little general agreement about the meaning of the term **personality.** One definition is that "personality may be said to encompass the characteristic traits and patterns of adjustment of the person in his inter-relationships with others and his environment."[4] And "personality is a holistic concept which is inclusive of those integrated qualities, impulses, habits, interests, ideals, and other characteristics that compose the individual as he exists in society."[5] Personality is the entire system of relatively permanent tendencies, both physical and mental, that are distinctive of a given individual, and determine his characteristic adjustments to his material and social surroundings."[6] Personality may be viewed as the pattern or organization of various responses made by individuals in the presence of general or specific stimuli. In other words, personality is what gives order and consistency to all the different kinds of behavior in which the individual engages. Personality mediates the adjustment of the individual. It consists of the varied and yet typical efforts at adjustment the individual carries out. Personality may also be equated with the unique or individual aspects of behavior. In this case, the term designates those things about the individual that are distinctive and set the person apart from other persons. Personality is also viewed as representing the essence of a person — what the person really is.

Some commentators have stated that no meaningful definition of personality can be applied with any generality. According to this view the definition of personality depends upon the theoretical preference of the definer. Thus, "personality consists concretely of a set of scores or descriptive terms which are used to describe the individual being studied according to the variables or dimensions which occupy a central position within the particular theory utilized."[7] It is certainly true that many definitions and theories of personality have been advanced by psychologists, psychiatrists, psychoanalysts, and others concerned with individual behavior. Moreover, each of these definitions and theories approaches the subject from a slightly different viewpoint. Of course, this book is mainly interested in how personality influences individual behavior in decision making. Therefore, the discussion to follow will present three general categories of personality theory with a view toward helping the reader understand this key concept as it operates within the integrated process of choice.

Biological, Subconscious, and Hereditary Forces

Sigmund Freud made a significant contribution to the knowledge of human behavior by developing the concept of the subconscious mind. Freud's theory emphasized the ideas of internal conflict, subconscious motivation, and defense mechanisms. He argued that (1) human beings are dominated by subconscious motives and emotions, and (2) the early stages of childhood form the most important basis for adult personality.[8] Freud also believed that people are governed by two basic drives: (1) **life instincts,** which include all activities that are positive and constructive, and (2) **death or hate instincts,** which are destructive. Life instincts are, for instance, hunger, thirst, and sex, and the energy involved in their activity is the **libido.** Freud paid most attention to the life instinct of sex, and he treated almost all behavior as originating from the sex drive.[9]

According to Freud, the human personality is made up of the **id,** the **ego,** and the **superego.** As McGuire explains:

> The id contains the basic drives for pleasure and aggression in their pure form. The ego . . . is the rational part of man's psychic system, which tries to satisfy the desires of the id while operating within the limits of the real world. The superego is the social and moral arbiter of the psychic system. Whereas the id is primarily biological, and the ego determined by physical reality, the superego is affected by society and culture.[10]

The three components of the Freudian psychic system continually conflict with one another. These conflicts are resolved by various adjustments in the conscious or subconscious. Defense mechanisms, such as rationalization, displacement, identification, and suppression, separately or together can relieve tension or reduce anxiety in the individual.

Freud's theory has been criticized as being too subjective and too vague to permit behavioral predictions. Moreover, his constant emphasis upon the sex drive as the primary life instinct is not universally agreed with. Personality theorists who have used the basic Freudian concepts but with different emphases include Alfred Adler, Carl Jung, and Erich Fromm. "The direction of change in each case was away from the biological, sexual, and subconscious forces motivating the individual and toward an emphasis upon the importance of social and cultural factors in the determination of personality and behavior."[11] In spite of its limitations, Freud's theory of personality is useful as a framework for understanding the psychological aspects of managerial decision making.[12]

Common Traits and Unique Individuality

Some theorists view personality as unique sets of traits possessed by every individual. A trait is a consistent pattern of action and reaction. Trait theorists want to predict as well as understand individual behavior. Traits have been classified in a number of ways. Designations include (1) "common" traits, such as aggressiveness, (2) "unique" traits, such as prudishness, (3) "surface" traits, such as tact, and (4) "depth" traits, such as intellectual capacity.[13]

The trait approach to personality permits the use of factor analysis for prediction. This analysis reduces a countless number of traits into a small and manageable number of basic and independent factors. However, in attempting to fragment the human personality into a number of isolated variables, trait theory overlooks the cohesive substance that organizes and integrates these factors into a single human personality.

Whereas some trait theorists have sought out the common elements of individual personalities, others have focused on the unique aspects of each individual. The rationale of the second approach is that personality would not exist if all persons thought, acted, and felt alike.[14] Although the trait theory, with its varying emphases on individual similarities and differences, is popular today, there is little agreement among psychologists as to which traits are significant. In this context, it is meaningful to note:

> Establishing the validity of the trait approach will require an extensive amount of research and development. The assessment of personality traits is not a unitary undertaking; techniques of assessment vary on several dimensions, which include: (a) self-description data versus the judgments of others, (b) structured or unstructured test stimuli, (c) structured or unstructured response options to the trait stimuli, (d) objective or subjective methods for scoring the responses, and, of course, (e) the topic of the trait itself.[15]

In summary, then, the trait approach to personality tends to hold the individual apart from the environment as a kind of composite of factors. One trait that is particularly important for managers is their willingness and/or ability to make risky decisions that usually involve discernible uncertainty as to the outcome. This trait is referred to as a manager's "tendency," "inclination," or "attitude" toward risk-taking behavior.[16] It is discussed extensively in the next major section of this chapter. However, the traditional emphasis on individual traits in managerial decision making is being augmented by a more holistic theory of personality.

Holistic Approaches to Personality

Holistic theories of personality emphasize the totality and interrelatedness of individual behavior The individual's grasp of objects and events, rather than the dictates of particular traits or stimuli, largely determines human behavior, which depends upon the individual's image of the world.[17] Maslow set forth a hierarchy of human needs developed from the study of people's positive and optimistic functions.[18] Carl Rogers proposed that the individual operates in a phenomenal field — the entire experience of the person.[19] And Lewin's concept of "field theory" is based on a complex psychological representation of an individual's perception of reality, which includes the interaction of forces internal and external to the person.[20]

Maslow's theory of personality is of particular interest here because research has shown that it is highly applicable to managerial behavior and thereby to decision making in formal organizations. As noted in earlier chapters, according to Maslow human beings are motivated by a hierarchy of needs, the highest of which is the need for self-actualization, or the need to become all that one is capable of becoming.[21] At the lower level of Maslow's hierarchy are such needs as food, water, sex, and security. These needs must be satisfied before those at the higher levels can be met. The highest-level need, self-actualization, may take many forms and be pursued with varying intensity, and the satisfaction of what is a lower-level need for one individual may represent a kind of ultimate fulfillment for another individual.[22]

Maslow set forth some general characteristics of a self-actualized person.[23] Such an individual will tend to:

1. Perceive reality accurately and accept it readily
2. Behave naturally and have a need for privacy
3. Show self-sufficiency as opposed to dependence
4. Appreciate and enjoy life and transcend the ordinary through peak experiences
5. Show brotherly love and social interest, including strong friends
6. Possess a democratic, egalitarian attitude
7. Be able to focus directly on problems
8. Express values and know the difference between right and wrong
9. Have a broad philosophical sense of humor
10. Be inventive and creative; see things in new ways
11. Resist the pressures of society to conform
12. Be well integrated, total, and entire
13. Transcend differences; bring together opposites

According to Maslow, individuals should feel good about themselves and should move upward, as they are destined to by their essential nature. Although it is probably true that not all managerial decision makers possess all the characteristics of Maslow's ideal self-actualized person, research does show that managers seek ultimate fulfillment of their personal needs. For example, Porter and Lawler's study of managers in seven organizations, both governmental and privately owned enterprises, showed that self-actualization was the strongest need among the managers.[24] M. Scott Myers's extensive study of motivation among 1,344 managers at all levels of the Texas Instruments Company in Dallas, Texas, showed that the managers' motivation is strongest (1) in pursuit of self-actualization, and (2) in the presence of opportunities to work toward meaningful goals.[25] These and other studies show managers' needs to be high on Maslow's hierarchy and reinforce the idea that managers are goal oriented.[26] Presumably, therefore, by virtue of the definition advanced in Chapter 3, managers also tend to be rational decision makers.

To summarize in terms of the three general categories of personality discussed, it seems apparent that the managerial decision maker:

1. In Freudian terms, tends to be ego-centered
2. In terms of discernible traits, tends to be highly motivated
3. In the context of Maslow's holistic theory, is oriented toward self-actualization through the attainment of goals and objectives

These general classifications of personality will become more meaningful through a brief review of several empirical studies that were directed toward gaining a broader perspective on the many dimensions of personality, with particular emphasis on the integrated process of decision making.

Empirical Perspectives on Personality

One of the best-known studies of the effect of selected variables on the decision-making process was published in 1962 by Orville C. Brim, Jr., and his associates. The study included two hundred adults and dealt with the decisions of parents regarding their children. Rather than focusing only on a set of personality variables, the researchers constructed three sets of variables as follows:

1. **Personality variables,** including the abilities, beliefs, attitudes, and motives of the individual

2. **Situational variables,** pertaining to the external, observable situations in which individuals find themselves

3. **Interactional variables,** which indicate the momentary state of the individual resulting from the interaction of a specific situation with characteristics of the individual's personality[27]

The rationale for this approach was to

> deal first with the direct effects of personality, regardless of the situation; second, to deal with the effects of situations, irrespective of personality; and third, to hypothesize that certain momentary states must have resulted from the interaction of these two sets of variables, and thus to look at the effects of interactions on the decisions.[28]

The approach used in the Brim study is a good example of a combination of the trait and holistic theories of personality. As such, its findings are useful to decision makers. The study's general implications for personality as a determinant in the decision-making process are as follows:

1. There is no reason to believe that any one person is equally proficient in all phases of the decision-making process. Instead the results suggest that some people will do well in one part of the process, whereas other people will do better in another part.

2. Different personality characteristics, such as the skill, intelligence, or training of the choice maker, may be associated with different decision-process factors.

3. The relation of personality to decision processes may vary for different social groups on the basis of factors like sex and social status.[29]

The Brim study is also significant in that it produced specific findings of more immediate use to managerial decision makers:

1. People who tend to be dependent on others will, in making their decisions, be somewhat more optimistic about the outcomes of their actions. They will consider fewer outcomes in evaluating alternatives and will be less rational when they rank actions according to their evaluations.

2. The characteristic of making extreme judgments in evaluating the desirability, probability, and time characteristics of outcomes was related to high effectiveness and to a general desire for certainty.

3. Individuals of middle-class social status tend to suppress their impulses and emotions more than lower-class individuals. They also think more about the future.

4. Individuals of lower-class social status seem less confident of their ability to control their personal destiny and environment, whereas middle-class individuals are more self-confident, self-sufficient, and dominant in their personal relations.[30]

The Brim study is also noteworthy for its findings about differences between males and females in the influence of personality on decision-making behavior. Such differences showed up after dividing the two hundred men and women into two groups of lower-class and middle-class individuals. Class distinctions were made on the basis of socioeconomic factors such as social position, occupation, education, and ancestry. The findings were as follows:

1. Middle-class males scored higher than their lower-class counterparts on the characteristics of pointing toward the future, belief in the predictability of life, independence of judgment, and verbal intelligence.

2. Lower-class males were more likely to believe in fate and the supernatural and to believe that "good things will happen" and "bad things won't happen." Lower-class males also tended to be more dependent on others than the middle-class males.

3. Middle-class males reported significantly more satisfaction with their life situations and scored higher on dominance in interpersonal relations.

4. Middle-class females were more intelligent, more satisfied, and less apathetic than lower-class females. They were also antitraditional, higher in independence of judgment, and higher in the belief that actions have many consequences. Middle-class females were also more autonomous than their lower-class counterparts.

5. There were noticeably few personality differences between lower-class males and lower-class females.

6. In the middle-class group, males scored higher than females on pointing toward the future, pessimism, dominance in interpersonal relations, self-confidence, and self-sufficiency. For their part, the middle-class females scored higher on fatalism, optimism, general satisfaction, nervousness, and the need for certainty.[31]

The main value of the Brim study is that it showed scientifically that decision making is influenced by the personal traits of the decision maker as well as by certain situational and interactional variables that are a part of the holistic theory of personality.

A study by Pollay, using students drawn from the upper-level and graduate classes at the University of California at Berkeley, provides additional insight into the effect of personality on the process of choice. Pollay hypothesized that "decision makers take longer to choose from four alternatives when two of the alternatives are easily rejected than when all four alternatives are equal." This study found that there was a strong correlation between the decision maker's achievement potential and willingness to make difficult choices from among equally attractive alternatives.[32]

In general, the study concluded the following:

> When discrimination between the best of a set of decision alternatives is difficult, experimental subjects take longer to reach a decision from a set of four alternatives including two easily rejected alternatives than they do when all four of the alternatives are equally attractive. When discrimination between the best of the alternatives is relatively easy, experimental subjects take longer when all of the alternatives are good than when some of the alternatives are inferior.[33]

In spite of the obvious effect of personality on the decision-making process, managers are noticeably reluctant to express their own feelings or recognize the feelings of others in the conduct of daily operations. Based on a survey of six companies that included interviews with 165 top managers, Chris Argyris reported that such managers rarely:

1. Take risks or experiment with new ideas or feelings
2. Help others to own up, be open, and take risks
3. Use a style of behavior that supports the norms of individuality and trust, as well as mistrust
4. Express feelings, either positive or negative[34]

Argyris did not interpret these findings to mean that the managers in the survey did not have any feelings. To the contrary, the survey revealed that many of the participants possessed very strong feelings on certain subjects. Still the overwhelming majority (84 percent) indicated that, in their opinion, it was a sign of immaturity to express sentiments openly during decision-making meetings.[35] Presumably it was more desirable to suppress personality traits and maintain an aura of complete objectivity about the decision at hand. However, the use of suppression mechanisms to inhibit feelings seems certain to result in a good deal of inner tension and personal frustration that may lead to conflict between the individual and the organization. Decision makers would do well to recognize the importance of personality in the process of choice.[36] Free expression can contribute positively to personal satisfaction and to outcomes that are accepted more enthusiastically by the affected individuals.

When personal values and organizational objectives conflict, undesirable consequences are likely to result from suppressed feelings:

> Usually we pretend that conflicts aren't present — act as though they were not part of us. We unconsciously repress them as though part of our personality protects us from unbearable hurt. . . . The conflict is repressed; the personality acts on feelings and usually gets itself in additional trouble and more conflicts and anxieties accumulate.[37]

Several additional studies have shown the influence of personality on decision making. For example, in a study of 357 college students Wallach and Kogan found "that women were more conservative than men when unsure of their decisions and more extreme than men when very sure of their decisions."[38] In another study of 79 industrial managers, Taylor and Dunnette found that personality attributes influenced styles or idiosyncrasies leading to a choice and were especially influential on behavior after the choice was made.[39] Stumph and Dunbar found that the personality of managers influences their strategic decisions.[40] Moussavi et al. determined that personality influences the way in which managers view strategic decisions and the approach that they take to make such decisions.[41] Still other studies suggest that personality significantly affects behavior in decision making.[42] It seems most instructive at this point to further elaborate on the many ways in which personality influences managerial decision making.

Personality Effects on Decision Making

The link between personality and decision making is not a simple one-to-one relationship. Managers do not merely act out their private motives in organizational affairs. Rather they transform childhood experiences, disappointments, and memories into action. In this transformation external reality is as important as the nonrational side of the decision maker's nature. Many managerial actions appear to be puzzling, inconsistent with organizational role, or simply incomprehensible. But such actions begin to make sense, and in fact can be seen to support a persistent inner direction, once the nature of the individual's inner conflicts and the defenses used to cope with these conflicts are uncovered.[43]

Managerial decision making represents a learned psychological process that is entangled with the decision maker's personality:

> Election of choices from among many alternatives clearly represents a psychological process that is learned, similar to other psychological processes. Man is not born with the ability to make decisions nor does he acquire this capacity very effectively simply through the process of trial-and-error in growing older. Rather, he develops competency in decision making by a series of carefully organized experiences that are properly paced to his development and psychological readiness.[44]

Numerous studies have confirmed the relationship between personality and managerial decision making. For example, Saunders and Stanton noted that the personality of managerial decision makers provides a general orientation toward goal attainment.[45] Arroba noted the tendency of managers to rely on feelings or wants in making "quite important" decisions.[46] Taylor's research showed that older managers tend to take longer to reach decisions and are generally less confident of their choices.[47] The study of executives by Henderson and Nutt demonstrated that the cognitive makeup (called "decision style") of managerial decision makers influenced the selection among alternative courses of action.[48] In their words: "Cognitive style influenced the choices made by executives in this study. The adoption prospects and perceptions of risk were found to be related to the executive's psychological makeup."[49] And, finally, numerous studies have shown the effects of stress on managerial decision makers in various phases of the decision-making process.[50]

In a practical sense, a managerial decision maker's personality may show its traits in the form of the following preferences:

1. A preference for high, low, or moderate risks and a preference to risk high or low amounts

2. A preference to look for problems and to keep control of the situation or, alternatively, a preference to give up control of the situation and to wait for problems to emerge on their own

3. A preference for innovation or for proven methods[51]

Personality attributes also influence the ability of the managerial decision maker to (1) accommodate large amounts of information, (2) deal with the pressures of a crisis, and (3) restructure ideas to relate specifically to the situation at hand. The decision maker may regard differences of opinion as a threat to his or her position and may react to a given situation temperamentally or with detachment. Moreover, personality attributes also act to shape the "rules" used by the decision maker, such as (1) what information is to be accepted, (2) what sequence of events must be followed, and (3) how many errors subordinates will be permitted to make. Finally, the managerial decision maker's personality shapes his or her style of leadership in a decision-making situation. Decision-making style includes the following variables:

1. Rules are made explicit or are never stated.

2. Proposals are evaluated on the basis of their intrinsic merit or their political acceptability.

3. Change is accomplished within the existing framework, the rules of the "game" are changed, or an entirely different "game" is attempted.

4. Leadership may be democratic, authoritarian, or laissez-faire.

5. Authority for a specific problem may be delegated directly to one individual or, for the purpose of retaining control, to different people.[52]

It is hard to dispute the influence of personality on the process of choice:

Effectiveness in decision making is directly related to the effectiveness of the executive personality. The successful personality makes decisions freely without the compelling forces of hidden personality factors. Thus, the successful decision maker knows how to prevent his own errors and works on himself to improve his decisions.[53]

Since it is not possible to isolate the influence of personality on the integrated process of arriving at a satisficing choice, decision makers in formal organizations should concentrate on improving their understanding of this complex phenomenon. By this means, they will convert its potentially unfavorable consequences into positive effects leading toward an outcome that will attain the original objective. Again, it should be noted that a decision is no less rational because it recognizes the influence of personality. To the contrary, such recognition is more likely to result in a choice that is truly satisficing.

WILLINGNESS TO ACCEPT RISK IN CHOICE BEHAVIOR

Risk is defined in the glossary of this book as "a common state or condition in decision making characterized by the possession of incomplete information regarding a probabilistic outcome." MacCrimmon and Wehrung identify three principal components of risk: (1) the magnitude of loss, (2) the chance of loss, and (3) the exposure to loss. They note that, to reduce riskiness in a decision-making situation, at least one of these components must be diminished. They also note that the degree of risk attendant on a given decision is directly proportional to the chance and size of the loss and to the degree of exposure of the decision maker to the loss.[54] The definition of risk advanced in this book relates the concept of risk to a decision and, more specifically, the outcome resulting from a decision. A risky situation is, therefore, one in which the decision maker is not sure which of several possible outcomes will occur. This uncertainty may lead to an erroneous choice, and, possibly, a financial loss.[55] A risky decision is one that is fraught with uncertainty regarding the likely outcomes of alternative choices in terms of the negative consequences attendant on such choices. The decision maker has some information but not perfect information. Acting in a managerial role, he or she is expected to cope with the uncertainty and to proceed with a choice that presumably reduces the risk to a level acceptable to both the managerial decision maker in a psychological sense and to the organization generally in an economic sense. This relationship explains why the willingness to accept risk is so important for managerial decision makers. They are expected to deal with risk and to make a decision that works to the best interest of the organization. That, in essence, is what it means to be a manager. The remainder of this section focuses on some relevant studies of individual decision making and on the psychological forces impacting a given manager as he or she goes about the process of making category II decisions. Chapter 11 presents some additional explanation of managerial risk acceptance/avoidance in the context of two major studies.

Empirical Perspectives on Risk Acceptance/Avoidance

Research has shown that individual decision makers vary considerably in their willingness to accept risk in the process of arriving at a choice.[56] For example, in a gambling experiment using dice, the researchers studied how the subjects' personalities affected their efforts to maximize expected gain. It was found that "people who are very much aware of objective probabilities and expected return are governed by other considerations in their risk-taking preferences."[57]

One personality variable in particular — the intelligence of the decision maker — was found to strongly influence acceptance or avoidance of risk. High intelligence was found to be related to low variability in risk taking. More intelligent subjects stayed with one particular risk strategy on the premise that if it was good in one situation, it would also be good in similar situations. The less bright subjects formed no particular strategy and tended to make choices at random or according to previous outcomes.[58]

Moreover, those subjects who elected a low payoff strategy, with moderate or minimal risks, did so because of strong values that belittled failure and placed a premium on modest success. Conversely, the high-payoff subjects reflected lower fear and a greater inclination to accept risks that might or might not result in greater rewards.

In summary, the following three conclusions of the study reflect the influence of personality on the willingness to accept risk in a choice situation:

1. Expected dollar value had little importance in determining betting preferences.
2. Intelligence was not significantly related to the degree of risk taking, but it was related to variability in risk taking.
3. Individuals who were sophisticated about probabilities and expected values were no more likely to maximize expected values than others.[59]

Another study, by Henry Morlock, was based on the hypothesis that "the strength of an expectation of an event varies positively with the desirability of the event." Morlock concluded:

> Under moderate levels of decision difficulty, less information is required to decide that a desirable event will occur than that an undesirable event will occur. Thus . . . the amount of information required for a decision can be affected by the values of outcomes that are independent of the decision.[60]

The results supported the hypothesis of this study.

Pruitt's study of the information required to make a decision showed that individuals tend to reduce risk by collecting information on the good and bad aspects of each alternative, but that once a decision is made, it takes considerably more information to cause the individual to adopt another alternative.[61] Presumably the subjects in this study had learned to cope with the risk associated with their first decision and were hesitant to accept different risks associated with another decision.

A study by Sieber and Lanzetta showed that individuals who deal easily with uncertainty are more able and willing to cope with complex or unsolvable problems than individuals who are generally averse to uncertainty.[62] Williams found that high-risk takers are more likely to accept the uncertainties of changing jobs than are low-risk takers. Williams also found that, while high-risk takers are not necessarily more satisfied on high-risk jobs than low-risk takers, they are definitely more dissatisfied on low-risk jobs than are their low-risk counterparts. Stated another way, the amount of risk in a given job is of great importance to the satisfaction of high-risk takers, but does not explain the job satisfaction of low-risk takers. The low-risk takers appeared more concerned with the physical effects of the work, whereas the high-risk takers placed a premium on the responsibilities of the job that presented a direct challenge to them.[63]

Another pertinent study, by Hendrick and his associates, showed that "there is a curvilinear relationship between the difficulty of a choice and decision time; decision time increases as difficulty increases until the choice becomes quite difficult and then decision time decreases." In this study, difficulty or complexity referred to the number of dimensions or attributes of the alternatives perceived as relevant to the choice. The more complex the alternatives, the more difficult the choice. Faced with alternatives with many attributes or many alternatives with few attributes, the decision maker may find the situation hopelessly complex and make an impulsive choice.[64]

Obviously different decision makers will accept different amounts of uncertainty and the conditions under which they will accept it vary a lot. Taylor and Dunnette found that individuals who readily accept risk reach a decision with much less information than other individuals who are inclined to avoid risk, although they tend to review the lesser amount of information very carefully.[65] A different view of the acceptance of risk was advanced by Slovic who stated that "the majority of the evidence argues against the existence of risk-taking propensity as a generalized characteristic of individuals."[66] Slovic feels that in previous experiences in risk-taking settings individuals learned to accept risk. Slovic assumes that such experiences are not part of a decision maker's personality, which is contrary to the view presented in this book.

Atkinson notes that high achievers tend to seek risk and low achievers tend to avoid it.[67] Several empirical studies have supported Atkinson's theory, so it deserves considerable respect.[68] Jones and Johnson found that the greater the delay in making a decision and experiencing its consequences, the greater the tendency to choose risky rather than conservative decision alternatives.[69] Jackson and his associates hypothesized a generalized model of risk taking involving monetary risk, physical risk, ethical risk, and social risk.[70] The results of their study tended to confirm this hypothesis. However, this study did not detract from the notion of risk taking as part of personality in decision making.

Brengelmann demonstrated the linkage between the personality of the decision maker and his or her willingness or ability to deal effectively with varying degrees of certainty in choice behavior.[71] Cummings and Harnett noted the willingness of decision makers to take greater risks if they are firmly committed to a given level of aspiration.[72] Berg documented the tendency of decision makers to form levels of aspiration by taking into account their need to achieve success along with their need to avoid failure.[73] Wallach and Kogan studied the relationship between the deterrence of the fear of failure and the impetus of anticipated success for decision makers of varying ages.[74] And Brown determined that business executives tend to be more accepting of risk than public school administrators.[75] Isen et al. found that the state of mind of the decision maker influences the process of choice.[76] Fagley and Miller concluded that the way in which a given decision is framed or presented affects the willingness of the decision maker to accept risk as well as the amount of risk likely to be accepted.[77] These studies show the many dimensions of individuals' tendencies to accept or avoid risk in decision making. These studies indicate that a conceptual model would be useful for illustrating the psychological aspects of risk acceptance or avoidance. Such a model appears in Figure 6.1 and is the subject of the discussion in the next section.

A Conceptual Model of Risk Acceptance/Avoidance

Think of the conceptual model in Figure 6.1 in terms of two decision makers who have completely opposite personalities. For convenience, we will call these two decision makers DM_1 and DM_2. DM_1 tends to accept risk and feels completely at home in the presence of a good deal of uncertainty. More important, DM_1 associates the acceptance of risk with a highly desirable outcome.

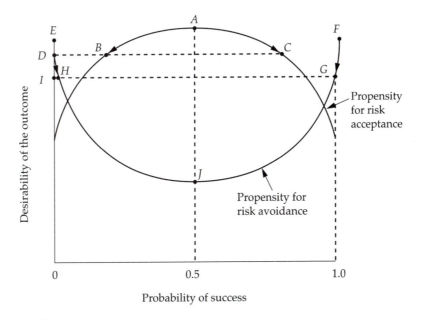

FIGURE 6.1

A Conceptual Model of Risk Acceptance/Avoidance

That is, DM_1 associates risk with reward up to a point where accepting further risk becomes intolerable. Accordingly, DM_1 prefers to make a choice where the reward will be the highest and where, at the same time, the uncertainty of success or failure is the greatest. Therefore, the preferred choice of DM_1 will be at point A in Figure 6.1. This point is the optimal combination for DM_1. The outcome is the most desirable and success is as likely as failure.

But the first decision maker's choices will only start at point A. DM_1 will continue to strive for the most desirable outcome, and as DM_1 gains more experience and information, he or she will tend to move away from point A toward either point B or point C. If the choices directed toward attaining DM_1's objective result in a lower probability of success with each succeeding trial, DM_1 will move from point A to point B. By this time the desirability of the expected outcome will be so low (point D) that DM_1 will be tempted to abandon the current objective in favor of one that promises a greater reward. Conversely, if DM_1's repeated choices result in a higher probability of success, DM_1 will move from point A to point C. At point C the less desirable outcome (point D) will cause DM_1 to abandon the current objective to pursue one that offers a higher expected outcome.

The lower desirability of the outcome in moving from point A to point C might seem contradictory in view of the higher probability of success. Remember, though, that DM_1 is highly motivated and associates great uncertainty or risk with high reward. As the uncertainty begins to decrease and the probability of success starts to rise, any of several variables will begin to make the outcome less attractive to DM_1: (1) the probability of success will, unless there are barriers, attract competitors who will share in the reward; (2) the increased likelihood of a successful outcome will reduce the challenge for the decision maker; or (3) the information and experience gained in the process of moving toward a higher probability of success will present new opportunities that appear to offer even greater rewards to the motivated decision maker. Therefore, DM_1 will abandon the current objective in pursuit of more desirable ends.

In summary, then, the line segment BAC on the parabolic curve represents the area of risk acceptance for DM_1. Point A, of course, is the preferred position of DM_1 on the parabolic curve and, theoretically at least, is the starting point for a series of decisions leading toward some desired end. DM_1 will continue to make decisions on the parabolic curve until encountering either point B or point C, at which time DM_1 will be disinclined to make further choices. This rationale assumes, of course, that DM_1 has alternative objectives. Thus DM_1 will seek another point A on a new parabolic curve.

The second decision maker, DM_2 in Figure 6.1, has a psychological aversion to risk of any sort. Therefore, DM_2 will tend to make choices when risk is lowest or when the outcome is most certain. On the scale for the probability of success in Figure 6.1, these states exist at point E and point F. At the former the probability of success is zero; what could be more certain? At the latter, the probability of success, of course, eliminates any uncertainty. At points E and F, then, the desirability of the outcome is the highest for the second decision maker, for it is at these points that DM_2 can avoid uncertainty or the acceptance of risk. And DM_2 would rather accept the certainty of known failure at point E than assume the risk of choices with a high probability of success, such as at point J. And, of course, DM_2 would willingly accept the perfect probability of a choice at point F.

Assuming that DM_2 elects a choice at point F, DM_2 might be tempted to try again, at which time he or she will move slightly away from perfect probability down the hyperbolic curve toward point G. If DM_2 continues all the way to point G, DM_2 will find the uncertainty intolerable. The desirability of the outcome will be reduced to point I, and DM_2 will abandon the current objective in favor of one with a more certain outcome. Alternatively, if DM_2 faces a probability with no visible chance of success, such as at point E, DM_2 might reject the apparent hopelessness of the situation and risk one or more trials that will move DM_2 down the hyperbolic curve toward point H. That is, with each succeeding trial DM_2 will gain more knowledge and experience, thereby increasing the probability of success. However, by the time DM_2 reaches point H, the uncertainty will have increased to an intolerable level. The desirability of the outcome will be reduced accordingly from point E to point I, and DM_2 will abandon the current objective in favor of one that offers less uncertainty. In summary, the line segment HJG on the hyperbolic curve is the area of risk avoidance for DM_2. Assuming that DM_2 has alternative objectives, points on the hyperbolic curve inside this area will be too unattractive for DM_2 to make further decisions.

Figure 6.1 is not intended to suggest that decision makers necessarily fall neatly into one of these two extremes of psychological behavior.[78] In reality, there are infinite gradations of risk acceptance and risk avoidance. Many of the variables analyzed in the previously cited psychological studies influence a person's degree of risk acceptance or avoidance. For example, willingness to accept risk is obviously influenced by at least the following variables: (1) the decision maker's motivation, (2) the decision maker's intelligence and other personality traits, (3) the decision maker's expectations, (4) the amount of information available to the decision maker, (5) the amount of time within which the choice must be made, and (6) the complexity (however defined) of the choice itself.[79]

The length of the line segment BAC, which constitutes DM_1's area of risk acceptance, and the length of the line segment HJG, which represents the area of risk avoidance for DM_2, will vary depending upon the role being enacted in the process of choice. For example, a decision maker such as DM_2, who is inclined to avoid uncertainty, may be willing to accept more uncertainty as a manager than in his or her personal life simply because of the demands of the managerial role. Similarly, a motivated decision maker such as DM_1, who prefers greater uncertainty, may have to make less risky choices, especially for greater probable success (point C), simply because he or she is committed to attaining managerial objectives.

Note that points B and C are not necessarily equidistant from point A for the motivated decision maker; and points H and G are not necessarily equidistant from points E and F, respectively, for the decision maker inclined to avoid risk. Again, the varying positions of these points depend upon the decision maker's role, the psychological forces acting during the decision-making process, and the situation surrounding the choice. To illustrate, a decision maker such as DM_2 may be very reluctant to leave the certainty of failure (point E) in the forlorn hope of achieving some probability of success (point H), but might easily venture forth from certain success (point F). It is obviously easier to move ahead from a position of success than to start from a point of failure, even though, in both cases, the degree of certainty may be the same.

Psychological studies tend to confirm the aforesaid rationale regarding possible variations in the risk-taking behavior of DM_1 and DM_2. For example, Lopes accurately noted that:

> Risk-averse people appear to be motivated by a desire for *security*, whereas risk-seeking people appear to be motivated by a desire for *potential*. The former motive values safety, and the latter, opportunity. . . . Risk-averse people look more at the downside and risk-seekers more at the upside. But risk-seekers may play it safe from time to time, and even the most risk-averse person will take chances — even big chances — when necessary.[80]

The conceptual model in Figure 6.1 is a useful illustration, because it provides a structure for analyzing psychological tendencies to accept or avoid risk. Such analysis can yield further insight into the behavioral aspects of the decision-making process.[81] Remember, too, that in considering the psychology of decision making the willingness to accept risk is influenced by the perception of the variables in the situation, as well as by the outcome that is likely to result from a choice.

PERCEPTION IN DECISION MAKING

Perception is being sensitive to and interpreting stimuli or facts. It includes the ability to fit a limited amount of facts and information into a whole picture. The greater the contact with the facts and the more information available, the more likely it is that a perception will be sharp and defined. Perceptions are also influenced by how people expect a person to enact a particular role. And, of course, reference groups — the groups with which a person relates or identifies — are a key in forming perceptions. Finally, a person's perception will be influenced by the vantage point from which he or she looks at a situation, a fact, or an act.[82] Note, for example, the following description of perception:

> Individuals are constantly bombarded by sensory stimulation. These are noises, sights, smells, tastes, and tactile sensations. Yet somehow we manage to process

this information without confusion. This process is known as perception. It may be defined as the experience people have as the immediate result of sensory inputs. The process is one of selection and organization of sensations to provide the meaningful entity we experience.[83]

There are two basic components in the foregoing definition. Perception is, first of all, a system of **selection,** or screening. Some information is received and processed, some is not. This screening helps individuals avoid processing irrelevant or disruptive information. The second component of perception is **organization.** The information received and processed must be ordered and categorized in some fashion that permits the individual to find meaning in the stimulus signals. These categories may be elaborate or they may be simple, but their central function is the reduction of complex information into simpler categories.[84]

Kolasa offers a comprehensive definition of perception in the following excerpt:

> It may be defined as the organization of material which comes in from the outside at one time or another. Perceptions may also be considered as the interpretation of the data that are received from inputs. The system, or organism, recognizes the information, assembles it, and makes comparisons with material previously stored, in the "central information processing storage.". . . It is a process that shapes whatever comes in from the outside; in turn, what is there is changed by what comes in.[85]

Given the decision maker's need to scan the environment in search of relevant alternatives, it is obvious that the perceptual process significantly affects the decision-making process.[86] In fact, the two processes are virtually inseparable. Still, the perceptual process has certain distinguishing characteristics that merit a more detailed analysis and discussion at this point.

The Perceptual Process

Litterer's concept of the perceptual process has three chief elements:

1. **Selectivity,** in which thresholds separate certain pieces of information for further consideration.
2. **Closure,** where bits of information are compiled into a meaningful whole.
3. **Interpretation,** where previous experiences aid in judging the information collected.[87]

These elements interact to create behavior based on the perception of the individual. In essence, the perceptual process calls forth a given response within the individual; the response is then translated into behavior based on the perceived consequences of the elected course of action. The individual then perceives the behavior's outcome and adjusts his or her response accordingly to attain the current objective. Thus, the perceptual process is a dynamic cycle. The process concludes only when the individual perceives that he or she has selected the correct information and has, as well as possible, anticipated the consequences of acting on such information.

Bergen divides the process of perception into four principal variables: (1) the stimulus characteristic observed, (2) the perceptual task of the observer, (3) the content categories of the stimulus observed, and (4) the sense modality through which the observation occurs. He defines these variables as follows:

1. **Stimulus characteristics** are the characteristics of external stimuli as perceived by an observer. Stimulus characteristics are composed of dimensions such as size, shape, and position.

2. A **perceptual task** is a set of requirements imposed on an observer. A perceptual task has three components: (a) the number and arrangement of stimuli, (b) the instructions to the observer, and (c) the behavior required of the observer. Variations in stimuli affect perception by altering what the perceiver can observe. Instructions influence what the observer expects as well as the observer's attention. Instructions also guide the observer's behavior when presented with the stimuli. In turn, the behavior required of the observer influences the manner in which the observer selects from the stimuli presented for observation.

3. **Content categories** are culturally determined classifications based on stimulus characteristics. The characteristic most extensively used in the definition of content categories is form.

4. **Sense modalities** refer to the sense or combination of senses through which information is processed. Each sense modality is responsible for processing a different kind of stimulus information. Accordingly each provides a different set of perceptual experiences. For example, one cannot hear noise with vision, and size and texture are both tactile and visual stimulus characteristics. Therefore, the stimulus at hand determines the combination of senses to be used.[88]

Perception is, first of all, a selective process. An individual selects a limited amount of information from the outside simply because he or she cannot handle all the information coming in. The individual may be undergoing many physical changes, but only certain stimuli are taken in and given a response.[89] The main factor in the selective process is attention. When an individual attends to a given situation, he or she focuses on a particular set of circumstances. This is the beginning of the perceptual process. The individual then attempts to order the stimuli into some meaningful whole, using sense modalities and the classifications determined by the stimulus characteristics. Then the individual interprets the stimuli, utilizing current impressions and past experiences, and uses these interpretations as the basis for actions directed toward the fulfillment of the current objectives.

Studies of perception and the perceptual process have been made by psychologists, social psychologists, and others in the behavioral sciences. Most of these studies aim toward measuring behavior.[90] The primary concern in this book is, of course, the influence of perception on managerial decision making. In any experimental situation, a researcher trying to measure perception must deal with two major classifications of variables. The first class may be termed **controllable variables** — that is, experimental conditions that the researcher can change. Among variables of this class that have been identified are (1) the measurement device, (2) the stimulus context, (3) the scenario, and (4) the actual stimuli.[91] The second class of variables influencing perception are **noncontrollable** by the researcher. Noncontrollable variables are defined as those that the individual brings into the experimental situation. These are the variables that give rise to true individual differences in perception. Included in this class of variables are (1) familiarity with the stimuli, (2) personal values, (3) personality, (4) cultural background, and (5) physiological characteristics.[92] Indeed, the web of uncontrollable variables affecting perception makes this process pervasive and significant in determining all the functions in the integrated process of decision making.

Characteristics of the Perceiver and the Perceived

In discussing the influence of perception on the decision-making process, one may find it useful to focus on the characteristics of the perceiver and the perceived.[93] This will make it easier to outline the interaction between these two principals in the perceptual process and to show how that process relates to the process of choice.

Because the perceiver begins the perceptual process, his or her characteristics assume a singular importance. Zalkind and Costello have summarized these characteristics as follows:

1. The perceiver may be influenced by unidentified responses to cues that are below the threshold of awareness.

2. When required to form difficult perceptual judgments, the perceiver may respond to irrelevant cues to arrive at a judgment.

3. In making abstract or intellectual judgments, the perceiver may be influenced by emotion; for instance, what is liked is perceived as correct.

4. The perceiver will weigh perceptual evidence coming from respected (or favored) sources more heavily than that coming from other sources.

5. The perceiver may not be able to identify all the factors on which his or her judgments are based. Even if aware of these factors, the perceiver is not likely to realize how much weight is given to them.[94]

Much current research indicates, also, that the individual tends to use self as the norm or standard by which to perceive or judge others. This suggests certain conclusions:

1. Knowing oneself makes it easier to see others accurately.

2. One's own characteristics affect the characteristics one is likely to see in others.

3. The person who accepts self is more likely to be able to see the good side of other people.

4. Accuracy in perceiving others is not a single skill. That is, the perceiver tends to interpret the feelings of others in terms of his or her feelings toward them.[95]

Most of the perceiver's characteristics are shared by the perceived. Still some special characteristics of the perceived person merit specific mention:

1. The status of the person perceived influences judgments about his or her behavior. Status differences between two perceived individuals can cause a perceiver to assign a different motivation to each individual's behavior.

2. High-status persons are judged as wanting to cooperate, whereas low-status persons are seen as having to cooperate.

3. The person of high status is better liked than the person of low status.

4. The perceived person's organizational role influences the judgment of the perceiver. For example, the perceiver may react differently to his or her own boss than to a person in another department with the same status.

5. Visibility of the traits being judged will influence the accuracy of the judgment. For example, evidence that the perceived likes the perceiver will influence the perceiver's judgment.[96]

The characteristics of the perceiver and the perceived are expressed as the perceiver forms impressions of others. As a result, a decision made is seldom free of preference, preconception, and prejudgment.

Forming Impressions of Others

Several things limit an individual's ability to form accurate impressions of others. For one thing, impressions are likely to be affected too much by the surroundings in which they are made and too little by the person or persons perceived. Many large companies, for example, wine and dine promising college recruits in the hope that the rich atmosphere will favorably affect the recruit's impression of the company. Further, although impressions are often based on a limited sample of the perceived person's behavior, the perceiver, more often than not, will make a sweeping generalization about the perceived.[97] This practice is called stereotyping and is discussed at length later.

Often the situation may not give the person perceived a chance to show behavior relevant to the traits about which impressions are being formed. For example, many organizations do not ask job applicants to demonstrate on-the-job performance. Applicants must be hired only on the basis of impressions gained from résumés, recommendations, and interviews.[98] Obviously, employers would increase their ability to predict an individual's performance if they arranged to observe the desired traits before reaching a decision to hire.

Finally, the perceiver's impressions of the person perceived may be grossly distorted by some highly personal reaction of the perceiver. If, for example, in the course of being observed the perceived uses a mannerism particularly offensive to the perceiver, the perceiver's view may be colored in a way that limits objectivity.[99]

There are many influences that distort the process of forming impressions. Some of the most important ones are (1) stereotyping, (2) the halo effect, (3) projection, and (4) perceptual defense.

Stereotyping   Kolasa defines a **stereotype** as "a 'simple picture in our head' which tells us 'all' about people in the particular group on which we are focusing."[100] It is a bias in perceiving people.[101] Bruner and his associates call stereotyping "prejudiced categorizing" in which conceptions of relationship and identity take too little account of the actual state of affairs. In short, stereotyping depends too much upon preferred but highly unreliable cues for achieving ends that are too narrowly defined.[102]

Stereotyping results from the act of categorizing:

> Categorization at the perceptual level consists of the process of identification, literally an act of placing a stimulus input by virtue of its defining attributes into a certain class. The act of identification involves a "fit" between the properties of a stimulus input and the specifications of a category.[103]

The perceiver finds the relevant attributes by judging the categorical identity of an object. However, it may well be that objects showing certain properties do not belong in the same category as other objects showing similar but not identical properties. In fact, one can never be certain what categorical identity a perceiver will give to a particular set of defining attributes.[104]

The best that can usually be done is categorization with *probabilistic cues*. That is, it may be said that in some percentage of the cases, an object showing a particular set of attributes belongs in a specific category. The important question then becomes how to identify the properties that permit the perceiver to place the object in a given category? Again, the evidence suggests that categorizations are based on cues revealed to the perceiver and that these categorizations are correct only part of the time. At this point, two more questions arise:

1. What general procedures does the perceiver follow in placing events in one category instead of another?

2. What specific procedures — what properties or attributes — does the perceiver use in placing a particular event in one category instead of another?[105]

One procedure for categorizing is to use the frequency of a given event as the only cue. This approach involves a search for attributes that are positioned in time such that the perceiver sees a cue in the relative frequency of occurrence. In other words, the position of a particular event in a series of events is the primary guide for categorizing. The only difference between one event and the next is timing. However, if the series of events to be categorized is truly random, then position in a series is not a valid attribute for categorizing. In this case the perceiver seizes on the only difference between two or more events and gives it a value that may have little basis in fact. Therefore, categorization using the frequency of a given event as its only cue can lead to misleading conclusions and wrong decisions.

A second and more common procedure for categorizing is to use partly valid attributes as cues. In other words, partly valid but not certain cues are present to guide the perceiver as to categorical identity. Still, the perceiver will treat these partly valid cues as if they were sure indicators and use them to make a judgment that is a stereotype.[106]

Several studies of categorizing based on partly valid attributes have confirmed that subjects tend to undervalue cues that are certain and overvalue partly valid cues.[107] For example, in one experiment subjects were asked to tell friendly from hostile aircraft on the basis of completely valid and partly valid attributes. The aircraft were identified more often from the less reliable cues. The subjects tended to focus on a partly valid cue and treat it as if it were certain while giving less attention to a completely reliable cue. In another experiment the subjects were asked to judge intelligence using assigned probabilities for certain facial features, such as brow, nose, and chin. This experiment revealed the same tendency to categorize on the basis of partly rather than completely valid attributes. For example, whatever probability was assigned the height of the brow, it tended to be treated as a perfect indicator of intelligence, whereas the length of the nose was treated as only a partly valid attribute, even when it was designated a completely valid indicator of intelligence.[108] Of course, the main conclusion from these studies is that despite the assigned probabilities for particular attributes, the subjects tended to stereotype or to depend too much on preferred but less reliable cues.

Other research has also revealed that perceivers tend to stereotype on the basis of cues resulting from partly valid attributes.[109] For example, in a study of how labor and management perceive one another, Mason Haire noted that managers tended to give higher values to pictures of individuals when they were labeled managers than when they were labeled union representatives. For their part, the union representatives gave higher values to those labeled union representatives. This study revealed "gross distortion in labor and management's perception of one another."[110]

In another study, by Haire and Grunes, college students experienced considerable difficulty in assigning intelligence to factory workers even when given the opportunity to do so.[111] This study reinforced the already cited studies in that the perceivers invariably tended to stereotype with cues from partly valid attributes.[112]

The Halo Effect   The term **halo effect** is used to describe a process in which a general impression that is favorable or unfavorable is used to evaluate specific traits — the "halo" serves as a screen that keeps the perceiver from actually seeing the trait being judged.[113] The halo effect is fairly common in rating employee performance. For example, a supervisor may single out one trait, good or bad, and use this trait as the basis for judging all other traits. Or a college professor with a strong belief in perfect attendance may downgrade the performance of students who attend class irregularly.

The halo effect is a classic example of categorizing on the basis of cues from partly valid attributes.[114] It may be more extreme when the perceiver is forming impressions of traits that are not important to cues in the perceived person's behavior, when the traits have moral overtones, or when the perceiver must judge traits with which he or she has had little experience.[115] The halo effect may be more pronounced if the perceiver knows the perceived, especially if they are friends.

"In evaluating the effect of halo on perceptual distortion . . . traits that correlate more highly with each other are more likely to lead to a halo effect than traits that are unrelated."[116] For example, a person who is aggressive is often assumed to have high energy, and a person who is generous is frequently assumed to have a good sense of humor.

Projection   The term **projection** refers broadly to the tendency to attribute one's own characteristics to other people. In the field of psychology, for example, the Rorschach, or "ink blot," test requires the perceiver to respond to an unstructured situation by structuring the stimulus according to the dynamics of his or her personality. In like manner the perceiver, in responding to cues of one sort or another, may assign personal attributes to the perceived. The perceptual process may be distorted through the perceiver's emotions or particular traits.

Perceptual Defense   Another distorter of the perceptual process is **perceptual defense.** This occurs when the perceiver is confronted with a fact or event that disagrees with any of his or her stereotypes. The perceiver cannot reconcile this inconsistency, makes an inaccurate perception, and thereby preserves his or her stereotypes. For example, the inability of the college students to perceive factory workers as intelligent was caused by perceptual defense.[117] Apparently the students had a preconception that factory workers are seldom intelligent or they wouldn't be working in a factory; even the suggestion by the researchers that intelligence was a personality trait was not enough to break the stereotype.

In summary, it seems obvious that impressions formed of others are highly subjective. They are generally made on the basis of cues resulting from partly valid attributes. Perceivers assign these attributes to the perceived on the basis of their preexisting or spontaneous stereotypes.

Situational Influences on Perception

Interpersonal relationships as well as the organizational setting greatly affect the perceptual process. "Social forces affect perception through group identification, social aspirations, and expectations of the perceiver. People are most inclined to accept perceptual evidence from sources with whom they identify."[118] Labor leaders, for example, frequently mistrust managers' motives and consequently give information provided by the company less weight than the facts suggest it deserves.

Dearborn and Simon found department identification to be a vital force in the perception of executives. Essentially they found that (1) sales executives tend to view problems with a sales bias, (2) production executives see large problems from a production point of view, and (3) finance managers see large problems in terms of finance.[119]

In the group or organizational setting, the similarity of the members' perceptions relates directly to their unity. Normally the greater the unity, the stronger the groupwide perceptual process.[120]

There is also, of course, a tendency to make the organization conform to the way the top executives perceive it. Thus management tends to select its new members on the basis of acceptable attributes.

Additional Empirical Perspectives on Perception

Perception is at best an imprecise phenomenon. That which is perceived is often not what it seems to be. Since perception affects all aspects of managerial decision making, its imprecision makes unstructured and complex choices something less than an exact science. Several studies show that perception often cannot be controlled, even under presumably controlled circumstances. One set of studies, for example, focused on the concept of "creeping determinism," which is the tendency among decision makers to perceive that which has happened (an outcome) as being relatively inevitable.[121] Two hypotheses were confirmed by these studies: (1) reporting an outcome's occurrence increases its perceived probability of occurrence, and (2) decision makers who receive knowledge about outcomes usually do not realize it changes their perceptions. These studies concluded with the following statement:

> Thus, undiagnosed creeping determinism not only biases people's impressions of what they would have known without outcome knowledge, but also their impressions of what they themselves and others actually *did* know in foresight.[122]

Another study of eighty college students showed that trait words reflecting unconventional, nonnormative behavior affect first impressions more than do words that actually describe people. This study noted:

> First impressions . . . involve more than simply a judgment of whether or not the person is likable. In forming an impression of another, we may want to know

whether he is intelligent or stupid, liberal or conservative, energetic or lazy, etc. A first impression, then, is a conglomerate of tentative judgments about another person, our attraction to him being only one . . . such component.[123]

Still another study, also involving college students, concluded that decision makers with a low level of dogmatism (dogmatism is a closed system of beliefs) were more accurate in their perceptions of how dogmatic other individuals are than were highly dogmatic decision makers.[124] This study indicates clearly that perception is at least partially shaped by the perceiver's personality, which in turn tends to influence the integrated functions of decision making.

A special group of studies has focused on the influence of perception in comparing and evaluating alternatives.[125] In general, these studies have found that perception's influence is stronger when two or more alternatives are a little different in attractiveness than when they are greatly different in attractiveness. In like manner, perception's influence on selecting among alternatives is stronger when certainty about the perceived attractiveness of alternatives is low. In summary, a decision maker must exercise more perceptual ability to arrive at a choice when there is little difference in the attractiveness of alternatives and the choice is made under conditions of low certainty. Although these relationships might seem obvious, their acceptance as effects of perception on decision making requires empirical validation.

Many other studies of the influence of perception on the behavior of decision makers could be cited.[126] The point is that the perceptual process is inextricably linked with all the functions that make up the integrated process of choice.

The perceptual process is important in decision making for several reasons. First, it provides a means of gathering information in the search for relevant alternatives. Moreover, as a result of not dealing with completely valid attributes, information flows are colored by the perceiver's biases or "filtering mechanisms." These mechanisms influence the search, the comparison and evaluation of alternatives, and, of course, the choice itself. But perception does not stop with the act of choice. It also influences the way in which the decision maker implements the choice, as well as the feedback and control required to ensure an outcome likely to meet the current objective. The perceptual process is interrelated with the decision-making process at each stage, and a recognition of this fact by managerial decision makers should result in more successful outcomes.[127]

SUBCONSCIOUS INFLUENCES ON DECISION MAKING

There is less than complete agreement regarding the influence of the subconscious mind on the behavior of the organizational decision maker. According to the Freudian theory of personality, almost every choice is guided by the interactions of the id, the ego, and the superego. Doubtless there are subconscious forces in some combination operating to some degree below the level of the decision maker's awareness. Unfortunately, a precise assessment of the influence these forces exert is impossible to make.

The managerial decision maker as seen by Freud and his successors might be characterized as follows:

> He is autistic; he distorts reality to suit inner needs and then makes his distorted picture of reality the premise of his actions. He is compulsive. He projects his own motives and reality views on others; represses powerful and urgent wants deep into the subconscious for fear of penalties from conscience or the responses of others, only to have his repressed wants unrecognizably displaced on other goals; acquires and displays exaggerated fears; colors the world with emotional tones of forgotten childhood; expresses hatreds and resentments from long-buried events; rationalizes all his actions; and throws a veil of hypocrisy and dishonesty not only over his outer behavior in order to deceive others but even over his innermost wishes in order to deceive himself.[128]

The foregoing quotation may seem a harsh caricature of the managerial decision maker; still, even if it were accurate, it need not impede the decision maker's pursuit of rational choices within the limits of bounded rationality. A satisficing decision made within the open decision model permits the subconscious to intrude without compromising the rationality of the choice.

Actually many levels of thought are involved in most human behavior. In this context it is useful to think of the mind as operating at conscious, subconscious (or unconscious), and preconscious levels. The preconscious level links the communicable processes of consciousness with the subconscious processes of anxiety and neurosis.

> Preconscious processes are assailed from both sides. From one side they are nagged and prodded into rigid distorted symbols by unconscious drives which are oriented away from reality and which consist of rigid compromise formations, lacking in fluid inventiveness. From the other side they are driven by literal conscious purpose, checked and corrected by conscious retrospective critique.[129]

The preconscious level of the human mind is described graphically in the following passage:

> Transient emotional impulses, as well as the more chronic types of emotional bias, are frequently not "unconscious" in the Freudian sense of the term, inasmuch as the person is capable of becoming at least partially aware of his feelings, if someone induces him to scrutinize his thoughts and behavior. Hence they can be characterized as "preconscious," the term used by Freud to designate those "wishes" or "impulses" that the person is unaware of at the time he takes action, but is capable of becoming aware of when he introspects or is given appropriate communication by others. Preconscious incentives are thus assumed to be susceptible to change through information and persuasion.[130]

Within the context of decision making, one of the most pervasive manifestations of the preconscious mind or the subconscious mind is **rationalization.** This term refers to the substitution of favorable motives for real motives below the level of conscious awareness.[131] In the following excerpt, Ferber describes how the process of rationalization occurs:

> On the conscious level we are aware of what we really think and can reason things out step by step. On the subconscious level or levels any number of physical or emotional influences can affect our thought processes. Then the person feels that a certain thought exists without knowing why. If this thought appears very desirable to the individual, rationalization occurs. In rationalization, the person tries, often subconsciously, to bring the subconscious thought into a pattern of conscious thought that will justify it.[132]

Managerial decision makers elect many rationalized choices. These choices can occur at the conscious, preconscious, or subconscious levels. Such decisions are for the most part self-centered, in that the decision maker rather than the organization stands to gain the most. Often, however, the decision maker is honestly convinced that a rationalized choice will benefit the organization when, upon close analysis, it is all too obvious that the decision maker alone will benefit. In such cases it is likely that the preconscious mind or the subconscious mind has intruded into the process of choice.[133]

In this connection, one final distinction is necessary. It is entirely possible that a rational decision — one that is objectives oriented — is also a rationalized decision made largely to benefit the decision maker rather than the organization. However, it is most unlikely that a nonrational decision — one that is made without heeding the consequences — is not also a rationalized decision. After all, why would a decision maker deliberately ignore the probable results of an action if not to gratify some subconscious force taking the form of an impulsive whim or emotional gesture? It may be true that relatively little is known about the influence of the preconscious or the subconscious mind on managerial decision makers' actions. But in the absence of evidence of objectives-oriented behavior, one can still make some educated guesses about the nonrationality of the actions.[134]

In recent years writers in the field of management have manifested increasing interest in the influence of the subconscious or preconscious mind on the making of decisions. A considerable literature has developed around the concept of intuitive choice.[135] According to one rather comprehensive perspective, intuition "characteristically does not advance in careful, well-planned steps. Indeed, it tends to involve maneuvers based seemingly on an implicit perception of the total problem. The [decision maker] arrives at an answer, which may be right or wrong, with little if any awareness of the process by which he reached it."[136] According to Jung, intuition is a kind of perception that cannot be traced directly back to conscious sensory experience. It is, in a manner of speaking, perception via the subconscious or preconscious mind.[137] Intuition shares certain properties with the creative process. In fact, many writers including Freud consider them essentially identical and group them together with dreams as prelogical experience as opposed to the logical processes of reason.[138]

Several writers have followed the lead of Jung in identifying intuition as one of the basic psychological functions.[139] (The others are thinking, feeling, and sensing.) Intuitive decision making has evolved into an identifiable style and is often contrasted with so-called analytical decision making. Analytical decision making occurs for the most part in the conscious mind through careful and deductive reasoning with a full awareness of the information and operations involved. Conversely, intuitive decision making results from information or images emanating from the unconscious or preconscious mind. Intuitive choice is the culmination of seeing the whole, or the gestalt, of the decision-making situation through the imagination. By definition intuitive decision making proceeds through a kind of fusion of the unconscious, preconscious, and conscious levels of thought. There is no precise dichotomy between analytical decision making and intuitive decision making.[140] As noted in the literature,[141] it is largely a matter of personal style conditioned by the decision maker's personality and constrained by the perennial boundaries of rational behavior in the open decision model culminating in satisficing choices.

Given the influence of many levels of thought in managerial decision making, it becomes more apparent why the best that a rational decision maker can hope for is a satisficing outcome. "Maximization, then, is not simply difficult and approximate, it is intrinsically impossible."[142] Actually, the rational decision maker seeks an objectives-oriented outcome within the context of psychological forces operating at and below the level of awareness:

> Man is possessed of an unconscious as well as a conscious level of being, and the former, judged against "rational" standards, is highly erratic in its influence on behavior. . . . His drives and ambitions are inevitably affected by both internal and external events. He is . . . conscious and subconscious, thinking and feeling, dreaming and coping, remembering and forgetting. . . . his present is simply the growing edge of his past.[143]

This passage describes the psychology of the managerial decision maker who is rational when in pursuit of a managerial objective but who, for the reasons discussed, can never be completely rational except at the conscious level of thought. In spite of the psychological forces operating on the managerial decision maker at the preconscious and subconscious levels, the principal concern in this book is with rational decision making as viewed at the level of awareness. Nonetheless it is important to understand the influence of those psychological forces within the decision maker that are not in evidence but that significantly affect his or her behavior. Such understanding can lead to more effective managerial decision making.

SUMMARY

This chapter noted that a great many variables compose the psychology of decision making. These variables, in differing combinations and at different times, affect the decision maker in ways that are difficult to see and even more difficult to control. For example, it was stated that the decision maker's many-sided personality, however defined, conditions his or her behavior throughout the integrated process of choice. Several studies were cited to support this phenomenon.

The decision maker's tendency to accept or avoid uncertainty was shown to depend upon his or her perception of the desirability of the outcome of a series of choices leading toward the fulfillment of an objective. The tendency to accept or avoid risk was thus noted as a significant psychological force, especially at the moment of choice. The decision maker who is psychologically disposed to accept uncertainty will prefer a decision situation where the outcome can go either way because, in this decision maker's view, high risk makes the outcome most desirable. In short, this decision maker associates the acceptance of risk with a large reward.

Conversely the decision maker who cannot, for any psychological reason, cope with uncertainty prefers a choice where the outcome is certain. This decision maker obviously covets a choice where the probability of success is perfect. However, such choices almost never exist in the real world of decision making. Moreover, the decision maker who tends to avoid risk also tends to make choices where the probability of success is zero — that is, choices for no decision. In essence this decision maker would rather accept the certainty of failure than attempt to cope with the uncertainty of only probable success. Apparently this decision maker finds it easier to rationalize no decision at all than to experience the anxiety of making a choice that might actually fall short of success.

It was also noted that the decision maker who seeks uncertain situations will pursue decisions toward the current objective only until it becomes apparent that the certainty of success or failure is becoming too great. At this time this decision maker will abandon the current objective and pursue another that offers more equal uncertainty and presumably a larger reward. Conversely, the risk-avoiding decision maker is reluctant to move away from choices involving complete certainty. Nevertheless, under some circumstances, this type of decision maker may be persuaded to make decisions that will move toward greater uncertainty, but only to the point where the risk becomes intolerable. At this time this decision maker will abandon the current objective and pursue one that promises complete certainty. The amount of certainty that will be accepted by the achievement-oriented decision maker and the amount of uncertainty that will be borne by the risk-averse decision maker are also influenced by the role being enacted and the situation surrounding the process of choice.

This chapter also described the process of perception and how it influences the integrated process of decision making. Decision makers are unable for many reasons to avoid inaccuracies in forming impressions of people, things, and events. Stereotyping, the halo effect, projection, and perceptual defense all operate in varying combinations to limit and distort the view of the decision maker. Several empirical studies were presented to illustrate the influence of perception on decision making.

Finally, the influences of the decision maker's preconscious and subconscious minds add to the psychological complex within which a choice is made. All these inner forces form the psychology of decision making. The process of choice is no less rational because of these phenomena. Still, decision making's imprecision must be apparent, even to the casual observer. To reiterate a continuing theme, the best that can be hoped for is a satisficing choice in the open decision model.

REVIEW AND DISCUSSION QUESTIONS

1. What are the major elements of Freud's theory of personality, and why has his theory been criticized so extensively?

2. The study of the influence of personality on decision making by Brim and his associates revealed some significant differences between male and female decision makers. What were these differences? Discuss.

3. What are the consequences likely to result from a continued suppression of feelings and emotions in the decision-making process? How can the decision maker limit the undesirable aspects of suppressed personality traits and forces?

4. What significant variables influence a given decision maker's tendency to accept or avoid risk in a choice situation? Discuss.

5. Use the theories, concepts, and studies presented in this chapter to evaluate this statement: Perception is, first of all, a selective process.

6. What are the significant characteristics of the perceiver and the perceived in the process of perception?

7. Discuss this statement: Perceivers often form impressions of others based on cues derived from partly valid attributes.

8. Why is perception important in the decision-making process, and how does it influence each part of that process?

9. Discuss this statement: A rational decision maker may make a rationalized decision, but it is unlikely that a nonrational decision will not be rationalized.

10. What can the decision maker do to cope with psychological forces operating below his or her level of awareness?

NOTES

1. See Charles R. Holloman, "Using Both Head and Heart in Managerial Decision Making," *Industrial Management* (November–December 1992), 7–10; and Herbert A. Simon, "Making Management Decisions: The Role of Intuition and Emotion," *Academy of Management Executive*, 1, No. 1 (February 1987), 57–64.

2. Charles L. Martin, "Feelings, Emotional Empathy, and Decision Making: Listening to the Voices of the Heart," *Journal of Management Development*, 12, No. 5 (1993), 43.

3. See Nigel Howard, "The Role of Emotions in Multi-Organizational Decision-Making," *Journal of the Operational Research Society*, 44, No. 6 (June 1993), 613–623; and Stephen A. Stumph and Roger L. M. Dunbar, "The Effects of Personality Type on Choices Made in Strategic Decision Situations," *Decision Sciences*, 22, No. 5 (November–December), 1991, 1047–1072.

4. Blair J. Kolasa, *Introduction to Behavioral Science for Business* (New York: Wiley, 1969), p. 243.

5. Joseph W. McGuire, *Theories of Business Behavior* (Englewood Cliffs, N.J.: Prentice-Hall, 1964), p. 195.

6. Gordon W. Allport, *Personality and Social Encounter* (Boston: Beacon Press, 1960), pp. 145–146.

7. Calvin S. Hall and Gardner Lindzey, *Theories of Personality*, 2nd ed. (New York: Wiley, 1970), p. 9.

8. McGuire, *Theories of Business Behavior*, p. 197.

9. Kolasa, *Behavioral Science for Business*, p. 243.

10. McGuire, *Theories of Business Behavior*, p. 197.

11. Ibid., p. 198.

12. See M. Kets de Vries and D. Miller, *The Neurotic Organization* (San Francisco: Jossey-Bass, 1984).

13. See the following references for a delineation of trait classifications: G. W. Allport and H. S. Odbert, "Trait Names: A Psychological Study," *Psychological Monographs*, 47, No. 211 (1936); G. W. Allport, *Personality: A Psychological Interpretation* (New York: Holt, Rinehart, 1937); and R. B. Cattell, *Personality: A Systematic, Theoretical and Factual Study* (New York: McGraw-Hill, 1950).

14. See M. Schoen, *Human Nature* (New York: Harper & Row, 1930).

15. John Gormly and Walter Edelberg, "Validity in Personality Trait Attribution," *American Psychologist*, 29 (March 1974), 189–193.

16. See Kenneth R. MacCrimmon and Donald A. Wehrung, *Taking Risks* (New York: Macmillan Co., 1986); and Zur Shapira, *Risk Taking: A Managerial Perspective* (New York: Sage, 1995).

17. Kenneth E. Boulding, *The Image* (Ann Arbor: University of Michigan Press, 1956).

18. Abraham H. Maslow, "A Theory of Human Motivation," *Psychological Review*, 50 (1943), 370–396.

19. Carl R. Rogers, *Client-Centered Therapy: Its Current Practice, Implications, and Theory* (Boston: Houghton Mifflin, 1951).

20. Kurt Lewin, *Field Theory in Social Science: Selected Theoretical Papers*, ed. D. Cartwright (New York: Harper & Row, 1951).

21. Maslow, "A Theory of Human Motivation."

22. Francis Heylighen, "A Cognitive-Systematic Reconstruction of Maslow's Theory of Self-Actualization," *Behavioral Science*, 37 (1992), 39–58.

23. A. H. Maslow, *Self-Actualizing People: A Study of Psychological Health* (New York: Grune & Stratton, 1950), pp. 156–174.

24. Lyman W. Porter and Edward E. Lawler III, *Managerial Attitudes and Performance* (Homewood, Ill.: Richard D. Irwin, 1968), p. 165.

25. M. Scott Meyers, "Conditions for Manager Motivation," *Harvard Business Review* (January–February 1966), 58–71.

26. I. D. Greig, "Basic Motivation and Decision Style in Organisation Management," *OMEGA, The International Journal of Management Science*, 12 (1984), 31–40.

27. Orville C. Brim, Jr., et al., *Personality and Decision Processes* (Stanford, Calif.: Stanford University Press, 1962), p. 46.

28. Ibid., p. 49.

29. Ibid., p. 103.

30. Ibid., pp. 122, 124.

31. Ibid., pp. 125–126.

32. Richard W. Pollay, "The Structure of Executive Decisions and Decision Times," *Administrative Science Quarterly*, 15 (December 1970), 459–471.

33. Ibid., pp. 469–470.

34. Chris Argyris, "Interpersonal Barriers to Decision Making," *Harvard Business Review* (March–April 1966), 86. Also see Chris Argyris, "Management Information Systems: The Challenge to

Rationality and Emotionality," *Management Science* (February 1971), B-275–B-292.

35. Ibid., p. 87.

36. See Holloman, "Using Both Head and Heart in Managerial Decision Making," pp. 57–64; and Martin, "Feelings, Emotional Empathy and Decision Making: Listening to the Voices of the Heart," pp. 33–45.

37. Howard K. Holland, "Decision Making and Personality," *Personnel Administration* (May–June 1968), 28.

38. Michael A. Wallach and Nathan Kogan, "Sex Differences and Judgment Processes," *Journal of Personality*, 27 (1959), 555–564.

39. Ronald N. Taylor and Marvin D. Dunnette, "Relative Contribution of Decision-Maker Attributes to Decision Processes," *Organizational Behavior and Human Performance*, 12 (October 1974), 286–298.

40. Stumph and Dunbar, "The Effects of Personality Type on Choices Made in Strategic Decision Situations."

41. Farzad Moussavi et al., "Explaining Strategic Managers' Choice of Decision Tools: Cognitive Style Representation Compatibility," *International Journal of Management*, 12, No. 3 (September 1995), 305–314.

42. See, for example, Gormly and Edelberg, "Validity in Personality Trait Attribution."

43. Sudhir Kakar, "Rationality and Irrationality in Business Leadership," *Journal of Business Policy*, 2 (Winter 1971–1972), 40–41.

44. Russell N. Cassel, *The Psychology of Decision Making* (North Quincy, Mass.: Christopher, 1973), pp. 79–80.

45. George B. Saunders and John L. Stanton, "Personality as Influencing Factor in Decision Making," *Organizational Behavior and Human Performance* (April 1976), 241–257.

46. Tanya Y. Arroba, "Decision-Making Style as a Function of Occupational Group, Decision Content, and Perceived Importance," *Journal of Occupational Psychology* (September 1978), 219–226.

47. Ronald N. Taylor, "Age and Experience as Determinants of Managerial Information Processing and Decision Making Performance," *Academy of Management Journal*, 18 (March 1975), 74–81.

48. John C. Henderson and Paul C. Nutt, "The Influence of Decision Style on Decision Making Behavior," *Management Science* (April 1980), 370–386.

49. Ibid., p. 384.

50. See, for example, Ole R. Holsti and Alexander L. George, "The Effects of Stress on the Performance of Foreign Policy Makers," in *Political Science Annual*, Vol. 6, ed. Cornelius P. Cotter (Indianapolis: Bobbs-Merrill, 1975), pp. 255–317; Irving L. Janis and Leon Mann, *Decision Making* (New York: Free Press, 1977); and Morris B. Holbrook and Michael J. Ryan, "Modeling Decision-Specific Stress: Some Methodological Considerations," *Administrative Science Quarterly*, 27 (1982), 243–258.

51. Joseph H. de Rivera, *The Psychological Dimension of Foreign Policy* (Columbus, Ohio: Merrill, 1968), p. 166.

52. Ibid., pp. 166–167.

53. Holland, "Decision Making and Personality," p. 29.

54. MacCrimmon and Wehrung, *Taking Risks*, p. 10.

55. Shapira, *Risk Taking: A Managerial Perspective*, p. 4.

56. Siegfried Streufer, "Individual Differences in Risk Taking," *Journal of Applied Social Psychology*, 16 (1986), 482–497.

57. Alvin Scodel, Philburn Ratoosh, and J. Sayer Minos, "Some Personality Correlates of Decision Making Under Conditions of Risk," *Behavioral Science* (January 1959), 26.

58. Ibid., p. 24.

59. Ibid., p. 27.

60. Henry Morlock, "The Effect of Outcome Desirability on Information Required for Decisions," *Behavioral Science* (July 1967), 296–300.

61. Dean G. Pruitt, "Informational Requirements in Making Decisions," *American Journal of Psychology*, 74 (1961), 433–439.

62. Joan E. Sieber and John T. Lanzetta, "Conflict and Conceptual Structure as Determinants of Decision Making Behavior," *Journal of Personality*, 32 (December 1964), 622–641.

63. Lawrence K. Williams, "Some Correlates of Risk Taking," *Personnel Psychology*, 18 (Autumn 1965), 297–309.

64. Clyde Hendrick, Judson Mills, and Charles A. Kiesler, "Decision Time as a Function of the Number and Complexity of Equally Attractive Alternatives," *Journal of Personality and Social Psychology*, 8 (1968), 317, 313–314.

65. Ronald N. Taylor and Marvin D. Dunnette, "Influence of Dogmatism, Risk-Taking Propensity,

and Intelligence on Decision-Making Strategies for a Sample of Industrial Managers," *Journal of Applied Psychology*, 59, No. 4 (1974), 420–423.

66. Paul Slovic, "Psychological Study of Human Judgment: Implications for Investment Decision Making," *Journal of Finance*, 27 (September 1972), 795.

67. J. W. Atkinson, "Motivational Determinants of Risk-Taking Behavior," *Psychological Review*, 64 (1957), 359–372.

68. See, for example, J. Ogden Hamilton, "Motivation and Risk Taking Behavior: A Test of Atkinson's Theory," *Journal of Personality and Social Psychology*, 29, No. 6 (1974), 856–864; Malcolm S. Weinstein, "Achievement Motivation and Risk Preference," *Journal of Personality and Social Psychology*, 13 (October 1969), 153–172; and John G. Hancock and Richard C. Teevan, "Fear of Failure and Risk-Taking Behavior," *Journal of Personality*, 32 (June 1964), 200–209.

69. Edward E. Jones and C. Anderson Johnson, "Delay of Consequences and the Riskiness of Decisions," *Journal of Personality*, 41 (December 1973), 613–637.

70. Douglas N. Jackson, Larry Hourany, and Neil J. Vidmar, "A Four-Dimensional Interpretation of Risk Taking," *Journal of Personality* (September 1972), 483–501.

71. J. C. Brengelmann, "Abnormal and Personality Correlates of Certainty," *Journal of Mental Sciences*, 105 (1959), 142–162.

72. Larry L. Cummings and Donald L. Harnett, "The Influence of Risk-Taking Propensity and Information Conditions on Bargaining Behavior," in *Papers and Proceedings of the 26th Annual Meeting of the Academy of Management* (San Francisco, 1966), 137–143.

73. Claus C. Berg, "Individual Decisions Concerning the Allocation of Resources for Projects with Uncertain Consequences," *Management Science*, 21 (September 1974), 98–105.

74. Michael A. Wallach and Nathan Kogan, "Aspects of Judgment and Decision Making: Interrelationships and Changes with Age," *Behavioral Science*, 6 (1961), 23–36.

75. Julius S. Brown, "Risk Propensity in Decision Making: A Comparison of Business and Public School Administrators," *Administrative Science Quarterly*, 15 (December 1970), 473–481.

76. Alice M. Isen, "Some Factors Influencing Decision-Making Strategy and Risk Taking," in *Affect and Cognition*, The Seventeenth Annual Carnegie Symposium on Cognition, ed. Margaret Syndor Clarke and Susan F. Fiske (Hillsdale, N.J.: Lawrence Erlbaum Associates, 1982), pp. 243–261.

77. N. S. Fagley and Paul M. Miller, "The Effects of Decision Framing on Choice of Risky vs. Certain Options," *Organizational Behavior and Human Decision Processes*, 39 (1987), 264–277.

78. See MacCrimmon and Wehrung, *Taking Risks*, pp. 34–36, for a discussion of the characteristics of risk accepters and risk avoiders.

79. See George Wright, ed., "Decisional Variance," in *Behavioral Decision Making* (New York: Plenum Press, 1985), pp. 43–59.

80. Lola L. Lopes, "Between Hope and Fear: The Psychology of Risk," *Advances in Experimental Social Psychology*, 20 (1987) 275 and 277.

81. See Daniel Kahneman and Dan Lovallo, "Timid Choices and Bold Forecasts: A Cognitive Perspective on Risk Taking," *Management Science*, 39, No. 1 (January 1993), 17–31; and J. Edward Russo and Paul J. H. Shoemaker, Managing Overconfidence," *Sloan Management Review*, 33, No. 2 (Winter 1992), 7–17.

82. Joseph A. Litterer, *The Analysis of Organizations* (New York: Wiley, 1965), pp. 62–63.

83. Ronald J. Ebert and Terence R. Mitchell, *Organizational Decision Processes* (New York: Crane, Russak, 1975), p. 76.

84. Ibid.

85. Kolasa, *Behavioral Science for Business*, p. 212.

86. See Alan J. Rowe and James D. Boulgarides, *Managerial Decision Making* (New York: Macmillan Co., 1992), pp. 63–73.

87. Litterer, *The Analysis of Organizations*, pp. 63–64.

88. John R. Bergen, "The Structure of Perception," *Journal of the Association for the Study of Perception* (Spring 1969), 1, 2–4.

89. Kolasa, *Behavioral Science for Business*, p. 213.

90. See, for example, Lewis R. Goldberg, "Man Versus Model of Man: A Rationale, Plus Some Evidence, for a Method of Improving on Clinical Inferences," *Psychological Bulletin*, 73, No. 6 (1970), 422–432.

91. See, for example, George S. Day, "Evaluating Models of Attitude Structure," *Journal of Marketing*

Research (August 1972), 279–286; and Paul E. Green, "Stimulus Context and Task Effects on Individuals' Similarity Judgments," in *Attitude Research Reaches New Heights*, ed. C. W. King and D. Tigert (Chicago: American Marketing Association, 1971), pp. 263–299.

92. See, for example, J. R. Brent Ritchie, "An Exploratory Analysis of the Nature and Extent of Individual Differences in Perception," *Journal of Marketing Research*, 11 (February 1974), 41–49; and M. Sherif and C. I. Hovland, *Social Judgment* (New Haven: Yale University Press, 1961).

93. See Sanford M. Dornbush et al., "The Perceiver and the Perceived: Their Relative Influence on the Categories of Interpersonal Cognition," *Journal of Personality and Social Psychology*, 1, No. 5 (1965), 434–440.

94. Sheldon S. Zalkind and Timothy W. Costello, "Perception: Some Recent Research and Implications for Administration," *Administrative Science Quarterly* (September 1962), 219–220.

95. Ibid., pp. 227–229.

96. Ibid., p 230.

97. See Samuel Fillenbaum, "Some Stylistic Aspects of Categorizing Behavior," *Journal of Personality*, 27 (1959), 187–195.

98. Robert E. Carlson, "Selection Interview Decisions: The Relative Influence of Appearance and Factual Written Information on an Interviewee's Final Rating," *Journal of Applied Psychology*, 51 (December 1967), 461–468.

99. Ibid., p. 222.

100. Kolasa, *Behavioral Science for Business*, p. 396.

101. Zalkind and Costello, "Perception," p. 227.

102. Jerome S. Bruner, Jacqueline J. Goodnow, and George A. Austin, *A Study of Thinking* (New York: Wiley, 1956), p. 204.

103. Ibid., p. 9.

104. Ibid., p. 182.

105. Ibid., p. 184.

106. Ibid., p. 195.

107. See, for example, Robert H. Ashton, "Cue Utilization and Expert Judgments: A Comparison of Independent Auditors with Other Judges," *Journal of Applied Psychology*, 59 (August 1974), 437–444; N. John Castellan, Jr., "Multiple-Cue Probability Learning with Irrelevant Cues," *Organizational Behavior and Human Performance*, 9 (February 1973),

16–29; and Hillel J. Einhorn, "Cue Definition and Residual Judgment," *Organizational Behavior and Human Performance*, 12 (August 1974), 30–49.

108. Bruner et al., *A Study of Thinking*, pp. 195–205.

109. See Sharon G. Watson, "Judgment of Emotion from Facial and Contextual Cue Combinations," *Journal of Personality and Social Psychology*, 24 (December 1972), 334–342.

110. Mason Haire, "Role-Perception in Labor-Management Relations: An Experimental Approach," in *Psychology in Administration*, ed. Timothy W. Costello and Sheldon S. Zalkind (Englewood Cliffs, N.J.: Prentice-Hall, 1963), pp. 25–33.

111. Mason Haire and Willa Freeman Grunes, "Perceptual Defenses: Processes Protecting an Organized Perception of Another Personality," in *Psychology in Administration*, ed. Timothy W. Costello and Sheldon S. Zalkind (Englewood Cliffs, N.J.: Prentice-Hall, 1963), pp. 37–44.

112. Also see Colin Camerer, "Illusory Correlations in Perceptions and Predictions of Organizational Traits," *Journal of Behavioral Decision Making*, 1 (1988), 77–94.

113. Haire and Grunes, "Perceptual Defenses," pp. 34–35.

114. Richard E. Nisbett and Timothy D. Wilson, "The Halo Effect: Evidence for Unconscious Alteration of Judgments," *Journal of Personality and Social Psychology*, 35 (1977), 250–256.

115. Zalkind and Costello, "Perception," p. 224.

116. Costello and Zalkind, *Psychology in Administration*, p. 36.

117. Haire and Grunes, "Perceptual Defenses," pp. 37–44.

118. Marcus Alexis and Charles Z. Wilson, eds., *Organizational Decision Making* (Englewood Cliffs, N.J.: Prentice-Hall, 1967), p. 69.

119. See DeWitt C. Dearborn and Herbert A. Simon, "Selective Perception: A Note on the Departmental Identifications of Executives," in *Psychology in Administration*, ed. Timothy W. Costello and Sheldon S. Zalkind (Englewood Cliffs, N.J.: Prentice-Hall, 1963), pp. 49–52.

120. Alexis and Wilson, *Organizational Decision Making*, p. 70.

121. Baruch Fischhoff, "Hindsight Foresight: The Effect of Outcome Knowledge on Judgment Under

Uncertainty," *Journal of Experimental Psychology*, 1 (August 1975), 288–299.

122. Ibid., p. 297.

123. David L. Hamilton and Leroy J. Huffman, "Generality of Impression — Formation Processes for Evaluative and Nonevaluative Judgments," *Journal of Personality and Social Psychology*, 20 (November 1971), 200–207.

124. Jacob Jacoby, "Interpersonal Perceptual Accuracy as a Function of Dogmatism," *Journal of Experimental Social Psychology*, 7 (March 1971), 221–236.

125. See, for example, John H. Harvey, "Determinants of the Perception of Choice," *Journal of Experimental Social Psychology*, 9 (March 1973), 164–179; and Jerald M. Jellison and John H. Harvey, "Determinants of Perceived Choice and the Relationship between Perceived Choice and Perceived Competence," *Journal of Personality and Social Psychology*, 28 (December 1973), 376–382.

126. See, for example, Einhorn, "Cue Definitions and Residual Judgment," and Watson, "Judgment of Emotion from Facial and Contextual Cue Combinations."

127. See Moussavi et al., "Explaining Strategic Managers' Choices of Decision Tools: Cognitive Style–Representation Compatibility."

128. Robert A. Dahl and Charles E. Lindblom, *Politics, Economics and Welfare* (New York: Harper & Row, 1953), p. 60.

129. Ulric Neisser, "The Multiplicity of Thought," *British Journal of Psychology* (February 1963), 4.

130. Irving L. Janis and Leo Mann, *Decision Making: A Psychological Analysis of Conflict, Choice, and Commitment* (New York: Free Press, 1977), p. 95.

131. McGuire, *Theories of Business Behavior*, p. 197.

132. Robert C. Ferber, "The Role of the Subconscious in Executive Decision-Making," *Management Science* (April 1967), B-520.

133. Ibid.

134. See Robert C. Ferber, "The Dark Side of Decision Making," *Management Review* (March 1971), 4–13.

135. See, for example, Paul J. H. Schoemaker and J. Edward Russo, "A Pyramid of Decision Approaches," *California Management Review* (Fall 1993), 9–31.

136. Neisser, "The Multiplicity of Thought," p. 3.

137. R. F. C. Hull, trans., *Psychological Types*, by C. G. Jung (Princeton, N.J.: Princeton University Press, 1971).

138. Neisser, "The Multiplicity of Thought," p. 3.

139. See, for example, Ralph H. Kilmann and Ian I. Mitroff, "Qualitative Versus Quantitative Analysis for Management Science: Different Forms for Different Psychological Types," *Interfaces* (February 1976), 17–27; and Don Hellriegel and John W. Slocum, Jr., "Managerial Problem-Solving Styles," *Business Horizons* (December 1975), 29–37.

140. See Richard E. Nisbett and Timothy D. Wilson, "Telling More Than We Can Know: Verbal Reports on Mental Processes," *Psychological Review* (May 1977), 231–259.

141. W. Agor, *Intuitive Management* (Englewood Cliffs, N.J.: Prentice-Hall, 1984); and Ian I. Mitroff and Ralph H. Kilmann, "On Evaluating Scientific Research: The Contribution of the Psychology of Science," *Technological Forecasting and Social Science*, 8 (1975), 163–174.

142. Ruth P. Mack, *Planning on Uncertainty* (New York: Wiley-Interscience, 1971), p. 62.

143. Ibid., pp. 62–63.

SUPPLEMENTAL REFERENCES

Beach, Lee Roy. "Decision Emergence: A Lewinian Perspective." *Acta Psychologica*, 45 (1980), 343–356.

Broadbent, D. E. "Aspects of Human Decision Making." *Advancement of Science*, 24 (September 1967), 53–64.

Bruner, Jerome. "The 'New Look' in Perception." In *Psychology in Administration.* Ed. Timothy W. Costello and Sheldon S. Zalkind. Englewood Cliffs, N.J.: Prentice-Hall, 1963, pp. 7–14.

Clark, R. D., III, and E. P. Willems. "Risk Preference as Related to Judged Consequences of Failure." *Psychological Reports*, 25 (1969), 827–830.

Cosier, Richard A., and John C. Aplin. "Intuition and Decision Making: Some Empirical Evidence." *Psychological Reports*, 51 (1982), 275–281.

Davis, Harry L., and E. K. Easton Ragsdale. *Limitations and Biases in Perceiving Others.* Chicago: Center for Decision Research, Graduate School of Business, University of Chicago, September 1983.

Einhorn, Hillel J., and Robin Hogarth. "Behavioral Decision Theory: Processes of Judgment and Choice." *Annual Review of Psychology*, 32 (1981), 53–88.

Frei, M. D. "Administrative and Socio-Psychological Constraints of the Business Decision-Making Process." *Management International Review*, 11, Nos. 2–3 (1971), 67–81.

Freud, Sigmund. *Civilization and Its Discontents.* New York: Norton, 1961.

Harvey, John H., and Shawn Johnston. "Determinants of Perceived Choice." *Journal of Experimental Social Psychology* (March 1973), 164–179.

Hill, Percy H., et al. *Making Decisions: A Multidisciplinary Introduction.* Reading, Mass.: Addison-Wesley, 1978.

Hogarth, Robin M. *Judgement and Choice.* New York: Wiley, 1980.

Kirkpatrick, Samuel A. "Psychological Views of Decision-Making." In *Political Science Annual.* Vol. 6. Ed. Cornelius P. Cotter. Indianapolis: Bobbs-Merrill, 1975, pp. 39–112.

Libby, Robert, and Peter C. Fishburn. "Behavioral Models of Risk Taking in Business Decisions: A Survey and Evaluation." *Journal of Accounting Research* (Autumn 1977), 272–291.

Linstone, Harold A. *Multiple Perspectives for Decision Making.* New York: North-Holland, 1984.

March, James G. *Decisions and Organizations.* New York: Blackwell, 1988.

MacCrimmon, Kenneth R., and Donald A. Wehrung. *Taking Risks.* New York: Free Press, 1986.

McKinney, John Paul. "The Development of Values: A Perceptual Interpretation." *Journal of Personality and Social Psychology*, 31 (1975), 801–807.

Mihalasky, John. "ESP in Decision Making." *Management Review* (April 1975), 32–37.

Nutt, Paul C. *Making Tough Decisions.* San Francisco: Jossey-Bass, 1989.

Nystrom, Harry. "Uncertainty, Information and Organizational Decision Making: A Cognitive Approach." *Swedish Journal of Economics*, 76 (March 1974), 131–139.

Parsons, J. A. "Decision Making Under Risk." *Journal of Systems Management* (July 1972), 42–43.

Rim, Y. "Risk-Taking and Need for Achievement." *Acta Psychologica*, 21 (1963), 108–115.

Saunders, George B., and John L. Stanton. "Personality as Influencing Factor in Decision Making." *Organizational Behavior and Human Performance* (April 1976), 241–257.

Shapira, Zir, ed. *Organizational Decision Making.* New York: Cambridge University Press, 1997.

Shubik, Martin. "Note on Decision Making and Replacing Sure Prospects with Uncertain Prospects." *Management Science* (February 1973), 711–712.

Siegel, Sheldon. "Level of Aspiration and Decision Making." *Psychological Review*, 64 (1957), 253–262.

Singer, Jerome L., and Dorothy G. Singer. "Personality." In *Annual Review of Psychology.* Ed. Paul H. Mussen and Mark R. Rosenzweig. Palo Alto, Calif.: Annual Reviews, 1972, pp. 375–412.

Sjoberg, Lennart. "Volitional Problems in Carrying Through a Difficult Decision." *Acta Psychologica*, 45 (1980), 123–132.

Sjoberg, Lennart, Tadeusz Tyszka, and James A. Wise, eds. *Human Decision Making.* Bodafors, Sweden: Bokforlaget Doxa, 1983.

Slovic, Paul. "Cue-Consistency and Cue-Utilization in Judgment." *American Journal of Psychology* (September 1966), 427–434.

Staw, Barry M., and Jerry Ross. "Commitment to a Policy Decision: A Multi-Theoretical Perspective." *Administrative Science Quarterly* (March 1978), 40–64.

Sutherland, Stuart. *Irrationality: Why We Don't Think Straight.* New Brunswick, N.J.: Rutgers University Press, 1992.

Taggart, William, Daniel Robey, and K. Galen Kroeck. "Managerial Decision Styles and Cerebral Dominance: An Empirical Study." *Journal of Management Studies* (March 1985), 175–192.

Taylor, Ronald N. "Perception of Problem Constraints." *Management Science*, 22 (September 1975), 22–29.

Tversky, Amos, and Daniel Kahneman. "The Framing of Decisions and the Psychology of Choice." *Science*, 211 (1981), 453–458.

Ulek, Charles, and Pieter-Jan Stallen. "Rational and Personal Aspects of Risk." *Acta Psychologica*, 45 (1980), 273–300.

Ungson, Gerardo R., and Daniel N. Braunstein, eds. *Decision Making: An Interdisciplinary Inquiry.* Boston: Kent, 1982.

Zey, Mary, ed. *Decision Making.* Newbury Park, Calif.: Sage, 1992.

The Sociology of Decision Making

*D*ecision making in organizations of all types takes place as a matter of course in groups such as teams, task forces, and committees. In fact, in most organizations of any size at all it is rather unusual to find decisions made regularly by one individual. This is especially true for category II decisions, which are nonroutine, nonrecurring, and uncertain of outcome.

There are various reasons group decision making prevails in formal organizations. For one thing, the increasing complexity of the managerial process, which requires more specialized knowledge than one individual usually possesses, calls for a collective approach to decision making. Further, once made and implemented, a choice has to be accepted by those directly and indirectly affected by it. This acceptance requires group participation throughout the decision-making process.

To reach a consensus, groups must foster open communication among members. In this process of interaction different personalities and viewpoints must somehow blend to produce a choice agreeable to all. This is the difference between a unilateral decision and one based on the collective judgment and consent of those who must transform the choice into an operational reality.

The theories and concepts set forth in this chapter apply to any assemblage that meets the defining characteristics of a group. Several people who interact in proximity in quest of a consensus regarding a common interest constitute a group. It is common in much of the current management literature to designate collective action or consensual decision making under the rubric of "teamwork." For purposes of this book, with its primary focus on managerial decision making in formal organizations, teams and committees are groups and are included in the vast literature on group decision making which, hopefully, is augmented by the content of this chapter.

Before we focus directly on group decision making, we should examine the anatomy of a group. Important subjects include (1) the profile of a group, (2) major theories of group behavior, (3) group norms and conformity, (4) group structure, (5) group communication, and (6) the characteristics of effective groups. Understanding these key subjects will help us illuminate the variables involved in arriving at a meeting of the minds within a decision-making group.

PROFILE OF A GROUP

George Homans advanced a general definition of a group in the following excerpt:

> We mean by a group a number of persons who communicate with one another often over a span of time, and who are few enough so that each person is able to communicate with all the others, not at secondhand, through other people, but face-to-face.[1]

Kast and Rosenzweig defined a group in essentially the same way: it is an "assemblage, cluster or aggregation of persons considered as being related in some way or united by common ties or interests — class, race, or occupation, for example."[2] Lawless stated that "a group (sometimes called a psychological group) consists of two or more persons interacting. This interaction requires that the behavior of each member influences the behavior of each other member and that the members share some common perceptions, beliefs, values, and objectives."[3]

Rather than relying on definitions to supply the profile of a group, we may find it more meaningful to describe a group in terms of its essential characteristics. Perhaps the most important characteristic of any group is **interpersonal consensus.** Essential to a group's effective functioning, it refers to agreement or harmony among the members with regard to the issue or objective at hand. Interpersonal consensus results from the second essential characteristic of a group, **interaction** among the members. In turn, interaction is facilitated by **communication** among the members, a group's third characteristic. All these characteristics presuppose a **common interest** among the members, which is the fourth essential characteristic of a group. The fifth and last is **proximity,** or nearness in place or location. The absence of any universal agreement regarding appropriate size keeps it from being an essential characteristic of a group. A small group is usually regarded as seven persons or less; large groups may have as many as twenty-five members.[4]

In addition to possessing these characteristics, groups develop norms or informal rules that guide the behavior of members. Further, when a group exists for any length of time, a structure develops that tends to place the members in different roles. The continued life of a group usually results, also, in the members developing attractions for other group members, for the group itself, and for the things for which it stands.[5]

In summary, then, the profile of a group shows a number of individuals who come together. Through close interaction and openness of communication they seek interpersonal consensus. And they assume membership roles, subject to informal rules and guidelines for acceptable conduct, that will ensure the attainment of the group's common purpose.

THEORIES OF GROUP BEHAVIOR

There are many theories of group behavior, each with its own particular emphasis. Some of these theories are especially important because, by virtue of their individual orientations, they open up new insight and understanding about the variables that characterize collective behavior. Such theories show the need to evaluate these variables properly if the group is to serve the common interest that gave rise to its formation.

Homans's system theory offers a solid foundation upon which to understand group behavior. **Activity, interaction,** and **sentiment** — the elementary forms of behavior — are the three basic concepts of his theory. Activities are basically the things people do with human or nonhuman objects, such as working, reading, writing, driving a car, and the like. Interaction is a special kind of activity directed toward another person and taking the other person's reaction or reciprocal behavior into account. Sentiments, of course, refer to feelings, attitudes, or beliefs. Homans made the point that these three concepts are so dynamically interrelated that a change in one will lead to a change in the others. For example, if the individual's activities change, the individual's pattern of interaction will also change. Or a change in sentiment may influence an individual's interaction by modifying his or her pattern of activities. Homans thought of a group as the basic unit in a social system characterized by the relationships shown in the activities, interactions, and sentiments of the group members. In other words, the behavior of members of a group must be considered as a *system* of behavior, not as separate actions unrelated to each other.[6]

Blau set forth a theory of social integration in which he sought to explain why and how individuals become accepted as members of groups. Acceptance in a group, according to Blau, depends on both **attractiveness** and **approachability.** A prospective new member must first impress the group with good personal qualities and then demonstrate personal approachability with well-chosen modesty. If the prospective new member shows weakness in things valued highly by the group, he or she will be perceived as unattractive. However, the prospective new member must guard against appearing too attractive or the group may view the prospect as unapproachable and a threat to the established relations among the members, in which case the prospect would not be accepted.[7]

Kelman developed a theory to describe how a group exerts social influence on the individual members.[8] He found three processes of influence that operate in group relations:

1. **Compliance,** in which people, to obtain favorable reaction from other persons, adopt attitudes or opinions the other persons want them to adopt.

2. **Identification,** in which individuals adopt attitudes or opinions of other persons because they identify with the other persons, take over their roles, and incorporate them in their self-image.

3. **Internalization,** in which people adopt attitudes or opinions of other persons because the attitudes or opinions agree with their perspectives or solve a problem for them.[9]

These three processes of influence operate in somewhat different ways. For example, compliance may be the kind of influence peers exert on each other. Identification may be the type of influence that authority figures exert over their admirers or supporters. Internalization may be the kind of influence that doctors exert over their patients or teachers over their students. Any of these processes may operate with varying intensity in a group.

Lewin's theory of **group dynamics** (frequently called **field theory**) is often used to explain and analyze group behavior.[10] Group dynamics assumes that

> a group has life space, it occupies a position relative to other objects in this life space; it is oriented toward goals; it locomotes in pursuit of these goals; and it may encounter barriers in the process of locomotion.[11]

In approaching the analysis of group behavior, the field theorist is essentially concerned with cohesion, the forces that bind members of a group to each other and to the group as a whole. These forces include:

1. The satisfaction that members obtain from being in a group

2. The degree of closeness and warmth the members of a group feel for each other

3. The pride felt by the members as a result of their membership in a group

4. The ability of the members to meet emergencies and crises that confront them as a group

5. The willingness of the members of a group to be frank and honest in their expression of ideas and feelings[12]

In the context of group dynamics, cohesion is directly related to the ability of a group to attain a level of interpersonal consensus that satisfies the members and their common interest. One indicator of cohesion is how a group arrives at a decision. For example, if cohesion is low, the members will probably make a decision by majority vote or by following the group leader. If cohesion is high, the decision will probably reflect the unanimous approval of the members, even though one or two of them may have some slight reservations about the outcome.

Where Lewin's group dynamics sheds useful light on group analysis, Bale's scheme of interaction-process analysis is a valuable tool for analyzing group behavior.[13] Bale's analytical scheme considers four main problems that confront a group:

1. *Adaptation* to factors outside the group that influence the group, such as the need to cooperate with another group or to consider the objectives of the larger organization of which the group is a part

2. *Instrumental control* over those things in the group that are relevant to performing its tasks, such as dividing the work or making decisions

3. The *expression and management of feelings* of the members, such as showing pleasure or dissatisfaction and relieving personal or interpersonal tensions

4. The *development and maintenance of integration* of the members with each other and of the group as a whole[14]

> The problems of adaptation and instrumental control are handled primarily by the expression of questions and answers. . . . The problems of the expression and management of feelings and the development and maintenance of integration are dealt with largely by the expression of positive and negative reactions.[15]

Within questions, most acts request information or opinions; within answers, most acts express opinions or information; within positive reactions, most acts express agreement or tension release; and within negative reactions, most acts express disagreement.

Analysis of the distribution of facts over time shows that the typical group emphasizes problems of orientation (facts and information) in the early phase of a meeting, problems of evaluation (opinions) in the middle phase, and problems of control and decisions (suggestions) in the final phase. In satisfied groups there are about twice as many suggestions and fewer requests for orientation than in dissatisfied groups. In terms of positive and negative reactions, dissatisfied groups have about three times as much disagreement and only about one-third as much agreement as satisfied groups.[16] Interaction-process analysis permits meaningful comparisons of satisfied and dissatisfied groups.[17] It also makes it easier to profile all groups. Such profiles help show the kind of balance among types of communicative acts that characterizes successful problem-solving groups. In this way, interaction-process analysis supplies a criterion for locating and avoiding trouble in group behavior.

Building on Lewin's theory of group dynamics, Jackson developed a two-dimensional theory to describe and analyze the basis of group membership. According to his theory, membership may be based on **attraction,** which is the force that leads an individual to join and remain in a group; or it may be based on **acceptance,** defined as the degree to which an individual's ability and behavior will fit the roles *defined* in a group. A member who has both positive attraction and acceptance is said to have **psychological membership** in a group. A member who has a positive attraction and close to no acceptance has a **preferential membership.** A member who has positive acceptance and little or no attraction to membership has a **marginal membership.** Finally, a member who has both negative attraction and negative acceptance has an **alienative membership.**[18] Like the other theories, Jackson's two-dimensional system offers a valuable analytical tool for gaining insight into the many variables that characterize group behavior.[19]

GROUP NORMS AND CONFORMITY

According to Homans, a norm is an idea in the minds of a group's members that can be stated to specify what the members are expected to do under given circumstances. The members' social standing in the group depends largely upon their compliance with established norms. Nonconformity is punished, and conformity is rewarded.[20] Homans set forth several hypotheses regarding the concept of norms in group behavior:

1. The higher a person's rank in the group, the more closely that person conforms to the norms of the group.

2. The higher a person's rank in the group, the more leeway that person has in conforming to the norms (the more likely nonconformity will be overlooked or will be interpreted as being in the interests of the group rather than a threat to the group).

3. The members of the group are pressed to maintain their established degree of conformity to the norms (and not to increase their conformity, since this might upset the hierarchy of rank).[21]

A norm is an agreement or consensus of group members concerning how individuals in the group should or should not behave. Norms are supported by group processes that ensure that actual behavior matches desired behavior.[22] Once norms are established, norm-sending encourages their observance. **Norm-sending** lets the members know what the group considers to be acceptable behavior. Norm-sending has three principal elements:

1. The definition of correct attitudes and fitting behavior (defining and agreeing upon perceptions and action in a particular situation).

2. Monitoring the degree of conformity to the norm (usually accomplished by observations of group members).

3. Application of sanctions (either reward or punishment applied for conformity or nonconformity).[23]

Once the norms have been sent, there are at least three social processes that aid in securing compliance with them: enforcement, internalization, and group pressure.[24]

The enforcement of group norms, in turn, consists of four principal elements: education, surveillance, warning, and disciplinary or rewarding actions. Education brings to the attention of the new member the important norms of the group. Surveillance usually takes the form of observations made by established group members. When a deviation is detected, group members increase interaction with the deviate, warning the person to comply with the norms. If the deviate does not heed the warning, the group may impose disciplinary action such as razzing, heckling, isolation, or outright expulsion.[25]

Norms set by a group may become personal standards of conduct that the member feels are right. In this case, the member is said to have internalized the group norms. The member acts in accordance with what he or she believes to be proper, rather than to earn rewards or avoid punishment.

Real or imagined social pressures are another means of enforcing group norms.[26] There are three principal elements that determine the influence of such pressures on the individual member: the existence of allies, the setting for the group pressure, and the personality of the member.[27]

Studies have shown the value of having a partner or ally when holding nonconforming opinions or beliefs as a member of a group.[28] In other words, when one member finds his or her beliefs, attitudes, or perceptions shared and supported by another member, both acquire psychological strength to withstand the pressure resulting from being different from the majority of the group. It is one thing to be a part of a group minority and quite another to stand alone against a strong majority.

The effect of group pressure also depends on the setting. Generally, the more ambiguous the situation, the more likely individuals are to question their own judgment and perhaps even to alter their perceptions. Conversely, in more concrete situations, individuals are not likely to change their perceptions or beliefs about the correctness of their position.[29]

Some individuals find it easier to conform than do others; the differences in such cases may stem largely from personality. One can pick out two basic personality types in group behavior: the independent individual who states an opinion or takes a position even though it may be different from the majority view, and the submissive individual who simply goes along with the majority opinion. Several studies have revealed some interesting personality traits for each of these types.[30]

Individuals with independent personalities often show the following characteristics in group behavior:

1. They may be quite confident that their perceptions are correct. Even though they know they are different from the group, they may still persist firmly in their opinions.

2. They often tend to be withdrawn from the group. They may be conspicuous for rigidly adhering to the principles of individuality, rather than vigorously claiming the accuracy of their perceptions.

3. They may feel a lot of tension and uncertainty about the differences in their perceptions, but still stick to their opinions because they honestly believe them necessary to get the job done.

Submissive individuals, on the other hand, are prone to display a somewhat different behavioral pattern in a group:

1. They may actually distort their perceptions and see the majority choices as the correct ones.

2. They may doubt the validity of their perceptions and demonstrate a lack of confidence in their own judgment.

3. They may perceive the situation quite accurately, but still go along with the majority because it is too uncomfortable to be different.[31]

Other personal attributes of the individual influence susceptibility to group pressure to conform. For example, research shows that older members of a group are less likely to conform than younger members. Women are more likely to conform, as are those with lesser intellectual ability. College graduates are less prone to conform than individuals with lower levels of education.[32]

Some people get a certain satisfaction from conforming to group norms not only because it helps to achieve goals but also because normative behavior satisfies certain of their personality needs. People with a strong need for affiliation, for example, enjoy normative behavior in friendly, cooperative groups. On the other hand, people with strong feelings of hostility may find that they can express this hostility by deviating. It is easy to see, therefore, that personality differences are largely responsible for different attitudes toward normative behavior in groups.[33]

Someone trying to change the norms of a group should keep in mind several important variables. First, norms are established mainly to control behavior so that the group can accomplish its tasks and achieve its goals. Second, the group rejects deviations from norms mainly because they threaten to interfere with the satisfaction of the members' needs and the group's ability to meet its goals. Finally, a change in norms that seems likely to help satisfy needs and achieve goals better will usually be accepted if properly introduced to the group, preferably by a member with high social status or personal influence.[34]

GROUP STRUCTURE

Another way to analyze group behavior is through a system of classifying groups on the basis of their structural variations. Of course, structure stems from the basic purpose of the group. An analysis of group structure shows the results expected from the group's composition and size as well as the reasons for the relationships among the members.

Classification of Groups

Groups that have been established under legal and formal authority to achieve specific goals or to undertake specific tasks are called **formal groups.** These groups have a visible structure and in that sense are organized with defined assignments of duties and relationships among the members. "Formal groups are those set up with relatively clear and official roles for members, rules for interaction, and goals for achievement. They reflect the psychological and administrative assumptions of those who designed them."[35]

In addition to following formal patterns of interaction, individuals usually form relationships that are not formally specified. These relationships soon crystallize into **informal groups.** Such groups may spring from simple physical factors such as location, or they may arise to fulfill the specific needs of a given set of individuals. Often, informal groups develop in a setting where a formal group already exists. In such cases, they result from the face-to-face contact and owe their existence only to the ongoing interaction among the individuals, rather than to the attention of someone with the ability to control.[36] Basically, informal groups are "those unplanned sets of subgroups, friendship relations, and other informal relationships which inevitably develop when a number of people are placed in necessary contact with one another."[37]

It is also useful to differentiate between **membership groups** and **reference groups.** A membership group is one in which a person actually belongs and has some duties and responsibilities. A reference group is one that a person identifies with or would like to belong to. In a reference group, the person's participation is vicarious rather than actual.

The term **primary groups** refers to individuals in a close, face-to-face relationship for a fairly long time. The sociology of decision making in this book focuses directly on the primary group. The importance of the primary group is that it fosters the development of a set of interpersonal relationships among the members. It is this set of interpersonal relationships that must be analyzed to gain a better understanding of group membership.[38]

Secondary groups are those in which the relationships are more general and remote. A secondary group combines individuals with common ties but without regular or direct interaction with other members in the group.[39] Secondary groups are not of much interest here; they are mentioned only in contrast with primary groups.

The principal focus in this book is on a special type of primary group that has the particular formal task of decision making.

> Decision-making groups comprise the bulk of all groups in most human organizations. Groups decide what new products will be manufactured, how they are to be designed, advertised, and sold. Groups decide which laws will serve to govern a society, how those laws will be enforced, how they are to be interpreted. . . . Our entire society functions through the organizations which comprise it. And each organization functions through decisions made by groups within that organization.[40]

In the current literature dealing with group decision making, it is common to see references to **teamwork** in ways that suggest that a team is somehow different from a group. For example, Rowe and Boulgarides state that "teams share a common goal and help to focus energy by emphasizing self-control on the part of the participants."[41] Presumably teams are collections of individuals who operate under inspired leadership to achieve highly positive outcomes.[42] However, these are essentially the same factors that characterize effective groups. Actually there is no significant difference between a group and a team. A team may be represented as something special in terms of its stated purpose or its distinctive performance. Nonetheless, a team is still simply a type of group and is, therefore, at least in this book, integral to the full range of theories and concepts dealing with group decision making.

Relationships Within the Group

Scott developed a meaningful analysis of group structure based on a technique called **sociometry.**[43] Sociometry identifies and measures relationships within groups.[44] According to Scott, a given group can be divided into three subsets. The first is the **primary set,** which is the group's focal point. The members of this subset establish and maintain the norms of the group; they are the prime movers for the group's efforts. The second subset is called the **fringe status.** The members of this subset support the members of the primary set but seldom, if ever, act on their own. They do not contribute firsthand to the group's output. The third subset is called **outstatus.** These individuals are isolated and are members of the group in name only. Individuals may acquire outstatus if they are persistently nonconforming or if the primary set feels their contribution may be against the best interests of the group. In terms of Jackson's two-dimensional system of group membership, the members of the primary set have a psychological membership in the group; the people with fringe status have a preferential or marginal membership; the people with outstatus hold an alienative membership.[45]

Group Size

Group size is probably the most significant element of group structure. Much of the literature on group behavior concerns the impact of size on the interactions and satisfaction of the members and on the ability of the group to achieve a lasting and meaningful consensus.

Several studies have found less satisfaction among members of larger groups than of smaller ones. It is easier to achieve consensus in small groups (five to seven persons) than in large ones (twelve to fifteen persons). Also, it is easier for all members to participate in smaller groups, and as group size increases the contribution of the less active members falls off noticeably.[46] This last phenomenon suggests that large groups harbor more unproductive members than small groups.[47]

Other things being equal, greater size means less group cohesiveness. One study of several thousand individuals in industry, for example, found that, as a rule, the cohesiveness of the group declined as its size increased, up to about twenty-five members.[48] One explanation for this is that as the size of the total group increases, subgroups tend to develop that direct the interactions of the members away from the common goal toward the local interests of the subgroups.

Research has shown that as group size increases, it becomes more difficult for each member of a group to keep every other member in mind as a separate person. The ability to view each member as an individual falls off steadily after six or seven. Moreover, the time available to each member during a regular meeting decreases as size increases. Therefore, it becomes progressively more difficult for each member to identify with the goals of the group, and subgroups tend to form to meet the need for personal interaction.[49]

As the size of the group increases and the intimacy of interactions decreases, more members are likely to feel threatened and reluctant to participate because of the growing impersonality of the situation. This feeling results from the increased complexity of the behavioral patterns and the distinct possibility of negative feedback from an enlarged membership. In this situation, the leader of the group communicates more actively, and the tendency toward factionalism and dissatisfaction increases.[50]

The relationship between group size and member interaction may be summarized as follows:

1. Member interaction tends to decrease with the group's growth.

2. Affective (emotional) relationships also decrease as the group grows.

3. Central, dominant leadership tends to increase with group size.

4. Enlarged group size tends to foster political rather than analytical solutions to disagreement.[51]

Despite the disadvantages of increasing group size, some undeniable benefits result from an enlarged membership: (1) expanded resources, such as more technical skills and energy; (2) greater input for problem solving, such as more information, critical judgments, and suggested solution strategies; and (3) broader participation in group deliberations, yielding more ready acceptance and support of forthcoming decisions.[52]

However, the benefits of increasing group size may be offset by (1) increased problems of coordination, (2) increased reluctance to participate because of the impersonality of expanded membership, (3) distraction from the common interest resulting from factionalism and subgroups, and (4) increased difficulty in reaching a consensus.[53]

Regardless of the group's classification, then, it seems that size is a variable that must be considered in determining group structure and the influence of the structure on the product of the total group effort.[54]

GROUP COMMUNICATION

It is essential to a group's effectiveness that there be a consensus among its members. Consensus results from interaction, which in turn is the product of open communication. Therefore, it seems obvious that, however defined, group effectiveness is directly or indirectly dependent upon open communication. In this context, communication is defined as the means (any means) by which information (of any type) is transmitted among the members of a group.

Communication within groups may be classified according to two dimensions: (1) the direction information flows in, that is, one way, two ways, or many ways; and (2) the structure of the network through which the information flows.

Three main factors determine the structure of communication networks in groups: (1) the formal organization, with its superior-subordinate reporting relationships; (2) the informal organization, with its unstructured relationships geared toward accomplishing tasks; and (3) the media used to transmit the information. Other, less important factors include (1) qualities of social status like age, education, and common background, (2) similar points of view, and (3) personal friendships.[55]

Research studies by Bavelas and others have revealed four basic types of communication networks: (1) the wheel network, (2) the chain network, (3) the circle network, and (4) the completely connected network.[56] These networks are illustrated in Figure 7.1.

The **wheel network,** with one member at the center and one member at the end of each of four or more spokes, is considered the most structured and hierarchical of the group communication networks. In this network each of the members on the edge can communicate with the person at the center, but with no one else. The person at the center can communicate with everyone directly. The other members have to go through the center to communicate with each other. Generally speaking, the wheel network is unsatisfying to all members except the individual at the center. However, it is very efficient for making routine and recurring (category I) decisions, especially where time and cost are important.

The **chain network** is close to the wheel in its central focus and its consequently unequal communication among the members. In this network there are two members who serve as end persons, each of whom can communicate directly with only one other person. The middle persons serve as relays, sending the information received from the end persons on to the next link in the chain toward the center. The person at the center of the chain receives information from both ends, decides on an answer, and sends it back through the relay persons toward the ends of the chain. Thus the end persons communicate directly with only one person, the relay persons with two persons, and the center person with two persons. However, the center person is in

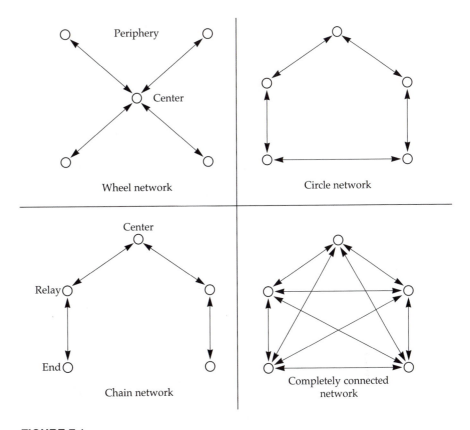

FIGURE 7.1

Communication Networks

closest contact with all members of the chain, and that person's position is not unlike that of the person at the center of the wheel. The chain network is highly unsatisfying to the end persons, somewhat more satisfying to the relay persons, and most satisfying to the center person. Like the wheel network, it is most adaptable to routine, recurring decisions with high certainty of outcome.

The **circle network** is a marked contrast to both the wheel and chain networks in that every member has an equal opportunity for communication. In the circle network information is passed around by all members, and each person acts as a decision-making center. In a study of wheel and circle networks, Cohen found that circle members were more satisfied with their roles than peripheral members of wheel networks.[57] On the other hand, it may take more time to transmit information through the circle network, largely because of the extra links.

In the **completely connected network,** there are no restrictions on any members. Groups in this network generally make decisions by having members communicate information to all directly, each member forming his or her own ideas and tentative alternatives.[58] It is the least restricted network and therefore affords the most personal satisfaction to the members. It is also the network that provides its members with the highest level of **information richness** because of the face-to-face communication.[59] This means that the information has a greater potential for meaning for the members; this, in turn, should contribute to higher levels of group performance. Like the circle, however, because of its many links, the completely connected network takes longer to convey information and allows a greater possibility for distortion of the original transmittal. Also like the circle, the completely connected network is best for decisions that are nonroutine, nonrecurring, and uncertain of outcome (category II decisions).

Highly centralized networks such as the wheel and the chain have the following principal characteristics:

1. They are efficient for routine and recurring decisions.
2. They strengthen the leadership position of the central member(s).
3. They result quickly in a stable set of interactions among the members.
4. They produce lower levels of satisfaction among members.[60]

Networks low in centralization, such as the circle and the completely connected network, may be characterized in the following ways:

1. They produce higher levels of satisfaction among members.
2. They facilitate nonroutine and nonrecurring decisions.
3. They are more likely to be open to innovative and creative solutions.[61]

The direction of communication within a group may flow one way, two ways, or many ways. For example, in the wheel network communication may flow only through the person at the center of the wheel; in the circle network communication almost certainly will flow among all members; and in the completely connected network, by definition, communication flows in every direction.

Communication that flows in more than one direction may be slower than a one-way flow of information, but it is usually more accurate. The senders in the flow of two or more directions feel less anxious and less threatened because the receivers respond to the original transmittal. Moreover, the receivers will feel more sure of themselves, since they get a better idea of whether they are correct in their judgments from the senders' responses. Communication in many directions may appear more disorderly and less efficient to the casual observer, but it generally works much better than a one-way flow.[62]

CHARACTERISTICS OF EFFECTIVE GROUPS

Group effectiveness is composed of at least two basic elements: (1) the attainment of the organizational goals that gave rise to the group's formation, and (2) the satisfaction of the needs of the people in the group.

Given these basic elements of group effectiveness, the question is: what are the characteristics of a group that is likely to be defined as effective? In general, the following characteristics stand out:

1. The group's procedures enable it to carry out systematically the several steps in the decision-making process, and its members have skills appropriate to the nature of the decision at hand.

2. The group has received training in decision-making strategies, and its efforts are appropriately motivated.

3. The group has a stable status system, familiar to all the members.

4. The group is large enough to accomplish the task but not so large that it distracts from the organizational goals.

5. The group is cohesive, with cooperative interaction among members possessing generally compatible personality characteristics.

6. The group is operating under mild or moderate, but not extreme, stress.[63]

McGregor has further outlined the characteristics of an effective group as follows:

1. The atmosphere tends to be informal, comfortable, and relaxed.

2. There is a lot of discussion in which nearly everyone participates, but the discussion stays relevant to the task.

3. The objectives are well understood and accepted by all members of the group.

4. The members listen to one another. Every idea is given a hearing. No one is afraid of being considered foolish by putting forward even extreme ideas.

5. There are disagreements, for disagreements are not overridden. The reasons for disagreement are examined, and there is an attempt to resolve them rather than suppress them.

6. Most decisions are reached by some form of consensus in which there is a general willingness to accept the decision. The group does not trust formal voting with a simple majority as the basis for best action.

7. Criticism is frequent and frank but comfortable and shows little evidence of personal attack.

8. Members feel free to express their feelings as well as their ideas not only on the decision to be made but also on the group's operation.

9. Assignments to members are clear and accepted.

10. The group leader does not dominate, nor is there evidence of a power struggle while the group works to achieve its task.

11. The group is self-conscious about its own operations.[64]

Kast and Rosenzweig have indicated that group effectiveness is the product of **cohesiveness** and the **internalization of organizational goals.**[65] Cohesiveness refers to a group quality that "includes individual pride, commitment, meaning, as well as the group's stick-togetherness, ability to weather crises, and ability to maintain itself over time."[66] "Internalization takes place when the person accepts an influence because the behavior induced is congruent with his value system."[67] Kast and Rosenzweig's rationale is simply that, in the presence of cohesiveness and internalization of organizational goals, a group will undertake behavior that is most likely to achieve the group's goals and meet the individual needs of the members.

"A feeling of cohesiveness among the members of a group is unquestionably the most influential determinant of the group's behavior as a group."[68] Research has shown, for example, that highly cohesive groups work harder than those with low cohesiveness. In addition to feeling a sense of cohesiveness, the members must also identify with or feel enthusiastic about the goals of the group.[69] In essence, a highly cohesive group is more likely to perform effectively than one characterized by internal competition and a general disregard for organizational goals.[70]

To be sure, groups may develop high cohesiveness based more on friendship than on effective performance.[71] In fact, under some circumstances cohesiveness may disrupt the output of a group.[72] Still, groups with high cohesiveness tend to develop norms demanding the contributions of the members to be equal. Such norms, in combination with an internalization of organizational goals, are more likely to result in effective performance. Uneven individual performance is less likely to occur in groups with high cohesiveness, because the norms will be enforced in one way or another. To the extent that such norms include reaching the organizational goals, the highly cohesive group should perform more effectively than its less cohesive counterpart. In sum, a high level of cohesiveness helps satisfy the individual needs of the members, and the group norms encourage the attainment of organizational goals.

Figure 7.2 reflects the seven characteristics of effective groups adopted in this book. Each of these characteristics is justified by ample research in the literature on group decision making.[73] A given characteristic may not weigh equally in the balance for a particular decision; but in most effective group decisions each characteristic will exert some degree of influence on the group's output. A brief description of each of the characteristics of effective groups as shown in Figure 7.2 is as follows:

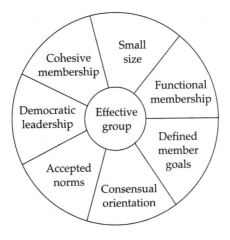

FIGURE 7.2

Characteristics of Effective Groups

1. *Small size.* The group has between five and ten members.
2. *Functional membership.* The individual and collective membership of the group possesses the knowledge and attributes necessary to make the required decision.
3. *Defined member goals.* The group understands and internalizes the goals set by the organization that will define its performance.
4. *Consensual orientation.* The group has a predisposition toward a meeting of the minds in its decision making.
5. *Accepted norms.* The standards for the group's behavior are known and accepted by the membership.
6. *Democratic leadership.* The group leadership does not attempt to dominate the group's decision-making process.
7. *Cohesive membership.* The group membership functions well together, and the group has a sense of esteem and confidence in its output without sacrificing member's egos or individuality.[74]

Depending on the nature of the decision at hand and taken together as a dynamic composite of varying proportional emphases, the aforesaid characteristics will imbue the group's decision with a high level of effectiveness.

GROUPTHINK

The term *groupthink* was coined by Irving Janis.[75] According to Janis, "high cohesiveness can in some circumstances be actively dysfunctional for the effectiveness of the group as a whole."[76] **Groupthink** refers to "a mode of thinking that people engage in when they are deeply involved in a cohesive ingroup, when the members' strivings for unanimity override their motivation to realistically appraise alternative courses of action. . . . Groupthink refers to a deterioration of mental efficiency, reality testing, and moral judgment that results from ingroup pressures."[77] "Defined simply, *groupthink* means that the more friendly and cooperative the members of a group, the greater the likelihood that independent critical thinking and objective moral judgment will be suspended in deference to group norms and in observance of group cohesiveness."[78] The resultant groupthink is fraught with potential for the following unfavorable consequences:

1. A belief in the group's basic morality that is so strong that ethical consequences of decisions are disregarded

2. A stereotypic view of some outside adversary or competitor as evil, weak, or stupid

3. A sense of invulnerability that encourages optimism and risk taking

4. Rationalized judgments that ignore warnings and disregard assumptions

5. Direct pressure on members not to express arguments against group positions under threat of being considered disloyal

6. Self-censorship to the point where doubts regarding the wisdom of the group consensus are suppressed

7. A shared sense of unanimity born out of the self-censorship and a view that silence signifies agreement

8. The emergence of certain members who protect the group from information that might interfere with the cohesion-induced groupthink syndrome[79]

Groupthink "represents a special kind of consensus pressure, resulting from a high level of group cohesiveness, with a corresponding failure to carefully examine options. The group gets locked into a particular decision, often the one abdicated by the leader, and chokes off attempts to look beyond that decision."[80] In one sense, groupthink is a kind of group pathology in that it tends to undermine the health, vitality, and objectivity of the group's decision-making capabilities. "The combination of high cohesiveness, isolation from alternative opinions and facts, group norms that stifle debate and the expression of minority views, and a directive leadership style that forces conformity produce the groupthink phenomenon."[81]

Groupthink tends to work against the effective accomplishment of the functions of decision making within the decision-making process that was illustrated in Figure 2.1.

For example:

1. Groupthink precludes a complete and open-minded consideration of opportunities and possibilities in developing managerial objectives.

2. Groupthink inhibits a meaningful search for information and imbues the search with a selective bias in analyzing and evaluating the information at hand.

3. Groupthink limits the ability of group members to impartially appraise alternative courses of action.

4. Groupthink often results in a failure to consider the possibility and the cost of failure, which, in turn, tends to produce choices with more risk than is warranted by the potential payoff.

5. Groupthink militates against the successful implementation of choices once made because of the group's inability and/or unwillingness to seriously consider obstacles and difficulties attendant upon execution.

6. The absence of contingency plans and fallback positions attributable to groupthink precludes actual outcomes from conforming to intended outcomes.[82]

Groupthink has been blamed for many faulty decisions, notably in the public sector. Raven, for example, notes that groupthink was evident in the Nixon group and contributed to Watergate.[83] Smith ascribes groupthink as a factor contributing to the failure of the Iranian hostage rescue attempt.[84] Esser and Lindoerfer,[85] Kruglanski,[86] and Harrison[87] cite groupthink as a partial explanation for the *Challenger* disaster. And Janis continues to attribute groupthink to a host of flawed decisions in the public sector.[88]

In spite of its increasing acceptance as a contributing factor in flawed decision making, groupthink is not without its detractors. It is regarded by some observers as only a partial or incomplete explanation of failed decisions.[89] Additional research is needed and is underway to further the evaluation of the concept of groupthink.[90]

GROUP DECISION-MAKING PERSPECTIVES

Group decision making continues to increase in organizations of all types. In many cases, for example, the top leadership of large corporations is no longer represented by a single executive making an unbroken series of unilateral decisions. Often there is a multiexecutive corporate office, where the burden of choice is shared by two or three top managers in the "office of the president."[91] Moreover, the drive for consensus at almost any cost has, as noted previously, led to a rise in groupthink among managers and administrators in all types of organizations.[92] An increasing incidence of group decision making among nonmanagers is reflected in the concept of *quality circles*, which originated in Japan and is gaining acceptance in the United States.[93] Whether one believes that group decisions are better or worse than decisions made by individuals, the fact remains that choice by consensus is rapidly becoming a way of life in many organizations. Accordingly, we shall analyze the theoretical foundations of group decision making and evaluate several empirical studies of how this theory applies to collective choice.

Theoretical Perspectives

According to the theory of group decision making, there are at least three ways to view a group:

1. A group is a *collective entity* independent of the properties of its members.
2. A group is a *set of individuals,* and group properties are functions of the properties of individual members.
3. A group is a *collective entity composed of a set of individuals,* and group behavior should be understood in terms of group properties *and* member properties.

The third perspective is by far the most comprehensive, and it is the focus of the discussion to follow. By adopting this perspective we are saying that it is necessary but not sufficient to define a group's properties in terms of its members' properties. We must also realize that groups do have minds of their own in the obvious sense that we can study the group's purposeful behavior independently of the characteristics of its members.[94] The notion of a group mind has been extended by Wegner through the concept of a transactive memory system.[95] In Wegner's words:

> The transactive memory system in a group involves the operation of the memory systems of the individuals and the processes of communication that occur within the group. Transactive memory is therefore not traceable to any of the individuals alone, nor can it be found somewhere "between" individuals. Rather it is a property of a group.[96]

In studying group behavior, then, the manager is

> not interested in deriving group action and values solely in terms of membership action and values; he uses the collective properties as well, and speaks of the "overall objectives of the company."[97]

A complete theory of group decision making should include a review of the assets and liabilities associated with efforts to reach a consensual choice. The assets of group decision making may be summarized as follows:

1. *Greater sum total of knowledge or information.* There is more information in a group than in any of its members. Therefore, decisions that require the use of knowledge should give groups an advantage over individuals.
2. *Greater number of approaches to a problem.* Individuals often fall into ruts in their thinking, and interaction with other members of the group who have different viewpoints should stimulate new thought and open up new intellectual horizons.
3. *Participation in decision making increases general acceptance of the final choice.* When groups make decisions, more people accept and feel responsible for making the decision work. A low-quality decision that has

acceptance can be more effective than a higher-quality choice that lacks general acceptance.

4. *Better comprehension of the decision.* There are fewer chances for failures in communication when the people who must work together to implement the decision have participated in making it.[98]

But the quest for a consensual choice also has the following general liabilities:

1. *Social pressure.* The desire to be a good group member and to be accepted tends to silence disagreement and favor consensus.

2. *Acceptance of solutions.* The first solution that appears to receive strong support from the majority of the members or even from a vocal minority tends to be accepted most of the time. Higher-quality solutions introduced after the first solution has been accepted have little chance of receiving real consideration.

3. *Individual domination.* In most leaderless groups a dominant individual emerges and exerts more than his or her share of influence on the decision. Even a leader who is appointed by the group tends to exert a major influence on the selection of a preferred alternative.

4. *Winning the decision.* The appearance of several alternatives often causes the members to support a particular position. These preferences often take precedence over finding the best solution and the result is a compromise decision of lower quality.[99]

The assets of group decision making can offset the liabilities if the number of members is held to a size conducive to effective interaction. In this regard, groups of five and, to a lesser extent, seven appear to offer the following advantages:

1. Given the odd number of members, a strict deadlock is not possible.

2. The group tends to split into a majority group and a minority group, and a minority position does not isolate a single member.

3. The group is large enough for the members to shift roles and withdraw from embarrassing positions, thus avoiding the problems of smaller groups.

4. The group is still small enough for the quieter members to play an active role in the discussion.[100]

A discussion of the theory of group decision making would be incomplete without a conceptual model for various strategies of choice. Table 7.1 relates the several dimensions of group behavior to three types of decision making.[101] The dimensions of group behavior may be summarized as follows:

1. **Group structure.** The organization of individual members

2. **Group roles.** The behavior required of individual members to facilitate the decision-making process

TABLE 7.1   Strategies for Group Decision Making

Dimensions	Strategy I Routine Decision Making	Strategy II Creative Decision Making	Strategy III Negotiated Decision Making
Group structure	Specialists with a coordinator (leader).	Heterogeneous, competent personnel; leader who facilitates creative processes.	Proportional representation of constituencies.
Group roles	Independent effort; specialist expertise.	All ideas are brought before the group for discussion.	Individual sees self as a representative of a faction.
Group process	Specify objectives; interaction among coordinators and specialists.	Problem-solving process with full participation, spontaneous communication, and considered judgment.	Orderly communication; formalized procedures; voting procedures.
Group style	High stress occasioned by quality and quantity commitments and time constraints.	Relaxed, nonstressful environment; ego-supportive; absence of sanctions.	Frankness and candor; acceptance of due process; avoidance of emotional hostility.
Group norms	Professionalism.	Openness in communication; consensus; supportive of originality; nonauthoritarian	Desire to reach agreement; constructive view of conflict; freedom to disagree; acceptance of compromise.

3. **Group process.** The manner of proceeding toward accomplishment of the group objective

4. **Group style.** The social-emotional tone of interpersonal relationships among the members

5. **Group norms.** The standards of conduct among the members

In Table 7.1 the objective of the group is the independent variable. The group can reach the objective by one of three types of decision-making strategies. The strategies represent the dependent variable. In effect, each strategy is a behavioral model embracing the multiple dimensions of group behavior. The strategy selected and used by the group depends upon the nature of the decision at hand.

The routine decision making in Table 7.1 is analogous to the programmed variety suggested by Simon and the generic type advanced by Drucker. Creative decision making in Table 7.1 is comparable to Gore's classification of innovative and Simon's nonprogrammed type. The negotiated decision making in Table 7.1 is generally similar to Gore's adaptive variety, with some elements of Drucker's classification of unique.

In routine decision making, the strategy emphasizes specialization, coordination, and individual expertise, with a strong commitment to professionalism. Creative decision making involves a strategy based on participative problem-solving techniques in a nonauthoritarian, unstructured environment. Finally, negotiated decision making stresses the formalized and disciplined representation of various constituencies in a context of established rules and procedures for arriving at a choice.

The primary value of Table 7.1 is that it provides a framework within which decision makers can adopt strategies for decision making that use the known dimensions of group behavior. By this means, group decisions should result in outcomes more likely to attain managerial objectives as well as the satisfaction of the members.

We should also note at this point that the classification of decisions and decision-making strategies in Table 7.1 basically elaborates on the categories of decision characteristics shown in Table 1.1. In effect, the tables are complementary. Table 1.1, though, has a broader application to the entire scope of decision making from the individual through the national levels. Table 7.1 applies mainly to achieving a consensual choice in a decision-making group.

Empirical Perspectives

There is empirical evidence to support the theory that a group is a collective entity composed of a set of individuals and that group behavior should be understood in terms of group properties and member properties. In the words of Clarkson and Tuggle: "In order to explain a group's decision behavior when it is engaged upon a specified task, . . . it is first necessary to know the decision processes with respect to the task of each member of the group."[102] This means that the behavior of a group is a direct consequence of how members make decisions. Certain additional group properties come to bear, such as norms and techniques for settling conflicts.

In a series of experiments involving competitive bidding among five groups, Clarkson and Tuggle showed that decisions made by groups can be analyzed through the decision-making sequence followed by individual members. However, the group decisions represented more than the simple product of member choices. In each case, group procedures were employed to resolve seemingly irreconcilable differences without seriously dissatisfying the participants.[103] These group procedures, if properly employed, can yield the obvious benefits of consensual choice.

Research has also shown that a decision based on high consensus among the members of a group is more likely to produce positive results than one based on low consensus.[104] Presumably the individual members, having gone through their own decision-making procedures, are more willing to commit themselves to a group choice in the face of a strong collective sentiment. Again, this finding shows that although group decision making can be studied in terms of how the members arrive at their personal choices, a more complete evaluation must also recognize group processes that blend individual differences into unified action.[105]

Other empirical perspectives on group decision making provide additional insight into this collective endeavor. For example, Kilduff notes that group decision making has a social context in which perceived similarities with other members influence individual participation in the group.[106] Maznevki observes that a diverse membership can enhance a group's performance if the diversity is properly integrated as a part of the group's behavior.[107] And Stasser et al. aver that group performance can be augmented if members are assigned expert roles for particular kinds of information.[108] Group decision-making perspectives lead logically to profiles of decision-making variables that can enhance our understanding of the complexities of collective choice.

GROUP DECISION-MAKING PROFILES

We have dwelt at some length on the sociology of decision-making groups and have discussed several views on various aspects of such groups. Now we present a specialized set of variables, or group decision-making profiles, that may increase the understanding of students and managers about the complex behavioral phenomena constituting the quest for consensual choices.

Classifications of Decision-Making Groups

The discussion up to this point has dealt entirely with the interacting group simply because this type of group grounds the sociology of groups for decision making and for most other purposes. However, there are at least two other types of collective decision-making entities that, although they may not be considered groups in the pure sense, must nonetheless be categorized as part of group decision making, at least as that activity is practiced by managers in formal organizations. The following summary describes the three primary types of decision-making groups:

1. **Interacting group technique.** Typically interacting group meetings begin with a statement of the problem by the group leader. This is followed by an unstructured group discussion to generate information and pool judgments among the participants. The meeting usually concludes with a majority vote on priorities, or a consensual decision.

2. **Nominal group technique.** This technique was developed by Delbecq and Van de Ven in 1968 from industrial engineering studies, social work studies, and social-psychological studies in the public sector.[109] The structured format of this technique proceeds this way: (a) individual members first silently and independently write down their ideas on a problem or task; (b) this is followed by a recorded round-robin in which every group member presents an idea to the group without discussion, and the ideas are summarized in short phrases and written on a blackboard or sheet of paper on the wall; (c) after all individuals have presented their ideas, there is a discussion to clarify and evaluate the recorded ideas; (d) the meeting concludes with a silent, independent vote on priorities by individuals through rank ordering or rating. The "group decision" is a pooled outcome of individual votes.[110]

3. **Delphi technique.** The delphi technique was developed by Norman Dalkey and his associates at the Rand Corporation.[111] This technique is particularly useful for (a) determining or developing a range of possible alternatives, (b) exploring or exposing underlying assumptions or information leading to various judgments, (c) seeking out information that may generate a consensus on the part of the group involved, or (d) correlating informed judgments on topics spanning several disciplines. Unlike either the interacting group or the nominal group decision-making processes, participants in the delphi process are physically dispersed and do not meet face to face for group decision making. The delphi technique provides for the systematic solicitation and collation of judgments on a particular topic through a set of carefully designed sequential questionnaires interspersed with summarized information and opinions derived from earlier responses. Usually only two repetitions of questionnaires and feedback reports are used to obtain a final opinion from the group.[112]

A good deal of research has been directed toward finding out whether the interacting group, nominal group, or delphi decision-making process is superior. There are some obvious differences among the three processes, but they appear to be more relative than absolute and, therefore, are not recounted here.[113]

Group Decision-Making Criteria

Doubtless there are many criteria by which the decisions made by groups can be evaluated. But for purposes of this book, three criteria are **quality, acceptance,** and **originality.** Quality is a generic characteristic that is desirable in most category II decisions. Decision quality includes most of the things that Trull associated with successfully implemented decisions in his study of one hundred organizations that was described in Chapter 2. Other dimensions of decision quality include (1) efficiency, or the ratio of output to input, (2) effects of failure, (3) ease of implementation, (4) the time period over which the decision will be effective, and (5) the estimated likelihood that the decision will attain key objectives.[114]

Decision acceptance means that the choice is agreeable to most of the parties that it will affect directly or indirectly. Obviously some decisions do not require acceptance, but without it, they can be made ineffective by overt blocking or covert subversion during the implementation stage.

The third criterion for group decision making is originality. In particular types of decision-making situations, an original choice may be desirable. In some situations a fresh, innovative decision is clearly the preferred course of action, and originality becomes an important criterion. Nonetheless, an original decision must still be acceptable to affected parties and be of reasonably high quality. The priority ranking for the criteria of group decision making is quality, acceptance, and originality in that order.

Situational Characteristics of Group Decision Making

Three characteristics of the group decision-making situation that are of primary importance are (1) **availability of expertise,** (2) **span of the decision,** and (3) **conflict within the group.** Obviously these characteristics affect the choice of group members and the actual functioning of the group.

The availability of expertise is important if the decision at hand requires specialized knowledge not normally available to the group's members. In such cases an outside expert or consultant must be brought in to obtain a high-quality decision.

The span of a decision refers to the number of persons, parties, or entities outside the control of the responsible manager who are likely to be affected by the group's decision. A decision with a narrow span might affect only internal parties, whereas a decision with a broad span might affect many external parties. In general, the broader the span of the decision the more important the criterion of acceptance in making a final choice.

Conflict in decision making is discussed in Chapter 8. In this specific context, conflict refers to how much group members are likely to disagree about a preferred choice. Obviously the group will want to reduce the negative effects of conflict and obtain as much benefit as possible from the differences that are bound to emerge among members.

Group Membership

For purposes of this book, there are three types of individuals who are likely to be appointed or elected to serve as members of decision-making groups. The first type is simply the **expert,** or the individual who has relevant knowledge, skill, or information to make a quality decision. The second type is the **representative,** or the individual who speaks for a particular constituency or special interest group. The third type is the **coworker,** who is an individual working within the unit in which the decision is being made. Depending upon the decision-making situation, then, group memberships will be composed of varying proportions of experts, representatives, and coworkers.

Conceptualized Profiles of Decision-Making Groups

Table 7.2 shows a set of three profiles — one for each of the major types of decision-making groups presented in this section. It should be noted that these profiles do not necessarily reflect how each type of decision-making group in the table will operate in *every* decision-making situation. Rather each profile is intended to idealize how a given type of decision-making group should operate in a typical decision-making situation, both as an entity in its own right and in relation to the other two types.

The interacting group is seen as the most effective type in terms of two out of three group decision criteria — quality and acceptance. The interacting group typically deals with decisions that have broad to intermediate spans with a moderate to high opportunity for conflict within the group. Membership in the interacting group usually includes coworkers, often includes representatives of parties interested in the decision, and occasionally includes experts. The principal weaknesses of the interacting group are that it generates few original decisions and may lose some of its effectiveness when harmful conflict occurs within the group.[115]

The delphi group is more of a technique than either of the other two types of decision-making groups. The delphi group relies rather heavily on expertise to generate original decisions that have an intermediate to narrow span. Interaction does not exist in the delphi group and there is no opportunity for conflict inside the group. This group is highly specialized and almost clinical in its approach to decision making. It is not used much in most types of formal organizations.

The nominal group seems to bridge the gap between the interacting group and the delphi group. For example, the nominal group tends to have moderate success in meeting all three group decision criteria; whereas the other two types of decision-making groups tend toward the extremes of high or low success. Again, with regard to the characteristics of the group decision-making situation, the nominal group tends to fall between the more extreme characteristics of the interacting group and the delphi group. The more moderate stance of the nominal group also shows in the mixed composition of

TABLE 7.2 Conceptualized Profiles of Decision-Making Groups

Profile Variables	Interacting Group	Nominal Group	Delphi Group
1. Group decision criteria:			
a. Quality	Moderate to high	Moderate	Low or moderate
b. Acceptance	Moderate to high	Moderate	Low to moderate
c. Originality	Low to moderate	Moderate	Moderate to high
2. Group situational characteristics:			
a. Availability of expertise	Low to moderate	Moderate	Moderate to high
b. Span of the decision	Intermediate to broad	Intermediate	Narrow to intermediate
c. Conflict within the group	Moderate to high	Low to moderate	Low
3. Group membership:			
a. Experts	Occasionally	Frequently	Usually
b. Representatives	Frequently	Occasionally	Seldom
c. Coworkers	Usually	Frequently	Occasionally

its membership, which often includes various proportions of experts, representatives, and coworkers. Indeed the nominal group appears to offer the lure of moderately good decisions with a minimum of structural and functional disadvantages to the decision makers. Nonetheless the interacting group's superiority in the areas of quality and acceptance, and the high originality of the delphi group's decisions lead many managers to favor these decision-making groups. To repeat, the interacting group is the principal vehicle for studying the sociology of decision making. It is the only decision-making entity that qualifies strictly as a group. The other two decision-making entities simply reinforce the interacting group as the ideal locus for studying consensual choice.

SUMMARY

This chapter has concentrated on the sociology of decision making. The profile of a group offered a set of primary characteristics, including (1) interpersonal consensus, (2) interaction, (3) communication, (4) common interest, and (5) proximity. Group size was also mentioned as being important, with small groups usually numbering seven individuals or less.

Several theories of group behavior were presented, among them Homans's theory of a group as a dynamic social system composed of the principal elements of activities, interaction, and sentiment.

Group norms and conformity were discussed, and it was stated that individuals who become members of a group must, as part of the price of acceptance by the others, adapt their personal preferences to the group's standards of conduct. Personality affects the extent to which an individual will make such modifications.

Group structure was examined in detail, with emphasis on the size of the group. Large groups have some advantages over small ones, but their disadvantages appear to be more significant, especially with regard to the personal satisfaction of the members. As a general rule, therefore, it may be said that group effectiveness decreases as group size grows.

Communication in groups must be open in all directions to foster the interaction necessary to achieve consensus. This chapter presented four basic types of communication networks. The wheel and chain networks, which are the most centralized, work best for category I decisions. The circle and completely connected networks, which are the most open, work best for category II decisions.

It was also noted that the most effective groups attain the objectives that gave rise to their formation and, at the same time, satisfy the needs of their members. A high level of cohesiveness helps satisfy the individual needs of the members, and the group norms encourage the attainment of the organizational goals. Figure 7.2 reflects the seven characteristics of effective groups adopted in this book. Cohesiveness has a negative as well as a positive dimension in group decision making. If carried to an extreme, cohesiveness can result in a condition called groupthink. Groupthink refers to a mode of thinking that people engage in when they are deeply involved in a cohesive ingroup and the members' strivings for unanimity override their motivation to appraise realistically alternative courses of action. Groupthink means that the more friendly and cooperative the members of a group, the greater the likelihood that independent critical thinking and objective moral judgment will be suspended in deference to group norms and in observance of group cohesiveness. Groupthink is characterized by (1) a strong belief in the group's morality, (2) a stereotypic view of adversaries or competitors, (3) a sense of group invulnerability, (4) rationalized member and group judgments, (5) pressure on members not to express arguments against group positions, (6) self-censorship of group consensus, (7) a shared sense of unanimity, and (8) group members who protect the cohesion-induced groupthink syndrome. Groupthink can militate against effective managerial decision making in groups.

Several theoretical perspectives on group decision making were presented and supported by selected empirical studies. Although group decision making can be studied in terms of the way individual members arrive at their personal choices, a more complete and meaningful study also requires recognition of the group processes that blend individual differences into unified action.

Three classifications of group decision-making entities were presented: the interacting group, the nominal group, and the delphi group. Three criteria for group decision making were identified: quality, acceptance, and originality. Three primary characteristics of decision-making situations were discussed: (1) availability of expertise, (2) span of the decision, and (3) conflict within the group. Finally, three types of members of decision-making groups were identified: the expert, the representative, and the coworker. A set of profiles for decision-making groups focusing on all these variables revealed that the interacting group has the most advantages and the fewest disadvantages; the delphi group has the fewest advantages and the most disadvantages; and the nominal group falls somewhere in between, depending on the decision-making situation. It was also noted that the interacting group, which is the main subject of this chapter, is the principal vehicle of study for the sociology of decision making.

REVIEW AND DISCUSSION QUESTIONS

1. There are several essential characteristics common to any group. What are they?

2. Homans conceived of a group as a dynamic social system. What are the parts of his system, and in what ways are they dynamic?

3. What does Jackson's two-dimensional concept tell us about the basis for group membership? Discuss.

4. Discuss the various ways in which group norms are enforced.

5. According to Scott's sociometric structure, what are the three subsets of a group, and what are their respective roles in the group's operation?

6. Contrast the four types of group communication networks in terms of reaching organizational goals and member satisfaction.

7. What are the three ways to view a group as a decision-making body, and how does each viewpoint influence the perspective of the decision maker?

8. Cite three strategies for group decision making, and indicate the profile of group behavior for which each strategy is best suited.

9. Discuss this statement: Interacting groups provide richer models for group decision making than do either nominal groups or delphi groups.

10. Why is an interacting group more likely to produce a decision that has a high level of acceptance? Why is acceptance important?

11. What is there in the nature of an interacting group that tends to work against its making original decisions?

12. In what specific ways does the phenomenon of groupthink work against rational decision making at the level of the group in formal organizations?

NOTES

1. George C. Homans, *The Human Group* (New York: Harcourt, Brace, 1950), p. 1.

2. Fremont E. Kast and James E. Rosenzweig, *Organization and Management: A Systems Approach* (New York: McGraw-Hill, 1970), p. 275.

3. David J. Lawless, *Effective Management: A Social Psychological Approach* (Englewood Cliffs, N.J.: Prentice-Hall, 1972), p. 106.

4. See Blair J. Kolasa, *Introduction to Behavioral Science for Business* (New York: Wiley, 1969), p. 446.

5. Joseph A. Litterer, *The Analysis of Organizations* (New York: Wiley, 1965), p. 107.

6. Homans, *The Human Group*, pp. 81–108.

7. Peter M. Blau, "A Theory of Social Integration," *American Journal of Sociology*, 65 (1960), 545–556.

8. Herbert C. Kelman, "Processes of Opinion Change," *Public Opinion Quarterly*, 25 (1961), 57–78.

9. Clovis R. Shepherd, *Small Groups: Some Sociological Perspectives* (Scranton, Pa.: Chandler, 1964), pp. 48–49.

10. Kurt Lewin, "Frontiers in Group Dynamics," *Human Relations*, 1 (1947), 5–41, 141–153.

11. Shepherd, *Small Groups*, p. 25.

12. Ibid., p. 26.

13. Robert F. Bales, *Interaction Process Analysis* (Reading, Mass.: Addison-Wesley, 1950).

14. Shepherd, *Small Groups*, p. 28.

15. Ibid.

16. Ibid., pp. 32, 34.

17. See Lawless, *Effective Management*, p. 224, for illustrative profiles of satisfied and dissatisfied groups.

18. Jay M. Jackson, "A Space for Conceptualizing Person-Group Relationships," *Human Relations*, 10 (1959), 3–15.

19. Lawrence S. Rothenberg, "Organizational Maintenance and the Retention Decision in Groups," *American Political Science Review* (December 1988), 1129–1152.

20. Homans, *The Human Group*, p. 123.

21. Shepherd, *Small Groups*, p. 41.

22. John W. Thibaut and Harold H. Kelley, *The Social Psychology of Groups* (New York: Wiley, 1959), p. 239.

23. Lawless, *Effective Management*, pp. 267–268.

24. Litterer, *The Analysis of Organizations*, pp. 109–112.

25. Charles E. Miller et al. "Some Social Psychological Effects of Group Decision Rules," *Journal of Personality and Social Psychology* (February 1987), 325–332.

26. Kolasa, *Behavioral Science for Business*, p. 458.

27. Litterer, *The Analysis of Organizations*, pp. 52–54; and Lawless, *Effective Management*, pp. 274–275.

28. See S. E. Asch, "Effects of Group Pressure Upon the Modification and Distortion of Judgments," in *Groups and Organizations: Integrated Readings in the Analysis of Social Behavior*, ed. Bernard L. Hinton and H. Joseph Reitz (Belmont, Calif.: Wadsworth, 1971), pp. 215–225.

29. Litterer, *The Analysis of Organizations*, p. 53.

30. See, for example, Asch, "Effects of Group Pressures," pp. 155–156; and Richard S. Crutchfield, "Conformity and Character," *American Psychologist*, 10 (1955), 191–198.

31. Litterer, *The Analysis of Organizations*, p. 53.

32. Kolasa, *Behavioral Science for Business*, pp. 459–460.

33. Lawless, *Effective Management*, pp. 274–275.

34. Ibid., pp. 278–279.

35. Ibid., pp. 106–107. Also see Joseph McCann and Thomas N. Gilmore, "Diagnosing Organizational Decision Making Through Responsibility Charting," *Sloan Management Review* (Winter 1983), 3–15.

36. Ibid., p. 107.

37. Kolasa, *Behavioral Science for Business*, pp. 450–451.

38. Ibid., p. 453.

39. B. Aubrey Fisher, *Small Group Decision Making: Communication and the Group Process* (New York: McGraw-Hill, 1974), p. 10.

40. Kast and Rosenzweig, *Organization and Management*, p. 277.

41. Alan J. Rowe and James D. Boulgarides, *Managerial Decision Making* (New York: Macmillan Co., 1992), p. 153.

42. Larry Van Meter, "Lead Before Managing — The Team Concept Approach," *Business Credit* (June 1995), 9–10.

43. William G. Scott, *Organization Theory* (Homewood, Ill.: Richard D. Irwin, 1967), p. 93.

44. Kolasa, *Behavioral Science for Business*, p. 66.

45. See Jackson, "Person-Group Relationships," p. 5.

46. See, for example, L. L. Cummings, George P. Huber, and Eugene Arendt, "Effects of Size and Spatial Arrangements on Group Decision Making," *Academy of Management Journal*, 17 (September 1974), 460–475; and George E. Manners, Jr., "Another Look at Group Size, Group Problem Solving, and Member Consensus," *Academy of Management Journal*, 18 (December 1975), 715–724.

47. Lawless, *Effective Management*, p. 121.

48. Litterer, *The Analysis of Organizations*, p. 93.

49. Fremont A. Shull, Jr., André L. Delbecq, and L. L. Cummings, *Organizational Decision Making* (New York: McGraw-Hill, 1970), p. 145.

50. Ibid., p. 146.

51. Ibid., p. 147.

52. Hsin-Ginn Hwang and Jan Guynes, "The Effect of Group Size on Group Performance in Computer-Supported Decision Making," *Information & Management*, 29 (1994), 189–198.

53. Ibid., p. 148.

54. See Edwin J. Thomas and Clinton F. Fink, "Effects of Group Size," *Psychological Bulletin*, 60 (1963), 371–384, for a compilation of research findings in the subject area.

55. Timothy W. Costello and Sheldon S. Zalkind, eds. *Psychology in Administration: A Research Orientation* (Englewood Cliffs, N.J.: Prentice-Hall, 1963), p. 456.

56. See A. Bavelas, "A Mathematical Model for Group Structures," *Applied Anthropology*, 7 (1948), 16–30; and H. Leavitt, "Some Effects of Certain Communication Patterns on Group Performance," *Journal of Abnormal and Social Psychology*, 46 (1951), 33–50.

57. Arthur M. Cohen, "Changing Small-Group Communication Networks," *Administrative Science Quarterly* (March 1962), 450–451.

58. Ibid., pp. 449–450.

59. For an extended discussion of information richness, see Mairead Browne, *Organizational Decision Making and Information* (Norwood, N.J.: Ablex, 1993), pp. 57–59; and Richard L. Daft and Robert H. Lengel, "Organizational Information Requirements, Media Richness, and Structural Design," *Management Science*, 32, No. 5 (May 1986), 554–571.

60. Costello and Zalkind, *Psychology in Administration*, p. 457.

61. Ibid.

62. George Katona, *Psychological Analysis of Economic Behavior* (New York: McGraw-Hill, 1963), p. 470.

63. Costello and Zalkind, *Psychology in Administration*, p. 444.

64. Douglas McGregor, *The Human Side of Enterprise* (New York: McGraw-Hill, 1960), pp. 232–235.

65. Kast and Rosenzweig, *Organization and Management*, pp. 284–285.

66. Shepherd, *Small Groups*, p. 88.

67. Lawless, *Effective Management*, p. 188.

68. Costello and Zalkind, *Psychology in Administration*, p. 444.

69. Ibid.

70. Katona, *Psychological Analysis of Economic Behavior*, p. 461; and Paul S. Goodman, Elizabeth Ravlin, and Marshall Schminke, "Understanding Behavior in Groups," in *Research in Organization Behavior*, Vol. 9, ed. Ricky W. Griffin (Greenwich, Conn.: JAI Press, 1987), pp. 121–173.

71. Deborah H. Gruenfeld et al., "Group Composition and Decision Making: How Member Familiarity and Information Distribution Affect Process and Performance," *Organizational Behavior and Human Decision Processes*, 67 (July 1996), pp. 1–15.

72. Shepherd, *Small Groups*, p. 91.

73. See David Jennings and Stuart Wattam, *Decision Making: An Integrated Approach* (London: Pitman, 1994), pp. 66–69.

74. See Janet A. Sniezek, "Groups Under Uncertainty: An Examination of Confidence in Group Decision Making," *Organizational Behavior and Human Decision Process*, 52 (1992), 124–155; and Batia M. Wiesenfeld, "Group Esteem: Positive Collective Evaluations in Task-Oriented Groups," Center for Decision Research, University of Chicago, Chicago, 1997.

75. Irving L. Janis, *Victims of Groupthink* (Boston: Houghton Mifflin, 1972).

76. J. Richard Hackman, "Group Influences on Individuals," in *Handbook of Industrial and Organizational Psychology*, ed. Marvin D. Dunnette (Chicago: Rand McNally, 1976), p. 1516.

77. Irving L. Janis, *Groupthink*, 2nd ed. (Boston: Houghton Mifflin, 1982), p. 9.

78. E. Frank Harrison, *Policy, Strategy, and Managerial Action* (Boston: Houghton Mifflin, 1986), p. 184.

79. Adapted with slight modifications from George A. Steiner and John B. Miner, *Management Policy and Strategy* (New York: Macmillan, 1977), pp. 191–192. Also see Janis, *Groupthink*, pp. 174–175.

80. Walter C. Swap, "Destructive Effects of Groups on Individuals," in *Group Decision Making*, ed. Walter C. Swap and Associates (Beverly Hills, Calif.: Sage, 1984), p. 80.

81. Ibid., p. 88.

82. See Daniel D. Wheeler and Irving L. Janis, *A Practical Guide for Making Decisions* (New York: Free Press, 1980), pp. 190–195.

83. Bertram H. Raven, "The Nixon Group," *Journal of Social Issues*, 30 (1974), 297–320.

84. Steve Smith, "Groupthink and the Hostage Rescue Mission," *British Journal of Political Science*, 15 (1984), 117–126.

85. James K. Esser and Joanne S. Lindoerfer. "Groupthink and the Space Shuttle *Challenger* Accident: Toward a Quantitative Case Analysis," *Journal of Behavioral Decision Making*, 2 (1989), 167–177.

86. A. W. Kruglanski, "Freeze-Think and the *Challenger*," *Psychology Today* (August 1986), 48–49.

87. E. Frank Harrison, "*Challenger*: The Anatomy of a Flawed Decision," *Technology in Society*, 15 (1993), 161–183.

88. See Paul 't Hart, "Irving L. Janis' Victims of Groupthink," *Political Psychology*, 12 (1991), 247–277.

89. See Jeanne Longley and Dean G. Pruitt, "Groupthink: A Critique of Janis's Theory," *Review of Personality and Social Psychology*, 1 (1980), 74–93; Gregory Moorhead and John R. Montanari, "An Empirical Investigation of the Groupthink Phenomenon," *Human Relations*, 39 (1986), 399–410; and Glen Whyte, "Groupthink Reconsidered," *The Academy of Management Review* (January 1989), 40–56.

90. Won-Won Park, "A Review of Research on Groupthink," *Journal of Behavioral Decision Making* (October–December 1990), 229–245.

91. See "Some Large Firms Find Operations Are Simplified by Group Takeover of the Chief Executive's Role," *Wall Street Journal* (July 7, 1972), 22.

92. See Irving L. Janis, "Groupthink," *Psychology Today* (November 1971), 43ff.

93. See Frank M. Gryna, Jr., *Quality Circles: A Team Approach to Problem Solving* (New York: AMACOM, 1981); and John Bank and Bernhard Wilpert, "What's So Special About Quality Circles?" *Journal of General Management*, 9, No. 1 (1983), 23–37.

94. For an illuminating discussion of the concept of the "group mind," see Fisher, *Small Group Decision Making*, pp. 201–203.

95. Daniel M. Wegner, "Transactive Memory: A Contemporary Analysis of the Group Mind," in *Theories of Group Behavior*, eds. Jon B. Mullen and G. R. Goethals (New York: Springer-Verlag, 1987), pp. 185–208.

96. Ibid., p. 191.

97. C. West Churchman, *Prediction and Optimal Decision* (Englewood Cliffs, N.J.: Prentice-Hall, 1961), pp. 300–302.

98. Norman R. F. Maier, "Assets and Liabilities in Group Problem Solving: The Need for an Integrative Function," in *Groups and Organizations: Integrated Readings in the Analysis of Social Behavior*, ed. Bernard L. Hinton and H. Joseph Reitz (Belmont, Calif.: Wadsworth, 1971), pp. 279–280.

99. Ibid., pp. 280–281.

100. Shull, Delbecq, and Cummings, *Organizational Decision Making*, p. 151.

101. Table 7.1 was adapted with modifications from André L. Delbecq, "The Management of Decision-Making within the Firm: Three Strategies for Three Types of Decision-Making," *Academy of Management Journal* (December 1967), 329–339.

102. Geoffrey P. E. Clarkson and Francis D. Tuggle, "Toward a Theory of Group-Decision Behavior," *Behavioral Science* (January 1966), 33.

103. Ibid., pp. 40–41.

104. See Edith Becker Bennett, "Discussion, Decision, Commitment and Consensus in 'Group Decision'" *Human Relations*, 8 (1955), 3–10; and Gruenfeld et al., "Group Composition and Decision Making: How Member Familiarity and Information Distribution Affect Process and Performance."

105. Mark Gradstein and Shmuel Nitzan, "Participation, Decision Aggregation and Internal Information Gathering in Organizational Decision Making," *Journal of Economic Behavior and Organization*, 10 (1988), 415–431.

106. Martin Kilduff, "The Interpersonal Structure of Decision Making: A Social Comparison Approach to Organizational Choice," *Organizational Behavior and Human Decision Processes*, 47 (1990), 270–288.

107. Martha L. Maznevski, "Understanding Our Differences: Performance in Decision-Making Groups with Diverse Members," *Human Relations*, 47, No. 5 (1994), 531–552.

108. Harold Stasser et al., "Experts Roles and Information Exchange During Discussion: The Importance of Knowing Who Knows What," *Journal of Experimental Social Psychology*, 31 (1995), 244–265.

109. See André L. Delbecq and Andrew H. Van de Ven, "A Group Process Model for Problem Identification and Program Planning," *Journal of Applied Behavioral Science*, 7 (1971), 466–492; and Andrew H. Van de Ven and André L. Delbecq, "Nominal Versus Interacting Group Processes for Committee Decision-Making Effectiveness," *Academy of Management Journal*, 14 (June 1971), 203–212.

110. Andrew H. Van de Ven and André L. Delbecq, "The Effectiveness of Nominal, Delphi, and Interacting Group Decision Making Processes," *Academy of Management Journal*, 17 (December 1974), 606.

111. See N. C. Dalkey, *The Delphi Method: An Experimental Study of Group Opinion* (Santa Monica, Calif.: Rand, 1969).

112. See Van de Ven and Delbecq, "The Effectiveness of Nominal, Delphi, and Interacting Group Decision Making Processes," p. 606. Also see Richard J. Tersine and Walter E. Riggs, "The Delphi Technique: A Long-Range Planning Tool," *Business Horizons*, 19 (April 1976), 51–56; and Harold A. Linstone and Murray Turoff, eds., *The Delphi Method* (Reading, Mass.: Addison-Wesley, 1976).

113. For an excellent comparative analysis, see Stephen A. Stumpf, Dale E. Zand, and Richard D. Freedman, "Designing Groups for Judgmental Decisions," *Academy of Management Review* (October 1979), 589–600; and Stephen A. Stumpf, Richard D. Freedman, and Dale E. Zand, "Judgmental Decisions: A Study of Interactions Among Group Membership, Group Functioning, and the Decision Situation," *Academy of Management Journal* (December 1979), 765–782. Also see Stephen G. Green and Thomas D. Faber, "The Effects of Three Social Decision Schemes on Decision Group Processes," *Organizational Behavior and Human Performance* (February 1980), 97–106.

114. Stumpf, Zand, and Freedman, "Designing Groups for Judgmental Decisions," p. 591.

115. See Randy Y. Hirokawa, "Why Informed Groups Make Faulty Decisions," *Small Group Behavior* (February 1987), 3–29.

SUPPLEMENTAL REFERENCES

Bass, Bernard M. *Organizational Decision Making*. Homewood, Ill.: Richard D. Irwin, 1983.

Bettenhausen, Kenneth, and J. Keith Murnighan. "The Emergence of Norms in Competitive Decision-Making Groups." *Administrative Science Quarterly* (September 1985), 350–372.

Burton, Gene E., Dev S. Pathak, and Ron M. Zigli. "Using Group Size to Improve the Decision-Making Ability of Nominal Groups." In *Academy of Management Proceedings*, 37th Annual Meeting. Ed. Robert L. Taylor et al. Orlando, Fla., August 14–17, 1977.

Butler, Richard. *Designing Organizations: A Decision-Making Perspective*. New York: Routledge, 1991.

Crutchfield, Richard S. "Conformity and Character." *American Psychologist*, 10 (1955), 191–198.

Ebert, Ronald J., and Terence R. Mitchell. *Organizational Decision Processes*. New York: Crane, Russak, 1975.

Feldman, Daniel C. "The Development and Enforcement of Group Norms." *Academy of Management Review* (January 1984), 47–53.

Fisher, B. Aubrey. "Decision Emergence: Phases in Group Decision Making." *Speech Monographs*, 38 (March 1970), 53–66.

Ford, Robert C., and Frank S. McLaughlin. "Effects of Group Composition on Search Activity." *Journal of Business Research*, 4 (February 1976), 15–24.

George, Alexander L. *Presidential Decision-Making in Foreign Policy: The Effective Use of Information and Advice*. Boulder, Colo.: Westview, 1980.

Gladstein, Deborah L. "Groups in Context: A Model of Task Group Effectiveness." *Administrative Science Quarterly* (December 1984), 499–517.

Green, Thad B. "An Empirical Analysis of Nominal and Interacting Groups." *Academy of Management Journal*, 18 (March 1975), 63–73.

Hackman, J. Richard, and Robert E. Kaplan. "Interventions into Group Process: An Approach to Improving the Effectiveness of Groups." *Decision Sciences* (July 1974), 459–480.

Hall, J., and V. O'Leary. "Getting Better Decisions from a Group." *Supervisory Management* (July 1971), 28–32.

Hare, A. Paul, ed. *Handbook of Small Group Research*. 2nd ed. New York: Free Press, 1976.

Herbert, Theodore T., and Edward B. Yost. "A Comparison of Decision Quality Under Nominal and Interacting Consensus Group Formats: The Case of the Structured Problem." *Decision Sciences* (July 1979), 358–370.

Hill, Percy H., et al. *Making Decisions: A Multidisciplinary Approach*. Reading, Mass.: Addison-Wesley, 1979.

Hollander, Edwin P., and Richard H. Willis. "Some Current Issues in the Psychology of Conformity and Nonconformity." In *Groups and Organizations: Integrated Readings in the Analysis of Social Behavior*. Ed. Bernard L. Hinton and H. Joseph Reitz. Belmont, Calif.: Wadsworth, 1971, pp. 232–248.

Holloman, Charles R., and Hal W. Hendrick. "Adequacy of Group Decisions as a Function of the Decision-Making Process." *Academy of Management Journal* (June 1972), 175–184.

Huber, George P., and André Delbecq. "Guidelines for Combining the Judgments of Individual Members in Group Conferences." *Academy of Management Journal*, 15 (June 1972), 161–174.

Janis, Irving L. *Crucial Decisions: Leadership in Policymaking and Crisis Management*. New York: Free Press, 1989.

Kast, Fremont E., and James E. Rosenzweig. *Organization & Management*. 4th ed. New York: McGraw-Hill, 1985.

Kiesler, Sara. *Interpersonal Processes in Groups and Organizations*. Arlington Heights, Ill.: AHM, 1978.

Kowitz, Albert C., and Thomas J. Knutson. *Decision Making in Small Groups*. Boston: Allyn & Bacon, 1980.

Longley, Jeanne, and Dean G. Pruitt. "Groupthink: A Critique of Janis's Theory." *Review of Personality and Social Psychology*, 1 (1980), 74–93.

Manners, George E., Jr., "Another Look at Group Size, Group Problem Solving, and Member Consensus." *Academy of Management Journal*, 18 (December 1975), 715–724.

Miner, Frederick C., Jr., "A Comparative Analysis of Three Diverse Decision Making Approaches." *Academy of Management Journal*, 22 (March 1979), 81–93.

Moskowitz, Herbert. "Some Observations on Theories of Collective Decisions." In *Utility, Probability, and Human Decision Making*. Ed. Dirk Wendt and Charles Vlek. Boston: D. Reidel, 1975, pp. 381–395.

Park, Margaret K. "Decision-Making Processes for Information Managers." *Special Libraries* (October 1981), 307–318.

Plott, Charles R., and Michael E. Levine. "A Model of Agenda Influence on Committee Decisions." *American Economic Review* (March 1978), 146–160.

Scott, William G., Terence R. Mitchell, and Philip H. Birnbaum. *Organization Theory: A Structural and Behavioral Analysis.* 4th ed. Homewood, Ill.: Richard D. Irwin, 1981.

Shaw, Marvin E. "Acceptance of Authority, Group Structure, and Effectiveness of Small Groups." *Journal of Personality*, 27 (1959), 196–210.

Shaw, Robert J. "Keeping the Commitment to Quality Circles." *Management Focus* (November–December 1982), 25–32.

Sommer, Robert. "Small Group Ecology." In *Groups and Organizations: Integrated Readings in the Analysis of Social Behavior.* Ed. Bernard L. Hinton and H. Joseph Reitz. Belmont, Calif.: Wadsworth, 1971, pp. 94–99.

Steiner, Ivan D. *Group Process and Productivity.* New York and London: Academic Press, 1972.

Takamiya, Susumu. "Group Decision-Making in Japanese Management." *International Studies of Management & Organization* (Summer 1972), 183–196.

Tetlock, Philip E. "Identifying Victims of Groupthink from Public Statements of Decision Makers." *Journal of Personality and Social Psychology*, 37, No. 8 (1979), 1314–1324.

Thomas, E. J., and C. F. Fink. "Effects of Group Size." *Psychological Bulletin*, 60, No. 4 (1963), 371–384.

Thompson, James D., and Donald R. Van Houten. *The Behavioral Sciences: An Interpretation.* Reading, Mass.: Addison-Wesley, 1970.

Ungson, Gerardo R., and Daniel N. Braunstein, eds. *Decision Making: An Interdisciplinary Inquiry.* Boston: Kent, 1982.

Van de Ven, Andrew A., and André L. Delbecq. "Nominal Versus Interacting Group Processes for Committee Decision-Making Effectiveness." *Academy of Management Journal*, 14 (June 1971), 203–212.

Wall, Victor D., Jr., Gloria J. Galanes, and Sue Beth Love. "Small, Task-Oriented Groups: Conflict, Conflict Management, Satisfaction, and Decision Quality." *Small Group Behavior* (February 1987), 31–55.

Ziller, R. C. "Group Size: A Determinant of Quality and Stability of Group Decisions." *Sociometry*, 20 (1957), 165–173.

CHAPTER EIGHT

The Social Psychology of Decision Making

*I*n one sense, this chapter represents a kind of composite of its two predecessor chapters. Chapter 6, for example, focuses on the emotional and behavioral characteristics of the individual decision maker as he or she accomplishes the several functions that constitute the managerial decision-making process. It is a basic premise of Chapter 6 that the psychological forces within decision makers affect their behavior throughout the entire integrated process of arriving at a satisficing choice. Subsequently, Chapter 7 focuses on the interactions that occur in groups as individuals come together in quest of a consensus that will attain their objectives. In this chapter the individual behavior of Chapter 6 blends with the social behavior of Chapter 7 in much the same way that the formal disciplines of psychology and sociology are fused to form the newer discipline of social psychology.

In still another sense, this chapter reflects a discernible configuration of its own in that it is composed of subject matter not commonly treated in the context of either psychology or sociology. Indeed the subject matter of this chapter does not fit neatly into either one of these traditional social sciences. Rather it consists of a newer and more advanced knowledge base that is reflective of the evolution of managerial decision making as it becomes increasingly eclectic through the assimilation of theories, concepts, and principles from other formal disciplines. The subjects of this chapter extend the traditional disciplines of psychology and sociology in much the same way that social psychology extends the entire range of the social sciences.

The first section of this chapter compares individual decision making with group decision making. A discussion of theoretical perspectives is followed by a series of empirical studies oriented toward the theory, with an emphasis on the relative advantages of each type of decision making. There follows a discussion of the so-called risky shift, which occurs when individuals become members of decision-making groups. Finally, the case for a composite individual and group emphasis through the managerial decision-making process is presented.

The second section deals with conflict in decision making. The subject is presented in the context of selected basic theories and concepts reflective of conflict's occurrence in all types of organizations with a special emphasis on managerial decision making. Topics covered include (1) the nature of conflict, (2) the determinants of conflict, (3) the indicators of conflict, and (4) the treatment of conflict.

The third section discusses participation in decision making. After a presentation of selected theoretical foundations of participative decision making, some empirical studies intended to confirm the theory are presented. The pervasive theme of this section is that participation in decision making is highly situational and is largely a matter of degree.

The final section presents a subject about which there is much opinion and little meaningful understanding: gender differences and similarities in managerial decision making. A series of empirical studies focusing first on gender differences and then on gender similarities is presented to develop a foundation of fact for the culminating advocacy of a fusion of gender strengths to arrive at satisficing choices in managing formal organizations.

INDIVIDUAL VERSUS GROUP DECISION MAKING

There is less than universal agreement regarding the relative effectiveness of managers functioning as individual decision makers or as members of decision-making groups. Much of the management literature increasingly extols the relative merits of collective decision making and consensual choice.[1] Some writers, however, point to the possible disadvantages inherent in the cohesiveness that is deemed essential for effective group decision making,[2] and others believe that exceptionally competent individuals are more likely to arrive at better decisions than the least-common-denominator consensus characteristic of collective choice.[3] Finally, there are those who assert that many individuals are more inclined to accept risk as members of groups than as decision makers in their own right.[4] This section focuses on these and related matters preparatory to advancing the case for a composite approach involving both individual and group decision-making efforts.

Theoretical Perspectives

Several psychological factors influence individuals making unilateral choices: (1) the profile of their unique personalities, (2) the mental images resulting from their perceptual processes, (3) their individual willingness and ability to accept varying degrees of uncertainty, and (4) the influence of their subconscious minds.

As members of decision-making groups, individuals are subject to the norms of the group and the need to communicate with each other in pursuit of a consensus.[5] Often the individual must compromise personal beliefs, attitudes, and values to accomplish the objectives of the group. Also, as a member of a group the individual is no longer solely responsible for the outcome of the choice that he or she has helped to make, which may affect the individual's willingness to accept uncertainty. In essence, the collective judgment of the group subordinates the individual's own preferences for quick decisions or procrastination. Rather than being a solitary decision maker, the individual is simply one among several choice makers, all of whom have their own personal preferences and objectives.

Groups usually take longer to arrive at a choice than individuals do.[6] Yet they bring more expertise to bear on a problem than any one person is likely to do. Further, the many perceptions blended in a group tend to neutralize the effect of individual bias. A group of open-minded decision makers may therefore be more likely to produce a less biased choice than an individual. Of course, it is possible for a group of closed-minded individuals with diverse value systems to arrive at a biased decision, but this is less likely than when one individual makes the decision.

Doubtless the best-known disadvantage of group decision making is the inordinate amount of time it often takes to achieve a consensus. "Research studies show that even when [decision-making] groups are clearly superior to individuals with regard to arriving at [satisficing choices] . . . the groups generally take longer than individuals do."[7] Other disadvantages of group decision making are potentially far more serious than the additional time taken to reach a meeting of the minds. "For example, the pooled judgments of a group tend to be *worse* than those of the best-qualified member when most other members are not competent to judge the issue. Group judgments tend to be superior only when most members are highly competent."[8]

The strengths of group decision making are a reflection of the potential weaknesses of individual decision making. For example, it seems fairly obvious that the sum total of the knowledge possessed by a given group will exceed the knowledge possessed by its most knowledgeable member.[9] What is less certain is that the collective knowledge of the group would be employed more effectively than would the personal knowledge of the most competent member in arriving at a satisficing choice. It is equally obvious that, in the usual case, a group can bring to bear a greater number of approaches to the process of choice.[10] But this process constitutes a multidimensional approach in its own right. It may well be, therefore, that the diverse viewpoints of a group are less advantageous within the generic and eclectic framework of the managerial decision-making process.

There is a general belief that greater participation in decision making tends to increase the acceptance of the final choice.[11] Presumably when more people are involved in the decision-making process there is an expanded sense of responsibility for making the decision work. If this presumption is accurate, group decision making should in the general case tend to elicit choices that have higher levels of acceptance than similar decisions made unilaterally by individual managers. It may also be true that a lot of participation in decision making is only a facade to obtain acceptance for choices that have actually been made unilaterally. A *perception* of participation may suffice to support an erroneous impression that a group made the decision.

Similarly, the apparent weaknesses of group decision making may reflect potential strengths for decision making by individuals. There is little doubt, for example, that "groups can and do exert powerful influences on their members. These influences are often destructive and must be understood and overcome to promote effective decision making."[12] One such influence is called **social loafing.** In many situations groups tend to impede the performance of highly motivated individuals. For example, the need to comply with group norms can easily inhibit the output of energetic members. It is somewhat paradoxical that in a decision-making group recognition and rewards can easily go to those members who behave according to social expectations.

Another more insidious negative influence on individuals functioning as members of decision-making groups is called **deindividuation,** which may be characterized as follows:

> People who are deindividuated have lost self-awareness and their personal identity in a group situation. Because they are prevented by the situation from awareness of themselves as individuals and from attention to their own behavior, deindividuated persons do not have the capacity for self-regulation and the ability to plan for the future. Thus . . . they become more reactive to immediate stimuli and emotions and are unresponsive to norms and the long-term consequences of their behavior.[13]

As noted above, deindividuation is characterized by a loss of objective self-awareness. Deindividuation can negate the possibility of making considered, intelligent decisions in groups. "Not only do deindividuated groups not carefully weigh alternatives, seek outside opinions, or otherwise critically assess decision alternatives but they seem immune to influences that might 'individuate' their members, and thereby make them sensitive to norms of appropriate behavior."[14] Many decision-making groups characterized by groupthink are firmly in the grip of deindividuation.[15]

A third dysfunctional influence on individuals functioning as members of decision-making groups is *pressure for group consensus*. There is always pressure to achieve consensus and, ideally, unanimity in decision-making groups. Presumably a group is more effective and its decisions more acceptable if it proceeds from unanimity. The majority rule that serves the judiciary so well is often regarded as an unacceptable deficiency in the smooth deliberations of a group. Social pressures and group norms are brought to bear in subtle and obvious ways to bring dissenters into line. "Members often censor their own ideas out of fear of being ridiculed or criticized by others in the group, especially when their ideas are somewhat novel or unorthodox and deviate from traditional ways of thinking. Instead of trying to come up with the best possible [alternative] and giving cogent arguments for it to the group, the member curtails his independent thinking because he is striving to live up to the expectations of the other members and to stay in their good graces."[16]

Apart from the potentially pernicious influences on the membership, the biggest comparative disadvantage of group decision making is the time required to reach a consensus. "In general, more time is required for a group to reach a decision than for a single individual to reach one. Insofar as some [situations] require quick decisions, individual decisions are favored."[17] "Research studies show that even when [decision-making] groups are clearly superior to individuals . . . the groups generally take longer than individuals do. . . . it may be much more efficient to have the very same people work independently after dividing up the tasks among them."[18]

"Few people have accused a group of being efficient. Referring a proposal to a committee to kill it is a well-known parliamentary tactic. Simple arithmetic should illustrate that in terms of man-hours expended, groups are destined to be more inefficient than individuals. . . . Compared to individuals groups are abominably slow."[19] Given the relative inefficiency of group decision making, one might be tempted to ask, "If groups are so slow and inefficient as a decision-making system, why bother with them at all? Let individuals make all the decisions."[20] The simple fact is that speed and efficiency are not the only criteria by which the comparative advantage of group decision making is judged. There is, for example, a deep-seated feeling that in many cases groups make better decisions than individuals. The jury system is based on the premise "that a group of peers is more likely to arrive at a better or more accurate verdict than a single individual, even a judge. . . . There is incontrovertible evidence that some situations virtually demand decisions made by groups and not by individuals."[21] In addition to the possibility of a higher-quality decision resulting from a group, there is the matter of acceptance of the decision by those who are affected by it. Many individuals are more amenable to accepting a decision in which they have had a direct voice or a representative vote. This phenomenon is likely the principal reason for the widespread incidence of group decision making. The matter of acceptance appears to overshadow the relative inefficiency of group choice.

Empirical Perspectives

"Research investigating group versus individual performance has a long history that is fraught with apparent inconsistencies."[22] "During the period preceding World War II, research into the productivity of groups was generally prompted by a desire to demonstrate the superiority of group action over individual action. . . . Needless to say, studies of this kind yielded a diverse assortment of findings. Groups were sometimes found to be more effective than individuals, but in other cases no significant differences were observed, or individuals seemed to be more productive than groups. . . . it became increasingly apparent that group performance was not consistently superior to that of individuals."[23]

Recent research into this subject has continued to yield inconclusive results. On balance, depending upon the nature of the task at hand, group decision making appears somewhat superior to individual choice.[24] It is also apparent, however, that highly competent individuals can produce decisions that are superior to the consensual outcomes of groups. Therefore, it is difficult if not inappropriate to assert the unvarying advantage of groups over individuals in managerial decision making. A cross-section of recent research findings will confirm this.

In a recent review of group versus individual performance, Hill pointed out that generalized comparisons are inappropriate and tend to simplify this extremely complex issue. His findings demonstrate that process and task differences influence any meaningful comparison.[25] Miner performed a study involving sixty-nine groups formed from 276 undergraduate students taking introductory courses in management.[26] The decision task used by Miner was a winter survival exercise. Survivors of a hypothetical plane crash are asked to decide individually or as a group whether to stay at the crash site or try to walk to a community known to be eighty miles away. (An attempt to walk out would mean almost certain death from freezing and exhaustion.) The findings of Miner's study showed that group decisions are better than *average* individual decisions and equal to the *best* individual decisions. Another study by Pfeiffer and Naglieri aimed to determine if special education placement decisions made by groups were superior to those made by individuals.[27] Their findings showed groups to be more effective decision makers than individuals where there exists one best alternative.

Still another study by McCormick, Lundgren, and Cecil focused on the approach taken by dyadic groups confronted with nonprogrammed decision-making tasks.[28] The results of this study showed that groups use approaches to category II decisions that are highly analogous to those used by individuals. Therefore, groups are not necessarily more effective than individuals in making nonroutine, nonrecurring decisions with uncertain outcomes. Zaleska's study of compared choices among solutions of a problem by individuals and groups from two populations also found no significant differences between individual and group decisions.[29]

A good deal of research supports an assertion of a greater willingness on the part of decision-making groups to assume more risk than individuals and more than may be warranted under the circumstances.[30] To this extent groups may be less effective decision makers than individuals (this is discussed in more detail later). Groups have also been shown to be less effective than individuals in making category I decisions.[31] Although relevant in a comparative context, this finding is less significant overall simply because groups are regarded as inappropriate entities for making routine, recurring decisions.

On balance, the empirical perspectives tend to support the theoretical perspectives on group versus individual decision making. Numerous other studies could be cited here,[32] but the evidence is already clear. It is far from axiomatic that group decision making is superior to that of individuals. The nature of the task at hand and the process used to arrive at a choice are determining variables in any meaningful comparison.[33] Groups are generally less efficient decision-making entities than are individuals. Groups may produce higher-quality decisions, however, and are more likely to produce more acceptable decisions. But groups are also likely to exert influences on their members that are conducive to varying degrees of deindividuation. Moreover, groups are totally inappropriate for category I choices that constitute the vast majority of decisions in most organizations. Finally, the tendency of groups to make riskier choices than would be made by their individual members further reduces any claim to their relative superiority.

The Risky Shift

Research has shown that some individuals functioning as members of groups are more likely to accept risk than they would as individual decision makers. For example, a study by Wallach and his associates revealed that "group interaction and achievement of consensus concerning decisions on matters of risk eventuate in a willingness to make decisions that are more risky than those that would be made in the absence of such interaction."[34] The tendency of some individuals to accept greater risk as members of groups is called the **risky shift** in the voluminous literature dealing with the subject.[35]

Explanations for the risky shift vary, but essentially there are three major categories of explanation. The first is the *interactive* explanation, which claims that risky shifts are due to interactions within the group as they relate to decision making and the emergence of leaders. This leadership aspect is supported by research, which indicates that members of the group who are higher in initial levels of risk taking are rated by other members as having the most influence on the group decision.[36] Moreover, risk-seeking individuals display higher confidence, need for achievement, and assertive abilities that are more likely to influence choices.[37] The decision-making aspect of this explanation holds that groups are better at making decisions than individuals[38] and that group discussion is a vital element in the risky shift.[39]

The second category presuming to explain the risky shift phenomenon consists of a set of *cognitive* hypotheses. One common cognitive explanation is that individuals tend to shift toward riskier positions as new information is obtained through group interaction, and the information is more important than the interaction in inducing the shift.[40] The other common cognitive explanation is based on the idea that group discussion causes a shift in the subjective expected utility of the individual who then moves toward a riskier position.[41]

The third and largest category that seeks to explain the risky shift phenomenon consists of a set of *affective* models that treat the effect that groups have on individuals in the presence of others. One of the most appealing affective explanations holds that risk is a value shaping the judgment of individuals.[42] A related explanation is based on the idea that the knowledge of another's risk level influences the extent to which an individual perceives himself or herself in relation to other members of the decision-making group.[43] A more recent view of value theory emphasizes the importance of ego self-esteem. According to this explanation, the individual's self-esteem and ego ideal cause the risky shift — that is, the individual moves closer to the position he or she personally values but was unable to approach before entering into group discussion.[44]

One of the earliest affective models relied on a so-called diffusion of responsibility hypothesis suggesting that individuals in a group view decisions from a collective perspective, thereby relieving themselves of individual responsibility for the decision and its consequences. This hypothesis may be summarized as follows:

> In a group situation the sense of personal responsibility for the decision is reduced to the extent that the decision is shared. This enables members of a group to anticipate that they will feel less blameworthy in case of failure than when they choose alone and must assume sole responsibility for the consequences. Presumably diffusion of responsibility occurs as a result of the group discussion where members can observe that each to some degree shares in determining the decision.[45]

In summary, there are many explanations that purport to account for the tendency of individuals to take riskier positions as members of groups than as decision makers in their own right. Although each explanation has some degree of cogency,[46] for purposes of this book the diffusion of responsibility hypothesis is adopted as most reflecting the author's perception of group decision making.

In another direction, groups are sometimes considered to be rather conservative decision makers. This may be because the need to arrive at a consensus may result in a choice that the most risk-averse member will accept.[47] The total group setting doubtlessly influences the behavior of individual members. If one person, for example, is entirely responsible for the outcome of his or her decision, that person may procrastinate in arriving at a choice. Membership in a group, however, tends to diffuse responsibility for the outcome, and the normally timid person may find temporary courage in the protection of the group.

Of course, it is also true that many motivated individuals will accept considerably more uncertainty than some groups. The group choice will often, therefore, tend to be more conservative than one made by an individual who covets risk in the belief that its acceptance will yield a reward. However, it is equally likely that the consensus of a group may produce a decision more risky than would be made by a risk-averse individual alone. The most that can be said, therefore, is that groups frequently tend to be more conservative than some risk-motivated individuals, and some risk-averse individuals tend to accept more uncertainty as members of a group.

A Composite Approach to Decision Making

Certain types of decisions may be best made by groups, whereas others may be better made by individuals.[48] Group decision making is suitable for the nonroutine, nonrecurring, highly uncertain choices requiring a judgmental strategy. Such decisions normally occur at the levels of middle and upper management. These managers also make category II decisions on a unilateral basis, but seemingly at a decreasing rate. Conversely, individual choice seems better suited to the routine, recurring, decision making involving a purely computational strategy. Normally such decisions are made by lower levels of management in the operating areas of the organization. This is a composite approach to decision making: the proper technique is matched with the decision at hand at the appropriate level of management.[49]

The numerous studies discussed in this section reflect mixed results with regard to the comparative advantage of group versus individual decision making. Nonetheless enough information is available to suggest some guidelines for managerial decision makers in formal organizations:

1. Group decision making is often better than the average individual's, but it is seldom better than the best individual's. In fact, the group's superior performance may result from the efforts of one superior decision maker.

2. The measure of a group's efficiency should be the total number of hours spent by each member in making the decision, not just the time spent by a group as compared to an individual.

3. Group decision making may be preferred to an individual choice, even though its superiority cannot be demonstrated. This may be especially true when acceptance of the decision is important or when organizational morale is a relevant consideration.[50]

A composite approach that utilizes to the fullest the strengths of both individual and group decision making is most likely to be achieved within the managerial decision-making process shown in Figure 2.1. In this context, the following rationale for group versus individual choice seems relevant:

1. In setting objectives groups may be selectively superior to individuals simply because more knowledge is available from the combined membership.

2. In the search for alternatives, many individual efforts, either by members of the group or by supporting staff, are necessary to ensure a broad search in the areas that apply.[51]

3. In evaluating the alternatives revealed mainly by individual efforts, the collective judgment of the group, with its broader range of critical viewpoints, has a definite potential to be superior.

4. The moment of choice in group decision making joins individuals who desire risk and those who wish to avoid it. The actual choice, therefore, may be more or less risky than one made by an individual, depending upon the individual's willingness to accept uncertainty. In any event, the group decision is more likely to be generally accepted as a result of the participation of those who will be affected by its consequences.

5. A decision made by an individual or a group must be implemented by individual managers who are personally responsible for the outcome of

their actions. It is well to recall that it is not practical to hold a group responsible for its choice. Therefore, responsibility falls on the individual manager.[52]

6. Follow-up and control procedures also must be carried out by individual managers at the point of implementation. Of course, a decision-making group can, and perhaps should, keep an eye on such procedures. Still, the direct responsibility to ensure an outcome that will meet the original objective lies with the individual manager.

CONFLICT IN DECISION MAKING

Conflict is inherent in all human interaction, and managerial decision making is no exception to the rule; opportunities for conflict abound in organizations of all types. Conflict, a vital and integrating aspect of human association, may contribute substantially to the perpetuation of the organization itself. The substantive issues of conflict arise from and have positive and negative consequences for the basic functioning of organizations.[53] An organization without conflict would be complacent, stagnant, and devoid of the dynamism that frequently stems from disagreement and dissonance.[54]

The Nature of Conflict

The literature suggests that conflict stems from one of several sources, including (1) competition for scarce resources (or rewards), (2) divergence of goals, and (3) drives for autonomy. In a broader context, the desire of one group or individual to dominate another entity is frequently cited as a basic source of conflict.[55]

In addition to the diversity of views regarding the sources of conflict, there is a wide variety of opinion as to its definition. Conflict has been identified as "behavior by organization members which is expended in opposition to other members."[56] Another conception suggests that conflict is "a type of behavior which occurs when two or more parties are in opposition or battle as a result of perceived relative deprivation from the activities of or interacting with another person or group."[57] In a generic sense, of course, conflict refers to all kinds of opposition or antagonistic interaction based on scarcity of power, resources, or social position as well as differing value structures.[58] "A conflict exists whenever incompatible activities occur."[59] Such activities may originate among persons, groups, or organizations. An activity that is incompatible with another activity prevents, obstructs, interferes, injures, or in some way makes the completion of the latter less likely or less effective.[60] Managerial decision making at all levels is fraught with the potential for incompatibilities and resultant conflict.[61]

It is a basic premise of this book that the greater the knowledge of the *determinants* and *indicators* of conflict, the greater the *understanding* of conflict, and the more likely that the *treatment* of conflict will have positive and beneficial effects. This relationship has been confirmed through empirical research.[62] It is conceptualized in Figure 8.1.

Determinants of Conflict

The determinants, or causal factors, of conflict are many. Any one or more can cause conflict in managerial decision making at any level.[63] One basic relationship in formal organizations that contributes greatly to the incidence of conflict is *interdependence between individuals or units.* Interdependence is the extent to which two or more entities depend on one another for assistance, information, compliance, or other coordinative acts in the performance of their respective tasks in the organization. Normally the higher the level of interdependence the greater the opportunity for conflict in arriving at decisions.[64] Another determinant of conflict in decision making relates to *performance criteria and rewards.* "The more the evaluations and rewards of higher management emphasize the separate performance of each department rather than their combined performance, the more conflict."[65] *Communication problems* are a third determinant of conflict. These problems may result from semantic difficulties, misunderstandings, and "noise" in the channels of communication.[66] *Role dissatisfaction* is another frequently cited determinant of conflict in managerial decision making. Frustrating task conditions such as work overload, underutilization of skills, and scarcity of resources contribute greatly to role dissatisfaction.

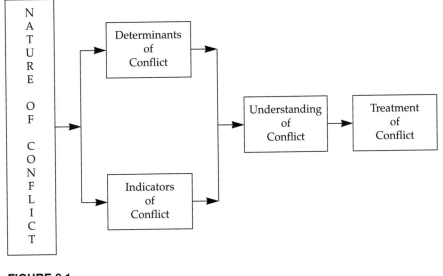

FIGURE 8.1

A Conceptual Model of Organizational Conflict

Research has found that certain *personality attributes* such as high authoritarianism, high dogmatism, and low self-esteem increase conflict behavior.[67] Individual idiosyncrasies and differing personal value systems fall into this same category. Moreover, to the extent that perception may be viewed as part of an individual's personality, *perceptual differences* also contribute to conflict in decision making. Still another significant determinant is a *divergence in goals or objectives*. Pondy has stated that "the major determinant of perceived interpersonal conflict is differentiation in the participants' goals for the organization."[68] And, of course, by definition, "a conflict relationship is one in which the parties can gain (relatively) only at each other's expense."[69]

A manager's knowledge of the determinants of conflict will contribute to his or her understanding and will result in more effective treatment of conflict. The understanding of conflict will also be enhanced by a knowledge of the indicators of conflict (see Figure 8.1).

Indicators of Conflict

The indicators of conflict are those observable and nonobservable symptoms that reflect the presence of conflict in formal organizations.[70] For example, in his study of high school teachers and administrators, Corwin used indices of *felt tension, reports of perceived disagreement,* and *overt disputes* as indicators of conflict.[71] In a comprehensive study of a telephone utility, Walton and his associates employed five indicators of conflict: (1) *interference*, or the lack of consideration shown and/or interference created between departments, (2) *overstatement*, or the tendency of a department to exaggerate its needs in order to influence another department, (3) *withholding of information*, or the tendency of one individual or department not to volunteer information useful to another entity in the organization, (4) *annoyance*, or the tendency for an individual in one department to become annoyed with the manager of another, and (5) *distrust*, or the level of feelings of distrust felt by a member of one department toward another department.[72]

Attitudinal correlates of conflict, such as *low trust, low friendliness,* and *low respect* between organizational entities, often lead to adverse manifest effects on performance in the form of tardiness, absenteeism, and resignation from the organization. Delivery schedules tend to be missed, rejection rates escalate, grievances mount, appeals proliferate, waste of resources increases, and overall efficiency and morale decline precipitously. These conditions are all tangible indicators of advanced conflict, more often than not undergirded by the more subtle and pervasive attitudinal factors.[73]

The indicators of conflict can, in a generic sense, be classified in terms of the extent to which the normal operation of the organization is interrupted. "This is the criterion of disruption."[74] There is, then, a threshold below which conflict may not be of significance to managerial decision making, although it may be quite significant to the individuals or other entities making up the total organization. Still, when the normal operation of the organization is constrained, deterred, impeded, or, in extreme cases, actually blocked, conflict in a manifest form does exist. Therefore, the essence of conflict in managerial decision making is the disruption of day-to-day operations. Potential disruptions can usually be averted and actual disruptions effectively treated through a better understanding occasioned by adequate knowledge of the determinants and indicators of conflict (see Figure 8.1).

Treatment of Conflict

Given the almost axiomatic incidence of varying degrees of conflict, the challenge becomes one of effective treatment to contain and reduce its dysfunctional effects. In this regard, the literature on conflict offers numerous suggestions.[75]

Boulding noted that the most important avenue of conflict resolution is the simple avoidance of conflict.[76] Goldman observed that organizations characterized by an absence of conflict suggest either noninteraction among human beings or a consensus about actions as they are occurring.[77] Clearly such a state is not reflective of managerial decision making in the real world.

In a more specific context, the use of *problem solving* is cited frequently as a particularly effective means for treating conflict.[78] This technique is based on the idea that conflict is essentially a common problem "in which the conflicting parties have the joint interest of reaching a mutually satisfactory solution."[79] However, problem solving is inherently weak in resolving conflicts based on differing value systems — one of the primary sources of conflict.[80] The **superordinate goal** is another technique often advanced for the treatment of conflict.[81] Essentially this technique involves inducing the conflicting parties into meaningful interaction through the presentation of some joint interest, collective benefit, or mutual advantage that stimulates them to resolve their differences for the common goal. In effect, the superordinate goal transcends the divisive issue of the moment and, by virtue of its compelling nature, overshadows conflicting viewpoints. It is very similar to another technique for treating conflict called **smoothing,** which means playing down differences while emphasizing common interests.[82]

Another technique often used to treat conflict is simply **making the system work.**[83] Basically this technique involves placing more emphasis on human relations to improve interaction among the conflicting parties. Improvement of communication, reassignment of personnel, and group therapy sessions are all part of this technique. A similar technique called *altering the human variable* was advanced by Robbins.[84]

In some cases of conflict, it may be necessary to *restructure the organization*.[85] Major options here include (1) creating coordinating positions, (2) developing an appeals system, (3) realigning departmental boundaries, and (4) changing individual responsibilities. The *expansion of resources* affords another means for treating conflict, especially when the conflict originates from a scarcity of resources. This technique is usually effective because, more often than not, it leaves the conflicting parties largely satisfied. Its principal disadvantage, of course, is the limited availability of resources for expansion.

Probably the most natural response to conflict is to avoid it. **Conflict avoidance** generally involves a withdrawal from the arena of confrontation. **Suppression** is also a form of conflict avoidance. This form is often used when withdrawal is not feasible or possible, as when interaction in a decision-making environment can't be avoided. The principal shortcoming of both these forms of conflict avoidance is that they merely conceal or mask the basic disagreements in the situation rather than resolve them in a positive, constructive way. As such, conflict avoidance, at least in a formal organization, is probably one of the least effective ways to treat conflict, except possibly on a very short-term basis.[86]

As a technique for treating conflict, **compromise** is the most frequently used.[87] Like conflict avoidance, compromise does not result in a decisive loser or winner. Unlike conflict avoidance, however, compromise does result in a decision, although it is seldom an optimal solution for any one party. The distinguishing characteristic of compromise is that each party to it must make some concession. Specific means for obtaining compromise solutions to conflictful situations include external or third-party intervention as well as internal mechanisms such as group and representative negotiation and voting.[88]

Pondy set forth the concept of **equilibrium** as an effective way to minimize conflict in formal organizations.[89] Presumably to the extent that subjectively valued inducements (such as benefits, status, recognition) exceed subjectively valued contributions (such as education, time, energy), there is less of an opportunity for conflictful situations to develop. Conversely, if contributions exceed inducements, a state of disequilibrium exists, and the opportunities for conflict are more plentiful. Obviously, then, the effective treatment of conflict necessitates minimizing the incidence of disequilibrium among individuals and units and between them and the organization itself.[90]

In summary, then, a better knowledge of its determinants and indicators leads to an improved understanding of conflict, which in turn contributes to a more effective treatment of conflict in the managerial decision making of formal organizations.[91]

PARTICIPATION IN DECISION MAKING

There is a voluminous literature dealing with the concept of participation in decision making. The concept seems to fascinate behaviorists and social scientists, who never tire of extolling its merits while tending to ignore its potential demerits. In the broader sense, participation refers to the active involvement of subordinates or followers in the making of decisions that directly affect them in the work place. Most of the theoretical perspectives and empirical studies cited here relate to this definition. A more precise concern of this book is with the actual accomplishment of functions and activities within the decision-making process by subordinate managers whose responsibilities are affected by choices made at higher levels of management.

Theoretical Perspectives

Participation in decision making is generally regarded as a sign of enlightened and democratic management.[92] Through the use of participation, individual members are involved in a wide range of the objective-setting, problem-solving, and decision-making activities of the organization. Participation in these activities is held to contribute to the effective integration of the individual's goals and the organization's objectives.[93] This integration is facilitated in two ways. "First, the process of participating will be directly satisfying to individuals whose personal goals include exerting control or contributing to policy formulation. Secondly, participation allows the individual to represent his unique needs and interests in the processes which actually define the nature of the organization. The outcome should be solutions, decisions, and objectives which have built into them provisions for attaining individual goals."[94]

Participation in decision making can be justified on several grounds. Presumably higher levels of management have a kind of moral obligation to encourage involvement in the decision-making process by lower levels of management. Participation is also frequently justified on the basis of improved efficiency and productivity as well as greater employee satisfaction. The actual mechanisms by which participation contributes to these outcomes, however, are by no means clear. "The very diversity in the outcomes from participation indicates that there may be a wide range of belief about the purpose of and rationales for participation. With a topic like participation, it is difficult to conceive of anyone who could not find an occasion when participation would be of value."[95]

Patchen has argued cogently that participation in decision making can lead to a closer identification with the organization.[96] As he explains it:

> When an individual participates in decisions that affect a group or organization to which he belongs, he comes to identify more with this organization. . . . we mean . . . that his role in the organization is an important and valuable part of his self-concept. . . . by virtue of participating in decision making, . . . the individual acquires a *higher status* in the organization. He is, by virtue of participating in decision-making, a more important member of the organization than he would otherwise be.[97]

Patchen further notes that "identification with the organization can lead to higher motivation to do the organization's work primarily because it makes the individual more susceptible to social pressures from organizational members."[98] In addition to greater susceptibility to social pressures, the participant in decision making should also be more responsive to organizational pressures for higher levels of performance from superiors in the managerial hierarchy. In theory, then, greater participation in decision making is conducive to higher levels of productivity and, presumably, a greater sense of self-fulfillment and satisfaction on the part of the individual, particularly if this increased output is recognized and rewarded equitably.[99]

"Participation in decision making generally produces favorable employee attitudes toward management, better relationships between supervisors and subordinates, better upward communication, and greater subordinate acceptance of superiors as their representatives. All these factors contribute to greater employee satisfaction."[100] Subordinates become more ego-involved in decisions they have influenced. When they have participated in the decision-making process, they tend to internalize the choice and feel personally responsible for carrying it out. Thus, the success or failure of a decision and subsequent action becomes their success or failure.

Participation by employees also tends to result in greater subordinate acceptance of decisions.[101] This is one of the principal arguments in favor of participative decision making. Because of the greater number of variables involved in the relationship between participation and productivity, it is a more complex phenomenon than the relationship between participation and satisfaction. In any event, higher levels of productivity and greater amounts of employee satisfaction are invariably preferred as the two principal advantages of participative decision making. A third advantage of a more subtle and political nature is the heightened acceptance of decisions in which subordinates have been involved.

There are some obvious potential disadvantages in participative decision making.[102] For example, as will be noted below, participation can be accomplished in varying degrees. If the degree of participation is less than is perceived to be genuine, the advantages might be transformed into disadvantages. For example, Argyris warns of the dangers of "pseudo-participation."[103] This is participation "which looks like, but is not, real participation. True participation means that the people can be observed to be spontaneous and free in their discussion. Participation, in the real sense of the word, also involves a group decision which leads the group to accept or reject some course of action."[104]

More obvious potential disadvantages of participative decision making include the time and effort required to involve several people in the process of choice. Where time is a primary constraint, participation may not be feasible. In such cases management should consider the trade-offs very carefully. Also some decisions, especially those of a highly confidential nature such as top-level strategic decisions, are necessarily limited to those who have a need to know. Participation in such decisions might compromise security and place the organization at a serious disadvantage vis-à-vis its principal competitors. Furthermore, some decisions such as those that require complex knowledge and professional judgment are simply not adaptable in any meaningful sense to participation for democratic purposes. Finally, it may well be that the decisions most amenable to participation by lower levels of management are those category I choices that should be made in the operating areas of the organization in any case. Participation in these decisions seems certain to be regarded as perfunctory at best. On balance, it may well be that the decisions in which subordinates would like to participate most are foreclosed to them, and the choices in which they ask to participate on a regular basis are the ones that should normally fall within their purview.

Perhaps the most significant potential disadvantage of participative decision making is the diffusion of accountability for results. Managers who practice participation do not relieve themselves of their responsibility to their superiors. Authority may be delegated, but responsibility may not. Higher levels of management are always accountable to their superiors for the performance of lower levels of management regardless of the degree of participation in decision making. This relationship is a basic tenet of management.

Williams advanced a thesis for participative decision making that, in light of the advantages and disadvantages of the approach, is adopted in this book:

> When compared with authoritarian [decision making], participative [decision making] expresses greater confidence in the subordinate's willingness and ability to assume responsibility, involves subordinates in [management] to a greater extent, and accepts more fully the notion that management has a responsibility to subordinates as well as to superiors. No manager can perform over an extended period of time without some degree of employee participation [in decision making].[105]

Clearly the actual advantages of participation in decision making appear to outweigh the potential disadvantages. In summary, the advantages are (1) improved decision making through collective judgment, (2) facilitation of change through broader acceptance of the choice, (3) closer identification of the participants with the organization's objectives and their personal goals, and (4) higher levels of achievement manifested in increased productivity and a greater sense of satisfaction and self-fulfillment. The potential disadvantages are likely to occur in the presence of (1) time pressures, which might be mitigated with more lead time, (2) confidential decisions where disclosure must be limited to a definite need to know, (3) complex decisions requiring highly specialized knowledge, and (4) misconceptions regarding the accountability of higher levels of management.

Participation in decision making, then, is highly situational and is largely a matter of degree. Depending upon the preferences of higher levels of management, the competencies of lower levels, the nature of the decision at hand, and the time and cost constraints of the moment, it seems reasonable to suggest a continuum of participation in decision making. From the least to the most participative decision making, this continuum is somewhat as follows:

1. The manager makes the decision and simply announces it.
2. The manager makes the decision and then tries to sell it.

3. The manager presents ideas, invites questions, and then makes the decision.

4. The manager presents a tentative decision subject to change.

5. The manager presents the decision-making situation, obtains suggestions and ideas, and then makes the decision.

6. The manager defines the limits and asks subordinates or the group to make the decision.

7. The manager permits the subordinates to make decisions freely within agreed limits.[106]

The precise degree of participation in decision making that is allowed by a given manager is a composite function of:

1. The importance of participation to the manager who is providing the opportunity for it

2. The manager's confidence in his or her subordinates

3. The manager's own decision-making style

4. The manager's willingness and ability to cope with the additional uncertainty attendant upon high degrees of participation[107]

Empirical Perspectives

Most of the empirical studies of participation in decision making are designed to show that involvement of subordinates in the process of choice tends to increase satisfaction and/or to raise productivity. A small group of empirical studies are oriented in a corollary fashion toward demonstrating that participative decision making begets acceptance and overcomes resistance to change. This section will briefly present a cross-section of these studies.

In a review of forty empirical studies from 1948 through 1969, Stogdill observed that participation in decision making does not always elicit increases in productivity, but for the most part increased participation is quite likely to result in higher levels of individual satisfaction.[108] Vroom also cited divergent effects on productivity as a result of increased participation in decision making.[109] One group of studies reported impressive gains in productivity and reduced resistance to change attributable to greater participation. Another smaller group of studies reported no increases in productivity as a result of greater participation in decision making.

As presented in Chapter 2, Trull's study found that participation in the decision-making process by managers who are directly involved in the implementation of a given choice tends to facilitate understanding and to elicit acceptance, which, in turn, contributes to decision success. Stagner's study of five hundred vice presidents in 125 large firms found that participation resulted in a good deal of executive satisfaction and contributed to higher levels of profitability.[110] In his words:

> Support is available for the positions taken by Likert (1967) and McGregor (1960) in favor of participative management. Involvement of all executives . . . and concern by the chief that all be satisfied . . . are associated with high executive morale, satisfaction with decision-making process, and profitability.[111]

Participation should in some degree occur in all the functions of the decision-making process rather than just in choice and implementation. "Participation of the executors of the decisions in diagnosis, search, and choice are . . . particularly important to implementation. Presumably learning and adaptability are enhanced by participative decision making."[112]

Research has shown consistently that managers use different degrees of participation at different times and with varying circumstances surrounding the decision-making situation.[113] For example, Heller's study of 260 senior managers in fifteen large successful American companies found that in a third of the decision-making situations, managers tended to make unilateral choices, whereas in another third of the situations, decisions were made by the leader after some consultation with his or her followers. In only one-fourth of the decisions were the followers given any appreciable voice in the outcome.[114] Heller concluded that, at best, no more than 50 percent of all decisions made received meaningful input from followers.[115] In other words, for a given choice it is far from certain that subordinates will have a significant voice in decisions directly affecting them.[116] Moreover, given the advantages frequently attributed to participative decision making, the degree of actual and meaningful involvement by subordinates in many organizations remains highly situational, especially for category II decisions.

Studies of participative decision making continue to abound in the literature of management.[117] For example, Driscoll studied the decision making of a small liberal arts college in upstate New York.[118] He found that "increasing levels of participation are associated with greater overall satisfaction with the organization as well as specific satisfaction with the participation itself."[119] Schuler's study of a large manufacturing firm revealed significant positive correlations between participation in decision making and satisfaction with the work situation.[120] A study by Abdel-Halim of 229 employees in a large retail drug company in the Midwest revealed that participation in nonrepetitive decision making by subjects with a high need for autonomy tended to improve performance and increase satisfaction.[121] And, finally, Harrison's study of research scientists in five laboratories revealed a strong desire on the part of the researchers to participate in the determination of their laboratory projects.[122]

Clearly there are different degrees of participation in decision making and different situations in which one degree may be chosen over another. One rather comprehensive summary of the findings from research on this subject states that:

1. Managers use decision processes providing greater opportunities for participation when the quality of the decision is important rather than when it is irrelevant.

2. Managers use decision processes providing less opportunity for participation when they possess all the necessary information to generate a high-quality decision rather than when they lack some of the needed information.

3. Managers use decision processes providing less opportunity for participation when the decision-making situation they face is well structured rather than when it is unstructured.

4. Managers use decision processes providing more opportunity for participation when the subordinate's acceptance of the decision is critical for its effective implementation and when the prior probability of acceptance of an autocratic decision is low rather than when either or both of these conditions are not satisfied.

5. Managers use decision processes providing a greater opportunity for participation when the subordinate's acceptance of the decision is critical for its effective implementation, when the manager trusts subordinates to pay attention to organizational rather than personal goals, and when conflict among subordinates is absent, rather than when one or more of these conditions is not satisfied.[123]

On balance it seems evident that the degree of participation in decision making afforded subordinates is influenced to a considerable extent by superiors' belief in the value of participation.[124] In this context a study of eighty-four top managers conducted by Dickson found that participation was practiced most frequently when some one or more of the following conditions prevailed: (1) acceptance of the decision by subordinates was important and was likely to be facilitated by participation, (2) the quality of the decision was likely to be improved through participation by subordinates, and (3) participation was regarded as a means of maintaining effective superior-subordinate communication.[125] Dickson emphasized the importance of the views of top managers with regard to participation in decision making as follows: "These persons are the principal power holders in their organizations, and their values and expectancies for participation will determine the form and process of participation and hence the likely outcomes from participation."[126] To reemphasize the principal theme of this section: participation in decision making is highly situational and is largely a matter of degree.[127]

GENDER DIFFERENCES AND SIMILARITIES IN DECISION MAKING

During the past twenty years the number of female managers in formal organizations more than doubled, while the number of male managers increased by much less. During this same period, the number of women enrolled in MBA programs throughout the nation increased threefold and continues to rise.

Today women constitute more than 45 percent of the entire work force in the United States.[128] The rise in the number of women in positions of actual or potential managerial responsibility has been accompanied by a proliferation of research and publications related to sex and gender. Several new journals, new chapters on sex roles in reference books, and new listings dealing with sex differences and sex roles have accelerated over the past twenty years.[129] One line of research investigates how men and women differ in a variety of behaviors, traits, and capabilities. A second and more recent research emphasis focuses on differences of a psychological rather than a demographic nature. Included in this category is an increasingly abundant literature on masculinity, femininity, and the newer concept of androgyny.[130] A third and still newer line of research deals with gender or sex as a social category. Here the focus is not on how men and women *actually* differ, but how people *think* they differ.[131]

In these three approaches to research on sex differences, comparisons are made between nonworking men and women, between working men and women, and between men and women occupying positions of managerial responsibility.[132] The primary concern in this book is with significant differences and similarities manifested by males and females enacting managerial roles including the making of decisions in formal organizations. The literature on this specialized group of individuals is sparse in relation to the proliferation of writings regarding differences between men and women in general. Still there is enough to provide a solid empirical foundation regarding gender differences and similarities in decision making, albeit, in many instances, the evidence is inferential. To this literature we now turn.

Gender Differences

Most of the differences attributed to gender relate to demographic, psychological, or social variations in behavior induced or observed under varying conditions. These variations do not for the most part deal directly with managerial decision making. The association must, therefore, be made by deduction or inference.

Kogan and Wallach's study of decision making by 114 male and 103 female undergraduates noted some differences in the risk-taking propensities of the subjects.[133] For example, "males exhibited greater confidence of judgments than females. Males, furthermore, were more extreme than females in their judgments at low and moderate confidence levels, but the reverse pattern obtained at higher confidence levels."[134] Given a high level of confidence, females tended to become more extreme in their judgments and quite bold in their willingness to make decisions. The researchers attributed this behavior on the part of the female subjects to a "counterphobic release of boldness."[135] In a study of 103 male and female students, Steers noted that in decision making "females tend to be more participative as a group and that different personality variables are associated with participation for each sex."[136] In still another study by Brenner and Vinacke of thirty-eight firms in

New York City, which included managers and nonmanagers, definite gender differences were manifested in that males tended to be exploitative in their behavior, whereas females tended to be accommodative.[137]

There is a good deal of research that shows significant differences in the values of males and females. Although these gender differences do not relate directly to decision making, they reflect a phenomenon to be reckoned with in gender choice. In a comprehensive study of 1,460 executives conducted under the auspices of the American Management Association, some unexpected differences surfaced between male and female managers.[138] Female managers, for example, ranked *good organization leadership* and *organizational stability* much higher than their male colleagues. Women managers placed a higher value on *ability, ambition, skill, cooperation,* and *flexibility.* Females considered *ability* to be the most important attribute. Males opted for *achievement.* Somewhat surprisingly, the survey indicated that *female managers are more career oriented than male managers.* Clearly this finding represents a refutation of stereotypic thinking. Another study by Deaux of male and female first-level managers in two organizations revealed that "males evaluated their performance more favorably than did women, and rated themselves as having more ability and greater intelligence."[139] And, finally, still another study of male and female decision makers revealed that the females preferred to provide student financial assistance on the basis of scholastic merit, whereas the males preferred to award financial aid on the basis of student need.[140] These studies suggest some discernible differences in the values of males and females that may be translated into differences in managerial decision making.

Numerous other writings focus on perceived gender differences, although not directly in decision making.[141] In this regard, it is well to recall two things: (1) differences in gender behavior that are only inferentially relatable to decision making are not the same thing as differences discerned in actually arriving at a choice, and (2) gender differences observed in the actual making of a decision can be a source of strength rather than a contribution to weakness. As a separate but significant point, it is well to recall that most studies show few if any significant differences in the direct decision-making behavior of males and females. To the contrary, it is not uncommon to find more similarities than differences between male and female decision makers.

Gender Similarities

In a study of two hundred male and female managers in several large metropolitan commercial banks, Humphreys and Shrode found more similarities than differences in the decision-making behavior of the subjects.[142] In a study of two hundred executives in federal agencies in Washington, D.C., there were no significant differences between the male and female executives on any of the decision task variables.[143] A study of undergraduate male and female students in New York City found no significant differences in their preferences for taking risks in decision making.[144]

In still another study of 130 actual and aspiring managers, Johnson and Powell found no differences in the decision-making style of the participants based on gender.[145] In their words, "No significant differences were found in this study in male and female decision quality or attitudes to risk."[146]

Other studies of the personal attributes of male and female managers also reveal few significant differences. For example, one study of one hundred males and one hundred females in senior management positions in Canadian business found more similarities than differences between the listings of success attributes provided by males and females in the study.[147] In this particular study, it is interesting to note that decision-making abilities were ranked higher by the males than by the females. In still another study of 513 executives by Barnett and Karson, the researchers noted a definite absence of significant decision-making differences attributable to gender. In their words, "there was no set of 'rules' of male or female behavior."[148] And finally, in an updating of the aforementioned study conducted under the auspices of the American Management Association, the researchers noted no significant difference stemming from the gender of the executive respondents.[149]

Clearly the evidence related to gender differences and similarities in decision making is mixed. "It is clear that many women have decision styles, personalities, and values that are closer to those of their male counterparts than to the stereotype of the female population."[150] Some writers even suggest that females possess certain advantages that give then an extra edge in management.[151] In any event, there is little basis in fact for most of the stereotypic thinking and behavior that surrounds women in management and decision making.[152]

In summary, the evidence surrounding differences and similarities in the demographic, psychological, and social behavior of males and females seems inconclusive at best and misleading at worst. There is little hard evidence to support a contention of significant differences in the behavior of males and females actually enacting managerial roles in formal organizations. Finally, the evidence adduced in the published studies of males and females enacting managerial roles and making managerial decisions reveals as many if not more similarities than differences. More significant, if there are differences in decision-making behavior, they may be attributable to the choice at hand or the environment of the decision rather than differences in gender.[153] There is no justification for many of the stereotypes held regarding female decision makers.[154] Whatever behavioral variations do exist can, through enlightened management, be meaningfully integrated so that organizations could benefit from the strengths of differences and dilute their weaknesses.

The place of women in management is well established in our society today. We benefit greatly from the decision-making attributes they bring to organizations of all types. With their male colleagues, these women managers will move managerial decision making to a new plateau of excellence.

SUMMARY

This chapter focused on four major subjects that fall within the discipline of social psychology and reflect the interdisciplinary nature of the managerial decision-making process.

Much management literature increasingly extols the relative merits of collective decision making and consensual choice. But some writers see the disadvantages inherent in the cohesiveness needed for effective group decision making. Others feel that competent individuals are more likely to arrive at better decisions than the least-common-denominator consensus characteristic of collective choice. Still others assert that many people are more inclined to accept risk as members of groups than as individual decision makers.

The advantages of group decision making include the fact that groups may have a larger and more varied knowledge base than any one individual. But there is some evidence that a highly competent individual can produce choices superior to those of a group. It is also asserted that group decisions are more likely to be accepted by those who must carry them out, especially if they had a voice in the decision. And, finally, group decision making can dilute biased or capricious behavior by individual decision makers.

Arguments against excessive reliance on group decision making include the inordinate amount of time it takes to achieve a consensus and the fact that pooled judgments tend to be worse than those of the most-qualified members when most members are not competent to judge an issue. Group judgments tend to be superior only when most members are highly competent.

Groups can exert powerful influences on their members, which tend to work against the initiative and intellect of the individual and to impede the performance of those who are highly motivated. Examples of pernicious group influences include (1) social loafing, (2) deindividuation, and (3) groupthink. The pressure to achieve a group consensus can be costly to individual members and the quality of the decision, which may offset any advantages of collective decision making.

The empirical evidence related to group versus individual decision making is inconclusive. The nature of the task at hand and the process used to arrive at a choice are determining variables in any meaningful comparison. Groups (1) are generally less efficient, (2) may produce high quality decisions, but are more likely to produce only more acceptable decisions, (3) are likely to exert influences on their members that are conducive to deindividuation, and (4) to make riskier choices. Moreover, groups are inappropriate for category I decisions. This book advocates a composite approach that draws upon the relative strengths of both individuals and groups.

Conflict is inherent in all human interaction. It has both positive and negative aspects. Although the tendency is to exaggerate the negative aspects, an organization without conflict would be complacent and stagnant. Conflict usually stems from the following sources: (1) competition for scarce resources, (2) divergence of goals, or (3) drives for autonomy. The desire of one party to dominate another is regarded as a primary source of conflict.

This book advances the premise that the greater the knowledge of the determinants and indicators of conflict the greater the understanding and the more likely the treatment of conflict will have positive effects (see Figure 8.1). The determinants (causes) of conflict include (1) interdependence between individuals or units, (2) performance criteria and rewards, (3) communication problems, (4) role dissatisfaction, (5) personality attributes, (6) perceptual differences, and (7) divergence in goals or objectives. The indicators (symptoms) of conflict include (1) felt tension, (2) perceived disagreements, (3) overt disputes, (4) overstatement of needs, (5) withholding of information, (6) annoyance, (7) low trust, (8) low friendliness, (9) low respect, and (10) disruption of operations. The extent of disruption is the indicator that tells management when it must take conflict seriously.

Techniques useful for treating conflict include (1) problem solving, (2) setting a superordinate goal, (3) smoothing, (4) making the system work, (5) restructuring the organization, (6) expanding resources, (7) avoiding conflict, (8) suppressing it, (9) compromising, and (10) maintaining equilibrium between inducements and contributions. Each situation must be assessed on its own merits in order to select the best approach to conflict resolution.

Participation refers to the active involvement of subordinates in the making of decisions that directly affect them. Participation is usually justified on the basis that it increases productivity, leads to greater employee satisfaction, and fulfills management's moral obligation to manage democratically. Participation in decision making is said to produce (1) favorable employee attitudes toward management, (2) better relations between supervisors and subordinates, (3) better upward communication, (4) greater acceptance by subordinates of superiors as their representatives, (5) heightened employee motivation, and (6) greater subordinate acceptance of decisions.

Disadvantages of participative decision making include the fact that unless it is genuine in intent, participation may be perceived as tokenism. Because participative decision making usually involves group effort, it can be time-consuming. Moreover, many decisions are confidential in nature, which tends to work against participation, as do decisions requiring high levels of specialized knowledge. Finally, the most significant disadvantage is the diffusion of accountability. Managers who practice participation do not relieve themselves of their responsibility to their superiors. Thus, participation in decision making is highly situational and is largely a matter of degree.

As the number of women in positions of managerial responsibility has increased, many studies have addressed the relative merits of male versus female decision making. But most of them that purport to reflect gender differences do not deal directly with decision-making behavior; differences tend to be demographic, psychological, and social in nature. In direct comparisons of males and females involved in comparable decision-making situations, the similarities are at least as numerous as the differences. Whatever differences do exist may be attributable to the choice at hand or the environment of the decision rather than to differences in gender. There is no justification for many of the stereotypes attributed to females in decision making.

REVIEW AND DISCUSSION QUESTIONS

1. In your opinion, what phenomena account for the increasing prevalence of group decision making? Discuss.

2. Make your own comparative evaluation of the relative merits of group versus individual decision making. What are your findings?

3. What are the relative advantages of group versus individual decision making within each of the decision-making functions?

4. What are the most likely determinants of conflict in managerial decision making in formal organizations?

5. Given the techniques discussed in this chapter, what are the three most effective means of treating a conflict in decision making?

6. Given the obvious disadvantages of participative decision making, how do you explain its increasingly expanded advocacy?

7. In your opinion what is the single most important advantage of participative decision making?

8. Need participative decision making always occur in groups?

9. If there are few significant differences or similarities resulting from comparisons of males or females directly involved in decision-making situations, how do you explain the increasing interest in the subject?

10. Human behavior in decision-making situations is the common thread running through the principal subjects of this chapter. Why is this an important phenomenon in the management of formal organizations?

NOTES

1. See "Decisions, Decisions, Decisions," *Psychology Today* (November 1971), 51ff.; and Donald L. Piper, "Decision Making: Decisions Made by Individuals vs. Those Made by Group Consensus or Group Participation," *Educational Administration Quarterly*, 10 (Spring 1974), 82–95. Also see Jay Hall, "Synergism in Group Decision Making," *Personnel Journal* (January 1979), 12–13.

2. See Irving L. Janis, *Groupthink*, 2nd ed. (Boston: Houghton Mifflin, 1982).

3. See John P. Campbell, "Individual Versus Group Problem Solving in an Industrial Sample," *Journal of Applied Psychology*, 52, No. 3 (1968), 205–210.

4. See James A. F. Stoner, "Risky and Cautious Shifts in Group Decisions: The Influence of Widely Held Values," *Journal of Experimental Social Psychology*, 4 (1968), 442–459.

5. Robert Tattersall, "In Defense of the Consensus Decision," *Financial Analysts Journal* (January/February 1984), 55–67.

6. Paul R. Timm, "Let's Not Have a Meeting," *Supervisory Management* (August 1982), 2–7.

7. Daniel D. Wheeler and Irving L. Janis, *A Practical Guide for Making Decisions* (New York: Free Press, 1980), p. 179.

8. Ibid., p. 180.

9. Raymond M. Wilmotte and Philip I. Morgan, "The Discipline Gap in Decision Making," *Managerial Review* (September 1984), 21–24.

10. J. Keith Murnighan, "Group Decision Making: What Strategies Should You Use?" *Management Review* (February 1981), 55–62.

11. Gene E. Burton, "The Group Process: Key to More Productive Management," *Management World* (May 1981), 12–15.

12. Walter C. Swap, "Destructive Effects of Groups on Individuals," in *Group Decision Making*, ed. Walter C. Swap and Associates (Beverly Hills, Calif.: Sage, 1984), p. 69.

13. E. Diener, "Deindividuation: The Absence of Self-Awareness and Self-Regulation in Group Members," in *Psychology of Group Influence*, ed. P. B. Paulus (Hillsdale, N.J.: Erlbaum, 1980), p. 210.

14. Swap, "Effects of Groups on Individuals," p. 74.

15. See Janis, *Groupthink*; and Wheeler and Janis, *A Practical Guide for Making Decisions*, pp. 188–195.

16. Wheeler and Janis, *A Practical Guide for Making Decisions*, p. 181.

17. Norman R. F. Maier, "Assets and Liabilities in Group Problem Solving: The Need for an Integrative Function," in *Groups and Organizations: Integrated Readings in the Analysis of Social Behavior*, ed. Bernard L. Hinton and H. Joseph Reitz (Belmont, Calif.: Wadsworth, 1971), p. 282.

18. Wheeler and Janis, *A Practical Guide for Making Decisions*, pp. 179–180.

19. B. Aubrey Fisher, *Small Group Decision Making: Communication and the Group Process* (New York: McGraw-Hill, 1974), p. 38.

20. Ibid.

21. Ibid., p. 39.

22. Frederick C. Miner, Jr., "Group versus Individual Decision Making: An Investigation of Performance Measures, Decision Strategies, and Process Losses/Gains," *Organizational Behavior and Human Performance*, 33 (1984), 112–124.

23. Ivan D. Steiner, *Group Process and Productivity* (New York: Academic Press, 1972), p. 10.

24. Larry K. Michelson et al., "A Realistic Test of Individual Versus Group Consensus Decision Making," *Journal of Applied Psychology*, 74, No. 5 (1989), 834–839.

25. G. W. Hill, "Group versus Individual Performance: Are N + 1 Heads Better Than One?" *Psychological Bulletin*, 91 (1982), 517–539.

26. Miner, "Group versus Individual Decision Making."

27. Steven I. Pfeiffer and Jack A. Naglieri, "An Investigation of Multi-Disciplinary Team Decision-Making," *Journal of Learning Disabilities* (December 1983), 588–590; and Steven I. Pfeiffer, "The Superiority of Team Decision Making," *Exceptional Children* (September 1982), 68–69.

28. Michael McCormick, Earl Lundgren, and Earl Cecil, "Group Search and Decision-Making Processes: A Laboratory Test of Soelberg's Confirmation Hypothesis," *Journal of Social Psychology* (February 1980), 79–86.

29. Maryla Zaleska, "Individual and Group Choices Among Solutions of a Problem When Solution Verifiability Is Moderate or Low," *European Journal of Social Psychology*, 8 (1978), 37–53.

30. See, for example, Patrick R. Laughlin and P. Christofer Earley, "Social Combination Models, Persuasive Arguments Theory, Social Comparison Theory, and Choice Shift," *Journal of Personality and Social Psychology* (February 1982), 273–280.

31. John C. Mowen and James Gentry, "Investigation of the Preference-Reversal Phenomenon in a New Product Introduction Task," *Journal of Applied Psychology* (December 1980), 715–722.

32. See, for example, John W. Dickson, "The Effect of Normative Models on Individual and Group Choice," *European Journal of Social Psychology*, 8 (1978), 91–107; and Joseph P. Forgas, "Responsibility Attribution by Groups and Individuals: The Effects of the Interaction Episode," *European Journal of Social Psychology* 11 (1981), 87–99.

33. Baruch Fischhoff, "Predicting Frames," *Journal of Experimental Psychology: Learning, Memory, and Cognition*, 9, (1983), 103–116.

34. Michael A. Wallach, Nathan Kogan, and Daryl J. Bem, "Group Influence on Individual Risk Taking," *Journal of Abnormal and Social Psychology*, 65, No. 2 (1962), 85.

35. For example, see D. G. Marquis, "Individual Responsibility and Group Decisions Involving Risk," *Industrial Management Review*, 3 (1962), 8–23; and S. Siegel and R. B. Zajonc, "Group Risk Taking in Professional Decisions," *Sociometry*, 30 (1967), 339–350.

36. Wallach, Kogan, and Bem, "Group Influence on Individual Risk Taking"; and Richard A. Lilienthal and Sam L. Hutchison, Jr., "Group Polarization (Risky Shift) in Led and Leaderless Groups," *Psychological Reports*, 45 (1979), 168.

37. See Y. Rim, "Risk-Taking and Need for Achievement," *Acta Psychologica*, 21 (1963), 108–115; and Eugene Burnstein, "An Analysis of Group Decisions Involving Risk ('The Risky Shift')," *Human Relations*, 22, No. 5 (1969), 381–395.

38. See William Faust, "Group Versus Individual Problem-Solving," *Journal of Abnormal and Social Psychology*, 59 (1959), 68–72.

39. Solomon Rettig, "Group Discussion and Predicted Ethical Risk Taking," *Journal of Personality and Social Psychology*, 3 (1966), 629–633.

40. See Nathan Kogan and Michael A. Wallach, "Risky Shift Phenomena in Small Decision-Making Groups: A Test of the Information Exchange Hypothesis," *Journal of Experimental Social Psychology*, 3 (1967), 75–84.

41. See Eugene Burnstein and Harold Miller, "Risky Shift Is Eminently Rational," *Journal of Personality and Social Psychology*, 20, No. 3 (1971), 462–471.

42. Roger Brown, *Social Psychology* (New York: Free Press, 1965), pp. 698–706; and Michael A. Wallach and Cliff W. Wing, Jr., "Is Risk a Value?" *Journal of Personality and Social Psychology*, 9 (1986), 101–106.

43. A. I. Teger and D. G. Pruitt, "Components of Group Risk Taking," *Journal of Experimental Social Psychology*, 3 (1967), 189–205.

44. H. Lamm, E. Schaude, and G. Trommsdorff, "Risky Shift as a Function of Group Members' Value of Risk and Need for Approval," *Journal of Personality and Social Psychology*, 20 (1971), 430–435.

45. Burnstein, "An Analysis of Group Decisions Involving Risk," p. 382.

46. Many of the references and much of the explanation related to the risky shift in this chapter is adapted with minor modifications from Samuel A. Kirkpatrick, "Psychological Views of Decision-Making," in *Political Science Annual*, Vol. 6, ed. Cornelius P. Cotter (Indianapolis: Bobbs-Merrill, 1975), pp. 83–87.

47. Fremont E. Kast and James E. Rosenzweig, *Organization and Management: A Systems Approach* (New York: McGraw-Hill, 1970), p. 421.

48. See John J. Sherwood and Florence M. Hoylman, "Individual versus Group Approaches to Decision Making," *Supervisory Management* (April 1978), 2–9.

49. See Patricia Doyle Corner et al., "Integrating Organization and Individual Information Processing Perspectives on Choice," *Organization Science*, 5, No. 3 (August 1994), 294–305.

50. Timothy W. Costello and Sheldon S. Zalkind, eds., *Psychology in Administration: A Research Orientation* (Englewood Cliffs, N.J.: Prentice-Hall, 1963), pp. 429–430.

51. Michael B. McCormick, Earl F. Lundgren, and Earl A. Cecil, "Group Search and Decision-Making Processes: A Laboratory Test of Soelberg's Confirmation Hypothesis," *Journal of Social Psychology*, (February 1980), 79–86.

52. For an excellent discussion of what it means to be a responsible individual, see John A. Dunn, Jr., "Organizational Decision Making," in *Group Decision Making*, ed. Walter C. Swap and Associates (Beverly Hills, Calif.: Sage, 1984), pp. 295–298.

53. Richard A. Cosier and Charles R. Schwenk, "Agreement and Thinking Alike: Ingredients for Poor Decisions," *The Executive* (February 1990), 69–74.

54. See E. Frank Harrison, "The Management of Organizational Conflict," *University of Michigan Business Review* (May 1979), 13–23; and E. Frank Harrison, "A Conceptual Model of Organizational Conflict," *Business and Society* (Winter 1980), 30–40.

55. See Ralf Dahrendorf, *Class and Class Conflict in Industrial Society* (Stanford, Calif.: Stanford University Press, 1959); and Harrison White, "Management Conflict and Sociometric Structures," *American Journal of Sociology* (September, 1961), 185–199.

56. James D. Thompson, "Organizational Management of Conflict," *Administrative Science Quarterly* (March 1960), 390.

57. Joseph A. Litterer, "Conflict in Organization: A Re-Examination," *Academy of Management Journal* (September 1966), 180.

58. See Stephen P. Robbins, *Managing Organizational Conflict* (Englewood Cliffs, N.J.: Prentice-Hall, 1974).

59. Morton Deutsch, *The Resolution of Conflict* (New Haven: Yale University Press, 1973), p. 10.

60. Ibid.

61. Charles R. Schwenk, "Conflict in Organizational Decision Making: An Exploratory Study of Its Effects in For-Profits and Not-For-Profit Organizations," *Management Science* (April 1990), 436–448.

62. See Harrison, "The Management of Organizational Conflict."

63. See Allen C. Amason, "Distinguishing the Effects of Functional and Dysfunctional Conflict on Strategic Decision Making: Resolving a Paradox for Top Management Teams," *Academy of Management Journal*, 39, No. 1 (1996), 123–148; and A. L. Minkes and A. E. Gear, "Process, Conflict, and Commitment in Organizational Decision

Making," *Journal of General Management*, 20, No. 2 (Winter 1994), 78–90.

64. See Louis R. Pondy, "A Systems Theory of Organizational Conflict," *Academy of Management Journal* (September 1966), 246–256; and Richard E. Walton and John Dutton, "The Management of Interdepartmental Conflict: A Model and Review," *Administrative Science Quarterly* (March 1969), 73–84.

65. Walton and Dutton, "The Management of Interdepartmental Conflict," p. 75.

66. Harrison, "A Conceptual Model of Organizational Conflict," p. 34.

67. Walton and Dutton, "The Management of Interdepartmental Conflict," p. 77.

68. Pondy, "A Systems Theory of Organizational Conflict," p. 256.

69. Ralph M. Goldman, "A Theory of Conflict Processes and Organizational Offices," *Journal of Conflict Resolution* (September 1966), 335.

70. Harrison, "A Conceptual Model of Organizational Conflict," p. 36.

71. Ronald G. Corwin, "Patterns of Organizational Conflict," *Administrative Science Quarterly* (December 1969), 507–520.

72. Richard E. Walton, John M. Dutton, and Thomas P. Cafferty, "Organizational Context and Interdepartmental Conflict," *Administrative Science Quarterly* (December 1969), 522–542.

73. John M. Dutton, "Analysis of Interdepartmental Decision-Making," in *Promising Research Directions*, Papers and Proceedings of the 27th Annual Meeting of the Academy of Management, ed. R. W. Millman and M. P. Hottenstein, Washington, D.C., December 27–29, 1967 (University Park: Pennsylvania State University, Commercial Printing, 1968), pp. 85–100.

74. A Beals and B. S. Siegel, *Divisiveness and Social Conflict* (Stanford, Calif.: Stanford University Press, 1966), p. 20.

75. See Barbara N. Kulieke, "Thinking Through Conflict," *Data Management* (September 1983), 28–29 and 37.

76. Kenneth Boulding, "Organization and Conflict," *Journal of Conflict Resolution* (June 1957), 122–134.

77. Goldman, "A Theory of Conflict Processes and Organizational Offices."

78. See Morton Deutsch, "Conflicts: Productive and Destructive," *Journal of Social Issues* (January 1969), 7–14; and Robbins, *Managing Organizational Conflict*.

79. Deutsch, *The Resolution of Conflict*, p. 23.

80. Robbins, *Managing Organizational Conflict*, p. 61.

81. See M. Sherif et al., *Intergroup Conflict and Cooperation: The Robbers Cave Experiment* (Norman, Okla.: University Book Exchange, 1961); and R. R. Blake and Jane S. Mouton, "Reactions to Intergroup Competition Under Win-Lose Conditions," *Management Science*, 7 (1961), 420–435.

82. Robbins, *Managing Organizational Conflict*, pp. 69–70.

83. Daniel Katz, "Approaches to Managing Conflict," in *Conflict Management and Organizations*, ed. Elise Boulding (Ann Arbor: Foundation for Research on Human Behavior and Center for Research on Conflict Resolution, University of Michigan, 1961), pp. 11–20; and Litterer, "Conflict in Organizations."

84. Robbins, *Managing Organizational Conflict*, pp. 72–73.

85. Katz, "Approaches to Managing Conflict"; Litterer, "Conflict in Organizations"; and Robbins, *Managing Organizational Conflict*.

86. Harrison, "A Conceptual Model of Organizational Conflict."

87. Georg Simmel, *Conflict and the Web of Group-Affiliations* (New York: Free Press, 1955); and Robbins, *Managing Organizational Conflict*.

88. Robbins, *Managing Organizational Conflict*, pp. 70–72.

89. Louis R. Pondy, "Organizational Conflict: Concepts and Models," *Administrative Science Quarterly* (September 1967).

90. Harrison, "A Conceptual Model of Organizational Conflict," pp. 37–38.

91. Victor D. Wall, Jr., Gloria J. Galanes, and Sue Beth Love, "Small, Task-Oriented Groups: Conflict, Conflict Management, Satisfaction, and Decision Quality," *Small Group Behavior* (February 1987), 31–55.

92. See Chris Argyris, *Integrating the Individual and the Organization* (New York: Wiley, 1964); Rensis Likert, *The Human Organization* (New York: McGraw-Hill, 1967); and Douglas McGregor, *The Human Side of Enterprise* (New York: McGraw-Hill, 1960).

93. Dean Tjosvold, "Effects of Shared Responsibility and Goal Interdependence on Controversy and

Decisionmaking Between Departments," *Journal of Social Psychology* (February 1988), 7–18.

94. John H. Barrett, *Individual Goals and Organizational Objectives: A Study of Integration Mechanisms* (Ann Arbor: University of Michigan Center for Research on Utilization of Scientific Knowledge, Institute for Social Research, 1970), p. 12.

95. John W. Dickson, "Top Managers' Beliefs and Rationales for Participation," *Human Relations*, 35, No. 3 (1982), 203.

96. Martin Patchen, "Participation in Decision-Making and Motivation: What Is the Relation?" in *Participative Management: Concepts, Theory, and Implementation*, ed. Ervin Williams (Atlanta: Georgia State University, 1976), pp. 31–41.

97. Ibid., p. 36.

98. Ibid., p. 37.

99. Katherine I. Miller and Peter R. Monge, "Participation, Satisfaction, and Productivity: A Meta-Analytic Review," *Academy of Management Journal*, 29 (1986), 727–753.

100. Kae H. Chung, *Motivational Theories and Practices* (Columbus, Ohio: Grid, 1977), p. 198.

101. Ibid.

102. See Michael L. Smith, "Decision Making for Project Managers: When to Involve Others," *Project Management Journal*, 24 (June 1993), 17–22; and Forrest A. Kessler, "How to Avoid Common Pitfalls of Consensus Decision Making," *Oil & Gas Journal* (September 27, 1993), 34 and 36.

103. Chris Argyris, *Personality and Organization* (New York: Harper & Row, 1957), p. 145.

104. Ibid.

105. J. Clifton Williams, *Human Behavior in Organizations* (Cincinnati: South-Western, 1978), p. 222.

106. See Robert Tannenbaum and Warren H. Schmidt, "How to Choose a Leadership Pattern," *Harvard Business Review* (March–April 1958), 95–101.

107. Williams, *Human Behavior in Organizations*, pp. 229–230.

108. Ralph M. Stogdill, ed., *Handbook of Leadership* (New York: Free Press, 1974), pp. 386–392.

109. Victor H. Vroom, "Leadership," in *Handbook of Industrial and Organizational Psychology*, ed. Marvin D. Dunnette (Chicago: Rand McNally, 1976), pp. 1527–1551.

110. Ross Stagner, "Corporate Decision Making: An Empirical Study," *Journal of Applied Psychology* (February 1969), 1–13.

111. Ibid., p. 12.

112. Bernard M. Bass, *Organizational Decision Making* (Homewood, Ill.: Richard D. Irwin, 1983), p. 96.

113. See J. A. Alutto and J. A. Belasco, "A Typology for Participation in Organizational Decision Making," *Administrative Science Quarterly* (March 1972), 117–125; and V. H. Vroom and P. W. Yetton, *Leadership Behavior on Standardized Cases*, Technical Report No. 3 (New Haven: Yale University Press, 1973).

114. Frank A. Heller, *Managerial Decision Making* (London: Tavistock, 1971).

115. Ibid., p. xvii.

116. Frank A. Heller, "Reality and Illusion in Senior Executive Decision Making," *Journal of Managerial Psychology*, 2 (1987), 23–27.

117. See Penny S. Ramsdell, "Staff Participation in Organizational Decision-Making: An Empirical Study," *Administration in Social Work*, 18, No. 4 (1994), 51–71; and Donde P. Ashmos and Reuben R. McDaniel, Jr., "Understanding the Participation of Critical Task Specialists in Strategic Decision Making," *Decision Sciences*, 27, No. 1 (Winter 1996), 103–121.

118. James W. Driscoll, "Trust and Participation in Organizational Decision Making as Predictors of Satisfaction," *Academy of Management Journal* (March 1978), 44–56.

119. Ibid., p. 49.

120. Randall S. Schuler, "A Role and Expectancy Perception Model of Participation in Decision Making," *Academy of Management Journal* (June 1980), 331–340.

121. Ahmed A. Abdel-Halim, "Effects of Task and Personality Characteristics on Subordinate Responses to Participative Decision Making," *Academy of Management Journal* (September 1983), 477–484.

122. E. Frank Harrison, "Organizational Correlates of Perceived Role Performance in the Research Laboratory," *IEEE Transactions on Engineering Management* (August 1984), 118–121.

123. Ronald J. Ebert and Terence R. Mitchell, *Organizational Decision Processes* (New York: Crane, Russak, 1975), pp. 260–266.

124. See John A. Parnell and Edward D. Bell, "The Propensity for Participative Decision Making Scale," *Administration & Society*, 25, No. 4 (February 1994), 518–530; and E. Frank Harrison and Monique A. Pelletier, "CEO Perceptions of

Strategic Leadership," *Journal of Managerial Issues*, 9, No. 3 (Fall 1997), 299–319.

125. John W. Dickson, "Top Managers' Beliefs and Rationale for Participation," *Human Relations*, 35, No. 3 (1982), 203–217. See also Teresa M. Harrison, "Communication and Participative Decision Making: An Exploratory Study," *Personnel Psychology*, 38 (1985), 93–115.

126. Ibid., p. 208.

127. Robert Maidment, "Decision Making: When Not to Involve Employees," *Supervisory Management* (October 1989), 33–35.

128. Howard N. Fullerton, Jr., "The 2005 Labor Force Growing But Slowly," *Monthly Labor Review* (November 1995), 29–44.

129. Kay Deaux, "From Individual Differences to Social Categories: Analysis of a Decade's Research on Gender," *American Psychologist* (February 1984), 105–116.

130. See S. L. Bem, "The Measurement of Psychological Androgyny," *Journal of Consulting and Clinical Psychology*, 42 (April 1974), 155–162.

131. Deaux, "From Individual Differences to Social Categories," pp. 105, 110.

132. See Gus Okanlawon, "Women as Strategic Decision Makers," *Women in Management Review*, 9, No. 4 (1994), 25–32; and J. Daniel Sherman et al., "Centralization of Decision Making and Accountability Based on Gender," *Group & Organization Studies*, 12, No. 4 (December 1987), 454–463.

133. Nathan Kogan and Michael A. Wallach, *Risk Taking* (New York: Holt, Rinehart, & Winston, 1964).

134. Ibid., p. 3.

135. Ibid.

136. Richard M. Steers, "Individual Differences in Participative Decision Making," *Human Relations*, 30, No. 9 (1977), 845.

137. Otto C. Brenner and W. Edgar Vinacke, "Accommodative and Exploitative Behavior of Males Versus Females and Managers Versus Nonmanagers as Measured by the Test of Strategy," *Social Psychology Quarterly*, 42, No. 3 (1979), 289–293.

138. Schmidt and Posner, *Managerial Values in Perspective*.

139. Kay Deaux, "Self-Evaluations of Male and Female Managers," *Sex Roles*, 5, No. 5 (1979), 571–580.

140. Frederick J. Klopfer and Thomas Moran, "Influences of Sex Composition, Decision Rule, and Decision Consequences in Small Group Policy Making," *Sex Roles*, 4, No. 6 (1978), 907–915.

141. See, for example, Virginia Ellen Schein, "The Relationship Between Sex Role Stereotypes and Requisite Management Characteristics," *Journal of Applied Psychology*, 57, No. 2 (1973), 95–100; and "Sex-Role Stereotypes and Requisite Management Characteristics: A Replication," *Sex Roles*, No. 5 (1979), 561–570.

142. Luther Wade Humphreys and William A. Shrode, "Decision-Making Profiles of Female and Male Managers," *MSU Business Topics* (Autumn 1978), 45–51.

143. Tressie W. Muldrow and James A. Bayton, "Men and Women Executives and Processes Related to Decision Accuracy," *Journal of Applied Psychology* (April 1979), 99–106.

144. Nathan Kogan and Karen Dorros, "Sex Differences in Risk Taking and Its Attribution," *Sex Roles*, 4, No. 5 (1978), 755–765.

145. J. E. V. Johnson and P. L. Powell, "Decision Making, Risk, and Gender: Are Managers Different?" *British Journal of Management*, 5 (1994), 123–138.

146. Ibid., p. 135.

147. Sandra Van Der Merwe, "What Personal Attributes It Takes to Make It in Management," *Business Quarterly* (Winter 1978), 28–35.

148. John H. Barnett and Marvin J. Karson, "Managers, Values, and Executive Decisions: An Exploration of the Role of Gender, Career Stage, Organizational Level, Function, and the Importance of Ethics, Relationships and Results in Managerial Decision-Making," *Journal of Business Ethics*, 8 (1989), 762.

149. Barry Z. Posner and Warren H. Schmidt, "Values and the American Manager: An Update Updated," (Spring 1992), 80–94.

150. Alan J. Rowe and James D. Boulgarides, *Managerial Decision Making: A Guide to Successful Business Decisions* (New York: Macmillan, 1992), p. 50.

151. Michael L. Johnson, "Women: Born to Manage," *Industry Week* (August 4, 1975), 22–26.

152. Stephen M. Brown, "Male Versus Female Leaders: A Comparison of Empirical Studies," *Sex Roles*, 5, No. 5 (1979), 595–611.

153. See "Women Directors Seen But Not Heard on Management Succession & Executive Compensation, Study Reports," Press Release, New York, Korn/Ferry International, October 21, 1997.

154. Gary N. Powell, "One More Time: Do Female and Male Managers Differ?" *The Executive* (August 1990), 68–75.

SUPPLEMENTAL REFERENCES

Adams, John R., Frederick P. Lawrence, and Sharla J. Cook. "Analyzing Stereotypes of Women in the Work Force." *Sex Roles*, 5, No. 5 (1979), 581–594.

Bazerman, Max H., Tom Giuliano, and Alan Appelman. "Escalation of Commitment in Individual and Group Decision Making." *Organizational Behavior and Human Performance*, 33 (1984), 141–152.

Belovicz, Meyer W., Frederick E. Finch, and Halsey Jones. "Do Groups Make Riskier Decisions Than Individuals?" In *Papers and Proceedings of the 28th Annual Meeting of the Academy of Management*, Chicago, December 26–28, 1968, pp. 73–85.

Clark, Russell D., III. "Group-Induced Shift Toward Risk." *Psychological Bulletin*, 76, No. 4 (1971), 252–270.

Coser, Lewis. *The Functions of Social Conflict*. New York: Free Press, 1956.

Duke, James F. *Conflict and Power in Social Life*. Provo, Utah: Brigham Young University Press, 1976.

Einhorn, Hillel J., Robin M. Hogarth, and Eric Klempner. "Quality of Group Judgment." *Psychological Bulletin*, 84, No. 1 (1977), 158–172.

Festinger, Leon. *Conflict, Decision, and Dissonance*. Stanford, Calif.: Stanford University Press, 1964.

Harren, Vincent A., et al. "Influence of Sex Role Attitudes and Cognitive Styles on Career Decision Making." *Journal of Counseling Psychology*, 25, No. 5 (1978), 390–398.

Hill, Gayle W. "Group Versus Individual Performance: Are N + 1 Heads Better Than One?" *Psychological Bulletin*, 91 (May 1982), 517–539.

Himes, Joseph S. *Conflict & Conflict Management*. Athens: University of Georgia Press, 1980.

Janis, Irving L., and Leon Mann. *Decision Making: A Psychological Analysis of Conflict, Choice, and Commitment*. New York: Free Press, 1977.

Kirkpatrick, Samuel A. "Psychological Views of Decision-Making." In *Political Science Annual*. Vol. 6. Ed. Cornelius P. Cotter (Indianapolis: Bobbs-Merrill, 1975), pp. 39–112.

Lannon, Judith M. "Male v. Female Values in Management." *Management International Review*, 17, No. 1 (1977), 9–12.

Lorge, Irving, et al. "A Survey of Studies Contrasting the Quality of Group Performance and Individual Performance, 1920–1957." *Psychological Bulletin*, 55 (November 1958), 337–372.

Mann, Leon, and Irving Janis. "Conflict Theory of Decision Making and the Expectancy-Value Approach." In *Expectations and Actions: Expectancy-Value Models in Psychology*. Ed. Norman F. Feather. Hillsdale, N.J.: Erlbaum, 1982, pp. 341–364.

March, James G. *A Primer on Decision Making*. New York: Free Press, 1994.

Mohr, Lawrence B. *Explaining Organizational Behavior*. San Francisco: Jossey-Bass, 1982.

Patchen, Martin. *Participation, Achievement, and Involvement on the Job*. Englewood Cliffs, N.J.: Prentice-Hall, 1970.

Pearson, Dick. "Inaccurate Perceptions About Women Managers." *Supervisory Management* (October 1984), 29–34.

Pruitt, Dean G. "Choice Shifts in Group Discussion: An Introductory Review." *Journal of Personality and Social Psychology*, 20, No. 3 (1971), 339–360.

Rosen, Benson, Thomas H. Jerdee. "Sex Stereotyping in the Executive Suite." *Harvard Business Review* (March 1974), 45–58.

Schellenberg, James A. *The Science of Conflict*. New York: Oxford University Press, 1982.

Steiner, Ivan D. *Group Processes and Productivity*. New York: Academic Press, 1972.

Terborg, James R. "Women in Management: A Research Review." *Journal of Applied Psychology*, 62, No. 6 (1977), 647–664.

Vaden, Richard E., and Naomi B. Lynn. "The Administrative Person: Will Women Bring a Differing Morality to Management?" *University of Michigan Business Review* (March 1974), 22–25.

Vroom, Victor H. *Work and Motivation*. New York: Wiley, 1964.

Vroom, Victor H., and Phillip W. Yetton. *Leadership and Decision Making*. Pittsburgh: University of Pittsburgh Press, 1973.

Worth, Leila F., Scott T. Allison, and David M. Messick. "Impact of a Group Decision on Perception of One's Own and Others' Attitudes." *Journal of Personality and Social Psychology* (October 1987), 673–682.

Wright, George. "Organizational, Group, and Individual Decision Making in Cross-Cultural Perspective." In *Behavioral Decision Making*. Ed. George Wright. New York: Plenum Press, 1985, pp. 149–164.

CHAPTER NINE

Political Aspects of Decision Making

W hether an individual is an executive in a large corporation, an administrator in a governmental agency, or a general or flag-rank officer in the armed forces, he or she is performing the basic functions of managerial decision making and is therefore a decision maker. Managers of large organizations in the United States today make countless decisions of varying significance that directly or indirectly determine the social and economic development of the nation, the prominence and prosperity of whole regions and individual communities, and the personal prospects and general well-being of the entire citizenry. Thus managerial decision makers possess and exercise considerable power. This power provides the foundation for the influence and determination of outcomes to the advantage of the organization. It is also the framework within which the political aspects of managerial decision making are accomplished. Of principal concern here is the idea that the decision makers of the largest corporations and governmental agencies, bureaus, and departments, including the armed forces, constitute a "new class." Dating the appearance of this class is of little consequence; the implications of its existence, given the concentration of power among its members, is of considerable significance. Indeed, the potential consequences of misuse of that power is sobering at best and frightening at worst.

This chapter will attempt to shed some light in an area where, in most writings about managerial decision making, darkness has prevailed. Because the political aspects of decision making are founded on power, the first section presents a profile of power, defining it and delineating the five common bases that give rise to it. The second section focuses on the new class of managerial decision makers. The conditions that precipitated their emergence, various concepts of management as a class of decision makers, and characteristics of managerial decision makers as a group are discussed in this section.

The third section presents the conceptual foundations of political power. The concept of politics is introduced and defined, and the concept of political power is presented as a mainstay of the political aspects of decision making. The fourth section focuses on significant profiles of political power in managerial decision making, including (1) divergence of goals and objectives,

(2) allocation of resources, and (3) dominance versus autonomy. The fifth section presents some salient dimensions of power in managerial decision making, and its scope in large corporations and government institutions is examined. The manifestations of power are revealed in the form of specific types of category II choices made by managerial decision makers in the command posts of these organizations. The final section of this chapter concentrates on the ways and means for constraining the power and influence of managerial decision makers, including both theoretical constraints and a selected group of operating constraints.

A PROFILE OF POWER

Although power is difficult to define and even more difficult to recognize in its subtler forms, it is pervasive in that, in one form or another, it touches everyone. It is essential, however, that power be defined in order to guard against its excesses and benefit from its responsible use. Goldhammer and Shils have defined the term this way:

> A person may be said to have *power* to the extent that he influences the behavior of others in accordance with his own intentions. . . . The power-holder exercises *force* when he influences behavior by physical manipulation . . . *domination* . . . by making explicit to others what he wants them to do . . . and *manipulation* without making explicit the behavior he thereby wants them to perform.[1]

According to this definition, then, the holder of power may influence behavior by any of three means. Power, although latent, always has a location. It does not float free and unattached, but resides with people in interaction. Individuals or groups have power if the consequences of their actions can be observed in the behavior of other people. Acts of power always involve the exercise of force, domination, or manipulation.[2] Force is a manifestation of power; power per se is the *ability* to employ force, not its actual employment. To possess power is to possess the ability to apply sanctions that require or prohibit the commission of an act; it is not the application of sanctions as such. The locus of power is in organizations and groups, and it expresses itself in interorganizational and intergroup relations; the locus of dominance is the individual, and it expresses itself in interpersonal relations. Power is a function of the organization and the status of the individual; dominance is a personal trait that manifests itself in the role played by the individual in the organization. Power may be dispensed through influence, but influence does not require power. However, if influence is dispensed to manipulate behavior, it becomes a means to exercise power. Manipulation may be exercised by utilizing symbols or by performing other acts to exercise power. Influence may or may not indicate such intentions, unless, of course, it is designed to manipulate behavior.[3]

Two principal criteria may be employed to measure the amount of power exercised by a given power holder: (1) the number of actions by any person, in a selected type of behavior, in which power is exercised successfully, and (2) the number of persons over whom such power is achieved.[4] By these criteria it is apparent that managerial decision makers in large organizations in the United States have ample opportunity to exercise a good deal of power. Of course, the potential for power is not power itself, but opportunities invariably invite responses from individuals inclined toward its acquisition.

Power, then, is "the ability of one party of a relationship to determine whether or not the other party is carried toward his goals or away from them, over and above the second party's own efforts."[5] It is the capacity of one person to prevent another from reaching a desired goal or it is the potential of one individual or group for influencing others to act or change in a given direction.[6]

Let us now examine the basis of power — that is, its source in a given relationship. It is uncommon to find power limited to one source. Normally a relationship will be characterized by several qualitatively different bases of power.[7] We may differentiate at least five common bases:

1. **Reward power.** This type of power reflects the ability to confer positive rewards of a monetary or psychological nature, as perceived by the potential beneficiary of the reward. The strength of this power varies with the expectation of the potential beneficiary that a particular kind of behavior will result in attainment of the reward. It also assumes that the reward is of some significance to the potential beneficiary.

2. **Coercive power.** This type of power is based on fear of undesirable consequences if a particular form of behavior is not forthcoming. The strength of this power varies with the expectation that punishment will follow as a result of nonconformance. It is the opposite of reward power.

3. **Legitimate power.** This type of power derives from position in the organizational hierarchy. Its strength varies with the legitimacy imputed to those who claim such power by those whose behavior will be modified by its acceptance. Thus legitimate power implies internalization of the right to exercise power and willingness to accept its constraints.

4. **Expert power.** This type of power is based on the possession of knowledge or skill for which a demand exists. The demand for expertise confers on its possessor power that usually results in the acceptance of advice or opinions and the rendering of compliant behavior. The strength of expert power varies with others' perceptions of the extent of knowledge or skill possessed by the expert.

5. **Referent power.** This type of power derives from identification with a particular individual or group possessing a high level of attractiveness for the identifier. The strength of this power varies with the degree of attractiveness, which in turn elicits a desire to associate with

individual or group. A desire *not* to associate because of unattractive-ness results in negative referent power.[8]

These bases of power may be organized into two major categories: (1) power based primarily on organizational factors, which include reward, coercive, and legitimate power; and (2) power based largely on personal factors, which include expert and referent power. Managerial decision-making power arises from the position a manager holds in the organizational hierarchy. *The higher the position in the formal structure of an organization and the greater the number of subordinates reporting to that position, the greater the opportunity for the exercise of managerial decision-making power by the incumbent.* This axiom explains this chapter's focus on high-level executives, administrators, and officers in the largest organizations in the United States. These positions hold a tremendous potential for the use of power. Though a given manager at any level may also possess expert or referent power, these types reside in the individual rather than in the position and therefore are not of primary concern here.

THE MANAGERIAL DECISION-MAKING CLASS

Compared with other nations, the United States is not a strongly class-conscious society. To be sure, its millions of inhabitants manifest innumer-able differences of origin, education, habits, and value systems. Moreover, in spite of the fact that all Americans have equal rights under the Constitution, their preferences in conjunction with their acquired perceptions of status and role lead them to seek out companions of similar extraction and background; such associations may be based on ethnic, economic, or societal factors. To the extent that people of similar origins and socioeconomic backgrounds associate in social groups and tend to erect socioeconomic barriers to out-siders, there are class distinctions in American society. As long as individuals perceive themselves and their chosen peers as occupying a given rung on a social ladder, such distinctions will persist. Of course, managerial decision makers are no different in this respect than anyone else. There is a certain commonality in the backgrounds of successful managers and a sameness in their values and perspectives. There is, in sum, a good deal of evidence to support the notion that there is a managerial decision-making class in the United States.

Emergence of the Managerial Decision-Making Class

It is obviously somewhat arbitrary to select a given point in time as marking the emergence of the managerial decision-making class in the United States. Tocqueville noted as early as 1831 the vast potential of the country for progress in industry because of the enormous ambition of its people and their strong devotion to profitable activity.[9] According to C. Wright Mills, the emergence of a managerial decision-making class began soon after the Civil War. In his view, the latter part of the nineteenth century marked the emergence of the "economic elite."[10] James Burnham dates the emergence of such a class to 1914.[11] Finally, Galbraith considers the last fifty years as marking the replacement of owner-managers by nonowner-managers — that is, the new class of managerial decision makers: "It is an occurrence of the last fifty years and it is still going on."[12]

Thus the advent of the twentieth century more or less marked the emergence of the managerial decision-making class in the United States. In the private sector, the initiating generation of entrepreneurs began to be displaced by the first generation of managerial decision makers soon after World War I. By the end of the 1930s this process was almost complete; today the managerial decision maker is firmly ensconced in the big corporations. The ascent of the managerial decision maker to a position of power in the large corporation was not a precipitous event. It transpired gradually through a kind of organizational metamorphosis, coincident with advancing technology and increasing size, which rendered organizations more complex to manage. The entrepreneur served a vital function in the development of the large corporations in the United States and then passed from the scene.[13]

The growth of big government in the 1930s under the Roosevelt administration created a new type of managerial decision maker — the federal executive, public administrator, or government bureaucrat. These individuals were very similar to the new managerial decision makers in the large corporations of the private sector.[14] Similarly, during World War II the organization of the American armed forces changed markedly, largely as a result of technological advances and increasing size. Managerial decision-making skills became essential for successful careers in the military; and the backgrounds of top officers were very similar to those of the managerial decision makers in private enterprise.[15]

It has been convincingly argued that there is a managerial decision-making class in the United States today. As the following discussion will show, there are several differing concepts of this class.

Concepts of the Managerial Decision-Making Class

The members of the managerial decision-making class include the top executives of the largest industrial and service corporations; the chief administrators of the largest government agencies, bureaus, and departments; and the senior general and flag-rank officers in the armed forces. "Essentially, it [includes] a very few senior executives at the top . . . perhaps only three or four, perhaps a dozen or so in a larger organization, but never very many. These are the oligarchy in whose hands is the power to shape the future course of the organization. . . ."[16] This type of decision-making power is the very essence of management. "It occurs in all forms of organization: in private firms, in large public [organizations], in local goverment, in hospitals, in universities, in whatever the organization may be."[17] This group includes most of the principal decision makers in the society. Many other individuals perform decision-making functions in big unions, large universities, school systems, and hospitals, although they might disclaim the label of manager. But for purposes of describing managerial decision makers as a class, the membership cited above seems sufficiently inclusive.

The Managerial Revolution   The theory of the managerial revolution, first espoused by James Burnham,[18] holds that the industrialized world is in a period of social transition characterized by an unusually rapid rate of change in the most important economic, social, political, and cultural institutions of society. The transition is essentially from a capitalist to a managerial society. Managers, as the term is employed by Burnham, should not be confused with engineers and technicians, although they may be either or both. In Burnham's words:

> I mean by managers, in short, those who for the most part in contemporary society are actually managing, on its technical side, the actual process of production, no matter what the legal and financial form — individual, corporate, governmental — of the process.[19]

According to Burnham's definition, managerial decision makers are found in any type of large organization, and their function is the organizations' direction and coordination. They make the difficult choices to commit the resources of the organization in fulfillment of its basic purposes. Burnham says that the growth of large organizations, particularly the giant corporations, brought into being a new class of managerial decision makers who are becoming the de facto controllers of society. Burnham stated in 1941 that the managerial revolution had begun at the time of World War I and would take almost fifty years to complete.[20] Although there is little evidence to support his contention that the United States is under the control of the managerial decision-making class, it is obvious nevertheless that the class is highly influential in making most of the significant decisions in the society.[21]

The Power Elite   The concept of the power elite originated with the renowned sociologist C. Wright Mills:

> The power elite are the men at the head of the great corporations, the armed forces, the state, the mass media of communication. They are the men who make the "big decisions" — whether to go to war, to drop a bomb, to make peace, to join an alliance, to adopt a new economic policy. And they have the power to make sure that the rest of society accepts their decisions, if, indeed, they bother to secure assent at all.[22]

Mills attributes power, then, to high managerial positions within big organizations. To be powerful is to be able to realize one's will even if others resist it. No one can be truly powerful without access to the command of major institutions, he says, "for it is over these institutional means of power that the truly powerful are, in the first instance, powerful."[23] Although the power enjoyed by this elite is vast, its membership is small.

"Power in Mills' terms is domination," Bell has commented.[24] Force is available, but it is seldom required. Manipulation through persuasion or other means is also available, but it is too time-consuming. The direct exercise of power by the power elite occurs through the dominance vested in the upper levels of the largest industrial, political, and military institutions. From a societal standpoint, Mills's identification of power as inhering in a top position in an organization, instead of in the individual by virtue of social origin or wealth, is a crucial distinction. "All means of power tend to become ends to an elite that is in command of them."[25]

Mills's power elite does not make all the decisions that affect society, only the critical ones. Such decisions have far-reaching consequences and touch the entire nation or a major segment of it in a significant way. "In our time the pivotal moment does arise, and at that moment, small circles do decide or fail to decide. In either cases, they are an elite of power."[26] The Cuban missile crisis exemplifies a critical decision; as Mills suggests it was made by a small group of powerful men.[27] Still, most of the operating decisions in organizations are made by managers who are not, by definition, part of the power elite. Consequently, the actual power of Mills's elite depends not on the number of decisions made but on how critical an individual decision is. Thus the power elite includes only the top level of management and is not totally reflective of the actual scope of managerial decision-making power.

The Marxist Theory Developed by Karl Marx in the 1840s and 1850s, Marxism was the first social theory to be identified with a particular social group — the working class. In Marxist theory, power is based on dominance by those who own and control the means of production over those whose services are purchased and exploited for the benefit of the power holders. It is the existence of private property and capital that transforms free activity into mere labor; and it is through capital that the capitalist exercises power of command over labor. Even the most favorable changes in the circumstances of the working class, however much they may improve workers' material existence, do not eliminate the basic antagonism between their interests and the interests of the capitalists.[28] The economic domination of the capitalist class thus flows directly from its legal right and physical ability to exploit the services of labor. "It is capital and its domination over labor which for Marx formed the axis of class power within capitalist society."[29]

In essence, then, Marx believed that power in society is held by those who supply capital and control the means of production. Their power within the enterprise is complete. Prices and wages are set in their interest. They dominate society and, through the pervasiveness of their power, set its moral tone. They also control the state, which becomes subordinate to the will and interest of the capitalist class. There is no possibility of power being associated with any other factor of production.[30]

Some significant differences among the theories of Burnham, Mills, and Marx merit discussion. To Marx, power resides in ownership. Ownership is the same as management; he made no distinction between these functions. Burnham, on the other hand, writing much later, saw a separation of ownership and management coincident with technological development and the growth of large organizations. "These changes have meant that to an ever-growing extent the managers are no longer, either as individuals or legally, or historically, the same as the capitalist."[31] Mills, writing still later, saw an increasing consolidation of managerial power at the very top levels of the biggest industrial, governmental, and military institutions — institutions that had grown larger and more complex since Burnham's time and that were immeasurably more advanced than the owner-manager enterprises of Marx's time. These institutions are still growing and becoming more complex; Galbraith has risen to the occasion by advancing the concept of the technostructure.

The Technostructure   Galbraith has written that the rise of the large corporation required by modern technology was accompanied by a divorce of the owner from control of the enterprise. In his view, "the entrepreneur no longer exists as an individual person in the mature industrial enterprise."[32] The entrepreneur has been replaced not by the management of the corporation but by a new entity that Galbraith designates the **technostructure**. According to him:

> This is a collective and imperfectly defined entity; in the large corporation it embraces chairman, president, those vice presidents with important staff or departmental responsibility, occupants of other major staff positions and, perhaps, division or department heads not included above. . . . It embraces all who bring specialized knowledge, talent, or experience to group decision making. This, not the management, is the guiding intelligence — the brain — of the enterprise.[33]

Galbraith declares that the truly large organization has outgrown the ability of one or even a few managers to control it. Increasing size has separated top managers from operations and operating information. Managers increasingly and necessarily deal with secondhand information that has been sifted many times on its way to the top. Moreover, accelerating technological change has placed a premium on the knowledge of specialists, who, by virtue of their expertise, possess very specialized information that is often critical in the decision-making process. Once again, the managers at the top are forced to rely on information passed upward from the operating units of the organization. In a de facto sense, then, according to Galbraith, decision making in the largest organizations has become a team effort simply because the size

and complexity of operations — and the attendant need for inf(
is fast, accurate, and specialized — has made it impossible f
manager to control the outcome of events.

Galbraith's technostructure obviously includes many groups outside of
management. In fact, he rejects the notion that the managers possess the real
power in organizations. In this respect, his theory differs from that of Burnham who sees power as having passed from the owners to the managers.
Galbraith is obviously at variance, too, with the Marxists, who equate power
with property ownership, and he departs radically from Mills by diffusing
power through a technostructure rather than concentrating it in the command posts of the very largest institutions. In fact, of all the concepts of managerial decision-making power presented in this section, only Burnham's
appears to have any real relevance to this context. There is a new class of
managerial decision makers, and they do have considerable power based
primarily on reward, coercion, and legitimacy. Still the acquisition of this
power did not come about by revolution. It was obtained gradually, through
the growth of large and complex organizations and the resultant separation
of ownership and control.

Having made the case for managerial decision makers as a class, let us
now examine some of the characteristics of its members.

Characteristics of the Managerial
Decision-Making Class

The managerial decision-making class in the United States today is a unique
social phenomenon. First of all, managers are much better educated than is
the average citizen. Second, they are increasingly mobile, both geographically and upwardly through the organizational hierarchy. Third, they have a
strong sense of identification with the organization — no one organization
in particular — as the ultimate source of satisfaction of their personal needs.
These attributes characterize managerial decision makers in all types of organizations — business, government, and military. It is unlikely that in all of
history there has ever been a class so committed to organized activity and so
well qualified to bring it about. A portrait of the modern managerial decision
maker is a portrait of organizational America.

The characteristics of this class have been documented in several noteworthy studies. Warner and Abegglen's study of the origins of several
thousand managers between 1928 and 1952 showed that the growth of large
organizations provided increasing opportunities for individuals whose
fathers had lower-status occupations to make it all the way to the top of the
hierarchy.[34] The same study found that managerial decision makers were
eight times as likely as the general population to have graduated from college,[35] and that the successful manager was a mobile individual who moved
with the opportunities, both geographically and hierarchically.[36] Newcomer's
classic study of 428 large organizations found significant changes in the

characteristics of managerial decision makers between 1900 and 1950 in the United States.[37] By 1950 it had become much easier for individuals of low social and economic origins to reach top positions in the very large organizations. This half-century coincided with the period during which the owner-manager gave way to the managerial decision maker as the head of most larger institutions. The key to advancement to a top position in management was found to be education. In 1900, for example, approximately one out of five managers had at least one college degree, whereas by 1950, almost one out of two had reached the baccalaureate level. Managers in 1900 were eight times as likely to have attended college as the general population; by 1950 managerial decision makers were twelve times as likely to have some college education.[38] By 1950, then, education had made it possible for the property-less individual to make it to the top of the biggest organizations.

A comprehensive study of several hundred government executives and military officers undertaken in 1959 tended to confirm the foregoing characterization of managerial decision makers.[39] This study made some interesting comparisons among managers in industry, government, and the military. Education, it found, was the principal preparation for advancement of government executives. Moreover, their origins, measured by the occupations of their fathers, tended to be middle class, as earlier studies had shown those of managerial decision makers in business to be. Similarly, the percentage of college graduates among the military officers in this study was very high; and the occupations of their fathers were very similar in the aggregate to those of the governmental executives.[40] The study showed "the backgrounds of the military and civilian executives are similar whether we are considering occupation, region or state of origin. They are also similar in level of education."[41] Moreover, American big business leaders and government executives "are far more alike than different in social and economic characteristics, including family and occupation as well as educational attainments."[42]

In general, then, the characteristics of managerial decision makers in business, government, and the military are similar in that they share (1) college education, (2) middle-class origin, (3) geographic and hierarchical mobility, and (4) a strong commitment to the organization. It is becoming increasingly less difficult for individuals from the lower levels of society to attain high positions as managerial decision makers. The evidence of growing social mobility at all levels of management in all institutions is unmistakable. The principal findings of a second study made by Newcomer in 1964 of twelve hundred top managerial decision makers further confirmed the increase in opportunities for the well-educated and motivated individual who aspired to a position of command in a large organization.[43] This latter study clearly showed that education, rather than wealth or social position, has become more than ever the key to achieving a top-level managerial decision-making post in the United States.

The results of Newcomer's landmark studies were validated by a survey published in 1976 by *Fortune*.[44] This survey included eight hundred chief executives, including the heads of the top five hundred industrial corporations and three hundred executives who run the largest commercial banks, life insurance firms, diversified financial enterprises, retail firms, transportation companies, and utilities in the United States. The survey's comprehensive empirical evidence corroborated the characteristics of the new class of managerial decision makers described above.

Finally, three more recent surveys further confirm and validate the aforementioned characteristics of managerial decision makers. The first survey conducted by Korn/Ferry International in 1986 elicited 1,362 responses to a comprehensive questionnaire from senior and executive vice presidents in a cross-section of Fortune 500 industrial and service companies.[45] The second survey was a global study of over 1,500 CEOs and senior executives in the United States, Western Europe, Japan, and Latin America. This survey was conducted jointly in 1989 by Korn/Ferry International and the Columbia University Graduate School of Business.[46] A third survey by Korn/Ferry International also in 1989 included responses from 698 senior executives in Fortune 500 companies.[47] All three of these surveys provided incontrovertible evidence of a new class of managerial decision makers. These top-level decision makers are well educated and are firmly committed to decisions that further the best interests of their respective organizations.[48] In the words of Mills, they constitute the "power elite" of the twenty-first century.[49]

CONCEPTUAL FOUNDATIONS OF POLITICAL POWER

We turn now to the political aspects of decision making. Two concepts are central to the notion of managerial decision makers wielding considerable amounts of power in politicizing the decision-making process. The first concept is that of politics, which, as previously noted, is based primarily on power. The second concept fuses the notions of power and politics into a new symbiotic concept of political power. Through the use of political power, managerial decision makers exert their influence on the process of choice, presumably to serve the basic purposes of their organizations.

The Concept of Politics

The concern with politics here is specific and related to the managerial decision-making process. There is no intention of discussing politics in the abstract or as a kind of generic concept. Still, prior to focusing on the effect of politics on the process of choice, we should develop a working definition for a term that has acquired a global image in the minds of most people.

Politics, however broadly defined, enters into most managerial decision making.[50] Various authors, in defining the term *politics*, see it as referring to efforts to influence people: "In all cases, politics specializes in achieving the behavior necessary to further a purpose."[51] "Politics is deciding who gets what. It is the decision-making process of any group that makes rules for its members. Politics is also the process of deciding who decides."[52] As decision makers, managers are faced with "a political universe in which who decides, what is to be decided upon, and according to what rules, become the core questions."[53] A more general definition notes that politics involves the use of influence to get what there is to get.[54] "Organizational politics involve intentional acts of influence to enhance or protect the self-interest of individuals or groups."[55] Organizationally, "politics refers to the structure and process of the use of authority and power to effect definitions of goals, directions, and other major parameters."[56] Organizational politics is also conceived as the use of power "to mobilize resources, energy, and information on behalf of a preferred goal or strategy."[57] Finally, organizational politics is defined as "behavior not formally sanctioned by the organization, which produces conflict and disharmony in the work environment by pitting individuals and/or groups against one another, or against the organization."[58]

Viewing politics in terms of the formal organization is more relevant for purposes of this book if only because managerial decision making takes place within organizations. Hayes asserts that managerial decision makers need to develop political competence if they are to operate effectively.[59] He suggests that organizations are

> political organisms within which individuals and groups attempt to influence each other in pursuit of self interest. Decisions and actions result from bargaining and negotiation between people who have different goals. Often they represent a compromise, they are the result of explicit or implicit working agreements that interested parties are prepared to live with, at least temporarily. When preferences conflict it is the power of the individuals and groups involved that determines the outcome of the decision process.[60]

Effective managerial decision makers, according to Hayes, possess a set of skills to influence others in the exercise of power within the organization. This is the meaning of political competence.[61]

A view of organizations as political entities is not a recent phenomenon. March, for example, suggested that organizations are political coalitions in which decisions are made and goals are set by bargaining processes,[62] and Zaleznik characterized organizations as political pyramids. In his words: "A political pyramid exists when people compete for power in an economy of scarcity. . . . people cannot get the power they want just for the asking. Instead, they have to enter into the decisions on how to distribute authority in a particular formal organization structure."[63] Mayes and Allen wrote that "organizational politics is the management of influence to obtain ends not sanctioned by the organization or to obtain sanctioned ends through non-sanctioned influence means."[64] Although somewhat simplistic, this definition is particularly cogent.

Mintzberg has attempted to go beyond most of the microcosmic definitions by describing the entire organization as a political arena.[65] He notes that "the system of politics may be described as reflecting power that is technically illegitimate (or, perhaps more accurately, 'alegitimate') in its means (and sometimes in its ends as well). In other words behavior termed political is neither formally authorized, widely accepted, or officially certified."[66] The means-ends orientation of Mintzberg is highly analogous to the definition advanced by Mayes and Allen.

Rather than assuming, as do many writers on the subject, that organizational politics is automatically dysfunctional to the organization, Mintzberg observes some potential functional benefits:

1. Politics in organizations may correct deficiencies in other more legitimate systems of influence and provide for certain necessary forms of flexibility not otherwise available.

2. Politics can act in a Darwinian manner to bring the strongest members of the organization into managerial decision-making roles.

3. Politics can often act to ensure an objective hearing of all sides of an issue when no other means is available.

4. Politics can often help to promote necessary organizational change blocked by more traditional means.

5. Politics can often facilitate the decision-making process, particularly the effective implementation of choices to serve particular interests.[67]

There are many other conceptions and definitions of politics in formal organizations. For example, organizational politics is often viewed as (1) actions that make a claim against the organization's resource-sharing system, (2) conflict regarding whose preferences will prevail in the determination of policy, (3) power tactics used by executives, (4) exploitation of resources to gain or extend control over others, and (5) behavior directed toward personal gain.[68]

Pfeffer tends to view power and politics as being virtually synonymous in managerial decision making. He notes that "politics involves activities which attempt to influence decisions over critical issues that are not readily resolved through the introduction of new data and in which there are differing points of view."[69] Pfeffer's definition of politics within formal organizations is founded on the use of power to influence and obtain preferred outcomes. His definition is unalterably part of the political aspects of managerial decision making and is, therefore, adopted for purposes of this book. The definition follows:

> Organizational politics involves those activities taken within organizations to acquire, develop, and use power and other resources to obtain one's preferred outcomes in a situation in which there is uncertainty or dissensus about choices.[70]

Given that politics is a way of life in formal organizations and managerial decision making, its effective use in the process of choice seems likely to work to the long-term best interests of the organization's principal stakeholders.

Clearly there is a need for competence in the use of politics in managerial decision making.[71] A good understanding of politics, political behavior, and political effects can limit the adverse consequences likely to ensue from the uninformed or irresponsible use of this form of power. Of even greater importance, skill and competence in the political aspects of decision making can result in numerous functional benefits that otherwise would materialize only by happenstance.

Politics and power are reciprocals of organizational life and are, therefore, endemic to the process of managerial decision making.[72] A more complete and meaningful perspective on politics in general and organizational politics in particular is afforded by fusing this concept with its counterpart concept. The result, of course, is the concept of political power, which is the most comprehensive aspect of the politics of decision making.

The Concept of Political Power

The concepts of power and politics find their ultimate and symbiotic expression in the form of political power permeating the process of managerial decision making. Although it is far more meaningful to discuss political power than to separate the two concepts, a more complete understanding of political power is likely if we first analyze its reciprocals.

Cogent explanations in the management literature of the relationship between power and politics are sparse. But one compelling theme running through the literature is that political behavior and power are closely related.[73] This is not to say, however, that they are identical. More accurately, organizational politics is a process of actual influence, whereas power is a reservoir of potential influence. By way of analogy, power may be viewed as similar to wealth and political behavior as similar to the cash flow by which wealth is accumulated or dispersed. Like wealth and cash flow, power and politics are closely related but distinguishable concepts. It is not necessary to have one to have the other, but it certainly helps. For example, one can behave politically without power, but to what end? In like manner one can possess power but not derive its full measure in the absence of political behavior. Power is the sought end and politics or political behavior is the means to increase the power base that enables the continual use of influence to determine outcomes.

To consider politics in the absence of power is a vacuous exercise; to consider power without the impetus of politics is to contemplate inertia. One must have a means to obtain an end; having obtained an end, one must still have a means to sustain and expand it. Such is the relationship between power and politics in managerial decision making. Consequently in discussing the political aspects of decision making, reference is necessarily made to political power — the symbiotic fulfillment of the reciprocal concepts of power and politics. Political power undergirds the organizational positions of managerial decision makers and permeates all their decision-making functions. Their base of political power is inherent in their positional power and in their legitimate power to reward and coerce in the accomplishment of organizational purposes. The exercise of managerial influence through formal and informal channels by legitimate and illegitimate means, then, is the manifestation of political power, which is employed to shape and make choices to accomplish ends in conformity with managerial preferences.[74] This is the dynamic aspect of political power in managerial decision making.[75]

If political power is to be effective, it must be employed through various means or tactics. One particularly good study of managers in the electronics industry in southern California revealed a set of tactics commonly ascribed to political behavior in formal organizations:

1. *Blaming or attacking others.* When something goes wrong, the emphasis is on "getting off the hook" by fixing the blame elsewhere.

2. *Manipulating information.* Information may be withheld, distorted, or used to overwhelm another.

3. *Creating and maintaining a favorable image.* This tactic is designed to promote self-interests.

4. *Developing a base of support.* This is accomplished by getting others to understand one's ideas before a decision is made, setting up a decision before a meeting is called, or getting others to contribute to an idea to ensure their commitment to it.

5. *Praising others or ingratiation.*

6. *Developing strong allies and forming power coalitions.*

7. *Associating with influential persons.*

8. *Creating obligations through reciprocity.*[76]

Managerial decision makers who have mastered the use of political power make frequent and selective use of these tactics as they seek to influence the outcome of significant choices, and they manifest high levels of competence in their use. At the very least, to survive as a respected member of the managerial decision-making class, a manager must recognize that power and politics constitute an integral part of organizational life.[77]

The locus of political power in formal organizations begins with top management. Only top management has continued access to the command posts of large organizations. Only top management has the inclination and information to exercise influence through political actions that affect all parts of the decision-making process. Only top management has the power of legitimacy, reward, and coercion to intervene in any part of the decision-making process to determine the tone and temper of significant choices. And only top management can apply or withhold the available resources from the most artfully crafted decision, thus causing it to either atrophy or flourish. Although top management may share power with middle management on occasion and even with operating management in a magnanimous moment, the locus of political power always resides in the positions of top management. It is one thing to speak of organizational democracy, participative decision making, consensual choice, and shared authority. It is something else to speak of ultimate accountability and responsibility that may not be delegated. Top management is the proper locus for political power in managerial decision making. It is necessary only that there be sufficient safeguards to preclude the misuse or abuse of this power.

Most of the political models of managerial decision making are based on some form of power. Allison's explanation of the Cuban missile crisis presents a government politics model in which power is the central ingredient.[78] He graphically describes the dynamics of power in the political model:

> Men share power. Men differ about what must be done. This milieu necessitates that government decisions and actions result from a political process. In this process, sometimes one group committed to a course of action triumphs over other groups fighting for other alternatives. Equally often, however, different groups pulling in different directions produce a result . . . — a mixture of conflicting preferences and unequal power of various individuals — distinct from what any person or group intended. In both cases, what moves the chess pieces is not simply the reasons that support a course of action, or the routines of organizations that enact an alternative, but the power and skill of proponents and opponents of the action in question.[79]

Other models of political decision making also emphasize the use of power to determine outcomes. For example, the political model of decision making presented in Chapter 5 posits a *dominant environment* that necessitates the presence and use of power. And Pfeffer, in discussing his political model of decision making, articulates the use of power to serve the political aspects of arriving at a choice. In his words:

> Political models of choice further presume that when preferences conflict, the power of the various social actors determines the outcome of the social process. Power models hypothesize that those interests, subunits, or individuals within the organization who possess the greatest power, will receive the greatest rewards from the interplay of organizational politics. . . . Power is used to overcome the resistance of others and to obtain one's way in the organization.[80]

The relationship between politics and power, then, is straightforward. A power base facilitates the use of politics to obtain more power. Power is both an end and a means — it is a terminal state and a means to extend itself. Politics is purely an instrumentality to secure, hold, and expand the base of power. Political behavior is a manifestation of power. In the absence of power, the substantive aspects of the politics of managerial decision making lose their significance. Effective managerial decision makers are aware of their power and use it judiciously through various forms of political behavior as they seek to influence and determine the outcomes of choice. This is the ethos of the new class of managerial decision makers.

PROFILES OF POLITICAL POWER IN DECISION MAKING

Profiles of political power represent conditions or circumstances within which the use of managerial decision-making power manifests itself. These profiles are not mutually exclusive. In fact the three principal profiles often overlap. A situation may, for example, include elements of divergence in goals or objectives and may also require enlarged allocations of resources, both conditions calling for the use of political power to resolve. Similarly a desire to constrain the autonomy of a given entity through dominance almost assuredly will result in a marked divergence of goals or objectives and doubtless some diminution in the allocation of resources for the dominated entity. Political power is a complex phenomenon that tends to defy analysis through unidimensional cause-and-effect relationships. The following profiles of political power are intended to further the understanding of this phenomenon.

Divergence of Goals and Objectives

Given the inevitable differences in values, expectations, and aspirations among managerial decision makers, it is reasonable to assume an occasional or even continuous divergence in goals and objectives underlying the process of choice. Etzioni notes that "goals [and objectives] are often set in a complicated power play involving various individuals and groups within and without the organization, and by reference to values which govern behavior in general and the specific behavior of the relevant individuals and groups in a particular society."[81] The divergence of goals and objectives is, in one sense, inherent in the nature of organizations. Cyert and March, for example, state that goals and objectives constitute a series of more or less independent constraints imposed on the organization through a process of bargaining among the members and elaborated over time in response to short-run pressures. They further note that goals and objectives arise in a divergent form because the organization is, in fact, a coalition of participants with disparate demands, changing focuses of attention, and limited ability to attend to all needs simultaneously.[82] Mohr observes that in the political model of managerial decision making, the primary choice mechanism is **domination**.[83] In other words, the goals and objectives most likely to be attained are those favored by the holders of power. Mohr further suggests that there is an integral goal incompatibility in the political model because the joint satisfaction of a number of mutually inconsistent goals and objectives is impossible. "If goal compatibility is extremely low, then the choice must be made by the flight of some participants or the domination of some by others."[84]

Often the setting of goals and objectives involves the translation of vague, nonoperational long-term aspirations into more specific short-term outcomes. This activity may be accomplished through the garnering and application of power.[85] The choice of goals and objectives to initiate the managerial decision-making process involves the use of political power. The key question is whose interests, whose goals and objectives, and whose preferences are to prevail at the outset and, ultimately, whose ends will be served by the outcomes. The political model of decision making emphasizes that organizational choices are consequences of the application of strategies and tactics by units seeking to influence decision processes in ways that will result in outcomes favorable to themselves. This model highlights the fact that different participants in the decision-making process often have different goals and objectives,[86] and that frequently these differences are resolved through the overt or unobtrusive application of power.[87] The manifestations of this power are usually revealed in various types of political behavior in which the managerial decision makers seek to have their values, expectations, and aspirations embedded in the goals and objectives of the process of choice as well as the outcomes resulting from the application of this process. In many instances, a divergence of goals and objectives in the decision-making process can lead to the use of power in attempting to influence the allocation of resources.

Allocation of Resources

The allocation of resources constitutes another profile within which political power is exercised in the managerial decision-making process. Ackoff notes that there are four primary types of resources: (1) money, (2) facilities and equipment, (3) materials, supplies, and services, and (4) personnel (manpower).[88] Planning for resources involves three principal phases: (1) determining how much of each type of resource will be required, (2) relating requirements to availabilities to obtain a balance, and (3) allocating resources to programs and organizational units.[89] It is in the third step that the use of political power comes into play. Because the resources required are invariably less than the resources available, those who control the supply have considerable power over those who have demands on the supply.

As part of their continuous interaction with the external environment, organizations require a steady stream of resources to consummate the ongoing flow of transactions with their customers, creditors, constituencies, and competitors. "Organizations require personnel, money, social legitimacy, customers, and a variety of technological and material inputs in order to continue to function. Some of these resources are relatively more critical to the organization's operations than others. Those subunits or individuals within the organization that can provide the most critical and difficult to obtain resources come to have power in the organization."[90] Resources are invariably inadequate to meet all the organization's legitimate requirements. Moreover, resources of varying types have varying degrees of criticality to individuals or units placing demands on the limited supply.

> The basic truth, so to speak, . . . is that there exists a restricted quantity of something of value that is coveted by some group or persons. The something of value, referred to as the resource pool, can be any tangible or intangible entity. . . . The only requirement is that the element be considered valuable by

members of the group and that the amount be restricted. . . . With respect to any resource pool some person or persons has or gains greater distribution prerogative over the pool than other persons who also want access to the same pool.[91]

Resources that serve as a basis for the use of political power through their allocation within the organization possess certain common characteristics. These are (1) need, (2) scarcity, (3) deployability, (4) convertibility, and (5) timing.[92] The *need* for a given resource may be determined by the degree of criticality. In extreme cases, individuals or units become totally dependent upon a particular resource, which gives the controllers of the supply an inordinate amount of power. *Scarcity* relates to the supply and availability of the resource. In general, if the users of a particular resource have ready access to a supply, that resource has a limited potential as a source of power. Resources must also be *deployable* to the situation if they are to serve as a power base. In other words, the resource must fill the need by fitting the situation. Resources that don't meet a specific need have little value as a source of power. The value of resources as a power base also increases as the *convertibility* increases. Limited resources or those with restricted use have a low power value. The *timing* of the availability of a given resource also adds to its value as a potential power base. In summary, then, resources increase in value as a power base through the medium of allocation to individuals or units within the organization when they are (1) critical to the task at hand, (2) in short supply or with limited access, (3) appropriate in form and content to the task at hand, (4) convertible to alternate uses, and (5) optimal with regard to timing.

A small number of comprehensive empirical studies has validated the allocation of resources as a standard profile of power in managerial decision making. A few studies of allocations through university budgets have confirmed that scarcity and criticality of the resources at hand directly influence the size of the power base.[93] In general, the more critical and scarce the resources being allocated, the greater the ability to use the allocation process as a power base for influencing the entire process of managerial decision making. Along with divergent goals and objectives, the allocation of resources in formal organizations affords the managerial decision-making class a definite profile within which power can be applied to influence outcomes.

Dominance Versus Autonomy

A power holder exercises domination in an attempt to influence behavior by making explicit to others what is expected of them. The means of exercising domination includes commands, instructions, directives, and the like. Dominance tends to constrain the individual who is its object and to limit, minimize, and, in many cases, eliminate the ability of the individual to attain any degree of independence, thus counteracting autonomy. In general, the higher the level of dominance the lower the level of autonomy. In a free society, much less a formal organization of any sort, both complete dominance and full autonomy are rare. Typically the use of dominance to constrain autonomy is a less common profile of power in managerial decision making. A divergence of goals or objectives is usually situational, and the use of the allocation of resources as a power base is frequently transitory from one distribution to the next. But the dichotomy of dominance versus autonomy is more deep-seated and intense. Once the balance is struck, the pendulum does not swing back without some counterforce to strike a new balance. Still the discussion of profiles of power would be incomplete in the absence of this dichotomy.

Dahrendorf noted that the desire of one individual or group to dominate another is the basic source of conflict.[94] Given that conflict in one form or another is endemic to all human interaction, managerial decision making is also open to disagreement and dissent. To the extent that conflict in managerial decision making escalates to overt or unobtrusive hostility, it may derive from the use of power to restrict autonomy in an attempt at domination. This profile of power is more chronic and dysfunctional than the first two. As such, a persistent condition of dominance at the expense of reasonable autonomy suggests a need for the use of one or more of the techniques for treating conflict presented in Chapter 8.

DIMENSIONS OF MANAGERIAL DECISION-MAKING POWER

Managerial decision makers at all levels in all types of organizations possess power, which varies with the individual's position in the hierarchy; it seldom inheres in the individual. Because it derives from position, managerial decision-making power is based on reward, coercion, and legitimacy. The discussion to follow will focus on the scope and manifestations of such power.

The Scope of Managerial Decision-Making Power

It is not difficult to ascertain the scope of managerial decision-making power as it is present in the large corporation. Management has a legal claim to the power of legitimacy by virtue of its position in the hierarchy. The bylaws of most corporations provide for the appointment of a chief executive whose powers are limited only by the board of directors, which is inclined to follow the lead of the chief executive in most matters. Moreover, the power of the chief executive can be strengthened by a judicious use of rewards and punishments. Through the process of delegation of authority, the chief executive's power is diffused to middle and lower levels of management throughout the hierarchy. In this context, formal authority may be seen as institutionalized power, a view that explains the internal structure of power in formal organizations.[95] Inside the corporation the power of the managerial decision makers is virtually unchallenged.[96]

It is the external aspect of managerial decision-making power that is viewed with criticism and suspicion by many elements of American society. This preoccupation with power stems from the fundamental belief that no group should be capable of dominating the society's decision-making processes. It is generally agreed that such processes should be open, to permit diverse social elements to participate democratically in the determination and implementation of public policy.[97]

In spite of the general concern in the United States with avoidance of concentrations of power, the nature of managerial decision making is such that power accrues to the decision makers. Indeed managerial decision making is synonymous with power. To the extent that its legitimacy confers on management the right to reward good decisions and penalize poor ones, it has power. Because power is inherent in the very process of managerial decision making, to undermine it is to vitiate the essential functions of the decision-making process.

Because of the nature of the capitalist system in the United States, managerial decision-making power resides primarily in the economic sphere. Although its use affects the politics of the nation, the social and cultural milieus, the rate of technological change, the physical environment, and the conditions under which people work, it still is basically economic in nature. As Epstein has said, "It is in fulfilling their economic role or maintaining an environment favorable to it that corporations extend their power to the noneconomic spheres."[98] Although it is doubtless easier to demonstrate in the private sector, a good deal of the power of managerial decision makers in the government and the military also lies in the economic sphere.

The decision-making power of managers in the government, like that of their counterparts in the private sector, is based primarily on aggregates of resources and the ability to command these resources to determine outcomes in keeping with the managers' objectives. *Resources* in this context means fiscal expenditures, number of employees, and concentrations of physical assets, all of which are increasing rapidly at all levels in government organizations. In fact, the rate of employment is increasing more rapidly in government organizations than in the private sector, and budgets at the federal, state, and local levels are expanding commensurately. Appropriations for expenditures are authorized by the legislative branch, but it is the executive branch that decides how and where and under what circumstances the expenditures will be made. This ability, derived from established position, to control the expenditure of billions of dollars of public funds gives the managerial decision makers in the government the same power of legitimacy, reward, and coercion as their counterparts in the private sector. To be sure, significant institutional differences between the two sectors exist, but managerial decision-making power is common to both. Indeed, in some instances, institutional differences tend to be overshadowed by the commonalities. Nowhere is this situation better exemplified than in the relationship between the Department of Defense and the aerospace industry.[99]

Let us turn now to the second dimension, the manifestations of managerial decision-making power. The possession of power is one thing; how it is used in the process of decision making is another.

Manifestations of Managerial Decision-Making Power

Manifestations of power can have good or bad effects; assuming a zero-sum situation, what is good for some is bad for others. Moreover, if there are advantages to be gained from the exercise of power, they will invariably redound to the benefit of the power holder. Our purpose here is not to pass judgment on the goodness or badness of managerial decision-making power, but simply to examine its effects.

In the private sector it is relatively simple to demonstrate the manifestations of managerial decision-making power. They occur primarily in the economic sphere with effects that often spill over into the political and social spheres. Moreover, power exercised within the large corporation usually reverberates in the community, the region, and, occasionally, at the level of the nation. The following list illustrates significant elements of managerial decision-making power in the large corporation:

1. *The power to decide the kind and quantity of jobs to be made available.* This power is not simply management's traditional power to hire and fire. It is also the power to decide what kinds of work individuals will do for a living. (In many cases, this power is to some extent shared with unions, but it is still a basic decision-making power of management.)

2. *The power to decide (within legal limits) where, when, and how the operations of the organization will be conducted.*

3. *The power to decide what services, supplies, or raw materials to buy from other firms or subcontractors; and the power to decide (within legal limits) how, where, and when to purchase them.*

4. *The power to decide the service to be provided or the product to be produced.*

5. *The power (within legal limits) to set and administer prices.*

6. *The power to decide the amount of new investment and how, where, and when to invest it.* "Management alone decides when to invest — in new capital equipment, in new locations, in new processes, products, and personnel. It need not receive the approval of any governmental agency, and no such agency can compel a corporation to go ahead with an investment program if it feels like retrenching. . . . The power to make investment decisions is concentrated in a few hands, and it is the power to decide what kind of a nation America will be."[100]

7. *The power to shape and temper the value systems of the nation's population through sponsorship of the mass media.*

8. *The power to influence the administration of existing legislation and the preparation and passage of new legislation by supporting candidates for political office and lobbying.*

9. *The power to influence the general health and welfare of entire communities and of the general population through the use of technology and processes that product noxious and irritating emissions.*

10. *The power to pay or withhold dividends.*

11. *The power to decide the amount of resources (if any) to be given to educational and philanthropic institutions and how, where, and when to make such gifts.*

12. *The power to withhold power.* Managers are free to decide when the considerable power at their disposal will not be used, either partially or completely.[101]

The manifestations of managerial decision-making power in the federal government are essentially the same as those in the private sector, except for a somewhat different range of power options. Government managers decide the jobs to be performed within their agencies and departments. Within limits, they also decide where, how, and when their operations will be conducted. Government managers purchase land and buildings, which is technically a kind of investment but not the capital formation found in the private sector. Because government agencies' services are prescribed by law, managers have little power in this area. And, of course, prices for services rendered, to the extent that they exist at all, are not a primary concern of government managers. The regulated use of government funds largely precludes donations or contributions, and the same restrictions limit the use of the mass media to influence the value system of the population. Moreover, for the most part, government installations do not pose a threat to environmental conditions comparable to that of private industrial firms. By definition, the payment of dividends is not a concern of governmental managers. However, a good deal of decision-making power is wielded by public-sector managers through their capacity to decide what services, supplies, or raw materials to purchase from the private sector and (within legal limits) how, where, and when to purchase them.

Government agencies, especially those with a mission to regulate certain activities in the private sector, also exercise a good deal of decision-making power in the process of administering and enforcing legislation enacted to protect the public interest. There are countless governmental regulatory agencies at the federal, state, and local levels that exercise considerable power over the activities of business organizations. By virtue of their proximity to legislative bodies, government agencies are also in an excellent position to exert influence over the shape and substance of emerging legislation. Outside of the legislative and judicial areas, government managers exercise tremendous influence through existing legislation, policies, and procedures, all of which exist in great profusion. This power, in combination with whatever influence can be brought to bear to determine new legislation, makes the decision-making power of government managers formidable indeed. In addition to maintaining national security, law and order, and the health, education, and welfare of the general population, a good deal of this power is used to control activities in the private sector. The decision-making power of government managers is extended even further into the private sector by the annual procurement of products, supplies, and raw materials in enormous quantities.

Thus managerial decision-making power is broad in scope in both the private and the public sectors, which leads logically to the question: What are the constraints on the power of managers to make decisions?

CONSTRAINTS ON MANAGERIAL DECISION-MAKING POWER

There are several ways to approach the subject of constraints on managerial decision-making power. In the interest of simplicity, the following discussion will be divided into two parts. The first will deal with two theoretical constraints that originated for the most part in the social sciences. The second part will treat a more tangible group of operating constraints of varying effectiveness in limiting the considerable decision-making powers of managers.

Theoretical Constraints

The theoretical constraints on managerial decision-making power are, for the most part, based on the idea that management is only one of several significant power groups in the society and that there is no need to be concerned about a managerial revolution or a power elite. The existence of other groups with formidable power of their own will diffuse or neutralize the power of the managerial decision makers, or at least countervail against it.

The Theory of Pluralism   Pluralism is the idea that power in society is balanced and diffused among a multiplicity of organizations and groups. "The notion of pluralism has historically been considered basic to our sort of democratic society, for so long as power is diffused and allegiances to groups and organizations dispersed, individuals will find that they possess freedom of action and expression."[102] In a pluralistic society, no single organization or group is supreme in the sense that it has command over all others.

Unlike Mills's theory of the power elite, the pluralism theory involves a diversified and balanced plurality of interest groups characterized by an increasing dispersion rather than a concentration of power. The power to determine policy shifts among the centers of power depending on the issue at hand, and there is a kind of monopolistic competition among groups and organizations. As a consequence, no single group or class is favored significantly over others. In a pluralistic society each organized group has struggled for and attained the power to block developments inimical to its interests.[103]

The benefits of pluralism to the preservation of democracy in the United States are summed up well in the following statement:

> The major safeguard for our pluralistic democracy is actually the competition for power among economic groups within our system — a competition including a sufficient number of groups that compromise — and consensus among all is required to create public policy.[104]

Pluralism, then, is a theory of the power structure in which power is conceived of as dispersed, and different elites are dominant in different issue areas.[105] According to the theory of pluralism, the managerial decision makers in the United States constitute only one of several groups with power.

The Theory of Countervailing Power   This theory formulated by Galbraith[106] involves the market power of large corporations. The theory of countervailing power is based on the idea that the market power of big business is overstated, since there exist numerous other centers of power that can offset it. According to the theory, a kind of self-generating quality is inherent in countervailing power. The mere existence of great power tends to breed an opposing power that will hold it in check.[107] For example, in the absence of antitrust action by the government to stop the growth of big business, the effectiveness of business power will soon be checked as other power groups in the society rise to block business. Moreover, according to Galbraith, government policy should be directed at reinforcing and preserving the centers of countervailing power. Slichter shares Galbraith's theory and argues that the real power holders in America are big business, big unions, and big government.[108]

Whether one argues from a pluralistic perspective or subscribes to the ideal of some degree of countervailing power — which may or may not countervail — the fact remains that there are centers of power in America. The pluralist would say that power is diffused among many competing centers of power; the countervailist would argue that power is concentrated in fewer hands but that there is still no single dominant group. Still it is difficult to deny that the leader of a pluralist group is also a manger; and few would question the dominance of managers in big business, big unions, and big government. Therefore, decision-making power in the United States resides primarily in the hands of the managers of organized groups and large organizations. The theories of pluralism and countervailing power do not challenge the primacy of managerial decision-making power; in many ways, they tend to reinforce it. In a theoretical sense, then, there are few effective constraints on the power of the managerial decision makers. It may be, however, that some constraints exist in the operating areas of management.

Operating Constraints

The operating constraints on managerial decision-making power, to the extent that they exist at all, may be subdivided into internal and external constraints. Most operating constraints exist in the private sector because it is there that the power of the managerial decision makers is most extensive. In the public sector, operating constraints affect a somewhat narrower range of managerial decision-making power.

Within the large corporation there are three sources of possible constraints on the power of management: (1) stockholders, (2) boards of directors, and

(3) employees. **Managerial control** means that no large concentrated stock-holding group maintains a close working relationship with the management of the corporation or is capable of challenging it.[109] Theoretically, of course, it is possible to challenge the top executives of a given corporation through the board of directors if the board is not, as is so frequently the case, dominated by the managers. But the act of challenge is awesome to contemplate, formidable to undertake, expensive to prosecute, and problematic in outcome. The incidence of such challenges is therefore quite small. Managerial control is the norm in industry now. Nominal power resides with the widely dispersed small stockholders, but actual power resides in the managerial decision-making class.[110]

The board of directors clearly provides no check on the power of the managerial decision makers. In many instances the board is composed of officers of the company as well as executives of other companies who hold interlocking memberships on several boards — making the board a rubber stamp for the projects of the managerial decision makers. Gordon and others have suggested that the board of directors should begin to perform as the theoretical model provides — that is, to act as a reviewing and consultative body with the power to remove any of the corporate officers for proper cause.[111] To date, however, there is little indication that any significant change in the existing state of affairs will occur.

The third possible source of constraint on managerial decision-making power within the corporation is the employees. However, given its capacity to hire, fire, promote, or otherwise reward or punish, management's decision-making power over the employees is virtually unassailable. The evidence shows that, in true pluralistic tradition, any power exercised by the employees derives from organizing into bargaining groups — that is, from outside the corporation through the offices of unions and similar associations. It thus seems apparent that there are few, if any, constraints on managerial decision-making power within the large corporation in the United States.

Opportunities for constraining managerial decision-making power from outside the large corporation appear to be more numerous. Government regulatory agencies tend to limit managerial decision making within the bounds of enacted legislation. Moreover, government procurement actions force the managers of large corporations to conform rigorously to detailed regulations governing the award of government contracts. It is difficult to gainsay the power of government in this respect. In fact, it appears that government at all levels is increasingly intruding into the affairs of business, both large and small.

Organized labor acts as a partial counterforce to managerial decision-making power in one critical area — the terms and conditions of employment. Efforts by labor leaders to extend constraints to other areas have been largely unsuccessful. Indeed, only with the advent of big government and enabling legislation in the 1930s was organized labor able to attain any real power at all. The power of organized labor vis-à-vis that of the managers of large corporations is considerably less extensive than that possessed by the government. Moreover, the power of organized labor is primarily economic, though it has some political influence; the government, on the other hand, possesses massive political power and considerable influence in the economic sphere through procurement actions and regulatory activities.

Special interest groups may, at various times and in various ways, possess limited power that competes with the decision-making power of management. If, for example, a commodity or service supplied to a corporation is of particular importance, and if the supply is subject to unified control, the interest group providing the commodity or service may be able to wield considerable power. Power may also be acquired by a group when its contractual rights in a company are threatened. The importance of creditor groups in a corporate reorganization is a case in point. An interest group is also likely to possess a significant measure of power if, for any of a number of reasons, an especially close relationship exists between it and the management of the firm. One of the strongest interest groups is composed of members of the financial community, notably insurance companies and big banks. At certain times bankers can exert considerable power and influence on the managerial decision-making class in debtor companies. Nevertheless, it is important to realize that most special interest groups are ad hoc by nature — that is, they coalesce to serve a special purpose related to the protection of their interests and then revert to their normally bland role in the affairs of the corporation. Such groups can hardly be considered an effective continuing counterforce to the decision-making power inherent in the managerial decision-making class.

Prior to the emergence of the giant corporation, competition was viewed as a constraint on decision making by managers in private enterprise. But the atomistic society of Adam Smith is no longer relevant in a corporate universe. As Berle has pointed out, "In blunt fact, competition in an industry dominated by two or three large units is not the same as competition among thousands of small units."[112] Thus the evidence at hand strongly suggests that competition per se is not a significant constraint on managerial decision-making power in industries dominated by large corporations.

One other possible external constraint is the public. Yet the means available to the public to counterbalance managerial decision-making power are limited and indirect. Economic boycotts, propaganda campaigns, and the like will not move the giant corporations. In fact, the power of the public is significant only when large numbers organize into groups and move against management in the political sphere. Even then the action is protracted and the results uncertain at best.

On balance, it appears that there are virtually no constraints on managerial decision-making power *within* the giant corporation; and with the possible exception of governmental power administered through legislation, most potentially constraining forces *outside* the corporation are relatively ineffective or effective only in specialized areas and for limited periods of time.

Managerial decision-making power within any given governmental institution, including military organizations, is constrained in the first instance by the legislation that empowered the department, agency, or bureau. The daily exercise of managerial decision making within the public sector is constrained by policies and procedures that circumscribe the actions of management much more than in the private sector. Still there is considerable latitude for the exercise of managerial decision-making power even within procedures as in the case of the Armed Services Procurement Regulations, which govern procurement action by the Department of Defense. External pressures to constrain the decision-making power of managers in government institutions may originate with the public and work their way through the political system to the legislative branch, which might then act to curtail the managerial decision-making power in the executive branch; or such pressures may originate with the legislative branch and be applied directly to the managers in the executive branch. In any event, it appears that the decision-making power of managers in government institutions is subject to considerably more constraints than is that of their counterparts in the private sector.

SUMMARY

Managerial decision makers possess and exercise considerable power. This power provides the foundation for the influence and determination of outcomes to the advantage of the organization. It is also the framework within which the political aspects of managerial decision making are accomplished.

Power may be defined as the ability to influence the behavior of others in accordance with one's intentions. Power may be applied by force, domination, or manipulation. Two principal criteria by which to measure the amount of power exercised by a given power holder include (1) the number of actions on the part of any person, in each of any number of selected types of behavior, in which power is exercised successfully, and (2) the number of persons over whom such power is achieved. By these criteria, it is apparent that the managerial decision makers in large organizations in the United States have ample opportunity to exercise a good deal of power. The usual bases of managerial decision-making power are legitimacy, reward, and coercion; managers less commonly possess expert power or referent power. Managerial decision-making power inheres in the position within the hierarchy of management rather than in the individual.

The emergence of managerial decision makers as a class may be seen in the context of the evolution of management thought and rapid advances in technology, which, along with the concomitant appearance of the large corporation and the virtual disappearance of the entrepreneur, gave rise to a new class of managerial decision makers committed to the organization. The development of the managerial decision-making class in the public sector was given impetus by the appearance of large government institutions in the 1930s. There are several theories of the managerial decision-making class: (1) Burnham's theory of the managerial revolution, (2) Mills's concept of the power elite, (3) Marxist theory, and (4) Galbraith's theory of the technostructure. Although no managerial revolution is apparent, the concept of a managerial decision-making class advanced in this book is probably closer to Burnham's formulation than any of the others. The principal identifying characteristics of the managerial decision-making class are (1) college education, (2) middle-class origin, (3) geographic and hierarchical mobility, and (4) a strong sense of commitment to the organization.

Politics involves the use of influence to get what there is to get. Organizational politics involves intentional acts of influence to enhance or protect the actor's self-interest. It is also concerned with the use of power to mobilize resources, energy, and information on behalf of a preferred goal or strategy. For purposes of this book, organizational politics involves those activities taken within organizations to acquire, develop, and use power and other resources to obtain one's preferred outcomes in a situation in which there is uncertainty or dissensus about choices. Clearly there is a need for competence in the use of politics for managerial decision making. A good understanding of politics, political behavior, and political effects can limit the adverse consequences likely to ensue from the uninformed or irresponsible use of this form of power. Politics and power are reciprocals of organizational life and are, therefore, endemic to the process of managerial decision making.

The concepts of power and politics find their ultimate and symbiotic expression in the form of political power permeating the process of managerial decision making. Organizational politics is a process of actual influence; power is a reservoir of potential influence. The two are closely related but clearly distinguishable concepts. Political power is employed by managerial decision makers in the shaping and making of choices to accomplish predetermined ends in conformity with managerial preferences.

The locus of political power in formal organizations begins with top management. Only top management has the power of legitimacy, reward, and coercion to intervene in any part of the decision-making process to determine the tone and temper of significant choices. The relationship between politics and power is straightforward. A power base facilitates the use of politics to obtain more power. Power is both an end and a means. It is a terminal state and an instrumentality to extend itself. In the absence of power, the substantive aspects of the politics of managerial decision making are lessened. Effective managerial decision makers are aware of their considerable power and use it judiciously as they seek to influence and determine the outcome of choices.

Profiles of political power represent conditions or circumstances within which the use of managerial decision-making power manifests itself. The three principal profiles of political power are (1) divergence of goals and objectives, (2) allocation of resources, and (3) dominance versus autonomy. These profiles are not mutually exclusive. There is a good deal of overlap or intersection between them. For example, a given situation involving the use of political power may include elements of divergence in goals and objectives, which in turn manifests itself in the use of political power to obtain enlarged allocations of resources. In other cases individuals or units may come to require a particular resource that gives the controllers of the resource a point of leverage to obtain dominance over those who are dependent on the resource. Resources that are critical to the task at hand or that are in short supply tend to have a high value as a power base. Finally, it should be noted that dominance tends to limit the ability of any submissive entity to make a self-determination in terms of setting goals and objectives or in obtaining resources for nearly any purpose. Clearly the profiles of political power are highly interdependent.

To the extent that its legitimacy confers on management the right to reward good performance and penalize poor performance, it has decision-making power. It is inherent in the very process of management. The basic decision-making power of management is economic in nature; it is the ability to command the allocation, use, and outcome of resources. Managerial decision-making power in the large corporations is facilitated by substantial concentrations of assets and the separation of the ownership of these assets from their control. Managerial decision makers determine outcomes apart from any ownership they may have in the corporation. In the public sector, managerial decision-making power is also reflected in substantial concentrations of resources and in the procurement actions of large government institutions, such as the Department of Defense, whose decisions influence the economic well-being of large and small companies in the private sector and the general prosperity of entire states and communities.

The manifestations of managerial decision-making power in the private sector are awesome to contemplate. For example, the power to determine the amount of new investment and to decide how, where, and when to make it is doubtless the most sovereign and significant of all managerial decision-making powers in the large corporations. In the public sector, managerial decision-making power manifests itself in the administration and enforcement of existing legislation and in the influence applied to shape and mold emerging legislation.

There are virtually no constraints on managerial decision-making power in the large corporation. The bulk of the shareholders are diffused and diffident, and their ownership shares are inconsequential; the board of directors is often only a rubber stamp for management; and the employees can apply influence only through unions and similar associations. Externally, the decision-making power of management is constrained primarily by law and by the efforts of government regulatory agencies. Unions exercise some limited power, with government support, on the terms and conditions of employment. Special interest groups may influence management for short periods in times of financial difficulty. Competition is scarcely a deterrent for large corporations in oligopolistic industries, and the influence of the public on corporate affairs is tangential at best.

Managerial decision-making power within government institutions is constrained to some degree by legislation, regulations, and procedures. Externally, such decision-making power is constrained primarily by the legislature operating on its own initiative or with an impetus provided by the public.

There can be little doubt that the decision-making power of management is significant in our society. But such power, if used responsibly in carrying out the functions of managerial decision making, can be a positive force contributing to progress for individuals, organizations, and the general community. This is the goal of a democracy and it should be kept uppermost in mind.

REVIEW AND DISCUSSION QUESTIONS

1. Discuss the general concept of power and the several bases of power, with particular emphasis on the decision-making power of management.

2. Do you agree or disagree with the notion that decision-making power is synonymous with management in all kinds of formal organizations? Defend your arguments with the materials presented in this chapter.

3. Is there really a managerial decision-making class in the United States? If so, what are its characteristics and what are the implications of its existence?

4. What are the significant differences among (a) Burnham's concept of the managerial revolution, (b) Mills's theory of the power elite, (c) the Marxist theory, and (d) Galbraith's ideal of the technostructure?

5. What are the significant potential benefits that may accrue to an organization through the political aspects of managerial decision making?

6. Discuss this statement: Politics, however broadly defined, enters into most managerial decision making.

7. Why does the locus of political power in formal organizations begin with top management?

8. What are the principal profiles of political power in managerial decision making and how do they overlap or intersect?

9. What are the principal manifestations of managerial decision-making power in the private sector? in the public sector?

10. Is there any power in American society that can effectively countervail against the decision-making power of top management in the private sector? in the public sector?

NOTES

1. Herbert Goldhammer and Edward A. Shils, "Types of Power," in *Human Relations in Administration*, ed. Robert Dubin (New York: Prentice-Hall, 1951), p. 182.

2. Robert Dubin, ed., *Human Relations in Administration* (New York: Prentice-Hall, 1951), p. 181.

3. For a more detailed discussion of these relationships, see Robert Bierstedt, "Power and Social Organization," in *Human Relations in Administration*, ed. Dubin, pp. 173–181.

4. Goldhammer and Shils, "Types of Power," pp. 185–186.

5. Arthur R. Cohen, "Situational Structure, Self-Esteem and Threat-Oriented Reactions to Power," in *Studies in Social Power*, ed. Dorwin Cartwright (Ann Arbor: University of Michigan Research Center for Group Dynamics, Institute for Social Research, 1959), p. 36.

6. George Levinger, "The Development of Perceptions and Behavior in Newly Formed Social Power Relationships," in *Studies in Social Power*, ed. Cartwright, p. 83.

7. John R. P. French, Jr., and Bertram Raven, "The Bases of Social Power," in *Studies in Social Power*, ed. Cartwright, pp. 150–167.

8. Ibid., pp. 155–164.

9. Alexis de Tocqueville, *Democracy in America*, trans. Richard D. Heffner (New York: New American Library, 1956), p. 17.

10. C. Wright Mills, *The Power Elite* (London: Oxford University Press, 1956), p. 271.

11. James Burnham, *The Managerial Revolution* (New York: John Day, 1941), p. 177.

12. John Kenneth Galbraith, *The New Industrial State* (Boston: Houghton Mifflin, 1967), p. 58.

13. See Orvis F. Collins and David G. Moore, *The Enterprising Man* (East Lansing: Michigan State University, 1964).

14. W. Lloyd Warner et al., *The American Federal Executive* (New Haven: Yale University Press, 1963).

15. See Morris Janowitz, ed., *The New Military* (New York: Norton, 1964).

16. David J. Hickson, ed., *Managerial Decision Making* (England: Dartmouth, 1995), p. xi.

17. Ibid.

18. Burnham, *The Managerial Revolution*.

19. Ibid., p. 80.

20. Ibid., p. 71.

21. See Albert A. Canella, Jr., "Executives and Shareholders: A Shift in the Relationship," *Human Resource Management*, 34, No. 3 (Spring 1995), 165–184.

22. Ralph Miliband, "C. Wright Mills," in *C. Wright Mills and the Power Elite*, ed. G. William Domhoff and Hoyt B. Ballard (Boston: Beacon Press, 1968), p. 16.

23. Mills, *The Power Elite*, p. 9.

24. Daniel Bell, ed., *The End of Ideology*, rev. ed. (New York: Free Press, 1960), p. 52.

25. Mills, *The Power Elite*, p. 23.

26. Ibid., p. 22.

27. See Roger Hilsman, *To Move a Nation* (New York: Dell, 1967).

28. Alan Swingewood, *Marx and Modern Social Theory* (London: Macmillan, 1975), pp. 140–141.

29. Ibid., p. 165.

30. Galbraith, *The New Industrial State*, p. 48.

31. Burnham, *The Managerial Revolution*, p. 82.

32. Galbraith, *The New Industrial State*, p. 71.

33. Ibid.

34. W. Lloyd Warner and James C. Abegglen, *Big Business Leaders in America Today* (New York: Columbia University Press, 1955).

35. Ibid., pp. 34–35.

36. Ibid., pp. 66–83.

37. Mabel Newcomer, *The Big Business Executive* (New York: Columbia University Press, 1955).

38. Ibid., pp. 68–70.

39. Warner et al., *American Federal Executive*.

40. Ibid., pp. 10–17.

41. Ibid., p. 18.

42. Ibid.

43. Mabel Newcomer, *The Big Business Executive/1964* (New York: Scientific American, 1965).

44. Charles G. Burck, "A Group Profile of the Fortune 500 Chief Executive," *Fortune* (May 1976), pp. 173ff.

45. *Korn/Ferry International's Executive Profile: A Survey of Corporate Leaders in the Eighties* (New York: Korn/Ferry International, 1986).

46. *Reinventing the CEO* (New York: Korn/Ferry International and Columbia University Graduate School of Business, 1989).

47. *Korn/Ferry International's Executive Profile: A Decade of Change in Corporate Leadership* (New York: Korn/Ferry International, 1990).

48. See "Portrait of a CEO," *Business Week* (October 11, 1983), 64–65; also see Deepak K. Datta and James P. Guthrie, "Executive Succession: Organizational Antecedents of CEO Characteristics," *Strategic Management Journal*, 15 (1994), 569–577, and James P. Guthrie and Deepak K. Datta, "Contextual Influences on Executive Selection: Firm Characteristics and CEO Experience," *Journal of Management Studies* (July 1997), 537–560.

49. Mills, *The Power Elite*.

50. See Andrew Kakabadse, "Organizational Politics," *Management Decision*, 25 (1987) 33–37; and "The Politics of Decision Making," *Meeting & Conventions* (October 1986), 42–54.

51. Ruth P. Mack, *Planning on Uncertainty* (New York: Wiley-Interscience, 1971), p. 171.

52. Percy H. Hill et al., *Making Decisions: A Multidisciplinary Introduction* (Reading, Mass.: Addison-Wesley, 1978), p. 82.

53. Ibid.

54. Harold D. Lasswell, "Politics — Who Gets What, When, How," in *The Political Writings of Harold D. Lasswell* (Glencoe, Ill.: Free Press, 1951).

55. Robert W. Allen et al., "Organizational Politics: Tactics and Characteristics of Its Actors," *California Management Review* (Fall 1979), 77.

56. Michael L. Tushman, "A Political Approach to Organizations: A Review and Rationale," *Academy of Management Review* (April 1977), 207.

57. Gerald F. Cavanagh, Dennis J. Moberg, and Manuel Velasquez, "The Ethics of Organizational Politics," *Academy of Management Review* (July 1981), 363.

58. Gerald R. Ferris et al., "Perceptions of Organizational Politics: Prediction, Stress-Related Implications, and Outcomes," *Human Relations,* 49, No. 2 (1996), 234.

59. John Hayes, "The Politically Competent Manager," *Journal of General Management* (Autumn 1984), 24–33.

60. Ibid., p. 26.

61. Don R. Beeman and Thomas W. Sharkey, "The Use and Abuse of Corporate Politics," *Business Horizons* (March / April 1987), 54–57.

62. James G. March, "The Business Firm as a Political Coalition," *Journal of Politics,* 24 (1962), 662–678.

63. Abraham Zaleznik, "Power and Politics in Organizational Life," *Harvard Business Review* (May-June 1970), 48.

64. Bronston T. Mayes and Robert W. Allen, "Toward a Definition of Organizational Politics," *Academy of Management Review* (October 1977), 675.

65. Henry Mintzberg, "The Organization as Political Arena," *Journal of Management Studies* (March 1985), 133–154.

66. Ibid., p. 134.

67. Ibid., pp. 148–150.

68. For a more complete account of definitions of organizational politics, see Mayes and Allen, "Toward a Definition of Organizational Politics," pp. 672–678.

69. Jeffrey Pfeffer, *Power in Organizations* (Marshfield, Mass.: Pitman, 1981), p. 6.

70. Ibid., p. 7.

71. Amos Drory and Tsilia Romm, "Politics in Organization and Its Perception within the Organization," *Organization Studies,* 9, (1988), 165–179.

72. Gerald R. Ferris and K. Michele Kacmar, "Perceptions of Organizational Politics," *Journal of Management,* 18, No. 1 (1992), 93–116; also see Samuel B. Bacharach et al., " Strategic and Tactical Logics of Decision Justification: Power and Decision Criteria in Organizations," *Human Relations,* 48, No. 5 (1995), 447–488.

73. See Dan L. Madison et al., "Organizational Politics: An Exploration of Managers' Perceptions," *Human Relations,* 33, No. 2 (1980), 79–100, for a comprehensive presentation of this relationship. Much of the rationale for the discussion to follow is derived from this source.

74. Steven P. Feldman, "Secrecy, Information, and Politics: An Essay on Organizational Decision Making," *Human Relations,* 41 (1988), 73–90.

75. Christopher Rowe, "Analysing Management Decision-Making: Further Thoughts After the Bradford Studies," *Journal of Management Studies* (January 1989), 29–46.

76. Allen et al., "Organizational Politics," pp. 78–80.

77. Raaj K. Sah, "Fallibility in Human Organizations and Political Systems," *Journal of Economic Perspectives* (Spring 1991), 67–68.

78. Graham T. Allison, *Essence of Decision: Explaining the Cuban Missile Crisis* (Boston: Little, Brown, 1971).

79. Ibid., p. 145.

80. Pfeffer, *Power in Organizations,* p. 28.

81. Amitai Etzioni, *Modern Organizations* (Englewood Cliffs, N.J.: Prentice-Hall, 1964), pp. 7–8.

82. Richard N. Cyert and James G. March, *A Behavioral Theory of the Firm* (Englewood Cliffs, N.J.: Prentice-Hall, 1963), p. 43.

83. Lawrence B. Mohr, "Organizations, Decisions, and Courts," *Law and Society* (Summer 1976), 621–641.

84. Ibid., p. 635.

85. Charles A. O'Reilly III, "The Use of Information in Organizational Decision Making," in *Research in Organizational Behavior,* Vol. 5, ed. L. L. Cummings and Barry M. Staw (Greenwich, Conn.: JAI Press, 1983), pp. 103–139.

86. Gerardo R. Ungson and Daniel N. Braunstein, eds., *Decision Making* (Boston: Kent, 1982), p. 255.

87. See Cynthia Hardy, "The Nature of Unobtrusive Power," *Journal of Management Studies* (July 1985), 384–399.

88. Russell L. Ackoff, *A Concept of Corporate Planning* (New York: Wiley-Interscience, 1970).

89. Ibid., pp. 75–76.

90. Pfeffer, *Power in Organizations*, p. 101.

91. Paul G. Swingle, *The Management of Power* (New York: Wiley, 1976), pp. 79–80.

92. Ian MacMillan and Patricia E. Jones, *Strategy Foundation*, 2nd ed. (St. Paul, Minn.: West, 1986), p. 15.

93. See Jeffrey Pfeffer and Gerald R. Salancik, "Organizational Decision Making as a Political Process: The Case of a University Budget," *Administrative Science Quarterly* (June 1974), 135–151; Gerald R. Salancik and Jeffrey Pfeffer, "The Bases and Use of Power in Organizational Decision Making: The Case of a University," *Administrative Science Quarterly* (December 1974), 453–473; and Frederick S. Hills and Thomas A. Mahoney, "University Budgets and Organizational Decision Making," *Administrative Science Quarterly* (September 1978), 454–465.

94. Ralf Dahrendorf, *Class and Class Conflict in Industrial Society* (Stanford, Calif.: Stanford University Press, 1959), p. 4.

95. See Bierstadt, "Power and Social Organization," p. 177.

96. See Edward S. Mason, ed., *The Corporation in Modern Society* (Cambridge, Mass.: Harvard University Press, 1959), p. 4.

97. Edwin P. Epstein, "Dimensions of Corporate Power, Part 1," *California Management Review* (Winter 1973), p. 10.

98. Ibid., p. 15.

99. See Seymour Melman, *Pentagon Capitalism* (New York: McGraw-Hill, 1970).

100. Andrew Hacker, "Power to Do What?" in *The New Sociology*, ed. Irving Louis Horowitz (New York: Oxford University Press, 1964), p. 139.

101. Ibid., p. 140.

102. Joseph W. McGuire, *Business and Society* (New York: McGraw-Hill, 1963), p. 130.

103. See David Reisman, Nathan Glazer, and Reuel Denny, *The Lonely Crowd* (New York: Doubleday, 1950), pp. 239–259; and William Kornhauser, "'Power Elite' or 'Veto Group,'" in *C. Wright Mills and the Power Elite*, ed. William Domhoff and Hoyt B. Ballard (Boston: Beacon Press, 1968), pp. 37–59.

104. R. Joseph Monson, Jr., and Mark W. Cannon, *The Makers of Public Policy: American Power Groups and Their Ideologies* (New York: McGraw-Hill, 1965), p. 310.

105. Arnold M. Rose, *The Power Structure: Political Process in American Society* (New York: Oxford University Press, 1967), p. 282.

106. John Kenneth Galbraith, *American Capitalism: The Concept of Countervailing Power* (Boston: Houghton Mifflin, 1952), pp. 108–153.

107. Howard D. Marshall, ed., *Business and Government: The Problem of Power* (Lexington, Mass.: Heath, 1970), pp. 54–78.

108. Sumner H. Slichter, "The Power Holders in the American Economy," *Saturday Evening Post* (December 15, 1958), 34ff.

109. Robert J. Larner, *Management Control and the Large Corporation* (New York: Dunellen, 1970).

110. Adolph A. Berle, Jr., *Power Without Property* (New York: Harcourt, Brace, 1959), pp. 70–71.

111. Robert Aaron Gordon, *Business Leadership in the Large Corporation* (Berkeley: University of California Press, 1961). Also see Larner, *Management Control and the Large Corporation*.

112. A. A. Berle, Jr., *The Twentieth Century Capitalistic Revolution* (New York: Harcourt, Brace, 1954), p. 51.

SUPPLEMENTAL REFERENCES

Bacharach, Samuel B., and Edward J. Lawler. *Power and Politics in Organizations*. San Francisco: Jossey-Bass, 1980.

Bass, Bernard M. *Organizational Decision Making*. Homewood, Ill.: Richard D. Irwin, 1983.

Braybrooke, David, and Charles E. Lindblom. *A Strategy of Decision*. New York: Free Press, 1963.

Butler, Richard. *Designing Organizations: A Decision-Making Perspective*. New York: Routledge, 1991.

Cartwright, Dorwin, ed. *Studies in Social Power*. Ann Arbor: University of Michigan Research Center for Group Dynamics, Institute for Social Research, 1959.

Clegg, Stewart. *Power, Rule and Domination*. London and Boston: Routledge & Kegan Paul, 1975.

Dahl, Robert A., and Charles E. Lindblom. *Politics, Economics, and Welfare*. New York: Harper & Row, 1953.

Ebert, Ronald J., and Terence R. Mitchell. *Organizational Decision Processes*. New York: Crane, Russak, 1975.

Eulau, Heinz. "Problematics of Decisional Models in Political Contexts." *American Behavioral Scientist* (September–October 1976), 127–144.

Filley, A. C., and A. J. Grimes. "The Bases of Power in Decision Processes." *Papers and Proceedings of the 27th Annual Meeting of the Academy of Management, December 27–29, 1967, Washington, D.C.*, pp. 133–160.

George, Alexander L. "Adaptation to Stress in Political Decision Making: The Individual, Small Group, and Organizational Contexts." In *Coping and Adaptation*. Ed. George V. Coelho et al. New York: Basic Books, 1974, pp. 176–245.

———. *Presidential Decisionmaking in Foreign Policy: The Effective Use of Information and Advice*. Boulder, Colo.: Westview, 1980.

Heller, Robert. *The Decision Makers*. New York: Penguin Books, 1991.

Hickson, David J., et al. *Top Decisions: Strategic Decision-Making in Organizations*. San Francisco: Jossey-Bass, 1986.

Janis, Irving L. *Groupthink*. 2nd ed. Boston: Houghton Mifflin, 1982.

Kirkpatrick, Samuel A., Dwight A. Davis, and Rody D. Robertson. "The Process of Political Decision Making in Groups: Search Behavior and Choice Shifts." *American Behavioral Scientist* (September–October 1976), 33–64.

Lerner, Allan W. *The Politics of Decision-Making*. Beverly Hills, Calif.: Sage, 1976.

Lindblom, Charles E. *The Policy-Making Process*. Englewood Cliffs, N.J.: Prentice-Hall, 1968.

March, James G. "The Business Firm as a Political Coalition." *Journal of Politics*, 24 (1962), 662–678.

March, James G. *A Primer on Decision Making*. New York: Free Press, 1994.

———, ed. *Decisions and Organizations*. London: Blackwell, 1988.

March, James G. and Herbert A. Simon. *Organizations*. New York: Wiley, 1958.

March, James G., and Roger Weissinger-Baylon. *Ambiguity and Command*. Marshfield, Mass.: Pitman, 1986.

Mechanic, David. "Sources of Power of Lower Participants in Complex Organizations." In *Readings in Organization Theory: A Behavioral Approach*. Ed. Walter A. Hill and Douglas M. Egan. Boston: Allyn & Bacon, 1966, pp. 196–206.

Pettigrew, Andrew M. "Strategy Formulation as a Political Process." *International Studies of Management & Organization* (Summer 1977), 78–87.

———. *The Politics of Organizational Decision-Making*. London: Tavistock, 1973.

Pfeffer, Jeffrey. *Managing with Power*. Boston: Harvard Business School Press, 1992.

Pfeffer, Jeffrey. "The Micropolitics of Organizations." In *Environments and Organizations*. Ed. Marshall W. Meyer and Associates. San Francisco: Jossey-Bass, 1978.

Radford, K. J. *Complex Decision Problems*. Reston, Va.: Reston, 1977.

Saaty, Thomas L. *Decision Making for Leaders*. Belmont, Calif.: Wadsworth, 1982.

Salancik, Gerald R., and Jeffrey Pfeffer. "Who Gets Power — And How They Hold on to It: A Strategic-Contingency Model of Power." *Organizational Dynamics* (Winter 1977), 3–21.

Steinbruner, John D. *The Cybernetic Theory of Decision*. Princeton, N.J.: Princeton University Press, 1974.

Tushman, Michael L. "A Political Approach to Organizations: A Review and Rationale." *Academy of Management Review* (April 1977), 206–216.

Walker, Thomas G. "Microanalytic Approaches to Political Decision-Making: Methodological Issues and Research Strategies." *American Behavioral Scientist* (September–October 1976), 93–110.

Yoffie, David B., and Joseph L. Badaracco, Jr. "A Rational Model of Corporate Political Strategies," Harvard Business School, Working Paper No. 9-785-018. Boston: HBS Case Services, 1985.

PART THREE

Foundations of Strategic Decision Making

Strategic Decision Perspectives

*T*his chapter marks a shift in focus from managerial decision making in general to strategic decision making at the top of the organization. As noted in Chapter 1, the primary emphasis in this book is on category II decisions, which are nonroutine, nonrecurring, and have a good deal of uncertainty attendant on the outcome (see Table 1.1). Strategic decisions constitute a special variety of category II choices with their own set of unique characteristics. Mainly because of their significance and complexity, strategic decisions require a good deal of study and analysis if they are to be understood and improved in organizations of all types. The facilitation of this understanding and improvement constitutes the rationale for the remaining chapters of this book.

This chapter commences with an explanation of the unique nature of strategic decisions. While most of this explanation is directed toward making strategic decisions in private enterprise, it is important to emphasize the generic aspects of strategic choice in that they are made at the executive level in both private enterprise and the public sector. In fact, three of the eight major cases presented in the later chapters of this book deal with strategic decisions made in the public sector at the federal level. The second major section of this chapter is devoted to the external environment of the organizations in which strategic decisions are made. The external environment is particularly important because it is invariably the point of origin for the need to make a strategic decision and the point of destination for the outcome of a strategic choice once it is made. Strategic decisions are influenced primarily by the organization's external environment and their acceptance or nonacceptance is directly dependent on a constellation of external forces.

By definition, strategic decisions are oriented toward the future and are, therefore, fraught with the uncertainty of outcomes yet to be realized. The third major section of this chapter focuses on uncertainty in strategic decision making. Uncertainty originates with change over time in the external

---

Note: This chapter contains selected materials used from E. Frank Harrison, "The Concept of Strategic Gap," *Journal of General Management*, 15 (Winter 1989), 57–72. Used with permission of the Braybrooke Press Ltd. and Henly Management College, Greenlands, Henley-on-the-Thames, Oxfordshire, England.

environment of the organization. Managers can reduce but never eliminate uncertainty in arriving at and implementing a strategic choice. The fourth and fifth sections constitute the centerpiece of this chapter. These sections present a detailed explanation of the concept of strategic gap, which is one of the primary frameworks for the evaluation of strategic decision success. The use of gap analysis is fundamental to a meaningful assessment of strategic choice in private enterprise. As such, it richly deserves and receives a full exposition. Gap analysis is somewhat less meaningful for assessing strategic decision success in the public sector where other considerations usually take precedence for the decision makers.[1] The sixth and final major section of this chapter presents the strategic decision-making process, which is a combination of the managerial decision-making process (Figure 2.1) and the concept of strategic gap (Figure 10.2). This subject concludes the presentation of strategic decision perspectives and leads logically to the evaluative frameworks for assessing strategic decision success presented in Chapter 11.

THE NATURE OF STRATEGIC DECISIONS

Mintzberg and his associates have noted the distinctive characteristics of strategic decisions in the following passage:

> A strategic decision process is characterized by novelty, complexity, and open-endedness, by the fact that the organization usually begins with little understanding of the decision situation it faces or the route to its solution, and only a vague idea of what that solution might be and how it will be evaluated when it is developed. Only by groping through a recursive, discontinuous process involving many difficult steps and a host of dynamic factors over a considerable period of time is a final choice made. This is not the decision making under *uncertainty* of the textbook, where alternatives are given even if their consequences are not, but decision making under *ambiguity*, where almost nothing is given or easily determined.[2]

Given that strategic decisions are highly complex and involve a host of dynamic variables, their preeminent characteristic is significance. "Strategic decisions deal with the long-term health of the enterprise."[3] Drucker notes the overriding significance of strategic decisions as follows:

> Effective executives do not make a great many decisions. They concentrate on the important ones. They try to think through what is strategic and what is generic rather than "solve problems." They make a few important decisions on the highest level of conceptual understanding.[4]

According to Hambrick and Snow, "Strategic decisions are those which normally fall within the purview of top management. Broadly speaking, strategic decisions are those which are 'important' to the organization — either through the scope of their impact and/or through their long-term implications. Because of their importance, strategic decisions must be closely linked with each other to form a consistent pattern for unifying and directing the organization."[5] This pattern of decisions reflects the strategy of the organization, which, by definition, is aimed at effectively matching or aligning organizational resources with environmental opportunities and threats.

Strategic decisions may be classified into at least three broad categories: (1) decisions related to the product/service domain of a given organization, (2) decisions related to the development and implementation of a technology for serving the product/service domain, and (3) decisions related to the differentiation and integration of an organizational structure.[6] "Strategic decisions are seldom made by chief executives acting alone — they are usually the product of the dominant coalition, the most influential members of the top management group."[7] Strategic decisions are made by the application of managerial perceptions conditioned by managerial values and experience to information obtained largely from the external environment within the prevailing internal constraints of power and policy.[8]

In a very real sense, strategy is the determination of the basic purposes and managerial objectives of the organization along with the adoption of courses of action and the choice of resource allocations to accomplish the purposes and attain the objectives. Strategic choice is the critical variable in strategic management.[9] It is the means by which perennially scarce resources are rationally committed to fulfill managerial expectations for success. "Decisions to launch radically new or different products, to expand into other areas of business or nonbusiness, or decisions to invest in new technology, for example, all contribute substantially to fashion the characteristics of our organized society. These decisions help to determine for instance, which international markets are entered, which services are available to the public, or decree how coming generations are to be educated."[10] Specific examples of strategic decisions include (1) mergers and acquisitions, (2) diversifications and divestitures, (3) expansions and retrenchment, (4) reorganization and reengineering, (5) joint ventures and alliances, and (6) new product development.[11]

Largely because of their complexity and long-range significance, strategic decisions compose a metalevel of category II choices. Inherent in the overall process of managerial decision making (Figure 2.1) is the need for strategic decisions, which integrate the following sequence of significant events in strategic management:

1. Judgments made in assessing the need for managerial strategy

2. Choices made to organize for strategy

3. Judgments made in formulating (and reformulating) strategic alternatives

4. Actions taken to select a primary managerial strategy

5. Decisions made in the subprocess of implementing a chosen managerial strategy

6. Judgments made to evaluate and choices made to control the implemented managerial strategy[12]

Moreover, strategic decision making involves the pursuit of individual goals as well as managerial objectives. Sometimes individual goals are shared by several people who form coalitions, whereas at other times they reflect personal values. In some cases, individual goals may come into conflict with the managerial objectives being pursued through strategic decisions. Management needs to be mindful of the influence of individual goals on the strategy of the organization. Long-term benefits to the organization may result from short-term accommodation to provide for individual goals. A viable fusion of managerial expectations and individual aspirations is desirable for effective strategic decision making.[13]

Following are five principal criteria for use in identifying and making a strategic decision:

1. The decision must be directed toward defining the organization's relationship to its environment . . . a strategic decision is externally-oriented and concerned with articulating the nature of the interface between the organization and its total environment . . . strategic decisions focus fundamentally on what business the [organization] is in or is to be in and the kind of [organization] it is or is to be. . . .

2. The decision must take the organization as a whole as the unit of analysis. . . .

3. The decision must be multifunctional in character, that is, it must depend on inputs from a variety of functional areas. . . .

4. The decision must provide direction for, and constraints on, administrative and operational activities throughout the [organization]. . . .

5. The decision must be [critically] important to the success of the organization.[14]

Although the making of strategic decisions properly falls within the purview of top management, the locus of choice for decisions of all types spans the entire hierarchy of management in formal organizations.

THE ENVIRONMENT OF STRATEGIC DECISION MAKING

Organizations do not exist in a vacuum. They are part of larger bodies such as the economic system, the political system, and the social system of a nation. Therefore, strategic decision makers must take account of the environment's influences in arriving at a choice, and they must consider the effects of that choice on the many forces that make up the environment. The acceptance and successful outcome of a strategic choice made without considering environmental forces is most unlikely.

The Concept of Environment

The **environment** includes all the conditions, circumstances, and influences surrounding and affecting the total organization or any of its internal systems. The environment contains forces that are variously dynamic and complex under different circumstances. Barnard characterizes the diverse, dynamic, and complex nature of the environment as follows:

> It consists of atoms and molecules, agglomerations of things in motion, alive, of men and emotions; of physical laws and social laws; social ideas, norms of action, of forces and resistances. Their number is infinite and they are always present. They are always changing.[15]

The forces that make up the environment confront management with the need to make decisions under considerable uncertainty. Changeable variables that are seldom well identified or understood tend to limit management's control over the outcome of events initiated within the organization. Consequently, executives need to "spend a large fraction of their time surveying the economic, technical, political, and social environment to identify new conditions that call for new actions."[16]

The Environmental System

In forming an image of the environment of a given formal organization, it is useful to think in terms of an **environmental system** within which the organization (a system in its own right) functions as a subsystem. In other words, a formal organization is a set of interdependent parts that together equal a whole. Each part contributes something to and receives something from the whole, which is in turn an interdependent part of the larger environment.[17] This relationship is conceptualized in Figure 10.1.

The organization as described here is one essential element in a large environmental system. The organization obtains inputs from the environment and transforms them into outputs, which by way of a feedback process are judged acceptable or unacceptable by the many forces that make up the environment. The concept of the environment as a system within which the organization functions is compatible with the concept of bounded rationality presented and illustrated in Chapter 3. In the latter concept, a rational strategic decision maker pursues satisficing choices in the process decision model responsive and sensitive to external forces. Indeed the environment exerts a pervasive and unrelenting influence over the dynamics of the total decision-making process and the activation of the subprocesses, such as the renewal of the search in the event that an implemented choice is rejected by external forces. To be sure, the influence of the environment starts with the setting of objectives and continues through the act of choice into the implementation stage, at which time the success or failure of the selected alternative is made known to management by positive or negative feedback.

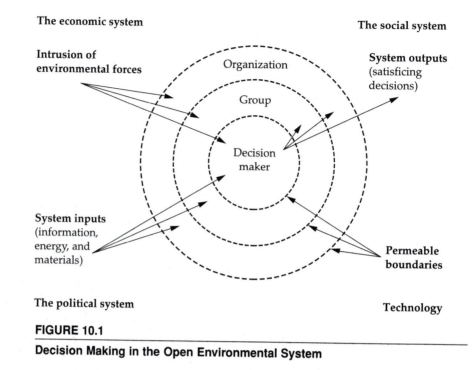

FIGURE 10.1

Decision Making in the Open Environmental System

A formal organization and its external environment interact across *organizational boundaries*. The concept of organizational boundaries is an integral part of the notion of an environmental system. Many organizations deal with organizational boundaries by designating specialists to perform at the cutting edge of the border between the organization and its environment. These specialists in organizational-environmental interaction are often referred to as "boundary personnel."[18] This category includes positions within the organizational structure in which a significant part of the duties and responsibilities of the incumbents are oriented toward some one or all of the relevant groups in the external environment. Examples include community relations, public relations, many functions within the human resources department, legal staff, marketing research, and many top executive positions.[19] The use of boundary personnel acts to strengthen the linkage between the organization and its external environment and, thereby, facilitates the making and implementing of strategic decisions.

Environmental Domains

Every organization establishes an **environmental domain.** Transactions and interactions take place across organizational boundaries and between the organization and its environmental domain. One definition of environmental domain encompasses the points at which the organization is dependent on inputs from the environment.[20] Another definition conceives a domain as consisting of little more than a combination or federation of organizations.[21] Domain provides the rationale and justification for policy agreements and extraorganizational roles from which flow standardized patterns of interaction.[22] Domain defines the mission that the organization claims as its unique purpose.

For purposes of this book, the environmental domain is also presumed to include the organization's **stakeholders.** This term is well established in the literature of strategic management. By common definition, stakeholders include those entities that have a tangible claim on the organization. In other words, stakeholders have a vested interest in the outcome of strategic decisions made within a given organization. Ansoff includes managers, workers, stockholders, suppliers, and vendors in his list of stakeholders.[23] Rhenman uses the term to designate the individuals or groups that depend on the organization for the realization of their personal goals and on whom the organization is dependent.[24] In this sense, stakeholders include employees, owners, customers, suppliers, and creditors. King and Cleland define stakeholders as individuals, groups, or institutions who have a demand for something due from the organizations.[25] Their list of stakeholders is very broad and includes stockholders, creditors, employees, customers, suppliers, governments, unions, competitors, local communities, and the general public. In this book, the environmental domain is viewed as that part of the environment most relevant to basic organizational purposes which, by definition, is populated by stakeholder groups in constant transaction and interaction with the organization across its boundaries.

An environmental domain is usually established by *domain consensus*. Domain consensus exists when the organization's stakeholders agree that it ought to do what it is doing.[26] In other words, if the relevant entities, external to the organization accept its domain, domain consensus exists. Domain consensus may also be used to identify the criteria by which an organization is judged, such as how the organization contributes to the larger environmental system.[27]

In summary, the concepts of environmental domain and domain consensus, which position stakeholder groups in various attitudes of transaction and interaction across organizational boundaries, clearly establish the organization as an integral part of its larger environmental system. This relationship posits acceptance by stakeholder groups as imperative for strategic decision success.

Environmental Forces

The four principal environmental forces are (1) the economic system, (2) the political system, (3) the social system, and (4) technology. The environments of all types of organizations contain these forces. The impact of a given environmental force on different organizations may change; but all organizations are subject to varying degrees of influence from each one.

The Economic System   The **economic system** includes employees, customers, competitors, and other industries. It also includes the federal government's regulation of business activities to protect the public interest and its use of monetary and fiscal policy to influence the availability of money and the cost of capital. The economic system may be thought of as a marketplace in which buyers and sellers do business and establish the prevailing price structure for a wide and varied range of goods and services.

The international market has emerged in recent years as a significant part of the global economic system.[28] As companies have expanded their operations abroad, they have had to contend with increasing uncertainty in their commercial transactions. Learning to do business in foreign countries continues to pose a challenge to organizations in this market. Both the need to decentralize operations to allow for on-the-spot decisions and the common requirement that the host country participate to some degree in the management of local operations introduce additional uncertainty into the external environment.

The trend in the international market is toward increased dynamism and complexity in the years ahead.[29] Competition in world markets is definitely on the increase as other industrialized nations continue to challenge the commercial leadership of the United States. This is the market in which effective interaction with environmental forces is essential for success and, in some cases, even for survival.

The Political System   A second major environmental force with which organizations must contend is the political system. The political system is founded on the concept of **governance,** which may be defined as "the exercise of an authority that seeks not merely the right to direct and to lead but to control."[30] The political system counterbalances unilateral or capricious decisions that might harm the public. Laws and regulatory agencies established to protect the public are very much in keeping with a democratic form of government, as are safeguards of the rights and freedom of the individual. Thus managers in formal organizations are obliged to consider the political system in making choices that affect the public, special interest groups, and any level of government.

The Social System   Parsons and Shils define the social system as

> a system of the actions of individuals, the principal units of which are roles and constellations of roles. It is a system of differentiated actions organized into a system of differentiated roles. . . . It is a condition of the existence of the system that the differentiated roles must be coordinated either negatively, in the sense of the avoidance of disruptive interference with each other, or positively, in the

sense of contributing to the realization of certain shared collective goals through collaborated activity.[31]

Change is an essential part of all social systems. Strategic decision makers should seek to identify the social problems and social conditions with which they must deal in the future.

> Decisions by management will . . . be influenced significantly by the social problems apparent, suspected, or expected in the [society]. . . . Irrespective of the decision situation, social problems will increase the level of uncertainty and risk in the decision making process.[32]

Whatever the arguments for and against the social responsibility of the formal organization, it is apparent that successful decisions must take cognizance of the myriad forces that make up the social system.

Technology   Of all the environmental forces, technology is the one most likely to confront the organization with unexpected and rapid change. Changes in technology can be sudden and dramatic. A major part of a given organization's product mix, for example, may be outmoded because of a single innovation by a major competitor. This possibility is particularly threatening for organizations in the so-called high technology industries such as aerospace, electronics, computers, and communications. In combination with the economic system, the political system, and the social system, technology confronts strategic decision makers with an imposing array of environmental forces that persistently intrude into the organization at all levels and in a multitude of ways. This is, of course, the primary reason why the external environment constitutes the most significant variable in strategic decision making.[33]

UNCERTAINTY IN STRATEGIC DECISION MAKING

As a term commonly used in decision theory and strategic decision making, there is no generally accepted definition of uncertainty.[34] In particular, the perceived stability or instability of the organizational environment tends to create feelings of relative certainty or uncertainty in the minds of management about whether a given decision will have positive or negative environmental effects. Uncertainty is likely to result from expectations of change in the environment, the degree of uncertainty rising with the rate of environmental change. The relationship between the rate of change and the degree of uncertainty in the environment of an organization may be summarized as follows:

1. Uncertainty or lack of knowledge about future conditions is inherent in the potential for change toward such conditions.

2. The potential for change exists to some degree in most organizational environments depending, of course, on how dynamic a given environment is.

3. Therefore, some degree of uncertainty is a characteristic of most organizational environments.

4. Uncertainty comes principally from the rate of change in a given environment and to a lesser extent from the complexity of that environment.[35]

Uncertainty may be defined as "the lack of certainty or certitude that may range from a mere falling short of these to an almost complete lack of knowledge or conviction especially about the result or outcome of something."[36] Thus, uncertainty is a matter of degree. Complete uncertainty — total lack of knowledge about a particular subject — is as unlikely as complete certainty — perfect knowledge of every aspect of a particular subject. In the real world of decision making, knowledge tends to be imperfect rather than nonexistent or complete. Consequently, decisions tend to be made under conditions of imperfect information or varying degrees of uncertainty. "Uncertainty is the complement of knowledge. It is the gap between what is known and what needs to be known to make correct decisions."[37] Decision makers attempt to bridge the gap by obtaining additional information and thus reducing uncertainty. However, uncertainty is never eliminated completely. The decision maker is unlikely to obtain all the information relevant to a given decision, and the information he or she does obtain from the environment must be tested for validity.

Most of the management literature dealing with the organizational environment cites **complexity** and **rate of change** as the most significant variables. For example, in advancing their concept of **environmental texture,** Emery and Trist emphasize the importance and interrelatedness of these variables.[38] According to them, environmental texture is a joint product of rate of change and complexity. Research suggests that the rate of change, or stability, of the environment is a dominant factor in producing uncertainty in decision making. Complexity is a significant factor, mainly in combination with rate of change. Much of the management literature avers that, for the most part, uncertainty originates in the external environment of the organization.[39] Another segment of the management literature places the origin of uncertainty squarely in the future.[40] And still another segment declares that uncertainty is inherent in inevitable change originating, for the most part, outside the organization.[41]

For purposes of this book uncertainty is conceived as the product of (1) change about which there is less than complete knowledge and (2) time through which change is manifested in any one or more of several forms. Indeed the basic premise here is that uncertainty originates with change over time; and both change and time occur in gradations. In general, the more rapid the degree of change, the higher the level of uncertainty. Time spans its own dimension between the present and the future. The further into the future that time is projected, the higher the level of uncertainty. In essence, as reflected in the following typology, uncertainty is a joint product of both change and time.

1. **Slow change/present time.** This condition indicates some degree of on-going gradual change. Because it can usually be observed and measured, it is reflective of a *high level of certainty* such as is found in most category I choices.

2. **Rapid change/present time.** Decision makers operating in this state confront a *low level of uncertainty*. There is some uncertainty emanating from the change; but it can usually be accommodated because the decision maker and the organization can adapt accordingly. The continuance of decision making in this state indicates that the organization is practicing crisis management rather than rational decision making as that term is defined in this book.

3. **Slow change/future time.** This state is characterized by gradual change over time. In this condition, decision makers must operate with a *low level of certainty*. However, the futurity of the gradual rate of change normally permits the decision maker to anticipate its occurrence and to position the organization to adapt in an effective manner. Most category II and strategic choices are made in this state. It is reflective of the type of uncertainty that constitutes the milieu of strategic decision making as advanced in this book.

4. **Rapid change/future time.** This state confronts the strategic decision maker with the worst of all possible conditions; that is, a *high level of uncertainty*. Most of the phenomena in this condition cannot be anticipated; for example, acts of God, manmade disasters, and technological breakthroughs. Consequently, organizations can only buffer themselves to a very limited extent from such eventualities. To do otherwise would be cost ineffective.[42]

Uncertainty as an environmental constraint is not the same for all types of decisions and for different levels of management. Category I decisions are, largely because of their routine, recurring nature, less susceptible to uncertainty. Such decisions tend, for the most part, to be made by operating management in the technical system and by middle management in the normal administrative processes of the organization. Conversely, category II decisions and, especially, strategic choices tend, by virtue of their nonroutine, nonrecurring nature, to be made by top management and are, therefore, highly susceptible to uncertainty regarding their outcomes. These decisions invariably confront the decision maker with an undefined set of cause-and-effect relationships, as well as undeveloped channels of information. In particular, it is essential to carefully consider environmental effects when making strategic decisions. Uncertainty can never be eliminated; but its occurrence can be reduced to acceptable proportions.

A summary on the effects of uncertainty on strategic decision making should note the following:

1. Uncertainty originates, for the most part, in the external environment of the organization.

2. Uncertainty results from the effects of change over time. The more rapid the change and the more distant the time, the greater the uncertainty.

3. Strategic decision making is concerned primarily with gradual change in future time. Lower-level decisions are properly addressed to most types of change in present time; and rapid change in future time is generally unanticipatable.

4. Uncertainty limits the ability of a given organization to control the outcomes of its strategic decisions. However, the adverse effects of uncertainty can usually be anticipated to an acceptable degree by developing alternative courses of action, and can be further mitigated by taking timely and appropriate corrective action following implementation of a preferred alternative.

THE CONCEPT OF STRATEGIC GAP

By virtue of their intrinsic nature, strategic decisions are oriented toward the relationship between a given organization and its external environment. This relationship is epitomized by the concept of *strategic gap*, which focuses on the fit between the capabilities of the organization and its most significant external entities. As used in this book, the term strategic gap is represented as a holistic concept that encompasses the principal factors that management should consider in making a strategic choice. The definition adopted herein is close to the one set forth by Hofer and Schendel, who define a strategic gap as "a comparison of the organization's objectives, strategy, and resources against the opportunities and threats in its external environment. . . ."[43] More simply, the definition advanced here views the strategic gap as the "imbalance between the current strategic position of the organization and its desired strategic position."[44] This definition is broad enough to accommodate the principal factors internal and external to the organization that should be considered by management in making its strategic choices. It is also specific enough to afford a meaningful focus for those managers who seek firmer foundations on which to make future strategic choices. As conceived in this book, the concept of strategic gap is intended for primary use in private enterprise, specifically medium-size and large corporations. Its selective use in strategic decision evaluations in subsequent chapters reflects this intention.

In one sense, the strategic gap is a measure of the perennially imperfect fit between the organization and its external environment. If the capabilities of the organization were fully committed to exploiting all perceived opportunities and warding off all discerned threats, there would be no strategic gap. For reasons to be discussed later, this eventuality is highly unlikely. The strategic gap is conceptualized in Figure 10.2.

Organizational Assessment

For the simple reason that strategic decisions founded on a balance of internal weakness seem certain to fail, gap analysis properly begins with an assessment of the major capabilities of the total organization.[45] The most successful strategy choices are likely to result when the principal strengths of the organization are being used to further its current advantage and its weaknesses or deficiencies are being corrected or reduced to enhance its future advantage.[46] This optimal state of affairs requires a systematic analysis of the generic and unique capabilities of the organization for capitalizing on opportunities, coping with threats, complying with requirements, and fulfilling responsibilities.

One rather common approach to organization assessment involves the development of a *capability profile* that permits management to conduct an in-depth appraisal of organizational *strengths and weaknesses*. This appraisal should discern areas of *distinctive competence* for the total organization; that is, its points of primary leverage where its principal strength and competitive advantage lie. There are at least three reasons why a capability profile of

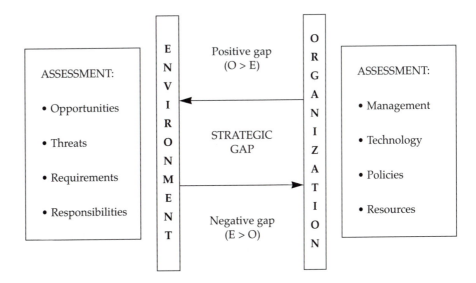

FIGURE 10.2

The Concept of Strategic Gap

strengths and weaknesses is important in measuring the strategic gap of a given organization:

1. Capitalizing on external opportunities usually signifies effective use of internal strengths.

2. Protecting the organization from environmental threats requires knowledge of internal weaknesses as well as strengths in order to erect adequate defenses.

3. Few organizations excel in all areas.[47]

"Thus [strategic decisions] ultimately are a compromise between offense and defense with the optimum balance dependent on awareness of external conditions and skillful utilization of internal resources."[48] Therefore, "in the process of [making strategic decisions], the ultimate objective of the internal analysis is to draw a profile of the entity and its resources and capabilities that provides both a segmented and integrated internal picture of the strengths and weaknesses of the entire organization."[49]

Management   The principal factors of organizational strengths and weaknesses are reflected in Figure 10.2. The first and foremost factor is management itself. Management is the vital force that makes the organization go, and good management is the key factor in the successful performance of the organization. Managerial values and experience find their expression in the application of managerial judgment; and good managerial judgment is necessary for successful strategic decisions.

Technology   Any assessment of the capabilities of an organization must include a review of its technology. By definition, technology means the systematic application of scientific or other organized knowledge to practical tasks.[50] Technology is a set of principles and techniques useful to bring about change toward desired ends.[51] Technology is knowledge of how to do things, how to accomplish human goals.[52] By its very nature technology implies change, and it is the phenomenon of technological change that concerns management in making strategic decisions. Consequently, management must constantly scan the environment for areas of technological advantage and must remain vigilant against the threat of technological obsolescence.[53] In the words of Erich Bloch:

> Today, success in the global marketplace means creating and applying new knowledge — which is to say new technology — faster than one's competitors. That is the fundamental law in this competitive world.[54]

Policies   Organizational policies provide a framework within which to make strategic decisions. The alternatives of strategic choice indicate the courses of action available to management. Prevailing policy indicates whether these courses of action can and should be pursued within the guidelines provided at the highest levels of the organization. On balance, organizational policies provide an essential underpinning of organizational assessment in developing a capability profile preparatory to strategic choice.

Resources   Organizational assessment has been completed when a measurement of the available resources has been taken. For our purposes resources may be divided into the following four categories: (1) **institutional resources,** which include stakeholders, goodwill, image, political competence, and social responsiveness; (2) **fiscal resources,** which include money and its near-equivalent, credit; (3) **physical resources,** which include facilities, equipment, supplies, and raw materials; and (4) **human resources,** which include time, energy, and intellect.[55] Resource adequacies and availabilities should be evaluated by management at the time of developing alternative courses of action and preparatory to making and implementing a given strategic choice.

Environmental Assessment

Once management has completed a capability profile to ascertain the strengths and weaknesses of the principal factors of organizational capability, the next step is to assess the external environment with a view toward determining the nature and the magnitude of the organization's strategic gap.

Opportunities   Doubtless the factor of greatest importance in the external environment for making strategic decisions is an actual or potential opportunity. Opportunities are external situations likely to work to the long-term benefit of the organization. Opportunities presume that the organization has the capability for capitalizing on them. The management, technology, and resources of the organization must be adequate for it to realize its opportunities, and there must be a willingness to accept the associated risk.

Threats   Along with opportunities, information obtained from the external environment helps management to ascertain threats to the organization. Threats include all exogenous forces with a potential for intruding on the organization at any level and in any way. "These externally imposed threats may stem from possible new technological developments, the advent of new substitute products, adverse economic trends, government action, changing consumer values and lifestyles, projections of natural resource depletions, unfavorable demographic shifts, new sources of strong competition, and the like."[56] A sustainable competitive advantage based on a balance of organizational strength and distinctive competence affords the best protection against threats from the external environment.[57]

Sociopolitical Factors   Two additional categories complete the assessment of the organization's environment. The first category constitutes **requirements,** largely of a legal nature with appropriate recognition of the governance aspects of the political system. Examples of requirements include legal codes, statutory restrictions, and emerging legislation. The second category of sociopolitical factors constitutes **responsibilities,** which are expectations on the part of some stakeholder group or external entity that a given strategic decision will not work to its disadvantage. Included in this second category is the more pervasive concept of **social responsibility.** This concept presumes an obligation on the part of the organization to consider the social welfare or the public interest in making its strategic choices.[58]

THE VARIATIONS OF STRATEGIC GAP

There are three conceivable variations of strategic gap: (1) positive strategic gap, (2) negative strategic gap, and (3) no strategic gap. The first two variations individually reflect the actual condition of a given organization at different points in time — that is, the organization has either a positive or a negative strategic gap; and management is advised to consider the type and size of the gap in making its strategic choices. The third variation of no strategic gap does not exist in the real world of organizations. It is a variation only in theory.

Positive Strategic Gap

If a concurrent assessment of the organization and its external environment reveals that the sum of internal capabilities is clearly greater than the total of significant external factors, a positive strategic gap exists. In other words, as symbolized in Figure 10.2, if O > E, the strategic gap is balanced in favor of the organization. In this state, the management, technology, policies, and resources of the organization are more than adequate to exploit any opportunity, cope with any threat, or meet any requirement or responsibility emanating from the external environment. With a positive strategic gap, the organization has a clear advantage vis-à-vis its external environment. However, this advantage is one of degree, which is to say that it is curvilinear rather than linear. As the positive gap tends to increase, the organization begins to incur the opportunity cost of underutilized management, technology, or resources. If not arrested, this opportunity cost can result in negative consequences for the organization. It is a paradox of the concept of strategic gap that too large a positive gap can parallel the disadvantages inherent in a negative gap. The best long-term condition is a small positive gap that reflects some reserve capability within the organization to exploit unexpected opportunities or to cope with unanticipated threats.

The ideal type of strategic gap exists when external opportunities are abundant and there is considerable (but not excessive) strength in internal capabilities. This is the optimal condition for successful strategic decisions. Management is effective; technology is advanced; policies are comprehensive; and resources are productively utilized in every sense. The capabilities of the organization are fully committed (with some reserves) in pursuit of attractive external opportunities across the full spectrum of time frames. On balance, the organization has a small positive strategic gap. Idle and non-productive resources are minimized, and opportunity costs are insignificant. Specific strategic decisions for the total organization are made rationally with appropriate consideration for trade-off values, present values, expected values, cost effectiveness, opportunity costs, and organizational priorities. This state of affairs is the hallmark of an effectively managed organization. It should be the quest of managers everywhere.

Negative Strategic Gap

A negative strategic gap occurs when the significant environmental factors are greater than the internal capabilities of the organization. This type, symbolized by E > O in Figure 10.2, means that the organization is unable to exploit available opportunities, deal with competition or technological threats, meet its legal requirements, or fulfill its expected responsibilities. In short, the organization is at a significant strategic disadvantage vis-à-vis its external environment. Obviously a negative strategic gap necessitates prompt and effective corrective action by management to redress the unacceptable balance. If the negative strategic gap of the organization is small, management should act to bolster or buttress the areas of internal weakness and to raise the capabilities of the organization to a level where it can begin to take advantage of attractive external opportunities. For example, corrective action by management might involve (1) a change in top management along with attendant restructuring of the organization, (2) an advancement of increasingly obsolescent technology, (3) a comprehensive revision of organizational policies, or (4) a reconfiguration and reallocation of organizational resources. If management's efforts are successful, the organization will move from a small negative to a small positive strategic gap. If management is negligent or uncertain about taking corrective action, a small negative gap will develop into a more negative situation requiring drastic action and draconian measures.

The equilibrium position for management is always a small positive strategic gap. Large positive strategic gaps clearly indicate underutilization of organizational capabilities and militate for development of attractive external opportunities to reduce a large positive gap to a more desirable small positive gap. In the presence of a small negative gap, management should concentrate on transforming internal weakness into strength, thereby moving from a small negative gap to a small positive gap. Managerial apathy or incompetence will surely foreclose any new external opportunities until timely and appropriate internal corrective action is forthcoming.

Zero Strategic Gap

There will always be a strategic gap between the organization and its external environment. The notion of a zero strategic gap is incomprehensible. There will never be a perfect interface between the capabilities of a given organization and the significant forces in its environmental domain. Factors such as imperfect information, time delays in responding to externally induced change, technological breakthroughs, and managerial incompetence all contribute to the unavoidability of the strategic gap. There is, in other words, a level of strategic gap, hopefully on the positive side, that is irreducible for any organization. Indeed it is not cost effective to try to create a perfect interface between the organization and its external environment. When, in the judgment of management, the strategic gap approaches an irreducible minimum, the organization has achieved a good **strategic fit.** This is a cost effective state that is both desirable and sustainable and one that should be sought by most organizations.[59]

THE STRATEGIC DECISION-MAKING PROCESS

Figure 10.3 conceptualizes the strategic decision-making process advanced in this book. This figure is a composite of the managerial decision-making process (Figure 2.1) and the concept of strategic gap (Figure 10.2). As such, it has many generic factors that have been fully explained in previous parts of this book. Figure 10.3 also reflects some unique factors that warrant a separate explanation preparatory to its use as an evaluative framework for real-world strategic decisions in later chapters of this book.

Flows of the Process

There are three types of process flows in Figure 10.3, each of which contributes to the interrelated dynamic of the total process.

Primary Flow   The **primary flow** encompasses the main functions of the process. These functions cannot be prematurely or arbitrarily circumvented without seriously compromising the integrity of the total process. The primary flow proceeds sequentially through the process. Information received from the external environment is used to assess the strengths and weaknesses of the organization along with the opportunities and threats in the external environment. These assessments result in a materialized strategic gap which is subjected to a gap analysis to discern the size and positive or negative nature of the gap. The results of the gap analysis are used by management to set or reset the managerial objectives that trigger the managerial decision-making process (see Figure 2.1). The managerial objectives constitute the ends for which the means of making and implementing a strategic choice are accomplished. The outputs of the implemented choice elicit feedback from the external environment permitting management to assess the outcome of its choice and take necessary corrective action, thereby ensuring attainment of the managerial objectives. The continuous evaluation of implemented choices is supplemented by periodic reviews with an annual updating of the strategic gap and the managerial objectives.

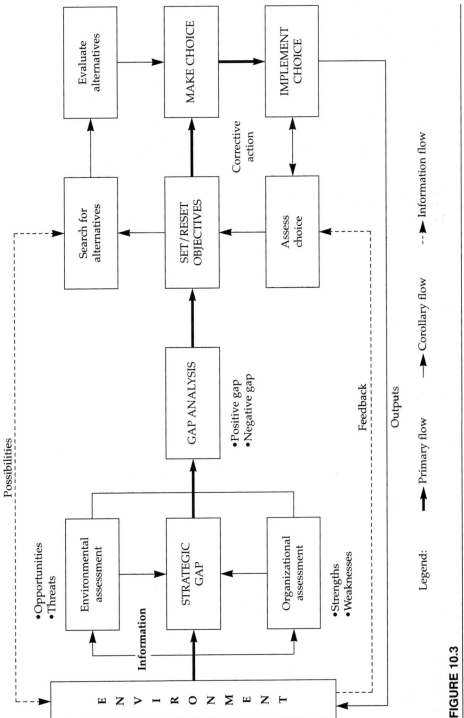

FIGURE 10.3

The Strategic Decision-Making Process

Corollary Flow   The **corollary flow** constitutes the ancillary functions of the process. These functions can be abridged or bypassed but not without some impairment of the total process. For example, a search may be circumscribed but possibly at the cost of an inadequate set of alternatives, or the assessment of an implemented choice may be accomplished less frequently than necessary at the price of a less successful outcome. An outcome of some sort is virtually assured with a primary flow; however, in combination with a corollary flow, a primary flow is much more likely to yield a successful outcome.

Information Flow   As shown in Figure 10.3, **information flow** constitutes the exploration of possibilities in the search for alternatives or the feedback of information from the external environment signifying the acceptance or nonacceptance of the implemented strategic choice. As such, information flow makes its own specialized contribution to strategic decision success. Information flow also permits management to identify possibilities for various courses of action in developing alternatives for strategic choice.

Application of the Process

The strategic decision-making process conceptualized in Figure 10.3 is applicable to strategic choices made in all kinds of organizations.[60, 61] However, it is somewhat more applicable to organizations in the private sector than to those in the public sector. It is, for example, much more relevant to consummate a gap analysis for a large corporation than for a state or the federal government. Assessments of the internal strengths and weaknesses of organizations in the public sector are fraught with political overtones; whereas the marketplace and financial orientation of the corporation lends itself rather nicely to gap analysis. Environmental assessments of states and nation states normally involve geopolitical factors and matters of sovereignty rather than the economic considerations of competition and technological obsolescence that are characteristic of private enterprise at the national or global level.

However, the primary orientation of the strategic gap in Figure 10.3 to corporations does not reduce the value of the total process as a framework for the evaluation of strategic decisions in the public sector. Environmental information is, for example, of critical importance in the strategic decision making of any type of organization; and the decision-making functions in Figure 10.3 are applicable to strategic choice in either the private or the public sector. The selective use of this figure as an evaluative framework will be evident in later chapters of this book.

SUMMARY

This chapter presented a set of strategic decision perspectives that reflects the significance and complexity of this type of choice in organizations of all types. In combination with the material presented in the first nine chapters of this book, this chapter and the next chapter are intended to imbue the student and practitioner of management with the insight and understanding necessary to share in the evaluation of strategic decision-making cases in the last four chapters and, ultimately, to make more successful strategic choices in the real world of organizations.

By their nature strategic decisions deal with the long-term health and vitality of the total organization. These are the most important decisions that executives make, and, therefore, normally fall within the purview of top management. Because of their overriding significance, strategic decisions tend to be closely linked to form a consistent pattern for unifying and directing the organization. This pattern of top-level choices represents the overall strategy of the organization. It is aimed at effectively aligning the aggregate capabilities of the total organization with the opportunities and threats in its external environment.

The acceptance and successful outcome of a strategic choice made without considering environmental forces is most unlikely. This chapter delineated and defined the concept of environment, and postured the organization as a subsystem operating within the large environmental system (see Figure 10.1). It was stated that a given organization interacts regularly with the stakeholder groups in its environmental domain across organizational boundaries. Organizational members designated "boundary personnel" represent the organization in these interactions. Environmental domain is the relevant part of the organization's total external environment. Domain defines the mission that the organization claims as its unique purpose. An environmental domain is usually established by domain consensus among the organization's stakeholder groups. Stakeholder groups are external entities that have a vested interest in and a tangible claim on the basic outputs of the organization. The four principal environmental forces are (1) the economic system, (2) the political system, (3) the social system, and (4) technology.

Because of their futuristic orientation, strategic decisions are characterized by a high level of uncertainty. Uncertainty originates, for the most part, in the rate of change over time in the external environment of the organization. Uncertainty limits the ability of an organization to control the outcomes of its strategic decisions. Strategic decision makers often try to reduce uncertainty with additional information and the use of quantitative techniques. But their complexity and futurity in combination with the external rate of change inherent in strategic choices imbues their outcomes with an unending plethora of unknowns. The adverse effects of uncertainty can usually be anticipated by developing alternative courses of action and can be partially mitigated by taking timely and appropriate corrective action following implementation of a preferred alternative.

The concept of strategic gap was presented in its entirety in this chapter. The strategic gap was defined as a comparison of the organization's capabilities against the opportunities and threats in its external environment. Organizational capabilities include (1) management, (2) technology, (3) policies, and (4) resources. An assessment of these capabilities yields a capability profile, which is a balance of the organization's strengths and weaknesses. An assessment of the external environment of the organization is focused primarily on opportunities and threats with corollary concerns for legal requirements and social responsibilities. If the organization's capabilities are greater than the external opportunities and threats, the strategic gap is positive and the strategic decision makers should concern themselves with sufficient attractive external opportunities to profitably commit the capabilities of the organization except for a small strategic reserve. This state of affairs is called a small strategic gap and it is the hallmark of effective strategic management. Conversely, if the organization's internal capabilities are not sufficient to exploit external opportunities and to protect it from internal threats, a negative gap is said to exist. In this event, management should take timely and appropriate corrective action to transform internal weakness into strength thereby permitting the organization to focus on existing opportunities or to develop new opportunities.

The best efforts of management notwithstanding, a zero strategic gap is an unlikely condition. Factors such as imperfect information, time delays in responding to externally induced change, technological breakthroughs, and managerial incompetence all contribute to the unavoidability of the strategic gap.

This chapter also presented the strategic decision-making process in Figure 10.3. This process is a composite of the managerial decision-making process (Figure 2.1) and the concept of strategic gap (Figure 10.2).

REVIEW AND DISCUSSION QUESTIONS

1. What are the most important characteristics of strategic decisions? Attempt to prioritize these characteristics.

2. In what specific ways is a view of the organization as a subsystem of a larger environmental system likely to improve its strategic decision making? Discuss.

3. Who defines and delineates the environmental domain of a given organization and how is this activity accomplished? Discuss.

4. How does uncertainty act to limit the ability of a given organization to control the outcome of its strategic decisions?

5. Does gap analysis start in the organization with an assessment of its strengths and weaknesses or in its external environment with an assessment of opportunities and threats?

6. Why is a small positive strategic gap the hallmark of effective strategic management?

7. Why is the notion of a zero strategic gap without merit?

8. What actions are required by management in the presence of a negative strategic gap?

9. How likely is management to acknowledge the existence of a negative strategic gap? Why or why not?

10. In what specific ways can the strategic decision-making process in Figure 10.3 reduce uncertainty and contribute to more successful strategic decisions? Discuss.

NOTES

1. Gregory Streib, "Applying Strategic Decision Making in Local Government," *Public Productivity and Management Review,* 15, No. 3 (Spring 1992), 341–353.

2. Henry Mintzberg, Duru Raisinghani, and Andre Theoret, "The Structure of 'Unstructured' Decision Processes," *Administrative Science Quarterly,* 21 (June 1976), 250–251.

3. Bernard M. Bass, *Organizational Decision Making* (Homewood, Ill.: Richard D. Irwin, 1983), p. 16.

4. Peter Drucker, *The Effective Executive* (New York: Harper & Row, 1967), p. 113.

5. Donald C. Hambrick and Charles C. Snow, "A Conceptual Model of Strategic Decision Making in Organizations," in *Proceedings of the Academy of Management,* ed. Robert L. Taylor et al. (Colorado Springs: University of Colorado, 1977), p. 109.

6. Ibid.

7. Ibid.

8. Ibid. See also E. Frank Harrison, *Policy, Strategy, and Managerial Action* (Boston: Houghton Mifflin, 1986).

9. See Alfred D. Chandler, Jr., *Strategy and Structure* (Cambridge, Mass.: MIT Press, 1962); and John Child, "Organizational Structure, Environment, and Performance: The Role of Choice," *Sociology,* 6 (January 1972), 1–22.

10. W. Graham Astley et al., "Complexity and Cleavage: Dual Explanations of Strategic Decision-Making," *Journal of Management Studies* (October 1982), 357.

11. David J. Hickson et al., "Decision and Organization — Processes of Strategic Decision Making and Their Explanation," in *Managerial Decision Making,* ed. David J. Hickson (England: Dartmouth, 1995), 77–94.

12. See Harrison, *Policy, Strategy, and Managerial Action,* pp. 159–194.

13. See George F. Farris, "The Informal Organization in Strategic Decision Making," *International Studies of Management & Organization* (Winter 1979–1980), 37–62; and D. E. Dimick and V. V. Murray, "Personnel Policy as a Form of Strategic Decision Making," *International Studies of Management & Organization* (Winter 1979–1980), 78–97.

14. Robert C. Shirley, "Limiting the Scope of Strategy: A Decision-based Approach," *Academy of Management Review* (April 1982), 264–265.

15. Chester Barnard, *The Functions of the Executive* (Cambridge, Mass.: Harvard University Press, 1938), p. 197.

16. Herbert A. Simon, *The New Science of Management Decision* (New York: Harper & Row, 1960), p. 2.

17. James D. Thompson, *Organizations in Action* (New York: McGraw-Hill, 1967), p. 6.

18. William M. Evan, "The Organization-Set: Toward a Theory of Interorganizational Relations," in *Approaches to Organizational Design,* ed. James D. Thompson (Pittsburgh: University of Pittsburgh Press, 1966), p. 180.

19. J. Eugene Haas and Thomas E. Drabek, *Complex Organizations: A Sociological Perspective* (New York: Macmillan, 1973), p. 220.

20. Thompson, *Organizations in Action,* p. 27.

21. George F. Wieland and Robert A. Ulbrich, *Organizations: Behavior, Design, and Change* (Homewood, Ill.: Richard D. Irwin, 1973), p. 202.

22. Haas and Drabek, *Complex Organizations,* pp. 215–217.

23. H. J. Ansoff, *Corporate Strategy* (New York: McGraw-Hill, 1965).

24. E. Rhenman, *Industrial Democracy* and *Industry Management* (London: Tavestock, 1968).

25. W. R. King and D. I. Cleland, *Strategic Planning and Policy* (New York: Van Nostrand Reinhold, 1978); see also R. Edward Freeman, "Strategic Management: A Stakeholder Approach," in *Advances in Strategic Management,* Vol. 1, ed. Robert Lamb (Greenwich, Conn.: JAI Press, 1983), pp. 31–60.

26. Thompson, *Organizations in Action*, p. 29.

27. Wieland and Ulbrich, *Organizations*, p. 202

28. W. Chan Kim and Renee A. Mauborgne, "Making Global Strategies Work," *Sloan Management Review* (Spring 1993), 11–27.

29. Robert E. Jones et al., "Strategic Decision Processes in International Firms" *Management International Review,* 32 (1992–93), 219–236.

30. Richard Eells and Clarence Walton, *Conceptual Foundations of Business*, rev. ed. (Homewood, Ill.: Richard D. Irwin, 1969), p. 405.

31. Talcott Parsons and Edward A. Shils, eds., *Toward a General Theory of Action* (New York: Harper & Row, 1951), p. 197.

32. Francis J. Bridges, Kenneth W. Olm, and J. Allison Barnhill, *Management Decisions and Organizational Policy* (Boston: Allyn & Bacon, 1971), p. 3.

33. David B. Jemison, "Organization versus Environmental Sources of Influence in Strategic Decision Making," *Strategic Management Journal,* 2 (1981), 77–89.

34. E. Frank Harrison, "Perspectives on Uncertainty in Successful Strategic Choice at the CEO Level," *OMEGA, The International Journal of Management Science*, 20 (1992), 105–116; and Patrick F. Gibbons and Lai Hong Chung, "Uncertainty: The Implications for Strategic Management," *Irish Business and Administrative Research*, 16 (1995), 17–31.

35. Harrison, *Policy, Strategy, and Managerial Action*, p. 114.

36. Webster's New Dictionary of Synonyms (Springfield, Mass.: G. & C. Merriam, 1973), p. 964.

37. Ruth P. Mack, *Planning on Uncertainty* (New York: Wiley, 1971), p. 1.

38. F. E. Emery and E. L. Trist, "The Casual Texture of Organizational Environments," in *Readings in Organization Theory: Open System Approaches*, ed. John Maurer (New York: Random House, 1971), pp. 46–57.

39. See Harrison, *Policy, Strategy, and Managerial Action*; L. R. Jauch and K. L. Kraft, "Strategic Management of Uncertainty," *Academy of Management Review*, 11, 777–790; and W. R. King and D. I. Cleland, *Strategic Planning and Management Handbook* (New York: Van Nostrand Reinhold, 1987).

40. See J. D. Braverman, *Management Decision Making* (New York: AMACOM, 1980); P. H. Hill et al., *Making Decisions: A Multidisciplinary Introduction* (Reading, Mass.: Addison-Wesley, 1980); and

D. D. Wheeler and I. L. Janis, *A Practical Guide of Making Decisions* (New York: Free Press, 1980).

41. P. Greenwood and H. Thomas, "A Review of Analytical Models in Strategic Planning," *OMEGA, The International Journal of Management Science*, 9 (1981), 397–417; and J. M. Pennings and Associates, *Organizational Strategy and Change* (San Francisco: Jossey-Bass, 1985).

42. Harrison, "Perspectives on Uncertainty," pp. 106–107.

43. C. W. Hofer and D. Schendel, *Strategy Formulation: Analytical Concepts* (St. Paul, Minn.: West Publishing Co., 1978), p. 47.

44. Harrison, *Policy, Strategy, and Managerial Action,* p. 383.

45. Stuart Hart, "How Strategy-Making Processes Can Make a Difference," *Strategic Management Journal*, 15 (1994), 251–269.

46. Margaret Ryan, "Human Resource Management and the Politics of Knowledge: Linking the Essential Knowledge Base of the Organization to Strategic Decision Making," *Leadership & Organization Development Juornal*, 16, No. 5, (1996), 3–10.

47. M. Leontiades, *Policy, Strategy, and Plans* (Boston: Little, Brown, 1982).

48. Ibid., p. 123.

49. D. J. McCarthy, R. J. Minichiello, and J. R. Curran, *Business Policy and Strategy: Concepts and Readings* (Homewood, Ill.: Richard D. Irwin, 1975), p. 107.

50. John Galbraith, *The New Industrial State* (Boston: Houghton Mifflin, 1967), p. 12.

51. J. Taylor, *Technology and Planned Organizational Change* (Ann Arbor: University of Michigan Institute for Social Research, 1970).

52. H. A. Simon, "Technology and Environment," in *Emerging Concepts in Management*, 2nd ed., M. S. Wortman and F. Luthans, eds. (New York: Macmillan, 1975), p. 4.

53. See Edward B. Roberts, "Benchmarking the Strategic Management of Technology — I," *Research-Technology Management* (January–February 1995), 44–56; and Edward B. Roberts, "Benchmarking the Strategic Management of Technology — II," *Research-Technology Management* (March–April, 1995), 18–26.

54. Erich Bloch, quoted in Robert M. Price, "Technology and Strategic Advantage," *California Management Review*, 38, No. 3 (Spring 1996), 38.

55. E. Frank Harrison, *Management and Organizations* (Boston: Houghton Mifflin, 1978).

56. A. A. Thompson, Jr., and A. J. Strickland, III, *Strategy Formulation and Implementation*, rev. ed. (Plano, Tex.: Business Publications, 1983), pp. 89–90.

57. Augustine A. Lado, "A Competency Based Model of Sustainable Competitive Advantage: Toward a Conceptual Integration," *Journal of Management*, 18, No. 1 (1992), 77–91.

58. Keith Davis, "The Case For and Against Business Assumption of Social Responsibility," *Academy of Management Journal*, 16 (1973), 312–322.

59. E. Frank Harrison, "The Concept of Strategic Gap," *Journal of General Management*, 15 (Winter 1989), 57–72.

60. Michael J. Harrison and Bruce Phillips, "Strategic Decision Making: An Integrative Explanation," *Research in the Sociology of Organizations* (Greenwhich, Conn.: JAJ Press, 1991), pp. 319–358.

61. Robert E. Jones et al., "Strategic Decision Processes in Matrix Organizations," *European Journal of Operational Research*, 78 (1994), 192–203.

SUPPLEMENTAL REFERENCES

Ansoff, H. Igor. "General Management in Turbulent Environments." *Practicing Manager*, 11 (Summer 1990), 6–27.

Bronner, Rolf. "Perception of Complexity in Decision-Making Processes: Findings of Experimental Investigations. In *Empirical Research on Organizational Decision-Making*. Ed. E. Witte and H. J. Zimmermann. New York: Elsevier, 1986, pp. 45–64.

Chorn, Norman H. "The 'Alignment' Theory: Creating Strategic Fit." *Management Decision*, 29 (1991), 20–24.

Fahey, Liam. *The Strategic Planning Management Reader*. Englewood Cliffs, N.J.: Prentice-Hall, 1989.

Cray, David, et al. "Explaining Decision Processes." *Journal of Management Studies* (May 1991), 227–253.

Grant, Robert M. "The Resource-Based Theory of Competitive Advantage: Implications for Strategy Formulation." *California Management Review* (Spring 1991), 114–135.

Hougland, James G., Jr. "Organizational and Individual Responses to Environmental Uncertainty." In *Uncertainty*. Ed. Seymour Fiddle. New York: Praeger, 1980, pp. 102–119.

Jackson, Susan E., and Jane E. Dutton. "Discerning Threats and Opportunities." *Administrative Science Quarterly*, 33 (1988), 370–387.

Jemison, David B. "Organizational versus Environmental Sources of Influence in Strategic Decision Making." *Strategic Management Journal*, 2 (1981), 77–89.

March, James G. *A Primer on Decision Making*. New York: Free Press, 1994.

———. *Decisions and Organizations*. New York: Blackwell, 1988.

Mazzolini, Renato. "Real-World Decision Making: The Limits of Top Management Power." *Journal of Business Strategy* (Fall 1980), 3–8.

Nutt, Paul C. *Making Tough Decisions*. San Francisco: Jossey-Bass, 1989.

Schenk, Charles R. *The Essence of Strategic Decision Making*. Lexington, Mass.: D. C. Heath, 1988

Shapira, Zur, ed. *Organizational Decision Making*. New York: Cambridge University Press, 1997.

Subramanian, S. K. "Technology, Productivity, and Organization." *Technological Forecasting and Social Change* (July 1987), 359–371.

Waterman, Robert H., Jr. "The Seven Elements of Strategic Fit." *Journal of Business Strategy* (Winter 1982), 68–72.

Weber, C. E. Edward. "Strategic Thinking — Dealing with Uncertainty." *Long-Range Planning*, 17 (1984), 60–70.

CHAPTER ELEVEN

Strategic Decision Success

*T*he focus in this chapter is on the factors and frameworks that contribute directly to successful outcomes for strategic decisions made by managers in all kinds of organizations. Strategic decision making is the most significant activity engaged in by managers who invariably are at or near the top of the organization. Because strategic decisions are so important to the long-term health of the total organization, it is imperative that they be successful most of the time. This requirement places a lot of pressure on strategic decision makers to produce beneficial decision outcomes. In fact there is a tacit expectation on the part of most of the organization's stakeholder groups that management should not fail in its strategic decision making. Failed decisions invariably elicit criticism and rejection while successful decisions are quickly internalized in the normal course of events. Consequently, strategic decision success assumes incomparable significance for the reputations, careers, and material well-being of executives who regularly make such decisions. These individuals, along with professors and students of management, should find this chapter of inestimable value. Now for the first time there is a broad variety of factors and frameworks for selective use in making strategic decisions. Several factors and frameworks have already been introduced in previous chapters. This chapter integrates and further explicates them with a view toward expanding the organizational record of strategic decision success. The final chapters of this book present and evaluate four pairs of strategic decision cases drawn from the public and private sectors. These cases are intended to further demonstrate the real-world applicability of the concepts and constructs presented in all the previous chapters of the book.

The first section of this chapter presents a short profile of strategic decision success. Selected studies of strategic decision success and failure are

Note: This chapter contains selected materials from the following sources: E. Frank Harrison, "Some Factors Involved in Determining Strategic Decision Success," *Journal of General Management*, 17 (Spring 1992), 72–87. Used with permission of the Braybrooke Press Ltd. and Henley Management College, Greenlands, Henley-on-the-Thames, Oxfordshire, England; and E. Frank Harrison and Monique A. Pelletier, "A Typology of Strategic Choice," *Technological Forecasting & Social Change*, 44 (1993), 245–263. Copyright 1993 by Elsevier Science Publishing Co., Inc.; reprinted by permission of the publisher.

noted and a working definition of strategic decision success for this book is advanced. The second section presents on analytical comparison of two studies of some factors involved in determining decision success. The first study in the 1960s of 100 case examples of organizations from five general areas by Samuel Trull was briefly described in the context of implementing managerial decisions in Chapter 2.[1] The second and more recent (1990) study of CEOs in 108 organizations in the San Francisco Bay area (hereinafter known as the Bay area study) was accomplished by the author to update and extend the results of the Trull study.[2] The comparative analysis of these two studies yields some firm indications of managerial strengths and weaknesses in successful strategic decision making. The third section is the culmination of this chapter and, in one sense, the entire book. This section presents a matrix model for use in making and evaluating strategic decisions.[3] This model embodies most of the important theories, concepts, and frameworks presented in the previous chapters. Specific examples of real-world strategic decision successes and failures are briefly described to support the classification of strategic decision types advanced in the matrix model. The fourth and final section delineates a composite approach to the evaluation of strategic decision success. This section is the gateway to the evaluation of the four pairs of strategic decision cases that end the book. Evaluative frameworks and concepts are reviewed and specific profiles for the evaluation of these cases are suggested.

A PROFILE OF DECISION SUCCESS

Given the significance of strategic choices for the long-term health of the total organization, it would seem that the literature of management would abound with studies of the determinants of successful outcomes resulting from such decisions. This, however, is far from the case. Management scholars continue to note the lack of empirical research on the making of strategic choices.[4] In particular, there is a paucity of recent research that focuses directly on factors determining the success of strategic choices made at the top management or CEO level. Noteworthy exceptions to this impoverished area of research include (1) Stagner's study of 500 vice presidents in 125 different business firms,[5] (2) Mintzberg, Raisinghani, and Theoret's study of 25 strategic decision processes,[6] (3) Peters and Waterman's study of a cross section of America's best run companies,[7] and (4) Donaldson and Lorsch's study of 12 mature corporations.[8] Another significant contribution is the comprehensive Bradford studies of strategic decision making conducted in Britain.[9]

Another group of studies and writings focuses mainly on failed strategic decisions and attempts to explain the reasons for the failures. For example, Weitzel and Johnson tell us what went wrong at W.T. Grant and Sears, Roebuck.[10] Whyte explains why decision fiascos occur and how to prevent them.[11] Hartley evaluates a cross section of managerial decision-making mistakes.[12] Nutt provides several examples of debacles in decision making.[13] March advances the notion that flawed organizational decisions often emanate from the ambiguity of a garbage can model of decision making.[14] Janis continues to aver that groupthink flaws many decisions made at the highest levels of government.[15] Crozier declares that the DeLorean decision failed because the objective was rendered unattainable from the outset by the decision makers who disregarded several significant constraints.[16] Huxham and Dando suggest that failed strategic decisions may result from bounded vision on the part of the decision makers.[17] And Makridakis observes that failed strategic decisions often result from organizational aging and conservation; and, paradoxically, decision failure frequently results from decision success.[18] Regrettably, few if any of these case studies of strategic decision failure or allegedly flawed approaches to decision making propound any new models or new approaches the use of which is likely to improve the chances for strategic decision success. That, of course, is the purpose of this book and, more specifically, this chapter.

Still another group of studies tends to reinforce the basic hypothesis of this book that a comprehensive process approach to strategic decision making is more likely to result in a successful outcome. For example, Jones et al. studied 70 U.S.-based international firms and found that a strategic decision-making process produced higher-quality decisions and more favorable organizational outcomes.[19] In another study of 27 matrix organizations Jones and a different set of co-researchers found that a process approach to strategic decision making yielded better strategic results for the organization.[20] In a study of 53 cases of decision making in eight British organizations, Rodrigues and Hickson found that a successful decision in a business firm is more likely to ensue from a strategic decision-making process.[21] And, finally, Nutt's study of 177 cases of managerial decisions revealed that a process model of decision making is more apt to be successful.[22] It seems apparent that strategic decision success can be largely attributed to a decision made within the comprehensive structure of a process such as those set forth in Figure 2.1 and Figure 10.3.

Before proceeding to present the two studies of factors determining strategic decision success, it seems advisable to set forth a definition of success for the choices normally made at the highest levels of management. For our purposes, *a successful strategic decision is one that results in the attainment of the objective that gave rise to the decision within the constraints that had to be observed to bring about such attainment.* For example, a strategic choice resulting in the attainment of its objective within time, cost, and environmental constraints is most likely to be designated successful. Conversely, another strategic choice resulting in the attainment of its objective at the expense of the organization or some of its principal stakeholders is less likely to be viewed as successful. And strategic choice that doesn't result in the attainment of its objective in any case is likely to be judged a failure, even in the presence of extenuating circumstances. On balance, the notion of intended ends that are accomplished within designated means seems defensible as a definition for strategic decision success.

DETERMINANTS OF STRATEGIC DECISION SUCCESS

Strategic decision success can only be anticipated in the act of choosing among alternative courses of action. Only when a preferred course of action has been selected and implemented can management begin to assess the prospects for a successful outcome. Implementation is that function in the decision-making process that reveals impediments, obstacles, deficiencies, and flaws not readily apparent to management in the comparison and evaluation of alternatives and the act of choice. Attempts to anticipate factors and conditions likely to work against success through techniques such as scenarios, simulation, and sequential implementation promise only limited information and little reduction of uncertainty. In most strategic decisions, management must make a substantial commitment of resources at the time of implementation to accurately ascertain the prospects for success. Reversals of such commitments can only be made at substantial cost to the organization. Consequently, management should focus its attention on those factors that are most likely to be significant determinants of strategic decision success before committing the organization to a course of action that is difficult or impossible to complete. Corrective action following implementation is intended to remedy operational difficulties in bringing an alternative to fruition. If an alternative is incapable of successful implementation, then the only recourse may be a renewal of the search, which means additional cost and a diminution of the opportunity sought by the organization. Clearly the best approach for management is to improve the prospects for strategic decision success through a more informed choice and implementation of a preferred alternative.

Studies of Strategic Decision Success

This section deals with two comprehensive studies of the determinants of decision success. The first study of 100 complex organizations by Samuel Trull in the 1960s was briefly described in Chapter 2 under the rubric of implementing managerial decisions. As noted there, Trull hypothesized that the success of a decision is a function of its quality and its implementation. A decision's quality in turn, is judged by (1) its compatibility with existing operating constraints, or the established way of doing business, (2) its timeliness, (3) its incorporation of the optimum amount of information, and (4) the decision maker's influence on it. And successful decision implementation is a product of (1) the avoidance of conflict of interest, (2) a positive risk-reward factor, and (3) how well the decision is understood by those who must carry it out.

The purpose of the second study in 1990 was to replicate Trull's study and thereby extend the knowledge base of key factors in determining the success of strategic decisions. This study encompassed 108 organizations from a broad cross section of private enterprise in the San Francisco Bay area. The participants in the Bay area study were all CEOs of their respective corporations. A comprehensive questionnaire was administered to the CEOs and 61 of them or 56 percent of the surveyed target responded. While this response does not seem particularly large in its own right, it is well above the average for questionnaires at the CEO level.

The Bay area study differs from Trull's study in two important respects. One, it included only respondents at the CEO level, whereas Trull's input was obtained from several executive and administrative levels; and two, it encompassed only strategic decisions in the literal meaning of that term, whereas Trull's study encompassed a cross section of managerial decisions. In spite of these differences, however, both studies deal essentially with top management decisions and are intended to ascertain factors involved in determining decision success. Therefore, they are quite suitable for comparative analysis in the context of strategic decision success.

The findings of the Bay area study are set forth in Table 11.1. The discussion to follow in this section will parallel the factors outlined above in the Trull study. Specific findings, replications, and conclusions will be presented for each factor. A final commentary will summarize the essence and implications of both studies for practitioners and students of management.

Decision Quality

The factors thought to affect strategic choice can be grouped according to decision quality and decision implementation. The first four factors listed in Table 11.1 are thought to affect decision quality.

Compatibility with Existing Operating Constraints   It seems reasonable to assume that, in the general case, successful decisions are more likely to result within the established way of doing business. Prevailing policies, procedures, and practices constitute an organizational framework with which to govern and guide the managerial decision-making process. In one sense, the existing operating constraints provide parameters to channel strategic choices toward the fulfillment of the institutional mission and the attainment of long-range managerial objectives.

Table 11.1 reflects a generally satisfactory degree of compatibility with the established way of doing business for successfully implemented strategic decisions among the respondents in the Bay area study. Twenty-seven of them rated such compatibility as good or better and thirty-four of them rated it as satisfactory or worse. On balance, this finding is somewhat at variance with

TABLE 11.1 Actual Distribution of Responses for Selected Factors of Strategic Choice at the CEO Level[a]

Decision Factors	CEO Responses[b]					
	Excellent	Good	Satisfactory	Marginal	Unsatisfactory	Mean Response
Compatibility with Operating Contraints	2	25	28	6	0	2.62
Nearness to Optimum Timing	4	35	17	4	1	2.39
Proximity to Optimum Amount of Information	6	45	9	1	0	2.08
Decision Maker's Influence	9	24	21	7	0	2.43
Risk-Reward Factor	10	36	11	4	0	2.15
Degree of Understanding	10	33	14	4	0	2.21
Total Actual Responses	41	198	100	26	1	

[a] n = 61 CEOs.
[b] Values of CEO responses: 1 = Excellent; 2 = Good; 3 = Satisfactory; 4 = Marginal; and 5 = Unsatisfactory.

the results of Trull's study. Trull found that the majority of successful managerial decisions were highly compatible with existing operating constraints. The finding in the Bay area study reflects an equally likely probability of good compatibility or just satisfactory compatibility. Apparently the CEOs in the Bay area study did not regard the established way of doing business as a particularly strong boundary condition for successful strategic decisions.

Proximity to Optimum Time for Decision   Clearly there is an optimal time in which to make a strategic decision. The precise point of optimality will approximate the zenith of the opportunity to be capitalized or the advantage to be gained by the organization. Time is an immutable constraint in most strategic decision-making situations in that it constitutes a defined interval within or a precise point at which action must be taken to commit scarce organizational resources.[23] Time also constitutes one of the invariable limitations on decision making under conditions of bounded rationality.[24] It is an integral part of the phase theorem of managerial decision making.[25] In essence, timing can be good or bad. If it is bad, it can be too early or too late. "A premature rush to the market can destroy potential larger opportunitities for the rushing organization. And an extended procrastination may prove to be too late. Timing must be optimized just like any other strategic decision criterion."[26] Ford's classic blunder in the Edsel decision affords an excellent example of the penalties resulting from being too late and missing the market. Coca Cola's decision to jettison old Coke in favor of new Coke is an example of erring on the early side through a premature and unjustified choice. Surely the Cuban missile crisis ranks as a paragon of optimum timing for a decision with potentially catastrophic consequences.

The respondent CEOs in the Bay area study were asked the following question:

> How would you describe the timing of your successful strategic decisions in terms of capitalizing on opportunities or solving problems?

As shown in Table 11.1, two-thirds of the respondent CEOs rated nearness to optimum timing as good or better. However, one-third of the respondents rated timing as only satisfactory or worse. The resultant mean was closer to satisfactory than to good. This finding tends to replicate the results of Trull's study in which he said that "it was clear that the decision makers displayed no conscious effort to determine the optimum time for making the judgment. . . ."[27] Strategic decisions are more likely to be successful if they are regularly made and implemented in proximity to the optimum time for such decisions. Timing constituted a definite need for improvement in both studies.

Proximity to Optimum Amount of Information   The respondent CEOs in the Bay area study for the most part indicated that the amount of information that they required to make their successful strategic decisions was generally adequate, but not excessive. Table 11.1 shows that fifty-one out of sixty-one CEOs rated the proximity to the optimum amount of information as good or excellent. Only ten respondents rated the amount of information as less than good. This finding is directly contrary to the results of Trull's study where the managers apparently continued to gather information mindless and heedless of the attendant costs in relation to the payoff.[28] As Trull observed, "generally, the decision makers were unaware of the costs associated with obtaining information."[29] To their great credit, most of the respondent CEOs in the Bay area study were obviously aware of the amount of information necessary to make a successful strategic choice and were willing and able to ascertain informational adequacy in relation to the expected outcome of the choice. In other words, these CEOs were mindful of the exponential rise in cost and the reciprocal decline in the marginal value of additional units of information (see Figure 2.2).

Decision Maker's Influence on the Decision   Trull's study found that "the perceived authority of the person making the decision tended to have an important influence on the decision-making process. The greater the perceived authority of the decision maker, the greater the extent of informal effort expended by the organization to ensure decision success."[30] Trull's findings tend to be confirmed by much of the literature on management which notes that successful decisions, especially those of a strategic nature, tend to be made by the chief executive officer or the top management team which usually includes the CEO and those executives reporting directly to the CEO. The CEO is usually considered to be the architect of corporate purpose.[31] As an individual, the CEO exerts more influence on strategic decisions than any other executive.[32] In some organizations, influential decision making is extended by the CEO to include the top management team.[33] The consensus among many management theorists is that significant and complex decisions are more likely to be made at the top of the organization; and top management involvement and approval increases the likelihood of a successful strategic decision.[34]

As shown in Table 11.1, the respondent CEOs in the Bay area study departed from the conventional wisdom of top management influence on strategic choice. About half the respondents did not perceive any particular need to exert the influence of their office in pursuit of a successful outcome. The other half generally got involved in some part of the implementation phase. In fact, the responses from these CEOs indicated a marked tendency toward only the occasional use of influence to ensure decision success rather than the ongoing involvement suggested by the findings of Trull's study and the bulk of the management literature. Clearly the respondent CEOs in the Bay area study favor a rather passive leadership role in the implementation of successful strategic decisions. Obviously many of them believe that active leadership is not necessary for a successful outcome.

Decision Implementation

The last two factors listed in Table 11.1 come under decision implementation.

Trull's study also included the avoidance of conflict of interest as a factor based on the seemingly defensible premise that conflict of interest can only work against decision success. However, his findings regarding conflict of interest were indeterminate and it was excluded from the Bay area study.

Risk-Reward Factor   Much of the economic literature posits a positive correlation between risk and return.[35] According to classical economic theory, most organizations are averse to risk; and risk aversion means that high-risk decisions demand high-return outcomes.[36] The offset of high risk, therefore, is high return. It is assumed that managerial decision makers are rational if the potential gain from their decisions increases as the risk of potential loss also increases. This is the concept of economic man who seeks to maximize outcomes commensurate with the probability of loss. The greater the amount of potential loss and the higher the attendant probability of such loss, the larger the imperative for a compensating return. "From Adam Smith on, it has been accepted that reasonable [or rational] men act to maximize their own pecuniary advantage and in most economic models even the potential for irrationality is ignored."[37]

The assumptions of classical economic theory constituted the underpinning of Trull's study. "In actuality it appeared that this straightforward theoretical formulation of rationality was ignored to a large extent."[38] In essence, Trull found that managerial decision makers did not behave like rational economic men in the model advanced by the classical economic literature. Risk identification, risk evaluation, and risk acceptance were not systematically observed in their managerial decision making.[39]

Contrary to the findings of Trull's study, the results of the Bay area study suggest that the respondent CEOs are very aware of the relationship between risk and reward. As shown in Table 11.1, three out of every four respondent CEOs perceived the risk-reward factor to be good or excellent for their successful strategic decisions. In this context, it is also significant to note that five out of every six respondent CEOs indicated that they had adequate information from which to make their decisions. Given the obvious relationship between the amount of information required to assess the risk-reward factor in a given choice and the willingness of the decision maker to accept the perceived risk in relation to the expected outcome, it seems altogether reasonable to assume that the respondent CEOs were quite comfortable with their perceptions of risk. Clearly the respondent CEOs in the Bay area study were considerably more sophisticated regarding the risk-reward factor than the managerial decision makers in Trull's study. The latter group manifested a highly contradictory tendency to demand unending quantities of information from which to accept risks unjustified by expected payoffs. Conversely, the CEOs in the Bay area study were consistent in requesting an optimum amount of information from which to internalize the risk inherent in attractive outcomes.

Degree of Understanding   Trull posited that "one of the most important variables in the relative success of any decision is the . . . degree to which the individuals involved in implementing the decision understand the basis upon which the decision was made, the means or agencies that are to carry out the decision, and the implications that stem from the decision."[40] Trull found that, in general, some degree of preparation for or participation in the making of the decision enhanced the likelihood of decision success. This finding is consistent with much of the management literature dealing with participative decision making. Ideally, participation to facilitate the degree of understanding should in some degree occur in all of the functions of the managerial decision-making process.[41] Research has consistently shown that managers use different degrees of participation at different times and with varying circumstances surrounding the decision-making situation.[42] "Participation of the executors of the decisions in diagnosis, search, and choice are also seen as particularly important to implementation. Presumably learning and adaptability are enhanced by participative decision making."[43]

The results of Trull's study anticipated the findings of the Bay area study regarding the assumed benefits of obtaining a high degree of understanding from those individuals responsible for the implementation of a given managerial decision. As shown in Table 11.1, nearly three out of every four respondent CEOs rated the degree of understanding among their decision implementors as good or excellent. The findings of both studies tend to confirm many of the prevailing theories of participative decision making.

A Profile of Study Results

The results of the Bay area study did not fully replicate the findings of Trull's study in the sense of completely agreeing with his results. It did, however, extend and update the knowledge base of several key factors involved in determining strategic decision success. A final assessment of the six key factors is as follows:

1. Contrary to the results of Trull's study, the respondent CEOs in the Bay area study were generally not bounded by the current operating constraints of the organization in making and implementing their successful strategic decisions. This is a factor that should be studied at greater length if only to ascertain the influence of prevailing policy on the formulation and selection of strategic choice.

2. The optimum timing for successful strategic choice is easily the most significant factor deserving of improvement. Since the time of Trull's study, more than 30 years ago, this factor continues to mystify and elude managerial decision makers. The Bay area study, of just nine years ago, found one-third of the respondent CEOs perceiving the timing of their successful strategic decisions as just satisfactory. The incidence and magnitude of strategic decision success can only benefit from better timing to capitalize on opportunities and to ward off actual and impending threats.

3. The quest for an optimum amount of information from which to obtain decision success is both costly and illusory. There is, for example, no way of ascertaining the definitive acquisition of some optimum amount of information. Therefore, the best that should be sought is some acceptable amount of information from which to internalize unavoidable uncertainty and to proceed with a choice that is good enough to meet management's objective. Contrary to the decision makers in Trull's study, the respondent CEOs in the Bay area study proceeded on this basis. This is a factor that, along with optimum timing, is richly deserving of additional research and publication.

4. The influence of the decision maker is customarily assumed to exert a positive effect on the outcome of strategic decisions. Top managers have traditionally been expected to exercise an active leadership role in making and implementing strategic choices. The decision makers in Trull's study tended to follow this conventional approach. The respondent

CEOs in the Bay area study chose a rather passive leadership role for their successful strategic decisions. No doubt this is a finding that should and will elicit future empirical research.

5. Trull's study showed that managers accept more risk than is justified by available rewards from a successful decision. Several recent comprehensive studies of managerial attitudes toward the acknowledgment and acceptance of risk provide cogent explanations of Trull's findings for the risk-reward factor.[44] In fact managers are very much aware of risk in their strategic decision making, but they are not put off in their choices because of it. Rather, managerial decision makers have a mind set that permits them to cope with risk through the use of various behavioral strategies. Usually (1) they seek to minimize or avoid risk without compromising the perceived attractiveness of the outcome, or (2) they simply acknowledge and accept the risk, confident in their ability to cope with it or to overcome it. They do not attempt to reduce the uncertainty, thereby making the risk more acceptable, through the use of quantitative analysis. Essentially the coping mechanisms of managerial decision makers for dealing with risk are behavioral rather than quantitative.

   Managerial decision makers have grown considerably since Trull's study in terms of their willingness and ability to deal with the risk-reward factor in strategic choice. They have evolved from the maximizing mode of classical economic theory to a satisficing mode of managerial process theory. They require only acceptable amounts of information from which to make decisions embodying risks that are presumed to be avoidable or controllable. The Bay area study extends and confirms the current literature of management for this critical factor of strategic decision making.

6. The Bay area study along with the results of Trull's study and the current literature on management all agree that there should be an acceptable degree of understanding on the part of decision implementors regarding what is expected of them in the decision-making process.

A MODEL FOR STRATEGIC DECISION SUCCESS

The primary thesis of this book is that managerial decision making is best accomplished within a process model embodying the interrelated functions of decision making. This model was presented in Figure 2.1 and, again, coupled with the concept of strategic gap, in Figure 10.3. The point of emphasis here is that this decision-making process has been empirically justified as demonstrably contributing to successful strategic outcomes.[45] Along with a small number of studies at the level of the nation-state, there is hard evidence to support a contention that a process model of decision making is more likely to yield a positive result.[46]

The purpose of this chapter and the remaining chapters of this book is to extend the body of knowledge in this significant area of managerial activity. Using a strategic decision matrix with a two-dimensional focus and four basic types of decision making, several high-visibility strategic decisions from different large organizations are evaluated to support the hypothesis that *a formal decision-making process is conducive to successful strategic decision outcomes.* The results of this evaluation clearly indicate that in the absence of any process or in the presence of an underdeveloped or misused process for strategic decisions, successful outcomes occur mainly by happenstance. Moreover, although a process-oriented approach to strategic choice affords no guarantee of a successful outcome, the likelihood of this occurrence tends to increase with such an approach.

Managerial Attitudes Toward the Decision-Making Process

Managerial attitudes toward the decision-making process are centered on two primary factors: (1) the attainability of the managerial objectives that undergird the process and (2) the openness of the process to the external environment and the numerous constraints that tend to limit the alternatives of the strategic decision makers.

Significance of the Objectives As noted in several preceding chapters of this book, the foundation of the decision-making process lies in the managerial objectives that give it purpose, direction, and continuity. A given objective represents an end point toward which management directs its decision making. Harvey states the case for the primacy of well-defined objectives in making strategic choices as follows:

> The strategic [decision-making] process involves the formulation of a set of . . . objectives for organizational performance. Strategic [choice] is based on results so [objectives] initiate the . . . process. This is true because it is difficult to [select] strategy if the manager does not know what results he is seeking to achieve.[47]

Several recent studies place well-defined objectives at the top of the list of chief executive responsibilities.[48] Most of these studies agree that objectives define the tasks that are essential for successful strategic decisions.[49] Objectives may be perfectly clear to management; but it is essential that they fall within the boundary of attainability. Objectives that are beyond the reach of the organization or those that exceed the state of the art provide a flawed foundation for strategic decision making. Successful strategic choices are not likely to result from such objectives. Yet, as strange as it may seem, managers often exhibit a tendency to set objectives of questionable feasibility.

Openness of the Process Many of the widely accepted guides in economics and statistics are based on closed decision models. Such models are considered closed "because of the minimal weight given to the environment of the decision maker, and [the underestimation of] the act of choice as such."[50] (Note: Closed models and open models of decision making were discussed extensively in Chapter 3 of this book. They are repeated here in summary form by way of review preparatory to introduction of the strategic decision matrix in Figure 11.1 on page 359). The principal assumptions underlying the closed decision model are as follows:

1. The strategic decision maker has only one objective and it tends to be fixed.

2. The information available to the strategic decision maker is unlimited and is completely quantifiable without any time or cost constraints.

3. The strategic decision maker has unlimited cognitive capacity to consider endless alternatives and combinations of alternatives.

4. Most of the key variables in the decision-making situation are within the knowledge and control of the strategic decision maker.

5. The outcome of the closed decision model is presumed to be maximized in terms of benefits to the strategic decision maker or the total organization.

6. The external environment is not considered as a significant variable by the strategic decision maker in the closed decision model.

7. Given the foregoing assumptions, it is a relatively simple matter for the strategic decision maker to select the alternative that promises to maximize the outcome in terms of a fixed objective.

The assumptions of the closed decision model completely constrict the openness of the strategic decision-making process (Figure 10.3). The closed model bespeaks a mindset toward strategic decisions that is antithetical to successful outcomes. Yet it is an approach that all too frequently characterizes management's behavior in making strategic choices.

The open decision model affords a complete contrast to the closed model. The following differences between the open and the closed model of decision making are most significant:

1. The open model replaces the fixed and predetermined objectives of the closed model with dynamic objectives and levels of aspiration.

2. Alternatives and outcomes are not predetermined in the open model; neither are the relations between specific alternatives and outcomes always assumed to be defined.

3. The ordering of all alternatives in the closed model is replaced in the open model by a search that considers fewer than all alternatives because of imperfect information, time and cost constraints, and cognitive limitations of the strategic decision maker.

4. The quest for a maximized outcome in the closed model is replaced in the open model by an outcome that meets the objectives.

5. The open model is characterized by interaction with the numerous stakeholder groups in the external environment of the organization.[51]

All things considered, the open model along with a set of attainable strategic objectives constitutes the optimal attitude toward the strategic decision-making process. Still it must be recognized that managers frequently do pursue strategic choices founded on unattainable objectives set in the closed decision model. But the strategic decision maker's attitude toward the process of arriving at a strategic choice is only one-half the equation. The other one-half relates to the manager's attitude toward the outcome of the strategic decision itself. (Note: In the context of the strategic decision matrix set forth in Figure 11.1, the open and closed models of decision making will be referred to as the open and closed decision-making processes.)

Managerial Attitudes Toward the Decision

Managerial attitudes toward a given strategic decision are also centered on two primary factors: (1) the judgmental or computational qualities of the decision-making strategy itself and (2) the maximizing or satisficing nature of the outcome that management hopes to obtain through the use of a given decision-making strategy.

The Strategies of Strategic Choice   Thompson and Tuden in 1959 and Thompson again in a later work noted that the basic variables of the choice itself are (1) preferences regarding possible outcomes and (2) presumed knowledge regarding a given outcome.[52] These two variables are scaled from certain to uncertain along a two-dimensional continuum that gives rise to a quadratic matrix of strategic choice.[53] A basic premise of this book is that managers making strategic choices acknowledge little uncertainty regarding their preferences for a given outcome. Hence, most strategic decisions are made with a presumption of high levels of certainty regarding a preferred outcome. However, it is the presumption of knowledge regarding a given outcome that is most significant in terms of certainty. Quite simply, a given manager may have a degree of knowledge regarding particular outcomes ranging from complete certainty to complete uncertainty. In most strategic choices, the preference of the manager is highly certain. There is a strategic objective and the manager clearly prefers a choice that will obtain the desired result. On the other hand, there is seldom perfect knowledge regarding the outcome of a given choice. If there were such knowledge, the choice would not be strategic. Consequently, a manager must proceed toward the strategic outcome in the presence of considerable (but not complete) uncertainty and choose a given alternative based on judgment applied to information that is less than perfect. This model of strategic decision making is called a **judgmental strategy,** and it is characteristic of most successful strategic choices.

There are times, however, when a manager presumes to know enough about the outcome to attempt an optimal alternative or one that will result in the highest possible level of attainment for the strategic objective. This model of decision making is called a **computational strategy** and, because of its simplistically quantitative emphasis, it seldom results in a successful strategic choice. In essence, a computational decision-making strategy tends to underestimate the complexity of the decision-making situation and to overrate the knowledge and capacity of the decision maker. Conversely, a judgmental decision-making strategy acknowledges the uncertainty attendant on most strategic choices and accepts the constraints on the human decision maker. Both strategies reflect strong preferences for desirable outcomes as is the case with most managers. However, the computational strategy is based on a nonexistent level of certainty, whereas the judgmental strategy is grounded in the reality of omnipresent uncertainty.

The Outcomes of Strategic Choice   An outcome is a state of affairs that exists as a consequence of a given alternative having been chosen by a strategic decision maker. Strategic outcomes normally involve significant change within the organization or between the organization and its principal stakeholders. *Strategic objectives operating through the process of strategic choice give rise to strategic outcomes.* There are two principal variations of strategic outcomes that are the main focus of this book. The first variation is called a **maximized outcome,** and it presumes the capability for attaining the best possible result in pursuit of a strategic objective. If the outcome of a given strategic choice is less than optimal, it is not a maximized result and, therefore, it is unacceptable to the maximizing strategic decision maker. For a maximizer, only an optimal result denotes a successful outcome. Anything less than optimal is only second or third best. Essentially maximizers tend to pursue optimal outcomes through a computational decision-making strategy. Maximizing behavior tends to be most common in business organizations with a particular emphasis on sales, market share, profits, and growth in resources. Many managers seek to maximize outcomes because it is what managers are expected to do. The problem is that maximizing is an illusion rather than a reality. The untenable presumptions of perfect information, unlimited time and resources, and limitless cognition by the strategic decision maker render a maximized outcome completely unattainable in strategic decision making. Maximizing involves a futile quest for unattainable objectives through the closed decision-making process. In point of fact, the best outcome that a strategic decision maker should seek is one that simply meets a strategic objective. There is no need to exceed a given objective. If a higher level of attainment is sought, simply escalate the objective, but not beyond the point of attainability. This variation is called a **satisficing outcome,** and it is recommended for all strategic choices. Satisficing outcomes normally result from a judgmental model of strategic decision making in which the manager's strong preference for a desirable result is complemented by an acceptance of less-than-perfect knowledge regarding the outcome. Strategic choices are more likely to be successful if they are geared to the attainment of realistic strategic objectives through the open decision-making process. This is the principle of satisficing in strategic decision making.

Types of Strategic Decisions

Figure 11.1 reflects a quadratic matrix of strategic decision-making classifications. Each classification is a composite of managerial attitudes toward the decision-making process and the decision itself. As shown in the figure, there are four basic types of strategic decisions. Type A has the best set of attitudes for a successful strategic choice. Decision making is characterized by attainable objectives pursued through an open decision-making process, and the decision results in a satisficing outcome obtained through a judgmental strategy. Type D has the worst set of attitudes for strategic decision making. Here the approach is characterized by a set of unattainable objectives developed within a closed decision-making process, and the decision maker uses a computational strategy in quest of a maximized outcome. Type D has an untenable attitude for both process and outcome, and is, therefore, virtually assured to fail. Conversely, Type A, with an open approach and expectations keyed to the realization of attainable objectives, is much more likely to result in strategic decision success.

Whereas Types A and D constitute the most positive and negative classifications in Figure 11.1, Types B and C represent mixed classifications. Type B, for example, has a realistic attitude toward the decision which is negated by a pursuit of unattainable objectives in a closed decision-making process. There is no possibility of satisficing the outcome for Type B simply

Attitude toward the decision	Attitude toward the decision-making process	
	Attainable objectives / Open DM process	Unattainable objectives / Closed DM process
Judgmental DM strategy / Satisficing outcome	Type A	Type B
Computational DM strategy / Maximizing outcome	Type C	Type D

FIGURE 11.1

Strategic Decision Matrix

because the objectives are out of sight; and the closed process of decision making is incompatible with a judgmental strategy of strategic choice. Type C, on the other hand, involves pursuing attainable objectives through the open decision-making process; but the use of a computational strategy in an unrealistic quest for a maximized outcome almost assures a lack of decision success. With a major adjustment in managerial attitude toward the decision itself and the acceptance of a satisficing outcome obtained through a judgmental decision-making strategy, a Type C choice may be transformed into a successful Type A choice.

An overall assessment of the prospects for successful outcomes though the strategic decision types classified in Figure 11.1 is as follows:

Type A: Success is not a sure thing; but the likelihood is much greater than for the other types.
Type B: Success is virtually foreclosed by unattainable objectives in a closed decision-making process.
Type C: Limited possibilities for success that would be enhanced by a more realistic attitude toward the decision itself. Attitude adjustment may transform the decision into Type A with escalated prospects for a successful outcome.
Type D: Untenable attitudes toward both the process and the decision itself virtually guarantee a failed strategic choice.

It is important to note at this point that strategic choices do not always fit neatly into a given strategic type. However, the primary characteristics set forth in Figure 11.1 normally permit a reasonably accurate classification.

Strategic Decision Applications

This section presents selected real-world applications of the strategic decision types set forth in Figure 11.1. These examples are intended to validate the strategic decision matrix as a meaningful construct for the assessment of successful outcomes.

Type A Applications   Of all the strategic decision-making classifications, Type A is the easiest one to present simply because it usually reflects a successful strategic choice. If the choice were not successful, close scrutiny would probably indicate some other decision-making classification. In a Type A decision, the objectives are attainable, the open decision-making process is used, a judgmental strategy is adopted, and the result is a satisficing strategic choice. The following strategic decisions are regarded as good examples of Type A choices:

1. PepsiCo's decision in 1997 to spin off its restaurant division (Taco Bell, Pizza Hut, and Kentucky Fried Chicken) as a publicly traded company

2. The restructuring of Hewlett-Packard in 1992

3. The decision of Microsoft in 1993 to develop and market its operating system, Windows NT

4. Sears's decision in 1995 to divest its acquired businesses to focus completely on its retailing operations

5. IBM's decision in 1995 to acquire Lotus Development Corporation

6. The decision by Mercedes-Benz in 1993 to broaden its consumer appeal by developing and marketing a C-class compact automobile

Type B Applications   The decision maker's attitude toward a Type B choice is characterized by a judgmental decision-making strategy in quest of a satisficing outcome. This attitude toward the decision itself normally promises a positive result, except in this case it is negated by the decision maker's attitude toward the strategic objective and the decision-making process. The wrong process is unlikely to yield the right decision, and a Type B choice epitomizes this negative relationship. Unattainable strategic objectives pursued within a closed decision-making process will not yield satisficing outcomes. Therein lies the deficiency inherent in a Type B classification. A cross section of Type B choices would include the following:

1. Seagram's purchase of MCA/Universal Studios in 1995

2. The strategic alliance in 1991 of IBM, Motorola, and Apple Computer

3. American Express's decision in 1987 to enter the revolving credit market with the Optima Card

4. General Motors's decision to acquire Hughes Aircraft in 1985

5. Eastern Airline's decision in 1985 to be acquired by Texas Air

6. General Motors's decision in 1983 to produce and market the Saturn automobile to outsell foreign competitors

Type C Applications   As shown in Figure 11.1, Type C strategic choices begin with attainable strategic objectives pursued through an open decision-making process. This category of strategic choice tends to fail because management presumes a high level of knowledge regarding the outcome and uses a computational decision-making strategy in quest of a maximized result. The all-too-frequent tendency of management to underestimate or ignore the uncertainty inherent in the outcome of a given strategic choice and to proceed computationally, oblivious to the risk attendant on a given strategic objective, is almost certain to produce a failure. The following applications exemplify this relationship:

1. Wells Fargo's acquisition of First Interstate Bank in 1996

2. Southwest Airline's decision in 1996 to expand its operations to the eastern and southeastern regions of the United States

3. AT&T's divestiture of Lucent and NCR in 1995

4. The merger of Chase Manhattan and Chemical Bank in 1995

5. Time-Warner's acquisition of Turner Broadcasting System, Inc., in 1995

6. Continental Oil Company's decision in 1992 to develop existing oil reserves in Ecuador's rain forest

Type D Applications   Again, with reference to Figure 11.1, Type D decisions constitute a double negative in strategic choice. In this category, the decision maker is seeking an unattainable strategic objective fashioned in the closed decision-making process through the use of a computational decision-making strategy oriented toward a maximized outcome. Essentially, Type D strategic decision epitomizes the wrong means directed toward the wrong ends. As such, this category is marked for failure from the outset. Most students and practitioners of management have their own list of Type D decisions. The applications of this category enumerated below are clearly representative, but they are far from being exhaustive.

1. Apple Computer's decision made in the late 1980s and confirmed in the early 1990s not to license its computer technology[54]

2. The decision of SEGA Enterprises, Ltd., in 1994 to diversify its product line

3. Sears's decision in 1993 to eliminate its catalog division

4. General Motors's failed 1992 joint venture with Jinbei Automobile Company, Ltd., in China

5. Coca-Cola's decision in 1985 to substitute new Coke for old Coke

6. The decision of R. H. Macy in the 1980s to become America's largest department store chain

A COMPOSITE APPROACH TO THE EVALUATION OF STRATEGIC DECISION SUCCESS

This chapter has brought into a composite focus a set of evaluative frameworks and concepts that were delineated at various places in this book. This composite approach to the evaluation of strategic choices is reflected in the cases presented in the final four chapters of the book. Preparatory to these evaluations, it is desirable to present a final review of frameworks and concepts.

Evaluative Frameworks

There are at least five major evaluative frameworks available to the student or practitioner of management for use in evaluating strategic choices made in formal organizations. These frameworks are as follows:

1. *The managerial decision-making process* (Figure 2.1). This framework is the evaluative centerpiece of this book. It is ideal for making, implementing, and evaluating any type of category II choice in any kind of organization.

2. *Bounded rationality* (Figure 3.1). This evaluative framework embodies most of the constraints that limit a rational managerial decision maker to a satisficing outcome.

3. *The concept of strategic gap* (Figure 10.2). This framework is most applicable as a foundation preparatory to the making of strategic decisions. It is most applicable in private enterprise, although it may have some applications in the public sector.

4. *The strategic decision-making process* (Figure 10.3). This framework is a composite of the managerial decision-making process and the concept of strategic gap. As such, its primary application is in private enterprise, but not to the exclusion of organizations in the public sector.

5. *Determinants of strategic decision success* (Table 11.1). This framework is composed of a set of evaluative factors validated in the Trull study in the 1960s and the Bay area study in 1990. These factors are especially applicable to implementing strategic decisions.

6. *The strategic decision-making matrix* (Figure 11.1). In one sense, this framework embodies most of the evaluative concepts advanced in this book. As such, it is applicable to the assessment of strategic choices made and implemented in any kind of organization.

Evaluative Concepts

At a later point in this book, there is a glossary of specialized terms that should be assimilated by the student or practitioner of managerial decision making. The short list of evaluative concepts to follow represents terms that are inherent in the basic themes of this book. They are also inherent in most of the preceding evaluative frameworks.

1. *Judgmental versus computational decision-making strategies.* These strategies differ primarily in the presumptions of the decision maker regarding his or her knowledge of the outcome likely to ensue from the decision at hand. If the presumption is based on a high level of knowledge regarding the outcome, the strategy is computational. Given the constraints and the uncertainty inherent in most category II choices and virtually all strategic decisions, the prospective outcome invariably militates for a judgmental strategy; that is, based on a low level of knowledge regarding the outcome.

2. *Satisficing versus maximizing outcomes.* In classical economic theory, a maximized outcome is the optimal result of a set of unattainable assumptions. In the real world of managerial decision-making, a satisficing outcome is

one that meets the organization's objectives. It is preferable because it is the only type that is attainable.

3. *Open versus closed decision making processes.* The closed process is the route of the maximizer using a computational strategy and generally oblivious to environmental effects. The open process employs a judgmental strategy in quest of a satisficing outcome with a full consideration of environmental effects.

4. *Attainable versus unattainable objectives.* Objectives may be unattainable because they are simply not feasible or they are set beyond the capability of the organization. Objectives may also be rendered unattainable by the actions of decision makers. In any case, successful strategic outcomes necessitate attainable objectives from the inception to the completion of the decision-making process.

SUMMARY

The basic orientation of this chapter is toward strategic decision success. The consequences of unsuccessful strategic choices can work against the long-term health of any organization. Given the significance and complexity of strategic decisions, they merit all the energy and expertise that management can bring to bear in a quest for a successful outcome. Anything more is probably not possible; anything less is unacceptable, especially if management is to fulfill its ultimate responsibility to the organization.

This chapter began with a profile of decision success in which it was noted that this subject is deserving of much more attention than it has received in the management literature. A successful strategic decision was defined as *one that results in the attainment of the objective that gave rise to the decision within the constraints that must be observed to bring about such attainment.* In essence, decision success signifies intended ends accomplished within designated means.

Studies of factors determining or influencing decision success are relatively rare in the management literature. This chapter presented the comparative results of two comprehensive studies in this area: the study by Trull in the mid 1960s and the Bay area study consummated in 1990. The findings of the Bay area study showed some significant changes, mostly of a positive nature, since the Trull study, and a mixed profile of constancy in two significant factors over a span of twenty-five years. An abstract of the comparative findings by factor is as follows:

1. *Operating constraints.* Bay area respondent CEOs were not bound by operating constraints in making successful decisions as were the decision makers in the Trull study. *Essentially this is a positive change.*

2. *Optimum timing.* There was no change and, therefore, no improvement in this factor between the two studies. *This is a negative constant.*

3. *Optimum amount of information.* Bay area respondent CEOs required much less information to make successful strategic decisions than did the decision makers in the Trull study. *This is also a positive change.*

4. *Influence of the decision maker.* Bay area respondent CEOs were much less inclined to use the prominence of their respective offices to influence successful strategic choices than were the decision makers in the Trull study. This finding appears to be a change that deserves additional research to fully ascertain its nature. *At this point, it seems to be a potentially negative change.*

5. *Risk-reward factors.* The Bay area study indicates that managerial decision makers have evolved from classical maximizers to prudent satisficers since the Trull study. *This is a positive change.*

6. *Degree of understanding.* Both studies agreed that understanding by those who must implement a given decision with regard to what is expected of them can only facilitate successful managerial choices. *This is a positive constant.*

On balance, the Bay area study indicates a growth in the sophistication of managerial decision makers since the 1960s that requires much additional research. However, the current level of knowledge is more than adequate to evaluate current strategic decisions in terms of their prospects for and their record of success.

This chapter also introduced a comprehensive model of successful strategic choice, which is reflected in Figure 11.1. With regard to Figure 11.1, it was hypothesized that *a formal decision-making process is conducive to successful strategic decision outcomes.* Successful strategic outcomes constitute a joint function of managerial attitudes toward the decision-making process along with managerial attitudes toward the decision itself. This relationship was conceptualized in Figure 11.1 as a strategic decision matrix. In this matrix, four types of strategic choices were identified and set forth as Type A, Type B, Type C, and Type D. Type A has the best set of attitudes for successful strategic decisions. Type D has virtually no chance for success because its decision makers are using a computational decision-making strategy in quest of maximized outcomes for unattainable objectives conceived within a closed decision-making process. Types B and C are classifications with mixed prospects for success largely because of incompatible attitudes on the part of the managerial decision makers. For example, decision makers using a Type B approach have a positive attitude toward the decision itself which is negated in pursuit of unattainable objectives set within a closed decision-making process. Conversely, decision makers employing a Type C approach tend to seek attainable objectives that defy realization because of a computational decision-making strategy oriented toward a maximized outcome.

Each classification of strategic choice in Figure 11.1 was validated by six real-world strategic decisions whose outcomes are known or anticipated. *Therefore, the hypothesis that a formal decision-making process is conducive to strategic decision success is accepted with the understanding that it requires much additional research.*

A final section of this chapter set forth a composite approach to the evaluation of strategic decision success using evaluative frameworks and concepts advanced at various places in the book. Such evaluations constitute the subject of the remaining four chapters.

REVIEW AND DISCUSSION QUESTIONS

1. Why is it important to include the means as well as the ends in any definition of strategic decision success? Discuss.

2. Why is timing such an important factor as a determinant of strategic decision success?

3. What are the positive and negative factors of change and constancy between the Trull study and the Bay area study? Discuss.

4. In your opinion, why did the respondent CEOs in the Bay area study manifest a low-profile influence of their respective offices on successful strategic decisions? Is this finding a positive or a negative change from the results of Trull's study? Discuss.

5. Do you or do you not believe that a formal decision-making process is more conducive to a successful strategic decision? Discuss.

6. In what specific ways is a Type A decision more likely to result in a successful outcome?

7. What is there about a Type D decision that virtually dooms it from the outset?

8. What changes in managerial attitudes might cause a Type C decision to be transformed into a Type A decision?

9. In what specific ways might managerial decision makers transform an otherwise attainable objective into a highly improbable end?

10. Do you believe that the majority of strategic decisions in all kinds of organizations should be classified as Type A? Why or why not? Discuss.

NOTES

1. S. G. Trull, "Some Factors Involved in Determining Total Decision Success," *Management Science* (February 1966), B-270–B-280.

2. E. Frank Harrison, "Some Factors Involved in Determining Strategic Decision Success," *Journal of General Management* (Spring 1992), 72–87.

3. E. Frank Harrison and Monique A. Pelletier, "A Typology of Strategic Choice," *Technological Forecasting and Social Change*, 44 (1993), 245–263.

4. See L. J. Bourgeois, "Performance and Consensus," *Strategic Management Journal*, 1 (1980), 227–248; R. A. Cosier, "Dialectical Inquiry in Strategic

Planning: A Case of Premature Acceptance? *Academy of Management Review*, 6 (1981), 643–648; and H. Mintzberg, "Patterns in Strategic Formation," *Management Science*, 24 (1978), 934–949.

5. R. Stagner, "Corporate Decision Making: An Empirical Study," *Journal of Applied Psychology* (February 1969), 1–13.

6. H. Mintzberg, D. Raisinghani, and A. Theoret, "The Structure of 'Unstructured' Decision Processes," *Administrative Science Quarterly* (June 1976), 246–275.

7. T. J. Peters and R. H. Waterman, Jr., *In Search of Excellence* (New York: Harper & Row, 1982).

8. G. Donaldson and J. W. Lorsch, *Decision Making at the Top* (New York: Basic Books, 1983).

9. D. J. Hickson et al., *Top Decisions: Strategic Decision Making* (Oxford: Blackwell, 1986).

10. William Weitzel and Ellen Johnson, "Reversing the Downward Spiral: Lessons from W. T. Grant and Sears, Roebuck," *The Executive* (August 1991), 7–22.

11. Glen Whyte, "Decision Fiascoes: Why They Occur and How to Prevent Them," *The Executive* (August 1991), 23–31.

12. Robert F. Hartley, *Management Mistakes & Successes*, 3rd ed. (New York: Wiley, 1991).

13. Paul C. Nutt, *Making Tough Decisions* (San Francisco: Jossey-Bass, 1989).

14. James G. March and Roger Weissinger-Babylon, *Ambiguity and Command* (Marshfield, Mass.: Pitman, 1986).

15. Irving L. Janis, *Crucial Decisions: Leadership in Policymaking and Crisis Management* (New York: Free Press, 1989).

16. Ray Crozier, "Postdecisional Justification: The Case of DeLorean," in *Process and Structure in Human Decision Making*, ed. H. Montgomery and O. Svenson (New York: Wiley, 1989), pp. 275–292.

17. C. S. Huxham and M. R. Dando, "Is Bounded-Vision an Adequate Explanation of Strategic Decision-Making Failure?" *OMEGA, The International Journal of Management Science*, 9 (1981), 371–379.

18. Spyros Makridakis, "What Can We Learn from Corporate Failure?" *Long-Range Planning*, 24 (August 1991), 115–126.

19. Robert E. Jones et al., "Strategic Decision Processes in International Firms," *Management International Review*, 32 (1992–93), 219–236.

20. Robert E. Jones et al., "Strategic Decision Processes in Matrix Organizations," *European Journal of Operational Research*, 78 (1994), 192–203.

21. Suzana Braga Rodrigues and David J. Hickson, "Success in Decision Making: Different Organizations, Differing Reasons for Success," *Journal of Management Studies*, 32, No. 5 (1995), 655–678.

22. Paul C. Nutt, "Formulation Tactics and the Success of Organizational Decision Making," *Decision Sciences*, 23 (1992), 519–540.

23. R. Bronner, *Decision Making Under Time Pressure* (Lexington, Mass.: D. C. Heath, 1982).

24. H. A. Simon, "A Behavioral Model of Rational Choice," *Quarterly Journal of Economics* (February 1955), 99–118.

25. E. Witte, "Field Research on Complex Decision-Making Processes — The Phase Theorem," *International Studies of Management and Organization* (Summer 1972), 156–182.

26. R. Ray Gehani, "Time-Based Management of Technology," *International Journal of Operations & Production Management*, 15, No. 2 (1995), 19–35.

27. Trull, "Some Factors Involved in Determining Total Decision Success," p. B-275.

28. See Figure 2.2 in Chapter 2 of this book for an analysis of the rapid decline in the marginal value of additional information.

29. Trull, "Some Factors Involved in Determining Total Decision Success," p. B-276.

30. Ibid., p. B-278.

31. K. R. Andrews, *The Concept of Corporate Strategy*, rev. ed. (Homewood, Ill.: Irwin, 1980).

32. W. H. Hegarty and R. C. Hoffman, "Who Influences Strategic Decision?" *Long-Range Planning*, 20 (1987), 75–85.

33. D. C. Hambrick, "The Top Management Team: Key to Strategic Success, *California Management Review*, 30 (1987), 88–108.

34. D. C. Hambrick, "Strategic Awareness Within Top Management Teams," *Strategic Management Journal*, 2 (1981), 263–279.

35. See H. O. Armour and D. J. Teece, "Organization Structure and Economic Performance: A Test of Multi-Dimensional Hypothesis," *Bell Journal of Economics*, 9 (1978), 106–122; N. Fisher and G. R. Hall, "Risk and Corporate Rates of Return," *Quarterly Journal of Economics*, 83 (1969), 79–92; and W. G. Shepherd, *The Economics of Industrial Organization* (Englewood Cliffs, N. J.: Prentice-Hall, 1969).

36. Jitendra V. Singh, "Performance, Slack, and Risk Taking in Organizational Decision Making," *Academy of Management Journal*, 29 (1986), 562–585.

37. Edward E. Williams and Findlay M. Chapman, III, "A Reconsideration of the Rationality Postulate: 'Right Hemisphere Thinking' in Economics," *American Journal of Economics and Sociology*, 40 (1981), 17. Also see Chapter 3 of this book for a complete presentation of economic man and the economic model of rational choice.

38. Trull, "Some Factors Involved in Determining Total Decision Success," p. B-278.

39. Inga Baird and Howard Thomas, "Toward a Contingency Model of Strategic Decision Making," *Academy of Management Review*, 10 (1986), 230–243.

40. Trull, "Some Factors Involved in Determining Total Decision Success," p. B-279.

41. See Chapter 8 for some theoretical and empirical perspectives on participation in decision making.

42. See J. A. Alutto and J. A. Belasco, "A Typology for Participation in Organizational Decision Making," *Administrative Science Quarterly* (March 1972), 117–125; and V. H. Vroom and P. W. Yetton, *Leadership Behavior on Standardized Cases*, Technical Report No. 3 (New Haven: Yale University Press, 1973).

43. Bernard M. Bass, *Organizational Decision Making*, (Homewood, Ill.: Irwin, 1983), p. 96.

44. See James G. March and Zur Shapira, "Managerial Perspectives on Risk and Risk Taking," *Management Science*, 33 (1987), 1404–1418; Kenneth R. MacCrimmon and Donald A. Wehrung, *Taking Risks: The Management of Uncertainty* (New York: Free Press, 1986); and Zur Shapira, "Risk in Managerial Decision Making," unpublished manuscript, Hebrew University, 1986.

45. See notes 19 through 22 for studies that attribute strategic decision success to the use of a comprehensive process model of strategic decision making.

46. See Z. Maoz, "The Decision to Raid Entebbe," *Journal of Conflict Resolution*, 25 (1981), 677–707; and G. M. Herek, I. L. Janis, and P. Huth, "Decision Making During International Crises: Is Quality of Process Related to Outcome?" *Journal of Conflict Resolution*, 31 (1987), 202–226.

47. D. F. Harvey, *Strategic Management* (Columbus, Ohio: Merrill, 1982), pp. 64–65.

48. See A. Noel, "Strategic Cores and Magnificent Obsessions: Discovering Strategy Formation Through Daily Activities of CEOs," *Strategic Management Journal*, 10 (1989), 33–49; and A. van der Merwe and S. van der Merwe, "Strategic Leadership of the Chief Executive," *Long-Range Planning*, 18 (1985), 100–111.

49. L. F. Hosmer, "The Importance of Strategic Leadership," *Journal of Business Strategy* (Fall 1982), 47–57.

50. C. Z. Wilson and M. Alexis, "Basic Frameworks for Decisions," *Academy of Management Journal* (August 1962), 152.

51. Ibid., p. 162.

52. J. D. Thompson and A. Tuden, "Strategies, Structures and Processes of Organizational Decisions," in *Comparative Studies in Administration*, ed. J. D. Thompson (Pittsburgh, Pa: University of Pittsburgh, 1959), pp. 195–216; and J. D. Thompson, *Organizations in Action* (New York: McGraw-Hill, 1967).

53. R. Butler, *Designing Organizations: A Decision-Making Approach* (New York: Routledge, 1991), pp. 59–61.

54. Jim Carlton, *Apple: The Inside Story of Intrigue, Egomania, and Business Blunders* (New York: Time Business, 1997).

SUPPLEMENTAL REFERENCES

Armstrong, J. Scott. "The Value of Formal Planning for Strategic Decisions: Review of Empirical Research." *Strategic Management Journal*, 3 (1982), 197–211.

Derkinderen, Frans G. J., and Roy L. Crum. "The Development and Empirical Validation of Strategic Decision Models." *International Studies of Management & Organization*, 18 (1988), 29–59.

Estrin, Teviah L. "The Roles of Information Providers in Decision Making." *Journal of General Management* (Spring 1990), 80–95.

Harrison, E. Frank. "Perspectives on Uncertainty in Successful Strategic Choice at the CEO Level." *OMEGA, the International Journal of Management Science*, 20 (1992), 105–116.

Heller, Robert. *The Decision Makers*. New York: Penguin Books, 1989.

Hickson, D. J., ed. *Managerial Decision Making*. England: Dartmouth, 1995.

Hickson, D. J., et al. *Top Decisions: Strategic Decision Making*. Oxford: Blackwell, 1986.

Hitt, Michael, and Beverly B. Tyler. "Strategic Decision Models: Integrating Different Perspectives." *Strategic Management Journal*, 12 (1991), 327–351.

Lippman, Steven A., and Kevin F. McCardle. "Does Cheaper, Faster, or Better Imply Sooner in the Timing of Innovation Decisions?" *Management Science* (August 1987), 1058–1064.

MacCrimmon, Kenneth R., and Donald A. Wehrung. "Characteristics of Risk Taking Executives." *Management Science* (April 1990), 422–435.

Norburn, D. "The Chief Executive: A Breed Apart." *Strategic Management Journal*, 10 (1989), 1–5.

Sinka, Deepak K. "The Contribution of Formal Planning to Decisions." *Strategic Management Journal* (1990), 479–492.

Wiseman, Robert M., and Philip Bromiley. "Risk-Return Associations: Paradox or Artifact? An Empirically Tested Explanation." *Strategic Management Journal*, 12 (1991), 231–241.

PART FOUR

Implementing Strategic Decisions

Case Set No. 1: The Cuban Missile Crisis and the Iranian Hostage Crisis

*T*he purpose of this chapter and the next three chapters in this book is to demonstrate the managerial attitudes toward the decision-making process and toward the decision itself that are most likely to result in strategic decision success. The second purpose is to illustrate the empirical use of selected evaluative frameworks and concepts advanced at various places in this book. The appropriate application of these frameworks and concepts along with the right managerial attitudes toward the process of choice and the strategic decision itself is shown to result in successful strategic outcomes. Conversely, the disregard or misuse of the evaluative frameworks and concepts in combination with the wrong managerial attitudes is shown to result in strategic decision failures.

The first case in this chapter — the Cuban missile crisis — is an excellent example of successful strategic decision making at the level of the nation state under inflexible constraints and in the presence of awesome potential consequences. After nearly forty years the Cuban missile crisis remains the most documented, evaluated, and publicized case of strategic decision making at the level of the nation-state. In the fields of political science and foreign policy in particular, this case is a classic example of the evaluative concepts and frameworks set forth in this book. Moreover, the case represents one of the high points of the tragically ended presidency of John F. Kennedy. It is, by any definition, an example of strategic decision making in which the decision makers had little margin for error. The second case — the Iranian hostage crisis — illustrates a different approach to strategic decision making, also at the level of the nation state, which, primarily because of the managerial attitudes manifested by the decision makers, resulted in a failed strategic outcome. The Iranian hostage crisis is nearly twenty years old. Like the Cuban missile crisis, it has become a classic in strategic decision making, albeit how the wrong approach begets the wrong decision. Unlike the Cuban missile crisis, however, the Iranian hostage crisis can recur at any time. Yesterday the miscreant was Iran, today it is Iraq, tomorrow it will be another nation. The Middle East remains an area fraught with ferment and fanaticism. Hopefully, the past will not influence how to proceed under similar circumstances in the future.

In order to broaden the reader's perspective, the significant events underlying each case will be presented in sufficient detail to facilitate understanding of the critical factors and relationships in the decision-making situation. Subsequently, these events will be related to each major step in the decision-making process to demonstrate the application of the process to decision making in the real world. Each case will then be analyzed and evaluated using conceptual frameworks selected especially to fit the profile of the case. The general approach to case evaluation in each chapter will use essentially the same evaluative frameworks and concepts for each case with special provision for significant variations in case profiles. For example, the Cuban missile crisis will, because of its high profile at the time of the case, receive a special evaluation in addition to the ones used for the Iranian hostage crisis. However, both of these cases will be evaluated comparatively using the determinant factors for strategic decision success in Trull's study and updated in the Bay area study as well as the classifications for strategic decision success set forth in Figure 11.1. Also, in recognition of the differences between organizations in the public sector and those in private enterprise, each corporation will receive a special analysis of its strategic gap. All of these evaluations are intended to demonstrate that successful strategic decisions invariably ensue from managerial attitudes embodying the right approach to the decision-making process and the right attitude toward the decision itself. In essence, this purpose suggests the need to pursue attainable objectives through the open decision-making process using a judgmental decision-making strategy in quest of satisficing outcomes.

THE CUBAN MISSILE CRISIS: A PERSPECTIVE

The Cuban missile crisis marks the closest the world has come to nuclear destruction. For six harrowing days in 1962, from the time President John F. Kennedy informed the nation of the Soviet missile buildup in Cuba until Nikita Khrushchev agreed to pull back, the American people lived under the threat of disaster.[1]

The Soviet decision to deploy long-range nuclear missiles in Cuba must have been reached some time during the spring of 1962, and certainly no later than early summer.[2]

> Leading Sovietologists have concluded that the introduction of strategic missiles into Cuba was motivated chiefly by the Soviet leaders' desire to overcome . . . the existing margin of U.S. strategic superiority.[3]

The noted historian Arthur Schlesinger, Jr., described the Soviet gambit in the following terms:

> In a general sense, the decision obviously represented the supreme probe of American intentions. . . . It was a staggering project — staggering in its recklessness, staggering in its misconception of the American response, staggering in its rejection of the ground-rules for coexistence among the superpowers.[4]

Even though the motive for the Soviet decision was strategic in the broad sense, it included political advantages as well because a general improvement in the Soviet military position offered enticing prospects for specific gains in foreign policy. For example, if the move in Cuba were successful and the overall Soviet position strengthened, Soviet leverage on Berlin would be improved. Moreover, NATO would surely be affected, and the chances that the United States would successfully create a multilateral nuclear force would be reduced. And in Latin America, other potential Castros might be encouraged. At the very least, American power would be less impressive and American protection less sought, and some Latin American countries might move in the Soviet direction even if their governments were not overthrown. Finally, a successful move in Cuba might strengthen the Soviet claim vis-à-vis the Chinese Communists for world leadership of the Communist movement.

The Soviet plan was based on "cover and deception."[5] Secrecy and speed were essential to the success of the operation. It had been known since 1960 that the Soviets were supplying Castro with conventional armaments. In the Soviet view, the movement of new weapons, including defensive and offensive missiles, was to be acknowledged as a continuation of the shipments of conventional armaments to help Cuba meet the threat from "aggressive imperialist quarters."[6]

There were to be four ballistic missile complexes, including some forty launching pads for thousand-mile, medium-range ballistic missiles. In close support of these missile complexes there were to be several batteries of surface-to-air missiles, one hundred MIG fighters, harbor defenses, and patrol boats armed with surface-to-surface missiles.[7] All in all, it was to be a major military deployment providing a nuclear strike capability that would threaten almost every major city in the United States.

The priority accorded secrecy and speed by the Soviets is reflected in the following passage:

> Very few ports were used. Cubans living near the docks were evacuated. High fences were put up and guarded by the Russians. . . . The equipment was landed at night, readied for transport by road, and moved out in night convoys to make room for the next shipment. Sites had been readied in remote areas. . . . And once the equipment reached the sites . . . no attempt was made to camouflage until after a weapon was operational. . . . Even the . . . nuclear storage magazines were prefabricated — cast in the Soviet Union and shipped the whole fantastic distance to Cuba.[8]

Table 12.1 contains a chronology of significant events in the Cuban missile crisis. As shown in the table, the Soviet buildup for placing offensive missile sites in Cuba began in the spring of 1962; when their presence was revealed a few months later, on October 14, 1962, they were nearly operational. During this period, however, the Kennedy administration was generally aware of Soviet intentions in Cuba, so that when aerial reconnaissance photographs and other sources of intelligence confirmed what was already suspected, the response was rapid and to the point. In fact, it was only two

TABLE 12.1   The Cuban Missile Crisis: A Chronology of Significant Events

Date	Event
Summer 1960	First shipments of Soviet arms began arriving in Cuba.
July 26, 1962, to August 24, 1962	Soviet arms shipments to Cuba were escalated.
Spring 1962	The Soviet Union decided to place long-range ballistic missiles in Cuba. The Cuban missile crisis had begun.
September 4, 1962	President John Kennedy released a public statement reflecting United States knowledge of surface-to-air missiles in Cuba.
September 7, 1962	President Kennedy sent a request to Congress for standby authority to call up reserve troops.
September 11, 1962	The Soviet Union publicly disclaimed any movement to place offensive weapons in Cuba.
September 13, 1962	President Kennedy made a major public statement warning the Soviets against placing offensive missiles in Cuba.
September 22, 1962	The Soviet Union publicly acknowledged that it had agreed to deliver defensive armaments and provide training specialists to the Cuban government.
September 25, 1962	Premier Fidel Castro announced an agreement with the Soviet Union to construct a "fishing port" in Cuba.
September 20, 1962, to September 28, 1962	Various intelligence sources (refugees, agents, and reconnaissance flights) indicated the installation of missile bases in Cuba.
October 3, 1962, to October 14, 1962	Spokesmen for the Kennedy administration assured the Congress and the general public that the Soviet arms buildup in Cuba was purely defensive. Soviet diplomats made similar assurances to the Kennedy administration.

weeks from discovery of the missile sites on October 14, 1962, until October 28, 1962, when Premier Nikita Khrushchev announced that the Soviets would execute a complete military withdrawal from Cuba. Of course, each day during this two-week period was filled with a terrible sense of urgency born of the imminence of potential nuclear destruction. The actions of the Kennedy administration in making and implementing its decision proceeded generally in accordance with the decision-making process set forth in this book.

TABLE 12.1   *(continued)*

Date	Event
October 14, 1962	The Kennedy administration first learned positively that the Soviet Union had placed offensive medium-range ballistic missiles in Cuba.
October 17, 1962, to October 19, 1962	The Executive Committee of the U.S. National Security Council met to consider alternatives directed toward removal of the missiles from Cuba.
October 21, 1962	President Kennedy and the Executive Committee decided a blockade of Cuba was the best alternative.
October 22, 1962	President Kennedy delivered a major public address in which he spoke of the awesome consequences that would result if missiles in Cuba were not removed immediately.
October 23, 1962	President Kennedy officially imposed the blockade on Cuba (it was actually put into effect on October 24, 1962).
October 26, 1962	The Soviet Union indicated, through formal and informal channels, its willingness to back away from the confrontation.
October 27, 1962	The Executive Committee responded to the Soviet overtures through formal channels.
October 28, 1962	Premier Khrushchev announced publicly the decision of the Soviet Union to withdraw its missiles from Cuba.
November 20, 1962	Premier Khrushchev also agreed to remove Soviet aircraft and personnel from Cuba.
October 28, 1962, to March 1963	Aerial reconnaissance and other means were employed by the United States to verify a complete Soviet withdrawal from Cuba. The Cuban missile crisis was over.

THE DECISION-MAKING PROCESS IN
THE CUBAN MISSILE CRISIS

The Objectives

The first and foremost American objective was to have the Soviet missiles removed from Cuba.[9] "The missiles must be removed. The alternatives of 'doing nothing' or 'taking a diplomatic approach' could not have been less relevant to this problem."[10] The United States could stand a gradual balancing of the strategic equation with the Soviet Union that would permit both political adjustments and agreements on a whole range of matters, including arms control. But a sudden, swift, and secret shifting of that balance was intolerable. The missiles had to go!

Of course, there were other purposes that had to be served in the process of removing the missiles. It was essential, for example, that the world power balance remain in favor of the United States. Moreover, while the defense of the Western Hemisphere had to be preserved, it was also necessary not to alienate neutral nations who might be inclined to move into the Communist camp. In addition, the politics of the moment dictated that the Kennedy administration respond in a way that would retain the favor of public opinion in the United States. Finally, the American response had to be made in a way that would not strengthen the relationship between the Soviets and the Communist Chinese. The adversary position of these two powers, who were vying for leadership of Communists around the world, could only work to the advantage of the United States and its allies. It was important that the decision not result in a permanent rupture in relations with the Soviet Union. Nonetheless, overriding these considerations was the need to effect an immediate removal of the missiles from Cuba. The task at hand was to decide how best to accomplish this end.

The Search for Alternatives

The search for alternatives in the Cuban missile crisis took place within a context of bounded rationality. The primary objective was clear-cut, but the limitations imposed on the decision makers in the Executive Committee of the National Security Council were appreciable. The complex set of interrelationships among nations, international organizations, and domestic politics created an extremely sensitive situation. Added to this complexity was the high degree of uncertainty accompanying the selection of a particular alternative — an uncertainty made terrifying because of the potential for nuclear war.

The Executive Committee was also constrained by limited information. To be sure, it was known that offensive missiles were being placed in Cuba, but the full extent of the Soviet plan and the timetable were unknown. Intelligence sources were limited to (1) general shipping reports, (2) sketchy information obtained from Cuban refugees, (3) unverified reports from agents of the Central Intelligence Agency, and most important (4) U-2 aerial reconnaissance flights that required reasonably good weather. All in all, it was a highly uncertain situation.

Perhaps the biggest constraint was time. Every day the Soviets were permitted to complete the missile sites was a day closer to their capture of a strategic advantage in the Western Hemisphere, with a threat of nuclear destruction. During the four days from October 17, 1962, to October 21, 1962, during which President Kennedy and the Executive Committee systematically searched for alternatives and finally decided on a blockade, time had a significance rarely found in the decision-making process.

Moreover, the critical nature of the decision before the Executive Committee further constrained the search activity. Taking no action was not a feasible alternative; a temporizing action was unacceptable; only a positive action effectively implemented could meet the challenge. In summary, cost was not a factor; time was of the essence; information was incomplete, which rendered probable outcomes highly uncertain; and environmental pressures dictated a positive response with the most beneficial consequences. It is doubtful if ever a group of human decision makers were called on to make a more fateful decision under such excruciating and binding constraints.

The Comparison and Evaluation of Alternatives

The action of the Executive Committee in selecting, comparing, and evaluating alternatives was influenced by the primary objective of immediately removing the missiles from Cuba in a way that would preserve the world balance of power and not work to the political disadvantage of the United States. In addition, the Executive Committee was forced, by the constraints discussed in connection with the search activity, to operate in a context of bounded rationality. Essentially six alternatives were considered.

1. *Do nothing.* This was an alternative by definition only. Under the circumstances it was not feasible. The arguments for a do-nothing response failed for at least two reasons: (a) they grossly underestimated the military and strategic significance of the Soviet move, and (b) they completely disregarded the political significance — both domestic and international — of inaction by the United States.

2. *Diplomatic pressures.* Several types of pressure were considered, such as (a) an appeal to the United Nations or the Organization of American States for inspection teams, (b) a secret or direct approach to Khrushchev, possibly at a summit meeting, or (c) withdrawal of the United States Jupiter missiles in Turkey in exchange for Soviet withdrawal from Cuba. President Kennedy rejected this last alternative from the outset simply because the time required would permit the Soviets to render the missile bases in Cuba completely operational, which would in turn increase the

danger to the United States and make it more difficult than ever to induce a complete withdrawal.[11]

3. *Various approaches to Castro.* The rationale here was to approach Castro secretly in an attempt to induce him to split with the Soviet Union. However, the depth of Soviet involvement in Cuba indicated that the removal of the missiles was basically a Soviet decision.[12] Therefore, this alternative was also rejected.

4. *Invasion.* The United States could use the crisis as an occasion to remove Castro as well as the missiles. In fact, preparations were made for an invasion of Cuba but only as a last resort. It was the general opinion of President Kennedy and the members of the Executive Committee "that an invasion — more than any other course — risked a world war, a Soviet retaliation at Berlin or elsewhere, a wreckage of our Latin-American policy and the indictment of history for our aggression."[13] An alternative with such portentous implications had to be dismissed, except as a last resort.

5. *Surgical air strikes.* This alternative called for a clean, swift removal of the missile sites by a conventional air attack. Although it was initially attractive to many members of the Executive Committee, on closer reflection this course of action contained many imperfections: (a) the U.S. Air Force could not guarantee complete destruction of all the missile sites, which, of course, made it rather likely that some missiles would be launched against the United States during or soon after the attack; (b) an air strike would almost certainly kill hundreds of Soviets in and around the missile sites, which would doubtless result in Soviet retaliation in Berlin, Turkey, or elsewhere; and (c) an attack without advance warning (which was militarily sound) would render the United States open to charges of a "Pearl Harbor in reverse."[14]

6. *Blockade.* As the Executive Committee considered the alternatives, indirect military action in the form of a blockade became more attractive. A blockade could be applied to offensive weapons only, or to all armaments, or to all strategic materials, including petroleum, on which the Cuban economy was very dependent.[15] A blockade offered both advantages and disadvantages, but the former outweighed the latter, and it was the choice of President Kennedy and the Executive Committee.

The Choice

One of the disadvantages of a blockade was that it might precipitate Soviet retaliation in Berlin. In that event, an impasse would result and the United States would be forced to lift the blockade of Cuba without accomplishing removal of the missiles. Another drawback of a blockade was the need to take direct action if the Soviet ships elected not to stop when so directed by the U.S. Navy. Further, a blockade might be held illegal, in violation of traditional freedom of the seas, unless the United States could obtain a two-thirds vote in the Organization of American States in favor of the blockade. Finally, the greatest single drawback of a blockade was time. It did not present Khrushchev and the rest of the world with a fait accompli. Rather, it offered a prolonged and agonizing approach, uncertain in its effect, indefinite in its duration, enabling the missiles to become operational, subjecting the United States to counterthreats by Khrushchev, and giving the Communists a worldwide propaganda advantage.

In spite of the several disadvantages presented by a blockade, it offered several very desirable benefits to the United States under the extreme constraints of the moment. A blockade was a middle course between inaction and attack. It was aggressive enough to signify firmness of intention but not so precipitous as an air strike. Moreover, it offered the Soviets the choice of avoiding a direct military clash by keeping their ships away. By this means, the Soviets had the last clear choice. The blockade also provided the United States a situation in which it had immediate superiority of land, sea, and air forces. In fact, no possible military confrontation could have been more acceptable to the United States than a naval engagement in the Caribbean. Finally, a blockade permitted the United States, by flexing its muscle, to exploit the threat of subsequent nonnuclear steps in each of which the United States would have substantial superiority.[16] The choice of a blockade to meet the Soviet threat is well explained in the following passage:

> American nuclear superiority could be counted on to paralyze Soviet nuclear power; Soviet transgression of the nuclear threshold in response to an American use of lower levels of violence would be wildly irrational since it would mean virtual destruction of the Soviet Communist system and Russian nation. American local superiority was overwhelming; it could be initiated at a low level while threatening with high credibility an ascending sequence of steps short of the nuclear threshold. All that was required was for the United States to bring to bear its local and strategic superiority in such a way that American determination to see the missiles moved would be demonstrated, while at the same time allowing Moscow time and room to retreat without humiliation. The naval blockade . . . did just that.[17]

Implementation of the Decision

The blockade went into effect early on October 24, 1962. The U.S. Navy deployed a task force of nineteen ships to set up a picket line in the Atlantic 500 miles from Cuba. The task force was prepared to intercept any Soviet ships that might be carrying missiles to the island. At this time American reconnaissance aircraft had already identified twenty-five Russian ships steaming toward the blockade line around Cuba. The Soviet vessels were joined by six Russian submarines. The situation was becoming more critical.

President Kennedy was determined to control events and issued orders that there was to be no shooting. The Soviet ships were to be kept in view, but none was to be boarded until he issued the orders. In spite of strong objections from the U.S. Navy, President Kennedy wanted the blockade line to be drawn close to Cuba so that Khrushchev would have plenty of time to change his mind.[18]

Late on October 24, 1962, it was reported that twelve of the Soviet ships — the ones suspected of carrying offensive missiles — had turned around and were headed back toward the Soviet Union. However, the oil tanker continued to proceed toward Cuba. Two ships actually penetrated the blockade; one was hailed and then waved on, and the second was boarded, searched, and allowed to continue on toward Cuba. At this time, it became apparent that the Soviets had no intention of precipitating a naval encounter in the Caribbean. For the time being, at least, the blockade seemed to be an effective choice. Still the Soviets pressed forward with their plan to make the missile sites in Cuba operational.

On October 26, 1962, the first break came in the crisis. A cable through formal channels to President Kennedy from Premier Khrushchev indicated the Soviets' willingness to negotiate for the withdrawal of the missiles from Cuba. At the same time, the Soviets also let it be known through informal channels that they had no desire to push toward nuclear confrontation.

After a day of serious deliberation with the members of the Executive Committee, President Kennedy sent a cable on October 27, 1962, to Premier Khrushchev in which he agreed to remove the blockade with the withdrawal of Soviet missiles from Cuba. On October 28, 1962, Premier Khrushchev cabled a reply to President Kennedy in which he agreed to dismantle and remove all missiles from Cuba in the full assurance that there would be no attack, no invasion of Cuba by the United States or any other nation in the Western Hemisphere. At noon on the same day, President Kennedy released a statement to the press in which he acknowledged Khrushchev's decision to withdraw from Cuba. The climax was over. A nuclear holocaust had been narrowly averted. All that remained was the follow-up to ensure control of the outcome — that the missiles were in fact removed.

Follow-up and Control

Fidel Castro refused to permit any on-site inspection by UN officials or anyone else of the dismantling, loading, and return shipment of Soviet armaments in Cuba, in spite of repeated requests by the Soviets and the United Nations. The United States had to rely on visual aerial inspection at sea as Soviet captains pulled back tarpaulins to reveal the missiles lashed to the decks of their ships.

On November 20, 1962, Premier Khrushchev also agreed to remove Soviet aircraft and personnel from Cuba. The United States also observed the departure of this last part of the Soviet deployment by aerial reconnaissance. By March 1963 "there was no doubt that President Kennedy had achieved a foreign policy victory of historical proportions."[19] The Cuban missile crisis had become a classic case of decision making under extreme constraints at the national level.

SPECIAL EVALUATION OF THE
CUBAN MISSILE CRISIS

On balance, it appears that the decision by President Kennedy and the Executive Committee to impose a blockade on Cuba was the best choice among the available alternatives. Table 12.2 shows a decision matrix in which the alternatives are related to specific objectives. For purposes of illustration, the objectives are weighted equally, although as a practical matter the immediate removal of the missiles from Cuba had top priority in the U.S. decision. Still it is doubtful that an action to remove the missiles would have been taken if it would have jeopardized the power balance in favor of the United States or reduced U.S. hemispheric defenses. Moreover, the Kennedy administration was very mindful of world political opinion, especially among neutral nations, and the political sentiment of the American public was always a significant factor. The relationship between the Soviet Union and Communist China, and between the Soviet Union and the United States, may have been of lesser importance only because it was not as demanding as the other objectives.

The six alternatives in Table 12.2 are the ones considered by the Kennedy administration in arriving at a choice. The number at the intersection of each alternative with a particular objective represents the assumed advantage to the United States resulting from the adoption of that course of action. The higher the value of the advantage, the more favorable the outcome to the United States. The last row in Table 12.2 is, because the objectives are weighted equally, the total point value of the simple arithmetic sum of all the advantages accruing to the United States with the selection of a given alternative in relation to each of the specific objectives sought by the United States. It should be noted that Table 12.2 is a special evaluative framework designed to fit the unique profile of the Cuban missile crisis in which the high level of uncertainty makes it difficult to assign anything other than equal weight to the several objectives of the decision-making process.

An analysis of the point values assigned to each alternative in Table 12.2 reveals the following:

1. The first three alternatives — do nothing, diplomatic approach to Castro, and diplomatic pressures — were relatively ineffective in terms of meeting all the objectives.

2. The fourth and fifth alternatives — invasion and air strikes — were especially appealing in terms of removing the missiles immediately, maintaining the world power balance in favor of the United States, and preserving hemispheric defenses. But these two alternatives have little or no point value in relation to the other objectives.

3. Only the sixth alternative — a blockade — has consistently high point values over the full range of objectives.

TABLE 12.2   Decision Matrix: The Cuban Missile Crisis

Objectives	Alternatives					
	Do nothing	Diplomatic approach to Castro	Diplomatic pressures	Invasion	Air strikes	Blockade
1. Missiles are removed immediately	0*	2	2	8	8	4
2. World power balance remains in favor of United States	1	4	2	8	8	6
3. U.S. hemispheric defenses are preserved	1	1	2	8	8	8
4. World opinion remains favorable toward United States	4	2	4	0	2	8
5. Sentiment of U.S. public remains favorable toward administration	2	2	3	2	2	10
6. Sino-Soviet relationship is not strengthened	5	5	5	2	2	8
7. U.S. relationship with Soviet Union is not worsened	2	4	4	0	0	6
Total point value	**15**	**20**	**22**	**28**	**30**	**50**

*Advantages are based on a point value system of 0 to 10.

Clearly, in view of the objectives underlying the decision as well as the un-quantifiable but excruciating constraints of the moment, a blockade was the best choice.

It is not so important that the student agree with the analysis reflected in Table 12.2. What is important is that he or she recognizes (1) the need for a systematic review of the alternatives in light of the objectives at hand and (2) the benefits that accrue from a rational approach to weighing the likely consequences of a particular alternative.

The Cuban missile crisis represents a decision-making situation that is obviously one of a kind; we hope a similar situation will never recur. But it is clear that under such circumstances of complexity and uncertainty, the entire integrated decision-making process is the most meaningful framework for analysis and evaluation of the choice. In this case, the need for immediate action overshadowed any reluctance on the part of the decision makers to cope with uncertainty. The group norm clearly favored decisive action. There was little time for developing a quantitative model or employing sophisti-cated statistical techniques to arrive at a choice.

The behavior of the decision makers was very rational in that they never lost sight of the objectives. The choice was made in the face of environ-mental pressures and very limited, incomplete information. Of course, the overriding constraint was the limited time available to the decision makers, who operated with the knowledge that a wrong step anywhere in the process of arriving at a choice could have drastic consequences. The Cuban missile crisis is a unique and historic example of reaching a satisficing choice in the open decision model.

THE IRANIAN HOSTAGE CRISIS: A PERSPECTIVE

There are many ways to describe the Iranian hostage crisis. Clearly it was an embarrassment for the United States. In retrospect it is apparent that not only were fifty-three individuals held hostage by Iranian militants for 444 days; America was, too. It was an extraordinary event that will be the subject of much analysis and evaluation by students of American foreign policy in the years to come. The Iranian hostage crisis was also a political disaster for President Jimmy Carter. The crisis contributed to a loss of confidence in Carter's leadership and to his defeat at the polls. For purposes of this book, the Iranian hostage crisis will be described as a decision-making situation that occurred at the national level.

After it has been analyzed and evaluated in the context of the decision-making process introduced in Chapter 2, it will be compared with the Cuban missile crisis in the context of the special evaluation frameworks presented in Chapter 11.

Table 12.3 presents a chronology of significant events in the Iranian hostage crisis when viewed as a case study in managerial decision making.[20] As it shows, the crisis began on November 4, 1979, with the seizure of the U.S. embassy in Tehran along with sixty-six hostages. The crisis ended on January 20, 1981, with the release of the remaining fifty-two hostages. The decision-making process in the Iranian hostage crisis began on November 6, 1979, when the Carter administration and the Joint Chiefs of Staff commenced planning to rescue the hostages. Between that date and April 11, 1980, when President Carter decided to proceed with an airborne rescue effort, the administration reviewed and evaluated several alternatives. During this five-month period, the administration was increasingly frustrated by its inability to resolve the crisis; and the patience of the American public began to wear thin. There was a growing sentiment at home and abroad that Carter was unable to provide the leadership necessary to effect a release of the hostages.

Carter's decision of April 11, 1980, to proceed with an airborne rescue attempt was implemented unsuccessfully and with enormously unfortunate consequences on April 24–25, 1980. Once Carter announced on April 26, 1980, that the rescue attempt had failed and eight American servicemen had been killed in a mishap at the rescue site, the disenchantment of the American public escalated. During the protracted negotiations with the Iranian government over the remainder of 1980, defeat at the polls seemed assured for Carter. The decision-making case presented in this book ended with

TABLE 12.3   Iranian Hostage Crisis: A Chronology of Significant Events

Date	Event
November 4, 1979	U.S. embassy in Tehran was seized by Iranian militants who took sixty-six U.S. diplomatic personnel and visitors prisoner.
November 5, 1979	Iran canceled treaties with the United States and the Soviet Union that gave the superpowers the right to intervene in Iran militarily under certain conditions.
November 6, 1979	Ayatollah Ruholla Khomeini and the Revolutionary Council took control of the Iranian government. Khomeini publicly endorsed the seizure of the hostages and refused to meet with any American emissaries.
November 6, 1979	Carter's administration and the Joint Chiefs of Staff commenced planning to rescue the hostages.
November 8, 1979	U.S. military commanders briefed the administration on the tentative rescue plan involving helicopters and airplanes.
November 9, 1979	Carter blocked delivery of $300 million worth of military equipment and spare parts to Iran.
November 10, 1979	Carter ordered deportation procedures to begin against Iranian students found to be in the United States illegally.
November 12, 1979	Carter suspended oil imports from Iran.
November 14, 1979	Carter declared a national emergency and froze all Iranian assets held in domestic and overseas branches of U.S. banks.
November 19–20, 1979	Thirteen blacks and females were released, reducing the number of hostages still held to fifty-three.
December 4, 1979	The UN Security Council unanimously called for the hostages' release.
February 11, 1980	Iran set conditions for the release of the hostages, which mainly involved the return to Iran of the former shah and his fortune.
March 21– April 11, 1980	The decision to rescue the hostages crystallized within the Carter administration.
April 2, 1980	A military plane reconnoitered the proposed rescue site in Iran and reported favorable terrain and conditions.
April 7, 1980	Carter severed diplomatic relations with Iran and imposed an embargo on American exports to Iran with the exception of food and medicine.

TABLE 12.3 *(continued)*

Date	Event
April 11, 1980	Carter decided to proceed with an airborne rescue of the hostages.
April 11–24, 1980	Final preparations were completed for the rescue mission.
April 24, 1980	The rescue mission began.
April 25, 1980	The rescue mission was aborted by Carter because of equipment failures in the Iranian desert. Eight Americans were killed in an accident at the rescue site.
April 26, 1980	Carter made a formal statement to the U.S. Congress and the American people in which he explained what had happened to the rescue mission and accepted full responsibility for the outcome.
April 26, 1980	Iran announced the dispersion of the hostages to discourage further rescue attempts.
May 18, 1980	Most Common Market countries imposed limited economic sanctions against Iran.
May 24, 1980	The International Court of Justice ordered Iran to release the hostages and pay reparations.
July 11, 1980	Iran released one hostage because of illness. The number held was reduced to fifty-two.
July 27, 1980	The deposed shah of Iran died in Cairo.
September 12, 1980	Khomeini reset the terms for release of the hostages; they now included (1) relinquishment of the property and assets of the shah, (2) cancellation of all financial claims against Iran, (3) release of the frozen Iranian assets, and (4) a promise not to interfere in Iran's internal affairs.
November 3, 1980	Militants holding the hostages relinquished responsibility to the Iranian government.
November 20, 1980	The Carter administration accepted the Iranian terms for the release of the hostages in principle.
November 20–January 18, 1981	Negotiations over details of a settlement agreement took place between the United States and Iran.
January 19, 1981	Carter announced to the American public that the Iranian hostage crisis was resolved.
January 20, 1981	The fifty-two hostages were released by Iran. The Iranian hostage crisis was ended.

the aborting of the rescue mission on April 25, 1980. For President Carter, however, the process continued for another nine months until, just before Ronald Reagan became president of the United States, the remaining fifty-two hostages were released.

THE DECISION-MAKING PROCESS IN
THE IRANIAN HOSTAGE CRISIS

The Objectives

The first and foremost objective in the Iranian hostage crisis was to obtain the release of the hostages. Anything less was unacceptable; anything else was unthinkable. The indignation and rage of America at being held hostage by Iranian militants demanded a quick and unequivocal release of all the hostages. Of course, there were corollary objectives and other serious considerations. For example, in its dealings with the Iranian government, the United States obviously did not wish to incur the displeasure of other oil-producing Islamic nations. Moreover, the United States did not wish to precipitate adversarial moves by the Soviet Union in any attempt by the latter to assert its superpower status in the area. Carter's administration was also mindful of the imminence of the presidential elections in 1980. The hostage crisis had to be resolved to help Carter's reelection. With the possible exception of the urgent need to remove the missiles from Cuba in the Cuban missile crisis, it is doubtful if any situation in recent times was more embarrassing and painful to America than the knowledge that fifty-two of its citizens were held in Iran at Khomeini's pleasure.

The hostages had to be returned; and two days after the seizure of the American embassy in Tehran on November 4, 1979, the Carter administration began planning their rescue. Regrettably it took five months to select and implement an alternative course of action that failed in the breach.

The Search for Alternatives

The chronology in Table 12.3 indicates that the Carter administration began searching for alternatives as soon as the hostages were seized. Planning for a formal rescue attempt started on November 6, 1979. As in the case of most complex decision-making situations, the search for alternatives in the Iranian hostage crisis took place within a context of bounded rationality. The primary objective was clear-cut, but there were limitations imposed on the Carter administration. The external environment was characterized by a good deal of complexity and a high level of volatility. The complexity was ascribable to a set of labyrinthine interrelationships among Iran, the United States, the Soviet Union, the major countries of Europe, and the principal nations in the Islamic world. For example, the high level of dependence of the Western nations on oil imported from the Middle Eastern countries was always a complicating factor in diplomacy and trade. The volatility in the hostage crisis was attributable to the revolutionary nature of Iranian politics, the incursions of the Soviet Union into neighboring Afghanistan, and the possibility that the United States might retaliate against Iran in a way that would escalate to conflict at the national level. Added to these obvious sensitivities was the chronically adversarial relationship between Israel and its neighboring Islamic countries. This complexity and volatility contributed to a high degree of uncertainty attendant upon any forceful action the United States might take to bring about the return of the hostages. There was, in short, a considerable amount of concern associated with any drastic action along with a growing realization that such an action might be the only way to break the impasse.

The Carter administration was also constrained by information that was often incomplete, inaccurate, or untimely. Intelligence sources were limited to (1) agents of the American government, (2) sympathizers with the United States, (3) official satellite photographs, and (4) unconfirmed reports from a variety of sources. There was a good deal of information available to the decision makers, but much of it was of questionable validity and unknown reliability. The imperfection of available information added to the uncertainty associated with the alternatives considered by the Carter administration.

Time and cost constraints invariably limit or condition the choices of decision makers. Cost was not a factor in the Iranian hostage crisis. When national security or national prestige is a major factor in a decision-making situation, efficiency is not a factor. Such was the case in the Cuban missile crisis, and the Iranian hostage crisis followed the pattern. Conversely, time was a dominant constraint that continually beset the Carter administration. Every day the hostages languished in Iranian detention was another nail in the coffin of Carter's political career. The high degree of visibility accorded the hostage crisis in the media around the world and the heightening expectation that the United States would act swiftly and decisively placed an inordinate amount of pressure on the decision makers. For five months the Carter administration tried a combination of negotiations, sanctions, and embargoes, all to no avail. More drastic alternatives were studied and restudied as the crisis evolved into an apparent impasse.

The escalating urgency to release the hostages imparted a high level of criticality to the situation confronting the administration. Indeed the critical nature of the decision that President Carter was being called upon to make further constrained the search for alternatives. Whatever action was forthcoming had to be successful. But the uncertainty of the outcome surrounding a given course of action indicated clearly that success was only a probability. There was also a reciprocal probability of failure that had to be considered by the decision makers.

In summary, the complexity and volatility of the environment confronted the decision makers with a good deal of uncertainty with regard to the probable consequences of a given course of action. The information available to the decision makers was incomplete, inaccurate, and untimely in varying degrees at different times, which added to the uncertainty. Cost was not a significant factor, but timing was of the essence. Cognitive limitations were present but not in any extraordinary degree. For example, the decision makers were not subjected to information overload nor did they need to deal with a large number of complex alternatives. Indeed as the weeks wore on, the alternatives seemed more and more apparent to the Carter administration.

The Comparison and Evaluation of Alternatives

The Carter administration tried a number of actions to secure the release of the hostages before settling on an airborne rescue attempt. Table 12.3 provides a recap of these actions. Along with the continual condemnation of the Iranian government for condoning the seizure of the hostages, the United States tried repeatedly through diplomatic channels to bring about their release. Moreover, Carter suspended oil imports from Iran, blocked the delivery of U.S. military equipment to Iran, and froze all Iranian assets held in U.S. banks anywhere in the world. On April 7, 1980, having seriously considered more direct and drastic actions for several weeks, the Carter administration severed diplomatic relations with Iran and embargoed all American exports to that country except food and medicine. Operating within a context of bounded rationality, the salient choices available to the decision makers in April 1980 were as follows:

1. *Do nothing.* As in most decision-making situations of crisis proportions at the national level, doing nothing was an alternative in name only. Moreover, in spite of actions taken by the Carter administration after the hostages were seized on November 4, 1979, there was a growing sentiment at home and abroad that the United States was already engaged in the do-nothing alternative. Clearly some form of definite and positive action was needed to bring about a release of the hostages.

2. *Continue negotiations.* Direct negotiations with Iran were not possible. Carter had severed diplomatic relations, and the Ayatollah Khomeini had refused since November 6, 1979, to treat with any American emissary. Negotiations would, therefore, have to take place through third-party nations who would agree to serve in this capacity. Another variation of this alternative was to negotiate under the auspices of the United Nations. Given the protracted detention of the American hostages, negotiations appeared to the administration to be an inadequate alternative. The situation called for a more decisive approach to resolve the crisis. As President Jimmy Carter noted on April 10, 1980: "We could no longer afford to depend on diplomacy. I decided to act."[21]

3. *Blockade.* A blockade of Iranian harbors was one of four major military options considered to resolve the crisis. The United States had substantial military presence in the area. In the Indian Ocean alone was a U.S.

task force of twenty-five ships including about two hundred combat planes on two aircraft carriers and an assault force of eighteen hundred marines on landing ships. It appeared to many observers that the United States was muscle-bound.[22]

A blockade appeared to be a logical choice. It would signify firmness of intentions by the United States without necessarily precipitating immediate and irreversible escalation. A blockade had proved successful in the Cuban missile crisis. But this wasn't Cuba. The Caribbean offered many more logistical advantages to the United States when compared with the Arabian Sea or the Persian Gulf. Moreover, a blockade of Iranian harbors would make it difficult or impossible for Saudi Arabia, Iraq, the United Arab Emirates, and other Persian Gulf countries to conduct their own trade through the Strait of Hormuz.[23] Finally, of course, a blockade might require some period of time to take effect, and there was a strong feeling in most quarters that the release of the hostages was long overdue. President Carter was not predisposed toward imposing a blockade on Iranian harbors. In his words: "A naval blockade of surface ships might have been . . . effective, but it would have involved repeated confrontations between us and ships of many other nations, some of which might have been damaged or sunk of they tried to run the blockade."[24] Therefore, this alternative was rejected by the decision makers.

4. *Mine Iranian harbors.* In combination with or apart from a blockade by U.S. warships, another military option involved mining Iranian harbors with explosive devices that would disrupt the flow of commerce and trade to Iran on the high seas. President Carter was inclined toward this alternative. In his words: "My own judgment was that the best and surest way to stop all ship traffic would be to mine the entrance to all Iranian seaports. We are capable of doing it immediately and without delay or serious threat to our own forces. Effective minesweeping operations by Iran or its potential supporters would be almost impossible."[25] Besides the fact that the mining of Iranian harbors might be construed as an act of war on the part of the United States, inviting retaliation in some form by the Soviet Union, there was also no way to ensure that the ships of allies or countries important to the United States might not be inadvertently sunk. Most important of all, mining Iranian harbors was simply another military option that could easily lead to a protraction of the impasse in obtaining the release of the hostages. As such, this alternative was also unacceptable to the decision makers.

5. *Surgical air strikes.* The use of surgical air strikes to apply swift and decisive pressure intended to elicit immediate capitulation was seriously considered at several times during the crisis. It was decided, however, that "air strikes against selected Iranian cities would be indiscriminate attacks on the population and must therefore be weighed against political consideration. . . . Another alternative would be an attack on certain military facilities such as the [airforce] bases."[26] Additional possibilities included "the bombing of Kharg Island, the site of Iran's main oil-export facility, and air strikes on the huge refinery at Abadan, which produces most of the country's fuel for

internal use."[27] In his memoirs Carter declares that he seriously considered the possibility of surgical air strikes. But can air strikes always be made surgically? This option was rejected in the Cuban missile crisis because the military commanders could not guarantee a surgical result. Perhaps for the same reason, air strikes were not chosen in the Iranian hostage crisis. One can only speculate that this alternative did not sit well with President Carter. His philosophy regarding the ideal outcome of any punitive action against Iran is stated in the following passage: "We want it to be quick, incisive, surgical, no loss of American lives, not involve any other country, minimal suffering of the Iranian people themselves, to increase their reliance on imports, sure of success, and unpredictable."[28] Clearly Carter wanted an ideal outcome to ensue from a perfect process. Such a result is most unlikely in a highly imperfect world. In all fairness, of course, it must be conceded that air strikes, surgical or otherwise, increase the likelihood of escalation particularly if, as in some scenarios, they are accompanied by ground assault forces. In any case, this option didn't get off the ground.

6. *Airborne rescue mission.* The fourth military option and the last major alternative considered in the crisis was an airborne rescue mission. This option had been presented to the administration by military commanders four days after the hostages were seized on November 4, 1979. At that time there was inadequate information regarding the disposition of the hostages as well as some substantial and complex problems of logistics. For example, the U.S. embassy in Tehran was distant from the United States and remote from any American-controlled facilities; helicopters were not usually used for a long-distance assault mission.[29] Between March 21 and April 11, 1980, the decision to try an airborne rescue of the hostages crystallized in the Carter administration. In his memoirs, President Carter noted that on "April 2, I received a report that our small plane had flown hundreds of miles into Iran at a very low altitude, landed in the desert, examined the possible rescue staging site and returned without detection. The pilot reported that it was an ideal place — a smooth and firm surface, adequately isolated with only a seldom-used country road nearby."[30]

The airborne rescue mission had much to commend it. It was a selective option and one in which failure need not result in immediate escalation of the conflict. The American presence was reduced to the absolute mission minimum, which tended to reduce the risk of loss of human life. It was a rapier thrust rather than a blunt-instrument assault by a world power. The size of the complement of personnel involved in the mission made for a high level of confidentiality. An elite force composed of the very best personnel and equipment that America could command was assembled into a rescue team. Once the rescue was accomplished, world praise would surely follow. The United States as the aggrieved nation was well within its rights to invade Iran on a singular mission to rescue its citizens held hostage by a militant Iranian group.

The airborne rescue mission was an alternative that appealed to a president who had a great veneration for humanity in general and human life in particular. It would restore the luster of his administration in the eyes of observers at home and abroad. It had only to succeed; and there was no belief that it would not. It appeared to be an optimal choice among numerous suboptimal possibilities. The airborne rescue mission was the response of civilized people to an uncivilized act carried out by militants, sanctified by revolutionaries, and supported by governmental inaction.

The Choice

The choice of an airborne rescue mission promised to bring a swift and successful conclusion to five months of suffering in the richest country on earth. The small number of individuals in the highest offices in the Carter administration who were involved in the decision felt a sense of relief at the prospect of an end to the crisis. There was virtually no doubt about the success of the mission. Because action had been so long in coming and because the wait had been so agonizing, the probability of mission failure did not occur to the decision makers. President Carter was particularly elated at the prospect of success. As he said in his memoirs: "Although I felt the weight of the responsibility and was properly concerned about what the future might hold, I had no doubt that the time was ripe. Because I was so clear in my resolve, I looked forward to the mission."[31]

Much of the writing about the Iranian hostage crisis relates to the implementation phase of the rescue attempt. As originally conceived, the choice involved the following sequence of operations:

> The plan . . . involved a two-day operation. Eight helicopters would rendezvous with three C-130's in the middle of the Persian desert during the first night, to be refueled and to transfer the assault team; the helicopters would then continue to a site near Tehran, where the team would conceal itself for a full day. The actual assault would take place during the second night, with the team transported by vehicles that were previously prepared. . . . Following the well-rehearsed penetration of the Embassy compound, all of the hostages, and perhaps some prisoners, would be moved to a nearby stadium, from which the helicopters would move the entire group to an airport near Tehran, which in the meantime would have been occupied in the course of a sudden landing by American military transport aircraft. The extrication of the entire mission would be completed in darkness.[32]

President Carter took a personal interest in all the details for the preparation of the mission. Brzezinski, in particular, was impressed with Carter's thoroughness in familiarizing himself with the details. "Carter's performance was very impressive. He . . . carefully examined every aspect of the mission."[33] Carter himself observed: "I was particularly impressed with the mission commanders. . . . In their meticulous description of every facet of the operation, I received satisfactory answers to my many questions. I informed the military leaders that they had my complete confidence and support."[34]

Although the information possessed by the decision makers in the Iranian hostage crisis was usually incomplete, often inaccurate, and frequently untimely, prior to the launch of the airborne rescue mission there was some intelligence regarding the location of the hostages and the state of preparedness of the captors. The administration had blueprints of the embassy buildings in Tehran. Information from American agents indicated that the captors had grown lax in their surveillance of the hostages. Satellite photographs provided a pattern of the movement of vehicles in and out of the embassy grounds. "Life for the guards around the embassy grounds seemed to have settled into a relaxed and humdrum existence, perfectly designed for a lightning strike by a highly-trained and well-equipped force."[35] Or so it seemed to the decision makers.

Implementation of the Decision

From its optimistic start to its ill-fated conclusion, the attempted airborne rescue of the hostages took less than seven hours. Using Washington, D.C., time, a brief chronology of significant events in the implementation of the decision is as follows:

April 24, 1980

10:35 A.M.	A fleet of eight helicopters took off from the aircraft carrier *Nimitz*, which was cruising in the Arabian Sea near Iran. Concurrently six C-130 transport planes took off from Egypt to rendezvous with the helicopters at a predetermined site (Desert One) in Iran.
12:00 P.M.	Bad weather over the Iranian desert caused two helicopters to abort short of the landing site. One was forced down and the other returned to the carrier.
3:15 P.M.	Six C-130 transport planes and six helicopters landed at Desert One. Military personnel disembarked, commenced refueling operations, and began preparations for the next phases of the rescue mission.
4:45 P.M.	A third helicopter went out of commission because of hydraulic system problems. Only five helicopters remained operational. (The minimum mission requirement was six operational helicopters.)
4:57 P.M.	After receiving full reports and recommendations from all his military commanders, President Carter aborted the mission.
5:58 P.M.	Carter was informed that one helicopter had crashed into a C-130 transport aircraft. In the ensuing fire, eight American military personnel were killed and three were burned badly.

6:21 P.M.	All military personnel were loaded on the remaining five C-130 transport aircraft. All remaining equipment and helicopters were abandoned at Desert One. The eight dead American military personnel could not be safely removed from the crash. (They were left behind and their bodies were subsequently reclaimed by the United States.)
11:05 P.M.	All teams had returned to their bases.
11:55 P.M.	President Carter decided to make a public announcement in which he assumed full responsibility for the failed rescue mission.

In a shocking turn of events, it became painfully apparent that the airborne mission had failed. Although President Carter made a prompt and full disclosure of the rescue attempt, the question of what went wrong remained to be answered.

Follow-up and Control

In the case of the Iranian hostage crisis, the implemented choice of an airborne rescue mission proved unsuccessful almost immediately. There was little opportunity to control the outcome of events once the mission got underway. It seemed that the mission deteriorated so quickly there was no way to take corrective action before it failed completely. The lesson to be learned here is that follow-up and control really begin before the decision is made and implemented, at which time the decision makers should attempt to anticipate adversity by planning for failure as well as for success. Clearly this was not the approach taken by the Carter administration in the Iranian hostage crisis. Consequently the discussion to follow is concerned mainly with what went wrong with the mission and what might have been done by the decision makers to improve the chances of success.

President Carter was dismayed by the failure of the mission. In his words: "The cancellation of our mission was caused by a strange series of mishaps — almost completely unpredictable. The operation itself was well planned. The men were well trained. We had every possibility of success."[36] But was the mission really well planned? Good planning requires a recognition of the possibility of failure, and that was not considered here. When the mission began to fall apart, there was no back-up plan. In point of fact, the rescue mission was a maximizing choice based on a computational decision-making strategy. But the situation called for a satisficing choice founded on a judgmental decision-making strategy. The decision makers assumed a complete knowledge of the cause-and-effect relationships to the point where they tried to measure precisely the inputs required to obtain a maximized output. This kind of omniscience is seldom available to decision makers operating within the bounded rationality of a situation like the Iranian hostage crisis. Regrettably the decision makers sought to obtain a preferred outcome based on a single throw of the dice. Unlike professional gamblers, however, they seemed traumatized when the result backfired on them.

In May 1980, the Joint Chiefs of Staff commissioned a Special Operations Review Group to conduct a broad examination of the planning, organization, coordination, direction, and control of the Iranian hostage rescue mission. The group consisted of six senior military officers at the rank of admiral or general. It was determined that two factors contributed directly to the mission abort: unexpected helicopter failure rate and low-visibility flight conditions en route to the rendezvous site. Some of the conclusions of the review group regarding the nature of the rescue mission were as follows:

1. The concept of a small clandestine operation was sound. A larger overt attempt would probably have resulted in the death of the hostages before they could be reached.

2. The operation was feasible and probably represented the plan with the best chance of success at the time the mission was launched.

3. Despite all the complexities, the inherent difficulties, and the human and equipment performance required, the risks were manageable, the overall probability of success good, and the operation feasible.

4. The plan for the unexecuted portion of the mission was soundly conceived and capable of successful execution.

5. The rescue mission was clearly a high-risk operation. This was the case because people and equipment were called upon to perform at the upper limits of human capacity and equipment capability. There was little margin to compensate for mistakes or just plain bad luck. Moreover, measures to reduce the risk factor could conceivably introduce new elements of risks.[37]

On balance, in analyzing the conclusions of the review group, it seems apparent that the airborne rescue mission was (1) conceptually sound, (2) technically feasible, and (3) a high-risk operation. Moreover, it was possibly the best alternative available to the Carter administration at the time. Why then did it fail? Here the conclusions of the review group provide further insight:

1. Throughout the planning and executing phases of the mission, decisions were made and actions taken or not taken because of operations security that the review group believed could have been done differently.

2. Command and control was excellent at the upper echelons, but became more tenuous and fragile at the intermediate levels. Further down the operational chain, command relationships were less well defined and not as well understood.

3. Planning was not adequate regarding the number of helicopters and the provisions for weather contingencies.

4. Preparation for the mission did not provide for comprehensive, full-scale training.[38]

In essence, according to the review group, the airborne rescue mission failed because of inadequate planning and organization on the part of the top-level decision makers. For example, instead of utilizing existing joint task force organizations, the Joint Chiefs of Staff started literally from the beginning to (1) establish a new joint task force organization, (2) find a commander, (3) provide a staff, (4) develop a plan, (5) select the units, and (6) train the forces before attaining even the most rudimentary mission readiness. Additionally, the review group concluded that many things that could have been done to enhance the success of the mission were not done because of operations security. The review group further concluded that had there been better planning, most of these measures could have been incorporated without compromising operations security.[39] In essence the decision makers proceeded with a computational strategy toward a maximized outcome as though they had complete knowledge of the principal cause-and-effect relationships of the mission. But, because of faulty planning and lack of organization, the decision makers had considerably less than complete knowledge of the key factors in a highly complex situation. The rescue attempt called for a judgmental strategy directed toward a satisficing outcome. The appropriate basis for follow-up and control is effective planning and organization that begins early in the decision-making process just after the objective is established and well before a given alternative is selected for implementation. Such was not the case in the Iranian hostage crisis, and the tragic consequences speak to this serious omission.

COMPARATIVE CASE DETERMINANTS OF STRATEGIC DECISION SUCCESS

Having analyzed and evaluated the Cuban missile crisis and the Iranian hostage crisis as individual cases, the comparative evaluation in this section is based on the determinants of decision success set forth in Trull's study of 100 organizations and further advanced by the Bay area study of 108 organizations. According to the foundations of these two studies, the success of a decision is a function of the quality of the decision and its implementation. Decision quality, in turn, is composed of (1) compatibility with operating constraints, (2) nearness to optimum time for the decision, (3) proximity to the optimum amount of information, and (4) the decision maker's influence on the decision. Decision implementation is a product of (1) a risk-reward factor and (2) the degree of understanding by those who must carry out the decision. These six factors make up the essence of the analysis and evaluation to follow.

Compatibility with Operating Constraints

Operating constraints refer to institutionalized policies and procedures associated with an established way of doing business. However, there was no precedent for the Cuban missile crisis. It was the first and, we hope, the last of its kind. Consequently, there were no institutionalized policies directly applicable to the decision-making process in this case. Obviously, there was also no established way of doing business. To be sure, the normal procedures of government were employed by the decision makers. But these procedures were designed for and applied to many events and happenings quite apart from the missile crisis. Therefore, this case presented no operating constraints to the decision makers, at least as that term is normally used.

In like manner, the Iranian hostage crisis occurred in a relatively non-institutionalized context. Policies and procedures of national governments are not designed to deal with the release of seized hostages. Moreover, in the interest of operations security, the airborne rescue mission was developed apart from existing intermediate-level joint service commands with coordination accomplished only at the level of the Joint Chiefs of Staff. The Iranian hostage crisis did not fit existing policy and procedure in either the military or the civilian sectors of the federal government. It was a unique and, it is hoped, nonrecurring event.

Nearness to Optimum Time

Decisions have an optimum time at which the maximum probability for success occurs. The relative success of a decision is therefore directly related to its timing.

Time was of the essence in the Cuban missile crisis. The need for action was apparent and the decision makers rose to the occasion. Exactly one week passed from the time that the Kennedy administration learned of the presence of offensive missiles in Cuba to the time a decision was made to impose a blockade around the island. Clearly the timing was optimum in this case.

In the case of the Iranian hostage crisis, the time constraints were also tight on the Carter administration. It is interesting to note that, as shown in the next chapter, the Carter administration obviously found it much easier to decide in favor of loan guarantees for Chrysler than to select an airborne rescue mission for the hostages. In fact during the five months from the seizure of the hostages to the implementation of the ill-fated rescue attempt, the Carter administration seemed unable to settle on a decisive course of action that would free the hostages. Moreover, given the five-month period taken by the administration to reach a decision, the lack of comprehensive planning and organization for the airborne rescue mission seems even more inexcusable. Clearly, Carter and the military chiefs went well beyond the optimum time in deciding to rescue the hostages.

Optimum Amount of Information

As mentioned earlier, the decision makers in the Cuban missile crisis operated with very limited and generally unreliable information. For a decision of this magnitude, the uncertainty stemming from imperfect information was indeed formidable. All things considered, the information at hand was considerably less than optimum. Still the decision makers were able to fashion a choice that was implemented successfully.

The situation in the Iranian hostage crisis was also difficult, albeit in the presence of less awesome consequences. The information available to the decision makers was incomplete, frequently inaccurate, and often untimely. Sources were of questionable reliability and the validity of so-called official information was often in doubt. The decision makers had too little of the right kind of information and were unable to use effectively what they did have. In fact, one reason the Iranian hostage crisis was not successfully resolved was that the decision makers proceeded as though they had a complete knowledge of cause-and-effect relationships when in fact they were operating with generally inadequate information.

Decision Maker's Influence

The decision in the Cuban missile crisis was made at the highest levels of government. President Kennedy and the other members of the Executive Committee were the only principals involved in the choice. The success of the final decision, in terms of its effective implementation and satisficing outcome, must be attributed largely to the top-level priority given the situation from beginning to end.

In like manner, the decision in the Iranian hostage crisis was also made by the commander-in-chief in consultation with his principal advisers. The final decision to proceed with an airborne rescue mission was made by President Carter, but his influence on the outcome of the decision was rather insignificant. In retrospect it is not too surprising that the mission failed. Indeed it may well be that President Carter's close personal involvement in all aspects of the decision-making process worked against a favorable outcome. Conceivably the military chiefs relied too heavily on Carter's involvement to ensure success, whereas he relied too heavily on their technical expertise to accomplish heroic deeds.

Risk-Reward Factor

There was considerable risk in the Cuban missile crisis. The uncertainty resulting from incomplete and unreliable information, combined with the awesome consequences of a mistake, created a decision-making situation of unprecedented risk. The decision makers clearly considered the risk-reward relationship in comparing and evaluating the alternatives at hand. For example, air strikes against the missile sites were rejected partly because the risk of killing Soviet personnel was too high; an invasion was rejected because it might have precipitated a third world war. Of course, the obvious immediate reward was removal of the missiles from Cuba. The decision makers chose to accept a lesser amount of risk in imposing a blockade around

Cuba. In their view, the probability of obtaining the reward through a blockade was at least equal to that offered by air strikes or an invasion. Further, this alternative carried considerably less risk of escalating the conflict into a third world war. Given the tremendous uncertainty confronting the decision makers in the Cuban missile crisis, their choice of a blockade reflected a strong appreciation of the risk-reward relationship in the situation.

The Iranian hostage crisis was fraught with risk. The uncertainty stemming from the political turmoil within Iran coupled with the normally volatile nature of Middle East politics heightened the explosive nature of the situation. Moreover, the continued attempts of the Soviet Union to assert its influence in Iran along with the concerns of European countries dependent on imports of Iranian oil exacerbated the uncertainty. Finally, the escalating expectations of the American public for positive, decisive, and successful action by the Carter administration to obtain a release of the hostages further heightened the extreme sensitivity of the situation. The reward was to free the hostages. The question was how much risk to assume in the process.

The airborne rescue mission was a conceptually sound, technically feasible alternative with a high-risk profile. It was risky because of the limited information available to the decision makers; it was risky because there was little margin for equipment failure and virtually no margin for human error; it was risky because of the need for a series of well-coordinated actions between groups and individuals who were specialists in something other than coordination; and it was risky because of the imponderables associated with the conditions of captivity of the hostages and the exact state of readiness of their captors.

The decision makers assumed the high risks attendant on the mission. Granted that hindsight holds its own brand of clarity, it appears that the risks were needlessly large in relation to the potential rewards. Conceivably additional planning and improved organization along with an expanded consideration of the alternatives would have resulted in a successful mission. But time was working against the decision makers. Five months had elapsed and something had to be done to free the hostages. Seemingly it was better to take some positive action rather than continue to be crucified by allegations of inaction. Still, there was no need to proceed against highly unfavorable odds when the correct use of the open decision-making process would have immeasurably improved the prospects for success.

Degree of Understanding

If the understanding of those who must carry out a decision or those who are affected by it is elicited, an outcome that will attain the original objective is more likely. Understanding can be obtained by involving those concerned in the decision-making process through participation or consultation.

Because of the confidential nature normally associated with national security matters, participation in the Cuban missile crisis was limited to a few individuals at the highest levels of the government. Those who needed to know were actively and continuously involved; those who did not need to know learned of the decision through official channels. In this case, there was no alternative. The success of the outcome depended considerably on the implementers understanding only what was necessary for them to carry out their respective responsibilities. All in all, it was well done.

Confidentiality was also essential to the success of the airborne rescue mission in the Iranian hostage crisis. Numerous actions were taken and decisions made within the constraint of operations security. The great fear was that any knowledge of the rescue attempt obtained by the Iranian captors would endanger the lives of the hostages. Indeed the emphasis on operations security tended to work against effective planning and organization of the mission. The insistence on restricting information only to those with a need to know at a high level of security clearance clearly limited the degree of understanding among many of those who were responsible for implementing the decision. In this case, there appeared to be no other way to proceed. Still the idea that greater participation in the decision-making process is conducive to greater understanding of the decision, which, in turn, leads to a more effectively implemented decision was not diminished by the need for confidentiality in the attempted rescue of the hostages. To the contrary, it appears that greater participation would have led to improved coordination, which would have improved the chances for the success of the mission.

When these two cases are evaluated in the context of Trull's conceptual framework and the Bay area study, it becomes readily apparent why the Cuban missile crisis resulted in a resounding success and the Iranian crisis culminated in a tragic failure. Both cases were decided at the highest levels of government. The unique nature of both cases precluded institutionalized policies and procedures from constituting any sort of operating constraint on the decision makers. The propitious timing of the decision in the Cuban missile crisis permitted the decision makers to capitalize fully on the opportunities available to them; whereas the delayed timing in the Iranian hostage crisis resulted in a rescue attempt that was too little and too late. The decision makers in both cases had to contend with imperfect information. In the Cuban missile crisis, the successful strategic choice reflects a best use of available information. Conversely, in the Iranian hostage crisis, the failed mission indicates a worst use of available information. The ultimate decision maker in both cases was the president of the United States. In the Cuban missile crisis, this influence generally manifested itself through the normal chain of command. In the Iranian hostage crisis the chain of command was bypassed through ongoing personal involvement that reflected presidential micromanagement. The decision makers in the Cuban missile crisis tempered the extreme risk in the situation by selecting a decisive course of action that could be gradually escalated. In the Iranian hostage crisis the decision makers assumed far more risk than was required to accomplish the mission simply because they did not allow any margin for error in the face of numerous constraints and unknowns. The degree of understanding by the decision implementers was readily apparent in the Cuban missile crisis.

Conversely, the break in the chain of command at the operating level in the Iranian hostage crisis directly contributed to mission failure. Strict confidentiality at the level of choice should not detract from clear understanding and effective coordination of activities at the level of implementation.

COMPARATIVE CASE CLASSIFICATIONS OF STRATEGIC DECISION SUCCESS

The comparative case classifications of strategic decision success are derived from the strategic decision matrix set forth in Figure 11.1. As shown in the figure, a given classification is a joint product of two sets of managerial attitudes. The first set is composed of managerial attitudes toward the decision-making process. Subsets here include (1) attainable objectives and an open decision-making process and (2) unattainable objectives and a closed decision-making process. The second set is composed of managerial attitudes toward the decision itself. Subsets here include (1) a judgmental decision-making strategy and a satisficing outcome and (2) a computational decision-making strategy and a maximized outcome. A Type A strategic decision is most likely to succeed because it is composed of attainable objectives developed in the open decision-making process that are pursued through a judgmental decision-making strategy in quest of a satisficing outcome. A Type D decision is unlikely to succeed because it is formulated on unattainable objectives conceived in the closed decision-making process that are sought through a computational decision-making strategy in pursuit of a maximized outcome. Types B and C are less likely to succeed because of their incompatible managerial attitudes. Type B, for example, negates a positive attitude toward the decision itself with a subset of unattainable objectives cast in the closed decision-making process. For its part, Type C reduces its prospects for realizing the benefits of attainable objectives developed in the open decision-making process by using a computational decision-making strategy in a futile quest for a maximized outcome.

Each case in this chapter and the next three chapters is analyzed in the context of the two sets of managerial attitudes set forth in Figure 11.1, and is then assigned a strategic decision classification. The two cases evaluated in each chapter are intended to illustrate the managerial attitudes and actions that resulted in strategic decision success and strategic decision failure. With one or two exceptions, these cases reflect a direct comparison between Type A and Type D classifications. Because of their incompatible characteristics, Types B and C are somewhat less suitable for educational purposes. It should be recalled, however, that changes in managerial attitudes can result in changes in classifications with attendant shifts in the prospects for strategic decision success. For this reason, any one of the four classifications may be justifiably assigned to a given case.

Managerial Attitudes Toward the Decision-Making Process

The overriding objective in the Cuban missile crisis was to remove the existing missiles and to keep any new missiles from arriving in Cuba. In the process of attaining this primary objective, the decision makers were mindful of other corollary objectives (see Table 12.1). Moreover, the decision makers proceeded in the open decision-making process limited by time and imperfect information and subject to a host of environmental constraints. In essence, they proceeded within the permeable parameters of bounded rationality (see Figure 3.1).

The primary objective in the Iranian hostage crisis was to rescue the hostages. Given the right managerial attitude toward the decision-making process, this objective was attainable. The constraints imposed on the decision makers by the normal limitations of bounded rationality along with the extraordinary complexity and sensitivity of the hostage situation demanded openness in decision making. Regrettably the decision makers proceeded to use the closed decision-making process with a general disregard or at least a diminution of environmental constraints. Consequently, an objective that might otherwise have been attainable was rendered unattainable.

Managerial Attitude Toward the Decision

In the Cuban missile crisis the decision makers tempered their strong preference for a successful outcome with an acceptance of limited knowledge regarding such an outcome. They internalized the high level of uncertainty in the total decision-making situation by adopting a judgmental decision-making strategy. By acknowledging and accepting the uncertainty associated with a preferred outcome, they oriented themselves toward a satisficing result; that is, one that would achieve the primary objective. Their choice of a blockade, which signified decisive but not irreversible action, in combination with their emphasis on attainability and openness in the decision-making process virtually guaranteed a successful strategic outcome. The Cuban missile crisis affords a landmark example of Type A strategic choice.

Even if the primary objective in the Iranian hostage crisis had been attainable in the closed decision-making process (which it was not), the uncertainty regarding the cause-and-effect relationships associated with a probable outcome still called for a judgmental rather than a computational strategy and for a satisficing rather than a maximizing outcome. In effect, a computational strategy was imposed on an unattainable objective in a futile quest for a maximized outcome. Actually, in the Iranian hostage crisis, the decision makers waited too long to use the wrong approach to make the wrong decision. This case affords a tragic example of incorrect managerial attitudes toward both the process and the decision itself. It is, therefore, a classic Type D strategic choice.

SUMMARY

This chapter presented the first of four sets of comparative case evaluations using the frameworks and concepts presented in this book.

The Cuban missile crisis was presented as the epitomy of a Type A strategic decision. The decision makers in this case performed admirably under extreme time and environmental constraints. They evoked an attainable primary objective that, along with a set of corollary objectives, was attainable in the open decision-making process. The decision makers also observed the determinants of strategic decision success with a particularly laudatory appreciation of timing, optimum levels of information, influence of the decision maker, risk-reward factor, and degree of understanding by the decision implementers. Using a judgmental decision-making strategy the decision makers in the Cuban missile crisis produced a satisficing outcome thereby justifying a Type A designation for their landmark strategic success.

The decision makers in the Iranian hostage crisis were not prepared to make a choice. Given their managerial attitudes toward the process and the decision itself, complete success in rescuing the hostages was most unlikely. As they proceeded through a closed decision-making process, they rendered their primary objective increasingly unattainable. Failure was assured through an ill-advised attempt to obtain a maximized outcome by using a computational decision-making strategy.

The Iranian hostage crisis demanded a decision that was action-oriented and one that would be successful. Action was forthcoming; but success eluded the decision makers. In this crisis, the United States expected its leadership to take decisive and timely action to obtain the release of the hostages. Instead the Carter administration procrastinated for five months after the hostages were seized. Finally, when it became apparent that only a military option would accomplish the objective, Carter and the military chiefs selected an alternative of heroic proportions which, as is so often the case, failed in the breach. The decision makers in the Iranian hostage crisis also fell short in virtually every one of the determinants of strategic decision set forth in the Trull study and the Bay area study. On balance, this case is a tragic landmark of a strategic decision failure, and, as such, is the epitomy of a Type D strategic decision.

REVIEW AND DISCUSSION QUESTIONS

1. What were the major objectives of the Soviet Union in its decision to place offensive missiles in Cuba? Discuss.

2. The decision making of the Executive Committee in the Cuban missile crisis took place in the presence of several constraints. What were these constraints?

3. In what ways did the constraints in the Cuban missile crisis influence the choice of a blockade? Discuss.

4. What evidence shows that the decision makers in the Cuban missile crisis were using a judgmental decision-making strategy to obtain a satisficing outcome?

5. How did the Executive Committee deal with the risk-reward factor in the Cuban missile crisis?

6. What were the principal constraints in the Iranian hostage crisis? How did the decision makers deal with them?

7. In what specific ways is the Iranian hostage crisis a particularly good example of a Type D strategic decision?

8. Develop a scenario in which you consider the alternative of an airborne rescue mission in the open decision-making process using a judgmental decision-making strategy to obtain a satisficing outcome. Compare this scenario with the actual case.

9. Which one of the determinants of strategic decision success was particularly good in the Cuban missile crisis and particularly bad in the Iranian hostage crisis? Justify your answer.

10. Could the Iranian hostage crisis have been avoided? How? Discuss.

NOTES

1. Robert A. Divine, ed., *The Cuban Missile Crisis* (Chicago: Quadrangle, 1971), p. 3.
2. Roger Hilsman, *To Move a Nation* (New York: Delta, 1967), p. 159.
3. Graham T. Allison, "Conceptual Models and the Cuban Missile Crisis," *American Political Science Review* (September 1969), 692.
4. Arthur M. Schlesinger, Jr., *A Thousand Days* (Boston: Houghton Mifflin, 1965), pp. 796–797.
5. Hilsman, *To Move a Nation*, p. 165.
6. Ibid.
7. Ibid., p. 159.
8. Ibid., p. 165.
9. Ibid., p. 202.
10. Allison, "Conceptual Models and the Cuban Missile Crisis," p. 713.
11. Ibid., pp. 696–697.
12. Ibid., p. 697.
13. Divine, *The Cuban Missile Crisis*, p. 19.
14. Allison, "Conceptual Models and the Cuban Missile Crisis," p. 687.
15. Hilsman, *To Move a Nation*, p. 196.
16. Allison, "Conceptual Models and the Cuban Missile Crisis," p. 698.
17. Ibid., p. 696.
18. Hilsman, *To Move a Nation*, p. 215.
19. Ibid., p. 226.
20. See "Key Events in U.S.–Iranian Relations . . . During 444-Day Hostage Crisis," *Congressional Quarterly Almanac*, Vol. 36, 1980 (Washington, D.C.: Congressional Quarterly, 1981), pp. 352–353.
21. Jimmy Carter, *Keeping Faith*. (New York: Bantam Books, 1982), p. 506.
22. Kenneth H. Bacon, "U.S. Alternatives in Iran," *Wall Street Journal* (April 18, 1980), p. 20.
23. Edward Heath, "'Recipe for Catastrophe,'" *New York Times* (May 4, 1980), E 23.
24. Carter, *Keeping Faith*, p. 466.
25. Ibid.
26. David R. Griffiths, "Options on Iran Considered Slim," *Aviation Week & Space Technology* (December 10, 1979), 16.
27. Drew Middleton, "Going the Military Route," *New York Times Magazine* (May 17, 1981), 103.

28. Carter, *Keeping Faith*, p. 461.
29. Zbigniew Brzezinski, *Power and Principle* (New York: Farrar, Straus & Giroux, 1983), p. 488.
30. Carter, *Keeping Faith*, p. 504.
31. Ibid., pp. 507–508.
32. Brzezinski, *Power and Principle*, pp. 490–491.
33. Ibid., p. 495.
34. Carter, *Keeping Faith*, p. 507.

35. Ibid., p. 509.
36. Ibid., p. 518.
37. "Review Group's Conclusions Reported," *Aviation Week & Space Technology* (September 29, 1980), 90–91.
38. Ibid., p. 91.
39. Ibid.

SUPPLEMENTAL REFERENCES

Allison, Graham F. *Essence of Decision: Explaining the Cuban Missile Crisis*. Boston: Little, Brown, 1971.

Allyn, Bruce J., James G. Blight, and David A. Welch. "Essence of Revision: Moscow, Havana, and the Cuban Missile Crisis." *International Security*, 14 (Winter 1989/1990), 136–172.

Anderson, Paul A. "Decision Making by Objection and the Cuban Missile Crisis." *Administrative Science Quarterly* (June 1983), 201–222.

Bernstein, Barton J. "The Cuban Missile Crisis: Trading the Jupiters in Turkey?" *Political Science Quarterly*, 95 (1980), 97–125.

Burt, Richard. "Report Charges 'Major' Mistakes on Iran Mission." *New York Times* (June 6, 1986), 188.

Crane, Robert D. "The Cuban Missile Crisis: A Strategic Analysis of American and Soviet Policy." *Orbis* (Winter 1963), 528–563.

"Debacle in the Desert." *Time* (May 5, 1980), 12ff.

"Defense Dept. Issues Detailed Analysis." *Aviation Week & Space Technology* (May 19, 1980), 91–94.

Gabriel, Major R. A. "A Commando Operation that Was Wrong from the Start: The U.S. Rescue Mission Into Iran, April 1980." *Canadian Defense Quarterly*, 10 (Winter 1980–1981), 6–10.

Garthoff, Raymond L. *Reflections on the Cuban Missile Crisis*. Washington, D.C.: Brookings, 1987.

Hadley, Arthur F. *The Straw Giant*. New York: Random House, 1986.

Herek, Gregory M., Irving L. Janis, and Paul Hurth. "Decision Making During International Crises." *Journal of Conflict Resolution* (June 1987), 203–226.

Herek, Gregory M., Irving L. Janis, and Paul Hurth. "Quality of U.S. Decision Making During the Cuban Missile Crisis." *Journal of Conflict Resolution* (September 1989), 446–459.

Hilsman, Roger. "The Cuban Missile Crisis: How Close We Were to War." *Look* (August 25, 1964), 17–21.

Holsti, Ole R. "Time, Alternatives, and Communications: The 1914 and Cuban Missile Crises." In *International Crises: Insights from Behavioral Research*. Ed. Charles F. Hermann. New York: Free Press, 1972, pp. 58–80.

Horelick, Arnold L. "The Cuban Missile Crisis." *World Politics*, 16 (1964), 363–389. "The Jimmy Carter Desert Classic." *New Republic* (May 10, 1980), 7–9.

Jordan, Hamilton. *Crisis: The Last Year of the Carter Presidency*. New York: Putnam, 1982.

Larson, David L. *The "Cuban Crisis" of 1962*. 2nd ed. Lanham, Md.: University Press of America, Inc., 1986.

"The Lessons of the Cuban Missile Crisis." *Time* (September 27, 1982), 85.

Maoz, Zeev. "The Decision to Raid Entebbe." *Journal of Conflict Resolution* (December 1981), 677–707.

Nathan, James A. "The Missile Crisis: His Finest Hour Now." *World Politics*, 27 (1975), 256–281.

Neustadt, Richard E., and Ernest R. May. *Thinking in Time: The Uses of History for Decision Makers*. New York: Free Press, 1986.

Saaty, Thomas L. *Decision Making for Leaders*. Belmont, Calif.: Wadsworth, 1982.

Salinger, Pierre. *America Held Hostage*. New York: Doubleday, 1981.

———. *With Kennedy*. New York: Doubleday, 1966.

Scott, Alexander. "The Lessons of the Iranian Raid for American Military Policy." *Armed Forces Journal International* (June 1980), 26ff.

Sick, Gary. *All Fall Down*. New York: Random House, 1985.

Smith, Steve. "Groupthink and the Hostage Rescue Mission." *British Journal of Political Science*, 15 (1985), 117–126.

Steinberg, Blema S. "Shame and Humiliation in the Cuban Missile Crisis." *Political Psychology*, 12 (1991), 653–690.

Strasser, Steve, et al. "A Grim Postmortem Begins." *Newsweek* (May 12, 1980), 29ff.

"Tragedy in the Desert — Rescue That Failed." *U.S. News & World Report* (May 5, 1980), 6–7.

U.S. Congress, House, Committee on Foreign Affairs. *Use of U.S. Armed Forces in Attempted Rescue of Hostages in Iran*. Communication from the President of the United States, 96th Congress, 2nd Session, April 26, 1980. Washington, D.C.: U.S. Government Printing Office, 1980.

U.S. Congress, Senate, Committee on Foreign Relations. *The Situation in Iran*. Hearings, 96th Congress, 2nd Session, May 8, 1980. Washington, D.C.: U.S. Government Printing Office, 1980.

Welch, David A. "Crisis Decision Making Reconsidered." *Journal of Conflict Resolution* (September 1989), 430–445.

Wohlstetter, Roberta. "Cuba and Pearl Harbor: Hindsight and Foresight." *Foreign Affairs* (July 1965), 691–707.

Wohlstetter, Roberta, and Albert Wohlstetter. "Controlling the Risk in Cuba." *Adelphi Papers* (April 1965), 3–24.

CHAPTER THIRTEEN

Case Set No. 2: The Chrysler Bailout Decision and the Challenger *Disaster*

*T*his chapter continues the presentation of cases that demonstrate the managerial attitudes toward the decision-making process and toward the decision itself that are most likely to result in strategic decision success. This chapter also continues to illustrate the empirical use of selected evaluative frameworks and concepts advanced at various places in this book.

The first case in this chapter — the Chrysler bailout decision — affords an excellent example of the influence of the environment on a strategic decision that was crucial to the survival of one of America's largest corporations. In the late 1970s, Chrysler seemed destined for bankruptcy; in the late 1990s Chrysler is stronger than it has ever been. In the nearly twenty years since the decision was made by the federal government to bail out the Chrysler Corporation, the company has weathered some difficult times, but always on the road to higher levels of improvement. In 1997 Chrysler was designated one of America's best-managed companies. At no time in its history has Chrysler been so admired and successful. Clearly the decision made by the Carter administration in 1980 to rescue Chrysler was the right decision made in the right way. In fact, Chrysler's turnaround from imminent bankruptcy to ongoing success is one of the marvels of U.S. capitalism in the twentieth century. (Note: See the 1996 annual report of Chrysler for tangible evidence of this exemplary performance.)

The second case in this chapter is an example of a different kind of strategic decision. It was a decision made at a specific moment in time in which the catastrophic consequences were immediately manifest to the decision makers. Contrary to many strategic choices that unfold gradually at the top of the organization over some period of time, this decision was tragically apparent to the entire organization and the world within seconds of its making. It is considered strategic because of its potentially significant consequences which, at the time, threatened to retard the entire program for the U.S. exploration of outer space. It is also considered strategic because of its complexity borne of an advanced technology that makes each application a state-of-the-art experience. This second case is, of course, the *Challenger* disaster, a decision that we need to examine in full detail if only to preclude its calamitous recurrence.

Since 1986 there has been no disaster in NASA's space program. It would be easy to believe that the *Challenger* catastrophe left an indelible impression on the minds of NASA's decision makers. However, there is little tangible evidence to support this belief. Indications are that NASA is more cautious in its launch decisions; but this caution can always be subordinated to some higher priority. There is a discernible tendency in NASA to render activities and programs operational as soon as possible. For NASA the operational mode means that quantitative criteria tend to justify the decision at hand. This inclination toward a quantitative mind-set contributes directly to a search for maximized results in the closed decision-making process using a computational strategy. This, of course, is the mind-set that gave rise to the *Challenger* disaster. Hopefully, NASA will move toward an open decision-making process in quest of satisficing outcomes in its future space endeavors.

In keeping with the general format for these case chapters, the significant events surrounding each case will be presented in sufficient detail to facilitate understanding of the critical factors and relationships in the decision-making situation. Subsequently, these events will be related to each major step in the decision-making process. Each case will then be analyzed and evaluated using conceptual frameworks selected especially to fit the profile of the case. The general approach to each case evaluation will use essentially the same evaluative frameworks and concepts with a special provision for significant variation in case profiles. For example, because of its corporate strategic orientation, the Chrysler bailout decision will feature a short analysis of the company's strategic gap at the height of its difficulty in 1978. In the case of the *Challenger* disaster, a singular confluence of events negates the need for a chronology of significant events. Actually, the focus of the *Challenger* disaster is characterized by a highly concentrated sequence of occurrences that developed and disappeared with catastrophic rapidity. Hopefully, this case evaluation will preserve the lesson of *Challenger* as a deterrent for any subsequent calamity of similar proportions.

Both of these cases will be evaluated comparatively using the determinants for strategic decision success developed in Trull's study and the Bay area study as well as the classification for strategic decision success set forth in Figure 11.1. These evaluations are intended to demonstrate that successful strategic decisions invariably ensue from managerial attitudes embodying the right approach to the decision-making process and the right attitude toward the decision itself. As noted elsewhere in this book, this purpose suggests the need to pursue attainable objectives through the open decision-making process using a judgmental decision-making strategy in quest of satisficing outcomes.

THE CHRYSLER BAILOUT DECISION: A PERSPECTIVE

By the middle of 1979, the Chrysler Corporation was on the brink of financial disaster. Chrysler was the fourteenth largest company in America and a key partner in the powerful automobile industry — the nation's largest private employer and consumer of steel, glass, and rubber. If immediate substantial assistance of an extraordinary nature was not forthcoming, bankruptcy seemed inevitable. A principal manifestation of Chrysler's dire straits was its chronic financial problems. Chrysler had a high proportion of debt to equity, which, in the event of a decline in sales, exerted substantial downward pressure on profits. The company's perennial difficulties in maintaining adequate cash flow was attributable to numerous bad management practices. Chrysler's creditors were becoming increasingly disenchanted with the company's poor financial performance and its dim prospects for near-term future improvement. Key financial facts about Chrysler in mid-1979 included:

Total assets	$7 billion
Total liabilities	$4 billion
Share of new-car market	9.3% in 1979, compared with 16.1% in 1970
Sales	$8.9 billion for first nine months of 1979, compared with $9.6 billion in 1978
Earnings	Loss of $721.5 million in the first nine months of 1979; projected loss of $2.3 billion during 1978–1980; last profitable year: 1977[1]

Chrysler's management and supporters offered a broad spectrum of justifiable reasons for the company's plight. For example, Lee Iacocca was quick to point out the financial impact on Chrysler of complying with federal government regulations. As the smallest company of the so-called Big Three, Chrysler seemed most affected by the increasing encroachments of the government. In particular, Chrysler's management alleged that it was adversely affected by:

1. *The Clean Air Act of 1963* (amended in 1970 and 1977), which mandated the amount of pollutants that cars could emit

2. *The National Traffic and Motor Vehicle Safety Act of 1966*, which imposed certain safety standards on all American auto makers

3. *The Energy and Policy Conservation Act of 1975*, which mandated that by 1985 all automobile fleets must meet an average gasoline consumption standard of 27.5 miles per gallon

Although these legislative acts applied to all three major auto makers, Chrysler's management argued that the cost of compliance was unreasonable and unequal in its effect. Lee Iacocca alleged that a good part of Chrysler's financial problems resulted from the need to raise massive amounts of new capital to meet federal law.

Another significant factor in Chrysler's perennial shortage of cash stemmed from its unprofitable investments in the European automobile industry under its former chief executive officer, Lynn Townsend. Chrysler's investments in the French and English automobile industries in the late 1950s and early 1960s acted as a continuous drain on corporate liquidity; its overseas ventures were never successful. In its foreign operations, the firm had an unerring instinct for doing the wrong thing at the wrong time.

Even the most sympathetic of Chrysler's diminishing cadre of supporters acknowledged the overall mismanagement of the company. In fact, Chrysler had a well-deserved reputation for bad management. Consider, for example, some of the impressions of Lee Iacocca upon assuming office as Chrysler's president and chief operating officer in 1978:

> What I found at Chrysler was thirty-five vice presidents, each with his own turf. There was no real committee setup, no cement in the organizational chart, no system of meetings to get people talking to each other. . . . All of Chrysler's problems really boiled down to the same thing: nobody knew who was on first. There was no team, only a collection of independent players, many of whom hadn't yet mastered their positions. . . . Chrysler couldn't blame its condition on its founder, who came from another era. The Chrysler fiasco had occurred after thirty years of postwar, scientific management. That in 1978 a huge company could still be run like a small grocery store was incomprehensible. These problems didn't develop overnight. In Detroit auto circles, Chrysler's reputation had been sinking for years. The place became known as a last resort: if somebody couldn't hack it elsewhere, he could always go to Chrysler.[2]

Under the leadership of Iacocca in 1979, Chrysler was in the process of revitalizing its entire organizational structure. Positions at all levels of management were being eliminated and consolidated as part of a massive effort to reduce costs and save the company. As Iacocca graphically stated the case: "I had to get rid of the many people who didn't know what they were doing. . . . I needed a good team of experienced people who could work with me in turning this company around before it completely fell apart. My highest priority was to put that team together before it was too late."[3] When the very survival of a company is in doubt, it is obviously difficult to think beyond the next payroll or perhaps the next fiscal year. Such was the case at Chrysler in late 1979.

The external environment at Chrysler seemed increasingly hostile in 1979. To be sure, all the members of the Big Three were affected by the potential threat of a seemingly imminent recession in the presence of uncontrollable inflation, particularly for fuel costs. Foreign competition was taking a larger and larger share of a slow growth market for automobile sales in America. Government regulation kept additional pressures on costs, straining breakeven points and reducing the prospects for near-term profitability.

Chrysler seemed to suffer more than General Motors or Ford. Perhaps the internal reorganization under the leadership of Iacocca exacerbated Chrysler's misery in mid-1979. Perhaps the sins of omission and commission under a legacy of mismanagement contributed to Chrysler's seemingly endless panorama of problems, concerns, and imminent disaster. Perhaps it was the continuing intrusions of the federal government into the affairs of the automobile industry through various pieces of environmental legislation. Perhaps Chrysler's chronic misfortune was attributable to its status as the third banana in an industry dominated by General Motors with Ford in second place. The top management at Chrysler was undoubtedly frustrated and dismayed over the abysmal state of internal affairs. The lack of internal strength heightened Chrysler's inability to cope with the dynamics of an increasingly turbulent external environment.

Thus, Chrysler's management was confronted by at least four environmental threats in 1979: (1) increasing intrusions by the federal government into the specifications for the manufacture of trucks and automobiles, (2) emerging dependency on the federal government for assistance in the event of substantial economic adversity, (3) continuing dominance of the market for trucks and automobiles by General Motors with Chrysler following the leader to the point that it had no distinctive competence of its own, and (4) increasing competition from overseas sources, which Chrysler seemed unable to offset to its economic advantage. In late 1979 Chrysler was unable to identify and capitalize on these external threats. Immediate improvement was necessary if the company were to stay in business.

Table 13.1 contains a chronology of significant events in the Chrysler bailout decision. As shown in the table, Chrysler's management began lobbying the Carter administration early in 1978, or eighteen months before the formal request for a fiscal rescue on July 31, 1979. It seemed almost as if John J. Riccardo's statement that the company would lose $2.5 billion between 1978 and 1980 was a self-fulfilling prophecy. Chrysler's request for federal rescue evoked a storm of dissent from many leading corporate executives and numerous conservative ideologues. After some initial, short-lived objections to Chrysler's request, the administration succumbed to the political, economic, and social pressures. Congress held numerous hearings and finally acted favorably on the administration's proposal to assist Chrysler. Less than five months after its formal request for rescue from the brink of bankruptcy, Chrysler's bailout was a fait accompli. Clearly Chrysler and its supporters deserve high marks for political effectiveness and legislative expediency.

THE STRATEGIC GAP AT CHRYSLER

From the preceding perspective on Chrysler, the nature of the strategic gap for the entire corporation in 1978 must be readily apparent. Still it may be instructive to put this bleak perspective into a meaningful focus.

TABLE 13.1   The Chrysler Bailout Decision: Significant Events

Date	Event
February 1, 1978–July 30, 1979	John J. Riccardo, chairman and chief executive officer of the Chrysler Corporation, lobbied key officials in the Carter administration for various forms of financial relief.
November 2, 1978	Lee Iacocca joined Chrysler as president and chief operating officer.
July 31, 1979	John J. Riccardo formally requested the federal government to rescue Chrysler. It was apparent that the company would lose approximately $2.5 billion during the 1978–1980 period.
July 31, 1979	Chrysler requested a $1.0 billion advance from the U.S. Treasury to be applied to tax credits earned in future years and a delay in meeting federal air-pollution and fuel-efficiency standards.
August 2–5, 1979	The nation's leading newspapers (*New York Times, Wall Street Journal, Washington Post,* and *Los Angeles Times*) editorialized about a financial bailout for Chrysler.
August 2, 1979	Thomas A. Murphy, chairman of General Motors, publicly opposed financial assistance to Chrysler from the federal government.
August 10, 1979	G. William Miller, secretary of the treasury, publicly opposed financial support for Chrysler. Secretary Miller said the administration would consider loan guarantees for Chrysler if the company came up with a suitable financial plan.
September 15, 1979	Chrysler submitted a revised rescue package to the Carter administration requesting one-third of the needed $2.1 billion with the remainder to come from outside sources.
October 19–December 18, 1979	Extended hearings took place in the U.S. Congress regarding the need and form of financial assistance for Chrysler.
October 25, 1979	Chrysler and the United Auto Workers agreed to a $1.3 billion wage pact over the next three years.

(*continued on next page*)

TABLE 13.1 (*continued*)

Date	Event
November 1, 1979	The Carter administration proposed to Congress a $1.5 billion package of guaranteed loans for Chrysler, conditioned on matching concessions from Chrysler's banks, stockholders, dealers, suppliers, and employees, as well as other levels of government.
December 18, 1979	The U.S. House of Representatives approved the Chrysler Corporation Loan Guarantee Act of 1979 (vote: 241–124).
December 19, 1979	The U.S. Senate approved the Chrysler Corporation Loan Guarantee Act of 1979 (vote: 43–34).
December 21, 1979	Senate and House conferees approved a $3.5 billion aid package for the ailing Chrysler Corporation. The bill was cleared for President Carter's signature.
December 31, 1979	Chrysler reported a net loss for 1979 of $1.1 billion.
January 7, 1980	President Jimmy Carter signed the Chrysler Corporation Loan Guarantee Act of 1979 into law. The act called for $1.5 billion in guaranteed loans and $2.0 billion of matching funds to be provided by Chrysler's stakeholders.
June 24, 1980	Chrysler took down $.5 billion of guaranteed loans.
July 31, 1980	Chrysler took down $.3 billion of guaranteed loans.
December 31, 1980	Chrysler reported a net loss for 1980 of $1.7 billion.
February 2, 1981	Chrysler took down $.4 billion of guaranteed loans.
December 31, 1981	Chrysler reported a net loss of $.5 billion for 1981.
December 31, 1982	Chrysler reported a net loss of $69 million for 1982.
June 1983	Chrysler repaid $1.2 billion in federally guaranteed loans.
December 31, 1983	Chrysler reported a net profit of $.5 billion for 1983.

Organizational Assessment

The purpose of an organizational assessment is to ascertain the overall capabilities of the organization in the critical areas of (1) management, (2) technology, (3) policies, and (4) resources. This assessment involves ascertaining specific strengths and weaknesses in each of the critical areas and combining them into a composite balance designated a *capability profile*. The capability profile indicates whether management should concentrate on internal improvements to translate weaknesses into strengths or whether there are enough strengths in the critical areas to permit the organization to exploit existing opportunities and cope with actual threats in the external environment.

In the case of Chrysler, all of the critical areas manifested serious weaknesses. For example, Chrysler's management had achieved a high level of incompetence well before Iacocca's arrival on the scene in late 1978. Chrysler was regarded as the worst managed company in the automotive industry. Insofar as technology is concerned, Chrysler's engineering and production operations were well behind those of General Motors and Ford. Expenditures for research and development were virtually nonexistent and new product development was minimal at best. Chrysler's policies tended to follow the other domestic automobile companies. In areas such as human resources and finance, Chrysler lagged well behind the rest of the industry. In the area of resources, Chrysler's situation was equally dismal. Human resources were overstaffed and less than productive; fiscal resources were in short supply exacerbated by the company's inadequate cash flow and low credit rating; physical resources were badly maintained, underutilized, and bordering on obsolescence; and Chrysler's image and reputation was generally negative. On balance, at the time of Iacocca's arrival at Chrysler, the company was characterized by serious weaknesses in all the critical areas of capability. Chrysler was teetering on the edge of bankruptcy.

Environmental Assessment

Environmental assessment focuses primarily on opportunities and threats in the external domain of the organization. Chrysler's internal weaknesses were so pervasive that the company was literally precluded from exploiting any opportunities in the external environment. As noted earlier in this chapter, Chrysler was unable to protect itself from domestic and foreign competitors and was generally unable to comply with a variety of government regulations for the production of its automobiles and trucks. Essentially, Chrysler's dysfunctional internal weaknesses rendered the company vulnerable to a host of adverse environmental influences.

Gap Analysis

Chrysler's situation in late 1978 may be accurately characterized as a large negative strategic gap. The company was literally at the mercy of its external environment. The situation called for immediate internal corrective action to stop the fiscal hemorrhaging of the company and to reconstitute the corporation with a view toward its long-term survival. Seldom has the management of any organization confronted a challenge of the magnitude faced by Lee Iacocca and his management team in late 1978. This was the time to rescue Chrysler from bankruptcy through timely and open managerial decision making.

THE DECISION-MAKING PROCESS IN THE CHRYSLER BAILOUT DECISION

The Objectives

The first and foremost objective was to save the Chrysler Corporation. Chrysler was too important to the regional economy of Detroit and, to a lesser extent, the economy of the nation. It could not be allowed to fail. There are too many constituencies and too many stakeholders at risk when a corporation of Chrysler's size and importance begins to fail. Its sheer size begets a widespread vested interest in its survival. The Darwinian aspects of capitalism begin and end in the atomistic milieu of small business. This is an exception to the conventional wisdom of classical economics.

Another objective was that any assistance provided to Chrysler should not constitute an example. Capitalism must be preserved, and the public and private sectors must be kept separate. The private ownership of the means of production must not become subservient to or partners with the governance mechanisms of the total society. Clearly this potential contamination of capitalism was an objective in name only. In the fifteen years preceding Chrysler's request for assistance, other large organizations, both profit and nonprofit, had received aid from the federal government — for example, Penn Central, Lockheed, Consolidated Rail Corporation, and New York City.[4] The objective to save Chrysler, then, was not unprecedented. It was appropriate that it be judged on its intrinsic merits.

There were at least four principal reasons advanced by Chrysler's management and its stakeholders as to why the company should be saved:

1. *Jobs.* According to a Department of Transportation study, Chrysler provided 119,500 direct jobs and 292,000 indirect jobs (through dealers and suppliers) for a total of 411,500 jobs. If all these people were thrown out of work, they would cut back on their purchases, which would in turn affect more jobs. One worst-case scenario claimed that, assuming a total Chrysler shutdown, 500,000 direct and indirect jobs would be lost temporarily and about 200,000 permanently.[5]

2. *Competition.* Chrysler should be saved from bankruptcy in order to preserve competition in the automobile business. The argument here was that a Big Three is oligopolistic enough. The disappearance of one would be the death knell of competition in the industry. In testimony before Congress on November 14, 1979, Chrysler's chief executive officer, Lee Iacocca, noted that "we need domestic competition. I don't want an auto industry of only two firms. We need at least three."[6]

3. *Federal regulations.* Chrysler's problems, some said, were not of its own making but rather were attributable to federal regulations calling for cars that would produce less air pollution, would be safer, and would have greater fuel efficiency. Chrysler argued that a smaller company has to spend as much as a larger one to develop the technology to meet federal

requirements. But since Chrysler makes so many fewer cars than General Motors, the unit cost of that technology is much higher, putting Chrysler at a competitive disadvantage in the marketplace.[7] Presumably, therefore, because the federal government was a primary cause of Chrysler's crisis, the Carter administration should support some form of financial assistance to equalize the burden of excessive regulation among the Big Three.

4. *The economy.* It was assumed that a Chrysler failure would have substantial adverse economic effects on the country. An analysis of the economic impact of a Chrysler shutdown made by the staff of the Treasury Department revealed the following potential adverse economic consequences: (a) a reduction in the gross national product (GNP) in nominal terms in 1980 by about $4 billion or .15 percent and by about $6 billion or .2 percent in 1981; (b) an increase in the federal budget deficit of $1 billion in 1980 and $1.75 billion in 1981; (c) a loss of assumed output to foreign producers in the amount of 200,000 subcompacts and 50,000 other motor vehicles with adverse effects on the U.S. balance of payments; and (d) substantial adverse unemployment effects on the city of Detroit, the state of Michigan, and other states in which Chrysler's plants were operating; most of these areas already had appreciable unemployment.[8]

By almost any reckoning, Chrysler should be saved. The question was how to accomplish this objective.

The Search for Alternatives

The search for alternatives in the Chrysler bailout decision took place within a context of bounded rationality. The primary objective was apparent, but there were limitations placed on the primary decision makers — the U.S. Congress and the president of the United States.

The environment was characterized by a high level of turbulence. The Carter administration was confronted with an impending recession in the presence of an inflationary price spiral. Increasing foreign competition was placing new pressures on the balance of payments. Pockets of high unemployment among minority groups where Chrysler's plants were located added a social dimension to the complexity of the environment. Lobbying by Chrysler's executives, officials from the United Auto Workers, and political and social figures from Detroit and Michigan quickly attained sizable proportions. Congressional hearings were numerous, intense, and prolonged during the fall of 1979. The U.S. Congress was buffeted continuously by forces favorable to Chrysler's request for assistance. There were numerous advocates and few detractors of government assistance. Senator William Proxmire, an opponent of Chrysler's bailout, noted the paucity of dissent:

> Who is going to say that to bail out Chrysler would be a precedent that would haunt our system for many years to come as businesses lose the courage to accept the consequences of their mistakes? The answer: Virtually no one. . . . In fact, all the power, all the money, all the skilled lobbyists, all the labor clout

and business clout and banking clout, plus the force of hundreds of thousands of Americans who have an immediate stake in the decision, are on one side. The Chrysler bailout can't lose. But the American taxpayer can and will.[9]

Added to this environmental turbulence and complexity was some uncertainty regarding the outcome of assistance provided to Chrysler. Possibly, as Senator Proxmire believed, bankruptcy was the only realistic alternative. Moreover, there was considerable doubt that Chrysler could be saved in the absence of massive infusions of federal assistance, which was, of course, antithetical to the capitalist ethos. A detailed study of Chrysler by the Transportation Department indicated that even with federal aid, the company might remain in a precarious financial position.[10]

On the other hand, Congress was inundated with studies, statements, and scenarios dealing with the potentially adverse consequences of a Chrysler failure. There was, if anything, far too much information, mostly in favor of support to the ailing auto maker. Congress was suffering from information overload, which stretched the cognitive limitations of the lawmakers. Still it was less a matter of deciding whether to aid Chrysler than it was how and for how long. The fact of aid seemed virtually assured; only its form and duration were in doubt.

Another major constraint in the Chrysler bailout decision was time. There was a high sense of urgency, if not desperation, continually conveyed to Congress by Chrysler's management. It was as though the federal government were expected to remedy immediately a financial crisis that had been years in the making. Chrysler's numerous constituents and stakeholders also bombarded Congress with pleas for assistance, coupled with predictions of the calamitous consequences if the company were not helped. Cost, too, was a constraint in the search for alternatives. The company's request for tax credits and delays in complying with federal legislation was rejected by the administration. Chrysler's initial formal request for loan guarantees was rejected and then resubmitted to the administration in revised form. It was apparent that Congress was sensitive to its responsibility to safeguard the taxpayers' dollars. It was also apparent that whatever aid was forthcoming from the federal government would have to be at least matched by Chrysler's constituencies and stakeholders. Those who had a direct or indirect financial interest in the survival of the company were expected to reduce the financial participation of the public to minimal proportions.

The political nature and potential economic consequences of the decision before Congress imposed considerable environmental pressure on the decision makers. Taking no action was not a feasible alternative; a temporizing action promised little political acceptance and improbable economic benefits; only a positive action directed toward restoring the long-term health of Chrysler seemed acceptable under the circumstances.

In summary, cost was a significant factor; time was perceived to be of the essence; cognitive limitations of the decision makers were strained by information overload; and the environment was highly politicized and turbulent.

Clearly the situation called for a satisficing decision in the open decision-making process. The decision makers were operating in a condition of bounded rationality.

The Comparison and Evaluation of Alternatives

The decision makers in Congress and the administration considered several alternatives, but some of them were alternatives in name only. Nonetheless it is useful to review all of the possibilities considered by the decision makers if only to better assess the final choice. Six alternatives were considered:

1. *Do nothing.* This was an alternative in name only. The arguments for a do-nothing response failed for at least two reasons: (a) they grossly underestimated the political power of Chrysler and its supporters, and (b) they disregarded the potentially adverse economic consequences of letting Chrysler drift and very possibly fail.

2. *Bankruptcy.* Several influential figures, including Senator Proxmire, believed that Chrysler should be encouraged to go into bankruptcy. In Proxmire's words:

> What would bankruptcy mean? Would [Chrysler] evaporate overnight, leaving its plants idle and rusting, its workers, dealers and suppliers out on the street? . . . Under the [bankruptcy] law, the company goes to court to file for bankruptcy and gets an automatic stay of its debts while it tries to work out with its creditors a plan for getting back on the job. . . . What [bankruptcy] really means is a chance to save the healthy elements of a company, to give it a fresh start.[11]

Chrysler's management proffered numerous arguments against bankruptcy as a viable alternative for the company. Most of the arguments graphically depicted worst-case scenarios intended to evoke sympathy for the company's plight.

The decision makers also rejected bankruptcy for Chrysler. G. William Miller, secretary of the treasury, stated the case of the administration against bankruptcy in advocating matching federal loan guarantees in the amount of $1.5 billion for Chrysler. His assessment was summarized as follows:

> A Chrysler bankruptcy could cost the Federal Government more than $1.5 billion in 1980 and 1981 alone. We estimate the total cost for those years at a total of at least $2.75 billion, an amount that includes loss of revenues, unemployment claims, welfare costs, and other incidental costs. Furthermore, there would be a substantial cost to the state and local governments.[12]

In addition to these out-of-pocket costs, other serious adverse effects of bankruptcy included (a) substantial increases in unemployment with attendant economic and social distress, (b) negative effects on the U.S. balance of payments attributable to an increase in imported automobiles, and

(c) reduced competition in an already highly oligarchic industry. Needless to say, bankruptcy for Chrysler was ruled out of the question.

3. *Tax credits.* After posting its losses in the second quarter of 1979, Chrysler pressed President Carter for a $1.0 billion advance from the Treasury to be applied against tax credits it would earn in future years. That concession would have required special legislation from Congress. But Chrysler had no earnings and was projecting losses at least through 1982. Therefore, the foundation for such a request was temporarily nonexistent and its justification was unacceptable to the administration and Congress. In 1979 there was still doubt as to Chrysler's ability to regain profitability. Moreover, as Chrysler's need for financial support escalated from several hundred million to a few billion dollars, the magnitude of the assistance required to save the company further precluded serious consideration of tax credits. As the foundation of current financial need expanded, the possibility of repaying tax credits with future earnings became more illusory, and this alternative was dismissed.

4. *Delayed federal standards.* Chrysler "also asked the government for a delay in meeting federal air-pollution and fuel-efficiency standards — regulations it claims have cost $8.6 billion over the last five years."[13] The company estimated that its cost of compliance with federal legislation was twice that of General Motors or Ford. Presumably, therefore, the federal standards for fuel economy, exhaust emissions, and safety discriminated against the smallest producer of the Big Three auto makers. However, Chrysler seemed unable to explain why many smaller foreign competitors managed to meet these standards and still earn a profit. Chrysler's management also reminded Congress that during the 1970s American Motors received both tax credits and approved delays in implementing federal emission standards for its automobiles.[14] The administration rejected Chrysler's arguments to delay implementation of federal standards on its automobiles and trucks. Secretary of the Treasury Miller stated the opposition of the administration as follows:

a. It would raise difficult policy problems, both with respect to the purposes of the regulations and equity vis-à-vis other producers. . . .

b. Regulation is only one of the many elements and costs in the environment in which Chrysler operates. . . .

c. There has been no persuasive evidence that Chrysler would not be in the same dilemma now without these regulatory requirements.

d. Chrysler has been unable to quantify adequately the portion of its financing needs which relate to compliance with regulatory requirements.[15]

Delayed federal standards were, therefore, eliminated as a viable alternative.

5. *Loan guarantees.* Loan guarantees constituted an alterative for which there was ample precedent. In 1970, for example, the Penn Central Railroad received $125 million in loan guarantees to assist it through bankruptcy. In

1971, Congress authorized $250 million in bank loans for the ailing Lockheed Aircraft Corporation. In 1974 President Nixon authorized $1.5 billion in loan guarantees to save seven bankrupt railroads by consolidating them into a single profit-making corporation. And in 1975, New York City received $2.3 billion in annual loans at near-market interest rates from the U.S. Treasury in the face of threatened bankruptcy.

In addition to the precedent for loan guarantees, this form of assistance had much to commend it as a preferred choice for Chrysler. The principal advantages were as follows:

a. The loan guarantee agreement could be written in a way to protect the federal government from noncompliance or nonperformance, thereby acting as a strong incentive for Chrysler to improve its situation.

b. In the event of a business failure, loan guarantees would constitute a prior claim on assets at the very least senior to the claims of equity shareholders in the corporation.

c. Loan guarantees were not directly dependent on the generation of profits for repayment in the short term as in the case of advanced tax credits.

d. Loan guarantees would provide more security for and possibly more financial return to the federal government than delayed compliance with federal regulations, which would benefit only the company at the expense of the general society.

On balance, then, loan guarantees in some necessary amount for some reasonable period of time appeared to be the most rational approach to assisting Chrysler. There was, however, another element necessary to make loan guarantees a truly satisficing choice. This additional element entailed financial participation with the federal government in the rescue of Chrysler by those groups with a vested interest in the survival of the company.

6. *Matching loan guarantees.* The concept of matching loan guarantees has all the general advantages of unrestricted loan guarantees except that the borrower receives a proportional amount (usually dollar for dollar) from the guarantor to match some minimally specified amount to be obtained from other authorized sources. In the Chrysler bailout decision, there was a strong feeling in the Carter administration and the Congress that there were numerous stakeholders who stood to gain or lose from Chrysler's performance. They would be the direct beneficiaries if Chrysler survived through financial assistance by the federal government. If the nation and the taxpayers stood to benefit indirectly from a Chrysler bailout, the employees, creditors, dealers, shareholders, suppliers, and various state and local governments stood to benefit more directly and in much greater magnitude. Moreover, the concept of matching funds or, in this case, matching guarantees normally requires the guarantor to match funds after the fact. In other words, the stakeholders must signify their faith in the survival of the enterprise by an initial action involving commitment and risk after which the guarantor (in this case the federal

government) will match the stakeholder's investment. This additional commitment required in advance by the stakeholders is intended to protect the guarantor. More important, however, the commitment of stakeholders is intended to elicit improved performance and renewed long-term vitality for the ailing enterprise. It is designed to save the corporation and to revitalize it for long-term success. As such, the matching loan guarantee solution was an eminently satisficing choice for a Chrysler bailout in 1979.

The Choice

As shown in Table 13.1 Senate and House conferees approved the Chrysler Corporation Loan Guarantee Act of 1979 on December 21, 1979, and on January 7, 1980, President Jimmy Carter signed the bill into law. The choice was made. The alternative selected was loan guarantees with matching funds from all of Chrysler's stakeholders, including employees, stockholders, creditors, suppliers, and dealers as well as concerned state and local governments. The administration was insistent that Chrysler's stakeholders manifest their faith in the future of the corporation by making firm commitments with some risk. The government's loan guarantees were supplemental rather than primary in the Chrysler bailout, at least from the perspective of the administration and Congress. The Chrysler bill provided for $1.5 billion in guaranteed loans to the company. To obtain these loans, it was necessary for Chrysler to obtain $2.0 billion in nonfederal assistance in various forms from the principal stakeholders of the corporation. The administration had proposed that Chrysler provide $1.5 billion in nonfederal funds in exchange for a like amount of federally guaranteed loans. To its credit, Congress increased the nonfederal portion to $2.0 billion.

The Chrysler Corporation Loan Guarantee Act of 1979 was to be administered through the Loan Guarantee Board with voting memberships held by the secretary of the treasury, comptroller general, and chairman of the Federal Reserve Board. Nonvoting members included the secretaries of labor and transportation. The authority for loan guarantees was $1.5 billion to be drawn not later than December 1983 and repaid by the end of 1990. Loan fees were .5 percent per year on the daily balance. To qualify for federal guarantees, credit could not be otherwise available to Chrysler on reasonable terms. Merger or sale of the company to a foreign entity was prohibited and no stock dividends were to be paid while guaranteed loans were outstanding.

Although all the provisions of the Chrysler act cannot be listed here, some safeguards of particular interest included:

1. The act specified that there had to be "$1 of nonfederally guaranteed assistance in place for each dollar of guarantee."[16]

2. Before a guarantee commitment could be issued, Chrysler would be required to submit a satisfactory four-year operating plan for the period through 1983, to demonstrate that the company would emerge viable

and self-financing thereafter. The plan had to be updated annually as long as any guarantees were outstanding.

3. Maturities on the present financing commitments and the new commitments to be obtained could be no shorter than the maturities on federal guarantees involved. The guarantees could not be issued at a faster rate than the other commitments were utilized.

4. Before committing and issuing guarantees, the Loan Guarantee Board had to determine that there was a reasonable prospect for repayment of a loan.

5. To preclude Chrysler's dependency on long-term federal aid, the guaranteed loans had to mature by 1990.

6. Guarantee and loan agreements were to include all affirmative and negative covenants and other protective provisions that were usual and appropriate to transactions of this nature.

7. There had to be adequate assurance of repayment, security had to be obtained, existing loans had to be subordinated, and dividends were prohibited.

8. The government would receive an adequate return for its participation: at a minimum, it would receive a guarantee fee of at least one-half percent per annum. If the program were successful, it would produce no direct cost to the government.[17]

It was apparent that, in recommending matching loan guarantees to Congress as a preferred form of financial assistance for Chrysler, the administration was desirous of protecting and reducing the cost to the taxpayers. Secretary of the Treasury Miller set for the rationale of the administration as follows:

> First, the Administration believes that Federal financing assistance is justified in this case. Second, estimates of the Company's financing needs have been carefully prepared and appear reasonable. Finally, we have submitted responsible legislation which would adequately protect the Federal interest.[18]

The government's choice of matching loan guarantees was also acceptable to Chrysler's management. Lee Iacocca noted in congressional testimony that "the $1.5 billion in loan guarantees contained in the Administration Bill is adequate."[19] Apparently all the parties to the Chrysler bailout decision were convinced that it was a satisficing choice — one that would save Chrysler in the short run and renew its fiscal vitality in the long run. With effective implementation, this objective would be met.

Implementation of the Decision

Chrysler complied with all the requirements of the act and took down $800 million in loan guarantees in 1980 and another $400 million in 1981. Between 1979 and 1981 Chrysler declared net losses of $3.3 billion. In 1982 Chrysler nearly broke even with a small $69 million net loss. The company's turn-around gained real momentum in 1983, and in the summer of that year the company repaid the $1.2 billion of federally guaranteed loans. At the end of 1983 Chrysler reported a $.5 billion net profit. Now the Chrysler bailout decision was over; the decision-making process had run its course. The net profits at Chrysler were $1.5 billion in 1984 and $1.6 billion in 1985.

There was nothing especially noteworthy about the implementation phase in the Chrysler bailout decision. Under the leadership of Lee Iacocca, Chrysler completed its reorganization and internal cost-cutting efforts. Chrysler's management should receive high marks for its intense negotiations with all the stakeholders required by the act to provide nonfederal financing before the loan guarantees could be executed.[20] Under the leadership of President Ronald Reagan, the economy moved out of recession, and the lot of the American automobile industry improved commensurately. Whatever the reason, the implementation of the Chrysler bailout decision proceeded to accomplish the objective that gave rise to the decision-making process in mid-1979. Chrysler was saved. At least for the moment. The decision-making process began in the summer of 1979 when it was generally agreed that something had to be done to save Chrysler. The decision-making process ended in the summer of 1983 with Chrysler's repayment of $1.2 billion in federally guaranteed loans.

Follow-up and Control

The rather stringent provisions of the Chrysler Corporation Loan Guarantee Act provided a firm baseline for follow-up and control. The Chrysler Loan Guarantee Board maintained close and continuous surveillance over the financial management of Chrysler during the three-year period from 1980 to 1983 during which the company had outstanding federally guaranteed loans. Of course, the real credit for follow-up and control to a successful outcome in this case must go to Chrysler's management who complied with all the provisions of the bailout legislation while returning the company to a profitable state. Ineffective managerial decision making over several decades had led almost to corporate extinction in 1979. Effective managerial decision making in accomplishing a turn-around in less than four years rescued the company for the short run and gave it another chance to affirm its viability.

THE *CHALLENGER* DISASTER: A PERSPECTIVE

More than a decade has passed since January 28, 1986, when exactly 73.621 seconds after liftoff at 11:39 A.M., the space shuttle *Challenger* exploded killing all seven persons on board. With the destruction of *Challenger*, America's dream for a quick and easy conquest of outer space died.[21] A more obvious casualty of the *Challenger* disaster, the reputation of the National

Aeronautics and Space Administration (NASA) for spectacular and fail-safe space probes, was severely tarnished. The "can-do" attitude of NASA that crested with the culmination of the *Apollo* moon mission in 1969 and continued without major interruption for nearly a score of years was replaced by "can-fail" realism.[22] NASA's aura of invincible professionalism was suddenly replaced with an image of bureaucratic bungling and institutional fallibility. The nation was shocked and incensed at *Challenger*'s destruction. A presidential commission was immediately formed to investigate the cause of the accident. This commission (hereinafter referred to as the Rogers Commission) held extensive hearings and conducted countless interviews after which it issued a multi-volume report. With regard to the technical cause of the *Challenger* disaster, the Rogers Commission stated that it "was caused by a failure in the joint between the two lower segments of the right solid rocket motor. The specific failure was the destruction of the seals that are intended to prevent hot gases from leaking through the joint during the propellant burn of the rocket motor."[23] Commenting on the contributing cause of the accident, the Rogers Commission stated:

> The decision to launch the *Challenger* was flawed. Those who made the decision were unaware of the recent history of problems concerning the O-rings and the joint and were unaware of the initial written recommendation of the contractor advising against the launch at temperatures below 53 degrees Fahrenheit and the continuing opposition of the engineers at Thiokol after the management reversed its position. . . . If the decision makers had known all of the facts, it is highly unlikely that they would have decided to launch 51-L on January 28, 1986.[24]

This book agrees with the conclusion of the Rogers Commission that NASA's decision to launch *Challenger* was flawed. *It was flawed because the decision makers used the wrong approach to make the wrong decision.* Essentially NASA's decision makers disregarded the numerous constraints surrounding the *Challenger* launch and proceeded with the decision according to their own preference for the outcome. They chose not to consider any alternative course of action in spite of contrary advice and objections from their own contractor. The resultant catastrophe affords a stark experience in how not to make a significant managerial decision.

THE DECISION-MAKING PROCESS IN THE *CHALLENGER* DISASTER

The managerial decision-making process is designed for category II choices. Because of the tight coupling and the complexity of its numerous and intricate systems, the launch of *Challenger* or any manned spacecraft is definitely a category II choice. The high visibility and environmental impact of a spacecraft launch tend to qualify it as significant in the customary sense of that term.

Challenger was, therefore, both complex and significant in that each launch was a stand-alone, nonrecurring action demanding an open attitude toward the decision-making process. As the following sections reveal, NASA treated the *Challenger* launch more like a routine, recurring, highly certain category I decision which contributed directly to its fatal consequences.

The Objectives

The launch of *Challenger* was not an objective in its own right. It was a means to the attainment of a total space shuttle mission objective which was established by presidential decree in 1970 during the Nixon administration. Essentially the mission objective was to establish an Earth-orbiting space station linked to the Earth by a fleet of space shuttles thereby facilitating easy and economical access to further exploration of outer space.[25] *Challenger* was one of four space shuttles. The other three are *Columbia*, *Discovery*, and *Atlantis*. The entire space program was declared fully operational on July 7, 1982. At the time of the *Challenger* disaster, the space shuttle fleet had flown twenty-four successful missions: *Challenger*, nine; *Columbia*, seven; *Discovery*, six; and *Atlantis*, two.[26]

The facts in the case clearly indicate that the launch of *Challenger* which, along with the rest of the space shuttle fleet, was a means to an end became an end in itself. The space shuttle mission objective was displaced by the predetermination to launch *Challenger* at a given time regardless of obvious constraints. The attainment of managerial objectives is highest when displacement is minimal. In the case of *Challenger*, the displacement was very high and the means did not survive as an end. The tight coupling and complexity of each launch made it a stand-alone experience more than deserving of a category II designation. Moreover, the tight coupling and complexity of each launch confronted the NASA decision makers with more uncertainty than they cared to admit. Safety is always a major factor in manned space flight;[27] and there is always an unpredictable amount of fine-tuning to bolster components and systems designated as "critical."[28] In summary, then, the launch of *Challenger* was definitely a category II decision demanding the appropriate type of decision-making strategy.

The Search for Alternatives

In the open decision-making process, the decision maker engages in search activity and defines a limited number of alternatives and outcomes. By way of contrast, in the closed decision-making process, alternatives and outcomes are considered to be predetermined. New possibilities or different alternatives are not available in the closed decision-making process because this process tends to disregard the environment or it assumes that the environment is constant or controlled. In the *Challenger* case, there were several alternatives available to NASA's decision makers, but they did not consider them. These alternatives were as follows:

1. Delay *Challenger's* launch until environmental and other constraints were acceptable to the engineers and managers for both NASA and Morton Thiokol (the contractor).

2. Postpone the launch schedule until the O-rings and other critical items were fixed on all spacecraft.

3. Postpone the launch schedule to redesign all spacecraft to reduce the vulnerability of the O-rings and other critical items. Resume a revised launch schedule with fully retrofitted spacecraft.

The first alternative would have meant a delay of hours or days; the second alternative days or weeks; and the third alternative weeks or months. The worst scenario might have resulted in a rescheduling of the space shuttle mission objective, but with a reduced probability of disaster and a higher expectancy of success. This seems like a small price to pay in the exploration of outer space.

In NASA's mind the space shuttle launches had to continue, and it was *Challenger's* turn to fly. Like the process of decision making used by NASA, the subject of search was closed. The launch of *Challenger* was a fait accompli. NASA's decision had already been made in 1982 when the space shuttle program was declared operational. Individual spacecraft launches were simply means being executed like ends.

The Comparison and Evaluation of Alternatives

The number of alternatives depends on how much effort the decision maker puts into a search for them. For a category II decision such as the *Challenger* launch, judgment is the favored mode of developing, comparing, and evaluating alternatives. But NASA's decision makers were not using a judgmental decision-making strategy. Instead they relied on a computational strategy that presumed nearly perfect knowledge of critical cause-and-effect relationships. As such, they underestimated the complexity and potential consequences of the launch in the same way that they overestimated their own ability to control the outcome of events set in motion by their adherence to a closed decision-making process.

Decisions made without considering alternatives may have unfortunate consequences. Drucker made this point succinctly in the following passage:

> Whenever one has to judge, one must have alternatives among which one can choose. A judgment in which one can only say "yes" or "no" is no judgment at all. Only if there are alternatives can one hope to get insight into what is truly at stake. . . . A decision without an alternative is a desperate gambler's throw, no matter how carefully thought through it might be. . . . Without

such an alternative, one is likely to flounder dismally when reality proves a decision to be inoperative.[29]

Although written twenty years before the *Challenger* tragedy, Drucker's caveat proved prophetic for NASA's managerial decision makers.

In comparing and evaluating alternatives, managerial decision makers are bounded by a multitude of constraints that normally reduce the number of alternatives to a viable few. By internalizing the alternative to launch on schedule, NASA's decision makers not only disregarded other options but they blocked out the full set of constraints — both generic and unique — that limit the behavior of decision makers whatever the number of alternatives. For example, the concept of bounded rationality (see Figure 3.1) provides a set of generic constraints as follows: (1) imperfect information, (2) time and cost limitations, and (3) cognitive limitations. NASA's decision makers did not have perfect information and they used imperfectly the information that was available to them. Time and cost factors are always important; in the case of *Challenger*, NASA's decision makers were determined to launch on schedule, and, if it occurred to them at all, to retrofit the spacecraft at some later date. Moreover, NASA's decision makers disregarded their own cognitive limitations by selectively hearing only those facts that supported their preferred alternative.

In addition to ignoring most of the constraints inherent in the concept of bounded rationality, NASA's decision makers blatantly disregarded most of the unique constraints associated with the *Challenger* launch. These constraints are as follows:

1. *Environmental constraints* such as (a) freezing temperature with ice on the launch pad, (b) wind shear launch conditions, and (c) stormy seas in the spacecraft recovery area

2. *Political constraints* such as (a) the desire to retain and increase political favor with the administration and the Congress, (b) international political differences with the Soviet Union, and (c) internal political rivalries within NASA

3. *Organizational constraints* such as (a) unstable leadership at the top of NASA, (b) undefined accountability throughout NASA for unfavorable consequences or failure, and (c) a matrix organizational structure in NASA that was not working as it should

4. *Institutional or image constraints* such as (a) the public image of NASA, (b) the professional community image of NASA, and (c) NASA's image of itself

5. *Technical constraints* resulting from a complex technology overlaid on a tightly coupled and highly complex system (as discussed earlier)

Clearly the rationality of NASA's managerial decisions makers was bounded by a multitude of diverse constraints. For the *Challenger* launch, what was required was a satisficing choice made within the bounded rationality of the open decision-making process. What transpired was a maximizing decision made within the unjustifiable and untenable assumptions of the closed decision-making process. A computational decision-making strategy was superimposed on a category II decision and the consequences were predictably tragic.

The Choice

The act of choice is, in one sense, the high point of the decision-making process. The decision itself is normally the culmination of the process. Regardless of the objective, the alternatives, or the consequences to follow, once a decision is made, things begin to happen. Decisions trigger action, movement, and change. However, the act of choice is only part of the process, not, as in the case of *Challenger*, the entire process in itself. To focus solely on the act of choice is to disregard or minimize all the actions necessary to create the proper conditions of choice, not to mention the post-decision actions essential to transform the choice into acceptable results. In this case, the space shuttle mission objective was displaced by a predetermination to launch the *Challenger* spacecraft at a given time and place. The means to the end became an end in itself. There was no search for alternatives because the mind set of NASA's decision makers was embedded in the closed decision-making process; and, for this same reason there was no comparison and evaluation of alternatives. Essentially, the *Challenger* launch was reduced to a category I decision made with a "go" or "no go" mind set; and, with the act of choice, NASA's "can-do" self-image became a "can-fail" reality.

Implementing the Decision

The real value of a decision becomes apparent only after it is implemented. In the case of *Challenger*, the spacecraft exploded just 73.621 seconds after liftoff, killing all seven persons on board. Clearly this is a negatively valued outcome that must be avoided in the future. Given the fact that *Challenger* was a tightly coupled system of great complexity, once the launch was underway there was no aborting or reversing the process until the flight was recalled or the mission was completed. Given the irreversibility of the spacecraft launch after liftoff, it was incumbent on the decision makers to anticipate problems and obstacles and to take appropriate countermeasures. Such anticipation should have, in the case of *Challenger*, preceded the act of choice through the antecedent functions that constitute the open managerial decision-making process. At the very least, a judgmental decision-making strategy employed in the open process model in quest of a satisficing outcome within the constraints of bounded rationality might have averted the *Challenger* disaster. The implementation of the *Challenger* launch failed in the breach because the

NASA decision makers failed to use the correct attitudes in their actions lead-ing up to the launch. A closed decision-making process employing a compu-tational decision-making strategy for a definitive category II choice has a high probability of failure. The *Challenger* case reaffirms this principle.

Follow-up and Control

There was no need to follow up the implemented *Challenger* decision to en-sure an outcome in keeping with the launch objective. The NASA decision makers lost control at the moment of launch and the dream disintegrated.[30]

COMPARATIVE CASE DETERMINANTS OF STRATEGIC DECISION SUCCESS

Having analyzed and evaluated the Chrysler bailout decision and the *Chal-lenger* disaster as individual cases, the comparative evaluation in this section is based on the determinants of decision success set forth in Trull's study of 100 organizations and further advanced by the Bay area study of 108 organi-zations. According to the foundations of these two studies, the success of a decision is a function of the quality of the decision and its implementation. Decision quality, in turn, is composed of (1) compatibility with operating constraints, (2) nearness to optimum time for the decision, (3) proximity to the optimum amount of information, and (4) the decision maker's influence on the decision. Decision implementation is a product of (1) a risk-reward factor and (2) the degree of understanding by those who must carry out the decision. These six factors constitute the essence of the analysis and evalua-tion to follow.

Compatibility with Operating Constraints

Operating constraints refers to institutionalized policies and procedures asso-ciated with an established way of doing business. There was an established way of doing business in the Chrysler bailout decision, and there was some precedent for the financial assistance sought by Chrysler's management. The formal review was processed through the legislative and executive branches of the federal government in due course. In the Chrysler bailout decision, there were definite operating constraints that were meticulously observed by all parties to the decision.

There was also an established way of doing business in the *Challenger* dis-aster. NASA's operating procedures are highly bureaucratized, and most of NASA's employees follow them meticulously. With the possible exception of not communicating the concerns of Morton Thiokol's engineers to the high-est levels of NASA, it appears that policies and procedures were completely observed. If anything, there was a discernible tendency on the part of NASA's decision makers to treat the *Challenger* launch as too operational — that is, a category I rather than a category II decision.

Nearness to Optimum Time

Decisions have an optimum time at which the highest probability for success occurs. The relative success of a strategic decision is therefore directly related to its timing.

In the Chrysler bailout decision, there was an induced urgency created by the continued insistence of Chrysler's management that federal assistance was needed immediately to save the company. Chrysler was able to obtain passage of a bailout bill in just under five months. Apparently this decision was close to the optimum time for Chrysler because it precipitated a return to profitability for the company.

In the case of the *Challenger* disaster, NASA's decision makers imparted a set of distorted priorities to the time constraints. The primary time constraint was deemed by NASA to be the launch schedule for *Challenger*. Conceivably, there were managerial concerns with maintaining NASA's image for flawless operations with attendant concern for NASA's budgetary allocation to administer the space program. Regrettably there was too little concern with the need to give more time for the weather to clear or, better yet, to properly retrofit all four spacecraft. With the possible exception of a recurring launch window for the spacecraft itself, the time constraints in the *Challenger* disaster were an induced function of the institutional priorities and urgencies of NASA's decision makers.

Optimum Amount of Information

The optimum amount of information is just enough to make a cost effective choice that meets the objective. In general, decision makers tend to seek too much information, which tends in many cases to work against a good decision. In the Chrysler bailout decision, Congress and the president had all the information they needed to decide on loan guarantees to save the company. To their credit in this case, the decision makers were able to separate the wheat from the chaff fairly quickly and to use the truly significant information in the most effective way. Clearly the Chrysler bailout decision epitomized the optimum amount and the optimum use of available information.

In the *Challenger* case, NASA's decision makers had all the information that they needed to make the correct decision which was to delay or reschedule the spacecraft launch. The decision makers knew that the O-rings for the rocket boosters did not function at their best below 53 Fahrenheit. They also knew that the O-rings were on the critical parts list for all four spacecraft along with a host of other items which obviously militated for a complete retrofit of the entire fleet of spacecraft. The decision makers were directly and unequivocally advised not to launch by their subcontractor's engineers who were at the launch site. In essence, NASA's decision makers chose to make selective use of the considerable information that was available to them and to disregard information that was crucial to mission success. Consequently, the result was a catastrophe immediately after the launch of *Challenger*.

Decision Maker's Influence

The choice in the Chrysler bailout decision was made at the highest levels of federal government. Because the government was in effect underwriting, on a dollar-for-dollar participating basis, the financial recovery of the company, the influence of the decision maker was most significant in determining a favorable outcome. In fact, the overall success of the final decision, in terms of its effective implementation and satisficing outcome, must be attributed to the top-level priority given to Chrysler's financial plight from beginning to end.

The decision to launch *Challenger* was not made at the highest level of government or even the highest level in NASA. Presumably if the senior executives in the chain of command had been privy to the concerns of the engineers from Morton Thiokol or if they had been aware of the actual weather conditions on the launch pad, the *Challenger* disaster would not have occurred. Hopefully improved communication will be forthcoming in future launches.

Risk-Reward Factor

The decision makers anticipated the risks in the Chrysler bailout decision. A government loan without a protective covenant would have risked a company failure and possible loss of part or all of the government's funds. A government loan without participation by Chrysler's stakeholders would have placed the entire weight of the company's rescue on the shoulders of the taxpayers. The government foresaw these risks and wrote a comprehensive loan guarantee agreement to limit its participation and protect its interests. The rewards of success accrued to Chrysler and its stakeholders. The risks were correctly borne by them.

In the *Challenger* case, the decision makers disregarded the risk of mission failure in favor of the reward of an on-schedule launch. NASA's managers presumed a level of knowledge regarding the outcome of the launch that was completely unjustified in the presence of the numerous constraints surrounding the decision. They let their preference for a timely launch confine their actions to the closed decision-making process. For a decision that demanded judgment they substituted computation; for an outcome that militated for satisficing they sought maximizing. Predictably they failed.

Degree of Understanding

If the understanding of those who must carry out a decision or those who are affected by it is elicited, an outcome that will attain the original objective is more likely. Understanding can be obtained by involving those concerned in the decision-making process through participation or consultation.

In the Chrysler bailout decision all the major stakeholders in the corporation and the concerned departments and branches of government at the local, state, and federal levels were involved in some way in providing information or giving opinions to the decision makers or those who might influence the decision makers. There was no confidentiality; and Chrysler's management clearly wanted every American citizen to be aware of the worst-case scenario if the company failed. There was, in short, a nearly universal degree of understanding regarding the seriousness of Chrysler's financial situation. This high degree of understanding was translated into effective action by Chrysler's management and its stakeholders to rescue the corporation, once Congress approved the loan guarantee bill that was subsequently signed into law by President Carter. In this case understanding of the decision clearly facilitated its effective implementation.

If the decision implementers in the *Challenger* disaster were the astronauts who perished just after launch, the precise degree of their understanding of all the variables in the decision-making situation will never be known. Did they, for example, know about the concerns of Morton Thiokol's engineers? If so, what was their response? Were they aware of the exact environmental conditions circumscribing the launch? If so, did they agree to proceed in any event? If the decision implementers were the operating managers who actually made the decision to launch, then one can only wonder why their understanding was not translated into a delay of the launch.

COMPARATIVE CASE CLASSIFICATIONS
OF STRATEGIC DECISION SUCCESS

The comparative case classifications of strategic decision success are derived from the strategic decision matrix set forth in Figure 11.1. As shown in the figure, a given classification is a joint product of two sets of managerial attitudes. The first set is composed of managerial attitudes toward the decision-making process. Subsets here include (1) attainable objectives and an open decision-making process and (2) unattainable objectives and a closed decision-making process. The second set is composed of managerial attitudes toward the decision itself. Subsets here include (1) a judgmental decision-making strategy and a satisficing outcome and (2) a computational decision-making strategy and a maximized outcome. A Type A strategic decision is most likely to succeed because it is composed of attainable objectives developed in the open decision-making process that are pursued through a judgmental decision-making strategy in quest of a satisficing outcome. A Type D decision is unlikely to succeed because it is founded on unattainable objectives conceived in the closed decision-making process that are sought through a computational decision-making strategy in pursuit of a maximized outcome. Types B and C are less likely to succeed because of their incompatible managerial attitudes. Type B, for example, negates a positive attitude toward the decision itself with a subset of unattainable objectives cast in the closed decision-making process. For its part, Type C reduces its prospects for realizing the benefits of attainable objectives cast in the decision-making process by using a computational decision-making strategy in a futile quest for a maximized outcome.

Each case in this chapter is analyzed in the context of the two sets of managerial attitudes set forth in Figure 11.1, and is then assigned a strategic decision classification. The two cases evaluated in this chapter — Chrysler bailout decision and *Challenger* disaster — are intended to illustrate the managerial attitudes and actions that result in strategic decision success or strategic decision failure. Therefore, these two cases reflect a direct comparison between Type A and Type D classifications. It should be recalled, however, that changes in managerial attitudes can result in changes in classifications with attendant shifts in the prospects for strategic decision success.

Managerial Attitudes Toward
the Decision-Making Process

As noted previously in comments made by Senator William Proxmire, "all of the power, all of the money, all the skilled lobbyists, all the labor clout and business clout and banking clout, plus the force of hundreds of thousands of Americans who have an immediate stake in the decision" tended to favor a financial bailout for Chrysler.[31] The question was how to accomplish this end. The open decision-making process was accomplished jointly by the executive and legislative branches of the federal government. The executive branch did the staff work and made its recommendations to the legislative branch, which in turn authorized the choice to be implemented through the executive branch. In the context of the process propounded in this book, the functions of decision making were accomplished somewhat as follows:

1. The Carter administration, acting on inputs from numerous sources including members of Congress, set the objectives and accomplished the initial search for alternatives.

2. The administration also accomplished an initial comparison and evaluation of alternatives and presented a preferred choice to Congress in the form of a detailed recommendation.

3. For its part, Congress accomplished a legislative search for alternatives along with a comparison and evaluation of alternatives preparatory to accepting and slightly modifying the administration's preferred choice.

4. Congress formally approved the final legislative enactment, clearing the way for what was obviously a pro forma ratification by President Carter.

5. The implementation and follow-up and control phases in the Chrysler bailout decision were accomplished through the Loan Guarantee Board established by Congress and staffed by members of the administration.

The mission objective in the *Challenger* disaster was to establish an Earth-orbiting space station linked to the Earth by a fleet of space shuttles thereby facilitating easy and economical access to further exploration of outer space. In the process of trying to maximize this mission objective, NASA's decision makers effectively displaced it by predetermining individual spacecraft launches, each of which became a surrogate objective in its own right. In actuality, the means to the end became an end in itself by virtue of NASA's attempt to maximize the mission objective. Given the open decision-making process the mission objective appeared to be attainable. Given the displacement of the mission objective by predetermined launch objectives pursued in the closed decision-making process, the wrong decision was virtually assured. The constraints imposed on NASA's decision makers by the normal limitations of bounded rationality along with the tight coupling and complexity of individual spacecraft launches demanded openness in decision making. Regrettably NASA's decision makers disregarded environmental and other constraints and proceeded to overlay a computational decision-making strategy on a choice that demanded a judgmental approach in quest of a maximized outcome when the best that could be obtained was a satisficing result.

The decision to launch was wrong in the *Challenger* case because the surrogate launch objective was not attainable within the closed decision-making process. The situation called for judgment and openness, and NASA's decision makers provided predetermination and computation in a closed mind set. Obvious constraints were disregarded and alternatives were never considered. It was all "can do" and "condition go." Even with the displacement of the mission objective, it was possible for *Challenger* and other launches to be made successfully. Many objectives are displaced without disastrous consequences. However, once a displaced objective is enmeshed in the closed decision-making process involving a choice of great sensitivity and fragility such as the launch of a spacecraft, the probability of failure assumes frightening proportions. Even the alternatives not considered by NASA's decision makers would not have assured attainment of the mission objective. For example, a delay in the launch of *Challenger* would have lessened the environmental constraints. Postponement of the space shuttle flight schedule to retrofit the fleet would have lessened the technical constraints. But other constraints stemming from the concept of bounded rationality would have reduced the prospects for mission success and maintained a high probability of individual launch failure. NASA's tendency to proceed as though it had perfect information and its inclination to impose artificial and frequently unattainable time constraints militated against mission success. NASA's refusal to acknowledge its own cognitive limitations along with its institutional and image constraints also dampened the likelihood of mission success. NASA's decision makers proceeded as if there were no boundaries on their rationality. Consequently their surrogate launch objectives seemed certain to fail and mission success was illusory at best. Indeed the wrong decision does inevitably ensue from the wrong approach. The *Challenger* disaster exemplifies this relationship.

Managerial Attitudes Toward the Decision

The choice made in the Chrysler bailout decision was definitely right. Regardless of any philosophical reservations or conservative disinclination, it was economically and politically indefensible to ignore Chrysler's plight in 1979. Regardless of the original causes, which were undoubtedly attributable to ineffective managerial decision making rather than government interference or uncontrollable factors, Chrysler had to be saved, and the decision makers opted for an alternative that protected the public interest in about every way. If the objective in a decision-making situation is unattainable or if it is in some appreciable measure lacking in economic, social, and political merit and if this objective is pursued in the closed decision-making process, then the approach to decision making is doubtless wrong and the right decision to meet the need is unlikely to materialize. Such was certainly not true in the Chrysler bailout decision. The decision was right because it was made and implemented using a judgmental strategy in quest of a satisficing choice. Satisficing choices are suitable only for attainable objectives; and judgmental strategies belong within the interrelated functions of the managerial decision-making process. Any variation from these critical guidelines can lead to a wrong approach and a wrong decision. The right decision was virtually assured within the right approach by the use of a judgmental strategy in quest of a satisficing choice. If, for example, the decision makers had presumed anything approaching a perfect knowledge of cause-and-effect relationships and if they had attempted to maximize results through a malapropos computational strategy, even the right approach might have yielded the wrong decision. Fortunately the approach complemented the decision in that both were correct and the attainment of the primary objective attests to this correctness.

The Chrysler bailout decision is a splendid example of a Type A strategic choice, that is, one that was successful because the right managerial attitudes toward the decision-making process were combined with the best managerial attitudes toward the decision itself to produce a successful strategic decision.

In terms of its decision-making characteristics, the *Challenger* launch was a category II choice in that it was nonroutine and nonrecurring with a high level of uncertainty attendant on the outcome. Each launch was a high-risk operation principally because of the tightly coupled and highly complex systems of the spacecraft. Spacecraft launches can never be routinized; each one is a unique phenomenon demanding fail-safe procedures. There was considerable fine-timing in each launch to reduce the uncertainty and to minimize the risk of catastrophic system failure. Because the decision makers in a spacecraft launch never have complete knowledge of all the cause-and-effect relationships and because they have a strong preference for successful outcomes, the category II decision to launch should employ a judgmental decision-making strategy. This strategy is properly employed in the open decision-making process with its emphasis on (1) dynamic objectives, (2) alternatives and outcomes that are not predetermined, (3) acceptance of the boundaries of imperfect information, time and cost constraints, and cognitive limitations, (4) an outcome that satisfices or meets the objective, and (5) openness and responsiveness to environmental influences. The open decision-making process includes recognition of all of the constraints that limit the ability of the decision maker and precludes the possibility of anything approaching a maximized outcome. The best outcome that the decision maker can obtain in the open decision-making process is one that meets the objectives, which in the usual case is good enough for the intended purpose. The open decision-making process is designed to accommodate category II decisions of the *Challenger* type. The process provides for the use of a judgmental strategy within the bounded rationality of the decision maker with a view toward a satisficing outcome. Regrettably, NASA's decision makers employed a computational decision-making strategy in a calamitous quest for a maximized outcome. This is a portrait of a catastrophic decision-making failure, that is, a Type D strategic choice.

SUMMARY

In the best of all possible conditions for the decision maker, the right decision is made through the right approach. The objectives are attainable; the open decision-making process is used; a judgmental strategy is adopted; and the result is a satisficing choice.

This state of affairs is characteristic of the Chrysler bailout decision. The primary objective set by the Carter administration was attainable. The expected outcome was to rescue Chrysler in the short run and restore its financial health for the long run. In making his presentation of the administration's recommendation to Congress, Secretary of the Treasury Miller manifested a strong belief in the likelihood of meeting Chrysler's needs through the alternative of matching loan guarantees. While expressing a strong preference for a favorable outcome, he did not presume to have anything approaching perfect knowledge of the cause-and-effect relationships in Chrysler's situation. Indeed the administration manifested something less than complete certainty about the outcome by providing numerous safeguards to protect the government in the event the bailout did not succeed. Consequently, Secretary Miller and the other members of the administration used a judgmental rather than a computational strategy. Moreover, the administration's recommendation was intended to achieve a satisficing outcome rather than anything like a maximized result. Congress used this same combination by expressing a strong preference to save Chrysler but by showing less than perfect knowledge of all the variables in the situation. The numerous meetings and hearings held by both houses of Congress reflect a judgmental strategy in quest of a satisficing outcome. Consequently, the Chrysler bailout decision stands as an excellent example of a Type A strategic choice with a highly successful outcome.

In relating the facts of the *Challenger* case to the principal frameworks and concepts presented in this book, it is obvious that:

1. NASA's decision makers treated the *Challenger* launch as a category I rather than a category II decision.

2. NASA's decision makers employed a computational decision-making strategy to make a category II decision that demanded a judgmental decision-making strategy.

3. NASA's decision makers made the decision to launch *Challenger* in the closed decision-making process rather than in the open decision-making process.

4. NASA's decision makers completely disregarded the constraints of bounded rationality along with virtually every other constraint in the decision to launch *Challenger*.

In terms of the specific decision-making process presented in this book, it is also obvious that:

1. NASA's decision makers displaced the long-term mission objective with predetermined and fixed short-term launch objectives.

2. There was no search for alternatives by NASA's decision makers because the launch objective was fixed and presumed to be fully operationalized.

3. No alternatives were considered by NASA's decision makers because it was assumed that none was required.

4. NASA's decision makers erroneously dealt with the *Challenger* launch as a category I choice which was routine and recurring with virtual complete certainty as to the outcome.

5. NASA's decision makers handled the implementation of the decision to launch *Challenger* in a predominantly computational and procedural mode with little if any anticipation of problems or failure.

6. In this case, there was no need for follow-up and control except for the recovery of the *Challenger* spacecraft and the dead astronauts which was fully proceduralized and so executed.

Finally, in the context of the strategic decision matrix set forth in Figure 11.1, the *Challenger* disaster is clearly a Type D strategic choice. Actually the case reflects the double negative of (1) an objective rendered unattainable in the closed decision-making process and (2) a futile attempt to obtain a maximized outcome through a computational decision-making strategy. The *Challenger* disaster epitomizes the principle that the wrong approach invariably begets the wrong result.

REVIEW AND DISCUSSION QUESTIONS

1. Was it really necessary to save Chrysler in 1979? Why? Discuss.
2. The decision-making process in the Chrysler bailout decision took place in the presence of numerous constraints on the decision makers. What were these constraints and how did the decision makers deal with them?
3. In what specific ways is the Chrysler bailout decision a good example of a Type A strategic choice?
4. Why was the decision to launch *Challenger* a category II decision? Discuss.
5. Was a successful launch an attainable objective for the *Challenger* spacecraft? If so, what happened to render it unattainable?
6. What alternatives were disregarded and what constraints were ignored by NASA's decision makers in the *Challenger* case?
7. In what specific ways is the *Challenger* disaster a good example of a Type D strategic choice?
8. What are the similarities between the Cuban missile crisis and the Chrysler bailout decision? Discuss.
9. What are the similarities between the Iranian hostage crisis and the *Challenger* disaster? Discuss.
10. How likely is there to be another disaster of the type and magnitude of *Challenger*? Discuss.

NOTES

1. See "Will $3 Billion Be Enough to Save Chrysler?" *U.S. News & World Report* (November 12, 1979), 78–79.
2. Lee Iacocca, *Iacocca* (New York: Bantam Books, 1984), pp. 152, 157.
3. Ibid., pp. 155–156.
4. See Gail Gregg, "Hill Leaders Pledge Prompt Consideration of Chrysler Aid," *Congressional Quarterly* (August 18, 1979), 1698–1699, for a more detailed discussion of previous recipients of financial assistance from the federal government.
5. U.S. Congress, House, Committee on Banking, Finance and Urban Affairs, Subcommittee on Economic Stabilization, *The Chrysler Corporation Financial Situation*, Hearings, 96th Cong., 1st Sess., October 30; November 1, 7, and 13, 1979 (Washington, D.C.: U.S. Government Printing Office, 1979), pp. 930–932. Also see "If Chrysler Shuts Down," *Challenge* (November–December 1979), 47–53.
6. U.S. Congress, Senate, Committee on Banking, Housing, and Urban Affairs, *Chrysler Corporation Loan Guarantee Act of 1979*, Hearings, 96th Cong.,

1st Sess., November 14 and 15, 1979 (Washington, D.C.: U.S. Government Printing Office, 1979), p. 661.

7. U.S. Congress, House, *The Chrysler Corporation Financial Situation*, p. 931.

8. See U.S. Congress, Senate, *Chrysler Corporation Loan Guarantee Act of 1979*, pp. 218–236.

9. U.S. Congress, House, *The Chrysler Corporation Financial Situation*, p. 932.

10. Robert H. Samuelson, "Will Federal Aid Be Enough to Put Chrysler Together Again?" *National Journal* (August 25, 1979), 1401–1403.

11. U.S. Congress, House, *The Chrysler Corporation Financial Situation*, p. 929.

12. U.S. Congress, Senate, *Chrysler Corporation Loan Guarantee Act of 1979*, p. 179.

13. Gregg, "Hill Leaders Pledge Prompt Consideration of Chrysler Aid," 1695.

14. U.S. Congress, Senate, *Chrysler Corporation Loan Guarantee Act of 1979*, p. 625.

15. U.S. Congress, House, *The Chrysler Corporation Financial Situation*, p. 1042.

16. Robert A. Comerford and Dennis W. Callaghan, *Strategic Management* (Boston, Mass.: Kent, 1985), p. 239.

17. U.S. Congress, Senate, *Chrysler Corporation Loan Guarantee Act of 1979*, pp. 191–192.

18. Ibid., p. 193.

19. Ibid., p. 634.

20. For extensive discussion of the implementation phase, see Robert B. Reich and John D. Donahue, *New Deals: The Chrysler Revival and the American System* (New York: Time Books, 1985), pp. 206–263.

21. G. H. Stine, "The Dream Is Down," *Analog Science Fiction/Science Fact*, 107 (February 1987), 57–91.

22. N. Hickey, "The *Challenger* Tragedy: It Exposed TV's Failures as Well as NASA's," *TV Guide*, 35 (January 24, 1984), 2ff; and S. A. Marshall, "NASA after *Challenger:* The Public Affairs Perspective," *Public Relations Journal*, 42 (August 1986), 17ff.

23. *Report of the Presidential Commission on the Space Shuttle* Challenger *Accident*, Vol. I (Washington, D.C.: U.S. Government Printing Office, 1986), p. 40.

24. Ibid., p. 82.

25. Ibid., p. 2.

26. Ibid., p. 6.

27. T. E. Bell and K. Esch, "The Fatal Flaw in Flight S1-L," *IEEE Spectrum* (February 1987), 36–81.

28. W. H. Starbuck and F. J. Milliken, "*Challenger:* Fine Tuning the Odds Until Something Breaks," *Journal of Management Studies*, 26 (July 1988), 319–340.

29. Peter F. Drucker, *The Effective Executive* (New York: Harper & Row, 1967), pp. 147 and 150.

30. Stine, "The Dream Is Down."

31. U.S. Congress, House, *The Chrysler Corporation Financial Situation*, p. 932.

SUPPLEMENTAL REFERENCES

Banks, H. "It's Time to Bust Up NASA." *Forbes* (February 8, 1988), 101–108.

Biddle, W. "What Destroyed *Challenger*?" *Discover* (April 1986), 40–47.

Bohr, Peter. "Chrysler's Pie-in-the-Sky Plan for Survival." *Fortune* (October 22, 1979), 46ff.

Brady, M. "NASA's Challenge: Ending Isolation at the Top." *Fortune* (May 12, 1986), 26 ff.

Chrysler Corporation Report to Shareholders, 1992. Highland Park, Mich.: Chrysler Corporation, 1992.

Cook, R. C. "The Rogers Commission Failed." *The Washington Monthly*, 18 (November 1986), 13–21.

Esser, James K., and Joanne S. Lindoerfer. "Groupthink and the Space Shuttle *Challenger* Accident: Toward a Quantitative Case Analysis." *Journal of Behavioral Decision Making*, 2 (1989), 167–177.

Flint, Jerry. "Company of the Year: Chrysler." *Forbes* (Jan. 13, 1997), 83–86.

Hirokawa, Randy Y., Dennis S. Gouran, and Amy E. Martz. "Understanding the Sources of Faulty Group Decision Making: A Lesson from the *Challenger* Disaster." *Small Group Behavior* (November 1988), 411–433.

Hunsucker, J. L., and J. S. Law, "Disaster on Flight 51-L: An IE Perspective on the *Challenger* Accident." *Industrial Management*, 28 (September–October 1986), 8–13.

"Is Chrysler the Prototype?" *Business Week* (August 20, 1979), 102ff.

Malley, J. C., V. D. Arnold, and R. L. Whorton, "Organizational Communication: A Disaster for *Challenger*," *Arkansas Business and Economic Review*, 21 (1988), 11–18.

McConnell, M. Challenger: *A Major Malfunction*. New York: Doubleday, 1987.

Moritz, Michael, and Barret Seaman. *Going for Broke: The Chrysler Story*. New York: Doubleday, 1981.

National Aeronautics and Space Administration, *Report to the President: Actions to Implement the Recommendations of the Presidential Commission on the Space Shuttle* Challenger *Accident*, Vol. I. Washington, D.C.: U.S. Government Printing Office, 1986.

Perrow, Charles. *Normal Accidents: Living with High-Risk Technologies*. New York: Basic Books, 1984.

Romzek, B. S., and M. J. Dubnick. "Accountability in the Public Sector: Lessons from the ·*Challenger* Tragedy." *Public Administration Review*, 47 (May/June 1987), 227–238.

Schwartz, H. S. "On the Psychodynamics of Organizational Disaster: The Case of the Space Shuttle *Challenger*." *The Columbian Journal of World Business*, 22 (Spring 1987), 59–67.

"Should Taxpayers Bail Out Chrysler?" *U.S. News and World Report* (November 28, 1979), 99–100.

Stockman, David A. "Chrysler Bailout: Regarding Failure?" *Wall Street Journal* (September 4, 1979), 15.

Stuart, Reginald. *Bailout*. South Bend, Indiana: Reginald Stuart, 1980.

Trento, J. J. *Prescription for Disaster*. New York: Crown Publishers, 1987.

U.S. Congress, House, Report No. 99-1016, *Investigation of the* Challenger *Accident*, 99th Congress, 2nd Sess., 1986. Washington, D.C.: U.S. Government Printing Office, 1986.

U.S. Congress, Senate, Subcommittee on Science, Technology, and Space of the Committee on Commerce, Science, and Transportation, *Space Shuttle Accident*, Hearings, 99th Congress, 2nd Sess., February 18, June 10 and 17, 1986. Washington, D.C.: U.S. Government Printing Office, 1986.

Vaughn, D. "Autonomy, Interdependence, and Social Control: NASA and the Space Shuttle *Challenger*." *Administrative Science Quarterly*, 35 (June 1990), 225–257.

Vaughn, D. *The* Challenger *Launch Decision*. Chicago: University of Chicago Press, 1996.

"Was the Chrysler Bailout Worth It?" *Business Week* (May 20, 1985), 23ff.

Case Set No. 3: General Motors and Philip Morris

*T*his chapter continues the presentation of cases that demonstrate the managerial attitudes toward the decision-making process and toward the decision itself that are most likely to result in strategic decision success. This chapter also continues the illustration of the empirical use of selected evaluative frameworks and concepts advanced at various places in this book.

The first case in this chapter — General Motors — affords an excellent example of the axiom that success in one period of time does not necessarily lead to continued success in subsequent periods of time. Since its inception in 1931, General Motors (GM) has epitomized corporate success. In the 1970s GM began to falter in its unbroken record of growth and prosperity. In 1978 GM embarked on a long-range strategy intended to protect the corporation from domestic and foreign competitors and to preserve its worldwide position of automotive preeminence. In 1997, after nearly twenty years and the expenditure of multiple billions of dollars, GM's market share has declined from just under one-half to less than one-third of the U.S. automobile market. In the interim, with the exception of 1994 to 1996, the corporation has hemorrhaged financially and downsized substantially, while at least three additional strategic decisions stemming from the 1978 strategic choice flounder in various stages of failure. By almost any definition, GM's long-term strategy yielded nothing but negative results for the corporation. The 1978 strategic choice to expend $40 billion stands as a monument to unsuccessful strategic decision making. This case is intended to explain how and why failure grew out of success.

The second case in this chapter also involves a strategic choice intended to attain a long-range strategic objective. In 1984, Philip Morris established a strategic objective to diversify out of its high level of dependence on tobacco products as its primary source of revenue and earnings. By 1993 the company's strategic objective had been successfully accomplished. In 1997 tobacco products still provide about two-thirds of profits, but food products provide nearly one-half of sales with excellent prospects for growth and additional profits. Philip Morris (PM) emerged from the 1980s as a highly profitable growth-oriented corporation with virtually unlimited possibilities to capitalize on additional opportunities that seem certain to materialize. In essence, PM is a marvelous example of strategic decision success over the long term. As such, it stands as a perfect counterpoise to the failure recorded by GM in essentially the same period of time.

In keeping with the general format for these case chapters, the significant events surrounding each case will be presented in sufficient detail to facilitate understanding of the critical factors and relationships in the decision-making situation. Each corporation will be subjected to a detailed gap analysis at the time of its strategic decision, that is, 1978 for GM and 1984 for PM. Subsequently the critical factors in each case will be related to each major step in the decision-making process. Both of these cases will be evaluated comparatively using the determinants for strategic decision success developed in Trull's study and the Bay area study as well as the classifications for strategic decision success set forth in Figure 11.1. These evaluations are intended to demonstrate that successful strategic decisions invariably ensue from managerial attitudes embodying the right approach to the decision-making process and the right attitude toward the decision itself. As noted at several places in this book, this purpose suggests the need to pursue attainable objectives through the open decision-making process using a judgmental decision-making strategy in quest of satisficing outcomes.

GENERAL MOTORS: A PERSPECTIVE

Table 14.1 on page 445 reflects a chronology of significant events for GM since 1978. In 1978 then CEO Thomas A. Murphy set a long-range strategic objective to use $40 billion to spend the competition into the ground. In actuality the objective was to protect GM's market share and to preserve the corporation's worldwide reputation as the leader in automotive production. Although GM's strategic objective appeared offensive in that it was intended to destroy the competition, it was defensive in that it reflected competitive and other environmental pressures being brought to bear on the world's largest producer of automobiles and trucks. Foreign competition, increased government regulation, and the world energy crisis converged in 1978 to create tremendous pressure on the Big Three domestic automobile producers. Using its vastly superior cash flow and cash reserves, GM intended to literally "reinvent" the corporation.

The strategic objective originated at the top of the corporation. GM's top management was buoyed by the company's past successes and was determined to use the full might of GM's balance sheet, technical know-how, and economies of scale. Clearly it was a strategy only GM could afford. Over the decade of the 1980s, GM would essentially start from scratch to redesign every one of its cars and factories. The cost was estimated at 40 billion; but by 1990 it was closer to $60 billion, and by 1997 it had substantially exceeded that amount. As conceived, GM's factories would turn out a vast assemblage of economical, smaller cars with front-wheel drive and quality to match any in the world. High technology and high volume would enable GM to produce cars cheaper than anyone.[1] In one incredibly bold master stroke, GM would dispose of its foreign competitors and leap years ahead of its domestic rivals. Unfortunately, for reasons to be elaborated in this case, GM's strategic objective was literally unattainable.

Table 14.1 reveals a chronology of strategic actions taken and decisions made by GM in a futile quest for its overall strategic objective formulated in 1978. For example, the decision to produce the Saturn automobile (classified as Type B in Chapter 11) was made in 1982 and the vehicle was brought to market in 1990. During this eight-year interval, the market for a Saturn vehicle changed considerably and several new competitive vehicles appeared that had not been anticipated in 1982. Consequently, the prospects for a financial break-even on the Saturn project is beyond hope; and the best that can be expected is an accounting break-even in a given calendar year. In short, the timing of Saturn negated the prospect of long-term profitability for the automobile.[2] Table 14.1 also reflects the purchase of Hughes Aircraft in 1983 ostensibly to imbue GM's automobiles with the technological aura of the future. Regrettably, there has been little if any technology transfer from Hughes to GM. In fact, the transfer has been one of financial support from GM to Hughes to pay for the latter's downsizing coincident with the shrinkage of defense contracting.

The jury is still out on the long-term benefits ascribable to GM's joint venture with Toyota (NUMMI) in 1983 or its purchase of Electronic Data Systems (EDS) in 1984 to end a shotgun marriage with Ross Perot. GM's management has found it difficult to assimilate the lessons of Japanese-style production management which is the basis of NUMMI. Consequently, the tangible benefits of this merger with Toyota seem negligible at this time. In like manner, the benefits from EDS to the long-term health of GM are difficult to ascertain. GM is in the business of producing automobiles and trucks, not developing management systems. And, finally, the massive reorganization of GM in 1984 did little to awaken a sleeping giant. Once the initial flow of layoffs and retirements was abated, GM had essentially the same number of management levels and managers. It was much like a game of corporate dominoes. Each time the dominoes are thrown, the resultant pattern is different. The problem from a corporate standpoint is that there is no change in the number of dominoes.

On balance, then, in view of the preceding remarks related largely to the chronology of significant events in Table 14.1, it is readily apparent why GM did not and will not achieve its strategic objective set by Thomas A. Murphy in 1978. In fact, GM is still in a kind of organizational free-fall. Market share

TABLE 14.1   General Motors: A Chronology of Significant Events

Date	Event
1978	GM's CEO Thomas A. Murphy establishes a long-range strategic objective to use $40 billion to spend the "competition into the ground."
1981	Roger B. Smith succeeds Thomas A. Murphy as GM's CEO.
1982	Roger Smith conceives the Saturn automobile.
1983	GM enters into a joint venture with Toyota (NUMMI).
1983	GM creates the Saturn Corporation and earmarks $5.1 billion to produce the Saturn automobile.
1984	GM purchases Electronic Data Systems (EDS) from Ross Perot for $2.5 billion.
1984	GM undertakes a vast internal reorganization.
1985	GM purchases Hughes Aircraft for $5.2 billion in cash and stock.
1986	GM commences production of the Saturn automobile.
1990	The Saturn automobile comes to market.
1990	Roger B. Smith retires as GM's CEO.
1990	Robert C. Stempel is named GM's CEO.
1992	Robert C. Stempel steps down as GM's CEO.
1992	John (Jack) Smith, Jr. is named GM's CEO.

has gone from just under 50 percent of the U.S. market in 1978 to just over 30 percent in 1997. Foreign market shares in Canada, Europe, and Asia are drifting. Only Mexico and Latin America show signs of growth. On balance the entire international market share is level at about 9 percent. Profits were higher in 1994 to 1996 but are still under cost pressure especially in North American operations. Ford and Chrysler are more profitable than GM, especially on a per-vehicle basis. Productivity at GM remains low; this makes it the highest-cost domestic automobile producer. Quality is suspect and new product development is lagging; this hurts GM's image with loyal customers and prospective buyers. Headcount has fallen and continues to decline. Excess production workers are easy to identify and costly to separate. Redundant white collar workers are more difficult to ascertain and somewhat less expensive to exit. Expendable supervisors and managers are even more difficult to identify especially at higher levels; and responsible executives invariably find it easier to cut at the bottom rather than reduce the top. GM needs improvement in all these areas. Hopefully, the analysis to follow will assist in this end.

THE STRATEGIC GAP AT GENERAL MOTORS IN 1978

Since GM's strategic objective to reinvent itself through the expenditure of $40 billion was set in 1978, it is instructive to focus on the corporation's strategic gap in that year.

Organizational Assessment

The purpose of an organizational assessment is to ascertain the overall capabilities of the organization in the critical areas of (1) management, (2) technology, (3) policies, and (4) resources. This assessment involves ascertaining specific strengths and weaknesses in each of the critical areas and combining them into a composite balance designated a *capability profile*. The capability profile indicates whether management should concentrate on internal improvements to translate weaknesses into strengths or whether there are enough strengths in the critical areas to permit the organization to exploit existing opportunities and to cope with actual threats in the external environment.

Management   The irony of GM is that its long-term strength has become its principal weakness. Since its inception in 1931, GM has epitomized the best in corporate management. More than any corporation in the world, GM was regarded as the leader in organizational performance. By 1978 excellence had become mediocrity; GM's management was characterized by a bloated, bureaucratic structure that impeded any attempt to improve the corporation. Objectives were ambiguous or poorly defined; lines of authority were compromised or negated; accountability for results was negligible or disregarded; and the personal interests of individual managers took precedence over the long-term best interests of the corporation.

When Alfred Sloan became CEO of GM in 1937, "he dealt effectively with GM's size by making its subsidiaries autonomous profit centers, and tying the decentralized [units] into a cohesive whole under the direction of a corporate management team."[3] By 1978, the product division structure created by Alfred Sloan was breaking down. Divisions had different and conflicting goals; disputes had to be taken to the top of the corporation for resolution; the bureaucracy was a quagmire of outmoded procedures choking off progress and productivity. "Many of the problems were tied up in GM's no-risk management environment, where individuals were not held accountable for the decisions they made . . . they were generally left unchallenged; in spite of the fiercely competitive nature of the industry, the [managers] were not prodded to be more efficient or innovative. The structure of the company and the corporate culture which valued conformity more than creativity prevented that from happening."[4] The reorganization instigated by Roger Smith in 1984 did little to reduce this organizational malaise.

Policies   Policies tend to flow from a clearly defined mission and well-defined managerial objectives both of which were absent from GM in 1978. The highly bureaucratized organizational structure of GM was replete with outmoded and obsolete procedures that did more to hinder than to help progress and productivity. The organizational malaise that characterized the product division structure of GM impeded the necessary revitalizing and updating of corporate policy and, derivatively, the operating procedures of the company. Along with management, policies at GM were a negative factor in 1978.

Technology   In 1978 GM looked to technology to improve its productivity, reduce its costs and increase its competitive position. Much of the $40 billion to finance the long-term strategic objective of GM was intended to replace labor with high technology and automation. Actually over the next fifteen years, GM would spend more than $60 billion on new technology to modernize its manufacturing plants and automotive products. Labor would be displaced by automated equipment including robots in many of GM's production areas; and GM's management would concentrate on increasing productivity and reducing unit costs of manufacture. This emphasis continued throughout the 1980s into the 1990s. The net result was little if any advantage gained in competitive costs of production and a steady diminution in market share. By the late 1980s, GM's emphasis on high technology was backfiring.

1. The company was said to produce too many look-alike cars.
2. The prevalent use of GM-made parts offset many of the cost advantages inherent in GM's new technology.
3. GM encountered many difficulties in integrating its new technology into existing operations.
4. Managerial and organizational problems tended to negate the full value of GM's new technology.
5. Competitors were also using new technology with the result that GM's costs remained high and its image of quality with existing and prospective customers continued to decline.[5]

On balance, then, in 1978 technology was a negative factor in GM's strategic gap; and indications are that it did not improve appreciably by 1997 in spite of the expenditure of more than $60 billion by the company.

Resources   Resources in the strategic gap are of four types: (1) human resources, (2) fiscal resources, (3) physical resources, and (4) institutional resources. In 1978 GM had more human resources than the company could support especially in view of its declared intention to increase productivity and reduce unit costs. Moreover, many of these human resources were essentially obsolete in that they were still doing things the way GM did in the

1950s and the 1960s. On balance, human resources at GM in 1978 were in over supply and were inadequate for the new technology desired by management. As such, human resources were a negative factor in GM's strategic gap.

Fiscal resources were a positive factor at GM in 1978. The company was awash in cash flow, cash reserves, and lines of credit. In fact, in 1978, GM recorded $63 million in sales with a phenomenal $3.5 billion in earnings and an astronomical $7 billion in cash flow. There is little doubt that this plethora of corporate riches contributed to the perception of GM's management that it could buy perpetual industry leadership.

GM's physical resources were badly in need of modernization or re-placement in 1978. Plants were obsolete and underutilized; equipment was worn and outmoded; and technology was far behind the state of the art. This, of course, was a primary concern of GM's management as they set out to reinvent the productive capability of the entire corporation.

Institutional resources are composed of (1) company reputation, (2) insti-tutional image, and (3) demonstrable goodwill for the corporation from most of its stakeholder groups. By this definition GM had an abundance of institu-tional resources in 1978. The 1970s were a good decade for GM. The company still enjoyed its reputation as the world's preeminent producer of automotive products. Foreign competitors were nibbling at the edges of GM's formidable image, but nothing like that which would materialize in the 1980s. Still in 1978, GM's capability profile showed a preponderance of internal weak-nesses that required corrective action before the corporation could success-fully exploit available opportunities in the external environment.

Environmental Assessment

As noted above, GM's capability profile reflected several significant weak-nesses. In fact, the only real strength was the corporation's fiscal resources which, in the absence of overdue corrective action, would steadily diminish. The company's external image was still positive; however the onset of qual-ity problems and productivity declines would surely cause GM to lose favor with actual and potential customers. The biggest weakness was GM's man-agement, which was the victim of nearly fifty years of industry leadership. Until management underwent a complete metamorphosis, GM was unable to exploit any external opportunity. Managerial weaknesses had to be trans-formed into managerial strengths if the corporation was to remain the industry leader. Whatever opportunities GM sought to exploit or create would surely flounder on a structure of pervasive managerial weakness. In 1978 there were no external opportunities for GM, only internal problems demanding immediate corrective action. Unfortunately this view was not shared by GM's top management. Of course it is difficult for any manage-ment group — especially one with GM's illustrious track record — to acknowledge that it is the source of the corporation's weakness. Conse-quently, GM proceeded to try to reinvent everything in the corporation except the one thing that really needed reinventing. This, of course, is the primary reason why GM failed to achieve its long-term strategic objective. The company simply didn't have the objectivity and the insight to focus on the real problem.

Apart from a lack of external opportunities in 1978, GM faced a host of external threats, the foremost of which included foreign competition and government regulation. As noted in the Chrysler case, GM's management was affected by the following federal legislation:

1. *The Clean Air Act of 1963* (amended in 1970 and 1977), which mandated the amount of pollutants that cars could emit

2. *The National Traffic and Motor Vehicle Safety Act of 1966*, which imposed safety standards on all American auto makers

3. *The Energy and Policy Conservation Act of 1975*, which mandated that by 1985 all automobile fleets must meet an average gasoline consumption of 27.5 mile per gallon

While the cost of compliance with the aforesaid legislation added substantially to the unit price of motor vehicles, GM's biggest threat in the external environment was foreign competition. In particular, Japanese car manufacturers were becoming a significant factor in the American market. This was the case because the general public was coming to accept the idea that Japanese products were superior to their American counterparts. By comparison, for example, GM's cars built in outmoded plants with an old technology were losing their distinctive qualities as desirable products. This growing loss of competitiveness was something that GM intended to address immediately and forcefully with the $40 billion earmarked for that purpose in 1978. In fact, the joint venture with Toyota (NUMMI) and the Saturn automobile both created in 1983 were directed at neutralizing the increasing inroads of foreign competition. Unfortunately, GM's management was never able to incorporate NUMMI's production successes into the mainstream of the entire corporation; and the delays and production problems associated with Saturn tended to reduce the value of that project as a role model for all of GM.

Gap Analysis

GM's situation in 1978 may be accurately characterized as a large negative gap. In particular, the situation called for a complete overhaul of GM's organizational structure with a substantial reduction in its size and incumbents. Instead GM chose to use its substantial fiscal resources in a futile attempt to revitalize and, in a sense, to reinvent the corporation. Unfortunately such a sweeping change must begin with substantial modifications in the managerial ethos of the corporation. GM sought to do the undoable by trying to change everything except its management. The failure of this closed decision-making process is reflected in the derivative strategic choices set forth in Table 14.1. For example, the joint venture with Toyota did not cause GM's management to adopt the most successful aspects of Japanese production methods. The Saturn automobile will never recover anything like its startup costs and has yet to prove itself consistently profitable. The technological promise seen by Roger Smith in the purchase of Hughes Aircraft has yet to materialize. (Note: Both Saturn and Hughes Aircraft were designated Type B strategic choices in Chapter 11.) And, finally, the purchase of EDS, accomplished mainly to remove Ross Perot from GM's board of directors, is of questionable long-term value to the corporation.[6] On balance, at least three out of the four strategic choices made by GM during the 1980s in pursuit of its 1978 strategic objective have failed or have not attained their intended strategic result.

As of this date, GM is still struggling to hold market share in the United States and in most foreign automobile markets. In the early part of the 1990s, the corporation lost money every year. In 1992, for example, GM lost more money than any other U.S. corporation.[7] GM's profit revival in 1994 to 1996 may be attributed to a healthy U.S. economy and a strong automobile market. Clearly the gap analysis of 1978 was substantially negative, but so is the gap analysis of 1997, albeit at a lower level of negativism, and the prospects for an immediate and lasting transformation to a positive strategic gap seem tenuous at best.

THE DECISION-MAKING PROCESS AT GENERAL MOTORS

The Objectives

While GM's nominal long-range strategic objective was "to use its vast financial resources to spend its competitors right into the ground," the actual objective was to protect and preserve the preeminence of the corporation.[8] In other words, while ostensibly offensive in its thrust, GM's strategic objective was set in defense of the corporation's industry leadership. In light of its large negative strategic gap, GM's management was correct in its emphasis on internal improvement. But rather than focus on the corporation's technology, quality, and productivity, all of which are important, the place to start was at the top of the corporation with a complete overhaul of the managerial ethos and the organizational structure. In the absence of draconian managerial modifications, GM's strategic objective had little chance for success.

Moreover, the objective was cast in the closed decision-making process which meant that internal and external constraints were largely ignored. Time was of some importance; but there was no limit on cost, and GM's managers acknowledged no cognitive limitations regarding the means to the end. The objective was unbelievably narrow in scope failing to assign necessary weight to environmental factors and the response capability of competitors.

In setting its objectives, GM also incorrectly assumed that automated production would axiomatically result in lower production costs. Consequently, a long-term program turned into a nightmare of problems with industrial robots and computer-controlled manufacturing systems. In essence, "GM tried to go too far too fast with its implementation of a factory of the future concepts."[9] Also in setting their long-range strategic objective, GM's managers did not satisfy the criterion of flexibility. They did not ask the question: Is the objective sufficiently flexible or is the organization likely to find itself locked into a fixed course of action? As it turned out, because of their fixed mind set with regard to their objective, GM's managers found themselves locked into an escalating spending plan during the 1980s that was obviously not going to be successful. Moreover, the magnitude of the expenditure originally set at $40 billion was enough to boggle the mind. The actual expenditure exceeded $60 billion. Was there any intention of recovering these expenditures? If not, who was accountable? Given GM's difficulty in identifying and controlling their costs during the 1980s, it is unlikely that anyone seriously tried to match expenditures with value received. In essence, there was no accountability for results.

On balance, it is apparent that GM's long-range strategic objective was doomed from the outset. Not only was the objective set mindless and heedless of most constraints, but it fell short on the critical characteristics of practicability, flexibility, cost effectiveness, and accountability.[10]

The Search for Alternatives

The available evidence indicates that GM did not search outside the corporation for any alternative courses of action. Reference to the strategic decision-making process in Figure 10.3 indicates that once a gap analysis is completed and the resultant strategic objective has been established, management necessarily begins to look for possibilities in the external environment from which to develop a set of alternatives. GM's strategic objective was established at the top of the organization by its CEO, Thomas A. Murphy. There was little done by way of a realistic strategic gap analysis. It was assumed that whatever GM sought GM would get. As GM's CEO stated, "If we are competing aggressively then whatever share we obtain is properly ours."[11] In other words, GM would do about anything it pleased as long as it did not break the law. Clearly this is a managerial attitude oriented toward a fixed objective in the closed decision-making process. Such an attitude does not produce a search for alternatives.

The Comparison and Evaluation of Alternatives

Because GM did not conduct a search for alternatives in the external environment of the corporation, there was no comparison and evaluation of alternatives. GM's managers blatantly disregarded most of the constraints that normally bound rational decision makers. Given the presence of a preferred alternative about which top management had no doubt regarding the outcome, there was an unjustifiable presumption of perfect information and complete knowledge. As noted earlier, time was of some importance, but cost had no limit, and cognitive limitations would never have been acknowledged. Simple modifications that might have facilitated implementation of a unilateral strategic choice were not considered. There was, for example, no perceived need for a pilot program to proceed incrementally and fine tune the choice based on continuous feedback. There was certainly no perceived need to institute any form of participation in the implementation phase of the decision. Everything was conceived at the top of the organization and implemented by fiat through the managerial hierarchy.

The Strategic Choice

The strategic decision to spend $40 billion to destroy the competition was the only choice considered by GM's decision makers. It was the best choice because it was their preferred choice. There was no doubt in their minds that it would succeed in the same way that GM had always succeeded. Failure was not considered because failure was not a characteristic of GM. Decisions made by other organizations may fail, but not those made by GM. In this regard, GM was caught up in a kind of organizational narcissism much like NASA in the catastrophic launch of the *Challenger* spacecraft.[12] Like NASA, GM was seduced by an organizational ideal that was totally divorced from reality. The NASA of 1986 was not the NASA of 1969, and the GM of 1978 was not the GM of the 1950s and 1960s. Times had changed; but GM was still operating from an organizational ideal that no longer existed. It may have been true as stated at one time by a former GM CEO that whatever is good for GM is good for the country; but it was certainly far from true that GM would succeed in whatever it believed was good for the corporation.

Implementation of the Decision

Implementation of GM's strategic decision to spend $40 billion to protect and preserve its industry leadership took place through the managerial hierarchy and the budgeting mechanisms of the corporation. Task assignments related to implementing high technology in the company's production operations were made through the normal chain of command. Resource allocations to finance the new emphasis on smaller cars and automated or robotized manufacturing processes were made in accordance with the task assignments. While GM was implementing its primary strategic decision to use new technology to produce an armada of fuel-saving cars with front-wheel drives, other decisions also of a strategic nature were made to attain the long-term strategic objective set in 1978. These corollary strategic decisions are reflected in Table 14.1. They include (1) a joint venture with Toyota, 1983, (2) creation of the Saturn Corporation, 1983, (3) purchase of EDS, 1984, (4) communication of a major internal reorganization, 1984, and (5) purchase of Hughes Aircraft, 1985.

Further evaluation of GM's implementation phase will constitute the subject of a comparative case assessment of determinants of strategic decision success set forth in a subsequent section of this chapter.

Follow-up and Control

Essentially there was no follow-up and control of GM's strategic decision to spend $40 billion to perpetuate its industry leadership. As billions of dollars were expended during the 1980s, GM's productivity continued to languish and its unit costs continued well above the industry average. The more money that GM spent, the more their market share declined. Most analysts and observers had concluded by 1987 that GM's strategic decision made in 1978 was a complete failure.[13] In one sense, GM was already out of control when it set its strategic objective. The futile pursuit of that objective simply made the actual state of affairs within GM more obvious to everyone, including GM's board of directors.

PHILIP MORRIS: A PERSPECTIVE

Philip Morris (PM) is widely regarded as the leading manufacturer and marketer of cigarettes in the United States. In 1996 it had a 49.4 percent retail share of a $74 billion industry.[14] For the past thirty years, PM has grown through a strategy of acquisition that in 1984 became one of acquisition and diversification. For the most part from 1944 to 1985, PM's acquisitions were in the cigarette industry. Notable exceptions were the acquisition of Miller Brewing Company in 1969 and the Seven-Up Company in 1977. In 1984, PM's CEO set a long-range strategic objective to lessen the company's dependence on cigarettes as its primary source of profits. This strategic objective resulted in a deliberate strategic choice to diversify PM into the food processing industry. With diversification, PM's subsequent strategic objective was to become and remain the most successful consumer packaged goods company in the world.[15]

When Hamish Maxwell became CEO of PM in 1984, the company was already eminently successful. In 1983, PM had surpassed R.J. Reynolds as the leading producer of cigarettes in America. PM was the darling of Wall Street in that the price of its common stock had doubled since 1980. Profits were increasing dramatically; and PM's market share was 35 percent of the U.S. cigarette market of which, Marlboro, the company's leading brand had 21 percent.

Still with all of this financial success for PM, there were dark clouds on the horizon for the cigarette industry. Between 1982 and 1985, for example, cigarette sales declined 5 percent in the United States. This decline was occasioned by numerous antismoking campaigns decrying cigarettes as injurious to personal health. This antismoking sentiment resulted in congressional legislation requiring cigarette manufacturers to place warning labels on their products. In essence, the cigarette industry found itself under siege from powerful health care groups that posed a continuing threat to cigarette sales. Another threat to the declining cigarette industry was the emergence of "generic" or "economy-priced" cigarette brands. Such brands could only lead to diminishing profits and reduced prospects for company and industry growth.

In spite of these significant threats to the cigarette industry, PM was performing well. The company was showing small annual increases in sales and a steady growth in profits. PM's profits were sustained by the simple expedient of raising cigarette prices. Because cigarettes have a good deal of price elasticity, smokers usually paid the higher prices which, of course, facilitated market entry by lower-priced discount brands. Although PM produced its own discount brands, their very presence detracted from sales of higher-priced cigarettes and placed continuing pressure on profits.

One of PM's primary concerns was its extreme dependence on cigarettes as a source of profits. In fact, cigarettes accounted for 92 percent of profits in 1984. Moreover, PM's Seven-Up Company lost $10 million in 1983, and PM's Miller Brewing Company was expected to post a 25 percent reduction in profits in 1984. Nonetheless, PM's CEO decided to hold onto these diverse businesses and to move the company deeply into the food processing industry.

In 1984, then, the long-range strategic objective for PM was to lessen the company's overdependence on profits from cigarettes through diversification into the food processing industry. The objective was truly long range in that it had a ten-year planning horizon. There would be a series of interim strategic decisions that would lead to the ultimate attainment of the strategic objective. These interim decisions would gradually lessen PM's dependence on tobacco profits and would result in a successful outcome for the primary strategic choice in 1984.

The aim of PM was to replace risky tobacco profits with more stable food processing profits. Food processing was chosen because it permitted PM to stay within the meta industry of consumer packaged goods, a stable industry in which PM already had considerable experience. Moreover, there were few external threats to the profits of the food processing industry. It was a stable, slow growth, less profitable industry that provided PM with an offset to the beleaguered and declining high-profit tobacco industry.

As noted earlier, PM had a history of expansion by acquisition in the tobacco industry. Since 1984 this emphasis has shifted to one of diversification by acquisition. PM already owned Miller Brewing Company and the Seven-Up Company. In recent years, PM has made several minor and major acquisitions in the food processing industry. The major acquisitions are few in number but significant in terms of their impact on the company's long-range strategic objective. These acquisitions are as follows:

November 1985	Purchased General Foods for $5.6 billion
December 1988	Acquired Kraft for approximately $12.9 billion
August 1990	Purchased Swiss-based coffee and confectionery company Jacobs Suchard AG for $4.1 billion

This emphasis on diversification by acquisition continues today in PM. The overall impact on PM's sales and profits indicates that, by most definitions, the company has attained its long-term strategic objective set in 1984. In 1984, for example, tobacco products accounted for 92 percent of PM's income from operations. By 1992 this proportion had dropped to 68 percent. Along with this steady diminution in dependence on income from tobacco products, PM steadily increased its market share in an overall declining tobacco industry. Tobacco products are obviously more profitable than processed foods. In 1996, for example, tobacco products accounted for 53 percent of PM's sales while contributing 67 percent of the company's profits.[16] The relative profitability of tobacco products explains why PM keeps increasing its market share of the tobacco industry. After all, PM's long-term strategic objective is to reduce the company's overdependence on profits from tobacco products, not to reduce profits absolutely. A diminution in tobacco's share of PM's profits from 92 to 67 percent in twelve years is prima facie evidence of the attainment of a strategic objective set in 1984 with a ten-year maturity.

On April 2, 1993, PM made a strategic decision to reduce the price of Marlboro, its leading brand of cigarettes, by 40 cents a pack. PM's management estimated that this price reduction would reduce pretax profits from tobacco products in 1993 as much as $2 billion.[17] This reduction in retail price reflected a decision intended to increase sales, profits, and market share in tobacco products and, therefore, was not part of PM's strategy to attain its 1984 long-range strategic objective. However, the overall effect would certainly increase the proportion of profits from processed foods in 1993 and possibly beyond. Even a 67/33 percent split in profits between tobacco and processed foods is a long way from the 92 percent held by tobacco products in 1984. Again, it seems obvious that PM's strategic choice in 1984 resulted in an eminently successful outcome.

THE STRATEGIC GAP AT PHILIP MORRIS IN 1984

Since PM's strategic objective to reduce its overdependence on profits from tobacco products was set in 1984, it is instructive to focus on the corporation's strategic gap in that year.

Organizational Assessment

The purpose of an organizational assessment is to ascertain the overall capabilities of the organization in the critical areas of (1) management, (2) technology, (3) policies, and (4) resources. This assessment involves ascertaining specific strengths and weaknesses in each of the critical areas and combining them into a composite balance designated a *capability profile*. The capability profile indicates whether management should concentrate on internal improvements to translate weaknesses into strengths or whether there are enough strengths in the critical areas to permit the organization to exploit existing opportunities and to cope with actual threats in the external environment.

In 1984 PM's capability profile was characterized by an abundance of strengths and only one significant weakness. The weakness of 1984 is still a weakness today. PM has too much cash flow and cash reserve. Primarily because of the high rate of profit on cigarettes and PM's continued growth in market share in the declining tobacco industry, the company is awash with excess cash.[18] In fact, PM normally generates more free cash flow than most any other corporation in the United States.[19] The management was highly effective in 1984. PM had just displaced RJR Nabisco as the leading producer of cigarettes in America. The company had a new CEO, Hamish Maxwell, who was obviously oriented toward company growth. The company's technology in the production of cigarettes was first rate. Its costs were under control and productivity was increasing. Policies were comprehensive in all of the units of PM and at the corporate level.

Resources of all types were in a positive state. The human resource at PM was generally challenged and satisfied. Labor-management relations were positive and internal opportunities for promotion were not lacking. Physical resources in the form of land, buildings, and machinery were modern and fully utilized; and the institutional resource of company image and goodwill were positive. Again, the only weakness at PM was a surfeit of liquidity which posed a continuing challenge to management to ensure its profitable use. Idle or underutilized fiscal resources for a company like PM carry a high opportunity cost; and it is incumbent on management to minimize cash reserves such that large balances are nonexistent. In spite of this potent weakness, PM's capability profile was replete with a balance of strength in nearly every critical factor.

Environmental Assessment

Given its vast internal strength along with its abundant cash flow and cash reserves, PM had more than sufficient capability to exploit existing opportunities and to develop new opportunities. The opportunities of interest to PM's management were those that would reduce the company's overdependence on profits from the declining tobacco industry. The threats in PM's external environment were (1) smoking and health-related issues, (2) anti-smoking litigation and legislation, (3) continuing declines in the total sales of cigarettes in the United States, and (4) the emergence of discount brands of generic cigarettes as a counter to steadily increasing prices for regular brands of name cigarettes. These threats represented a composite of environmental forces from the economic, social, and political areas. As such they were beyond the ability of any company — even one as powerful and profitable as PM — to control. The only viable strategy for PM was to continue to assert its concern for health-related issues to forestall harmful litigation and legislation and to bolster its market share in a declining industry by extolling the merits of its regular brands of cigarettes while joining the industry trend toward discount brands. Obviously the confluence of significant threats in its external environment is what caused PM to use its internal strengths to protect itself through diversification by acquisitions outside of the tobacco industry.

Gap Analysis

PM's situation in 1984 may be accurately characterized as a large positive gap. In particular the situation called for a strategy to reduce PM's dependence on profits from a declining and beleaguered industry by diversification into an industry that was both compatible and stable with reasonable prospects for moderate profits and growth. PM had both the management and the fiscal resources to accomplish this strategy. Its strategic choice in 1984 to diversify into the food processing industry was a logical culmination of this rationale. The decision to diversify and the choice of a target industry for diversification were totally compatible with the large positive strategic gap at PM in 1984. Management accurately assessed the situation, comprehended the need, and instigated timely and appropriate action to protect the long-term best interests of PM.

THE DECISION-MAKING PROCESS
AT PHILIP MORRIS

The Objectives

As stated previously, PM's long-range strategic objective was to reduce its overdependence on profits from a declining and beleaguered cigarette industry. Given PM's history of growth by acquisition in the cigarette industry, it was likely that the overdependence on cigarette profits would be reduced by diversification through acquisition. PM's objective was essentially defensive in that it sought to protect the company from further industry declines occasioned by antismoking sentiment and legislation. The objective sought to offset a possible loss of profits from cigarettes with new profits from other industries with a more stable outlook for a reasonable amount of growth.

PM's objective was both practical and timely in that its management obviously perceived a need to protect the company from actual and emerging threats in the external environment. The tobacco industry obviously affords a good-size target for many health care groups. For PM, it was prudent to seek to diversify into a product area where the company's production and marketing expertise would yield synergistic results. PM's objective was also flexible in that it contemplated a ten-year maturity. Ten years is a long time to seek and obtain balanced diversification for any company. PM's objective was cost effective in that the company's excess cash flow and cash reserves would be productively utilized in an attempt to sustain increasing profitability and nurture long-term growth. If, perchance, the diversification attempt should fail (which, given PM's capability profile, was most unlikely), PM's top management would be patently accountable. After all, the long-range strategic objective was of their making.

The Search for Alternatives

The search for alternatives is derived from the strategic long-range objective which necessitates a strategic choice and implemented decision from which to secure attainment of the objective. PM had a world of alternatives to shield the company from the numerous threats in the external environment. In this context, it is well to recall that the objective was to reduce PM's overdependence on profits from the tobacco industry. Almost by definition this objective suggests a need for diversification. There is a need to continue the company somewhat in its present trajectory of growth and to buffer the company's profits from hostile external forces in its present industry. In the case of PM, this need suggested some kind of diversification into consumer products, an area in which the company had already demonstrated remarkable proficiency. Considerations of profit margins and industry stability guided PM's search for a suitable diversification candidate. Ideally, the diversification should produce synergistic benefits for both parties. PM, for example, would be shielded from the hostile external environment of the tobacco industry with a minimal loss of growth and profitability, whereas the other party to diversification would benefit from PM's ample fiscal resources and proven managerial expertise.

Overall the search took place within the concept of bounded rationality. PM's decision makers acknowledged that they were proceeding with imperfect information and a good deal of uncertainty associated with the outcome. There were also mindful of time and cost constraints on the need to take some decisive action. And they were also sensitive to their own cognitive limitations in that they considered a rather small number of alternatives.

The Comparison and Evaluation of Alternatives

The search soon dwindled down to a precious few possibilities. The diversification strategy should build on PM's considerable strength and provide added impetus to the company's abundant future prospects. The choice should be complementary and yet provide for compatibility and consistency in fulfilling PM's overall corporate mission. Consumer products in general and consumer packaged products in particular were the primary candidates of choice. Again, mindful of the constraints of bounded rationality, PM's decision makers screened the possible industries and companies with strong preferences for a favorable outcome, but with an agonizing sense of uncertainty occasioned by a host of imponderables in the situation.

The Choice

The strategic choice of the food processing industry as the target for PM's diversification thrust was eminently rational. Food processing is a stable industry with a low profit margin and a slow rate of growth. Conversely, the tobacco industry is an increasingly threatened industry with a high profit margin and, until the 1980s, a rather rapid rate of growth. The two industries seem divergent, but they have some significant similarities. Both tobacco products and processed foods, for example, use essentially the same kind of production technology and both are purveyed to the ultimate consumer through a vast and diversified distribution system. These similarities mean that both industries require the kind of managerial know-how that is characteristic of most consumer packaged goods producers, and PM is one of the best of this kind. Finally, PM might have been influenced by the knowledge that its principal competitor, R.J. Reynolds, was also moving toward diversification into the food processing industry. In fact, Reynolds acquired Nabisco and became RJR Nabisco in 1985 when PM acquired General Foods.

On balance, the choice of the food processing industry was a satisficing strategic choice, that is, one that met but did not necessarily exceed PM's long-range strategic objective. It was made in the open decision-making process using a judgmental decision-making strategy. As such, it seemed virtually assured of a successful outcome.

Implementation of the Decision

Implementation of PM's strategic decision to diversify into the food processing industry essentially took place at the top of the corporation with a series of strategic decisions to buy several major companies in the food processing industry. As noted earlier, these acquisitions included (1) General Foods in 1985 for $5.6 billion, (2) Kraft in 1988 for $12.9 billion, and (3) Jacobs Suchard

AG (Swiss) in 1990 for $4.1 billion. These are only the major acquisitions in the food processing industry made by PM since 1984. Other acquisitions are being contemplated in pursuit of the company's long-term strategic objective.

Further evaluation of PM's implementation phase will constitute the subject of a comparative case assessment of determinants of strategic decision success set forth in the next major section of this chapter.

Follow-up and Control

The effectiveness of follow-up and control by PM to ensure a successful outcome for its strategic choice is attested to by the company's ability to successfully assimilate its major acquisitions while increasing its market share and enhancing its industry leadership in the beleaguered and declining tobacco industry. Since 1984, for example, PM has recorded substantial growth in both sales and profits. PM is regularly listed among America's top 200 growth companies.[20] And in 1992, PM led all U.S. corporations with a net income of $4.9 billion.[21] Somewhat ironically, in the context of this book, PM was the biggest money maker and GM was the biggest money loser among U.S. corporations in 1992.[22] (Note: By 1996 GM had returned to profitability but was only 40 percent as profitable as PM.)

Effective follow-up and control normally results in the attainment of the objective that gave rise to the decision that is being followed up. In PM's case the attainment of its long-range strategic objective is obvious; and, like any other successful strategic choice, such attainment necessarily resulted from effective follow-up and control to ensure a positive result.

COMPARATIVE CASE DETERMINANTS
OF STRATEGIC DECISION SUCCESS

Having analyzed and evaluated General Motors and Philip Morris as individual cases, the comparative evaluation in this section is based on the determinants of decision success set forth in Trull's study of 100 organizations and further advanced by the Bay area study of 108 organizations. According to the foundations of these two studies, the success of a given decision is a function of the quality of the decision and its implementation. Decision quality, in turn, is composed of (1) compatibility with operating constraints, (2) nearness to optimum time for the decision, (3) proximity to the optimum amount of information, and (4) the decision maker's influence on the decision. Decision implementation is a product of (1) a risk-reward factor and (2) the degree of understanding by those who must carry out the decision. These six factors make up the essence of the analysis and evaluation to follow.

Compatibility with Operating Constraints

Operating constraints are organizational policies and procedures associated with an established way of doing business. Trull's study found that, in the majority of cases, successful decisions were highly compatible with existing operating constraints. Conversely, the Bay area study found that the respondent CEOs did not regard the established way of doing business as a particularly strong boundary condition for their successful strategic choices. The evaluation of GM and PM in this chapter agrees with the findings of the Bay area study. Neither one of these corporations appeared to depart significantly from the established way of doing business in their respective industries, and the results of their respective strategic choices are markedly divergent. This divergence must be attributable to factors other than the established way of doing business.

Nearness to Optimum Time

Both Trull's study and the Bay area study found that nearness to optimum time was the factor deserving of the most improvement in seeking a successful strategic choice. Clearly there is an optimal time in which to make a strategic decision. The precise point of optimality will approximate the zenith of the opportunity to be capitalized or the advantage to be gained by the decision maker. Time is an immutable constraint in most strategic decision-making situations in that it constitutes a defined interval within or a precise point at which action must be taken to commit scarce resources. Time also constitutes one of the immutable constraints of strategic decision making under conditions of bounded rationality (see Figure 3.1). In essence, timing can be good or bad.[23]

In the case of PM, top management clearly picked the optimal time to diversify into the food processing industry. Cigarette consumption in the United States peaked in 1982 and in 1984 the outlook called for slow steady declines in future consumption. In 1983 PM passed R.J. Reynolds as the number one producer of cigarettes in the United States Litigation and legislation threatened to impede future growth in the tobacco industry. PM was the leader in a beleaguered and declining industry. The time was right to diversify; and PM chose a ten-year maturity for its strategic objective within which to make diversified acquisitions for the long-term benefit of the company. PM attained its long-range strategic objective within its own time horizon while observing the time constraints imposed by threatening environmental forces. The company's strategic choice was made and implemented within the optimal time.

For its part, GM also made its strategic choice at the optimal time. GM had a good decade in the 1970s; the company was still regarded as economically impregnable. Foreign competition was increasing, but GM still had just under one-half of the U.S. car and truck market. GM's top management knew that it was time for a change so they made their strategic choice to spend $40 billion. GM's decision fell apart in its implementation. Without a massive revitalization of GM's management, its strategic choice had no chance for success. GM's timing was bad in that it put the cart before the horse. First change management; then reinvent the corporation.

GM's timing for Saturn was also erroneous. Saturn was conceived in 1982; the Saturn Corporation was established in 1983; Saturn went into production in 1986; and the roll out of the first Saturn automobile occurred in 1990. Meanwhile the competition was producing automobiles that would usurp Saturn's potential customers. Eight years from conception to roll out is simply too much time in the highly competitive automobile industry.

On balance, GM's timing was fatally flawed in that the corporation attempted to implement its strategic choice with a bureaucratic managerial hierarchy in a bloated organizational structure, which resulted in numerous errors in timing throughout the 1980s and ultimately caused its long-range strategy to fail. GM was its own worst enemy in this undertaking.

Optimum Amount of Information

The results of Trull's study found that managerial decision makers do not fully appreciate the futility of seeking the optimum amount of information. Conversely, the CEOs in the Bay area study for the most part indicated that the amount of information that they required to make their successful strategic decisions was generally adequate. For their part, PM's decision makers operated in the open decision-making process. They knew that they did not have anything like perfect information; but they made good use of the information available to them. PM's decision makers made a satisficing choice within the omnipresent constraints of bounded rationality.

In a contrary fashion, GM's decision makers erroneously assumed they had all of the relevant information necessary to make and implement their strategic choice. This assumption was perfectly natural for them because they operated in the closed decision-making process. They assumed a high level of knowledge regarding the outcome over the course of a decade that was the most competitive period in U.S. automotive history. On balance, GM's use of available information was flawed, and its assumptions regarding the accessibility of additional information was deficient. Consequently, GM proceeded on the basis of a level of certainty regarding the outcome of its strategic choice made in 1978 that was totally unjustified. Clearly this was a formula for failure.

Decision Maker's Influence

Trull's study found that the perceived authority of the person making the decision tended to have an important influence on the outcome of the choice. Conversely, the respondent CEOs in the Bay area study indicated that the authority of their respective offices was not highly influential in determining strategic decision success.

The results of the two cases presented in this chapter tend to validate the findings of the Bay area study. At GM in 1978 and again at PM in 1984, the subject strategic choices were made by the CEOs of these corporations, and the results were totally divergent. GM's strategic failure was offset by PM's strategic success. Ironically, in 1992 PM was the profit leader and GM was the loss leader among all U.S. corporations. With regard to these two case studies, the influence of the decision maker on the outcome of the strategic choices appears negligible.

Risk-Reward Factor

Contrary to the findings of Trull's study, the Bay area study revealed that the respondent CEOs were very aware of the relationship between risk and reward. In the classical economic model, decision makers accept additional risk only with the inducement of additional reward. Satisficing decision makers seldom seek additional increments of risk even in the presence of off-setting reward. It is only necessary to accept enough risk to attain the objective. For the satisficer, there is no need to aspire to some unattainable achievement. Conversely, the maximizer is always seeking the highest possible outcome and often will accept considerably more risk than the potential rewards justify.

GM, for example, was clearly trying to maximize its strategic choice to spend $40 billion to preserve its industry leadership without first drastically changing its managerial ethos and its organizational structure. GM made its strategic choice in the closed decision-making process using a computational decision-making strategy that transformed its strategic objective into an unattainable result. There was no thought given to risk because GM would never have entertained the notion of possible failure and because the corporation had so much excess cash that financial loss was not a threat for it. In 1978 the risk-reward relationship was completely ignored by GM's decision makers. There was no perceived risk for GM and, consequently, there proved to be no actual reward.

Conversely, PM was very mindful of its risk-reward relationship. PM's management was keenly aware of the numerous threats in its external environment. The threats promised to retard PM's long-term growth and to reduce its annual profits. PM's management carefully considered the possibilities of continuing to concentrate in the tobacco industry or diversifying into some other industry that would provide an offset to reduced growth, declining unit sales, diminishing profits, and increasing legislation and litigation. The choice of the food processing industry was clearly a satisficing decision. The industry was characterized by slow growth and low profits. Still it provided PM with a source of long-term balance and equilibrium. PM manifested a high regard for its risk-reward factor and was rewarded with a successful outcome.

Degree of Understanding

Both the Trull study and the Bay area study agree that there should be an acceptable degree of understanding on the part of the decision implementors regarding what is expected of them. Neither of the cases in this chapter confirmed or refuted these findings. The strategic choices were made by top management and implemented through the chain of command and the normal budgetary allocation process. It seems reasonable to assume, therefore, that there was a requisite degree of understanding.

When these two cases are evaluated in the context of the Trull study and the Bay area study, it becomes more apparent why GM's strategic choice was a resounding failure and PM's strategic choice was a noteworthy success. PM observed every one of the six critical factors that constitute the determinants of strategic decision success. Some of these factors were less important than others, but PM did not disregard any of them. For its part, GM fell short on three of the six critical factors. First, GM's timing was less than optimal, especially in attempting to implement its strategic choice in the presence of weak management. Second, GM's management proceeded on the basis of a level of certainty regarding the outcome of its strategic choice that erroneously presumed an optimum amount of information. Finally, GM's management totally disregarded the risk-reward factor by completely dismissing any concern about recovering the $40 billion that it intended to spend.

COMPARATIVE CASE CLASSIFICATIONS OF STRATEGIC DECISION SUCCESS

The comparative case classifications of strategic decision success are derived from the strategic decision matrix set forth in Figure 11.1 and discussed completely in Chapter 11. As shown in the figure, a Type A strategic decision is most likely to succeed because it is composed of attainable objectives developed in the open decision-making process that are pursued through a judgmental decision-making strategy in quest of a satisficing outcome. Conversely, a Type D strategic decision is unlikely to succeed because it is founded on unattainable objectives conceived in the closed decision-making process that are sought through a computational decision-making strategy in pursuit of a maximized outcome.

Managerial Attitude Toward the Decision-Making Process

The overriding objective in the GM case was to preserve the industry leadership of the corporation. GM's CEO set this objective in the closed decision-making process oblivious to the constraints of bounded rationality. There was an erroneous presumption of perfect information along with a sense of complete knowledge regarding the outcome of the strategic choice. If GM was going to spend $40 billion to bury the competition, how could it not be successful? Time and cost constraints were also disregarded. After all, GM was still the industry leader with seemingly limitless fiscal resources. The disregard of a realistic design and production schedule for the Saturn automobile is prima facie evidence of GM's blatant disregard of the time constraint. Insofar as the cognitive limitations of the decision makers are concerned, GM would never acknowledge any sort of limitation on its top management. Presumably they were both omniscient and prescient in their decision making. In fact, however, the biggest single factor in GM strategic decision failure was its management. Nearly fifty years of managerial strength had by 1978 become GM's greatest weakness. In essence, the use of the closed decision-making process by GM rendered unattainable an objective that otherwise might have been attained.

PM's long-range strategic objective was simply to reduce its overdependence on profits from the tobacco industry. Given PM's internal strengths and minimal weaknesses, this objective was eminently realistic. Moreover, the objective was set in the open decision-making process in that the decision makers were extremely sensitive to a host of hostile environmental forces. PM's decision makers also operated within the several constraints of bounded rationality. Imperfect information was acknowledged; time and cost constraints were observed; and cognitive limitations were accepted. PM exhibited a positive set of managerial attitudes toward the strategic decision-making process.

Managerial Attitudes Toward the Decision

GM pursued a computational decision-making strategy in seeking to maximize its unattainable objective. It was simply a matter of spending billions to reinvent GM and overpower the competition. GM was clearly seeking a maximized result. There was no perceived limit on the corporation's aspirations. Any behavior was acceptable as long as it was legal; any benefit redounding to GM was the corporation's just due. GM started out in 1978 as the biggest and the best of its kind; and GM's decision makers intended that the end result of their labors would perpetuate this state of affairs. Regrettably and predictably, GM's negative strategic gap was much larger in 1993 than it was in 1978. By 1996 GM had made some progress in reducing its negative strategic gap; but the gap was still negative and the GM of 1996 was not the corporation of 1978.[24] GM could look back on eighteen years of futility and failure. Clearly GM's decision is the epitome of a Type D strategic choice.

For its part, PM pursued a judgmental decision-making strategy in seeking to satisfice its attainable objective. PM's decision makers obviously had a strong preference for a favorable outcome, but they also internalized a low level of knowledge regarding the outcome. In other words they accepted the uncertainty inherent in the outcome of a strategic choice intended to attain a long-range strategic objective. Moreover, PM's decision makers simply wanted to achieve their objective. They wanted to make the corporation less dependent on profits from the tobacco industry rather than independent of such profits. PM sought a satisficing outcome which is most appropriate for any strategic choice; and they were demonstrably successful. As such, PM provides an excellent example of a Type A strategic choice.

SUMMARY

This chapter presented the third of four sets of comparative case evaluations using the frameworks and concepts presented in this book.

General Motors (GM) was presented as highly illustrative of a Type D strategic choice. GM set a long-range strategic objective in 1978 to preserve and protect its industry leadership by reinventing the corporation. Eighteen years later GM still had a negative strategic gap. During the 1980s, GM spent upwards of $60 billion to reinvent itself; its market share declined from just under one-half of the U.S. automobile and truck market to scarcely one-third of that market. In the early 1990s GM recorded substantial financial losses. In 1992 GM was the U.S. corporate financial loss leader. By 1996 GM had returned to profitability, but at a lower level than during its halcyon years in the 1950s, 1960s, and 1970s. A substantially reduced market share along with a rigid cost structure severely impacted GM's profitability in the 1990s.

This chapter demonstrated that GM transformed an objective that was difficult to attain into one that was impossible to attain by using the closed decision-making process. GM's decision makers did not seriously consider a range of viable alternatives, and they ignored the many constraints that limited their decision-making endeavors. GM proceeded with a sense of complete certainty regarding the outcome of its strategic choice in a situation that was replete with uncertainty. The corporation's organizational narcissism deceived its management into expecting an ideal outcome simply because it was GM.

Philip Morris (PM) was presented as the epitome of a Type A strategic choice. PM set a long-range strategic objective in 1984 to reduce its overdependence on profits from the tobacco industry. This decision resulted in PM's diversification into the food processing industry. By 1996 tobacco profits were reduced from 92 percent of PM's total to just 67 percent with every indication of further declines in subsequent years. Moreover, in every year of the 1990s, PM has been a U.S. corporate profit leader.

This chapter demonstrated that PM facilitated the attainment of its long-term strategic objective by using the open decision-making process. Contrary to GM's decision makers, PM considered several alternatives and observed a full set of decision-making constraints in making its decision to diversify into the food processing industry. PM's decision makers proceeded mindful and heedful of the uncertainty inherent in making and implementing a strategic choice. This positive approach resulted in a highly successful strategic outcome for PM.

This chapter also demonstrated that GM ignored virtually every one of the determinants of decision success that were used in the Trull study and the Bay area study. In particular, GM was deficient in (1) proximity to optimum timing for implementing the decision, (2) proximity to the optimum amount of information for making the decision, and (3) observance of the risk-reward factor. In a contrary fashion, PM scored high marks on all of the determinants of strategic decision success.

Finally, a comprehensive evaluation of both corporations in the context of the strategic decision matrix set forth in Figure 11.1 revealed that GM was the archetype of a Type D strategic choice and PM was the quintessence of a Type A strategic choice.

REVIEW AND DISCUSSION QUESTIONS

1. How could GM possibly overlook the acute need to reinvent its management before undertaking the reinvention of the entire corporation?

2. Was GM's long-range strategic objective attainable under any circumstances? Discuss.

3. In what specific ways did GM's decision makers confine themselves to the closed decision-making process?

4. How did GM deal with the risk-reward factor in its strategic choice?

5. What evidence is there to place GM squarely in the Type D category of strategic choice?

6. In what specific ways did PM's decision makers operate in the open decision-making process?

7. How did PM deal with the timing factor in its strategic choice?

8. Under what circumstances might PM's long-range strategic objective have become unattainable? Discuss.

9. What evidence is there to place PM squarely in the Type A category of strategic choice?

10. Under what circumstances might PM have become a Type C strategic choice? Discuss?

NOTES

1. See "General Motors: What Went Wrong?" *Business Week* (March 16, 1987), 102–110.
2. See "Here Comes GM's Saturn," *Business Week* (April 9, 1990), 56–62.
3. Maryann Keller, *Rude Awakening: The Rise, Fall, and Struggle for Recovery of General Motors* (New York: William Morrow, 1989), p. 46.
4. Ibid., pp. 106–107.
5. "General Motors: What Went Wrong?" p. 104.
6. Doron P. Levin, *Irreconcilable Differences: Ross Perot versus General Motors* (New York: Penguin Books, 1990).
7. General Motors Annual Report, 1992 (Detroit, Mich.: General Motors Corporation, 1992).

8. "General Motors: What Went Wrong?" p. 103.

9. Brian S. Moskal, "Is GM Getting a Bum Rap?" *Industry Week* (January 12, 1987), 42.

10. E. Frank Harrison, *Management and Organizations* (Boston: Houghton Mifflin, 1978), pp. 81–91.

11. "General Motors: What Went Wrong?" p. 103.

12. See Howard S. Schwartz, *Narcissistic Process and Corporate Decay: The Theory of the Organizational Ideal* (New York: New York University Press, 1990).

13. See "General Motors: What Went Wrong?" and Keller, *Rude Awakening*.

14. John A. Pearce, II, and Richard B. Robinson, Jr., *Strategic Management: Formulation, Implementation, and Control*, 5th ed. (Burr Ridge, Ill.: Irwin, 1994), p. 565.

15. *Philip Morris Companies, Inc. 1996 Annual Report* (New York: Philip Morris, 1992), p. 6.

16. Ibid., p. 21.

17. Eben, Shapiro, "Cigarette Burn: Price Cut on Marlboro Upsets Rosy Notions About Tobacco Products," *Wall Street Journal* (April 6, 1993), B3.

18. See Patricia Sellers, "Can He Keep Philip Morris Growing," *Fortune* (April 6, 1992), 86–92.

19. Ibid.

20. Michael Ozanian et al., "America's Top 200 Growth Companies," *Financial World* (August 4, 1992), 32–34.

21. Edmund Faltermayer,"Poised for a Comeback," *Fortune* (April 19, 1993), 174ff.

22. Ibid.

23. See R. Bronner, *Decision Making Under Time Pressure* (Lexington, Mass.: D. C. Heath, 1982).

24. Raymond E. Miles et al., "Keys to Success in Corporate Redesign," *California Management Review*, 37, No. 3 (Spring 1995), 128–145.

SUPPLEMENTAL REFERENCES

Chakravarty, Subrata N. "Philip Morris Is Still Hungry." *Forbes* (April 2, 1990), 96–101.

Dunkin, Amy, et al. "Beyond Marlboro Country." *Business Week* (August 1988), 54–58.

Flint, Jerry. "Darkness Before Dawn." *Forbes* (November 23, 1992), 42–44.

"GM Board Pours on Heat." *Automotive* (October 28, 1992), 1ff.

Kerwin, Kathleen, et al. "Can Jack Smith Fix GM?" *Business Week* (November 1993), 126–134.

Kerwin, Kathleen, et al. "Crisis at GM." *Business Week* (November 9, 1992), 84–87.

Koerner, Elaine. "Technology Planning at General Motors." *Long-Range Planning*, 22 (1989), 9–19.

Leinster, Colin. "Is Bigger Better for Philip Morris?" *Fortune* (May 8, 1989), 66–69.

Moreau, Dan. "The Big, Wide World of Philip Morris." *Kiplinger's Personal Finance Magazine* (July 1992), 28.

Nulty, Peter. "Living with the Limits of Marlboro Magic." *Fortune* (March 18, 1985), 24ff.

Robert, Michel. "The Do's and Dont's of Strategic Alliances." *Journal of Business Strategy* (March/April 1992), 50–53.

Saporito, Bill. "Who Wins in the Hugest Deals?" *Fortune* (November 21, 1988), 83ff.

Seligmon, Daniel. "Don't Bet Against Cigarette Makers." *Fortune* (August 17, 1987), 70ff.

Sellers, Patricia. "Can He Keep Philip Morris Growing?" *Fortune* (April 6, 1992), 87–92.

Solomon, J. "Can GM Fix Itself?" *Newsweek* (November 9, 1992), 54ff.

Taylor, Alex, III. "The Road Ahead at General Motors." *Fortune* (May 4, 1992), 94–95.

———. "The Tasks Facing General Motors." *Fortune* (March 13, 1989), 52ff.

———. "What's Ahead for GM's New Team?" *Fortune* (November 30, 1992), 52–61.

Therrien, Lois. "From Chuck Wagon to Trail Boss of Marlboro Country." *Business Week* (April 15, 1991), 60–66.

Treece, James B. "Here Comes GM's Saturn." *Business Week* (April 9, 1990), 56–62.

White, Joseph B., and Neal Templin. "GM's U.S. Loss Said to Approach $2 Billion in 1993." *Wall Street Journal* (October 11, 1993), A3 and A6.

White, Joseph B., and Neal Templin. "Uphill Road." *Wall Street Journal* (October 26, 1993), 1ff.

Zinn, Laura. "Even Philip Morris Feels the Pull of Gravity." *Business Week* (February 15, 1993), 60–62.

Case Set No. 4: The Walt Disney Company

*T*his chapter concludes the presentation of cases that demonstrate the managerial attitudes toward the decision-making process and toward the decision itself that are most likely to result in strategic decision success. This chapter also concludes the illustration of the empirical use of selected evaluative frameworks and concepts advanced at various places in this book. Finally, this chapter is different from its predecessors in that it presents and evaluates two separate strategic decisions made by a single corporation at two different points in time. The managerial decision makers in these two cases are the top executives of the Walt Disney Company. Given the closeness in time of the two decisions, the decision makers constitute the same set of executives. In particular, the chief executive officer (CEO) of the Walt Disney Company is the same individual, Michael Eisner. For reasons to be elaborated in subsequent sections of this chapter, Eisner is the primary strategic decision maker for Disney. However, this chapter is not about Eisner or any of his top executive team. Rather, it is about two strategic decisions made by the Disney organization, of which one has proved less than successful and the other has prospects for success if Disney's management does not take action to preclude it.

The first case in this chapter — Eurodisney — affords an excellent example of the thesis that the use of a computational decision-making strategy in quest of a maximized outcome militates against decision success even if the objective is attainable and the decision maker operates in the open decision-making process. By 1996, four years after the start of Eurodisney, the enterprise is barely profitable and then only because interest payments have been deferred and management fees have been reduced. By almost any definition, Eurodisney has not made a positive contribution to the parent Disney organization. In fact Disney's management rarely refers to Eurodisney probably because the prospects for its eventual success look bleak.

The second case in this chapter involves a strategic decision that is much larger and more complex than Eurodisney. It is a strategic decision that promises to vastly extend the organizational reach of Disney, and one that appears to have made the corporation a planetary powerhouse in the production and distribution of entertainment. The decision involves the acquisition by Disney of Capital Cities/ABC in 1995 for the colossal sum of $19 billion. As a result of this strategic choice, Disney is now advantageously positioned to produce its own forms of entertainment and to accomplish the distribution of these entertainment modules through a vast network that is owned and controlled by Disney. In 1998 the acquisition by Disney of Capital Cities/ABC appears headed toward a successful outcome. The decision itself seems to be capable of achieving Disney's strategic objectives. Still after three years, the process of implementation is far from completed. An evaluation of the decision at this time has to be cautiously optimistic. In that context it is well to recall that the Disney decision makers for Capital Cities/ABC are the same ones who made the Eurodisney decision. Hopefully, they have learned their lesson.

In keeping with the general format of these case chapters, the significant events surrounding each case will be presented in sufficient detail to facilitate understanding of the critical factors and relationships in the decision-making situation. Disney will be subjected to a detailed gap analysis at the time of the Eurodisney decision in 1990 with an updated gap analysis at the time of the Capital Cities/ABC acquisition in 1995. Subsequently the critical factors in each case will be related to each major step in the decision-making process. Both of the cases will be evaluated comparatively using the determinants for strategic decision success developed in Trull's study and the Bay area study as well as the classifications for strategic decision success set forth in Figure 11.1. These evaluations demonstrate that successful strategic decisions invariably ensue from the open decision-making process with a judgmental decision-making strategy in quest of a satisficing outcome.

THE WALT DISNEY COMPANY: A PERSPECTIVE

The Walt Disney Company has a unique character in that it is an integral part of American folklore. Disney projects a larger-than-life image that is replete with fantasylands, magic kingdoms, and fictional personalities. Disney plays to the dreams of America's children and buffers the daily frustrations and disappointments of its adults who, for the most part, grew up on a steady diet of Disney scenarios and storybook figures. *Disney is the great American escape.* It is the fantasy world that transcends reality. It is the tranquilizer for vanquished hopes and shattered ambitions. Disney also provides a place to share the fulfillment of real-life accomplishments in the universe of virtual reality created and projected by Disney's technical magicians. When asked how one plans to celebrate a significant achievement, the common response is: "I'm going to Disneyland." A trip to Disneyland is a kind of psychic reward in its own right. This profile is what gives Disney its unique place in the United States. No other company has created a perception of its ability to uplift the human spirit in happiness or despair. This is the magical world of Disney.

This chapter is not about the unique place of Disney in American folklore. Rather it deals with two strategic decisions made by Disney's top executives that were intended to expand Disney's magic kingdom to a larger and ultimately global platform. Make no mistake about it; Disney is committed to a global presence and one that is as influential abroad as it is in America.[1] Disney has come a long way since 1929 when Walt Disney, creator of Mickey Mouse and Donald Duck, started out as a motion-picture producer.[2] His phenomenal success led to the opening of an amusement park based entirely on his film characters. This park, called Disneyland, opened in Anaheim, California, in 1955. A similar park, Disney World, opened in 1971 in Orlando, Florida. The first international venture, called Tokyo Disneyland, opened in 1983. It was followed in 1992 by Eurodisney which opened in France. Today the Walt Disney Company is a multinational enterprise in the entertainment industry concentrating on creating films, television programs, and theme parks. With the acquisition of Capital Cities/ABC in 1995 for $19 billion, Disney became a major player in the distribution as well as the production of entertainment modules. Without doubt Disney is currently the world's largest fully integrated entertainment company.

In the mid-1980s the Walt Disney company underwent a major internal restructuring beginning with the acquisition a new management. In 1984 Michael Eisner became the chief executive officer (CEO). The strategic decisions to launch Eurodisney and to acquire Capital Cities/ABC were the products of Eisner and his top management team. They were the principal decision makers in both of these strategic choices. Consequently, the credit for success or the accountability for failure may be ascribed to them. In this context the evaluations of success or failure reflect only the opinions of the author. These cases were written only for educational purposes, not to find fault or ascribe blame.

THE STRATEGIC GAP AT DISNEY IN 1990

Disney's top management conceived Eurodisney as early as 1985. In that year a letter of intent was signed confirming France as the host country. (Note: Eurodisney has been renamed Disneyland Paris by the parent corporation. However, in this case it will be designated by its original name.) The major commitment of resources by the Walt Disney Company to Eurodisney did not begin until about 1990. Eurodisney was opened to the public in April 1992. Therefore, it is instructive to focus on Disney's strategic gap at the beginning of the 1990s. It is also instructive to note that Disney's strategic objective to establish and project a major global presence manifested itself in the 1980s and steadily gained momentum into the 1990s.[3]

Organizational Assessment

The purpose of an organizational assessment is to ascertain the overall capabilities of the organization in the critical areas of (1) management, (2) technology, (3) policies, and (4) resources. This assessment involves ascertaining specific strengths and weaknesses in each of the critical areas and combining them into a composite balance designated a *capability profile*. The capability profile indicates whether management should concentrate on internal improvements to translate weaknesses into strengths or there are enough strengths in the critical areas to permit the organization to exploit existing opportunities and to cope with actual threats in the external environment.

Management   The first and foremost factor is management itself. Management is the vital force that makes the organization go, and good management is the key factor in the successful performance of the organization. Managerial values and experience find their expression in the application of managerial judgment; and good managerial judgment is necessary for successful strategic decisions.

In the case of Disney, management in 1990 was still relatively new. The centralization of decision making and the turnover of key executives had not begun to manifest itself. Eisner and his top management team were still characterized by overall strength at this point in time.

Policies   Organizational policies provide a framework within which to make strategic decisions. The alternatives of strategic choice indicate the courses of action available to management. Prevailing policy indicates whether these courses of action can and should be pursued within the guidelines provided at the highest levels of the organization. Policies provide guidance for strategy and governance for behavior in formal organizations.

In an organizational sense, Disney is strongly committed to its policies which began with its founder, Walt Disney, and which continue under its current management. All Disney employees are required to assimilate and manifest the Disney core concepts of self-image and ideology. All Disney employees attend orientation seminars. There is a special glossary of acceptable Disney words, and Disney employees are required to dress, speak, and behave in ways acceptable to the company. Disney's intensive screening and indoctrination of its employees is accompanied by a corporate obsession with secrecy and control and the unending cultivation of a Disney image and mystique. When Michael Eisner and his management team took over in 1984, the core policies of Disney continued and formed the bedrock of Disney's resurgence in the following decade.[4]

On balance, whether one agrees with them or not, Disney must be given good marks for the completeness of and compliance with its policies.

Technology   Technology means the systematic application of scientific or other organized knowledge to practical tasks.[5] Technology is a set of principles and techniques useful to bring about change toward desired ends.[6] Technology is knowledge of how to do things, how to accomplish human goals.[7] Technology implies change, and it is the phenomenon of technological change that concerns management in making strategic decisions.

By the 1990s Disney had become an industry leader in the technology of entertainment. Disney's reputation for special effects, scenarios, and animation were second to none. The virtual reality of fantasylands, magic kingdoms, and lifelike fictional characters was and is a principal strength of Disney.

Resources   Organizational assessment has been completed when a measurement of the available resources has been taken. Resources may be divided into the following four categories: (1) *institutional resources,* which include stakeholders, goodwill, image, political competence, and social responsiveness; (2) *fiscal resources,* which include money and its near-equivalent, credit; (3) *physical resources,* which include facilities, equipment, supplies, and new materials; and (4) *human resources* which include time, energy, and intellect.[8]

Disney's resources were very strong at the beginning of the 1990s. Since Eisner and his top management team took over in 1984, fiscal resources had grown at a substantial rate. The targeted annual rate of return on stockholders equity was 20 percent, and Disney hit the target regularly. There was approximately $1 billion of excess cash flow generated every year from Disney's operations which required continuing investment in new ventures. Disney's physical resources in the form of land holdings, real estate developments, and theme park assets were substantial and contributed substantially to the company's large annual cash flow. Disney's human resources in the form of management and employees were also a source of considerable strength for the company. Disney demanded loyalty and commitment from all its employees. Good performance was rewarded with recognition and opportunities for advancement. Turnover of employees was low and there was satisfaction with working conditions and relationships in the company. Institutional resources in the form of a positive image and considerable goodwill among stakeholder groups were very strong in the early 1990s. Disney had always maintained a positive rapport with its external environment. On balance, all forms of resources were conducive to a positive strategic gap.

Environmental Assessment

Once management has completed a capability profile to ascertain the strengths and weaknesses of the principal factors of organizational capability, the next step is to assess the external environment with a view toward determining the nature and the magnitude of the organization's strategic gap. In the case of Disney, the capability profile in the early 1990s showed considerable strength in all the factors of organizational capability. Disney was in a good position to develop and exploit external opportunities with more than enough strength to protect itself from external threats.

Opportunities   In searching for opportunities in the external environment, Disney sought situations that promised long-term benefits for the company. The U.S. theme park market generated $4 billion annually and had been growing at an annual rate of 10 percent for at least a decade. Moreover, the financial success of Tokyo Disneyland opened in 1983 suggested considerable opportunities in overseas markets. At this time there was a substantial growth in European tourism, and a Disney theme park in Europe seemed a logical extension of the company's global orientation. In fact, the possibilities for a Eurodisney seemed endless, and the venture promised a fruitful outlet for the company's substantial annual cash flow.

Threats   Disney was more than able to deal with any external threats to its position as the world's largest entertainment company. There was competition to be sure; but Disney had met and mastered most of its competitors. The competition in Europe did not seem formidable in terms of its ability to outperform a Disney theme park. With regard to the threat of technological obsolescence, Disney is not competing in a high-tech industry. Moreover, as noted in its capability profile, Disney is at the forefront of new technology in its industry. For example, at this time Disney has been awarded over 45 Academy Awards, not only for its movies but for its technical and scientific contribution to film making.[9]

Gap Analysis in 1990

Disney's situation in 1990 may be accurately characterized as a large positive gap. Disney's capability profile revealed virtually no internal weaknesses. In fact all Disney's categories of capability showed considerable strength. There were no significant threats in Disney's external environment. However, the company was compelled by virtue of its large cash flow to seek external opportunities for expansion. Such opportunities had to meet at least two principal criteria: (1) be compatible with Disney's aspirations for global expansion of its theme parks and (2) yield a return comparable with the rest of Disney's operations, that is, a 20 percent return on stockholders' equity. At this juncture, it appeared that a Disney theme park in Europe was a logical strategic choice.

THE DECISION-MAKING PROCESS FOR EURODISNEY

The Objectives

Disney's primary objective in the Eurodisney decision was to continue its substantial rate of financial growth through an expansion of its international theme parks. There were at least two corollary objectives also of a financial nature: (1) to invest some of Disney's excess cash flow from its other operations in ways that would contribute to the long-term benefit of the company and (2) to earn a return on the company's investment (specifically the stock-holders' equity) equivalent to the internal standard of 20 percent. It is important to note that in 1990, all Disney's objectives with regard to Eurodisney were attainable. Later in the decision-making process, the actions of Disney's decision makers tended to compromise the attainability of their objectives. It is also important to note that once a decision was made to build a theme park in Europe, the decisions to accomplish the objectives dealt with the questions of where, when, and how Eurodisney would materialize. The answer to the "when" question was as soon as possible. The answer to the "how" question was in ways advantageous to the Walt Disney Company. The remaining question of "where" constitutes the object of the decision-making process in this chapter.

The Search for Alternatives

In the search for a suitable location for Eurodisney, over 200 possible locations were considered.[10] The search quickly narrowed itself to a contest between two primary locations: Barcelona, Spain, and Paris, France. Spain boasted 40 million tourists annually, whereas France brought in 34 million in the same period. The site in Spain would be on the Mediterranean, which indisputably had superior weather. The site in France would be at Marne-la-Vallee outside Paris, which would necessitate an indoor theme park because of the French winter. Disney's decision makers were also concerned about the hospitality of the French and the ability of the Spanish to provide speedy, efficient services. The competition between Spain and France for the Eurodisney theme park lasted two years. Thousands of jobs and millions of dollars in foreign exchange revenues were at stake. Both countries offered substantial tax exemptions and other concessions. The final choice of location required a contract that would definitely work to the long-term advantage of the Walt Disney Company. For that to happen more concessions were required.

Comparison and Evaluation of Alternatives

In comparing and evaluating Spain and France as possible sites, Disney was influenced by the population potential of a location near Paris. The following numbers helped the Disney decision makers in choosing their French site:

1. Seventeen million people within a two-hour drive
2. Forty-one million people within a four-hour drive
3. One hundred and nine million people within a six-hour drive
4. Three hundred and ten million people within a two-hour flight[11]

To obtain the theme park of Eurodisney, the French government gave many concessions. Apart from money, it offered subsidized loans, 5,000 acres of land at 1971 prices and sufficient additional land to permit expansion of the project to meet increasing demand, road and rail links giving ready access to the site, tax breaks, and reduced taxes on ticket sales.[12]

Before deciding to locate Eurodisney in France, Disney's decision makers demanded and received other concessions that promised to benefit the company over the long run. Such concessions included:

1. Disney owns only 49 percent of the common stock of Eurodisney. The remaining 51 percent was sold to the European Community on organized stock exchanges.

2. Disney has full operational control of the theme park and any land development around it.

3. Disney gets tax benefits from accelerated depreciation charges and low-cost interest payments.

4. Disney obtains royalties amounting to 7 percent of all revenues from rides, merchandise, and hotels.

5. Disney's management fees range from 3 to 6 percent of all park revenues.

6. Higher attendance levels increase Disney's cash flows by virtue of a graduated royalty and management fee structure.

7. Disney also obtains 49 percent of total park revenues apart from all royalties and fees by virtue of its stock ownership.

8. At about the $500 million annual revenue level, Disney obtains about one-half of the total cash flow from Disneyland. Higher levels of revenue should result in larger proportions of cash flow for Disney.[13]

(Note: The refinancing agreement consummated by Disney with its creditors for Eurodisney in 1994 delayed or deferred the receipt of part of the above cash flow. In some cases fees, royalties, and interest payments were temporarily reduced. Disney's ownership proportion was reduced to 39 percent. However, the original basic agreement is still in effect, especially with regard to Disney's interest payments on approximately $3 billion of debt financing.)[14]

The Choice

The choice of France as the site for Eurodisney was motivated primarily by economic and monetary considerations. Disney's investment in Eurodisney was minimal in relation to the concessions exacted from the French government. The immediate investment by the Walt Disney Company approximated $200 million for its 49 percent share of Eurodisney. Much of the debt for which Disney is liable is to be paid off by sale and lease-back agreements on the several hotels in Eurodisney. The financial exposure of the parent company is minimal in relation to the total earnings potential of the theme park. It is a classic case of minimizing the risk of financial loss while maximizing the possibility of handsome financial benefits. All that was necessary to transform this ideal arrangement into tangible financial benefits for Disney was a smooth and successful implementation of the decision to start Eurodisney.

Implementation of the Decision

Eurodisney opened its magic doors on April 2, 1992. From the very first day, the theme park was beset by problems and disappointments. The opening was marred by technical failures, long queues, striking railway employees, and the opposition of some of the French intellectuals who described Eurodisney as a cultural Chernobyl. "It soon became terribly evident that everyone, bankers, brokers, and even government had been blinded by the glamour and that all the projections that had been made four years before had been horribly off the mark."[15]

It became apparent very quickly that the actual attendance at Eurodisney was significantly below the projections made by Disney's management consultants. The attendance potential was said to be somewhere between 12 million and 17 million with an annual growth rate of 5 percent in the first five years of operations.[16] The actual attendance started at 11 million with little growth in sight. The principal reason for the low level of attendance was the belief on the part of the visitors that Disney's prices were too high. Admission prices, concession prices, hotel prices, food prices, and merchandise prices were much higher than the European competitors and more in keeping with the price structure of Disney's American theme parks. Cultural problems with employees contributed to high and costly levels of turnover. A recession in France resulted in declining land values for Disney. And Eurodisney's stockholders soon perceived that they had paid too much for their equity investment. Nothing went right for Eurodisney from the beginning. It soon became apparent that Disney had overestimated the market and underestimated the cost of starting Eurodisney as well as the cost of operating a theme park in France.[17]

Disney's problems in implementing its strategic decision for Eurodisney were essentially of six major types:

1. *Management hubris.* Disney's executives projected a managerial style that was invariably brash, frequently insensitive, and often overbearing.

2. *Cultural differences.* Disney's decision makers manifested a gross misunderstanding of European lifestyles which resulted in numerous and costly mistakes in the daily operations of Eurodisney.

3. *Environmental and location factors.* Basically Eurodisney was sited in a location with good weather only six months a year; and considerable effort was required to maintain an acceptable level of annual attendance.

4. *French labor issues.* Differences between U.S. and European labor laws meant that Disney could not operate the theme park as efficiently and as cost-effectively as it desired.

5. *Financing and the initial business plan.* Essentially the beginning financial plan for Eurodisney was highly optimistic and extraordinary complex. It was based on an ideal set of assumptions which did not work out and the pricing structure for all aspects of operations was unsustainably high. Disney rather than the investors in Eurodisney was the primary beneficiary in the original financial plan. A restructuring or a major modification of the financing arrangements was recommended by Disney's consultants.

6. *Competition from U.S. Disney parks.* Disney's decision makers overlooked the differences in currency values with regard to traveling to the United States rather than paying the high prices at Eurodisney.[18]

In terms of its effect on the bottom line for Eurodisney as a separate business venture, the results for the first three years of operations were disheartening. In 1992 the theme park lost 339 million French francs; in 1993 it lost 5,337 million French francs, and in 1994 it lost 1,797 million French francs.[19] Using a rough conversion rate of 5 French francs to 1 U.S. dollar during this period, the losses were (1) $67.8 million in 1992 (for six months), (2) $1,067.5 million in 1993, and (3) $359.4 million in 1994. These unacceptable results clearly militated for immediate corrective action; and it was forthcoming in 1994.

Follow-up and Control

A system of follow-up and control is essential to ensure that the results agree with those expected at the time the decision was made. In the case of Eurodisney the feedback to management of problems and obstacles to a successful implementation was immediate. Eurodisney's management instituted various forms of corrective action but to no avail. In 1992 financial results were shocking, but they could be rationalized as attributable to the newness of the theme park. The 1993 results were really horrendous and demanded immediate corrective action. By 1994, corrective action was taken but not in time to avert another unacceptable financial loss for Eurodisney.

On March 14, 1994, Disney's shareholders agreed to the following restructuring of the original financial plan for Eurodisney:

1. Disney would obtain a standby line of credit in the approximate amount of $225 million for ten years at the current market rate.

2. Disney would spend an additional $280 million buying certain Eurodisney assets which would eventually be leased back.

3. Disney would waive royalties on entrance fees and food and merchandise and would suspend management fees for five years.

4. Disney agreed to subscribe to 49 percent of a right to convert $603 million of newly issued bonds to common stock at the market price at the time of maturity.

For their part, the banks agreed to:

1. Underwrite the remaining 51 percent of the rights issue of common stock attached to the proposed issue of bonds.

2. Accept a moratorium on the payment of interest by Disney for eighteen months.

3. Defer principal payments on Eurodisney's debt for three years.[20]

The terms of the restructuring agreement were intended to give Eurodisney some financial breathing room.[21] After all, the theme park had run out of cash at the end of 1993 at which time Eisner had threatened to close Eurodisney rather than renegotiate with the banks. The situation was desperate, and for a time it seemed that Eurodisney would perish. However, in June 1994, Eurodisney received some unexpected outside financial support. Saudi Prince Al-Walid bin Talal agreed to invest $430 million of new equity capital in Eurodisney.[22] This unexpected development along with the aforesaid restructuring agreement was approved by Disney's stockholders. The parent company's equity investment in Eurodisney was reduced from 49 to 39 percent.

Given this infusion of new equity capital along with the deferrals and postponements of various payments, one would have expected immediate improvement in Eurodisney's financial performance. Attendance at Eurodisney reached nearly 12 million customers in 1996 with a 72 percent occupancy rate in Eurodisney's hotels. However, the entire price structure at Eurodisney has been reduced since 1993 which, while bolstering attendance and occupancies, tends to depress profits. Using a rough ratio of 5 French francs to 1 U.S. dollar, Eurodisney did make a small $22.8 million profit in 1995 and a $40.4 million profit in 1996.[23] These levels of profit will not begin to offset the losses recorded at Eurodisney during 1992 to 1994. Moreover, in 1997 Eurodisney resumed payments on its outstanding debt along with accompanying interest payments which were resumed in 1996. Eurodisney will not receive any royalties or management fees until 1999 and may be required to contribute more equity capital if the holders of its $603 million in convertible bonds opt to become common stock owners.[24]

On balance, it is far from certain that Eurodisney will emerge from the 1990s as a financially robust theme park. Further, it seems even less likely that Eurodisney will ever achieve the 20 percent return on shareholder's equity that the Walt Disney Company has come to regard as its norm.

THE STRATEGIC GAP AT DISNEY IN 1995

A review of Disney's capability profile in 1995 reveals that, with one significant exception, the strengths noted in the above gap analysis in 1990 were greater than ever. In the intervening five years since the Eurodisney decision, the Walt Disney Company had prospered to the point where even the outright failure of this theme park would not severely damage the parent corporation. For example, between 1993 and 1995, Disney's aggregate revenue from all sources increased from $8.5 billion to $12.1 billion, a 42 percent increase. In terms of Disney's three major categories of revenue, the highest rate of increase was in filmed entertainment at 63 percent. Consumer products was next at 52 percent while theme parks and resorts were number three at just 15 percent. The same rankings carried over into the operating income generated from each category of revenue. While theme parks were important at 32.7 percent of total revenue in 1995, this was the least-profitable category of Disney activity. As such, the financial problems of Eurodisney were only tangential to Disney's overall financial success.

In fact, with the exception of management, all the categories of capability for Disney showed a definite growth in strength between 1990 and 1995. Four contributing factors tended to reduce the strength of management at Disney in the 1990s:

1. As the decade wore on, the decision making at Disney became more centralized in the person of the CEO, Michael Eisner.

2. Beginning in 1994, the top management team at Disney began to desert the company and was replaced by executives of lesser experience and/or competence.

3. Given Eisner's major heart surgery in 1994, there was no executive designated or being groomed as his successor.

4. In 1995 Disney's board of directors came under heavy fire as a pawn of Eisner ready to rubber stamp whatever he requested.

It is no secret that Eisner rules Disney with an iron fist.[25] All strategic decisions at Disney tend to be made by the CEO including the Eurodisney decision and the decision to acquire Cap Cities/ABC. Basically Eisner tends to operate as a unilateral decision maker with limited and selective participation by this top management team. In 1994 the Disney top management team began to unravel.[26] Eisner's top executives began to leave Disney when they noticed his reluctance to promote them. Eisner has also resisted any attempt to designate one of his executives as heir apparent.[27]

Perhaps the most serious managerial shortcoming at Disney is the allegation that Eisner has the board of directors in his pocket. In 1997, for example, the Disney board was designated by *Business Week* as the worst in the United States.[28] Specifically, Disney's board was scorned for being "a meek, handpicked group with long-standing ties to Eisner or the company."[29] Included among the 16 members of Disney's board are: (1) four current Disney executives, including Eisner, (2) three former Disney executives, and (3) a miscellany of outside directors including Eisner's personal lawyer, his children's former elementary school principal, an architect who has done work for Disney, an actor, an investment banker for the Disney family, a priest/administrator, a former U.S. senator, a current outside CEO, and the former CEO of Cap Cities/ABC.[30] For his part, Eisner defends the

composition of his board by citing Disney's favorable financial performance. Eisner's view that Disney's shareholders should be able to live without a strong governance structure has been criticized as follows:

> Chairman Michael Eisner's view that Disney shareholders should be willing to
> live without a strong governance structure is akin to taking them on a financial
> ride without seat belts.[31]

Given the aforesaid problems in Disney's management, it appears that
management has emerged in recent years as a possible area of weakness or
at least a factor requiring immediate improvement. On balance, however,
given the obvious strength in Disney's other categories of capability, the
company seems to be operating from an overall position of strength, with
some managerial weaknesses.

Environmental Assessment

Disney's external environment did not change significantly between 1990
and 1995. Disney became stronger, but so did its competition. Technology
continued to advance in the entertainment industry, but Disney was at the
forefront of such advancement. On balance, Disney was trying to create new
opportunities while protecting itself from external threats. A change in the
regulations of the Federal Communications Commission (FCC) opened new
areas of opportunity for Disney and other producers of entertainment by
permitting them to own both the content of their product and the means for
its distribution.[32] Without this recent change in Federal regulations the
acquisition of Capital Cities/ABC by Disney would not have been possible.[33]

Gap Analysis in 1995

Disney's capability profile in 1995 was characterized by considerable
strength that was nearly offset by some weakness in management. Disney
was ready to create new opportunities for itself, and it was quite capable of
coping with threats from the external environment. In essence, Disney was
operating with a small positive gap, whereas in 1990 its strategic gap was
more positive because the weakness in its management had not surfaced.

THE DECISION-MAKING PROCESS
FOR CAPITAL CITIES/ABC

The Objectives

In the early 1990s, Disney was trying to use its internal strengths to create
external opportunities. Given the slowdown in the development of theme
parks and the infusion of cash from successful films, Disney needed an out-
let for its surfeit of fiscal resources. Moreover, Disney also required new

opportunities for continued growth and the attainment of its targeted 20 percent return on shareholders equity.[34] Disney also desired an opportunity for profitable growth and expansion that would enhance its image as the global leader in the entertainment industry.[35] Finally, Disney was seeking opportunities that would combine its demonstrated creativity in the production of entertainment with a means to distribute its entertainment to worldwide audiences.[36] Given the forthcoming removal of the FCC regulation against combining the production and distribution of entertainment under the same ownership, the way was open for Disney to acquire one of the major television networks.[37] On balance, Disney's decision to acquire Capital Cities/ABC was undergirded by multiple objectives which translated into power, prestige, and profits with plenty of potential for growth in all areas.

The Search for Alternatives

For Disney to become quickly engaged in the distribution of its entertainment modules on a scale that would meet its multiple objectives, the acquisition of a major network was required. Eisner had been discussing the acquisition of or a merger with Capital Cities/ABC since 1993. Agreement on a financial deal was still under consideration in 1995. Eisner had walked away from a deal with NBC because of demands that he was not willing to meet.[38] The Fox network was obviously not for sale, and CBS was an overpriced network with years of rebuilding ahead of it.[39] Having been an executive at ABC earlier in his career and recognizing the distribution capability and overall profitability of Capital Cities/ABC, Eisner was disposed toward reaching an agreement with that company.

The Comparison and Evaluation of Alternatives

Having narrowed the alternatives that would meet Disney's multiple objectives for the acquisition of a major network and having focused on Capital Cities/ABC as the most desirable alternative, Eisner took a closer look at this possibility. Capital Cities/ABC was the preferred choice but it was expensive. Moreover, what was the best way to proceed? A strategic alliance would provide a workable fusion of entertainment content and distribution. A merger would provide the same benefits, but with more of an ownership commitment. And, finally, the outright acquisition of Capital Cities/ABC by Disney would provide both benefits and control to the acquiring company. Capital Cities/ABC was the result of a merger in March 1985. It owns the most profitable television network, eight of the best-managed television stations in the country which reach 25 percent of the nation's viewers, 31 radio stations, the ESPN sports cable network, trade magazines, and an interest in cable networks. It also owns 225 affiliate broadcasters and a newspaper group.[40] Moreover, the acquisition of Capital Cities/ABC would make Disney the first media company with a major presence in four distribution systems: (1) filmed entertainment, (2) cable television, (3) broadcasting through network television and radio, and (4) telephone communication through its joint ventures with three regional phone companies.[41]

The Choice

On August 7, 1995, Disney announced that it had acquired Capital Cities/ABC in a stock and cash agreement valued at $19 billion.[42] The Disney deal created the largest entertainment company in the world. It was approved by the shareholders of both companies. In the aggregate, the financial terms of the deal called for $10 billion in cash, which Disney had to borrow, and $9 billion in Disney stock. The stock part of the transaction resulted in a dilution of existing Disney equity through a 30 percent increase in the number of outstanding shares. Disney's financial liquidity was somewhat reduced and its credit rating declined slightly because of its new $10 billion debt. However, there were numerous financial offsets to the apparent cost of the acquisition. For example, the 1996 Disney annual report showed a 54 percent increase in revenues to $18.7 billion from 1995.[43] During this same period Disney's net earnings increased 11 percent. With the acquisition of Capital Cities/ABC, Disney jumped from a $12 billion entertainment company leading the industry in producing entertainment modules to a $19 billion vertically integrated entertainment company leading the industry in both content and distribution.[44]

The term *synergy* means that what was formerly differentiated is now optimally integrated.[45] After the acquisition of Capital Cities/ABC, Disney was supposed to derive synergistic benefits resulting from a fusion of the number one entertainment company with the number one distribution company. Synergy would result from the control that Disney would exercise over its entertainment modules from their origin to the ultimate consumer.[46] "Eisner now runs a company that manufactures a product, owns the network distribution system for it, and controls how long the product stays on the network. . . ."[47] Conversely, there are those who say the benefit of synergy is overstated:

> There aren't a lot of synergies between these two companies . . . I think this deal got more credit than it deserved. I'm not sure it buys a lot.[48]

Still others believe that even if there is synergy to be gained, it was not necessary for Disney to acquire Capital Cities/ABC:

> There's nothing in the Disney-ABC get together that couldn't be better achieved by a strategic alliance. Creating product and distributing it are two distinct businesses. The two partners have been superbly managed. They would have been better off if they had remained single.[49]

Given these disparate opinions regarding Disney's strategic choice, it remains for the implementation to establish the record.

Implementation of the Decision

It has been more than three years since Disney acquired Capital Cities/ABC. For acquisitions even of this size, the process of implementation should be virtually completed. Granted that $19 billion is a substantial sum to pay and the new company is enormously large and complex, one would normally expect considerable progress with the implementation of the strategic choice. For the most part the expected benefits of synergy remain illusive.[50] Since August 7, 1995, there has been a very high rate of turnover among top Disney executives. Eisner has manifested considerable reluctance to delegate the authority to achieve synergy. In the first few months after the acquisition, Disney made a real effort to integrate its TV operations with those of ABC.[51] In an effort to accomplish an effective reorganization, Eisner got directly involved in Disney's TV division in early 1996.[52] The result of this micromanagement was a decline in ABC's network ratings from number one to number three in fall 1996 as it recorded some of the most miserable ratings in broadcast history.[53]

Perhaps, as Eisner has noted, there is no quick payoff from the purchase of Capital Cities/ABC:

> You won't begin to see a payoff in the first year, not for two or three years . . . and the real earnings explosion won't come for five or six years.[54]

Still given the magnitude of the deal and the assertions of synergistic benefits, one would expect implementation to be much further along. The analysis and preparation for implementation begins with the comparison and evaluation of alternatives in an attempt to anticipate and prepare for expected obstacles and difficulties in transforming the decision from an abstraction to a reality. Apparently such was not true in this case. There was no intention to streamline operations or to reduce costs with the acquisition of Capital Cities/ABC. One wonders what the actual costs and the opportunity costs are as Disney moves glacially through implementation.

Follow-up and Control

In this case there is a definite need for follow-up and control if only to accelerate the implementation of the decision in pursuit of Disney's objectives. By any measure, Disney has been dilatory in its implementation of a decision involving a $19 billion acquisition. One can only speculate at the possibilities for synergies of all types in the presence of committed managerial action.

COMPARATIVE CASE DETERMINANTS
OF STRATEGIC DECISION SUCCESS

Having analyzed and evaluated the Eurodisney decision and Disney's acquisition of Capital Cities/ABC as separate cases, the comparative evaluation in this section is based on the determinants of decision success in Trull's study of 100 organizations and further advanced by the Bay area study of 108 organizations. These determining factors constitute the essence of the analysis and evaluation to follow.

Compatibility with Operating Constraints

Operating constraints refer to institutionalized policies and procedures associated with an established way of doing business. There is an established way of doing business in the entertainment industry. The Eurodisney decision did not appear to depart from Disney's way of doing business. Its problems after implementation were attributable to other factors to be discussed below. In many ways, Disney's acquisition of Capital Cities/ABC also was accomplished within established policies and procedures. However, the delays and procrastination in accomplishing a full implementation of this decision appear to depart from Disney's usual efficiency. At the very least, good business practice is being compromised.

Nearness to Optimum Time

Both Trull's study and the Bay area study found that nearness to optimum time was the factor deserving of the most improvement in seeking a successful strategic choice. The Eurodisney decision was especially propitious in that it recognized several factors that contributed to good timing: (1) Disney's large cash flows in 1990 militated for immediate new investment opportunities, (2) there was room for another theme park in Europe in 1990, and (3) Disney's decision makers anticipated some benefits from the expected unification of the European community in 1992 and the opening of the English Channel to underseas transportation in 1993. With regard to the Capital Cities/ABC acquisition Disney's sense of timing was equally good. Important factors in this decision included: (1) a continuing need for new investment opportunities, (2) elimination of the legal restrictions imposed by the FCC regarding ownership of both the production and the distribution of entertainment modules, and (3) Capital Cities/ABC's riding the crest of a steady improvement in its earnings. Disney may be losing some of the benefits of its good timing by delaying the full implementation of the Capital Cities/ABC acquisition. However, on balance, Disney deserves high marks for excellent timing in both decisions.

Optimum Amount of Information

The optimum amount of information is just enough to make a cost effective choice that meets the objective. In general, decision makers tend to seek too much information; this tends in many cases to work against a good decision. In the case of Eurodisney, the decision makers tended to assume that they had a high level of knowledge regarding the outcome. Essentially with their high preference for a profitable outcome and their unjustified presumption of complete knowledge regarding the outcome, Disney's decision makers used a computational strategy in quest of a maximized result. Disney spent an inordinate amount of effort on the legal and financial aspects of Eurodisney to ensure maximum benefits for the parent company. Too little effort was spent on marketing and cultural difference research especially on European lifestyles and French labor laws. Disney's unidimensional focus on financial results to the virtual exclusion or diminution of other types of information worked against a successful outcome for Eurodisney.

In the acquisition of Capital Cities/ABC, Disney had the optimal amount of information. Eisner had contemplated the acquisition of a major network for at least three years before purchasing Capital Cities/ABC. Moreover, as a former executive with Capital Cities/ABC, Eisner knew the strengths and weaknesses of his targeted acquisition. Further Eisner was very knowledgeable regarding the actions of his major competitors and the need for Disney to move quickly to secure a competitive advantage in both the production and distribution of entertainment modules. The unidimensional focus of Eurodisney was replaced by a comprehensive assessment of an optimal amount of information in the acquisition of Capital Cities/ABC.

Decision Maker's Influence

The strategic decisions presented in this chapter were made at the highest executive level in Disney. On the basis of previous remarks, it is reasonable to assume that Disney's board of directors was not a significant factor in either decision. In point of fact, the decision maker was the CEO, Michael Eisner. The top-level priority given to Eurodisney in the early 1990s was not sufficient to offset the significant oversights and omissions that contributed to the financial losses in 1992 to 1994. In the case of Capital Cities/ABC, the decision makers' influence is threatening to turn potential decision success into probable decision failure as the continued procrastination in the implementation phase increasingly militates against the attainment of Disney's objectives in making the acquisition. In both cases, Disney merits low marks for the influence of its decision maker.

Risk-Reward Factor

Maximizers normally find it necessary to accept risks somewhat commensurate with their expected rate of return. Generally the higher the anticipated return, the greater the amount of risk that must be borne by the decision maker. In the Eurodisney case, the parent company attempted to negate this well-established relationship. Disney attempted to preclude the possibility of any financial loss from Eurodisney by crafting a financial agreement that couldn't lose for anyone except the European investors. In fact, Disney was programmed to receive its royalties and management fees from ticket and merchandise sales right off the top even if the public stockholders received only paper losses. Using a computational strategy in pursuit of a maximized outcome, Disney sought unsuccessfully to repudiate the risk-reward factor in Eurodisney.

The Capital Cities/ABC acquisition involved a more traditional risk-reward relationship. Given Disney's cash flow and borrowing power, the $19 billion purchase price did not seem excessive. Capital Cities/ABC's earnings and the expected synergies would offset the $10 billion in new debt and the $9 million dilution in shareholder's equity. Disney had the financial resources and the credit rating to consummate a purchase that was as big as Disney itself. There was no expectation on Disney's part that its normal 20 percent return on equity for Disney's shareholders would be impaired by the acquisition. Still the delay in making a full implementation including synergies, economies, efficiencies, and greater productivity are working against the financial return from the acquisition. Clearly there must be duplications, redundancies, and overlapping responsibilities that cry for elimination. At best, the risk-reward factor is questionable for Capital Cities/ABC. As Disney overcompensated unsuccessfully in the case of Eurodisney, it may be undercompensating for Capital Cities/ABC.

Degree of Understanding

Both the Trull study and the Bay area study agreed that there should be an acceptable degree of understanding on the part of the decision implementers regarding what is expected of them. The evidence indicates clearly that in the case of Eurodisney, the decision makers failed to inform the decision implementers regarding what was expected of them. In part this omission was attributable to insufficient knowledge regarding European lifestyles, French culture, and French labor laws. The inordinate emphasis on the financial dimension contributed to a neglect of requisite degrees of understanding in other critical areas.

In the case of the Capital Cities/ABC acquisition, the decision was made by Eisner and its implementation is presently paced by Eisner. The rest of the Disney organization has little if any knowledge of what is expected of them. This lack of understanding can only work against the success of this strategic decision.

When these two cases are evaluated in the context of the Trull study and the Bay area study, the prospects for their success or failure become more apparent. In the case of the Eurodisney decision, the compatibility with operating constraints and the timing factor are both positive. Regrettably, the remaining four determinants of information, decision maker's influence, risk-reward factor, and degree of understanding are negative. Consequently, the prospects for Eurodisney militate for failure. It remains to be seen if the corrective action taken in 1994 will change the outlook for this decision. An analysis of the Capital Cities/ABC acquisition results in a positive rating for all six of the determinants of strategic decision success. Regrettably, the continued delay in accomplishing a full implementation of this decision tends to work against some of the factors such as timing and risk-reward relationship.

COMPARATIVE CASE CLASSIFICATIONS
OF STRATEGIC DECISION SUCCESS

The comparative case classifications of strategic decision success are derived from the strategic decision matrix set forth in Figure 11.1 and discussed completely in Chapter 11. As shown in the figure, a Type A strategic decision is most likely to succeed because it is composed of attainable objectives developed in the open decision-making process that are pursued through a judgmental decision-making strategy in quest of a satisficing outcome. Conversely, a Type C strategic decision is less likely to succeed because although it is founded on attainable objectives crafted in the open decision-making process, they are sought using a computational decision-making strategy in pursuit of a maximized outcome.

Managerial Attitude Toward the Decision-Making Process

Disney's primary objective in the Eurodisney case was to continue its substantial rate of financial growth through an international expansion of its theme parks. Given Disney's considerable internal strengths, this objective was eminently attainable. Disney's objective was compromised to some degree in that the decision-making process used by Disney was not completely open. Disney's decision makers accepted only part of the constraints of bounded rationality. Time and cost constraints were observed, imperfect information was disregarded, cognitive limitations were acknowledged, and only the economic aspects of the external environment were considered. This reduction of the decision-making process from completely open to partially open tended to diminish the attainability of an otherwise easily attainable objective.

Disney had multiple objectives in the acquisition of Capital Cities / ABC. Again Disney's internal strengths were more than sufficient to attain these objectives. In this case, Disney's decision maker accepted the constraints of bounded rationality. The external environment was scanned for other opportunities and possible threats. Imperfect information was acknowledged, time and cost constraints were observed, and cognitive limitations were accepted. Disney had a set of positive attitudes toward the decision-making process in the Capital Cities / ABC acquisition if only because it was vastly bigger and infinitely more complex than Eurodisney.

Managerial Attitudes Toward the Decision

In the Eurodisney case, Disney pursued a computational decision-making strategy in an ill-advised attempt to maximize an otherwise attainable objective. Disney's inordinate emphasis on the financial agreement with European banks and the company's insistence that it benefit even at the expense of European stockholders is prima facie evidence of maximization. Disney had substantial cash flow but chose to limit its investment and to seek unlimited returns. The company sought to minimize its risk and to maximize its return on a small investment. In this way Disney would be assured of providing its shareholders with their customary 20 percent return on invested capital. Moreover, Disney insisted that its price structure be substantially above the competition and that every important item in its financial agreement with the European banks have a number assigned to it. This attitude bespoke a deep commitment to maximization.

With regard to its computational decision-making strategy, Disney's unyielding preference for high returns was based on a presumption of the ability to control the outcome of its decision. For Disney there was little uncertainty as to the consequences of its actions because it was in charge of its destiny. In essence, anything that couldn't be quantified was disregarded as immaterial or simply diminished in importance. Because of Disney's mind set toward the decision-making process and the decision itself, the Eurodisney case is the epitome of a Type C strategic decision, which is to say one that was unlikely to succeed from the outset and, even after considerable corrective action, is unlikely to succeed in the future.

In the acquisition of Capital Cities / ABC, Disney began with a judgmental decision-making strategy in quest of a satisficing outcome. Given that the decision-making process in this case was only partially open, Disney proceeded to make the right choice in the right way up to the point of implementation. In the implementation phase, the decision-making process comes to a halt. This diminution in the overall decision-making process is serious because converting the choice into action is a major element in the process. In fact, a brilliantly conceived decision can prove worthless without effective implementation. To put it another way, a satisficing outcome is unlikely in the absence of effective action in the implementation and the follow-up and control phases of the decision-making process. In the case of the Capital Cities / ABC decision, the positive managerial attitudes of Disney's decision maker may be nullified by continued inaction in consummating the choice throughout the full decision-making process.

SUMMARY

This chapter presented the last of four sets of comparative case evaluations using the frameworks and concepts presented in this book. This chapter is somewhat innovative in that it used one company with two cases to demonstrate the determining factors for strategic decision success or failure. The two cases involve strategic decisions made by the Walt Disney Company. The first decision dealt with the establishment of the Eurodisney theme park in France in the early 1990s. The second decision involved the acquisition of Disney of Capital Cities/ABC in 1995 for the colossal sum of $19 billion, making it the second biggest acquisition in U.S. corporate history.

In retrospect, Eurodisney was destined to have problems from its very inception. Eurodisney began with an attainable objective and a timely decision and quickly devolved into a quagmire of problems occasioned by Disney's disregard of environmental influences and its preoccupation with profit to the exclusion of other equally important items. Corrective action in 1994 in the form of a modified financial agreement with European banks along with an unexpected investment by a Saudi prince gave Eurodisney's management some breathing room. Very small profits in 1995–1996 offer little lasting assurance that Eurodisney will recover from its financial losses during 1992 to 1994. This was a classic Type C strategic decision in which Disney needlessly and mindlessly sought to maximize a very attainable objective using a computational decision-making strategy. Given a different mind set with a judgmental strategy in quest of a satisficing outcome, Eurodisney might have been part of the Disney family in perpetuity.

The acquisition of Capital Cities/ABC by Disney in August 1995 was heralded as the ideal fusion of the number one entertainment company with the number one distributor of entertainment modules, that is, an idyllic blending of content and distribution. This decision showed positive in every one of the contributing determinants of decision success set forth in the Trull study and the Bay area study. Apart from the fact that the decision was made by one person with little consultation and with no plan for implementation, it promised handsome benefits for Disney in the form of synergies resulting from the compatibility of the two companies. To date these synergies have not materialized. In fact, there are few if any realized benefits from this marriage made in heaven. The evidence suggests that Eisner is delaying the implementation by insisting that he be involved in every detail. After three years the decision is still not implemented fully. Until such implementation takes place, the Capital Cities/ABC acquisition is a successful decision in concept but not in practice. It may be a Type A decision ready to materialize in some tangibly measurable fashion. Or it may be a latent Type C decision like its Eurodisney predecessor in which top management transforms attainable objectives into unattainable ends. This is a decision that requires much additional research and publication, if only because of its potentially lasting impact on the entertainment industry. At this time, it seems like a Type A strategic choice in the throes of metamorphosis.

In concluding a book of this magnitude and scope, a short note hardly seems adequate. Still, if we recall that decision making in general and strategic decision making in particular constitute the major activities that differentiate management from all other endeavors in our society and if we resolve to use the content of this book to improve these core managerial endeavors, then better decision making and more successful outcomes will assuredly reward our efforts.

REVIEW AND DISCUSSION QUESTIONS

1. What is there about the Eurodisney decision that makes it the epitome of a Type C strategic decision?

2. In what specific ways did Disney's decision makers disregard the absence of complete information in the Eurodisney case?

3. What factors militate against the attainment of the objective for Eurodisney in spite of the restructuring of the financial agreement with European banks in 1994?

4. How did Disney deal with the traditional risk-reward relationship in the Eurodisney case?

5. In your opinion what is the future for Eurodisney? Discuss.

6. Why was it reasonable to expect some synergies from Disney's acquisition of Capital Cities/ABC? Discuss.

7. What evidence is there in the case to confirm that Disney used a judgmental decision-making strategy in quest of a satisficing outcome in the acquisition of Capital Cities/ABC?

8. Use the determining factors in the Trull study and the Bay area study to make your own comparative case assessment of strategic decision success for the two cases in this chapter. Discuss.

9. What are the key differences and similarities between the two cases in this chapter?

10. In your opinion how likely is the Capital Cities/ABC acquisition to remain a Type A strategic decision? Justify your answer.

NOTES

1. See "Disney's World," *Newsweek* (August 14, 1995), 21; and Paul R. Michaud, "Wild Kingdom," *World Trade* (October 1992), 46–50.

2. Ron Grover, *The Disney Touch* (Burr Ridge, Ill.: Irwin, 1997), p. 2.

3. See "Disney Global Goals," *International Marketing* (May 17, 1990), 22–26.

4. See James C. Collins and Jerry J. Porras, *Built to Last: Successful Habits of Visionary Companies* (New York: Harper Collins, 1994), pp. 127–131.

5. John Galbraith, *The New Industrial State* (Boston: Houghton Mifflin, 1967), p. 12.

6. J. Taylor, *Technology and Planned Organizational Change* (Ann Arbor: University of Michigan Institute for Social Research, 1970).

7. H. A. Simon, "Technology and Environment," in *Emerging Concepts in Management*, 2nd ed.,

M. S. Wortman and F. Luthans, eds. (New York: Macmillan Co., 1975), p. 4.

8. E. Frank Harrison, *Management and Organizations* (Boston: Houghton Mifflin, 1978).

9. "Getting Mickey Organized," *Business Month* (December 1987), 29.

10. Grace Wagner, "It's a Small World After All," *Lodging Hospitality* (April 1992), 26–31.

11. Richard F. Babcock, "Mickey a la Mode," *Planning* (April 1991), 18–21.

12. Roger Mills et al., "Euro Disney: A Mickey Mouse Project?" *European Management Journal*, 12, No. 3 (September 1994), 306–314.

13. Robert Wrubel, "Le Defi Mickey Mouse," *Financial World* (October 1989), 18 and 21.

14. Victoria Griffith, "Mortgaging the Mouse," *CFO* (August 1997), 71–73.

15. Mills et al., "Euro Disney: A Mickey Mouse Project," p. 308.
16. Ibid.
17. See Rita Gunther McGrath and Ian C. MacMillan, "Discovery-Driven," *Harvard Business Review* (July–August 1995), 44–54.
18. Warren J. Keegan, *Global Marketing Management*, 5th ed. (Englewood Cliffs, N.J.: Prentice-Hall, 1995), pp. 67–74.
19. Euro Disney S. C. A., *1995 Annual Report*, Paris, France, 1995.
20. Mills, et al., "Euro Disney: A Mickey Mouse Project," p. 312.
21. John McGrath, "The Lawyers Who Rebuilt Eurodisney," *International Financial Law Review* (May 1994), 10–12.
22. See "Eurodisney's Prince Charming?" *Business Week* (June 13, 1994), 42; and John Rossant, "How Disney Snared a Princely Sum," *Business Week* (June 20, 1994), 61–62.
23. Eurodisney S. C. A., *1996 Annual Report*, Paris, France, 1996.
24. Victory Griffith, "Mortgaging the Mouse," *CFO* (August 1997), 71–73.
25. Debra Sparks, "Off to See the Wizards," *Financial World* (November 7, 1995), 28–33.
26. Ken Auletta, "Awesome," *New Yorker* (August 14, 1995), 29–32, and "The Company Eisner Keeps," *Mediaweek* (August 7, 1995), 14–22.
27. See Michael Meyer and Stryker McGuire, "How Eisner Saved Disney — and Himself," *Newsweek* (August 14, 1995), 28 and 30.
28. John A. Byrne et al., "The Best and Worst Boards," *Business Week* (December 8, 1997), 90–104.
29. Ibid., p. 90.
30. Bruce Orwall and Joann S. Lublin, "If a Company Prospers, Should Its Directors Behave by the Book?" *Wall Street Journal* (February 24, 1997), 1 and 8.
31. Dana R. Hermanson, "Eisner Takes Shareholders on a Daredevil Ride." *Wall Street Journal* (March 13, 1997), 15.
32. Stratford Sherman, "Why Disney Had to Buy ABC," *Fortune* (September 4, 1995), 80.
33. Kathryn Harris, "Lights! Camera! Regulation!" *Fortune* (September 4, 1995), 83–86.
34. See Michael Oneal et al., "Disney's Kingdom," *Business Week* (August 14, 1995), 30–34.
35. See Paul McCann, "Disney Acquires ABC for $19Bn," *Marketing Week* (August 2, 1996), 7.
36. See Auletta, "Awesome," p. 31.
37. See Sherman, "Why Disney Had to Buy ABC," and Harris, "Lights! Camera! Regulation!"
38. Glover, *The Disney Touch*, p. 285.
39. Ibid.
40. "Disney to Acquire Capital Cities / ABC," *Corporate Growth Weekly Report* (August 7, 1995), 7975–7976.
41. Ibid.
42. Ibid.
43. Walt Disney Company, *1996 Annual Report*, Burbank, Calif., 1996.
44. Chris McConnell, "Mega-Merger Gets FCC Nod," *Broadcasting & Cable* (February 12, 1996), 9.
45. E. Frank Harrison, *Policy, Strategy, and Managerial Action* (Prospect Heights, Ill.: Waveland, 1994), pp. 149 and 383.
46. Kevin Maney, "Companies Are Going Vertical / Media Firms Shift to Gain Product Control," *Money* (September 14, 1995), 18.
47. Auletta, "Awesome," p. 31.
48. Debra Sparks, "Off to See the Wizards," p. 32.
49. "Re Disney-ABC," *Forbes* (August 28, 1995), 24.
50. Bruce Orwall and Kyle Pope, "Disney, ABC Promised 'Synergy' in Merger: So, What Happened?" *Wall Street Journal* (May 16, 1997), A1 and A9.
51. Cynthia Littleton, "Disney ABC Integrates TV Operations," *Broadcasting & Cable* (April 22, 1996), 33–34.
52. T. L. Stanley, "Definite Difference at Disney," *Mediaweek* (April 22, 1996), 5–6.
53. Orwall and Pope, "Disney, ABC Promised 'Synergy' in Merger: So, What Happened?" p. A1.
54. Maggie Mahar, "Magic Kingdom?" *Barron's* (August 7, 1995), 14–15.

SUPPLEMENTAL REFERENCES

"A Saudi Prince Comes to EuroDisney's Aid." *Corporate Growth Weekly Report* (June 13, 1994), 7291 and 7302.

Belsky, Gary, et al. "Mirror, Mirror on the Wall, Who's Fairer Than Disney?" *Money* (September 1995), 66–68.

Carr, Josephine, et al. "The Deals of 1989." *International Financial Law Review* (January 1990), 9–11.

Crumley, Bruce, and Christy Fisher. "EuroDisney Tries to End Evil Spell." *Advertising Age* (February 7, 1994), 39.

Curwen, Peter. "EuroDisney: The Mouse That Roared (Not!)." *European Business Review,* 95, No. 5 (1995), 15–20.

"Easy as ABC." *CFO* (October 1995), 34–38.

Gottesman, Alan. "The Analyst's Couch." *Mediaweek* (August 7, 1995), 24–25.

Grover, Ron. "Thrills and Chills at Disney." *Business Week* (June 21, 1993), 73–74.

Gubernick, Lisa. "Mickey n'est pas fini." *Forbes* (February 14, 1994), 42–43.

Kets de Vries, F. R. "Toppling the Cultural Tower of Babel." *Chief Executive* (May 1994), 68–71.

Michaud, Paul R. "Wild Kingdom." *World Trade* (October 1992), 46–50.

Pitcher, George. "Disney's Road to Damascus." *Marketing Week* (August 11, 1995), 25.

Saseen, Jane. "Disney's Bungle Book." *International Management* (July–August 1993) 26–27.

Saseen, Jane. "Mickey Mania." *International Management* (November 1989), 32–34.

Scimone, Diana. "Bonjour, Mickey Mouse." *Europe* (July–August 1989), 46–47.

Sharkey, Betsy. "The Magic Kingdom," *Mediaweek* (August 7, 1995), 10–12.

"The Kingdom Inside a Republic." *Economist* (April 13, 1996), 66–67.

Toy, Stewart, and Paula Dwyer. "Is Disney Headed for the Euro-Trash Heap?" *Business Week* (January 24, 1994), 32.

Toy, Stewart, et al. "The Mouse Isn't Roaring." *Business Week* (April 24, 1992), 38.

Walker, Angela. "Eurodisney Woes Likely to Continue After Fiscal Boosts." *Hotel & Management* (July 5, 1994), 1 and 32.

Glossary

Adaptive decision   A decision that deals with problems rather than the recurring tasks of a routine decision.

Alternative   A course of action whose selection may result in an outcome that will attain the original objective.

Boundary personnel   Individuals in the organization who are enacting output roles with the external environment.

Bounded rationality   A conceptual framework for describing, understanding, and evaluating decision making based on satisficing behavior in the open decision-making process.

Capability profile   A comprehensive assessment of the total organization showing its aggregate strengths and weaknesses in designated critical factors vis-à-vis the opportunities and threats in its external environment.

Category I decision   A decision that is basically routine and recurring and has a high degree of certainty related to the outcome.

Category II decision   A decision that is basically nonroutine and nonrecurring and has a high degree of uncertainty attached to the outcome.

Certainty   An uncommon state of nature characterized by the possession of perfect information related to a known outcome.

Chain network   A communication network characterized by a high degree of centrality and a low level of personal satisfaction for the people at the end of the chain.

Circle network   A communication network characterized by a two-way flow of information around the perimeter and a good deal of personal satisfaction among the individuals in the network.

Closed decision-making process   A decision-making process that ignores the constraints of bounded rationality and is essentially closed to the external environment.

Closed decision model   A conceptual framework for decision making based on maximizing the outcome of a decision.

Cognition   The act or process of knowing, including both awareness and judgment.

Cognitive strain   A psychological phenomenon characterized by an overload of information confronting a decision maker and exceeding the person's cognitive capacity.

Completely connected network   A communication network characterized by a multidirectional flow of information and a high level of personal satisfaction among the individuals in the network.

Compromise strategy   A strategy used in choosing among alternatives when there is a high level of certainty and a weak preference associated with an outcome.

Computational strategy   A strategy used in choosing among alternatives when there is a high degree of certainty and a strong preference associated with an outcome.

Conditional viewing   The act of scanning a more or less clearly identified area or type of information without actively searching.

Conflict   Oppositional or antagonistic interaction based on scarcity of power, resources, or social position as well as differing value structures.

Conflict determinants   The basic causes of conflict.

Conflict indicators   Observable and nonobservable symptoms that reflect the presence of conflict.

Conflict treatment   Any one or some combination of a number of techniques to resolve conflict or to reduce it to some acceptable level.

Conjunctive model   A model of choice in which the decision maker sets certain cut-off points on the dimensions so that any alternatives falling below a point are eliminated.

Conscious mind   That part of thought at the threshold of awareness.

Cost effectiveness   A state or condition in which the benefits associated with a particular outcome clearly exceed the cost of obtaining the outcome.

Countervailing power   Power that limits other power and is, in turn, limited by other power.

Creative decision   A decision made without the benefit of an existing agreed-upon approach.

Decision   A moment of choice in an ongoing process of evaluating alternatives with a view to selecting one or some combination of them to attain the desired end.

Decision-making process   A series of six interrelated functions of decision making commencing with the setting of objectives and culminating, through a continuous cycle, with the attainment of such objectives.

Decision span   The number of persons, parties, or entities outside the control of the responsible manager who are likely to be affected by a group decision.

Decision success   A measure signifying partial or complete attainment of the objective that gave rise to the decision-making process.

Deindividuation   A loss of self-awareness and a sense of personal identity in a group decision-making situation.

Delphi group   A group decision-making technique that provides for the systematic solicitation and collation of judgments on a topic through the use of questionnaires and feedback.

Disjunctive model   A model of choice in which alternatives are evaluated according to their best attribute regardless of the levels of other attributes.

Distinctive competence   The points of primary leverage within an organization where its principal strengths and competitive advantage lie.

Domain consensus   A set of expectations regarding what the organization will and will not do in interacting with its environmental domain.

Ego   Freud's term for the rational part of the human psychic system, which tries to satisfy the basic drives (generated by the id) with the constraints of the real world.

Elimination-by-aspects model   A model of choice in which alternatives are eliminated if they do not possess requisite amounts of predetermined important aspects or characteristics.

Environment   A framework conceived as an open system composed of external forces in some interconnected spatial arrangement with which the organization must interact in arriving at a satisficing choice in the open decision-making process.

Environmental assessment   A comprehensive appraisal of the forces, entities, and conditions in the organization's external environment.

Environmental boundaries   The interface between a given organization and its external environment.

Environmental domain   The points at which the organization is dependent on inputs from the external environment.

Environmental system   The external environment conceived as a system within which a given organization functions as an integral subsystem.

Environmental texture   A conceptualization of the external environment as the product of its rate of change and complexity.

Ethical   Conforming to principles of human conduct; according to common usage, the following terms are synonymous with ethical: *moral, good, right, just,* and *honest.*

Ethical standards   Principles or ideals of human conduct.

Ethics   Standards for decision making; the application of values to the process of choice; the study of the morality of human actions; the standards for these actions.

Feedback   The process of receiving, evaluating, and using information about past performance in an attempt to judge future actions.

Fiscal resources   Money and its near-equivalent, credit.

Follow-up and control   The stage in the decision-making process immediately following the implementation of a choice; at this stage surveillance procedures are applied to ensure an outcome that meets the original objective.

Formal group   A group that has been established under legal and formal authority to achieve specific goals or to undertake particular tasks.

Formal search   A structured type of search usually following a preestablished plan, procedure, or methodology to obtain specific information related to a particular issue.

Fringe status A part of the structure of a formal group composed of individuals who support the primary set but seldom, if ever, initiate any action themselves.

Gender A set of two categories of masculine and feminine used here to distinguish the decision-making behavior of men and women.

Generic decision A decision that is routine and repetitive; a definite procedure exists for handling it. See *programmed decision*.

Goal A subset of an objective expressed in terms of one or more specific dimensions.

Group A small number of individuals who come together with a common interest for the purpose of making a decision that will attain the objective of the group while satisfying the personal needs of the individual members.

Groupthink A coined term that means that members of a given group have a tendency to suspend independent critical thinking and objective moral judgment in deference to group norms and in observance of group cohesiveness.

Halo effect A process in which a general impression that is favorable or unfavorable is used to evaluate the specific traits of an individual.

Heuristic A simplifying strategy or a rule of thumb useful in making decisions primarily of a category I type or, possibly, a search for alternatives in making a category II decision.

Human resources Time, intellect, and energy.

Id According to Freud, a component of the human psychic system containing the basic drives for pleasure and aggression.

Implementation The stage in the decision-making process immediately after the selection of an alternative during which the choice is put into effect.

Informal group A group that comes into existence on an unplanned basis as a result of friendship or some other informal relationship that develops when several people are placed in contact with one another.

Informal search A relatively limited and unstructured type of search to obtain specific information for a particular purpose.

Information Knowledge intended to reduce uncertainty in the making of a given decision.

Innovative decision A decision that is concerned with major changes in activities and operations that lead to changes in goals, purposes, or policies.

Inspirational strategy A strategy used for choosing among alternatives when there is a good deal of uncertainty and a rather weak preference associated with an outcome.

Institutional resources Goodwill, image, political competence, and social responsiveness.

Instrumental values Desirable modes of conduct.

Integrative decision making A principle that emphasizes the inseparability of the several stages in the total decision-making process.

Interacting group A group in which there is interaction in pursuit of a consensus.

Interdisciplinary decision making A principle that emphasizes the fusion of the quantitative disciplines and the behavioral sciences as well as the influence of the environment in decision making.

Interlocking decision making A principle that emphasizes the limitations and constraints imposed on the rational decision maker from both inside and outside the organization as he or she pursues a satisficing choice in the open decision-making process.

Interrelational decision making A principle that emphasizes the interrelatedness of decision making to all functions of the manager, with particular emphasis on planning and control.

Irrational A breakdown in the normal reasoning process; a tendency toward illogic; a lack of the customary clarity of thinking.

Judgment The evaluation or categorizing of a person, object, or event.

Judgmental strategy A strategy used in choosing among alternatives when there is a good deal of uncertainty and a strong preference associated with an outcome.

Lexicographic model A model of choice in which the attributes or characteristics of greatest importance are selected, and the alternative with the highest ranking on the most important characteristic is the logical choice.

Linear model A model of choice in which the evaluation of each alternative is based on the sum of its weighted values on all its dimensions, and the alternative with the greatest sum is the obvious choice.

Managerial control   A situation in which no large concentrated stockholding is capable of challenging the management of the corporation.

Marginal value   The value of the next unit of whatever item is being measured.

Maximized outcome   An optimal result embodying the highest possible value for which a given decision is made.

Maximizing behavior   An approach to decision making oriented toward obtaining an outcome of the highest quantity or value.

Membership group   A group to which an individual actually belongs and in which he or she has some duties and responsibilities.

Model   A physical or abstract representation of some part of the real world that is used to describe, explain, and predict behavior.

Morality   The property of an action by means of which it conforms to a norm of human conduct.

Negative strategic gap   A state in which the capabilities of an organization are more than sufficient to take advantage of external opportunities and to ward off external threats.

Negotiated decision   A decision made when opposing factions confront each other concerning either ends or means or both; for instance, union and management in a labor negotiation.

Nominal group   A group decision-making technique in which the decision is the pooled outcome of individual votes.

Nonprogrammed decision   A decision that is novel, unstructured, and consequential; no cut-and-dried method for making the choice exists. See *unique decision.*

Nonrational behavior   Behavior not in accordance with one's best estimate of the costs, gains, and probabilities regarding a decision and not mindful of the consequences likely to result from taking a particular action.

Norm   An idea in the minds of the members of a group that can be put in the form of a statement specifying what the members ought to do or are expected to do under given circumstances.

Objective   The end point toward which management directs its decision making.

Open decision-making process   A decision-making process that observes the constraints of bounded rationality and that is open to the external environment.

Open decision model   A conceptual framework for decision making based on obtaining a satisficing outcome from a given choice.

Open system   A conceptual framework in which an environment is seen as a network of external forces, with varying spatial relationships, providing informational inputs to the organization through permeable boundaries and evaluating outputs in the form of satisficing decisions.

Operating constraints   Institutionalized policies and procedures that reflect the established way of doing business.

Opportunities   External situations likely to work to the long-term advantage of the organization.

Opportunity cost   The cost of the next best alternative that is sacrificed to select what appears to be the best alternative.

Optimal amount of information   A hypothetical point on the marginal value curve where the next unit of information will decline in its marginal value and one less unit will result in a loss in marginal value. See Figure 2.2.

Optimal timing   A hypothetical point or interval at which the opportunity to be capitalized or the advantage to be gained appears to be at its zenith.

Organizational assessment   A comprehensive appraisal of the aggregate strengths and weaknesses in the critical factors used to make a capability profile. See *capability profile.*

Organizational boundary   The interface between the organization and its external environment.

Organizational model   A neoclassical model that combines the behavioral disciplines with the quantitative aspects of decision making to arrive at a choice that recognizes most decision-making constraints.

Output role   A role enacted by one or more individuals in relating the organization to its external environment.

Outstatus   A term applied to a subset of a formal group composed of individuals who are essentially isolated and members of the formal group in name only.

Participative decision making   A prechoice situation in which there is meaningful involvement in the decision-making process by those who are responsible for implementing the choice or are directly or indirectly affected by it.

Perception   A process that entails being sensitized to and developing certain interpretations of stimuli or facts.

Perceptual defense   A type of behavior that occurs when a perceiver is confronted with a fact or event that is inconsistent with one or more of his or her stereotypes; because the individual is unable to reconcile this inconsistency, he or she makes an inaccurate perception, thereby preserving the stereotype.

Perceptual process   A process in which selected pieces of information are compiled into a meaningful whole for interpretation and use as the basis for action in decision making.

Physical resources   Land, buildings, machinery, equipment, and raw materials.

Pluralism   The idea that power in society is balanced and diffused among a multiplicity of organizations and groups.

Point of optimality   The most desirable point on the marginal value curve for the acquisition of additional information at which the value of the last unit acquired is highest in relation to its cost of acquisition.

Policy   A verbal, written, or implied overall guide setting up boundaries that supply the general limits and directions in which managerial actions will take place.

Political model   A behavioral decision-making model that involves incremental steps within a loosely structured process in which the acceptance of the outcome is the overriding criterion.

Political power   The symbiotic union of the reciprocal concepts of power and politics. See *power; politics*.

Politics   The use of power to effect definitions or goals and directions and to mobilize resources, energy, and information on behalf of a preferred goal or strategy.

Positive strategic gap   A state in which the capabilities of an organization are more than sufficient to take advantage of external opportunities and to ward off external threats.

Power   The capacity of one person or group to prevent another person or group from reaching a goal.

Power elite   The individuals at the head of the giant corporations, the armed forces, the state, and the mass media of communication.

Preconscious mind   That part of thought that links the subconscious mind and the conscious mind.

Primary group   A number of individuals with a common interest interacting in a close face-to-face relationship over a relatively extended period of time in pursuit of a definable objective.

Primary set   A part of the structure of a formal group composed of the prime movers for the group's efforts.

Probability   The limits of the relative frequency of the occurrence of a given event over the long run.

Probability of the outcome   The percentage of times a given event would occur if a particular trial were repeated a great many times.

Problem   A barrier between a current and a desired state of affairs.

Problem solving   A process of thoughtfully and deliberately striving to overcome obstacles in the path toward a goal.

Process model   A model of the interdisciplinary decision-making process involving six highly integrated decision-making functions that are interrelated with the basic functions of the manager and take place in an interlocking mode.

Programmed decision   A decision that is routine and repetitive; a definite procedure exists for handling it. See *generic decision*.

Projection   The tendency to attribute one's own characteristics to other people.

Rational behavior   Behavior that is goal-oriented with regard to a decision at hand and that is guided by the consequences likely to result from the selection of a given alternative.

Rational decision   A choice made in the presence of an objective and that, in the view of the decision maker, promises to meet the objective.

Rationality   The selection of preferred behavior alternatives in terms of some system of values whereby the consequences of behavior can be evaluated.

Rationalization   A defensive mechanism in the conscious or subconscious mind that permits a decision maker to convince himself or herself that a choice is or was in the best interests of the organization.

Rational model   A normative model of decision making that is prescriptive rather than descriptive and that epitomizes the classical approach to decision theory.

Reference group   A group with which an individual identifies or to which he or she would like to belong.

Resources   Reserves, wealth, or capital possessed by an organization in the form of (1) fiscal resources, (2) physical resources, (3) human resources, or (4) institutional resources.

Risk   A common state or condition in decision making characterized by the possession of incomplete information regarding a probabilistic outcome.

Risk avoider   An individual who covets a sure thing and therefore may prefer the certainty of inaction or outright failure to the probabilistic success of a risk-laden choice or an uncertain outcome.

Risk-reward factor   A hypothetical factor based on a positive correlation between risk and reward; that is, risk should be offset with commensurate reward.

Risk seeker   A high achiever who equates the acceptance of risk with potential reward and looks for risky situations.

Risky shift   The manifested willingness of an individual to accept more risk as a member of a group than as a decision maker in his or her own right.

Routine decision   A decision made when the organization or group has agreed on the desired goal and the technology exists to achieve the goal.

Satisficing behavior   An approach to decision making based on obtaining an outcome that meets the objective.

Satisficing outcome   A satisfactory result that meets the objective for which a given managerial decision is made.

Search   A function of decision making in which information is sought from which to fashion alternative courses of action.

Secondary group   A group composed of individuals with common ties or interests but without regular or direct interaction.

Simulation model   A special type of abstract model that is analogous to a segment of the real world and contains a time dimension. It is used to explain and predict behavior as if it occurred in the real world.

Social loafing   A state in which the performance of highly motivated individuals is impeded by a felt need to comply with the output norms of a group.

Social responsibility   A presumed obligation for a given organization to consider the social welfare or the public good in making and implementing its managerial decisions.

Stakeholders   Those entities that have a vested interest in the outcome of events within a given organization.

Standards   Criteria against which the results of an implemented decision can be measured.

State of nature   A state or condition likely to prevail when a choice is made.

Stereotype   A prejudicial categorization in which conceptions of relationship and identity do not take the actual state of affairs sufficiently into account.

Strategic choice   The selection of a course of action involving an appreciable commitment of resources for the long-term advantage of the organization to capitalize on opportunities and to repel threats in the external environment.

Strategic control   A process designed to evaluate the effectiveness of an implemented strategic choice in terms of the attainment of its underlying long-range strategic objective.

Strategic decision   A special variety of category II decision that is of significance to the long-term health of the organization and falls within the purview of top management. See *category II decision; strategic choice.*

Strategic decision-making process   A conceptual framework consisting of the concept of strategic gap and the managerial decision-making process designed to facilitate the making of successful strategic choices. See Figure 10.2.

Strategic decision matrix   A conceptual framework used to classify strategic choices based on a set of managerial attitudes toward the decision-making process and the decision itself. See Figure 11.1.

Strategic decision success   A choice made by management that results in the attainment of the long-range strategic objective that gave rise to the decision within the constraints that must be observed to bring about such attainment; intended ends accomplished within designated means.

Strategic fit   The degree of compatibility between the capabilities of an organization and the opportunities and threats in its external environment.

Strategic gap   An imbalance between the internal capabilities of a given organization and the opportunities and threats in its external environment.

Strategic horizon The most distant point in time at which a strategic maturity can be established with a reasonable expectation of attainment.

Strategic management The continuous process of effectively using the capabilities of an organization to capitalize on the opportunities and to repel the threats in the external environment.

Strategic management process A series of inter-related strategy-based functions that employ externally derived information used by management to commit the organization's technology and resources toward the attainment of its long-range strategic objective.

Strategic maturity A long-range point in time at which a given strategic objective will be attained.

Strategic objective A long-range result established by top management and sought by one or more strategic choices committing the total organization toward its attainment.

Strategic position The relationship between a given organization and the significant forces in its external environment at a given moment in time.

Strategic surprise An event arising from a sudden, urgent, and unfamiliar change in the external environment of a given organization that threatens it with a major reversal or the loss of an important opportunity.

Strategy A conceptualization, expressed or implied, by management of (1) the long-term purposes of the organization, (2) the broad constraints and policies that restrict the scope of the organization's activities, and (3) the set of plans and near-term goals that have been adopted in the expectation they will contribute to the attainment of the long-range strategic objective.

Strategy-based information Information obtained largely from the external environment of a given organization and used to formulate, make, implement, and control strategic choices.

Subconscious mind That part of thought below the threshold of awareness.

Subjective probability The degree of confidence placed in the occurrence of an event by the decision maker based on available evidence.

Superego According to Freud, a component of the human psyche that is the social and moral arbiter of the individual.

Superordinate goal A joint interest, collective benefit, or mutual advantage that will accrue to members of a group if they abandon conflict and focus on the group objective; it is often presented to resolve intergroup or intragroup conflict.

Synergy The optimal integration of what was formerly differentiated as a result of cohesive interaction among the members of a group.

Technology The systematic application of scientific or other knowledge to practical tasks.

Technostructure All those individuals or groups who bring specialized knowledge, talent, or experience to bear on decision making in large corporations.

Terminal values Desirable modes of conduct.

Threats Unfavorable or potentially disadvantageous states of affairs or combinations of circumstances in the external environment of a given organization.

Time An unavoidable constraint in most strategic decision-making situations constituting a defined or precise interval or temporal point.

Timing An actual interval or temporal point in which a decision would be made to permit a given organization to capitalize on an opportunity or repel a threat in its external environment.

Trade-off value A value that exists when a given amount of one kind of performance may in some measure be substituted for another kind of performance.

Transitivity axiom A requirement that all preferences are transitive — for example, if A is preferred to B, and B is preferred to C, then A is preferred to C.

Two-person, zero-sum game A conceptual framework for decision making in a situation of conflict wherein two players (decision makers) compete to obtain a decisive advantage in a way that one player's gain is the other player's loss.

Type A strategic choice A choice with an attainable objective pursued in the open decision-making process using a judgmental decision-making strategy in quest of a satisficing outcome.

Type B strategic choice A choice with an unattainable objective pursued in a closed decision-making process using a judgmental decision-making strategy to obtain a satisficing outcome.

Type C strategic choice A choice with an attainable objective pursued in the open decision-making process using a computational decision-making strategy in quest of a maximized outcome.

Type D strategic choice A choice with an unattainable objective pursued in the closed decision-making process through a computational decision-making strategy to obtain a maximized outcome.

Uncertainty An uncommon state of nature characterized by the absence of any information related to a desired outcome; the complement of knowledge.

Unconditional probability The probability of the occurrence of a given event independent of the occurrence of any other event.

Undirected viewing The act of scanning for information without an active search and with no specific purpose in mind except perhaps exploration.

Unique decision A decision that is novel, unstructured, and consequential; no cut-and-dried method for making the choice exists. See *nonprogrammed decision*.

Utility Technically, want-satisfying power; it is often defined as the preference of the decision maker for a given outcome.

Value A conception, explicit or implicit, of what an individual, group, or organization regards as desirable.

Value judgment A special type of evaluation or categorization based primarily on values rather than facts.

Values The normative standards by which human beings and organizations are influenced in their choices.

Value system A relatively permanent perceptual framework that shapes and influences the general nature of an individual's behavior.

Wheel network A communication network characterized by a very high degree of centrality and a rather low level of satisfaction among the individuals on the periphery of the wheel.

Zero strategic gap A hypothetical situation characterized by a perfect balance between the capabilities of a given organization and the opportunities and threats in its external environment.

Zone of cost effectiveness An area on either side of the point of optimality on the marginal cost curve for the acquisition of additional information in which the last unit of information has a clear value in relation to its cost.

Bibliography

BOOKS

Abelson, Robert P., et al., eds. Theories of Cognitive Consistency: A Sourcebook. Chicago: Rand McNally, 1968.

Agor, W. *Intuitive Management.* Englewood Cliffs, N.J.: Prentice-Hall, 1984.

Aguilar, Francis Joseph. *Scanning the Business Environment.* New York: Macmillan, 1967.

Aitchison, John. *Choice Against Chance: An Introduction to Statistical Decision Theory.* Reading, Mass.: Addison-Wesley, 1970.

Albanese, Robert. *Managing: Toward Accountability for Performance.* 3rd ed. Homewood, Ill.: Richard D. Irwin, 1981.

Albers, Henry H. *Principles of Management: A Modern Approach.* 4th ed. New York: Wiley, 1974.

Alexis, Marcus, and Charles Z. Wilson, eds. *Organizational Decision Making.* Englewood Cliffs, N.J.: Prentice-Hall, 1967.

Allison, Graham T. *Essence of Decision: Explaining the Cuban Missile Crisis.* Boston: Little, Brown, 1971.

Amey, Lloyd R., ed. *Readings in Management Decision.* London: Longman, 1973.

Andrews, K. R. *The Concept of Corporate Strategy.* Rev. ed. Homewood, Ill.: Irwin, 1980.

Ansoff, H. J. *Corporate Strategy.* New York: McGraw-Hill, 1965.

Axelrod, Robert, ed. *Structure of Decision.* Princeton, N.J.: Princeton University Press, 1976.

Bahm, Archie, J. *Ethics as a Behavioral Science.* Springfield, Ill.: Charles C Thomas, 1974.

Bales, Robert F. *Interaction Process Analysis.* Reading Mass.: Addison-Wesley, 1950.

Barnard, Chester. *The Functions of the Executive.* Cambridge, Mass.: Harvard University Press, 1938.

Barnet, Richard J., and Ronald E. Muller. *Global Reach: The Power of the Multinational Corporations.* New York: Simon & Schuster, 1974.

Bass, Bernard M. *Organizational Decision Making.* Homewood, Ill.: Richard D. Irwin, 1983.

Baumhart, Raymond. *Ethics in Business.* New York: Holt, Rinehart & Winston, 1968.

Baumol, W. J. *Business Behavior, Value, and Growth.* rev. ed. New York: Harcourt, Brace & World, 1967.

Bazerman, Max H. *Judgment in Managerial Decision Making,* 3rd. ed. New York: Wiley, 1994.

Beach, Lee Roy. *Making the Right Decision.* Englewood Cliffs, N.J.: Prentice-Hall, 1993.

Benn, S. I., and G. W. Mortimore, eds. *Rationality and the Social Sciences.* London: Routledge & Kegan Paul, 1976.

Borcherding, K., O. J. Larichev, and D. M. Messick, eds. *Contemporary Issues in Decision Making.* New York: Elsevier Publishing Co., 1990.

Braverman, Jerome D. *Management Decision Making.* New York: AMACOM, 1980.

Braybrooke, David, and Charles E. Lindblom. *A Strategy of Decision.* New York: Free Press, 1963.

Brehmer, B., et al., eds. *New Directions in Research on Decision Making.* New York: Elsevier Publishing Co., 1986.

Bridges, Francis J., Kenneth W. Olm, and J. Allison Barnhill. *Management Decisions and Organizational Policy: Text, Cases, and Incidents.* 2nd ed. Boston: Allyn & Bacon, 1977.

Brim, Orville C., Jr., et al. *Personality and Decision Processes.* Stanford, Calif.: Stanford University Press, 1962.

Bronner, R. *Decision Making Under Time Pressure.* Lexington, Mass.: D. C. Heath, 1982.

Brown, Roger. *Social Psychology.* New York: Free Press, 1965.

Browne, Mairead. *Organizational Decision Making and Information.* Norwood, N.J.: Ablex, 1993.

Bruner, Jerome S., Jacquelyn J. Goodnow, and George A. Austin. *A Study of Thinking.* New York: Wiley, 1956.

Brunson, Nils. *The Irrational Organization.* New York: Wiley, 1985.

Brzezinski, Zbigniew. *Power and Principle.* New York: Farrar, Straus & Giroux, 1983.

Butler, Richard. *Designing Organizations: A Decision-Making Perspective.* New York: Routledge, 1991.

Carlton, Jim. *Apple: The Inside Story of Intrigue, Egomania, and Business Blunders,* New York: Time Business, 1997.

Carter, Jimmy. *Keeping Faith.* New York: Bantam Books, 1982.

Cartwright, Dorwin, ed. *Kurt Lewin: Field Theory in Social Science: Selected Theoretical Papers.* New York: Harper & Row, 1951.

———. *Studies in Social Power.* Ann Arbor: University of Michigan Research Center for Group Dynamics, Institute for Social Research, 1959.

Cartwright, Dorwin, and Alvin Zender, eds. *Group Dynamics: Research and Theory.* Evanston, Ill.: Ross Peterson, 1953.

Cassel, Russell N. *The Psychology of Decision Making.* North Quincy, Mass.: Christopher, 1973.

Cattell, R. B. *Personality: A Systematic, Theoretical, and Factual Study.* New York: McGraw-Hill, 1950.

Cavanaugh, Gerald F. *American Business Values with International Perspectives,* 4th ed. Upper Saddle River, N.J.: Prentice-Hall, 1998.

Chakraporty, S. K. *Managerial Transformation by Values: A Corporate Pilgrimage.* Newbury Park, Calif.: Sage, 1993.

Chandler, Alfred D., Jr. *Strategy and Structure.* Cambridge, Mass.: MIT Press, 1962.

Churchman, C. West. *Prediction and Optimal Decision.* Englewood Cliffs, N.J.: Prentice-Hall, 1961.

Clausen, G. "Risk Taking in Small Groups." Ph.D. diss., University of Michigan, 1965.

Cleland, David I., and William R. King. *Management: A Systems Approach.* New York: McGraw-Hill, 1972.

Collingridge, Daniel. *Critical Decision Making.* New York: St. Martin's Press, 1982.

Collins, B. E., and H. Guetzkow. *A Social Psychology of Group Processes for Decision Making.* New York: Wiley, 1964.

Collins, James C., and Jerry J. Porras. *Built to Last: Successful Habits of Visionary Companies.* New York: Harper Collins, 1994.

Collins, Orvis F., and David G. Moore. *The Enterprising Man.* East Lansing: Michigan State University, 1964.

Cook, Karen Schweers, and Margaret Levi, eds. *The Limits of Rationality.* Chicago: University of Chicago Press, 1990.

Cornell, Alexander H. *The Decision-Maker's Handbook.* Englewood Cliffs, N.J.: Prentice-Hall, 1980.

Corsini, Raymond J., ed. *Current Personality Theories.* Itasca, Ill.: F. E. Peacock, 1977.

Costello, Timothy W., and Sheldon S. Zalkind, eds. *Psychology in Administration: A Research Orientation.* Englewood Cliffs, N.J.: Prentice-Hall, 1963.

Cyert, Richard M., and James G. March. *A Behavioral Theory of the Firm.* Englewood Cliffs, N.J.: Prentice-Hall, 1963.

Dahrendorf, Ralf. *Class and Class Conflict in Industrial Society.* Stanford, Calif.: Stanford University Press, 1959.

Dawson, Roger. *The Confident Decision Maker.* New York: Morrow, 1993.

De Rivera, Joseph H. *The Psychological Dimension of Foreign Policy.* Columbus, Ohio: Merrill, 1968.

Deutsch, Morton. *The Resolution of Conflict.* New Haven: Yale University Press, 1973.

Divine, Robert A., ed. *The Cuban Missile Crisis.* Chicago: Quadrangle, 1971.

Domoff, G. William. *Who Rules America?* Englewood Cliffs, N.J.: Prentice-Hall, 1967.

Donaldson, Gordon, and Jay W. Lorsch. *Decision Making at the Top.* New York: Basic Books, 1983.

Driver, Michael J., et al. *The Dynamic Decision Maker.* San Francisco: Jossey-Bass, 1993.

Drucker, Peter. *The Effective Executive.* New York: Harper & Row, 1967.

Duncan, W. Jack. *Decision Making and Social Issues.* Hinsdale, Ill.: Dryden Press, 1973.

Ebert, Ronald J., and Terence R. Mitchell. *Organizational Decision Processes.* New York: Crane, Russak, 1975.

Eells, Ellery. *Rational Decision and Causality.* Cambridge: Cambridge University Press, 1982.

Eells, Richard, and Clarence Walton. *Conceptual Foundations of Business.* rev. ed. Homewood, Ill.: Richard D. Irwin, 1969.

Eilon, Samuel. *Management Control.* 2nd ed. New York: Pergamon, 1979.

Elbing, Alvar O. *Behavioral Decisions in Organizations.* 2nd ed. Glenview, Ill.: Scott, Foresman, 1978.

Elbing, Alvar O., and Carol J. Elbing. *The Value Issue of Business.* New York: McGraw-Hill, 1967.

Ellul, Jacques. *The Technological Society.* New York: Vintage Books, 1967.

Emory, C. William, and Powell Niland. *Making Management Decisions.* Boston: Houghton Mifflin, 1968.

Evans, William A. *Management Ethics*. Boston: Martinus Nijhoff, 1981.

Fahey, Liam. *The Strategic Planning Management Reader*. Englewood Cliffs, N.J.: Prentice-Hall, 1989.

Feather, Norman F., ed. *Expectations and Actions: Expectancy-Value Models in Psychology*. Hillsdale, N.J.: Lawrence Erlbaum Associates, 1982.

Festinger, Leon. *Conflict, Decision, and Dissonance*. Stanford, Calif.: Stanford University Press, 1964.

Fisher, B. Aubrey. *Small Group Decision Making: Communication and the Group Process*. New York: McGraw-Hill, 1974.

Fisk, George, ed. *The Psychology of Management Decision*. Lund, Sweden: CWK Gleerup, 1967.

Freud, Sigmund. *Civilization and Its Discontents*, New York: Norton, 1961.

Friedman, Myles I. *Rational Behavior*. Columbia: University of South Carolina Press, 1975.

Galbraith, John Kenneth. *American Capitalism: The Concept of Countervailing Power*. Boston: Houghton Mifflin, 1952.

———. *The New Industrial State*. Boston: Houghton Mifflin, 1967.

Garrett, Thomas M. *Business Ethics*. New York: Appleton-Century-Crofts, 1966.

Garthoff, Raymond L. *Reflections on the Cuban Missile Crisis*. Washington, D.C.: Brookings, 1987.

George, Alexander L. *Presidential Decisionmaking in Foreign Policy: The Effective Use of Information and Advice*. Boulder, Colo.: Westview, 1980.

George, Claude S., Jr. *The History of Management Thought*. 2nd ed. Englewood Cliffs, N.J.: Prentice-Hall, 1972.

Glover, Ron. *The Disney Touch*, rev. ed. Burr Ridge, IL: Irwin, 1997.

Gordon, Robert Aaron. *Business Leadership in the Large Corporation*. Berkeley: University of California Press, 1961.

Gore, William J. *Administrative Decision Making: A Heuristic Model*. New York: Wiley, 1964.

Goslin, L., and A. Rethans. *Basic Systems for Decision Making*. Dubuque, Iowa: Kendall/Hunt, 1980.

Greene, Richard M., Jr., ed. *Business Intelligence and Espionage*. Homewood, Ill.: Dow Jones-Irwin, 1966.

Greenwood, William T., ed. *Decision Theory and Information Systems*. Cincinnati: South-Western, 1969.

Griffin, Ricky W., ed. *Research in Organizational Behavior*. Vol. 9. Greenwich, Conn.: JAI Press, 1987.

Gryna, Frank M., Jr. *Quality Circles: A Team Approach to Problem Solving*. New York: AMACOM, 1981.

Haas, J. Eugene, and Thomas E. Drabek, *Complex Organizations: A Sociological Perspective*. New York: Macmillan, 1973.

Hadley, Arthur F. *The Straw Giant*. New York: Random House, 1986.

Hall, Calvin S., and Gardner Lindzey. *Theories of Personality*. 2nd ed. New York: Wiley, 1970.

Halter, Albert N., and Gerald W. Dean. *Decisions Under Uncertainty with Research Applications*. Cincinnati: South-Western, 1971.

Harrison, E. Frank. *Management and Organizations*. Boston: Houghton Mifflin, 1978.

———. *Policy, Strategy, and Managerial Action*. Boston: Houghton Mifflin, 1986.

Hartley, Robert F. *Management Mistakes & Successes*. 3rd ed. New York: Wiley, 1991.

Harvey, D. F. *Strategic Management*. Columbus, Ohio: Merrill, 1982.

Heermance, Edgar L. *The Ethics of Business*. New York: Harper, 1926.

Heller, Frank A. *Managerial Decision Making*. London: Tavistock, 1971.

Heller, Robert. *The Decision Makers*. New York: Penguin Books, 1991.

Herman, Charles F., ed. *In International Crises: Insights from Behavioral Research*. New York: Free Press, 1972.

Hickson, David J., ed. *Managerial Decision Making*. England: Dartmouth, 1995.

Hickson, David J., et al. *Top Decisions: Strategic Decision-Making in Organizations*. San Francisco: Jossey-Bass, 1986.

Hill, Percy H., et al. *Making Decisions: A Multidisciplinary Introduction*. Reading, Mass.: Addison-Wesley, 1978.

Hilsman, Roger. *To Move a Nation*. New York: Delta, 1967.

Hinton, Bernard L., and H. Joseph Reitz, eds. *Groups and Organizations: Integrated Readings in the Analysis of Social Behavior*. Belmont, Calif.: Wadsworth, 1971.

Hofer, C. W., and D. Schendel, *Strategy Formulation: Analytical Concepts*. St. Paul, Minn.: West Publishing Co., 1978.

Hogarth, Robin. *Judgement and Choice*. 2nd ed. New York: Wiley, 1987.

Homans, George C. *The Human Group*. New York: Harcourt, Brace, 1950.

Horowitz, Ira, ed. *Organization and Decision Theory.* Norwell, Mass.: Kluwer Academic Publishers, 1980.

Huber, George P. *Managerial Decision Making* Glenview, Ill.: Scott, Foresman, 1980.

Hull, R. F. C., trans. *Psychological Types,* by C. G. Jung. Princeton, N.J.: Princeton University Press, 1971.

Iacocca, Lee. *Iacocca.* New York: Bantam Books, 1984.

Janis, Irving L. *Crucial Decisions: Leadership in Policy-making and Crisis Management.* New York: Free Press, 1989.

———. *Groupthink,* 2nd ed. Boston: Houghton Mifflin, 1982.

———., and Leon Mann. *Decision Making: A Psychological Analysis of Conflict, Choice, and Commitment.* New York: Free Press, 1977.

Jennings, David, and Stuart Wattam. *Decision Making: An Integrated Approach,* London: Pitman, 1994.

Johnson, Eric J. *Deciding How to Decide: The Effort of Making a Decision.* Chicago: University of Chicago, Center for Decision Research, 1979.

Johnson, Rossall J. *Executive Decisions.* 2nd ed. Cincinnati: South-Western, 1970.

Jones, Manley Howe. *Executive Decision Making.* Homewood, Ill.: Richard D. Irwin, 1962.

Jordan, Hamilton. *Crisis: The Last Year of the Carter Presidency.* New York: Putman's, 1982.

Joshi, Madhudar V. *Management Science: A Survey of Quantitative Decision-Making Techniques.* Belmont, Calif.: Wadsworth, 1980.

Katona, George. *Psychological Analysis of Economic Behavior.* New York: McGraw-Hill, 1963.

Kazmier, Leonard J. *Statistical Analysis for Business and Economics.* 3rd ed. New York: McGraw-Hill, 1978.

Keegan, Warren J. *Global Marketing Management,* 5th ed. Englewood Cliffs, N.J.: Prentice-Hall, 1995.

Keller, Maryann. *Rude Awakening: The Rise, Fall, and Struggle for Recovery of General Motors.* New York: William Morrow, 1989.

Kepner, Charles, and Benjamin S. Tregoe. *The Rational Manager.* New York: McGraw-Hill, 1963.

Kets de Vries, F. R., and D. Miller. *The Neurotic Organization,* San FranciscoL Jossey-Bass, 1984.

Kiesler, Sara. *Interpersonal Processes in Groups and Organizations.* Arlington Heights, Ill.: AHM, 1978.

King, W. R., and D. I. Cleland. *Strategic Planning and Management Handbook.* New York: Van Nostrand Reinhold, 1987.

King, W. R., and D. I. Cleland. *Strategic Planning and Policy.* New York: Van Nostrand Reinhold, 1978.

Klein, George S. *Perception, Motives, and Personality.* New York: Alfred A. Knopf, 1970.

Knotts, Ulysses S., Jr., and Ernest W. Swift. *Management Science for Management Decisions.* Boston: Allyn & Bacon, 1978.

Kogan, N., and M. A. Wallach. *Risk-Taking: A Study in Cognition and Personality.* New York: Holt, Rinehart & Winston, 1964.

Kolasa, Blair J. *Introduction to Behavioral Science for Business.* New York: Wiley, 1969.

Kolko, Gabriel. *Wealth and Power in America.* New York: Praeger, 1962.

Koontz, Harold, Cyril O'Donnell, and Heinz Weihrich. *Essentials of Management.* 5th ed. New York: McGraw-Hill, 1990.

Korn/Ferry International's Executive Profile: A Decade of Change in Corporate Leadership. New York: Korn / Ferry International, 1990.

Korn/Ferry International's Executive Profile: A Survey of Corporate Leaders in the Eighties. New York: Korn / Ferry International, 1986.

Lamb, Robert, ed. *Advances in Strategic Management.* Vol. 1. Greenwich, Conn.: JAI Press, 1983.

Lamb, Robert Boyden, ed. *Competitive Strategic Management.* Englewood Cliffs, N.J.: Prentice-Hall, 1984.

Larner, Robert J. *Management Control and the Large Corporation.* New York: Dunellen, 1970.

Larson, David L. *The "Cuban Crisis" of 1962.* 2nd ed. Lanham, Md.: University Press of America, 1986.

Lawless, David J. *Effective Management: A Social Psychological Approach.* Englewood Cliffs, N.J.: Prentice-Hall, 1972.

Lee, Wayne. *Decision Theory and Human Behavior.* New York: Wiley, 1971.

Leontiades, M. *Policy, Strategy, and Plans.* Boston: Little, Brown, 1982.

Levin, Doron P. *Irreconcilable Differences: Ross Perot versus General Motors.* New York: Penguin Books, 1990.

Leys, Wayne A. R. *Ethics for Policy Decisions.* Englewood Cliffs, N.J.: Prentice-Hall, 1962.

Lillie, William. *An Introduction to Ethics.* New York: Barnes & Noble, 1964.

Lindley, D. V. *Making Decisions.* New York: Wiley-Interscience, 1971.

Linstone, Harold A. *Multiple Perspectives for Decision Making.* New York: North-Holland, 1984.

Linstone, Harold A., and Murray Turoff, eds. *The Delphi Method.* Reading, Mass.: Addison-Wesley, 1976.

Lorsch, Jay W., and Paul R. Lawrence, eds. *Studies in Organization Design*. Homewood, Ill.: Richard D. Irwin and Dorsey Press, 1970.

McCarthy, D. J., R. J. Minichiello, and J. R. Curran. *Business Policy and Strategy: Concepts and Readings*. Homewood, Ill.: Richard D. Irwin, 1975.

McConnell, M. *Challenger: A Major Malfunction*. New York: Doubleday, 1987.

MacCrimmon, Kenneth R., and Donald A. Wehrung. *Taking Risks: The Management of Uncertainty*. New York: Free Press, 1986.

McFarland, Dalton E. *Management: Formulations and Practices*. 5th ed. New York: Macmillan, 1979.

McGuire, Joseph W. *Theories of Business Behavior*. Englewood Cliffs, N.J.: Prentice-Hall, 1964.

Mack, Ruth P. *Planning on Uncertainty*. New York: Wiley-Interscience, 1971.

Maier, Norman R. F. *Problem Solving and Creativity in Individuals and Groups*. Belmont, Calif.: Brooks/Cole, 1970.

Mailick, Sidney, and Edward H. Van Ness, ed. *Concepts and Issues in Administrative Behavior*. Englewood Cliffs, N.J.: Prentice-Hall, 1962.

Mandler, G., ed. *New Directions in Psychology, III*. New York: Holt, Rinehart and Winston, 1967.

Mannheim, K. *Rational and Irrational Elements in Contemporary Society*. London: Oxford University Press, 1934.

March, James G. *A Primer on Decision Making*. New York: Free Press, 1994.

———. *Decisions and Organizations*. New York: Blackwell, 1988.

March, James G., and Johan P. Olsen. *Ambiguity and Choice in Organizations*. 2nd ed. Bergen, Norway: Universitetsforlaget, 1979.

March, James G., and Herbert A. Simon. *Organizations*. New York: Wiley, 1958.

March, James G., and Roger Weissinger-Baylon. *Ambiguity and Command*. Marshfield, Mass.: Pitman, 1986.

Marshall, Howard D., ed. *Business and Government: The Problem of Power*. Lexington, Mass.: Heath, 1970.

Matheson, James E. *Decision Analysis Practice: Examples and Insights*. Menlo Park, Calif.: Stanford Research Institute, 1969.

Miller, David W., and Martin K. Starr. *The Structure of Human Decisions*. Englewood Cliffs, N.J.: Prentice-Hall, 1967.

Mills, C. Wright. *The Power Elite*. London: Oxford University Press, 1956.

Mockler, Robert J. *Management Decision Making and Action in Behavioral Situations*. Austin, Texas: Austin Press, 1973.

Monsen, R. Joseph, Jr., and Mark W. Cannon. *The Makers of Public Policy: American Power Groups and Their Ideologies*. New York: McGraw-Hill, 1965.

Montgomery, H., and O. Swenson, eds. *Process and Structure in Human Decision Making*. New York: Wiley, 1989.

Moore, P. G. *The Business of Risk*. New York: Cambridge University Press, 1983.

Moritz, Michael, and Barrett Seaman. *Going for Broke: The Chrysler Story*. New York: Doubleday, 1981.

Nash, Manning. *Primitive and Peasant Economic Systems*. San Francisco: Chandler, 1966.

National Aeronautics and Space Administration. *Report to the President: Actions to Implement the Recommendations of the Presidential Commission on the Space Shuttle Challenger Accident*. Vol. I. Washington, D.C.: U.S. Government Printing Office, 1986.

Nelson, Richard R., and Sidney G. Winter. *An Evolutionary Theory of Economic Change*. Cambridge, Mass.: The Belknop Press of Harvard University Press, 1982.

Neustadt, Richard E., and Ernest R. May. *Thinking in Time: The Uses of History for Decision Makers*. New York: Free Press, 1986.

Newman, Joseph W. *Management Applications of Decision Theory*. New York: Harper & Row, 1971.

Nisbett, Richard, and Lee Ross. *Human Inference: Strategies and Shortcomings of Social Judgments*. Englewood Cliffs, N.J.: Prentice-Hall, 1980.

Nozik, Robert. *The Nature of Rationality*. Princeton, N.J.: Princeton University Press, 1993.

Nutt, Paul C. *Making Tough Decisions*. San Francisco: Jossey-Bass, 1989.

Ofstad, H. *An Inquiry into the Freedom of Decision*. Oslo: Norwegian Universities Press, 1961.

Parsons, Talcott, and Edward A. Shils, eds. *Toward a General Theory of Action*. New York: Harper & Row, 1951.

Pennings, J. M., and Associates, *Organizational Strategy and Change*. San Francisco: Jossey-Bass, 1985.

Perles, Benjamin, and Charles Sullivan, eds. *Modern Business Statistics*. Rev. ed. Englewood Cliffs, N.J.: Prentice-Hall, 1969.

Perrow, Charles. *Normal Accidents: Living with High-Risk Technologies*. New York: Basic Books, 1984.

Peters, T. J., and R. H. Waterman, Jr. *In Search of Excellence*. New York: Harper & Row, 1982.

Pfeffer, Jeffrey. *Managing with Power*. Boston, Mass.: Harvard Business School Press, 1992.

———. *Power in Organizations*. Marshfield, Mass.: Pitman, 1981.

Quade, E. S. *Analysis for Public Decisions*. 2nd ed. New York: North-Holland, 1982.

Rappaport, Alfred, ed. *Information for Decision Making: Quantitative and Behavioral Dimensions*. Englewood Cliffs, N.J.: Prentice-Hall, 1970.

Reich, Robert B., and John D. Donahue. *New Deals: The Chrysler Revival and the American System*. New York: Time Books, 1985.

Reinventing the CEO. New York: Korn/Ferry International and Columbia University Graduate School of Business, 1989.

Report of the Presidential Commission on the Space Shuttle Challenger Accident. Vol. I. Washington, D.C.: U.S. Government Printing Office, 1986.

Rhenman, E. *Industrial Democracy* and *Industry Management*. London: Tavistock, 1968.

Rice, George H., Jr., and Dean W. Bishoprick. *Conceptual Models of Organization*. New York: Appleton-Century-Crofts, 1971.

Robbins, Stephen P. *Managing Organizational Conflict*. Englewood Cliffs, N.J.: Prentice-Hall, 1974.

Rokeach, Milton. *Beliefs, Attitudes and Values*. San Francisco: Jossey-Bass, 1968.

———. *The Nature of Human Values*. New York: Free Press, 1973.

Rose, Arnold M. *The Power Structure: Political Process in American Society*. New York: Oxford University Press, 1934.

Rowe, Alan J., and James D. Boulgarides. *Managerial Decision Making: A Guide to Successful Business Decisions*. New York: Macmillan, 1992.

Russo, J. Edward, and Paul J. H. Schoemaker. *Decision Traps: The Ten Barriers to Brilliant Decision Making and How to Overcome Them*. New York: Simon & Schuster, 1989.

Saaty, Thomas L. *Decision Making for Leaders*. Belmont, Calif.: Wadsworth, 1982.

Salinger, Pierre. *America Held Hostage*. New York: Doubleday, 1981.

———. *With Kennedy*. New York: Doubleday, 1966.

Sanford, Edward, and Harvey Addman. *Management Decisions: A Behavioral Approach*. Cambridge, Mass.: Winthrop, 1977.

Schein, Edgar H. *Organizational Psychology*. 2nd ed. Englewood Cliffs, N.J.: Prentice-Hall, 1970.

Schlesinger, Arthur M., Jr. *A Thousand Days*. Boston: Houghton Mifflin, 1965.

Schoen, M. *Human Nature*. New York: Harper & Row, 1930.

Schwartz, Howard S. *Narcissistic Process and Corporate Decay: The Theory of the Organizational Ideal*. New York: New York University Press, 1990.

Schwenk, Charles R. T *Essence of Strategic Decision Making*. Lexington, Mass.: D. C. Heath, 1988.

Selekman, Benjamin M., and Sylvia K. Selekman. *Power and Morality in a Business Society*. New York: McGraw-Hill, 1956.

Servan-Schreiber, J. J. *The American Challenge*. New York: Atheneum, 1968.

Shackle, G. L. S. *The Nature of Economic Thought*. London: Cambridge University Press, 1966.

Shapira, Zur, ed. *Organizational Decision Making*. New York: Cambridge University Press, 1997.

———. *Risk Taking: A Managerial Perspective*. New York: Sage, 1995.

Shelly, Maynard W., III, and Glenn L. Bryan, ed. *Human Judgments and Optimality*. New York: Wiley, 1964.

Shepherd, Clovis R. *Small Groups: Some Sociological Perspectives*. San Francisco: Chandler, 1964.

Shepherd, W. G. *The Economics of Industrial Organization*. Englewood Cliffs, N.J.: Prentice-Hall, 1969.

Sherif, M., et al. *Intergroup Conflict and Cooperation: The Robbers Cave Experiment*. Norman, Okla.: University Book Exchange, 1961.

Sherif, Muzafer, and Carl I. Hovland. *Social Judgment*. New Haven: Yale University Press, 1961.

Shugan, Steven M. *The Cost of Thinking: Its Implications*. Chicago: University of Chicago, Center for Decision Research, 1980.

Shull, Fremont A., Jr., André L. Delbecq, and L. L. Cummings. *Organizational Decision Making*. New York: McGraw-Hill, 1970.

Sick, Gary. *All Fall Down*. New York: Random House, 1985.

Sidgwick, Henry. *The Methods of Ethics*. 7th ed. Chicago: University of Chicago Press, 1962.

Simon, Herbert A. *Administrative Behavior*. 3rd ed. New York: Free Press, 1976.

———., ed. *Models of Bounded Rationality: Behavioral Economics and Business Organization*. Vol. 2. Cambridge, Mass.: MIT Press, 1982.

———. *Models of Man*. New York: Wiley, 1957.

———. *The New Science of Management Decision*. Rev. ed. Englewood Cliffs, N.J.: Prentice-Hall, 1977.

Sjoberg, Lennart, Tadeusz Tyszka, and James A. Wise, eds. *Human Decision Making*. Bodafors, Sweden: Bokforlaget Doxa, 1983.

Smith, M. Brewster. *Social Psychology and Human Values*. Chicago: Aldine, 1969.

Snyder, Glenn H., and Paul Diesing. *Conflict Among Nations*. Princeton, N.J.: Princeton University Press, 1977.

Steinbruner, John D. *The Cybernetic Theory of Decision*. Princeton, N.J.: Princeton University Press, 1974.

Steiner, Ivan D. *Group Processes and Productivity*. New York: Academic Press, 1972.

Stuart, Reginald. *Bailout*. South Bend, Ind.: Reginald Stuart, 1980.

Stufflebeam, Daniel, et al. *Educational Evaluation and Decision Making*. Itasca, Ill.: Peacock Publishers, 1971.

Sutherland, John W. *Administrative Decision-Making: Extending the Bounds of Rationality*. New York: Van Nostrand Reinhold, 1977.

Sutherland, Stuart. *Irrationality: Why We Don't Think Straight*. New Brunswick. N.J.: Rutgers University Press, 1992.

Swap, Walter C., and Associates, eds. *Group Decision Making*. Beverly Hills, Calif.: Sage, 1984.

Swingle, Paul G. *The Management of Power*. New York: Wiley, 1976.

Taylor, J. *Technology and Planned Organizational Change*. Ann Arbor, Mich.: University of Michigan Institute for Social Research, 1970.

Terry, George R., and Stephen G. Franklin. *Principles of Management*. 8th ed. Homewood, Ill.: Richard D. Irwin, 1982.

Thibaut, John W., and Harold H. Kelley. *The Social Psychology of Groups*. New York: Wiley, 1959.

Thompson, A. A., Jr., and A. J. Strickland, III. *Strategy Formulation and Implementation*. Rev. ed. Plano, Tex.: Business Publications, 1983.

Thompson, James D. *Organizations in Action*. New York: McGraw-Hill, 1967.

———., ed. *Comparative Studies in Administration*. Pittsburgh: University of Pittsburgh Press, 1956.

———., ed. *Approaches to Organizational Design*. Pittsburgh: University of Pittsburgh Press, 1966.

Thompson, Victor A. *Bureaucracy and the Modern World*. Morristown, N.J.: General Learning Press, 1976.

Towle, Joseph W., ed. *Ethics and Standards in American Business*. Boston: Houghton Mifflin, 1964.

Trento, J. J. *Prescription for Disaster*. New York: Crown Publishers, 1987.

Tuite, Matthew, Roger Chisholm, and Michael Radnor, eds. *Interorganizational Decision Making*. Chicago: Aldine, 1972.

Ungson, Gerardo R., and Daniel N. Braunstein, eds. *Decision Making: An Interdisciplinary Inquiry*. Boston: Kent, 1982.

Vaughn, D. *The Challenger Launch Decision*. Chicago: University of Chicago Press, 1996.

Vroom, Victor H., and Phillip W. Yetton. *Leadership and Decision Making*. Pittsburgh: University of Pittsburgh Press, 1973.

Walker, Charles R., ed. *Technology, Industry, and Man: The Age of Acceleration*. New York: McGraw-Hill, 1968.

Watson, Donald S. *Price Theory and Its Uses*. 2nd ed. Boston: Houghton Mifflin, 1968.

Weber, C. Edward, and Gerald Peters. *Management Action: Models of Administrative Decisions*. Scranton, Pa.: International Textbook, 1969.

Webster's New Dictionary of Synonyms. Springfield, Mass.: G&C Merriam, 1973.

Wendt, D., and C. Vlek, eds. *Utility, Probability and Human Values*. Dordrecht, Holland: D. Riedel, 1975.

Wheeler, Daniel D., and Irving L. Janis. *A Practical Guide for Making Decisions*. New York: Free Press, 1980.

Wieland, George F., and Robert A. Ulbrich. *Organizations: Behavior, Design, and Change*. Homewood, Ill.: Richard D. Irwin, 1973.

Wilensky, Harold L. *Organizational Intelligence*. New York: Basic Books, 1967.

Witte, E., and H. J. Zimmerman, eds. *Empirical Research on Organizational Decision Making*. New York: Elsevier Publishing Co., 1986.

Wortman, M. S., and F. Luthans, eds. *Emerging Concepts in Management*. 2nd ed. New York: Macmillan, 1975.

Wren, Daniel A. *The Evolution of Management Thought*. New York: Ronald Press, 1972.

Wright, George, ed. *Behavioral Decision Making*. New York: Plenum Press, 1985.

Young, Roland, ed. *Approaches to the Study of Politics*. Evanston, Ill.: Northwestern University Press, 1958.

Young, Stanley. *Management: A Decision-Making Approach*. Belmont, Calif.: Dickenson, 1968.

Zey, Mary, ed. *Decision Making: Alternatives to Rational Choice*. Newbury Park, Calif.: Sage Publications, 1992.

ARTICLES

"A Saudi Prince Comes to EuroDisney's Aid." *Corporate Growth Weekly Report* (June 13, 1994) 7291 and 7302.

Abbasi, Sami M., and Kenneth W. Hollman. "An Exploratory Study of the Personal Value Systems of City Managers." *Journal of Business Ethics*, 6 (1987), 45–53.

Abdel-Halim, Ahmed A. "Effects of Task and Personality Characteristics on Subordinate Responses to Participative Decision Making." *Academy of Management Journal* (September 1983), 477–484.

Achampong, Francis K., and Wold Zemedkun. "An Empirical and Ethical Analysis of Factors Motivating Managers' Merger Decisions." *Journal of Business Ethics*, 14 (1995), 855–865.

Aldag, Ramon J., and Donald W. Jackson, Jr. "A Managerial Framework for Social Decision Making." *MSU Business Topics*, 23 (Spring 1975), 33–40.

Alexander, Ernest R. "The Design of Alternatives in Organizational Contexts." *Administrative Science Quarterly*, 24 (September 1979), 382–404.

Alker, H. A., and N. Kogan. "Effects of Norm-Oriented Group Discussion on Individual Verbal Risk Taking and Conservatism." *Human Relations*, 21 (1968), 393–405.

Allen, Robert W., et al. "Organizational Politics: Tactics and Characteristics of Its Actors." *California Management Review* (Fall 1979), 77–83.

Allison, Graham T. "Conceptual Models and the Cuban Missile Crisis." *American Political Science Review* (September 1969), 689–718.

Allport, G. W., and H. S. Odbert. "Trait Names: A Psychological Study." *Psychological Monographs*, 47, No. 211 (1936).

Allyn, Bruce J., James G. Blight, and David A. Welch. "Essence of Revision: Moscow, Havana, and the Cuban Missile Crisis." *International Security*, 14 (Winter 1989/1990), 136–172.

Alutto, J. A., and J. A. Belasco. "Typology for Participation in Organizational Decision Making." *Administrative Science Quarterly* (March 1972), 117–125.

Amason, Allen C. "Distinguishing the Effects of Functional and Dysfunctional Conflict on Strategic Decision Making: Resolving a Paradox for Top Management Teams." *Academy of Management Journal*, 39, No. 1 (1996), 123–148.

Anderson, Paul A. "Decision Making by Objection and the Cuban Missile Crisis." *Administrative Science Quarterly* (June 1983), 201–222.

Ansoff, H. Igor. "General Management in Turbulent Environments." *Practicing Manager*, 11 (Summer 1990), 6–27.

Argyris, Chris. "Interpersonal Barriers to Decision Making." *Harvard Business Review* (March–April 1966), 84–97.

———. "Management Information Systems: The Challenge to Rationality and Emotionality." *Management Science* (February 1971), B-275–B-292.

———. "Organization Man: Rational or Self-Actualizing." *Public Administration Review* (July–August 1973), 354–357.

———. "Some Limits of Rational Man Organization Theory." *Public Administration Review* (May–June 1973), 253–267.

Armour, H. O., and D. J. Teece. "Organization Structure and Economic Performance: A Test of Multi-Dimensional Hypothesis." *Bell Journal of Economics*, 9 (1978), 106–122.

Armstrong, J. Scott. "The Value of Formal Planning for Strategic Decisions: Review of Empirical Research." *Strategic Management Journal*, 3 (1982), 197–211.

Arroba, Tanya Y. "Decision-Making Style as a Function of Occupational Group, Decision Content, and Perceived Importance." *Journal of Occupational Psychology* (September 1978), 219–226.

Arrow, Kenneth J. "Rationality of Self and Others in an Economic System." *Journal of Business*, 59 (1986), S385–S399.

Asch, S. E. "Studies of Independence and Conformity: A Minority of One Against a Unanimous Majority." *Psychological Monographs*, 70 (1956).

Ashmos, Donde P., and Reuben R. McDaniel, Jr. "Understanding the Participation of Critical Task Specialists in Strategic Decision Making." *Decision Sciences*, 27, No 1 (Winter 1996), 103–121.

Ashton, Robert H. "Cue Utilization and Expert Judgments: A Comparison of Independent Auditors with Other Judges." *Journal of Applied Psychology*, 59 (August 1974), 437–444.

Astley, W. Graham, et al. "Complexity and Cleavage: Dual Explanations of Strategic Decision-Making." *Journal of Management Studies* (October 1982), 357–375.

Atkinson, J. W. "Motivational Determinants of Risk-Taking Behavior." *Psychological Review*, 64 (1957), 359–372.

Auletta, Ken. "Awesome." *New Yorker* (August 14, 1995), 29–32.

Babcock, Richard F. "Mickey a la Mode." *Planning* (April 1991), 18–21.

Bachrach, Peter, and Morton S. Baratz. "Decisions and Nondecisions." *American Political Science Review* (December 1967), 385–392.

———. "Decisions and Nondecisions: An Analytical Overview." *American Political Science Review* (May 1963), 632–642.

Bacharach, Samuel B., et al. "Strategic and Tactical Logics of Decision Justification: Power and Decision Criteria in Organizations." *Human Relations*, 48, No. 5 (1995), 447–488.

Back, Kurt W. "Decisions Under Uncertainty: Rational, Irrational, and Non-Rational." *American Behavioral Scientist*, 4 (February 1961), 14–19.

Bailey, Duncan, and Stanley E. Boyle. "Sales Revenue Maximization: An Empirical Vindication." *Industrial Organization Review*, 5, No. 1 (1977), 46–55.

Baird, Inga, and Howard Thomas. "Toward a Contingency Model of Strategic Decision Making." *Academy of Management Review*, 10 (1986), 230–243.

Bank, John, and Bernhard Wilpert. "What's So Special About Quality Circles?" *Journal of General Management*, 9 (1983), 21–37.

Banks, H. "It's Time to Bust Up NASA." *Forbes* (February 8, 1988), 101–108.

Barnett, John H., and Marvin J. Karson. "Managers, Values, and Executive Decisions: An Exploration of the Role of Gender, Career Stage, Organizational Level, Function, and the Importance of Ethics, Relationships and Results in Managerial Decision-Making." *Journal of Business Ethics*, 8 (1989), 747–771.

———. "Personal Values and Business Decisions: An Exploratory Investigation." *Journal of Business Ethics*, 6 (1987), 371–382.

Baron, Robert S., et al. "Group Consensus and Cultural Values as Determinants of Risk Taking." *Journal of Personality and Social Psychology*, 20 (1971), 446–455.

Baron, Robert S., Thomas C. Monson, and Penny H. Barron. "Conformity Pressure as a Determinant of Risk Taking: Replication and Extension." *Journal of Personality and Social Psychology*, 28 (1973), 406–413.

Baumol, William J., and Richard E. Quandt. "Rules of Thumb and Optimally Imperfect Decisions." *American Economic Review*, 54 (March 1964), 23–46.

Bavelas, A. "A Mathematical Model for Group Structures." *Applied Anthropology*, 7 (1948), 16–30.

Beach, Lee Roy, and Terence R. Mitchell. "A Contingency Model for the Selection of Decision Strategies." *Academy of Management Review* (July 1978), 439–449.

Becker, Gordon M., and Charles G. McClintock. "Value: Behavioral Decision Theory." In *Annual Review of Psychology*. Ed. Paul R. Farnsworth. Palo Alto, Calif.: Annual Reviews, 1967.

Beeman, Don R., and Thomas W. Sharkey. "The Use and Abuse of Corporate Politics." *Business Horizons* (March/April 1987), 54–57.

Bell, Paul R., and Bruce D. Jamieson. "Publicity of Initial Decisions and the Risky Shift Phenomenon." *Journal of Experimental Social Psychology*, 6 (July 1970), 329–345.

Bell, T. E., and K. Esch. "The Fatal Flaw in Flight S1-L." *IEEE Spectrum* (February 1987), 36–81.

Belovicz, Meyer W., Frederick E. Finch, and Halsey Jones. "Do Groups Make Riskier Decisions Than Individuals?" *Papers and Proceedings of the 28th Annual Meeting of the Academy of Management*, Chicago, December 26–28, 1968.

Belsky, Gary, et al. "Mirror, Mirror on the Wall, Who's Fairer Than Disney?" *Money* (September 1995), 66–68.

Bem, Sandra L. "The Measurement of Psychological Androgyny." *Journal of Consulting and Clinical Psychology*, 42 (April 1974), 155–162.

Bennett, Edith. "Discussion, Decision, Commitment, and Consensus in 'Group Decision.'" *Human Relations*, 8 (1955), 3–10.

Berg, Claus C. "Individual Decisions Concerning the Allocation of Resources for Projects with Uncertain Consequences." *Management Science*, 21 (September 1974), 98–105.

Bergen, John R. "The Structure of Perception." *Journal of the Association for the Study of Perception* (Spring 1969), 1–19.

Bernstein, Barton J. "The Cuban Missile Crisis: Trading the Jupiters in Turkey?" *Political Science Quarterly*, 95 (1980), 97–125.

Bernthal, Wilmar F. "Value Perspectives in Management Decisions." *Academy of Management Journal* (December 1962), 190–196.

Biddle, W. "What Destroyed Challenger?" *Discover* (April 1986), 40–47.

Bird, Frederick, and James A. Waters. "The Nature of Managerial Moral Standards." *Journal of Business Ethics*, 6 (January 1987), 1–13.

Bivins, Thomas H. "A Systems Model for Ethical Decision Making in Public Relations." *Public Relations Review*, 18, No. 4 (1992), 365–383.

Blascovich, Jim. "Sequence Effects on Choice Shifts Involving Risk." *Journal of Experimental Social Psychology*, 8 (May 1972), 260–265.

Blau, Peter M. "A Theory of Social Integration." *American Journal of Sociology*, 65 (1960), 545–556.

Bluedorn, Allen C., and Robert B. Denhardt. "Time and Organizations." *Journal of Management*, 14 (1988), 299–320.

Bohr, Peter. "Chrysler's Pie-in-the-Sky Plan for Survival." *Fortune* (October 22, 1979), 46ff.

Borgida, Eugene, and Richard E. Nisbett. "The Differential Impact of Abstract vs. Concrete Information on Decisions." *Journal of Applied Social Psychology*, 7 (1977), 258–271.

Boulding, Kenneth E. "The Ethics of Rational Decision." *Management Science*, 12 (February 1966), B-161–B-189.

Bourgeois, L. J. "Performance and Consensus." *Strategic Management Journal*, 1 (1980), 227–248.

Bower, Joseph L. "Group Decision Making: A Report of an Experimental Study." *Behavioral Science* (July 1965), 277–289.

———. "The Role of Conflict in Economic Decision-Making Groups: Some Empirical Results." *Quarterly Journal of Economics* (May 1965), 263–277.

Bowman, E. H. "Consistency and Optimality in Managerial Decision Making." *Management Science* (January 1963), 310–321.

Bowman, James S. "Managerial Ethics in Business and Government." *Business Horizons*, 19 (October 1976), 48–54.

Boxx, W. Randy, Randall Y. Odom, and Mark G. Dunn, "Organizational Values and Value Congruency and Their Impact on Satisfaction, Commitment, and Cohesion: An Empirical Examination Within the Public Sector." *Public Personnel Management*, 20 (Spring 1991), 195–205.

Brady, F. Neil. "Aesthetic Components of Management Ethics." *Academy of Management Review*, 11 (1986), 337–344.

Brady, M. "NASA's Challenge: Ending Isolation at the Top." *Fortune* (May 12, 1986), 26ff.

Brehm, Jack W., and Elena Rozen. "Attractiveness of Old Alternatives When a New Attractive Alternative Is Introduced." *Journal of Personality and Social Psychology*, 20 (1971), 261–266.

Brehmer, Berndt, and Goran Quarnstrom. "Information Integration and Subjective Weights in Multiple-Cue Judgments." *Organizational Behavior and Human Performance*, 17 (October 1976), 118–126.

Brengelmann, J. C. "Abnormal and Personality Correlates of Certainty." *Journal of Mental Sciences*, 105 (1959), 142–162.

Brenner, Otto C., and W. Edgar Vinacke. "Accommodative and Exploitative Behavior of Males Versus Females and Managers Versus Nonmanagers as Measured by the Test of Strategy." *Social Psychology Quarterly*, 42, No. 3 (1979), 289–293.

Brightman, Harvey J. "Differences in Ill-Structured Problem Solving Along the Organizational Hierarchy." *Decision Sciences*, 9 (January 1978), 1–18.

Broadbent, D. E. "Aspects of Human Decision Making." *Advancement of Science*, 24 (September 1967), 53–64.

Brockhoff, Klaus. "Decision Quality and Information." In *Empirical Research on Organizational Decision-Making*. Ed. E. Witte and H.-J.-Zimmerman. New York: Elsevier Science Inc., 1986, 249–265.

Bronner, Rolf. "Perception of Complexity in Decision-Making Processes: Findings of Experimental Investigations. In *Empirical Research on Organizational Decision-Making*. Ed. E. Witte and H.-J.-Zimmerman. New York: Elsevier Science, Inc., 1986, 45–64.

Brown, Harold I. "On Being Rational." *American Philosophical Quarterly* (October 1978), 241–248.

Brown, Julius S. "Risk Propensity in Decision Making: A Comparison of Business and Public School Administrators." *Administrative Science Quarterly*, 15 (December 1970), 473–481.

Brown, Martha A. "Values — A Necessary but Neglected Ingredient of Motivation on the Job." *Academy of Management Review*, 1 (October 1976), 15–23.

Brown, Stephen M. "Male Versus Female Leaders: A Comparison of Empirical Studies." *Sex Roles*, 5 (1979), 595–611.

Brunsson, Nils. "Deciding for Responsibility and Legitimation: Alternate Interpretations of Organizational Decision Making." *Accounting, Organizations and Society*, 15 (1990), 47–59.

———. "The Irrationality of Action and Action Rationality: Decision, Ideologies and Organizational Actions." *Journal of Management Studies* (January 1982), 29–44.

Burnstein, Eugene. "An Analysis of Group Decisions Involving Risk ('The Risky Shift')." *Human Relations*, 22, No. 5 (1969), 381–395.

Burnstein, Eugene, and Stuart Katz. "Individual Commitment to Risky and Conservative Choices as a Determinant of Shifts in Group Decisions." *Journal of Personality* (December 1971), 564–580.

Burnstein, Eugene, and Harold Miller. "Risky Shift Is Eminently Rational." *Journal of Personality and Social Psychology*, 20, No. 3 (1971), 462–471.

Burnstein, Eugene, and Amiram Vinokur. "Testing Two Classes of Theories About Group Induced Shifts in Individual Choice." *Journal of Experimental Social Psychology*, 9 (March 1973), 123–137.

Burnstein, Eugene, Amiram Vinokur, and Yaacov Trope. "Interpersonal Comparison Versus Persuasive Argumentation: A More Direct Test of Alternative Explanations for Group-Induced Shifts in Individual Choice." *Journal of Experimental Social Psychology*, 9 (May 1973), 236–245.

Burt, Richard. "Report Charges 'Major' Mistakes on Iran Mission." *New York Times* (June 6, 1986), 188.

Burton, Gene E. "The Group Process: Key to More Productive Management." *Management World* (May 1981), 12–15.

Burton, Gene E., Dev S. Pathak, and Ron M. Zigli. "Using Group Size to Improve the Decision-Making Ability of Nominal Groups." In *Academy of Management Proceedings*, 37th Annual Meeting. Ed. Robert L. Taylor et al. Orlando, Fla., August 14–17, 1977.

Byrne, John A., et al. "The Best and Worst Boards." *Business Week* (December 8, 1997), 90–104.

Camerer, Colin. "Illusory Correlations in Perceptions and Predictions of Organizational Traits." *Journal of Behavioral Decision Making*, 1 (1988), 77–94.

Campbell, John P. "Individual Versus Group Problem Solving in an Industrial Sample." *Journal of Applied Psychology*, 52, No. 3 (1968), 205–210.

Canella, Albert A., Jr. "Executives and Shareholders: A Shift in the Relationship." *Human Resource Management*, 34, No. 3 (Spring 1995), 165–184.

Carlson, Robert E. "Selection Interview Decisions." *Journal of Applied Psychology*, 51 (December 1967), 461–480.

Carr, Josephine, et al. "The Deals of 1989." *International Financial Law Review* (January 1990), 9–11.

Carroll, Archie B. "Managerial Ethics: A Post-Watergate View." *Business Horizons*, 18 (April 1975), 75–80.

Carson, J. "Taking Decisions by the Book." *International Management* (September 1972), 50ff.

Carter, E. Eugene. "The Behavioral Theory of the Firm and Top-Level Corporate Decisions." *Administrative Science Quarterly*, 16 (December 1971), 413–428.

Cartwright, Dorwin. "Risk Taking by Individuals and Groups: An Assessment of Research Employing Choice Dilemmas." *Journal of Personality and Social Psychology*, 20 (December 1971), 361–378.

Castellan, N. John, Jr. "Multiple-Cue Probability Learning with Irrelevant Cues." *Organizational Behavior and Human Performance*, 9 (February 1973), 16–29.

Cavanagh, Gerald F., Dennis J. Moberg, and Manuel Velasquez. "The Ethics of Organizational Politics." *Academy of Management Review* (July 1981), 363–374.

Cecil, Earl A., Larry L. Cummings, and Jerome M. Chertkoff. "Group Composition and Choice Shift: Implications for Administration." *Academy of Management Journal*, 16 (September 1973), 412–422.

Cecil, Earl A., and Earl F. Lundgren. "A Laboratory Study of Individual Search Patterns in a Decision-Making Situation." *Decision Sciences*, 9 (July 1978), 429–433.

Chia, Robert. "The Concept of Decision: A Deconstructive Analysis." *Journal of Management Studies*, 31, No. 6 (November 1994), 781–806.

Chiattello, Marion L., and Robert J. Waller. "Relativism as a Cultural Influence on Twentieth Century Decision Making." *Decision Sciences*, 5 (April 1974), 209–224.

Child, John. "Organizational Structure, Environment, and Performance: The Role of Choice." *Sociology*, 6 (January 1972), 1–22.

Chorn, Norman H. "The 'Alignment' Theory: Creating Strategic Fit." *Management Decision*, 29 (1991), 20–24.

Chrysler Corporation Report to Shareholders, 1992. Highland Park, Minn.: Chrysler Corporation, 1992.

Church, George J. "How Reagan Decides." *Time* (December 13, 1982), 12ff.

Churchman, C. West. "On Rational Decision Making." *Management Technology*, 2 (December 1962), 71–76.

Cifuentes, Carlos L. "Fundamentals of the Managerial Decision-Making Process." *International Studies of Management and Organization* (Summer 1972), 213–221.

Clark, Russell D., III. "Group-Induced Shift Toward Risk." *Psychological Bulletin*, 76, No. 4 (1971), 251–270.

Clark, Russell D., III, Walter H. Crockett, and Richard L. Archer. "Risk-as-Value Hypothesis: The Relationship Between Perception of Self, Others, and Risky Shift." *Journal of Personality and Social Psychology*, 20 (1971), 425–429.

Clark, Russell D., III, and E. P. Willems. "Risk Preference as Related to Judged Consequences of Failure." *Psychological Reports*, 25 (1969), 827–830.

———. "Where Is the Risky Shift?" *Journal of Personality and Social Psychology*, 13 (November 1969), 215–221.

Clark, Thomas D., Jr., and William A. Schrode. "Public-Sector Decision Structures: An Empirically-Based Description." *Public Administration Review* (July/August 1979), 343–354.

Clarkson, Geoffrey P. E., and Francis D. Tuggle. "Toward a Theory of Group Decision Behavior." *Behavioral Science* (January 1966), 33–42.

Cohen, Arthur M. "Changing Small-Group Communication Networks." *Administrative Science Quarterly* (March 1962), 443–462.

Cohen, L. Jonathan. "Can Human Irrationality Be Experimentally Demonstrated?" *The Behavioral and Brain Sciences*, 4 (September 1981), 317–370.

Cohen, Michael D., James G. March, and Johan P. Olsen. "A Garbage-Can Model of Organizational Choice." *Administrative Science Quarterly*, 17 (March 1972), 1–25.

Conant, Michael. "Systems Analysis in the Appellate Decision-Making Process." *Rutgers Law Review*, 24 (1970), 293–322.

Conner, Patrick E., et al. "A Cross-National Comparative Study of Managerial Values: United States, Canada, and Japan." *Advances in International Comparative Management*, 8 (1993), 3–29.

Conrath, David W. "Organizational Decision Making Behavior Under Varying Conditions of Uncertainty." *Management Science* (April 1967), B-489–B-500.

Cook, R. C. "The Rogers Commission Failed." *The Washington Monthly*, 18 (November 1986), 13–21.

Corner, Patricia Doyle, et al. "Integrating Organizational and Individual Information Processing Perspectives on Choice." *Organization Science*, 5, No. 3 (August 1994), 294–308.

Corwin, Ronald G. "Patterns of Organizational Conflict." *Administrative Science Quarterly* (December 1969), 507–520.

Cosier R. A. "Dialectical Inquiry in Strategic Planning: A Case of Premature Acceptance?" *Academy of Management Review*, 6 (1981), 643–648.

Cosier, Richard A., and Charles R. Schwenk. "Agreement and Thinking Alike: Ingredients for Poor Decisions." *The Executive* (February 1990), 69–74.

Crane, Robert D. "The Cuban Missile Crisis: A Strategic Analysis of American and Soviet Policy." *Orbis* (Winter 1963), 528–563.

Cravens, David W. "An Exploratory Analysis of Individual Information Processing." *Management Science* (June 1970), B-656–B-669.

Cray, David, et al. "Explaining Decision Processes." *Journal of Management Studies* (May 1991), 227–253.

Crozier, Ray. "Postdecisional Justification: The Case of DeLorean." In *Process and Structure in Human Decision Making*. Ed. H. Montgomery and O. Svenson. New York: Wiley, 1989.

Crumley, Bruce, and Christy Fisher. "EuroDisney Tries to End Evil Spell." *Advertising Age* (February 7, 1994), 39.

Crutchfield, Richard S. "Conformity and Character." *American Psychologist*, 10 (1955), 191–198.

Cummings, Larry L., George P. Huber, and Eugene Arendt. "Effects of Size and Spatial Arrangements on Group Decision Making." *Academy of Management Journal*, 17 (September 1974), 460–475.

Curwen, Peter. "EuroDisney: The Mouse That Roared (Not!)." *European Business Review*, 95, No. 5 (1995), 15–20.

Cyert, R. M., W. R. Dill, and J. G. March. "The Role of Expectations in Business Decision Making." *Administrative Science Quarterly* (December 1958), 307–340.

Daft, Richard L., and Robert H. Lengel. "Organizational Information Requirements, Media Richness, and Structural Design." *Management Science*, 32, No. 5 (May 1986), 554–571.

Daniel, D. Ronald. "Management Information Crisis." *Harvard Business Review* (September–October 1961), 111–121.

Datta, Deepak K., and James P. Guthrie. "Executive Succession: Organizational Antecedents of CEO Characteristics." *Strategic Management Journal*, 15 (1994), 569–577.

Davis, Keith. "The Case For and Against Business Assumption of Social Responsibility." *Academy of Management Journal*, 16 (1973), 312–322.

Deaux, Kay. "From Individual Differences to Social Categories: Analysis of a Decade's Research on Gender." *American Psychologist* (February 1984), 105–116.

———. "Self-Evaluations of Male and Female Managers." *Sex Roles*, 5 (1979), 571–580.

"Debacle in the Desert." *Time* (May 5, 1980), 12ff.

Deepak K. Sinka. "The Contribution of Formal Planning to Decisions." *Strategic Management Journal*, 11 (1990), 479–492.

"Defense Dept. Issues Detailed Analysis." *Aviation Week & Space Technology* (May 19, 1980), 91–94.

Delbecq, André L. "The Management of Decision-Making Within the Firm: Three Strategies for Three Types of Decision Making." *Academy of Management Journal* (December 1967), 329–339.

Derkinderen, Frans G. J., and Roy L. Crum. "The Development and Empirical Validation of Strategic Decision Models." *International Studies of Management & Organization*, 18 (1988), 29–59.

DeSalvia, Donald N., and Gary R. Gemmill. "An Exploratory Study of the Personal Value Systems of College Students and Managers." *Academy of Management Journal*, 14 (June 1971), 227–238.

Devinney, Timothy M. "Rationally Determined Irrationality: An Extension of the Thesis of Rationality as Anti-Entropic." *Journal of Economic Psychology*, 10 (1989), 303–319.

Dimick, D. E., and V. V. Murray. "Personnel Policy as a Form of Strategic Decision Making." *International Studies of Management & Organization* (Winter 1979–1980), 78–97.

Dion, Kenneth L., and Norman Miller. "An Analysis of the Familiarization Explanation of the Risky-Shift." *Journal of Experimental Social Psychology*, 7 (September 1971), 524–533.

Dion, Kenneth L., Norman Miller, and Mary Ann Magnon. "Cohesiveness and Responsibility as Determinants of Group Risk Taking." *Journal of Personality and Social Psychology*, 20 (1971), 400–406.

"Disney to Acquire Capital Cities / ABC." *Corporate Growth Weekly Report* (August 7, 1995), 7975–7976.

"Disney's Global Goals." *International Marketing* (May 17, 1990), 22–26.

"Disney's World." *Newsweek* (August 14, 1995), 21.

Doktor, Robert H., and William F. Hamilton. "Cognitive Style and the Acceptance of Management Science Recommendations." *Management Science* (April 1973), 884–894.

Dressel, Paul L. "Values Cognitive and Affective." *Journal of Higher Education*, 15, No. 42 (1971), 400–405.

Driscoll, James W. "Trust and Participation in Organizational Decision Making as Predictors of Satisfaction." *Academy of Management Journal* (March 1978), 44–56.

Dror, Yehezkel. "Muddling Through — Science or Inertia?" *Public Administration Review* (September 1964), 153–158.

Drory, Amos, and Tsilia Romm. "Politics in Organization and Its Perception Within the Organization." *Organization Studies*, 9 (1988), 165–179.

Drucker, Peter F. "The Effective Decision." *Harvard Business Review*, 45 (January–February 1967), 92–98.

Dudycha, Linda W., and James C. Naylor. "Characteristics of the Human Inference Process in Complex Choice Behavior Situations." *Organizational Behavior and Human Performance*, 1 (1956), 110–128.

Duncan, Robert B. "Characteristics of Organizational Environments and Perceived Organizational Uncertainty." *Administrative Science Quarterly*, 17 (September 1972), 313–327.

Dunn, John A., Jr. "Organizational Decision Making." In *Group Decision Making*. Eds. Walter C. Swap and Associates. Beverly Hills, Calif.: Sage Publications, 1984, 280–310.

"Easy as ABC." *CFO* (October 1995), 34–38.

Ebbesen, Ebbe B., and Richard J. Bowers. "Proportion of Risky to Conservative Arguments in a Group Discussion and Choice Shift." *Journal of Personality and Social Psychology*, 29 (1974), 316–327.

Ebert, R. J. "Environmental Structure and Programmed Decision Effectiveness." *Management Science* (December 1972), 435–445.

Eccles, A. J., and D. Wood. "How Do Managers Decide?" *Journal of Management Studies*, 9 (October 1972), 291–302.

Edland, Anne, and Ola Svenson. "Judgment and Decision Making Under Time Pressure." In *Time Pressure and Stress in Human Judgment and Decision Making*. Eds. A. John Maule and Ola Svenson. New York: Plenum, 1993, 27–40.

Edwards, Ward. "The Theory of Decision Making." *Psychological Bulletin,* 54, No. 4 (1954), 380–417.

Eilon, Samuel. "Goals and Constraints." *Journal of Management Studies,* 8 (October 1971), 292–303.

———. "What Is a Decision?" *Management Science* (December 1969), B-172–B-189.

Einhorn, Hillel J. "Cue Definition and Residual Judgment." *Organizational Behavior and Human Performance,* 12 (August 1974), 30–49.

Eisenhardt, Kathleen M. "Making Fast Strategic Decisions in High-Velocity Environments." *Academy of Management Journal,* 32 (1989), 543–576.

Elbing, Alvar O., Jr. "The Value Issue of Business: The Responsibility of the Businessman." *Academy of Management Journal,* 13 (March 1970), 79–89.

Elster, John. "Ulysses and the Sirens: A Theory of Imperfect Rationality." *Social Sciences Information,* 16, No. 5 (1977), 469–526.

Emery, F. E., and E. L. Trist. "The Casual Texture of Organizational Environments." In *Readings in Organization Theory: Open System Approaches.* Ed. John Maurer. New York: Random House, 1971.

England, George W. "Personal Value Systems of American Managers." *Academy of Management Journal* (March 1967), 53–68.

———. "Personal Value Systems of Managers and Administrators." *Academy of Management Proceedings* (August 1973), 81–88.

Ericson, Richard F. "The Impact of Cybernetic Information Technology on Management Value Systems." *Management Science* (October 1969), B-40–B-60.

———. "Rationality and Executive Motivation." *Journal of the Academy of Management* (April 1962), 7–23.

Esser, James K., and Joanne S. Lindoerfer. "Groupthink and the Space Shuttle Challenger Accident: Toward a Quantitative Case Analysis." *Journal of Behavioral Decision Making,* 2 (1989), 167–177.

Estrin, Teviah L. "The Roles of Information Providers in Decision Making." *Journal of General Management* (Spring 1990), 80–95.

Etzioni, Amitai. "Humble Decision Making." *Harvard Business Review* (July–August 1989), 122–126.

———. "How Rational We?" *Sociological Forum,* 2 (1987), 1–20.

———. "Guidance Rules and Rational Decision Making." *Social Science Quarterly* (December 1985), 755–769.

———. "Mixed-Scanning: A 'Third' Approach to Decision Making." *Public Administration Review* (December 1967), 385–392.

———. "Rationality is Anti-Entropic." *Journal of Economic Psychology,* 7 (1986), 17–36.

———. "Normative-Affective Factors: Toward a New Decision-Making Model." *Journal of Economic Psychology,* 9 (1988), 125–150.

Eurodisney S. C. A. *1995 Annual Report.* Paris: 1995.

Eurodisney S. C. A. *1996 Annual Report.* Paris: 1996.

"Eurodisney's Prince Charming?" *Business Week* (June 13, 1994), 42.

Evan, William M. "The Organization-Set: Toward a Theory of Interorganizational Relations." In *Approaches to Organizational Design.* Ed. James D. Thompson. Pittsburgh: University of Pittsburgh Press, 1966, 175–191.

Fagley, N. S., and Paul M. Miller. "The Effects of Decision Framing on Choice of Risky vs. Certain Options." *Organizational Behavior and Human Decision Processes,* 39 (1987), 264–277.

Faltermayer, Edmund. "Poised for a Comeback." *Fortune* (April 19, 1993), 174ff.

Farris, George F. "The Informal Organization in Strategic Decision-Making." *International Studies of Management & Organization* (Winter 1979–1980), 37–62.

Faust, W. L. "Group versus Individual Problem-Solving." *Journal of Abnormal and Social Psychology,* 59 (1959), 68–72.

Feldman, Steven P. "Secrecy, Information, and Politics: An Essay on Organizational Decision Making." *Human Relations,* 41 (1988), 73–90.

Feldman, Jack, and Michael K. Lindell. "On Rationality." In *Organization and Decision Theory.* Ed. Ira Horowitz. Norwell, Mass.: Kluwer Academic Publishers, 1990, 83–164.

Ferber, Robert C. "The Dark Side of Decision Making." *Management Review* (March 1971), 4–13.

———. "The Role of the Subconscious in Executive Decision Making." *Management Science* (April 1967), B-519–B-532.

Ference, Thomas P. "Organizational Communication Systems and the Decision Process." *Management Science,* 17 (October 1970), B-83–B-95.

Ferris, Gerald R., and K. Michele Kacmar. "Perceptions of Organizational Politics." *Journal of Management,* 18, No. 1 (1992), 93–116.

Ferris, Gerald R., et al. "Perceptions of Organizational Politics: Prediction, Stress-Related Implications, and Outcomes." *Human Relations*, 49, No. 2 (1996), 233–266.

Fillenbaum, Samuel. "Some Stylistic Aspects of Categorizing Behavior." *Journal of Personality*, 27 (1959), 187–195.

Fischhoff, Baruch. "Predicting Frames." *Journal of Experimental Psychology: Learning, Memory, and Cognition*, 9 (1983), 103–116.

———. "Hindsight Foresight: The Effect of Outcome Knowledge on Judgment Under Uncertainty." *Journal of Experimental Psychology*, 1 (August 1975), 288–299.

Fishburn, Peter C. "A Comparative Analysis of Group Decision Methods." *Behavioral Science*, 16 (November 1971), 538–544.

Fisher, B. Aubrey. "Decision Emergence: Phases in Group Decision Making." *Speech Monographs*, 38 (March 1970), 53–66.

Fisher N., and G. R. Hall. "Risk and Corporate Rates of Return." *Quarterly Journal of Economics*, 83 (1969), 79–92.

Flint, Jerry. "Company of the Year: Chrysler." *Forbes* (January 13, 1997), 83–86.

Floyd, Steven W., and Bill Wooldridge. "Managing Strategic Consensus: The Foundation of Effective Implementation." *Executive*, 6, No. 4 (November 1992), 27–39.

Ford, Robert C., and Frank S. McLaughlin. "Effects of Group Composition on Search Activity." *Journal of Business Research*, 4 (February 1976), 15–24.

Forgas, Joseph P. "Responsibility Attribution by Group and Individuals: The Effects of the Interaction Episode." *European Journal of Social Psychology*, 11 (1981), 87–99.

Fox, David J., and Irving Lorge. "The Relative Quality of Decisions Written by Individuals and by Groups as the Available Time for Problem Solving Is Increased." *Journal of Social Psychology*, 57 (June 1962), 227–242.

Frank, Robert H. "Shrewdly Rational." *Sociological Forum*, 2 (Winter 1987), 21–41.

Fredrikson, E. Bruce. "Noneconomic Criteria and the Decision Process." *Decision Sciences*, 2 (January 1971), 25–52.

Freeman, R. Edward. "Strategic Management: A Stakeholder Approach." In *Advances in Strategic Management*. Vol. 1. Ed. Robert Lamb. Greenwich, Conn.: JAI Press, 1983, 31–60.

Frei, Manfred-Dieter. "Administrative and Socio-Psychological Constraints of the Business Decision-Making Process." *Management International Review*, 11, Nos. 2–3 (1971), 67–81, 84–86.

Friedman, Milton, and L. J. Savage. "The Utility Analysis of Choices Involving Risk." *Journal of Political Economy* (August 1948), 279–304.

Friedman, Yorom, and Eli Segev. "The Decision to Decide." *Journal of Management Studies*, 14 (May 1977), 159–168.

Fritzsche, David J. "A Model of Decision-Making Incorporating Ethical Values." *Journal of Business Ethics*, 10, (1991), 841–852.

Fullerton, Howard N., Jr. "The 2005 Labor Force Growing But Slowly." *Monthly Labor Review* (November 1995), 29–44.

Gabriel, Major R. A. "A Commando Operation That Was Wrong from the Start: The U.S. Rescue Mission Into Iran, April 1980." *Canadian Defense Quarterly*, 10 (1980–1981), 6–10.

Gaeth, Gary J., and James Shanteau. "Reducing the Influence of Irrelevant Information on Experienced Decision Makers." *Organizational Behavior and Human Performance*, 33 (1984), 263–282.

Gandz, Jeffrey, and Nadine Hayes. "Teaching Business Ethics." *Journal of Business Ethics*, 7, (1988), 657–669.

Garfinkel, Harold. "The Rational Properties of Scientific and Common Sense Activities." In *Management: A Decision-Making Approach*. Ed. Stanley Young. Belmont, Calif.: Dickenson, 1968.

Gehani, R. Ray. "Time-Based Management of Technology." *International Journal of Operations & Production Management*, 15, No. 2 (1995), 19–35.

Geller, Scott, Charles P. Whitman, and William S. Beamon. "Effects of Expressed and Measured Value Preference on Decision Speed." *Psychonomic Science* (July 1971), 84–86.

Gemunden, Hans G., and Jurgen Hauschildt. "Number of Alternatives and Efficiency in Different Types of Top-Management Decisions." *European Journal of Operational Research*, 22 (1985), 178–190.

General Motors Annual Report, 1992. Detroit, Mich.: General Motors Corporation, 1992.

General Motors *1996 Annual Report.* Detroit, Mich.: General Motors Corporation, 1996.

"Getting Mickey Organized." *Business Month* (December 1987), 29.

Gibbons, Patrick F., and Lai Hong Chung. "Uncertainty: The Implications for Strategic Management." *Irish Business and Administrative Research*, 16 (1995), 17–31.

Glazer, Rashi, et al. "Locally Rational Decision Making: The Distracting Effect of Information on Managerial Performance." *Management Science*, 38, No. 2 (February 1992), 212–226.

Glueck, William F. "Decision Making: Organization Choice." *Personnel Psychology*, 27 (Spring 1974), 77–93.

Goldberg, Lewis R. "Man Versus Model of Man: A Rationale, plus Some Evidence for a Method of Improving on Clinical Inferences." *Psychological Bulletin*, 73, No. 6 (1970), 422–432.

Goldman, Ethel K. "Need Achievement as a Motivational Basis for the Risky Shift." *Journal of Personality*, 43 (June 1975), 346–355.

Goldman, Ralph M. "A Theory of Conflict Processes and Organizational Offices." *Journal of Conflict Resolution* (September 1966), 328–343.

Golightly, Henry O. "Needed: Decision Makers for Today's Business Environment." *Advanced Management Journal* (April 1974), 4–9.

Goodman, Paul S., Elizabeth Ravlin, and Marshall Schminke. "Understanding Behavior in Groups." In *Research in Organizational Behavior*. Vol. 9. Ed. Ricky W. Griffin. Greenwich, Conn.: JAI Press, 1987, 121–173.

Gore, William J. "Decision-Making Research: Some Prospects and Limitations." In *Concepts and Issues in Administrative Behavior*. Eds. Sidney Mailick and Edward H. Van Ness. Englewood Cliffs, N.J.: Prentice-Hall, 1962, 49–65.

Gormly, John, and Walter Edelberg. "Validity in Personality Trait Attribution." *American Psychologist*, 29 (March 1974), 189–193.

Gottesman, Alan. "The Analyst's Couch." *Mediaweek* (August 7, 1995), 24–25.

Gradstein, Mark, and Shmuel Nitzan. "Participation, Decision Aggregation and Internal Information Gathering in Organizational Decision Making." *Journal of Economic Behavior and Organization*, 10 (1988), 415–431.

Grandori, Anna. "A Prescriptive Contingency View of Organizational Decision Making." *Administrative Science Quarterly*, 29 (1984), 192–209.

Granger, Charles H. "The Hierarchy of Objectives." *Harvard Business Review* (May–June 1964), 63–74.

Grant, A. J. "Making Sense of Public Values: Environmental Controversies for Corporate Decision Makers." *Total Quality Environmental Management* (Summer 1995), 65–71.

Grant, Robert M. "The Resource-Based Theory of Competitive Advantage: Implications for Strategy Formulation." *California Management Review* (Spring 1991), 114–135.

Graves, Clare W. "Levels of Existence: An Open System Theory of Values." *Journal of Humanistic Psychology*, 10 (Fall 1970), 131–155.

Green, Stephen G., and Thomas D. Faber. "The Effects of Three Social Decision Schemes on Decision Group Processes." *Organizational Behavior and Human Performance* (February 1980), 77–108.

Green, Thad B. "An Empirical Analysis of Nominal and Interacting Groups." *Academy of Management Journal*, 18 (March 1975), 63–73.

Greenwood, P., and H. Thomas. "A Review of Analytical Models in Strategic Planning." *OMEGA, The International Journal of Management Science*, 9 (1981), 397–417.

Greig, I. D. "Basic Motivation and Decision Style in Organisation Management." *OMEGA, The International Journal of Management Science*, 12 (1984), 31–40.

Gremion, Catherine. "Toward a New Theory of Decision-Making?" *International Studies of Management and Organization* (Summer 1972), 125–141.

Griffith, Victoria. "Mortgaging the Mouse." *CFO* (August 1997), 71–73.

Grover, Ron. "Thrills and Chills at Disney." *Business Week* (June 21, 1993), 73–74.

Gruenfeld, Deborah H., et al. "Group Composition and Decision Making: How Member Familiarity and Information Distribution Affect Process and Performance." *Organizational Behavior and Human Decision Processes*, 67 (July 1996), 1–15.

Gubernick, Lisa. "Mickey n'est pas fini." *Forbes* (February 14, 1994), 42–43.

Guetzkow, Harold, and John Gyr. "An Analysis of Conflict in Decision-Making Groups." *Human Relations*, 7 (1954), 367–382.

Gustafson, David H., Ramesh K. Shukla, André Delbecq, and G. William Walster. "A Comparative Study of Differences in Subjective Likelihood Estimates Made by Individuals, Interacting Groups, Delphi Groups, and Nominal Groups."

Organizational Behavior and Human Performance, 9 (1973), 280–291.

Guth, William D., and Renato Tagiuri. "Personal Values and Corporate Strategies." *Harvard Business Review* (September–October 1965), 123–132.

Guthrie, James P., and Deepak K. Datta. "Contextual Influences on Executive Selection: Firm Characteristics and CEO Experience." *Journal of Management Studies* (July 1997), 537–560.

Haire, Mason, and Willa Freeman Grunes. "Perceptual Defenses: Processes Protecting an Organized Perception of Another Personality." In *Psychology in Administration*. Eds. Timothy W. Costello and Sheldon S. Zalkind. Englewood Cliffs, N.J.: Prentice-Hall, 1963, 37–44.

Haley, Hugh J., and Brendon G. Rule. "Group Composition Effects on Risk Taking." *Journal of Personality*, 39 (March 1971), 150–161.

Hall, J., and V. O'Leary. "Getting Better Decisions from a Group." *Supervisory Management* (July 1971), 28–32.

Hall, Jay. "Decisions, Decisions, Decisions." *Psychology Today* (November 1971), 51–54, 86–88.

———. "Synergism in Group Decision Making." *Personal Journal* (January 1979), 12–13.

Haltiwanger, John, and Michael Waldman. "Rational Expectations and the Limits of Rationality: An Analysis of Heterogeneity." *American Economic Review*, 75 (June 1985), 326–340.

Hambrick, D. C. "The Top Management Team: Key to Strategic Success." *California Management Review*, 30 (1987), 88–108.

———. "Strategic Awareness Within Top Management Teams." *Strategic Management Journal*, 2 (1981), 263–279.

Hambrick, Donald C., and Charles C. Snow. "A Conceptual Model of Strategic Decision Making in Organization." In *Proceedings of the Academy of Management*. Ed. Robert L. Taylor et al. Colorado Springs: University of Colorado, 1977, 109–112.

Hamilton, David L., and Leroy J. Huffman. "Generality of Impression — Formation Processes for Evaluative and Nonevaluative Judgments." *Journal of Personality and Social Psychology*, 20, No. 2 (1971), 200–207.

Hamilton, J. Ogden. "Motivation and Risk Taking Behavior: A Test of Atkinson's Theory." *Journal of Personality and Social Psychology*, 29, No. 6 (1974), 856–864.

Hampton, William J., and James R. Norman. "General Motors: What Went Wrong?" *Business Week* (March 16, 1987), 102–110.

Hancock, John G., and Richard C. Teevan. "Fear of Failure and Risk-Taking Behavior." *Journal of Personality*, 32 (June 1964), 200–209.

Hardy, Cynthia. "The Nature of Unobtrusive Power." *Journal of Management Studies* (July 1985), 384–399.

Harris, Ben, and John H. Harvey. "Self-Attributed Choice as a Function of the Consequence of a Decision." *Journal of Personality and Social Psychology* (June 1975), 1013–1019.

Harris, Kathryn. "Lights! Camera! Regulation!" *Fortune* (September 4, 1995), 83–86.

Harrison, E. Frank. "A Conceptual Model of Organizational Conflict." *Business and Society* (Winter 1980), 30–40.

———. "Challenger: The Anatomy of a Flawed Decision." *Technology in Society*, 15 (1993), 161–183.

———. "Interdisciplinary Models of Decision Making." *Management Decision*, 31 (1993), 27–33.

———. "Organizational Correlates of Perceived Role Performance at the University and College Level." *Academy of Management Journal* (June 1973), 227–238.

———. "Perspectives on Uncertainty in Successful Choice at the CEO Level." *OMEGA, The International Journal of Management Science*, 20 (1992), 105–116.

———. "Some Factors Involved in Determining Strategic Decision Success." *Journal of General Management* (Spring 1992), 72–87.

———. "The Concept of Strategic Gap." *Journal of General Management*, 15 (Winter 1989), 57–72.

———. "The Management of Organizational Conflict." *University of Michigan Business Review* (May 1979), 13–23.

Harrison, E. Frank, and Monique A. Pelletier. "A Typology of Strategic Choice." *Technological Forecasting and Social Change*, 44 (1993) 245–263.

Harrison, E. Frank, and Monique A. Pelletier. "CEO Perceptions of Strategic Leadership." *Journal of Managerial Issues*, 9, No. 3 (Fall 1997), 299–317.

Harrison, E. Frank, and James E. Rosenzweig. "Professional Norms and Organizational Goals: An Illusory Dichotomy." *California Management Review* (Spring 1972), 38–48.

Harrison, F. L. "Decision-Making in Conditions of Extreme Uncertainty." *Journal of Management Studies*, 14 (May 1977), 169–178.

Harrison, J. Richard, and James G. March. "Decision Making and Postdecision Surprises: The Politically Competent Manager." *Administrative Science Quarterly* (March 1984), 26–42.

Harrison, Michael J. and Bruce Phillips, "Strategic Decision Making: An Integrative Explanation." *Research in the Sociology of Organizations* (1991), 319–358.

Harrison, Teresa M. "Communication and Participative Decision Making: An Exploratory Study." *Personnel Psychology*, 38 (1985), 93–115.

Hart, Paul't. "Irving L. Janis' Victims of Groupthink." *Political Psychology*, 12 (1991), 247–277.

Hart, Stuart. "How Strategy-Making Processes Can Make a Difference." *Strategic Management Journal*, 15 (1994), 251–269.

Harvey, John H. "Determinants of the Perception of Choice." *Journal of Experimental Social Psychology*, 9 (March 1973), 164–179.

Hauschildt, Jurgen. "Goals and Problems-Solving in Innovative Decisions." In *Empirical Research on Organizational Decision-Making*. Ed. E. Witte and H.-J.-Zimmerman. New York: Elsevier Science, Inc., 1986.

Hayes, John. "The Politically Competent Manager." *Journal of General Management* (Autumn 1984), 24–33.

Hegarty, W. H., and R. C. Hoffman. "Who Influences Strategic Decision?" *Long-Range Planning*, 20 (1987), 75–85.

Heller, Frank A. "Reality and Illusion in Senior Executive Decision Making." *Journal of Managerial Psychology*, 2 (1987), 23–27.

Hellriegel, Don, and John W. Slocum, Jr. "Managerial Problem-Solving Styles." *Business Horizons* (December 1975), 29–37.

Hempel, Carl G. "Rational Action." In *Proceedings and Addresses of the American Philosophical Association*. Vol. 35. Yellow Springs, Ohio: Antioch Press, 1962, pp. 5–23.

Hems, John M. "The Limits of Decision." *Philosophy and Phenomenological Research* (June 1971), 527–539.

Henderson, John C., and Paul C. Nutt. "The Influence of Decision Style on Decision Making Behavior." *Management Science* (April 1980), 370–386.

Hendrick, Clyde, Judson Mills, and Charles A. Kiesler. "Decision Time as a Function of the Number and Complexity of Equally Attractive Alternatives." *Journal of Personality and Social Psychology*, 8 (1968), 313–318.

Herbert, Theodore T. "A Comparison of Decision Quality Under Nominal and Interacting Consensus Group Formats: The Case of the Structured Problem." *Decision Sciences*, 10 (July 1979), 358–370.

"Here Comes GM's Saturn." *Business Week* (April 9, 1990), 56–62.

Herek, Gregory M., Irving L. Janis, and Paul Hurth. "Quality of U.S. Decision Making During the Cuban Missile Crisis." *Journal of Conflict Resolution* (September 1989), 446–459.

———. "Decision Making During International Crises: Is Quality of Process Related to Outcome?" *Journal of Conflict Resolution*, 31 (1987), 202–226.

Hermanson, Dana R. "Eisner Takes Shareholders on a Daredevil Ride." *Wall Street Journal* (March 13, 1997), 15.

Heylighen, Francis. "A Cognitive-Systematic Reconstruction of Maslow's Theory of Self-Actualization." *Behavioral Science* (January 1992), 39–58.

Hickey, N. "The Challenger Tragedy: It Exposed TV's Failures as Well as NASA's." *TV Guide*, 35 (January 24, 1984), 2ff.

Hickson, David J., et al. "Decision and Organization—Processes of Strategic Decision Making and Their Explanation." In *Managerial Decision Making*. Ed. D. J. Hickson England: Dartmouth, 1995, 77–94.

Hill, G. W. "Groups Versus Individual Performance: Are N + 1 Heads Better Than One?" *Psychological Bulletin*, 91 (May 1982), 517–539.

Hills, Frederick S., and Thomas A. Mahoney. "University Budgets and Organizational Decision Making." *Administrative Science Quarterly* (September 1978), 454–465.

Hilsman, Roger. "The Cuban Missile Crisis: How Close We Were to War." *Look* (August 25, 1964), 17–21.

Hirokawa, Randy Y. "Why Informed Groups Make Faulty Decisions." *Small Group Behavior* (February 1987), 3–29.

Hirokawa, Randy Y., Dennis S. Gouran, and Amy E. Martz. "Understanding the Sources of Faulty Group Decision Making: A Lesson From the Challenger Disaster." *Small Group Behavior* (November 1988), 411–433.

Hitt, Michael, and Beverly B. Tyler. "Strategic Decision Models: Integrating Different Perspectives." *Strategic Management Journal*, 12 (1991), 327–351.

Hitt, William D. "Two Models of Man." *American Psychologist*, 24 (July 1969), 651–658.

Hogarth, Robin M. "Decision Time as a Function of Task Complexity." In *Utility, Probability, and Human Decision Making.* Ed. Dirk Wendt and Charles Vlek. Boston: D. Reidel, 1975.

Hogarth, Robin M., and Spyros Makridakis. "Forecasting and Planning: An Evaluation." *Management Science* (February 1981), 115–137.

Holbrook, Morris B., and Michael J. Ryan. "Modeling Decision-Specific Stress: Some Methodological Considerations." *Administrative Science Quarterly*, 27 (1982), 243–258.

Holland, Howard K. "Decision Making and Personality." *Personnel Administration* (May–June 1968), 24–29.

Holland, Jeffrey R. "The Value of Values: Shared Tasks for Business and Education in the 1980s." *Executive Speeches* (August–September 1994), 55–59.

Holloman, Charles R. "Using Both Head and Heart in Managerial Decision Making." *Industrial Management* (November–December 1992), 7–10.

Holloman, Charles R., and Hal. W. Hendrick. "Adequacy of Group Decisions as a Function of the Decision-Making Process." In *Academy of Management Proceedings*, August 15–18, 1971.

———. "Adequacy of Group Decisions as a Function of the Decision Making Process." *Academy of Management Journal* (June 1972), 175–184.

———. "Effects of Status and Individual Ability on Group Problem Solving." *Decision Sciences*, 3 (October 1972), 55–63.

Holsapple, Clyde W., and Herbert Moskowitz. "A Conceptual Framework for Studying Complex Decision Processes." *Policy Sciences*, 13 (1980), 83–104.

Holsti, Ole R. "Time, Alternatives, and Communications: The 1914 and Cuban Missile Crises." In *International Crises: Insights from Behavioral Research.* Ed. Charles F. Hermann. New York: Free Press, 1972.

Holsti, Ole R., and Alexander L. George. "The Effects of Stress on the Performance of Foreign Policy Makers." In *Political Science Annual.* Vol. 6. Ed. Cornelius P. Cotter. Indianapolis: Bobbs-Merrill, 1975, 255–317.

Horelick, Arnold L. "The Cuban Missile Crisis." *World Politics*, 16 (1964), 363–389.

Hosmer, L. F. "The Importance of Strategic Leadership." *Journal of Business Strategy* (Fall 1982), 47–57.

Hougland, James G., Jr. "Organizational and Individual Responses to Environmental Uncertainty." In *Uncertainty.* Ed. Seymour Fiddle. New York: Praeger, 1980, 102–119.

"How Objective Is Your Decision-Making?" *Industry Week* (January 8, 1973), 8.

Howard, Nigel. "The Role of Emotions in Multi-Organizational Decision-Making." *Journal of the Operational Research Society*, 44, No. 6 (June 1993), 613–623.

Hoyt, George C., and James A. Stoner. "Leadership and Group Decisions Involving Risk." *Journal of Experimental Social Psychology*, 4 (1968), 275–284.

Huber, George P., and André Delbecq. "Guidelines for Combining the Judgments of Individual Members in Decision Conferences." *Academy of Management Journal*, 15 (June 1972), 161–174.

Huber, Oswald. "Decision Making as a Problem Solving Process." In *New Directions in Research on Decision Making.* Ed. B. Brehmer et al. New York: Elsevier Publishing Co., 1986, 108–138.

Humble, John, et al. "The Strategic Power of Corporate Values." *Long-Range Planning*, 27, No 6 (1994), 28–42.

Humphreys, Luther W., and William A. Shrode. "Decision-Making Profiles of Male and Female Managers." *MSU Business Topics* (Autumn 1978), 45–51.

Hunsucker, J. L., and J. S. Law. "Disaster on Flight 51-L: An IE Perspective on the Challenger Accident." *Industrial Management*, 28 (September–October 1986), 8–13.

Huxham, C. S., and M. R. Dando. "Is Bounded-Vision an Adequate Explanation of Strategic Decision-Making Failure?" *OMEGA, The International Journal of Management Science*, 9 (1981), 371–379.

Hwang, Hsin-Ginn, and Jan Guynes. "The Effect of Group Size on Group Performance in Computer-Supported Decision Making." *Information & Management*, 29 (1994), 189–198.

"Is Chrysler the Prototype?" *Business Week* (August 20, 1979), 102ff.

Isen, Alice M. "Some Factors Influencing Decision-Making Strategy and Risk Taking." In *Affect and Cognition.* The Seventeenth Annual Carnegie Symposium on Cognition. Ed. Margaret Sydnor Clarke and Susan F. Fiske. Hillsdale, N.J.: Lawrence Erlbaum Associates, 1982, 243–261.

Jackson, Douglas N., and Neil J. Vidmar. "A Four-Dimensional Interpretation of Risk Taking." *Journal of Personality*, 40 (September 1972), 483–501.

Jackson, Jay M. "A Space for Conceptualizing Person-Group Relationships." *Human Relations*, 10 (1959), 3–15.

Jackson, Susan E., and Jane E. Dutton. "Discerning Threats and Opportunities." *Administrative Science Quarterly*, 33 (1988), 370–387.

Jacob, Philip E., James J. Flink, and Hedvah L. Schuchman. "Values and Their Function in Decision-Making." *Supplement to the American Behavioral Scientist*, 5 (May 1962), 1–34.

Jacoby, Jacob. "Interpersonal Perceptual Accuracy as a Function of Dogmatism." *Journal of Experimental Social Psychology*, 7 (March 1971), 221–236.

Jaffe, Yoram, and Yoel Yinon, "Retaliatory Aggression in Individuals and Groups." *European Journal of Social Psychology*, 9 (1979), 177–186.

Janis, Irving L. "Groupthink." *Psychology Today* (November 1971), 43ff.

Jauch, L. R., and K. L. Kraft. "Strategic Management of Uncertainty." *Academy of Management Review*, 11, 777–790.

Jellison, Jerald M., and John H. Harvey. "Determinants of Perceived Choice and the Relationship Between Perceived Choice and Perceived Competence." *Journal of Personality and Social Psychology*, 28, No. 3 (1973), 376–382.

Jemison, David B. "Organizational versus Environmental Sources of Influence in Strategic Decision Making." *Strategic Management Journal*, 2 (1981), 77–89.

Jensen, Michael C., and William H. Meckling. "Theory of the Firm: Managerial Behavior, Agency Costs and Ownership Structure." *Journal of Financial Economics*, 3 (1976), 305–360.

Johnson, H. H., and J. M. Torcivia. "Group and Individual Performance on a Single-Stage Task as a Function of Distribution of Individual Performance." *Journal of Experimental Social Psychology*, 3 (1967), 266–273.

Johnson, J. E. V., and P. L. Powell. "Decision Making, Risk, and Gender: Are Managers Different?" *British Journal of Management*, 5 (1994), 123–138.

Johnson, Michael L. "Women: Born to Manage." *Industry Week* (August 4, 1975), 22–26.

Johnson, Mitzi M.S. "Age Differences in Decision-Making: A Process Methodology for Examining Strategic Information Processing." *Journal of Gerontology, PSYCHOLOGICAL SCIENCES*, 45 (March 1990), 75–78.

Johnson, Rossall J. "Conflict Avoidance Through Acceptable Decisions." *Human Relations*, 27 (January 1974), 71–82.

Jones, Edward E., and C. Anderson Johnson. "Delay of Consequences and the Riskiness of Decisions." *Journal of Personality*, 41 (December 1973), 613–637.

Jones, Robert E., et al. "Strategic Decision Processes in Matrix Organizations." *European Journal of Operational Research*, 78 (1994), 192–203.

Jones, Robert E., et al. "Strategic Decision Processes in International Firms." *Management International Review*, 32 (1992–93), 219–236.

Kaflan, John. "Decision Theory and the Factfinding Process." *Stanford Law Review* (June 1968), 1065–1092.

Kahneman, Daniel, and Dan Lovallo. "Timid Choices and Bold Forecasts: A Cognitive Perspective on Risk Taking." *Management Science*, 39, No. 1 (January 1993), 17–31.

Kakabadse, Andrew. "Organizational Politics." *Management Decision*, 25 (1987), 33–37.

Kakar, Sudhir. "Rationality and Irrationality in Business Leadership." *Journal of Business Policy*, 2 (Winter 1971–1972), 39–44.

Karp, H. B., and Bob Abramms. "Doing the Right Things." *Training & Development* (August 1992), 37–41.

Kaufman, Bruce E. "A New Theory of Satisficing." *The Journal of Behavioral Economics*, 19 (1990), 35–51.

Kayaalp, Orhan. "Towards a General Theory of Managerial Decisions: A Critical Appraisal." *SAM Advanced Management Journal* (Spring 1987), 36–42.

Kelman, Herbert C. "Processes of Opinion Change." *Public Opinion Quarterly*, 25 (1961), 57–78.

Kessler, Forrest A. "How to Avoid Common Pitfalls of Consensus Decision Making." *Oil & Gas Journal* (September 27, 1993), 34 and 36.

Kets de Vries, F. R. "Toppling the Cultural Tower of Babel." *Chief Executive* (May 1994), 68–71.

Kharbanda, O. P., and E. A. Stallworthy. "Managerial Decision Making, Part I: Conventional Techniques." *Management Decision*, 28 (1990), 4–9.

———. "Managerial Decision Making, Part 2: The New Techniques." *Management Decision*, 28 (1990), 29–35.

Kickert, Walter J. M., and John P. van Gigch. "A Metasystem Approach to Organizational Decision-Making." *Management Science*, 25, No. 12 (December 1979), 1217–1231.

Kiesler, Charles A. "Conflict and the Number of Choice Alternatives." *Psychological Reports*, 18 (February 1966), 603–610.

Kilduff, Martin. "The Interpersonal Structure of Decision Making: A Social Comparison Approach to Organizational Choice." *Organizational Behavior and Human Decision Processes*, 47 (1990), 270–288.

Kilmann, Ralph H., and Ian I. Mitroff. "Qualitative Versus Quantitative Analysis for Different Psychological Types." *Interfaces* (February 1976), 17–27.

Kim, W. Chan, and Renee A. Mauborgne. "Making Global Strategies Work." *Sloan Management Review* (Spring 1993), 11–27.

Kinder, Donald R., and Janet A. Weiss. "In Lieu of Rationality: Psychological Perspectives on Foreign Policy Decision-Making." *Journal of Conflict Resolution* (December 1978), 707–735.

Kingley, Gordon A., and Pamela N. Reed. "Decision Process Models and Organizational Context: Level and Sector Make a Difference." *Public Productivity & Management Review* (Summer 1991), 397–413.

Kirchner, W. K. "Age Differences in Short-Term Retention of Rapidly Changing Information." *Journal of Experimental Psychology*, 55 (1958), 352–358.

Klopfer, Frederic J., and Thomas Moran. "Influences of Sex Composition, Decision Rule, and Decision Consequences in Small Group Policy Making." *Sex Roles*, 4, No. 6 (1978), 907–915.

Kogan, N., and M. A. Wallach. "Group Risk Taking as a Function of Members' Anxiety and Defensiveness Levels." *Journal of Personality*, 35 (1967), 50–63.

———. "Risk Taking as a Function of the Situation, the Person, and the Group." In *New Directions in Psychology, III.* Ed. G. Mandler. New York: Holt, Rinehart and Winston, 1967.

Kogan, Nathan, and Karen Dorros. "Sex Differences in Risk Taking and Its Attribution." *Sex Roles*, 4, No. 5 (1978), 755–765.

Kolaja, Jiri, et al. "An Organization Seen as a Structure of Decision Making." *Human Relations*, 16, No. 4 (1963), 351–357.

Koontz, Harold. "A Model for Analyzing the Universality and Transferability of Management." *Academy of Management Journal* (December 1969), 415–429.

———. "The Management Theory Jungle Revisited." *Academy of Management Review* (April 1980), 175–187.

Koplin, H. T. "The Profit Maximization Assumption." *Oxford Economic Papers*, 12, No. 2 (1963), 130–139.

Kozielecki, Jozef. "Elements of a Psychological Decision Theory." *Studia Psychologica*, 13 (1971), 53–60.

Kriger, Mark P., and Louis B. Barnes. "Organizational Decision-Making as Hierarchial Levels of Drama." *Journal of Management Studies* (July 1992), 439–457.

Krouse, C. G. "Complex Objectives, Decentralization, and the Decision Process of the Organization." *Administrative Science Quarterly* (December 1972), 544–554.

Kruglanski, A. W. "Freeze-Think and the Challenger." *Psychology Today* (August 1986), 48–49.

Kulieke, Barbara N. "Thinking Through Conflict." *Data Management* (September 1983), 28–29 and 37.

Laczniak, Gene R., and Edward J. Inderrieden. "The Influence of Stated Organizational Concern upon Ethical Decision Making." *Journal of Business Ethics*, 6 (1987), 297–307.

Lado, Augustine A. "A Competency Based Model of Sustainable Competitive Advantage: Toward a Conceptual Integration." *Journal of Management*, 18, No. 1 (1992), 77–91.

Lamm, Helmut, and Nathan Kogan. "Risk Taking in the Context of Intergroup Negotiation." *Journal of Experimental Social Psychology*, 6 (July 1970), 351–363.

Lamm, Helmut, Edith Schaude, and Gisela Trommsdorff. "Risky Shift as a Function of Group Members' Value of Risk and Need for Approval." *Journal of Personality and Social Psychology*, 20 (1971), 430–435.

Lanzetta, John T., and Vera T. Kanareff. "Information Cost, Amount of Payoff, and Level of Aspiration as Determinants of Information Seeking in Decision Making." *Behavioral Science*, 7 (October 1962), 459–473.

Latham, Gary P., and Glen Whyte. "The Futility of Utility Analysis." *Personnel Psychology*, 47 (1994), 31–46.

Learned, Edmund P., Arch R. Dooley, and Robert L. Katz. "Personal Values and Business Decisions." *Harvard Business Review* (March–April 1959), 111–120.

Leavitt, H. "Some Effects of Certain Communication Patterns on Group Performance." *Journal of Abnormal and Social Psychology*, 46 (1951), 38–50.

Lee, James A. "Changes in Managerial Values, 1965–1986." *Business Horizons*, 31 (July/August 1988), 29–37.

Leibenstein, Harvey. "On Relaxing the Maximization Postulate." *The Journal of Business Economics*, 15 (Winter 1986), 3–16.

Lewin, Kurt. "Frontiers in Group Dynamics." *Human Relations*, 1 (1947), 5–41, 141–153.

Liedtka, Jeanne M. "Value Congruence: The Interplay of Individual and Organizational Value Systems." *Journal of Business Ethics*, 8 (1989), 805–815.

Lilienthal, Richard A., and Sam L. Hutchison, Jr. "Group Polarization (Risky Shift) in Led and Leaderless Groups." *Psychological Reports*, 45 (1979), 168.

Lindblom, Charles E. "The Science of 'Muddling Through.'" *Public Administration Review*, 19 (Spring 1959), 79–88.

———. "Still Muddling, Not Yet Through." *Public Administration Review* (November–December 1979), 517–536.

Linder, Darwyn E., Camille B. Wortman, and Jack W. Brehm. "Temporal Change in Predecision Preferences Among Choice Alternatives." *Journal of Personality and Social Psychology*, 19 (1971), 282–284.

Lippman, Steven A., and Kevin F. McCardle. "Does Cheaper, Faster, or Better Imply Sooner in the Timing of Innovation Decisions?" *Management Science* (August 1987), 1058–1064.

Litterer, Joseph A. "Conflict in Organization: A Re-Examination." *Academy of Management Journal* (September 1966), 178–186.

Littleton, Cynthia. "Disney ABC Integrates TV Operations." *Broadcasting & Cable* (April 22, 1996), 33–34.

Longley, Jeanne, and Dean G. Pruitt. "Groupthink: A Critique of Janis's Theory." *Review of Personality and Social Psychology*, 1 (1980), 74–93.

Lopes, Lola L. "Between Hope and Fear: The Psychology of Risk." *Advances in Experimental Social Psychology*, 20 (1987), 255–295.

Lorge, Irving, et al. "A Survey of Studies Contrasting the Quality of Group Performance and Individual Performance, 1920–1957." *Psychological Bulletin*, 55 (November 1958), 337–372.

Lukes, Steven. "Some Problems About Rationality." *Archives Europeennes de Sociologie*, 8 (1967), 247–264.

Lusk, Edward J., and Bruce L. Oliver. "American Managers' Personal Value Systems — Revisited." *Academy of Management Journal*, 17 (September 1974), 549–554.

McCormick, Michael B., Earl F. Lundgren, and Earl A. Cecil. "Group Search and Decision-Making Processes: A Laboratory Test of Soelberg's Confirmation Hypothesis." *The Journal of Social Psychology*, 110 (1980), 79–86.

MacCrimmon, Kenneth R., and Donald A. Wehrung. "Characteristics of Risk Taking Executives." *Management Science* (April 1990), 422–435.

McGuire, William J. "A Syllogistic Analysis of Cognitive Relationships." In *Attitude Organization and Change*. Ed. Milton J. Rosenburg et al. Yale Studies in Attitude and Communication. Vol. 3. New Haven: Yale University Press, 1970.

Machina, Mark J. "Choice Under Uncertainty: Problems Solved and Unsolved." *Economic Perspectives*, 1 (Summer 1987), 121–154.

Machlup, Fritz. "Theories of the Firm: Marginalist, Behavioral, Managerial." *American Economic Review* (March 1957), 1–33.

MacKenzie, Kenneth D. "An Analysis of Risky Shift Experiments." *Organizational Behavior and Human Performance*, 6 (May 1971), 283–303.

———. "The Effects of Status upon Group Risk Taking." *Organizational Behavior and Human Performance*, 5 (November 1970), 517–541.

McMurray, Robert N. "Conflicts in Human Values." *Harvard Business Review* (May–June 1963), 130–145.

Madaras, George R., and Daryl J. Bem. "Risk and Conservatism in Group Decision-Making." *Journal of Experimental Social Psychology*, 4 (1968), 350–365.

Mahar, Maggie. "Magic Kingdom?" *Barron's* (August 7, 1995), 14–15.

Maidment, Robert. "Decision Making: When Not to Involve Employees." *Supervisory Management* (October 1989), 33–35.

"Make Decisions Under Pressure." *Management Information* (July 22, 1974), 2–4.

Makridakis, Spyros. "What Can We Learn from Corporate Failure?" *Long-Range Planning*, 24 (August 1991), 115–126.

Malley, J. C., V. D. Arnold, and R. L. Whorton. "Organizational Communication: A Disaster for Challenger." *Arkansas Business and Economic Review*, 21 (1988), 11–18.

Mandler, George. "The Structure of Value: Accounting for Taste." In *Affect and Cognition*. The Seventeenth Annual Carnegie Symposium on Cognition. Ed. Margaret Sydnor Clark and Susan F. Fiske. Hillsdale, N.J.: Lawrence Erlbaum Associates, 1992, 3–36.

Maney, Kevin. "Companies Are Going Vertical/Media Firms Shift to Gain Product Control." *Money* (September 14, 1995), 18.

Mann, Leon, and Irving Janis. "Conflict Theory of Decision Making and the Expectancy-Value Approach." In *Expectations and Actions: Expectancy-Value Models in Psychology*. Ed. Norman F. Feather. Hillsdale: N.J.: Erlbaum, 1982. pp. 341–364.

Manners, George E., Jr. "Another Look at Group Size, Group Problem Solving, and Member Consensus." *Academy of Management Journal*, 18 (December 1975), 715–724.

Maoz, Zeev. "The Decision to Raid Entebbe." *Journal of Conflict Resolution* (December 1981), 677–707.

March, James G. "Decision Making Perspective." In *Perspectives on Organization Design and Behavior*. Ed. A. H. Van de Ven and W. F. Joyce. New York: Wiley-Interscience, 1981, 205–248.

March, James G., and Zur Shapira. "Managerial Perspectives on Risk and Risk Taking." *Management Science*, 33 (1987), 1404–1418.

Markin, Ron J. "A Philosophy of Management." *University of Washington Business Review* (April 1963), 67–78.

Marquis, D. G. "Individual Responsibility and Group Decisions Involving Risk." *Industrial Management Review*, 3 (1962), 8–23.

Marquis, Donald G., and H. Joseph Reitz. "Effect of Uncertainty on Risk Taking in Individual and Group Decision Making." *Behavioral Science*, 14 (1969), 281–288.

Marris, Robin. "A Model of the 'Managerial' Enterprise." *Quarterly Journal of Economics* (May 1963), 185–209.

Marschak, Jacob. "Decision Making: Economic Aspects." In *International Encyclopedia of the Social Sciences*. Vol. 4. Ed. David L. Sills. New York: Macmillan and Free Press, 1968, pp. 42–65.

Marshall, S. A. "NASA After Challenger: The Public Affairs Perspective." *Public Relations Journal*, 42 (August 1986), 17ff.

Martin, Charles L. "Feelings, Emotional Empathy, and Decision Making: Listening to the Voices of the Heart." *Journal of Management Development*, 12, No. 5 (1993), 33–45.

Martin, James E., George B. Kleindorfer, and William R. Brashers, Jr. "The Theory of Bounded Rationality and Legitimation." *Journal for the Theory of Social Behaviour*, 17 (March 1987), 63–82.

Maslow, A. H. "A Theory of Human Motivation." *Psychological Review*, 50 (1943), 370–396.

Mattessich, Richard. "The Incorporation and Reduction of Value Judgments in Systems." *Management Science*, 21 (September 1974), 1–9.

Mayntz, Renate. "Conceptual Models of Organizational Decision-Making and Their Application to the Policy Process." In *European Contributions to Organization Theory*. Eds. G. Hofstede and M. S. Kassem. Amsterdam: Van Gorcum, 1976, 114–125.

Maznevski, Martha L. "Understanding Our Differences: Performance in Decision-Making Groups with Diverse Members." *Human Relations*, 47, No. 5 (1994), 531–552.

Mazzolini, Renato. "Real-World Decision Making: The Limits of Top Management Power." *Journal of Business Strategy* (Fall 1980), 3–8.

McCann, Joseph E., and Thomas N. Gilmore. "Diagnosing Organizational Decision Making Through Responsibility Charting." *Sloan Management Review* (Winter 1983), 3–15.

McCann Paul. "Disney Acquires ABC for $19Bn." *Marketing Week* (August 2, 1996), 7.

McClelland, David C. "How Motives, Skills, and Values Determine What People Do." *American Psychologist*, 40, No 7 (July 1985), 812–825.

McConnell, Chris. "Mega-Merger Gets FCC Nod." *Broadcasting & Cable* (February 12, 1996), 9.

McGrath, John. "The Lawyers Who Rebuild Eurodisney." *International Financial Law Review* (May 1994), 10–12.

McGrath, Rita Gunther, and Ian C. MacMillan. "Discovery-Driven." *Harvard Business Review,* (July–August 1995), 44–54.

McLaughlin, David. J. "Strengthening Executive Decision Making." *Human Resource Management,* 34, No. 3 (Fall 1995), 443–461.

Messick, David M., and Max H. Bazerman. "Ethical Leadership and the Psychology of Decision Making." *Sloan Management Review* (Winter 1996), 9–22.

Metzger, Michael B., and Charles R. Schwenk. "Decision Making Models: Devil's Advocacy and the Control of Corporate Crime." *American Business Law Journal*, 28 (Fall 1990), 323–377.

Meyer, Michael, and Stryker McGuire. "How Eisner Saved Disney—and Himself." *Newsweek* (August 14, 1995), 28 and 30.

Meyer, John W. "Sources and Effects of Decisions: A Comment on Brunsson." *Accounting, Organizations and Society*, 15, (1990), 61–65.

Michaud, Paul R. "Wild Kingdom." *World Trade* (October 1992), 46–50.

Michelson, Larry K., et al. "A Realistic Test of Individual Versus Group Consensus Decision Making." *Journal of Applied Psychology,* 74, No. 5 (1989), 834–839.

Mihalasky, John. "ESP in Decision Making." *Management Review* (April 1975), 32–37.

Miles, Raymond E., et al. "Keys to Success in Corporate Redesign." *California Management Review,* 37, No. 3 (Spring 1995), 128–145.

Miller, Charles E., et al. "Some Social Psychological Effects of Group Decision Rules." *Journal of Personality and Social Psychology* (February 1987), 325–332.

Miller, Katherine I., and Peter R. Monge. "Participation, Satisfaction, and Productivity: A Meta-Analytic Review." *Academy of Management Journal,* 29 (1986), 727–753.

Miller, Samuel H. "The Tangle of Ethics." *Harvard Business Review* (January–February 1960), 59–62.

Mills, Roger, et al. "Euro Disney: A Mickey Mouse Project?" *European Management Journal,* 12, No. 3 (September 1994), 306–314.

Miner, Frederick C., Jr. "A Comparative Analysis of Three Diverse Group Decision Making Approaches." *Academy of Management Journal,* 22 (March 1979), 81–93.

Minkes, A. L., and A. E. Gear. "Process, Conflict, and Commitment in Organizational Decision Making." *Journal of General Management,* 20, No. 2 (Winter 1994), 78–90.

Mintzberg, H. "Patterns in Strategic Formation." *Management Science,* 24 (1978), 934–949.

———. "The Organization as Political Arena." *Journal of Management Studies* (March 1985), 133–154.

Mintzberg, Henry, Duru Raisinghani, and André Theoret. "The Structure of 'Unstructured' Decision Processes." *Administrative Science Quarterly,* 21 (June 1976), 246–275.

Mitroff, J. J., and F. Betz. "Dialectical Decision Making: A Meta Theory of Decision Making." *Management Science* (September 1972), 11–24.

Mohr, Lawrence B. "Organizations, Decisions, and Courts." *Law and Society* (Summer 1976), 621–641.

Monsen, R. J., B. O. Saxberg, and R. A. Suterneister. "The Modern Manager: What Makes Him Run?" *Business Horizons* (Fall 1966), 23–34.

Montanari, John R. "Managerial Discretion: An Expanded Model of Organization Choice." *Academy of Management Review,* 3 (April 1978), 231–241.

Moorhead, Gregory, and John R. Montanari. "An Empirical Investigation of the Groupthink Phenomenon." *Human Relations,* 39 (1986), 399–410.

Morlock, Henry. "The Effect of Outcome Desirability on Information Required for Decisions." *Behavioral Science* (July 1967), 296–300.

Morrisey, George L. "The Decision Matrix." *Personnel Administrator,* 21 (September 1976), 37–39.

Morrison, J. H. "Making Better Decisions." *Industry Week* (November 20, 1972), 45–48.

Moskal, Brian S. "Is GM Getting a Bum Rap?" *Industry Week* (January 12, 1987), 42.

Moussavi, Farzad, et al. "Explaining Strategic Managers' Choice of Decision Tools: Cognitive Style Representation Compatibility." *International Journal of Management,* 12, No. 3 (September 1995), 305–314.

Muldrow, Tressie W., and James A. Bayton. "Men and Women Executives and Processes Related to Decision Accuracy." *Journal of Applied Psychology* (April 1979), 99–106.

Murnighan, J. Keith. "Group Decision Making: What Strategies Should You Use?" *Management Review* (February 1981), 55–62.

Myers, David G., Peter Murdoch, and Gene F. Smith. "Responsibility Diffusion and Drive Enhancement Effects on Risky Shift." *Journal of Personality,* 38 (September 1970), 448.

Nathan, James A. "The Missile Crisis: His Finest Hour Now." *World Politics,* 27 (1975), 256–281.

Neisser, Ulric. "The Multiplicity of Thought." *British Journal of Psychology,* 54 (February 1963), 1–14.

Newstrom, John W., and William A. Ruch. "The Ethics of Management and the Management of Ethics." *MSU Business Topics,* 23 (Winter 1975), 29–37.

Nisbett, Richard E., and Timothy D. Wilson. "Telling More Than We Can Know: Verbal Reports on Mental Processes." *Psychological Review,* 84 (1977), 231–259.

———. "The Halo Effect: Evidence for Unconscious Alteration of Judgments." *Journal of Personality and Social Psychology,* 35 (1977), 250–256.

Noel, A. "Strategic Cores and Magnificent Obsessions: Discovering Strategy Formation Through Daily Activities of CEOs." *Strategic Management Journal,* 10 (1989), 33–49.

Norburn, D. "The Chief Executive: A Breed Apart." *Strategic Management Journal,* 10 (1989), 1–5.

Nutt, Paul C. "Formulation Tactics and the Success of Organizational Decision Making." *Decision Sciences,* 23 (May/June 1992), 519–540.

———. "Influence of Decision Styles on the Use of Decision Models." *Technological Forecasting and Social Change*, 14 (1979), 77–93.

———. "Models for Decision Making in Organizations and Some Contextual Variables Which Stipulate Optimal Use." *Academy of Management Review*, 1 (April 1976), 84–98.

———. "Preventing Decision Debacles." *Technological Forecasting and Social Change*, 38 (September 1990), 159–174.

———. "The Influence of Direction Setting Tactics on Success in Organizational Decision Making." *European Journal of Operational Research*, 60 (1992), 19–30.

———. "Types of Organizational Decision Processes." *Administrative Science Quarterly* (September 1984), 414–450.

Nystrom, Harry. "Uncertainty, Information, and Organizational Decision Making: A Cognitive Approach." *Swedish Journal of Economics*, 76 (March 1974), 131–139.

Okanlawon, Gus. "Women as Strategic Decision Makers." *Women in Management Review*, 9, No. 4 (1994). 25–32.

Olander, Folke. "Search Behavior in Non-Simultaneous Choice Situations: Satisficing or Maximizing?" In *Utility, Probability, and Human Decision Making*. Eds. Dirk Wendt and Charles Vlek. Boston: D. Reidel, 1975.

Oneal, Michael, et al. "Disney's Kingdom." *Business Week* (August 14, 1995), 30–34.

O'Reilly, Charles, A., III. "The Use of Information in Organizational Decision Making: A Model and Some Propositions." In *Research in Organizational Behavior*. Vol. 5. Eds. L. L. Cummings and Barry M. Staw. Greenwich, Conn.: JAI Press, 1983, 103–139.

Orwall, Bruce, and Joann S. Lublin. "If a Company Prospers, Should Its Directors Behave by the Book?" *Wall Street Journal* (February 24, 1997), 1 and 8.

Orwall, Bruce, and Kyle Pope. "Disney, ABC Promised 'Synergy' in Merger: So, What Happened?" *Wall Street Journal* (May 16, 1997), A1 and A9.

Owens, B. D. "Decision Theory in Academic Administration." *Academy of Management Journal* (June 1968), 221–232.

Ozanian, Michael, et al., "America's Top 200 Growth Companies." *Financial World* (August 4, 1992), 32–44.

Palmer, David D., John F. Veiga, and Jay A. Voro. "Managerial Value Profiles as Predictors of Policy Decisions in a Cross-Cultural Setting." *Academy of Management Proceedings* (August 1979), 133–137.

Palumbo, Dennis J., and Paula J. Wright, "Decision Making and Evaluation Research." *Policy Studies Journal*, 8 (1980), 1170–1177.

Park, Margaret K. "Decision-Making Processes for Information Managers." *Special Libraries* (October 1981), 307–318.

Park, W-W. "A Review of Research on Groupthink." *Journal of Behavioral Decision Making* (October–December 1990), 229–245.

Parker, LeRoss. "Test Your Decisions with Follow-Up." *Administrative Management* (October 1967), 56–57.

Parnell, John A., and Edward D. Bell. "The Propensity for Participative Decision Making Scale." *Administration & Society*, 25, No. 4 (February 1994), 518–530.

Parsons, J. A. "Decision Making Under Risk." *Journal of Systems Management* (July 1972), 42–43.

Patchen, Martin. "Decision Theory in the Study of National Action: Problems and a Proposal." *Journal of Conflict Resolution* (June 1965), 165–176.

Pate, Larry E. "Using Theories as 'Overlays' for Improved Managerial Decision Making." *Management Decision*, 26 (1988), 36–40.

Pepitone, Albert. "The Role of Justice in Interdependent Decision Making." *Journal of Experimental Social Psychology*, 7 (January 1971), 144–156.

Petit, Thomas A. "A Behavioral Theory of Management." *Journal of the Academy of Management* (December 1967), 341–350.

Pfeffer, Jeffrey, and Gerald R. Salancik. "Organizational Decision Making as a Political Process: The Case of a University Budget." *Administrative Science Quarterly* (June 1974), 135–151.

Pfeiffer, Steven I. "The Superiority of Team Decision Making." *Exceptional Children* (September 1982), 68–69.

Pfeiffer, Steven I., and Jack A. Naglieri. "An Investigation of Multi-Disciplinary Team Decision-Making." *Journal of Learning Disabilities* (December 1983), 588–590.

Philip Morris Companies, Inc. 1992 Annual Report. New York: Philip Morris, 1992.

Phillips, Lawrence D. "Organizational Structure and Decision Technology." *Acta Psychologica*, 45 (1980), 247–264.

Piper, Donald L. "Decision Making: Decisions Made by Individuals vs. Those Made by Group Consensus or Group Participation." *Educational Administration Quarterly*, 10 (Spring 1974), 82–95.

Pitcher, George. "Disney's Road to Damascus." *Marketing Week* (August 11, 1995), 25.

Pollay, Richard W. "A Model of Decision Times in Difficult Decision Situations." *Psychological Review*, 77, No. 4 (1970), 274–281.

———. "The Structure of Executive Decisions and Decision Times." *Administrative Science Quarterly*, 15 (December 1970), 459–471.

Pollis, Nicholas P., and Carol A. Pollis. "Single and Array Stimuli as Determinants of Social Judgment." *Journal of Experimental Social Psychology*, 8 (November 1972), 549–557.

Pondy, Louis R. "Organizational Conflict: Concepts and Models." *Administrative Science Quarterly* (September 1967), 296–320.

"Portrait of a CEO." *Business Week* (October 11, 1983), 64–65.

Posner, Barry Z., W. Alan Randolph, and Warren H. Schmidt. "Managerial Values Across Functions." *Group & Organization Studies*, 12 (1987), 373–385.

Posner, Barry Z., and Warren H. Schmidt. "The Values of Business and General Government Executives: More Different Than Alike." *Public Personnel Management*, 25, No. 3 (Fall 1996), 277–289.

Posner, Barry Z., and Warren H. Schmidt. "Values and the American Manager: An Update." *California Management Review* (Spring 1984), 202–216.

———. "Values and the American Manager: An Update Updated." *California Management Review*, 34 (Spring 1992), 80–94.

———. "Value Congruence and Differences Between the Interplay of Personal and Organizational Value Systems." *Journal of Business Ethics*, 12 (1993), 341–347.

Powell, Gary N. "One More Time: Do Female and Male Managers Differ?" *The Executive* (August 1990), 68–75.

Price, Robert M. "Technology and Strategic Advantage." *California Management Review*, 38, No. 3 (Spring 1996), 38–56.

Pruitt, Dean G. "Choice Shifts in Group Discussion: An Introductory Review." *Journal of Personality and Social Psychology*, 20, No. 3 (1971), 339–360.

———. "Conclusions: Toward an Understanding of Choice Shifts in Group Discussion." *Journal of Personality and Social Psychology*, 20 (1973), 495–510.

Radner, Roy. "Satisficing." *Journal of Mathematical Economics*, 2 (1975), 253–262.

Rados, David L. "Selection and Evaluation of Alternatives in Repetitive Decision Making." *Administrative Science Quarterly*, 17 (June 1972), 196–206.

Rae, Douglas W. "Decision Rules and Individual Value in Constitutional Choice." *American Political Science Review*, 63, No. 1 (1969), 40–56.

Ralston, David A., et al. "The Impact of Managerial Values on Decision-Making Behaviour: A Comparison of the United States and Hong Kong." *Asia Pacific Journal of Management* (April 1993), 21–37.

Ramsdell, Penny S. "Staff Participation in Organizational Decision-Making: An Empirical Study." *Administration in Social Work*, 18, No. 4 (1994), 51–71.

Rapoport, Amnon, and Thomas S. Wallston. "Individual Decision Behavior." In *Annual Review of Psychology*. Ed. Mark R. Rosenzweig. Palo Alto, Calif.: Annual Reviews, 1972.

Raven, Bertram H. "The Nixon Group." *Journal of Social Issues*, 30 (1974), 297–320.

"Re Disney-ABC." *Forbes* (August 28, 1995), 24.

Reich, Robert B., and John D. Donahue. "Lessons from the Chrysler Bailout." *California Management Review* (Summer 1985), 157–183.

Rim, Y. "Leadership Attitudes and Decisions Involving Risk." *Personnel Psychology*, 18 (Winter 1965), 423–430.

———. "Risk-Taking and Need for Achievement." *Acta Psychologica*, 21 (1963), 108–115.

Ritchie, J. R. Brent. "An Exploratory Analysis of the Nature and Extent of Individual Differences in Perception." *Journal of Management Research*, 11 (February 1974), 41–49.

Roberts, Edward B. "Benchmarking the Strategic Management of Technology—I." *Research-Technology Management*, (January–February 1995), 44–56.

———. "Benchmarking the Strategic Management of Technology—II." *Research-Technology Management*, (March–April, 1995), 18–26.

Roberts, John C., and Carl H. Castore. "The Effects of Conformity, Information, and Confidence upon Subjects' Willingness to Take Risk Following a Group Discussion." *Organizational Behavior and Human Performance*, 8 (December 1972), 384–394.

Robinson, James A. "Decision Making: Political Aspects." In *International Encyclopedia of the Social Sciences*. Vol. 4. Ed. David L. Sills. New York: Macmillan and Free Press, 1968.

Rodrigues, Suzana Braga, and David J. Hickson. "Success in Decision Making: Different Organizations, Differing Reasons for Success." *Journal of Management Studies*, 32, No. 5 (1995), 655–678.

Romzek, B. S., and M. J. Dubnick. "Accountability in the Public Sector: Lessons from the Challenger Tragedy." *Public Administration Review*, 47 (May/June 1987), 227–238.

Rossant, John. "How Disney Snared a Princely Sum." *Business Week* (June 20, 1994), 61–62.

Rothenberg, Lawrence S. "Organizational Maintenance and the Retention Decision in Groups." *American Political Science Review* (December 1988), 1129–1152.

Rowe, Christopher. "Analysing Management Decision-Making: Further Thoughts After the Bradford Studies." *Journal of Management Studies* (January 1989), 29–46.

Runyan, David L. "The Group Risky-Shift Effect as a Function of Emotional Bonds, Actual Consequences, and Extent of Responsibility." *Journal of Personality and Social Psychology*, 29, No. 5 (1974), 670–676.

Russo, J. Edward, and Paul J. H. Schoemaker. "Managing Overconfidence." *Sloan Management Review* (Winter 1992), 7–17.

Ryan, Margaret. "Human Resource Management and the Politics of Knowledge: Linking the Essential Knowledge Base of the Organization to Strategic Decision Making." *Leadership & Organization Development Journal*, 16, No. 5, (1996), 3–10.

Ryan, William L. "Missile Crisis Rocked World Ten Years Ago." *Tacoma News Tribune* (October 22, 1972), B-3, B-4.

Sah, Raaj K. "Fallibility in Human Organizations and Political Systems." *Journal of Economic Perspectives* (Spring 1991), 67–88.

Salancik, Gerald R., and Jeffrey Pfeffer. "The Bases and Use of Power in Organizational Decision Making: The Case of a University." *Administrative Science Quarterly* (December 1974), 453–473.

Samuelson, William, and Richard Zelkhauser. "Status Quo Bias in Decision Making." *Journal of Risk and Uncertainty*, 1 (1988), 7–59.

Saseen, Jane. "Disney's Bungle Book." *International Management* (July–August 1993), 26–27.

———. "Mickey Mania." *International Management* (November 1989), 32–34.

Saunders, George B., and John L. Stanton. "Personality as Influencing Factor in Decision Making."

Organizational Behavior and Human Performance (April 1976), 241–257.

Scanlon, Burt K. "Make Sure Your Decisions Get Carried Out." *Business Management* (September 1967), 63–64.

Schein, Edgar H. "The Problem of Moral Education for the Business Manager." *Industrial Management Review*, 8 (1966), 3–14.

Schein, Virginia Ellen. "The Relationship Between Sex Role Stereotypes and Requisite Management Characteristics." *Journal of Applied Psychology*, 57, No. 2 (1973), 95–100.

———. "Sex-Role Stereotypes and Requisite Management Characteristics: A Replication." *Sex Roles*, No. 5 (1979), 561–570.

Schoemaker, Paul J. H. "Strategic Decisions in Organizations: Rational and Behavioural Views." *Journal of Management Studies* (January 1993), 107–129.

Schoemaker, Paul J. H., and J. Edward Russo. "A Pyramid of Decision Approaches." *California Management Review*, (Fall 1993), 9–31.

Schrenk, L. P. "Aiding the Decision Maker — A Decision Process Model." *Ergonomics*, 12 (July 1969), 543–557.

Schroeder, Harold E. "The Risky Shift as a General Choice Shift." *Journal of Personality and Social Psychology*, 27, No. 2 (1973), 279–300.

Schuler, Randall S. "A Role and Expectancy Perception Model of Participation in Decision Making." *Academy of Management Journal* (June 1980), 331–340.

Schwartz, H. S. "On the Psychodynamics of Organizational Disaster: The Case of the Space Shuttle Challenger." *The Columbian Journal of World Business*, 22 (Spring 1987), 59–67.

Schwenk, Charles R. "Conflict in Organizational Decision Making: An Exploratory Study of Its Effects in For-Profits and Not For Profit Organizations." *Management Science* (April 1990), 436–448.

Scimone, Diana. "Bonjour, Mickey Mouse." *Europe* (July–August 1989), 46–47.

Scodel, Alvin, Philburn Ratoosh, and J. Sayer Minos. "Some Personality Correlates of Decision Making Under Conditions of Risk." *Behavioral Science* (January 1959), 19–28.

Scott, Alexander. "The Lessons of the Iranian Raid for American Military Policy." *Armed Forces Journal International* (June 1980), 26ff.

Scott, William G., and David K. Hart. "The Moral Nature of Man in Organizations: A Comparative

Analysis." *Academy of Management Journal* (June 1971), 241–255.

Segal, Morley. "Organization and Environment: A Typology of Adaptability and Structure." *Public Administration Review* (May–June 1974), 212–220.

Sellers, Patricia. "Can He Keep Philip Morris Growing." *Fortune* (April 6, 1992), 86–92.

Senger, John. "Managers' Perceptions of Subordinates' Competence as a Function of Personal Value Orientations." *Academy of Management Journal*, 14 (December 1971), 415–423.

Shackle, G. L. S. "Decision: The Human Predicament." *Annals of the American Academy of Political and Social Science*, 412 (March 1974), 1–10.

Shapira, Zur. "Risk in Managerial Decision Making." Unpublished manuscript, Hebrew University, 1986.

Shapiro, Eben. "Cigarette Burn: Price Cut on Marlboro Upsets Rosy Notions About Tobacco Products." *Wall Street Journal* (April 6, 1993), B-3.

Sharkey, Betsy. "The Magic Kingdom." *Mediaweek* (August 7, 1995), 10–12.

Sharples, Brian. "Rational Decision-Making in Education: Some Concerns." *Educational Administration Quarterly*, 11 (Spring 1975), 55–65.

Shaw, Marvin E. "Acceptance of Authority, Group Structure, and Effectiveness of Small Groups." *Journal of Personality*, 27 (1959), 196–210.

Sherman, J. Daniel, et al. "Centralization of Decision Making and Accountability Based on Gender." *Group & Organization Studies*, 12, No. 4 (December 1987), 454–463.

Sherman, Stratford. "Why Disney Had to Buy ABC." *Fortune* (September 4, 1995), 80.

Sherwood, John J., and Florence M. Hoylman. "Individual versus Group Approaches to Decision Making." *Supervisory Management* (April 1978), 2–9.

Shirley, Robert C. "Limiting the Scope of Strategy: A Decision-Based Approach." *Academy of Management Review* (April 1982), 262–268.

"Should Taxpayers Bail Out Chrysler?" *U.S. News and World Report* (November 28, 1979), 99–100.

Shrode, William A., and Warren B. Brown. "A Study of Optimality in Recurrent Decision Making of Lower-Level Managers." *Academy of Management Journal*, 13 (December 1970), 389–401.

Shugan, Steven M. "The Cost of Thinking." *Journal of Consumer Research* (September 1980), 99–111.

Shuler, Cyril O. "How Good Are Decision Makers?" *Business Horizons*, 18 (April 1975), 89–93.

Shumway, C. R., et al. "Diffuse Decision-Making in Hierarchial Organizations: An Empirical Examination." *Management Science*, 21 (1975), 697–707.

Sieber, Joan E., and John T. Lanzetta. "Conflict and Conceptual Structure as Determinants of Decision-Making Behavior." *Journal of Personality*, 32 (December 1964), 622–641.

Siegel, Sheldon. "Level of Aspiration and Decision Making." *Psychological Review*, 64 (1957), 253–262.

Siegel, Sheldon, and Robert B. Zajonc. "Group Risk Taking in Professional Decisions." *Sociometry*, 30 (1967), 339–350.

Sikula, Andrew F. "The Values and Value Systems of Governmental Executives." *Public Personnel Management* (January–February 1973), 16–22.

———. "Values and Value Systems: Importance and Relationship to Managerial and Organizational Behavior." *Journal of Psychology*, 78 (July 1971), 277–286.

———. "Values, Value Systems, and Their Relationship to Organizational Effectiveness." In *Academy of Management Proceedings*, August 15–17, 1971.

Silver, William S., and Terence R. Mitchell. "The Status Quo Tendency in Decision Making." *Organizational Dynamics* (Spring 1990), 34–46.

Silverthorne, Colin P. "Information Input and the Group Shift Phenomenon in Risk Taking." *Journal of Personality and Social Psychology*, 20 (1973), 456–461.

Simon, Herbert A. "Administrative Decision Making." *Public Administration Review* (March 1965), 31–37.

———. "A Behavioral Model of Rational Choice." *Quarterly Journal of Economics*, 69 (February 1955), 99–118.

———. "Making Management Decisions: The Role of Intuition and Emotion." *Academy of Management Executive*, 1, No. 1 (February 1987), 57–64.

———. "On How to Decide What to Do." *Bell Journal of Economics* (Autumn 1978), 494–507.

———. "Organization Man: Rational or Self-Actualizing?" *Public Administration Review* (July–August 1973), 346–353.

———. "Rational Decision Making in Business Organizations." *American Economic Review* (September 1979), 493–513.

———. "Rationality." In *Models of Bounded Rationality: Behavioral Economics and Business Organization.* Vol. 2. Ed. Herbert A. Simon. Cambridge, Mass.: MIT Press, 1982, 318–355.

————. "Rationality as Process and as Product of Thought." *American Economic Review* (May 1978), 1–16.

————. "Technology and Environment." In *Emerging Concepts in Management.* 2nd ed. Eds. M. S. Wortman and F. Luthans. New York: Macmillan, 1975, 4–15.

————. "Theories of Decision-Making in Economics and Behavioral Science." In *Models of Bounded Rationality: Behavioral Economics and Business Organization.* Vol. 2. Ed. Herbert A. Simon. Cambridge, Mass.: MIT Press. 1982, 287–317.

————. "Theories of Bounded Rationality." In *Models of Bounded Rationality: Behavioral Economics and Business Organization.* Vol. 2. Ed. Herbert A. Simon. Cambridge, Mass.: MIT Press, 1982, 408–423..

Simon, Herbert A., and Michael Barenfeld. "Information-Processing Analysis of Perceptual Processes in Problem Solving." *Psychological Review,* 76 (1969), 473–483.

Simon, Herbert A., and A. Newell. "Heuristic Problem Solving: The Next Advance in Operations Research." *Operations Research* (January–February 1958), 1–10.

Simon, Walter B. "The Quest for Subjective Certainty." In *Management: A Decision-Making Approach.* Ed. Stanley Young. Belmont, Calif.: Dickenson, 1968.

Singer, J. David. "Inter-Nation Influence: A Formal Model." *American Political Science Review,* 57 (1963), 420–430.

Singer, Jerome L., and Dorothy G. Singer. "Personality." In *Annual Review of Psychology.* Eds. Paul H. Mussen and Mark R. Rosenzweig. Palo Alto, Calif.: Annual Reviews, 1972.

Singh, Jitendra V. "Performance, Slack, and Risk Taking in Organizational Decision Making." *Academy of Management Journal,* 29 (1986), 562–585.

Sinka, Deepak K. "The Contribution of Formal Planning to Decisions." *Strategic Management Journal* (1990), 479–492.

Slicter, Sumner H. "The Power Holders in the American Economy." *Saturday Evening Post* (18 December 1958), 34ff.

Slovic, Paul. *From Shakespeare to Simon: Speculations — and Some Evidence — About Man's Ability to Process Information.* Eugene: Oregon Research Institute, 1972.

Smith, Gerald F. "Towards a Theory of Managerial Problem Solving." *Decision Support Systems,* 8 (1992), 29–40.

Smith, Michael L. "Decision Making for Project Managers: When to Involve Others." *Project Management Journal,* 24 (June 1993), 17–22.

Smith, Steve. "Groupthink and the Hostage Rescue Mission." *British Journal of Political Science,* 15 (1984), 117–126.

Sniezek, Janet A. "Groups Under Uncertainty: An Examination of Confidence in Group Decision Making." *Organizational Behavior and Human Decision Process,* 52 (1992), 124–155.

Snyder, Glenn H. "Deterrence and Power." *Journal of Conflict Resolution* (June 1960), 163–178.

Snyder, Richard C. "A Decision-Making Approach to the Study of Political Phenomena." In *Approaches to the Study of Politics.* Ed. Roland Young. Evanston, Ill.: Northwestern University Press, 1958. pp. 3–38.

Soelberg, Peer. "Unprogrammed Decision Making." In *Studies in Managerial Process and Organizational Behavior.* Eds. John H. Turner, Allan C. Filley, and Robert H. House. Glenview, Ill.: Scott, Foresman, 1972, 135–144.

"Some Large Firms Find Operations Are Simplified by Group Takeover of the Chief Executive's Role." *Wall Street Journal* (July 7, 1972), 22.

Sondak, Arthur. "How to Answer the Question, 'What Should I Do?'." *Supervisory Management* (December 1992), 4–5.

Sparks, Debra. "Off to See the Wizards." *Financial World* (November 7, 1995), 28–33.

Springer, J. Fred. "Policy Analysis and Organizational Decisions." *Administration & Society,* 16, No. 4 (1985), 457–508.

Stagner, Ross. "Corporate Decision Making: An Empirical Study." *Journal of Applied Psychology* (February 1969), 1–13.

Stanley, T. L. "Definite Difference at Disney." *Mediaweek,* (April 22, 1996), 5–6.

Starbuck, W. H., and F. J. Milliken. "Challenger: Fine Tuning the Odds Until Something Breaks." *Journal of Management Studies,* 26 (July 1988), 319–340.

Stasser, Harold, et al. "Experts Roles and Information Exchange During Discussion: The Importance of Knowing Who Knows What." *Journal of Experimental Social Psychology,* 31 (1995), 244–265.

Staw, Barry M., and Frederick V. Fox. "Escalation: The Determinants of Commitment to a Chosen Course of Action." *Human Relations,* 30, No. 5 (1977), 431–450.

Steers, Richard M. "Individual Differences in Participative Decision Making." *Human Relations*, 30, No. 9 (1977), 837–847.

Stein, Jorge. "Strategic Decision Methods." *Human Relations*, 34, No. 11 (1981), 917–933.

Steinberg, Blema S. "Shame and Humiliation in the Cuban Missile Crisis." *Political Psychology*, 12 (1991), 653–690.

Stine, G. H. "The Dream Is Down." *Analog Science Fiction/Science Fact*, 107 (February 1987), 57–91.

Stockman, David A. "Chrysler Bailout: Regarding Failure?" *Wall Street Journal* (September 4, 1979), 15.

Stoner, J. A. F. "Risky and Cautious Shifts in Group Decisions: The Influence of Widely Held Values." *Journal of Experimental Social Psychology*, 4 (1968), 442–459.

Strasser, Steve, et al. "A Grim Postmortem Begins." *Newsweek* (May 12, 1980), 29ff.

Streufert, Siegfried. "Complexity and Complex Decision Making: Convergence Between Differentiation and Integration Approaches to the Prediction of Task Performance." *Journal of Experimental Social Psychology*, 6 (October 1970), 494–509.

———. "Individual Differences in Risk Taking." *Journal of Applied Social Psychology*, 16 (1986), 482–497.

———. "Success and Response Rate in Complex Decision Making." *Journal of Experimental Social Psychology*, 8 (September 1972), 382–403.

Streufert, Siegfried, and Carl H. Castore. "Information Search and the Effects of Failure: A Test of Complexity Theory." *Journal of Experimental Social Psychology*, 7 (January 1971), 125–143.

Streib, Gregory. "Applying Strategic Decision Making in Local Government." *Public Productivity and Management Review,* 15, No. 3 (Spring 1992), 341–353.

Stumph, Stephen A., and Roger L. M. Dunbar. "The Effects of Personality Type on Choices Made in Strategic Decision Situations." *Decision Sciences*, 22, No. 5 (November–December, 1991), 1047–1072.

Stumpf, Stephen A., Richard D. Freedman, and Dale E. Zand. "Judgmental Decisions: A Study of Interactions Among Group Membership, Group Functioning, and the Decision Situation." *Academy of Management Journal* (December 1979), 765–782.

Stumpf, Stephen A., Dale E. Zand, and Richard D. Freedman. "Designing Groups for Judgmental Decisions." *Academy of Management Review* (October 1979), 589–600.

Subramanian, S. K. "Technology, Productivity, and Organization." *Technological Forecasting and Social Change* (July 1987), 359–371.

Summers, Irvin, and Major David E. White. "Creativity Techniques: Toward Improvement of the Decision Process." *Academy of Management Review*, 1 (April 1976), 99–107.

Suppes, Patrick. "The Philosophical Relevance of Decision Theory." *Journal of Philosophy*, 58 (October 1961), 605–614.

Svenson, Ola. "Process Descriptions of Decision Making." *Organizational Behavior and Human Performance*, 23 (1979), 86–112.

———. "Some Propositions for the Classification of Decision Situations." In *Contemporary Issues in Decision Making*. Eds. K. Borcherding, O. I. Larichev, and D. M. Messick. New York: Elsevier Publishing Co., 1990, 149–157.

Szaniawski, Klemens. "Philosophy of Decision Making." *Acta Psychologica*, 45 (1980), 327–341.

Tattersall, Robert. "In Defense of the Consensus Decision." *Financial Analysts Journal* (January / February 1984), 55–67.

Taylor, Ronald N. "Age and Experience as Determinants of Managerial Information Processing and Decision Making Performance." *Academy of Management Journal*, 18 (March 1975), 74–81.

———. "Perceptions of Problem Constraints." *Management Science*, 22 (September 1975), 22–29.

———. "Psychological Determinants of Bounded Rationality: Implications for Decision-Making Strategies." *Decision Sciences*, 6 (July 1975), 409–429.

Taylor, Ronald N., and Marvin D. Dunnette. "Influence of Dogmatism, Risk-Taking, Propensity, and Intelligence on Decision-Making Strategies for a Sample of Industrial Managers." *Journal of Applied Psychology*, 59, No. 4 (1974), 420–423.

———. "Relative Contribution of Decision-Maker Attributes to Decision Processes." *Organizational Behavior and Human Performance*, 12 (October 1974), 286–298.

Teger, A. I., and D. G. Pruitt. "Components of Group Risk Taking." *Journal of Experimental Social Psychology*, 3 (1967), 189–205.

Tersine, Richard J., and Walter E. Riggs. "The Delphi Technique: A Long-Range Planning Tool." *Business Horizons*, 19 (April 1976), 51–56.

"The Company Eisner Keeps." *Mediaweek* (August 7, 1995), 14–22.

"The Jimmy Carter Desert Classic." *New Republic* (May 10, 1980), 7–9.

"The Kingdom Inside a Republic." *Economist* (April 13, 1996), 66–67.

"The Lessons of the Cuban Missile Crisis." *Time* (September 27, 1982), 85.

"The Politics of Decision Making." *Meeting & Conventions* (October 1986), 42–54.

The Walt Disney 131 Company. *1996 Annual Report.* Burbank, Calif.: 1996.

Thomas, Edwin J., and Clinton F. Fink. "Effects of Group Size." *Psychological Bulletin*, 60, No. 4 (1963), 371–384.

Thompson, Howard E. "Management Decisions in Perspective." In *Management in Perspective*. Eds. William E. Schlender, William G. Scott, and Alan C. Filley. Boston: Houghton Mifflin, 1965.

Thompson, James D., and Arthur Tuden. "Strategies, Structures, and Processes of Organizational Decision." In *Comparative Studies in Administration*. Eds. James D. Thompson et al. Pittsburgh: University of Pittsburgh Press, 1959. 195–216.

Timm, Paul R. "Let's Not Have a Meeting." *Supervisory Management* (August 1982), 2–7.

Tjosvold, Dean. "Effects of Shared Responsibility and Goal Interdependence on Controversy and Decisionmaking Between Departments." *Journal of Social Psychology* (February 1988), 7–18.

Toda, Masanao. "Emotion and Decision Making." *Acta Psychologica*, 45 (1980), 133–155.

———. "The Decision Process: A Perspective." *International Journal of General Systems*, 3 (1976), 79–88.

Toy, Stewart, and Paula Dwyer. "Is Disney Headed for the Euro-Trash Heap?" *Business Week* (January 24, 1994), 32.

Toy, Stewart, et al. "The Mouse Isn't Roaring." *Business Week* (April 24, 1992), 38.

"Tragedy in the Desert — Rescue That Failed." *U.S. News & World Report* (May 5, 1980), 6–7.

Trevino, Linda Klebe. "Ethical Decision Making in Organizations: A Person-Situation Interactionist Model." *Academy of Management Review*, 11 (1986), 601–617.

Trull, Samuel G. "Some Factors Involved in Determining Total Decision Success." *Management Science* (February 1966), B-270–B-280.

Tushman, Michael L. "A Political Approach to Organizations: A Review and Rationale." *Academy of Management Review* (April 1977), 206–216.

Tversky, A. "Elimination by Aspects: A Theory of Choice." *Psychology Review*, 79 (1972), 281–299.

U.S. Congress, House, Committee on Foreign Affairs. *Use of U.S. Armed Forces in Attempted Rescue of Hostages in Iran.* Communication from the President of the United States, 96th Congress, 2nd Sess., April 26, 1980. Washington, D.C.: U.S. Government Printing Office, 1980.

U.S. Congress, Senate, Committee on Foreign Relations. *The Situation in Iran.* Hearings, 96th Congress, 2nd Sess., May 8, 1980. Washington, D.C.: U.S. Government Printing Office, 1980.

U.S. Congress, House, Report No. 99-1016. *Investigation of the Challenger Accident.* 99th Congress, 2nd Sess., 1986, Washington, D.C.: U.S. Government Printing Office, 1986.

U.S. Congress, Senate, Subcommittee on Science, Technology, and Space of the Committee on Commerce, Science, and Transportation. *Space Shuttle Accident.* Hearings, 99th Congress, 2nd Sess., February 18, June 10 and 17, 1986. Washington, D.C.: U.S. Government Printing Office, 1986.

U.S. Congress, House, Committee on Banking, Finance and Urban Affairs, Subcommittee on Economic Stabilization. *The Chrysler Corporation Financial Situation.* Hearings, 96th Congress, 1st Sess., October 30, November 1, 7, and 13, 1979. Washington, D.C.: U.S. Government Printing Office, 1979.

U.S. Congress, Senate, Committee on Banking, Housing, and Urban Affairs. *Chrysler Corporation Loan Guarantee Act of 1979.* Hearings, 96th Congress, 1st Sess., November 14 and 15, 1979. Washington, D.C.: U.S. Government Printing Office, 1979.

van der Merwe, A., and S. van der Merwe. "Strategic Leadership of the Chief Executive." *Long-Range Planning*, 18 (1985), 100–111.

van der Merwe, Sandra. "What Personal Attributes It Takes to Make It in Management." *Business Quarterly* (Winter 1978), 28–35.

Van de Ven, Andrew H., and André L. Delbecq. "The Effectiveness of Nominal, Delphi, and Interactive Group Decision Making Processes." *Academy of Management Journal*, 17 (December 1974), 605–621.

———. "Nominal Versus Interacting Group Processes for Committee Decision-Making Effectiveness." *Academy of Management Journal*, 14 (June 1971), 203–212.

Van Meter, Larry. "Lead Before Managing — The Team Concept Approach." *Business Credit,* (June 1995), 9–10.

Vaughn, D. "Autonomy, Interdependence, and Social Control: NASA and the Space Shuttle Challenger." *Administrative Science Quarterly*, 35 (June 1990), 225–257.

Vidmar, Neil. "Group Composition and the Risky Shift." *Journal of Experimental Social Psychology*, 6 (April 1970), 153–166.

Vinokur, Amiram. "Cognitive and Affective Processes Influencing Risk-Taking in Groups: An Expected Utility Approach." *Journal of Personality and Social Psychology*, 20 (1971), 472–486.

———. "Distribution of Initial Risk Levels and Group Decisions Involving Risk." *Journal of Personality and Social Psychology*, 13 (November 1969), 207–214.

———. "Review and Theoretical Analysis of the Effects of Group Processes upon Individual and Group Decisions Involving Risk." *Psychological Bulletin*, 76 (October 1971), 231–250.

Vinokur, Amiram, and Eugene Burnstein. "Effects of Partially Shared Persuasive Arguments on Group-Induced Shift: A Group Problem-Solving Approach." *Journal of Personality and Social Psychology*, 29 (1974), 305–315.

Vinokur, Amiram, S. Katz, and J. Crowley. "Risky Shift Is Eminently Rational." *Journal of Personality and Social Psychology*, 20 (1973), 462–471.

Vroom, V. H., and P. W. Yetton. *Leadership Behavior on Standardized Cases*. Technical Report No. 3. New Haven: Yale University Press, 1973.

Waddell, William C. "Values: A Challenge to a Science of Management." *University of Washington Business Review*, 29 (Winter 1970), 28–39.

Wadia, Maneck S. "Management and the Behavioral Sciences: A Conceptual Scheme." *California Management Review* (Fall 1965), 65–72.

Wagner, Grace. "It's a Small World After All." *Lodging Hospitality* (April 1992), 26–31.

Walker, Angela. "Euro Disney Woes Likely to Continue After Fiscal Boosts." *Hotel & Management* (July 5, 1994), 1 and 32.

Wall, Victor D., Jr., Gloria J. Galanes, and Sue Beth Love. "Small, Task-Oriented Groups: Conflict, Conflict Management, Satisfaction, and Decision Quality." *Small Group Behavior* (February 1987), 31–55.

Wallach, Michael A. "Group Influence on Individual Risk Taking." *Journal of Abnormal and Social Psychology*, 65 (1962), 75–86.

Wallach, Michael A., and Nathan Kogan. "Sex Differences and Judgment Processes." *Journal of Personality*, 27 (1959), 555–564.

———. "Aspects of Judgment and Decision Making: Interrelationships and Changes with Age." *Behavioral Science*, 6 (1961), 23–36.

Wallach, Michael A., and Cliff W. Wing, Jr. "Is Risk a Value?" *Journal of Personality and Social Psychology*, 9 (1986), 101–106.

Wallach, Michael A., Nathan Kogan, and D. J. Bem. "Diffusion of Responsibility and Level of Risk Taking in Groups." *Journal of Abnormal and Social Psychology*, 68 (1964), 263–274.

Wallach, Michael A., Nathan Kogan, and Roger B. Burt. "Are Risk Takers More Persuasive Than Conservatives in Group Decisions?" *Journal of Experimental Social Psychology*, 4 (1968), 76–89.

Walton, Richard E., and John Dutton. "The Management of Interdepartmental Conflict: A Model and Review." *Administrative Science Quarterly* (March 1969), 73–84.

Walton, Richard E., and Robert B. McKersie. "Behavioral Dilemmas in Mixed-Motive Decision Making." *Behavioral Science*, 11, No. 5 (1966), 370–384.

"Was the Chrysler Bailout Worth It?" *Business Week* (May 2, 1985), 23ff.

Waterman, Robert H., Jr. "The Seven Elements of Strategic Fit." *Journal of Business Strategy* (Winter 1982), 68–72.

Watson, G. B. "Do Groups Think More Efficiently Than Individuals?" *Journal of Abnormal and Social Psychology*, 3 (1928), 328–336.

Watson, John G., and Sam Barone. "The Self-Concept, Personal Values, and Motivational Orientations of Black and White Managers." *Academy of Management Journal*, 19 (March 1976), 36–48.

Watson, Sharon G. "Judgment of Emotion from Facial and Contextual Cue Combinations." *Journal of Personality and Social Psychology*, 24, No. 3 (1972), 334–342.

Weber, C. E. Edward. "Strategic Thinking — Dealing with Uncertainty." *Long-Range Planning*, 17 (1984), 60–70.

Weber, James. "Managers' Moral Reasoning: Assessing Their Responses to Three Moral Dilemmas." *Human Relations*, 43 (1990), 687–707.

Wegner, Daniel M. "Transactive Memory: A Contemporary Analysis of the Group Mind." In *Theories of Group Behavior*. Eds. Jon B. Mullen and G. R. Goethals. New York: Springer-Verlag, 1987, 185–208.

Wehman, Paul, Melvin A. Goldstein, and Jeral R. Williams. "Effects of Different Leadership Styles on Individual Risk-Taking in Groups." *Human Relations*, 30 (March 1977), 249–259.

Weinstein, Malcolm S. "Achievement Motivation and Risk Preference." *Journal of Personality and Social Psychology*, 13 (October 1969), 153–172.

Weir, M. W. "Developmental Changes in Problem-Solving Strategies." *Psychological Review*, 71 (1964), 473–490.

Weiss, Janet A. "Coping with Complexity: An Experimental Study of Public Policy Decision-Making." *Journal of Policy Analysis and Management*, 2, No. 1 (1982), 66–67.

Weitzel, William, and Ellen Johnson. "Reversing the Downward Spiral: Lessons from W. T. Grant and Sears Roebuck." *The Executive* (August 1991), 7–22.

Welch, David A. "Crisis Decision Making Reconsidered." *Journal of Conflict Resolution* (September 1989), 430–445.

Whitely, William, and George W. England. "Managerial Values as a Reflection of Culture and the Process of Industrialization." *Academy of Management Journal*, 20 (September 1976), 439–453.

Whyte, Glen. "Decision Fiascoes: Why They Occur and How to Prevent Them." *The Executive* (August 1991), 23–31.

———. "Groupthink Reconsidered." *The Academy of Management Review* (January 1989), 40–56.

Wiberg, Hakan. "Rational and Non-Rational Models of Man." In *The Context of Social Psychology: A Critical Assessment*. Eds. Joachim Israel and Henri Tajfel. New York: Academic Press, 1972.

Wicklund, Robert A., and William J. Ickes. "The Effect of Objective Self-Awareness on Predecisional Exposure to Information." *Journal of Experimental Social Psychology*, 8 (July 1972), 378–387.

Wiesenfeld, Batia M. "Group Esteem: Positive Collective Evaluations in Task-Oriented Groups." Chicago: Center for Decision Research, University of Chicago, 1997.

Wiest W. M., L. W. Porter, and E. E. Ghiselli. "Relationship Between Individual Proficiency and Team Performance and Efficiency." *Journal of Applied Psychology*, 45 (1961), 435–440.

Wildavsky, Aaron. "Information as an Organizational Problem." *Journal of Management Studies* (January 1983), 29–40.

Willems, Edwin P., and Russell D. Clark, III. "Shift Toward Risk and Heterogeneity of Groups." *Journal of Experimental Social Psychology*, 7 (May 1971), 304–312.

Williams Edward E., and Finellay M. Chapman, III. "A Reconsideration of the Rationality Postulate: 'Right Hemisphere Thinking' in Economics." *American Journal of Economics and Sociology*, 40 (1981), 17.

Williams, Lawrence K. "Some Correlates of Risk Taking." *Personnel Psychology*, 18 (Autumn 1965), 297–310.

Williams, R. M., Jr. "Individual and Group Values." *Annals of the American Academy of Political and Social Science* (May 1967), 20–25.

Wilmotte, Raymond M., and Philip I. Morgan. "The Discipline Gap in Decision Making." *Managerial Review* (September 1984), 21–24.

Wilson, Charles Z., and Marcus Alexis. "Basic Frameworks for Decisions." *Journal of the Academy of Management* (August 1962), 150–164.

Wilson, Timothy D., et al. "Introspecting About Reasons Can Reduce Post-Choice Satisfaction." *Personality and Social Psychology Bulletin.* 19, No. 3 (June 1993), 331–339.

Winston, George C. "Imperfectly Rational Choice." *Journal of Economic Behavior and Organization*, 12 (1989), 67–86.

Wiseman, Robert M., and Philip Bromiley. "Risk-Return Associations: Paradox or Artifact? An Empirically Tested Explanation." *Strategic Management Journal*, 12 (1991), 231–241.

Witte, Eberhard. "Field Research on Complex Decision-Making Processes — The Phase Theorem." *International Studies of Management and Organization* (Summer 1972), 156–182.

Wohlstetter, Roberta. "Cuba and Pearl Harbor: Hindsight and Foresight." *Foreign Affairs* (July 1965), 691–707.

Wohlstetter, Roberta, and Albert Wohlstetter. "Controlling the Risk in Cuba." *Adelphi Papers* (April 1965), 3–24.

"Women Directors Seen But Not Heard on Management Succession & Executive Compensation, Study Reports." Press Release. New York: Korn/Ferry International, October 21, 1997.

Worth, Leila F., Scott T. Allison, and David M. Messick. "Impact of a Group Decision on Perception of One's Own and Others' Attitudes." *Journal of Personality and Social Psychology* (October 1987), 673–682.

Wright, George. "Decisional Variance." In *Behavioral Decision Making*. Ed. George Wright. New York: Plenum Press, 1985.

———. "Organizational, Group, and Individual Decision Making in Cross-Cultural Perspective. In *Behavioral Decision Making*. Ed. George Wright. New York: Plenum Press, 1985.

Wright, Peter. "The Harassed Decision Maker: Time Pressures, Distractions, and the Use of Evidence." *Journal of Applied Psychology*, 59 (1974), 555–561.

Wright, William F. "Cognitive Information Processing Biases: Implications for Producers and Users of Financial Information." *Decision Sciences*, 11 (April 1980), 284–298.

Wrubel, Robert. "Le Defi Mickey Mouse." *Financial World.* (October 1989), 18 and 21.

Zajonc, Robert B., Robert J. Wolosin, and Myrna A. Wolosin. "Group Risk-Taking Under Various Group Decision Schemes." *Journal of Experimental Social Psychology*, 8 (January 1972), 16–30.

———. "Group Risk-Taking Under Various Group Decision Schemes." *Journal of Experimental Social Psychology* (May 1972), 260–265.

Zakay, Dan, and Stuart Wooler. "Time Pressure, Training and Decision Effectiveness." *Ergonomics*, 27 (1984), 273–284.

Zaleska, Maryla. "Individual and Group Choices Among Solutions of a Problem When Solution Verifiability Is Moderate or Low." *European Journal of Social Psychology*, 8 (1978), 37–53.

Zaleznik, Abraham. "Power and Politics in Organizational Life." *Harvard Business Review* (May–June 1970), 47–60.

Zalkind, Sheldon S., and Timothy W. Costello. "Perceptions: Some Recent Research and Implications for Administration." *Administrative Science Quarterly* (September 1962), 218–235.

Ziller, R, C. "Group Size: A Determinant of Quality and Stability of Group Decisions." *Sociometry*, 20 (1957), 165–173.

Index

Abbasi, S.M., 120
ABC, *see* Walt Disney Company
Abdel-Halim, A.A., 267
Abegglen, J.C., 289
Ability
  characteristics of decision maker, 60
  cognitive strain, 94–95
  simplified cognitive structures, 87
Abramms, R., 130
Academic sector
  managerial class, 286
  participatory decision making, 267
Acceptance, social, 217
Acceptance of decision
  group behavior/dynamics, 223, 233
  group decision making, 254–255, 257
    decision making criteria, 238, 240t
    participatory decision making, 264, 268
Accountability
  decision task, 60
  managerial objectives, characteristics of, 45
  participatory decision making, 265
  see also Responsibility
Acquired values, 119
Action
  commitment to, 134
  corrective, *see* Corrective action
  group decision making, 14
  models of decision making, 150
  process of decision making, 37
  strategic management, 321
Adaptability, participatory decision making and, 267
Adaptation, group behavior/dynamics, 217
Adaptive decisions, 20, 234t, 235
Adaptive (political) model of decision making, 152t, 155–158, 296, 297–300
Adaptive process, problem solving as, 13
Adler, A., 178

Administration
  levels of decision making, 7–8
  values for, 125
Administrative theory, 96
Adopted values, 121
Aesthetic persons, 122
Affective models, 255
Age
  and cognitive strain, 95
  group behavior/dynamics, 224
Aggression
  managerial values, 123t
  psychology, 162
  see also Personality
Aguilar, F.G., 47
Albers, H.H., 8
Alexis, M., 46, 88, 90
Alienative membership, 218, 222
Allen, R.W., 292, 293
Allison, G.T., 149, 296
Allport, G., 117
Alternatives
  choosing among, *see* Choice
  complexity and decision time, 188
  group behavior/dynamics, 233
    deindividuation and, 252
    groupthink, 231
  interdisciplinary perspective, 26
    economics and statistics, 166, 167
    philosophy, 161
    sociology and social psychology, 163
  managerial decision making, 25
  models of decision making
    organizational, 155
    political model, 157
    rational, 150, 153
  open decision model, 90
  process of decision making, 37
  rational decision making, 76
    cognitive limitations and, 87
    optimal versus satisfactory, 90
    satisficing behavior, 96
  strategic, 321
  strategic decision success, 347

types of decision making
  group decision making, 14
  individual decision making, 12, 13
  organizational decision making, 16
value judgements, 113, 136
Alternatives, comparison and evaluation of, 10
  decision making, components of, 39
  group decision making, 257
  process model elements, 40f, 50–55
    anticipation of outcomes, 54–55
    multidimensional perspectives, 51–53
    typology of alternatives, 53
  strategic decision-making case sets
    Challenger disaster, 427–429
    Chrysler bailout, 419–422
    Cuban missile crisis, 379–380
    Disney, 1990, 475–476
    Disney, 1995, 482–483
    General Motors, 451–452
    Philip Morris, 459
Alternatives, evaluation and selection of
  psychology
    perception, 201
    personality characteristics, 183
  sociology and social psychology, 163
  values and, 127
Alternatives, search for
  decision making, components of, 38–39
  group decision making, 257
  process model elements, 45–50, 40f
    cost of additional information, 49–50
    imperfections in, 45–46
    perspectives on, 46–47
    structure of, 47–49
  strategic decision-making case sets
    Challenger disaster, 426–427
    Chrysler bailout, 417–417

Alternatives, search for (*continued*)
    Cuban missile crisis, 378–379
    Disney, 1990, 475
    Disney, 1995, 482
    General Motors, 451
    Philip Morris, 458
    strategic decision success, 356
Ambiguity, decision task, 60
American Express, 361
American Management Association
    (AMA) surveys, 124–125, 126,
    270
Analysis
    cause-effect relationships, 30
    cognitive limitations, 87
    evaluation of alternatives, 52–53
    group decision making, 14
    individual decision making, 12
    intuition and, 204
    mathematics and, 167–169
    organizational decision making,
    15
    political model, 157
Analytical decision making, 204
Analytic model, 149
Anderson, D.F., 149
Anthony, R.N., 85
Anthropology, 160f, 161–165
Apple Computer, 361, 362
Argyris, C., 183
Aristotle, 75
Arroba, T.Y., 184
Aspect, 13
Aspiration level
    cognitive strain, 95
    individual decision making, 13,
    162
    open decision model, 90, 92–93
    psychology, 162
    and risk acceptance/avoidance,
    188–189
    satisficing behavior, 89, 90, 90, 91
    and search activity, 48
    strategic decision success, 357
Atkinson, J.W., 188
AT&T, 361
Attitudes, 24, 301
    change, resistance to, 28
    group behavior/dynamics
    and conformity, 219
    norms, 218–220
    participatory decision making,
    264
    power, 301

Attitudes of managers toward
    decision-making process
    comparison of case sets
    Challenger disaster and Chrysler
    bailout, 434–436
    General Motors and Philip
    Morris, 464–465
    Disney, 488
    strategic decision success, 355–357
Attitudes of managers toward
    decisions
    comparison of case sets
    Challenger disaster and Chrysler
    bailout, 436–437
    Disney, 488–489
    General Motors and Philip
    Morris, 465–466
    strategic decision success, 357–359
Attractiveness
    group behavior/dynamics, 215,
    217, 218
    referent power, 283–284
Authority
    entrepreneurs versus managers
    and, 121
    implementation of decision, 61–62,
    62f
    personality and, 185
    and values, 114
Autonomy, managerial power elites,
    299–300
Average-value curve, 49f, 50
Avoidance of conflict, 262
Axioms
    models of decision making, 150
    utility theory, 54

Bahm, A.J., 118
Bale, R.F., 216–217
Banks, 307
Bargaining, 52
Barnett, J.H., 271
Bass, B.M., 6, 15, 39
Baumol, W.J., 82, 83
Bavelas, A., 224
Bay area study, 345, 348, 349, 349t,
    351, 352, 353, 354, 365, 401,
    461, 462, 463, 487
Becker, B.W., 125
Behavior
    group, *see* Group behavior and
    dynamics; Social psychology
    power, 282

Behavioral disciplines
    decision theory, 9
    interdisciplinary approaches to
    decision making, 159–165,
    160f, 169–170
    combined with quantitative
    disciplines, 169–170
    law, anthropology, and political
    science, 160f, 161–165
    philosophy, 160–161, 160f
    psychology, 160f, 161–162
    sociology and social psychology,
    160f, 162–164
Behavioral model, group behavior/
    dynamics, 234t, 235
Beliefs
    cognitive strain, 95
    group behavior/dynamics, 214
    and conformity, 219
    groupthink, 229–231
    individuals in groups, 250
    nonrational decision making,
    77–78
Bergen, J.R., 194
Berle, A.A. Jr., 307
Bernthal, W.F., 17, 114, 115, 116
Bias
    creeping determinism, 200–201
    group decision making, 251
    organizational decision making, 16
    perceptions, 199, 200
    search activity, 45, 46, 47
    stereotyping, 196, 197–198, 199, 270
    subconscious elements, 202
Biology
    and perception, 195
    and personality, 177–178
Bird, F. 119, 130
Bishoprick, D.W., 148
Bland alternatives, 53
Blau, P.M., 215
Bloch, E., 332
Boards of directors, constraints on
    managerial power, 305, 306
Boulgarides, J.D., 221
Boundaries
    scope of decision making, 11f
    strategic decision making, open
    environmental system, 324,
    324f
Bounded rationality, 94, 96, 97, 97f,
    98, 363
    interlocking decision making, 27
    time and, 349

Boxx, W.R., 120
Boycotts, constraints on managerial power, 307
Braverman, J.D., 5
Brenglemann, J.C., 188
Brenner, O.C., 269
Brim, O.C. Jr., 181–182
Brown, J.S., 189
Bruner, J.S., 197
Bureaucratic politics model, 149
Burnham, J., 285, 286, 288, 289

Calvinist ethic, 120, 126
Capability profile, 331–332
    Chrysler, 414–415
    Disney, 1990, 472, 473
Capital
    acceptable profit level, 87
    constraints on managerial power, 307
Capital Cities/ABC, see Walt Disney Company
Carter, J., see Chrysler bailout; Iranian hostage crisis
Castro, F., see Cuban missile crisis
Category I decisions, 30
    attributes and properties, 21, 21t
    group behavior/dynamics, 234t, 235
    group decision making, 254
    locus of choice, 22–23
    models of decision making, classical, 155
    participatory decision making and, 264–265
Category II decisions, 30, 42
    attributes and properties, 21, 21t
    choice, 56
    group, 226, 234t, 235
    group decision making, 254
    judgmental mode in, 52–53
    locus of decision making, 23–24
    properties of, 25
    value judgement in, 135–136
Cause-effect relationships, 30, 87
Cecil, E., 254
Centralized networks, 224–225, 225f, 226
Certainty
    locus of decision making, 23
    predictability of outcomes, 54–55
    routine decisions, 21. See also Category I decisions
    typology of decisions, 30

Chain network, 224–225, 225f
Challenger disaster, 425–437
    comparison with Chrysler bailout
        classification of success, 433–437
        determinants of success, 430–433
    decision-making process, 425–430
        alternatives, comparison and evaluation of, 427–429
        alternatives, search for, 426–427
        choice, 429
        follow-up and control, 430
        implementation, 429–430
        objectives, 426
    groupthink, 231
Change, 24, 25, 28
    managerial values, 123t
    organizational decision making, 16
    personality and, 185
    uncertainty, 328, 329
Chase Manhattan Bank, 362
Chemical Bank, 362
Chiu, J.S.Y., 83
Choice
    complexity and decision time, 188
    decision making, components of, 39, 40
    definitions of decision making, 5–6
    ethics, 130
    group decision making, 233–235, 234t, 238, 251
        composite approach, 257
        risky shift phenomenon, 256
    groupthink and, 231
    individual decision making, 12
    interdisciplinary framework
        economics and statistics, 166, 167
        philosophy, 161
    intuitive, 203–204
    justification of, 55
    managerial decision making, 25
    models of decision making
        political model, 157
        rational, 150
    participation in decision making and, 264
    process model elements, 40f, 55–60
        characteristics of, 59–60
        models of, 57–59
        multidimensional perspectives, 56–57
    process of decision making, 37, 38, 38

psychology
    perception, 201
    personality characteristics, 181, 182–183
strategic decision-making case sets
    Challenger disaster, 429
    Chrysler bailout, 422–423
    Cuban missile crisis, 380–381
    Disney, 1990, 476–477
    Disney, 1995, 483
    General Motors, 452
    Philip Morris, 459
strategic management, 321
subconscious elements, 203
values and, 112, 113, 128, 132
Chrysler bailout, 410–425, 430–437
    chronology, 413–414t
    comparison with *Challenger* disaster
        classification of success, 433–437
        determinants of success, 430–433
    decision-making process, 416–424
        alternatives, comparison and evaluation of, 419–422
        alternatives, search for, 417–417
        choice, 422–423
        follow-up and control, 424
        implementation, 423–424
        objectives, 416–417
    strategic gap, 412, 414–415
        environmental assessment, 415
        gap analysis, 415
        organizational assessment, 414–415
Churchman, C.W., 116
Circle network, 225, 225f
Clarkson, G.P.E., 235, 236
Classical economic theory, 351. *See also* Maximizing behavior
Classical model, 149, 150–151, 152t, 153, 157
Closed decision models, 355–356
    evaluative concepts, 364
    maximizing behavior and, 92
    strategic decision matrix, 357, 359f
Closure, perceptual process, 193
Closure axiom, 54, 150
Coca-Cola, 362
Code, ethical, 131
Coercive power, 283
Cognitive hypotheses, risky shift phenomenon, 255

Cognitive abilities/limitations
  group behavior/dynamics
    characteristics of effective
      groups, 229, 229f
    size of group and, 223
  group decision making, 251
  and judgement, 134
  open model, 356
  personality characteristics and,
    181, 182
  rational decision making, 150
    bounded rationality concept, 97,
      97f, 98–99
    maximizing behavior, 86
    satisficing behavior, 91, 99
  simplification of models, 46
  see also Information; Intelligence
Cognitive media of search, 48
Cognitive model, 149
Cognitive strain, 13, 94–95
Cognitive style (decision style), 61,
  184–185
Cohen, M.D., 149, 225
Collins, O.F., 121
Communication
  group behavior/dynamics, 214,
    216, 217, 224–226, 225f, 233,
    234t
    characteristics of effective
      groups, 227
    conflict, 259
    groupthink, 230
    participatory decision making,
      268
  satisficing behavior, 96
  sociology and social psychology,
    164
  of values, 112
Competence
  characteristics of decision maker, 60
  distinctive, 331
  and group decision quality, 251
Competence values, 119f, 120
Competition, economic, 97, 97f
  Chrysler bailout justification, 416
  constraints on managerial power,
    307
  Eurodisney, 478
Competition, interpersonal, 228
Completely connected network,
  225f, 226
Complexity
  bounded rationality concept, 98
  decision task, 60

and decision time, 188
  group decision making, 14
  individual decision making, 13
  models of decision making, 150
  organizational decision making, 15
  strategic decision making, 328
Compromise, conflict management,
  262
Compromise strategy, 20, 20f, 30
Computational decision making
  evaluative concepts, 363
  strategic decision making success,
    358
  strategic decision matrix, 359f
Computational strategy, 20, 20f, 30
Conceptual generality of values, 117
Conceptual model
  conflict, 259f
  group behavior/dynamics, 233
Conceptual nature of values, 117
Conditioned viewing, structure of
  search activity, 47
Conflict, 258–262, 259f
  determinants of, 259–260, 259f
  group behavior/dynamics, 217
    conformity, 219
    decision making, 236
    size of group and, 223
  group decision making, 238, 240t
  indicators of, 259f, 260–261
  managerial values, 123t
  nature of, 258–259, 259f
  perceptions, 199, 200
  personality and, 185
  politics in formal organizations,
    293
  personality and, 185
  sociology and social psychology,
    163
  treatment of, 259f, 261–262
  values and, 112
Conflict avoidance, 262
Conflicts of interest
  implementation of decision, 62f
  maximizing behavior, 85
Conformity
  group norms, 218–220
  managerial values, 123t
Conjunctive model of choice, 59
Connor, P.E., 125
Consensus
  domain, 325
  group behavior/dynamics, 214,
    215, 216

characteristics of effective
  groups, 229, 229f
  groupthink, 229–231
  norms, 218–220
  size of group and, 222–223
  group decision making, 236, 251
  implementation of decision, 61
  time to decision, 251
Consensus, interpersonal, 214, 215,
  216
Conservatism, group decision
  making, 255
Constituencies, 158. *See also*
  Stakeholders
Constraints
  operating, 348–349, 349t, 364
  on power, 304–308
    operating, 305–308
    theoretical, 304–305
  values as, 114
Content categories, perception, 194
Continental Oil, 362
Contingency model of choice, 59–60
Contingency planning, groupthink
  and, 231
Control
  group behavior/dynamics, 217
  locus of decision making, 23
  mathematics and, 169
  organizational decision making,
    16, 17
  personality and, 185
  see also Follow-up and control
Cooperation, characteristics of
  effective groups, 227
Cornell, A.H., 6, 7, 61
Corollary flow, strategic decision
  making, 337f, 338
Corrective action, 41, 347
  follow-up and control phase, 65
  organizational decision making,
    17
  strategic decision success, 347
Costello, T.W., 5, 195
Cost of additional information, 48,
  49–50
Costs
  managerial objectives and, 45
  rational decision making, 77
  see also Time and cost constraints
Costs/benefits
  Chrysler bailout, 419
  outcomes, 55
Cravens, D.W., 48–49

Creative decisions, 19, 21, 21t, 234t, 235. *See also* Category II decisions
Creativity
  group behavior/dynamics
    communication networks, 226
    theories, 232
  see also Innovation
Creeping determinism, 200
Criteria, group decision making, 238
Criteria set, 38
Criticism, 227
Crozier, R., 346
Cuban missile crisis, 296, 374–386, 376–377t, 397–403
  comparison with Iranian hostage crisis, 397–403
  decision making models, 149
  decision making process, 378–382
    alternatives, comparison and evaluation of, 379–380
    alternatives, search for, 378–379
    choice, 380–381
    follow-up and control, 382
    implementation, 381–382
    objectives, 378
  decision matrix, 384t
  evaluation of, 383–385, 384t
Cues, stereotyping, 197–198
Culture, 17
  ethical judgements, 129
  Eurodisney and, 477
  and maximizing behavior, 86
  and perception, 195
  power, managerial decision making, 301
  power elites, managerial decision makers, 302
Cummings, L.L., 61, 188
Cybernetic model, 149
Cyert, R.M., 45, 154, 297

Dahrendorf, R., 300
Dalkey, N., 237
Dando, M.R., 346
Dearborn, D.C., 200
Death instincts (Freudian model), 177
Decision, judgement versus, 134
Decision maker influence
  strategic decision case sets
    Challenger disaster, 432
    Disney, 1995, 486
    General Motors versus Philip Morris, 462–463

strategic decision making success, 365
  and strategic decision success, 62, 63f
Decision making process, 3–31
  decision theory, 9–10
  definitions, 4, 5
  entrepreneurs versus managers, 121
  as generic process, 8–9
  locus of choice, 22–24
  managerial aspects of, 24–25
  perspectives on, 25–28
    integrative, 26
    interdisciplinary, 26–27
    interlocking, 27
    interrelational, 27–28
  practice of, 28
  problem solving versus decision making, 5–6
  profile of decision, 4–5
  scope of, 10–18
  significance of decision making, 6–8
  typology of decisions, 18–22, 20f, 21t
  see also Process model
Decision matrix, Cuban missile crisis, 384t
Decision rule, 56, 90
Decisions
  manager attitudes toward, *see* Attitudes of managers toward decisions
  strategic management, 321
Decision styles, 61, 184–185
Decision theory, 9–10, 147
  comparing and evaluating alternatives, 52–53
  individual decision making and, 12
  typology of decisions, 18–22, 20f
Decision time
  group decision making, 251
  participation in decision making and, 264
  strategic decision quality, 349–350, 349t
  see also Time and cost constraints
Defense, perceptual, 199
Definitions, 4, 5
Deindividuation, 252, 255
Delbecq, A.L., 19, 61, 116, 237
Delphi group, 237, 239, 240t, 241
Dent, J.K., 122, 123
Determinism, creeping, 200

Deterministic models, 169
Development, strategic decisions, 321
Dickson, J.W., 268
Diffusion of responsibility hypothesis, 255
Discretion, bounded, 96
Disjointed incrementalism, 157
Disjunctive model of choice, 59
Disney, *see* Walt Disney Company
Dogma, 129, 130
Dogmatism, 95, 201
Doktor, R.H., 61
Domain consensus, 325
Domains
  environmental, 324–325
  strategic decisions, 321
Dominance
  managerial power elites, 299–300
  personality characteristics, 182
  see also Personality; Status
Dominant environment, 296
Domination, political power and, 282, 297
Donaldson, G., 345
Downs, A., 83
Driscoll, J.W., 267
Drucker, P.F., 7, 19, 53, 64, 84, 130, 235, 320
Dunbar, R.L.M., 184
Dunette, M.D., 184, 188
Dyadic groups, 254
Dynamic objectives, 357

Ebert, R.J., 48, 136
Eclectic (interdisciplinary)
  approaches to decision making, 26–27, 30–31, 147–170
  behavioral disciplines, 159–165, 160f, 169–170
  combined with quantitative disciplines, 169–170
  law, anthropology, and political science, 160f, 161–165
  philosophy, 160–161, 160f
  psychology, 160f, 161–162
  sociology and social psychology, 160f, 162–164
  group decision making, 251
  models of decision making, 148–159, 152t
  organizational (neoclassical), 152t, 153–155
  political (adaptive), 152t, 155–158

Eclectic (interdisciplinary)
  approaches to decision
  making (*continued*)
    process (managerial), 152t,
      158–159
    rational (classical), 150–151,
      152t, 153
  quantitative disciplines, 160f,
    165–169
    combined with behavioral
      disciplines, 169–170
    economics and statistics, 160f,
      166–167
    mathematics, 160f, 167–169
Economic boycotts, constraints on
  managerial power, 307
Economic elite, 285
Economic man, *see* Maximizing
  behavior
Economic persons, 120, 122
Economic power, 305
Economics
  interdisciplinary approaches to
    decision making, 160f, 166–167
  values, 116
Economic sectors/macroeconomy
  Chrysler bailout justification, 416,
    417
  generic nature of decision making,
    8–9
  metaorganizational decision
    making, 17
  power elites, 302
  strategic decision making
    environmental domain, 325, 326
    open environmental system,
      324f
    see also specific strategic decision
      implementation case sets
Economic theory, *see* Maximizing
  behavior
Education
  communication, 224
  managerial elite, 290
  values, appreciation of varying
    systems, 113
Education/instruction in group
  norms, 218, 219
Effectiveness
  group decision making, 253
  manager, 7
Efficiency
  group decision making, 14, 251,
    252–253

organizational decision making,
  16–17
personality characteristics, 182–183
see also Decision time
Ego, 178, 201
Eilon, S., 5, 38
Eisner, M., *see* Walt Disney Company
Elbing, A.O., 83, 116, 119
Elbing, C.J., 116, 119
Elements of decision making, *see*
  Decision making process
Elimination-by-aspects model of
  choice, 59
Emory, C.W., 4, 328
Emotion(s)
  group behavior/dynamics, 216,
    217, 223
  managerial values, 123t
  projection, 87
  psychology, 161–162
    personality characteristics, 182
    value conflicts, 183–184
  rational decision making, 76–77
  subconscious, 201–202
  see also Psychology
Employees
  acceptance of decision, *see*
    Acceptance of decision
  Chrysler bailout justification, 416
  constraints on managerial power,
    306
  Eurodisney, 477
  high profits, effects on wage
    demands, 87, 88
  managerial values, 120, 123t
  organizational decision making, 16
  power, managerial, 302
  strategic decision making
    human resources, assessment of,
      333
    understanding of process, 365
  see also Participatory decision
    making
End point, *see* Objectives
England, G., 112, 117–118, 121–122,
  125
Entrepreneurial decisions, 20
Entrepreneurs
  personality profiles, 121
  technostructure and, 288
Environment
  bounded rationality concept, 97, 97f
  decision making, components of,
    38–39

Eurodisney and, 477
group decision making, 235
law, anthropology, and political
  science, 164–165
models of decision making
  interdisciplinary framework, 160f
  process model, 158
scope of decision making, 11
search media, 48
strategic decision making, 322–327
  concept of, 323
  domains, 324–325
  forces, 325–327
  system, 323–324, 324f
Environment, organizational, 96
Environmental assessment
  decision making, components of,
    38–39
  strategic decision-making case sets
    Chrysler bailout, 415
    General Motors, 448–449
    Philip Morris, 456–457
    Walt Disney in 1990, 473–474
    Walt Disney in 1995, 481
  strategic gap analysis, 322, 331f
Environmental texture, 328
Epstein, 301
Equilibrium, conflict management, 262
Error, individual decision making, 12
Error tolerance, personality and, 185
Esser, J.K., 231
Ethic, Calvinist, 120, 126
Ethical, defined, 128
Ethical risk, 188
Ethics, 17, 127–131
  definitions, 128
  interdisciplinary framework
    law, anthropology, and political
      science, 165
    philosophy, 161
  maximizing behavior and, 85, 87
  models of decision making
    interdisciplinary framework,
      160f
    philosophy, 160, 161
  values and, 112
Etzioni, A., 149, 297
Eurodisney, *see* Walt Disney Company
Evaluation
  mathematics and, 167–169
  values and, 112
  see also Follow-up and control;
    Success
Ewing, D.W., 119

Executive management, *see* Hierarchy, organizational
Experiments, mathematics and, 167–169
Expertise
group decision making, 236, 238
group membership, 239, 240t
Expert power, 283

Fagley, N.S., 189
Feasibility studies, 169
Feedback, 155
Feelings, *see* Emotion(s)
Ference,, T.P. 48
Field theory, 179, 216
Finance sector, constraints on managerial power, 307
Fiscal resources
Disney, 473, 478
gap analysis, 333
Floyd, S.W., 61
Follow-up and control, 40
decision making, components of, 39
group decision making, 258
interdisciplinary framework
philosophy, 161
psychology, 162
process model elements, 40f, 64–65
strategic decision-making case sets
Challenger disaster, 430
Chrysler bailout, 424
Cuban missile crisis, 382
Disney, 1990, 478–479
Disney, 1995, 484
General Motors, 453
Philip Morris, 460
Force, and power, 282
Forces, environmental, 325–327
Formal search, 47
Fortune survey of 1976, 290–291
Fox, F.V., 61
Fredrikson, E.B., 38
Freud, S., 177
Freudian model of personality, 177–178, 180, 201
Friedman, M., 81, 82
Fringe status, 222
Fromm, E., 178

Galbraith, J.K., 83, 285, 288–289, 305
Gap analysis, *see* Strategic gap analysis
Garbage-can model, 149, 346

Gender, 268–271
differences, 269–270
personality characteristics, 181, 182, 184
similarities, 270–271
General Motors, 361, 362, 443–457, 460–466
chronology 1978–1992, 445t
comparison with Philip Morris
classification of success, 464–466
determinants of success, 460–464
decision-making process, 450–453
alternatives, search for, 451
choice, 452
comparison and evaluation of, 451–452
follow-up and control, 453
implementation, 452–453
objectives, 450–451
strategic gap, 446–450
environmental assessment, 448–449
gap analysis, 449–450
organizational assessment, 446–448
Generic decisions, *see* Category I decisions
Generic process, decision making as, 8–9
Geopolitical scale
scope of decision making, 11
strategic decision case sets, *see specific strategic decision implementation case sets*
George, A.L., 90
Gestalt, 204
Global economy, managerial class, 291
Goals
group behavior/dynamics, 228, 229, 229f
conflict, 260, 261
norms and conformity requirements, 220
managerial power elites, 297–298
managerial values, 123–124, 123t
mathematics and, 169
models of decision making
organizational, 154
political model, 156
objectives versus, 43
participatory decision making and, 268
personality theory, 180
rational decision making, 76–77

satisficing behavior, 90
value conflicts, 132
Goal-striving behavior, 88
Goal weighting function, 56
Goldhammer, 282
Good alternatives, 53
Gordon, R.A., 83
Gore, W.J., 19, 235
Government
generic nature of decision making, 8–9
law and political science, 164–165
managerial elites, 285, 290, 301, 303
managerial values in, 120
maximizing behavior, constraints on, 87
strategic decision making
environmental assessment, 333–334
environmental domain, 325, 326
see also specific strategic decision implementation case sets
see also Legislation; Public sector
Governmental (bureaucratic) politics model, 149
Government politics, 296
W.T. Grant, 345
Group behavior and dynamics, 213–242
characteristics of groups, 214–215
communication, 224–226, 225f
decision-making perspectives, 231–236, 234t
advantages and limitations, 232–233
strategies of choice, 233–235, 234t
theory, 232–235, 234t
decision-making profiles, 19, 236–241, 240t
classification of groups, 236–238
conceptualized, 239–241, 240t
locus of decision making, 23
membership, 239
situational characteristics, 238
effective groups, characteristics of, 227–229, 229f
group think, 229–231
interdisciplinary perspective, 26–27, 160f
norms and conformity, 218–220
psychology, *see* Social psychology
structure of groups, 220–223
theories of, 215–218

Group behavior and dynamics
(*continued*)
value conflicts, 131–133
values and, 115–116
Groups
definitions of, 214
managerial values, 123t
politics in formal organizations,
293, 295
size, 233
sociology and social psychology,
162–164
strategic decision making
environmental domain, 325
open environmental system, 324f
structure/classification of, 220–222
value conflicts, 131–133
Groupthink, 229–231, 251
Growth
managerial objectives and, 45
values, organizational, 116
Grunes, W.F., 198
Guth, W.D., 122

Haire, M., 198
Halo effect, 199
Hambrick, D.C., 320
Hamilton, W.F., 61
Happiness, 115
Harnett, D.L., 188
Harrison, E.F., 231, 267
Hartley, R.F., 346
Hasan, Z., 85
Hate instincts (Freudian model), 177
Hayes, J., 292
Heller, F.A., 267
Henderson, J.C., 184
Hendrick, C., 188
Herendeen, J.D., 83
Heuristic problem solving, 21, 21t.
See also Category II decisions
Hewlett-Packard, 360
Hickson, D.J., 346
Hierarchy, needs (Maslow), 11–12,
117, 179, 180
Hierarchy, organizational, 44
entrepreneurs versus managers,
121
Category I versus Category II
decisions, 21, 21t, 22
levels of decision making, 7–8
locus of choice, 22–24
politics in formal organizations,
295–296

power, managerial decision
making, 300
strategic decision making, 322
Hierarchy, power, 284
Hill, G.W., 254
Hitt, W.D., 74
Hogarth, R., 58
Hollman, K.W., 120
Holsapple, C.W., 38
Homans, G., 115, 214, 215, 218
Human resources
Disney, 1990, 473
gap analysis, 333
Humphreys, L.W., 270
Huntsman, B., 83
Huxham, C.S., 346

Iacocca, L., *see* Chrysler bailout
IBM, 361
Id, 178, 201
Identification
group behavior/dynamics, 216
size of group and, 223
participation in decision making,
263
and perception, 200
referent power, 283–284
Ideology
metaorganizational decision
making, 17
values, 111
Implementation, 6
decision making, components of,
39, 40
group behavior/dynamics
size of group and, 223
theories, 233
group decision making
composite approach, 257–258
participatory decision making
and, 264, 267, 268
groupthink and, 231
interdisciplinary framework
philosophy, 161
sociology and social psychology,
163
organizational decision making, 16
political model, 157
process model elements, 40f,
60–64, 63f
strategic decision-making case sets
Challenger disaster, 429–430, 433
Chrysler bailout, 423–424
Cuban missile crisis, 381–382

Disney, 1990, 477–478
Disney, 1995, 484, 487
General Motors, 452–453, 464
Philip Morris, 459–460, 464
strategic decision success, 347
quality of decision, 351–353
understanding of process by
employees, 352–353, 365
strategic management, 322
see also Acceptance of decision
Incrementalism, disjointed, 157
Incrementalism, logical, 157
Individual
group decision making, 14, 26–27
group dynamics, *see* Group
behavior and dynamics;
Social psychology
models of decision making, 149
value conflicts, 131–133
Individual attributes
managerial decision making, 25
variations in values, 112, 113
see also Intelligence
Individual decision making, 23–24
scope of, 10–11
versus group decision making,
250–258
composite approach, 256–258
empirical perspectives, 253–255
risky shift, 255–256
theoretical perspectives, 250–253
Individuality, 219
Industrial manager, 122
Influence
group behavior/dynamics,
215–216, 220
power elites, managerial decision
makers, 302
strategic decision-making case sets
Challenger disaster, 432
Disney, 1995, 486
General Motors and Philip
Morris, 462–463
strategic decision success, 62, 63f,
349t, 350–351, 365
Informal groups, 221
Informal search, 47
Information
additional, cost of, 48
Category I versus Category II
decisions, 21, 21t
cognitive strain, 94–95
complexity of decision task, 60
cost of additional, 49–50

group behavior/dynamics
 communication networks, 224–226, 225
 theories, 232
group decision making
 conflict indicators, 260
 interdisciplinary perspective, 26
groupthink, 231
individual decision making, 12, 13
managerial decision making, 25
maximizing behavior and, 86
and participatory decision making, 268
perception, components of, 193
politics in formal organizations, 295
process of decision making, 38
psychology
 personality and, 185
 risk reduction approaches, 187
and quality of decision, 61
rational decision making, 150
 bounded rationality concept, 97, 97f, 98
 satisficing behavior, 96
search activity, 45
selective perception of, 86
strategic decision case sets
 Disney, 1995, 485–486
 General Motors and Philip Morris, 462
strategic decision making
 flow of, 337f, 338
 open environmental system, 324f
strategic decision success, 62, 63f, 365
 Challenger disaster, 431–432
 open model, 356
 quality of decisions, 349t, 350
 suppression of data, 48
Innovation, 21, 21t
 group behavior/dynamics, 226
 organizational decision making, 16
 personality, 185
 see also Category II decisions
Inputs
 open environmental system, 324f
 process of decision making, 38
 scope of decision making, 11
Inspirational strategy, 20f, 21, 21, 21t, 30. *See also* Category II decisions
Institutional resources, Disney, 1990, 473
Instrumental control, 217

Instrumental values, 118, 119f
Insurance companies, 307
Integration
 group behavior/dynamics, 217
 social, 215
Integrative decision making, 26
Integrative principle, 30
Intelligence, 10, 87
 characteristics of decision maker, 60
 cognitive strain, 95
 and managerial decision making, 25
 and risk acceptance/avoidance, 187
 search media, 48
Intended values, 121
Interacting group, 237, 239, 240t, 241
Interaction
 Brim study, 181
 interpersonal, *see* Interpersonal interactions/relationships
 system theory, group behavior, 215
Interaction-process analysis, 216–217
Interdependence, and conflict, 259
Interdisciplinary decision making, *see* Eclectic (interdisciplinary) approaches to decision making
Interest groups, constraints on managerial power, 307
Interlocking decision making, 27, 31
Internalization, 216, 228
International politics, 11, *see specific strategic decision case sets*
Interpersonal consensus, 214, 215
Interpersonal interactions/ relationships
 entrepreneurs versus managers, 121
 group behavior/dynamics
 conflict, *see* Conflict
 consensus, 214, 215
 size of group and, 223
 and perception, 200
 values and, 112
Interpretation, perceptual process, 193
Interrelational decision making, 27–28, 31
Intuition, 203–204
Investors, 307, 473, 478
Iranian hostage crisis, 386–403
 chronology, 386–387t
 comparative case classifications of success, 402–403
 comparison with Cuban missile crisis, 397–403

compatibility with operating constraints, 397–398
 decision makers influence, 399
 information, 398–399
 risk-reward factor, 399–400
 timing, optimal, 398
 understanding by implementers, 385
decision making process, 388–397
 alternatives, comparison and evaluation of, 390–393
 alternatives, search for, 388–390
 choice, 393–394
 follow-up and control, 395–396
 implementation, 394–395
 objectives, 388
groupthink, 231
Isen, A.M. 189

Jackson, J.M., 188, 217–218, 222
Janis, I., 37, 51, 229
Japanese management, 231
Jensen, M.C., 85
Johnson, C.E., 345
Johnson, J.E.V., 271
Johnson, R.J., 100
Jones, M.H., 124
Jones, R.E., 346
Judgment, 133–136
 decision versus, 134
 evaluation of alternatives, 52–53
 group decision making, 256–257
 groupthink, 230
 perception, 195, 196
 personality characteristics, 181
 satisficing behavior, 97
 strategic gap analysis, 332
 strategic management, 321, 322
 values and, 112
 see also Choice
Judgmental decisions, 20, 20f, 21, 21t, 30, 359f
 evaluative concepts, 363
 strategic decision making success, 358
 see also Category II decisions
Jung, C., 178, 203, 204

Kahn, R.L., 86
Kakar, S., 75
Karp, H.B., 130
Karson, M.J., 271
Kast, F.E., 214, 228
Katona, G., 87

Katz, D., 86
Kelman, H.C., 215
Kennedy, J.F., *see* Cuban missile crisis
Khomeini, R., *see* Iranian hostage crisis
Khruschev, N., *see* Cuban missile crisis
Kickert, W.J.M, 38
Kilduff, M., 236
Knowledge
   characteristics of decision maker, 60
   decision-making strategy classification, 20, 20f
   expert power, 283
   group decision making
      interdisciplinary perspective, 26
      quality of decisions, 251
   technostructure, 288–289
Kogan, N., 184, 189, 269
Kolaja, J., 61
Kolasa, B., 193, 197
Koontz, H., 8, 64
Koplin, H.T. 82
Korn/Ferry International survey, 126, 130, 290–291
Kraft, *see* Philip Morris
Kruglanski, A.W., 231

Labor unions
   constraints on managerial power, 306–307
   new managerial class, 286
   perceptions, 199, 200
Lanzetta, J.T., 187
Law
   ethical judgements, 128, 130
   interdisciplinary approaches to decision making, 160f, 161–165
   power elites, managerial decision makers, 302, 303
   strategic decision making
      environmental assessment, 333–334
      environmental domain, 325, 326
      tobacco litigation, 461
   values and, 115
Lawler, E.E., 180
Lawless, D.J., 214
Leadership
   gender differences, 270
   group behavior/dynamics
      characteristics of effective groups, 228, 229, 229f
      communication networks, 226

decision-making profiles, 237
   size of group and, 223
   theories, 233
   group decision making, 235
   personality and, 185
   strategic decision quality, 350–351
Learning
   participatory decision making and, 267
   process of decision making, 38
Lee, J.A., 126
Legislation
   Chrysler bailout, 414t, 422
   and Chrysler problems, 410
   and General Motors, 449
   power elites, managerial decision makers, 302, 303
Legitimate power, 283
Level of management, *see* Hierarchy, organizational
Lewellen, W.G., 83
Lewin, K., 179, 216
Lexicographic model of choice, 59
Leys, W.A.R., 115
Libido, 177
Life instincts (Freudian model), 177
Likert, 267
Lillie, W., 128
Lindblom, C.E., 94, 149, 157
Lindoerfer, J.S., 231
Linear model of choice, 58–59
Linstone, H.A., 149
Litterer, J.A., 193
Locus of choice, 22–24. *See also* Hierarchy, organizational
Locus of responsibility, and satisficing behavior, 91
Logical incrementalism, 157
Long-term objectives
   cognitive limitations and, 87
   interrelational decision making, 27–28
   locus of decision making, 23
   models of decision making
      organizational, 155
      process model, 158
   satisficing behavior, 100
   see also Planning; Strategic decision making; Time frame
Lorsch, J.W., 345
Lotus Development Corporation, 361
Lucent, 361
Lundgren, E., 254
Lusk, E.J., 122

Mabry, B.D., 83
MacCrimmon, K.R., 186
Machlup, F., 80, 82
Mack, R.P., 135
Macy's, 362
Makridakis, S., 346
Management
   attitudes toward decision-making process, *see* Attitudes of managers toward decision-making process
   attitudes toward decisions, *see* Attitudes of managers toward decisions
   Eurodisney, 477
   strategic gap analysis, 331f, 332
   Disney in 1990, 472
   General Motors, 446–447
Managerial decision-making process, framework for evaluation, 363
Managerial model, *see* Process model
Managerial objectives, *see* Objectives
Managerial revolution (Burnham), 286
Managerial style, Eurodisney, 477
Managerial values, *see* Values, organizational/managerial
Managers
   entrepreneurs versus, 121
   functions, 16
   personality profiles (values), 121
Mann, L., 51
March, J.G., 45, 63, 86, 90, 149, 154, 292, 297, 346
Marginal membership, 218, 222
Marginal value curve, 49f, 50
Market power, 305
Marris, R., 83
Marx, K., 287–288
Marxism, 287–288
Maslow, A.
   needs hierarchy of, 11–12, 117, 179, 180
   theory of personality, 179–180
Masson, R.T., 83
Mathematics
   decision theory, 10
   interdisciplinary approaches to decision making, 160f, 167–169
Maximizing behavior, 79–89, 92
   concept, 79–81
   at Disney, 1995, 486
   evaluative concepts, 363–364
   features, 81–84

limitations, 84–89
managerial values, 123t, 124
models of decision making, 154, 155
strategic choice, 357–359
strategic decision matrix, 359f
utility, 166
Maximum profit, 87
Maxwell, H., *see* Philip Morris
Mayes, B.T., 292, 293
McCormick, M., 254
McGregor, D., 227, 267
McGuire, J.W., 83, 84, 85, 178
Means-ends chain, 44, 118
Means value, 118
Measurement
managerial objectives, quantifiability, 44
quantitative disciplines, 10, 160f, 165–169
Measures of performance, *see* Follow-up and control
Measures of success, 61
Mecking, W.H., 85
Medical sector, managerial class, 286
Membership, 239
group behavior/dynamics, 215, 216, 217
types of, 222
Membership groups, 221
Mercedes-Benz, 361
Mergers, 362
Metaorganizations, 11
Microsoft, 361
Middle management
categories of decisions, 23, 24
see also Hierarchy, organizational
Miller, G.W., 189, 419
Mills, C.W., 285, 286–287, 288, 291, 304
Miner, F.C. Jr., 254
Minimum effort principle, 59
Mintzberg, H., 20, 38, 55, 292–293, 320, 345
Mitchell, T.R., 48, 60, 136
Mixed alternatives, 53
Mixed-scanning model, 149
Modeling, mathematics and, 167–169
Models, decision-making, 148–159, 152t
interdisciplinary framework, 160f.
See also Eclectic (interdisciplinary) approaches to decision making

organizational (neoclassical), 152t, 153–155
politcal (adaptive), 152t, 155–158
process (managerial), 152t, 158–159
rational (classical), 150–151, 152t, 153
Models, risk taking, 188
Mohr, L.B., 297
Monetary risk, model of risk taking, 188
Monitoring
follow-up and control phase, 64. *See also* Follow-up and control
information, 64
Monsen, R.J. Jr., 83, 124
Moore, D.G., 121
Morality, 128, 129, 130
Moral values, 118, 119f
Morlock, H., 187
Moscowitz, H., 38
Motivation
characteristics of decision maker, 60
cognitive strain, 95
group behavior/dynamics, 227
participatory decision making, 263
personality theory, 179–180
politics in formal organizations, 293
psychological models, 11–12, 117, 179, 180
for search activity, 45
see also Aspiration levels
Motorola, 361
Moussavi, F., 184
Murphy, T.A., *see* General Motors
Myers, M.S., 180

Naglieri, J.A., 254
NASA, *see* *Challenger* disaster
NCR, 361
Needs hierarchy of Maslow, 179 get
Negotiated decisions, 19, 234t, 235
Neoclassical model, *see* Organizational model
Newcomer, M., 289, 290
Niland, P., 4
Nominal group, 237, 239, 240t, 241
Nonprogrammed decisions, 19
Nonrecurring choices, 423
Normative decision theory, 12
Norms
ethical judgements, 129, 130
group, 214, 218–220, 233, 234t, 235
characteristics of effective groups, 228, 229, 229f

decision making, 236
values and, 115–116
organizational, 86
values, 113, 115–116
Norm-sending, 218
Nutt, P.C., 149, 184, 346

Objectives
versus goal, 43
group behavior/dynamics, 214, 234t, 235
composite approach, 257
conflict, 260, 261
groupthink, 230
theories, 232
interdisciplinary framework
economics and statistics, 167
mathematics, 169
philosophy, 161
sociology and social psychology, 163
locus of decision making, 23
managerial decision making, 25
managerial power elites, 297–298
models of decision making
political model, 156, 157
process model, 158
rational, 150
organizational decision making, 17
process model elements, 38, 42–45, 40f
advantages, 43
characteristics, 44–45
hierarchy, 43–44
rational decision making
bounded rationality concept, 97, 97f, 98, 99
satisficing behavior, 99
revising, 41–42, 155
satisficing behavior, 91–92
standards for performance assessment, 65
strategic decision-making case sets
Challenger disaster, 426
Chrysler bailout, 416–417
Cuban missile crisis, 378
Disney in 1990, 474–475
Disney in 1995, 481–482
General Motors, 450–451
Philip Morris, 457–458
strategic decision success, 357
managerial attitudes toward decision making, 355

Objectives (*continued*)
  open model, 356
    strategic decision matrix, 359f
  subprocesses, 41–42
  values and, 183
Ofstad, H., 4
Oliver, B.L., 122
Olsen, J.P., 63, 149
Open decision models, 46, 92
  evaluative concepts, 364
  managerial attitudes toward decision making, 355–358, 359f
  satisficing behavior, 90
  subconscious elements, 202
Open systems, organizations as, 16
Operating constraints, 364
  Challenger disaster, 430–431
  Disney, 1995, 485
  General Motors and Philip Morris, 461
  strategic decision quality, 62, 63f, 348–349, 349t
Operating values, 121
Operations
  locus of decision making, 7–8, 23, 24
  organizational decision making, 17
Opportunism, ethics of, 130
Opportunities
  Disney, 1990, 474
  environmental assessment, 331, 332, 333
Opportunity cost, managerial decision making, 24–25
Optimal alternatives, 90
Optimal decision making, 95–96, 100
Optimality, point of, 49f, 50
Optimization, timing, 61
Optimizing decision rule, 90
Organizational assessment
  strategic gap analysis, 331f
  strategic decision-making case sets
    Chrysler bailout, 414–415
    Disney in 1990, 472–473
    Disney in 1995, 479–481
    General Motors, 446–448
    Philip Morris, 456
Organizational interests, values and, 112
Organizational (neoclassical) model, 92, 100, 149, 152t, 153–155
  comparison with political and classical models, 157
  comparison with process model, 158
Organizational myopia, 23

Organizational process model, 149
Organizational structure
  implementation of decision, 61
  strategic decision making, 321
Organizational values, *see* Values
Organization (enterprise)
  interrelational decision making, 27
  managerial decision making and, 24
  scope of decision making, 11
  strategic decision making
    gap analysis, 331f
    open environmental system, 324f
  see also Hierarchy, organizational
Organization (process), perception as, 193
Organized labor, *see* Labor unions
Originality
  group decision criteria, 238, 240t
  see also Creativity; Innovation
Outcomes, 30
  creeping determinism, 200
  decision making
    components of, 39
    strategy classification, 20, 20f
  groupthink and, 231
  interdisciplinary framework
    mathematics, 169
    psychology, 162
    sociology and social psychology, 164
  managerial decision making, 25
  models of decision making
    political model, 157
    rational, 153
  negative, revision of, 58
  open decision model, 90, 92–93
  optimal decision making, 95–96
  personality characteristics, 181
  politics in formal organizations, 293–294
  predictability of, 54–55
  process model elements, 54–55
  strategic decision success
    evaluative concepts, 363–364
    open model, 356
    strategic choice, 357–359
  typology of decisions, 30
  see also Quality of decisions; Success
Outstatus, 222

Parsons, T., 326
Participatory decision making, 262–268
  empirical approaches, 266–268

strategic decision success, 352
theory, 263–266
Passivity, 27
Patchen, M., 263
PepsiCo, 360
Perception, 192–201
  characteristics of perceiver and perceived, 195–196
  empirical perspectives, 200–201
  group behavior/dynamics, 16, 214, 215
    conflict, 260
    and conformity, 219, 220
  impressions of others, 196–199
  process, 193–195
  psychology, 161–162
  satisficing behavior, 97
  and search activity, 47
  search activity, 48
  selective, 86
  situational influences, 200
  and strategic decision implementation, 63
  utility, 91
  values and, 112
Perceptual defense, 199
Perceptual media of search, 48
Performance
  follow-up and control phase, 64–65
  organizational decision making, 17
Performance evaluation
  and conflict, 259
  managerial objectives, characteristics of, 45
Personal interactions, *see* Interpersonal interactions/relationships
Personality, 176–186
  biological, subconscious, and hereditary factors, 177–178
  Brim study, 181
  common traits and unique individuality, 178–179
  effects on decision making, 184–186
  empirical approaches, 181–184
  entrepreneurs versus managers, 121
  group behavior/dynamics
    characteristics of effective groups, 227
    and conformity, 219–220
  group decision making, 26–27
    conflict, 260
    interdisciplinary perspective, 26
  holistic approaches, 179–180

implementation of decision, 61–62, 62f
individual decision making, 13
and perception, 195
psychology, 161–162
significance in decision making, 61
and strategic decision success, 62, 63f
subconscious, 201–202
theories of, 177–178
and values, 113
Personal perspective, models of decision making, 149
Personal values, 118, 119f, 120
Personnel, boundary, 324
Peters, T.J., 345
Petit, T.A., 85
Pfeffer, J., 254, 293, 296
Phase theorem of managerial decision making, 349
Phenomenal field (Rogers' model), 179
Philip Morris, 443–457, 460–466
comparison with General Motors
classification of success, 464–466
determinants of success, 460–464
decision-making process, 457–460
strategic gap at, 455–457
Phillips, C,F, 81, 82
Phillips, L.D., 62
Philosophy, 160–161, 160f
Physical media of search, 48
Physical resources
Disney, 1990, 473
gap analysis, 333
Physical risk, model of risk taking, 188
Planning, 20
interrelational decision making, 27–28
locus of decision making, 23
models of decision making
organizational, 155
process model, 158
organizational decision making, 16
see also Long-term objectives; Strategic decisions
Pluralism, theory of, 304–305
Point of optimality, 49f, 50
Policy, organizational
group decision making difficulties, 14
models of decision making
organizational, 155

political model, 156, 157
process model, 158
satisficing behavior, 97
strategic gap analysis, 331f, 332–333
Disney in 1990, 472
General Motors, 447
Political aspects of decision making, 11, 30, 281–311
constraints on power, 304–308
operating, 305–308
theoretical, 304–305
dimensions of managerial decision making power, 300–304
manifestations, 302–304
scope, 300–301
political power in decision making, 297–300
divergence of goals and objectives, 297–298
dominance versus autonomy, 299–300
resource allocation, 298–299
power, nature of, 282–284
social class, decision makers as, 284–296
concepts of class, 285–284
concepts of power, 294–296
emergence of, 284–285
managerial revolution (Burnham), 286
Marxism, 287–288
power elite (Mills), 286–287
technostructure (Galbraith), 288–289
Political (adaptive) model of decision making, 152t, 155–158, 296, 297–300
Political persons, 123
Political science,160f, 161–165
Political solutions, 223
Political system
strategic decision case sets, see specific case sets
strategic decision making
environmental assessment, 333–334
environmental domain, 325, 326
open environmental system, 324f
Politics
metaorganizational decision making, 17
values, 111, 114, 117
Politics, organizational, 292–294
Politics model, 149

Pollay, R.W., 183
Poor alternatives, 53
Porter, L.W., 180
Posner, B.Z., 118, 130
Powell, P.L., 271
Power
concepts of power, 294–296
managerial values, 123t
nature of, 282–284
political personality and, 123t
significance in decision making, 61
see also Political aspects of decision making
Power elite, 286–287, 291, 304
Prasad, S.B., 83
Precedent, 97
organizational model, look 165
satisficing behavior, 97
Precision/imprecision, organizational decision making, 16
Predictive ability, 54–55
behavioral/psychological models, 178
interdisciplinary framework, 160f, 167–169
perceptions, 196–197
Preferences
decision-making strategy classification, 20, 20f
group decision making, 26
models of decision making, 150
personality and, 184, 185
typology of decisions, 30
Preferential membership, 217, 222
Preventive decision making, 63–64
Primary flow, strategic decision making, 336, 337f
Primary groups, 221
Primary set, 222
Principle of minimum effort, 59
Probabilistic approach, individual decision making, 13
Probabilistic cues, 197
Probabilistic models, 169
Probabilistic outcomes, 39
Probability, 77
individual decision making, 12
interdisciplinary framework, 160f, 166–167
Problem definition, 150
group behavior/dynamics, 237
political model, 157
process of decision making, 37
see also Analysis

Problem recognition, 37
Problem solving
  conflict management, 261
  versus decision making, 5–6
  entrepreneurs versus managers,
    121
  preventive decision making, 63–64
Process, group, 234t, 235
Processing, in perception, 193
Process model, 37–67, 149, 152t,
    158–159
  alternatives, comparing and evalu-
    ating, 40f, 50–55
    anticipation of outcomes, 54–55
    multidimensional perspectives,
      51–53
    typology of alternatives, 53
  alternatives, search for, 45–50, 40f
    cost of additional information,
      49–50
    inperfections in, 45–46
    perspectives on, 46–47
    structure of, 47–49
  choice, 40f, 55–60
    characteristics of, 59–60
    models of, 57–59
    multidimensional perspectives,
      56–57
  follow-up and control, 40f, 64–65
  implementation, 40f, 60–64, 63f
  nature of process, 37–42
    decision making as dynamic
      process, 41–42
    functions, 38–39
    interrelationships, 39–40, 40f
  objectives, setting, 42–45, 40f
    advantages, 43
    characteristics, 44–45
    hierarchy, 43–44
  strategic decision implementation,
    *see specific strategic decision im-
    plementation case sets*
Process of decision making, *see*
    Decision making process
Productivity, participatory decision
    making and, 266
Product/service domains, strategic
    decisions, 321
Profile of decision, 4–5
Profit
  criteria of successful decisions, 61
  managerial values, 123t, 125
  maximizing behavior, *see*
    Maximizing behavior

participatory decision making, 266
  values, organizational, 116
Programmed decisions, 15, 19, 21.
    See also Category I decisions
Programmed search, 47
Projection, 87, 199
Propaganda, 307
Proxmire, W., 417
Pruitt, D.G., 187
Psychological group, 214
Psychological membership, 217, 222
Psychology, 176–206
  cognitive limitations, 87
  cognitive strain, 94–95
  decision theory, 9
  entrepreneurs versus managers, 121
  group decision making, 26–27. *See
    also* Group behavior and
    dynamics; Social psychology
  interdisciplinary approaches to
    decision making, 26, 160f,
    161–162
  perception, 192–201
    characteristics of perceiver and
      perceived, 195–196
    empirical perspectives, 200–201
    impressions of others, 196–199
    process, 193–195
    situational influences, 200
  personality, 176–186
    biological, subconscious, and
      hereditary factors, 177–178
    common traits and unique indi-
      viduality, 178–179
    effects on decision making,
      184–186
    empirical approaches, 181–184
    holistic approaches, 179–180
  power, 283
  risk acceptance/aversion, 186–192
    conceptual model, 189–192, 189f
    empirical perspectives, 186–189
    and search activity, 48
  significance in decision making, 61
  subconscious influences, 201–204
  values, 114. *See also* Values
  see also Rational decision making
Public, constraints on managerial
    power, 307
Public sector
  constraints on managerial power,
    305
  law, anthropology, and political
    science, 164–165

managerial class, 285–286
  managerial elite, 290
  managerial values in, 120, 121
  political model, 158
  power constraints, 307–308
  typology of decisions, 30
  see also Government
Public service organizations, ethics
    survey, 130

Quality circles, 231
Quality of decision
  cognitive limitations, 87
  group decision making, 14, 251,
    254–255
    composite approach, 257
    criteria, 238, 240t
    deindividuation and, 252, 253
  managerial decision making, 25
  organizational decision making, 16
  participatory decision making, 268
  political model, 157
  strategic decision success, 348–351
  Trull model for evaluation of,
    61–62, 62f
  see also Outcomes; Success
Quantification, managerial objec-
    tives, 44
Quantitative disciplines, 160f,
    165–169
  decision theory, 10
  interdisciplinary approaches to
    decision making
    combined with behavioral
      disciplines, 169–170
    economics and statistics, 160f,
      166–167
    mathematics, 160f, 167–169
Quinn, J.B., 157

Raisinghani, D., 55, 345
Rand Corporation, 237
Rank
  and conformity requirements, 218
  personality characteristics, 181, 182
  see also Dominance; Status
Rational, defined, 75
Rational behavior
  versus nonrational behavior, 74–78
  utility, 166
Rational decision making, 74–100
  managerial values and, 124
  maximizing behavior, 79–89
  concept, 79–81

features, 81–84
limitations, 84–89
personality characteristics, 181
rational versus nonrational
    behavior, 74–78
satisficing behavior, 89–100
    concept, 89–93
    features, 93–99
    limitations, 99–100
    value judgement in, 135–136
Rationality, bounded, 94, 96, 349, 363
Rationalization, 203
Rational (classical) model, 149,
    150–151, 152t, 153, 157
Raven, B.H., 231
Recurring decisions, 21. *See also*
    Category I decisions
Reference groups, 221
Referent power, 283–284
Regulation
    Chrysler problems, 410, 416–417,
        420
    constraints on managerial power,
        305
    and General Motors, 449
    power elites, managerial decision
        makers, 303
    strategic decision making, 325,
        326
Relationships, entrepreneurs versus
    managers, 121
Relevance, search activity, 45
Religion, 128
Religious persons, 123
Repertoires, 155
Representation, group decision
    making, 14
Representative, group membership,
    239, 240t
Research managers, 122
Resources
    conflict management, 261
    implementation of decision, 61
    managerial decision making,
        24–25
    managerial power elites, 298–299
    metaorganizational decision
        making, 17
    politics in formal organizations,
        293
    strategic decision making, 333
    strategic gap analysis, 331f
        Disney in 1990, 473
        General Motors, 447–448

Responsibility
    group decision making, 14, 255
    participatory decision making, 265
    strategic decision making, 334
    see also Accountability
Restraints, values as, 114
Restructuring, conflict management,
    261
Results, *see* Follow-up and control
Reversibility, decision task, 60
Revision of objectives, 41–42
Reward power, 283
R.J. Reynolds, 461
Rhenman, E., 325
Rice, G.H., 148
Risk acceptance/aversion, 186–192
    cognitive strain, 95
    gender differences, 269
    group decision making
        interdisciplinary perspective, 26
        risky shift, 255–256
    groupthink, 230
    individual decision making, 13
    interdisciplinary framework
        economics and statistics, 166
        psychology, 162
    managerial values, 123t, 124
    outcomes, 54, 55
    predictability of outcomes, 54
    psychology
        conceptual model, 189–192, 189f
        empirical perspectives, 186–189
        personality, 179, 183, 185
    and search activity, 47
Risk-reward factor
    implementation of decision, 63,
        63f
    strategic decision case set
        comparisons
        Challenger disaster, 432
        Disney, 1995, 486–487
        General Motors and Philip
            Morris, 463
    strategic decision quality, 351–352,
        365
Robbins, S.P., 261
Rodrigues, S.B., 346
Rogers, C., 179
Rokeach, M., 118, 119, 120, 127
Roles, group behavior/dynamics,
    215, 217, 221, 233, 234t
Rosenzweig, J.E., 214, 228
Rostow, E.V., 81
Routine decisions, 19, 21

group, 234t, 235
management and, 22
see also Category I decisions
Rowe. A.J., 221
Rule-based decisions, 21. *See also*
    Category I decisions
Rules
    group behavior/dynamics, 214, 215
    and judgement, 135
    personality and, 185
Rules of thumb, 15, 21, 21t. *See also*
    Category II decisions

San Francisco Bay area study, 345,
    348, 349, 349t, 351, 352, 353,
    354, 365, 401, 461, 462, 463,
    487
Satisfaction
    goals of rational behavior, 76
    group decision making, 216, 234t,
        235
        communication networks, 226
        and conflict, 259
        size of group and, 222
        maximizing, *see* Maximizing
            behavior
    participatory decision making,
        266, 267
    personality and, 188
Satisfactory alternatives, 90
Satisficing behavior, 89–100, 466
    concept, 89–93
    features, 93–99
    group decision making, 251
    limitations, 99–100
    managerial values and, 124
    models of decision making, 154,
        155
    risk-reward factor, 463
    strategic decision making matrix,
        359f
    strategic decision making success
        evaluative concepts, 363–364
        strategic choice, 358
    subconscious elements, 202
    value judgements in, 136
    values and, 128
Saturn, *see* General Motors
Saunders, G.B.184
Saxberg, B.O., 124
Schlesinger, A., 375
Schlichter, S.H., 305
Schmidt, W.H., 118, 130
Schrenk, L.P., 37

Schuler, R.S., 267
Scientists
    participatory decision making, 267
    values, 122
Scott, W.G., 222
Seagram, 361
Search
    individual decision making, 13
    organizational decision making, 15
    structure of, 48–49
Search activity, 10
    interdisciplinary framework
        economics and statistics, 166
        mathematics, 169
        sociology and social psychology,
            163
    models of decision making
        organizational, 154
        political model, 157
        rational, 153
    rational decision making
        bounded rationality concept, 98
        satisficing behavior, 91, 96
    see also Alternatives, search for
Search rules, individual decision
            making, 13
Sears and Roebuck, 345, 361
Secondary groups, 221
SEGA Enterprise, 362
Selection, perception as, 193
Selective perception of information,
            86
Self-actualization, 11–12, 179–180
Self-assertion, 132
Self-censorship, 230
Self-evaluation, 113
Self-inhibition, 114
Self-interest
    ethical judgements, 129
    managerial values, 125
Sense modalities, perception, 194
Sentiment, 215
Shackle, G.L.S., 89
Shareholders
    maximizing behavior and, 85
    power elites, managerial decision
            makers, 303
Sharples, B., 20
Shils, E.A., 282, 326
Shrode, W.A., 270
Shull, F.A., 4, 61
Shumway, C.R., 61
Sieber, J.E., 187
Significance of decision making, 6–8

Significance of decisions, 7–8
Simon, H.A., 4, 17, 19, 37, 44, 55, 75,
            76, 86, 90, 91, 92, 93, 94, 96,
            100, 154, 200, 235
Simplification, search activity, 46
Simulations, mathematics and,
            167–169
Situational ethics, 130
Situational variables, Brim study, 181
Size of groups, 222–223, 229, 229f
Sloan, A., see General Motors
Slovic, P., 188
Smith, A., 79, 120, 126–127, 307, 351
Smith, R. 446
Smith, S., 231
Smoothing, conflict, 261
Snow, C.C., 320
Social class
    decision makers as, 284–296
        concepts of class, 285–284
        concepts of power, 294–296
        emergence of, 284–285
        managerial revolution
            (Burnham), 286
        Marxism, 287–288
        power elite (Mills), 286–287
        technostructure (Galbraith),
            288–289
    managerial elite origins, 290
    and personality characteristics, 182
Social factors
    group behavior/dynamics, 233
    group decision making, 26, 236
Social goals, value conflicts, 132
Social integration, theory of, 215
Social persons, 123
Social psychology, 249–273
    conflict, 258–262, 259f
        determinants of, 259–260, 259f
        indicators of, 259f, 260–261
        nature of, 258–259, 259f
        treatment of, 259f, 261–262
    decision theory, 9
    gender, 268–271
        differences, 269–270
        similarities, 270–271
    individual versus group decision
            making, 250–258
        composite approach, 256–258
        empirical perspectives, 253–255
        risky shift, 255–256
        theoretical perspectives, 250–253
    interdisciplinary approaches to de-
            cision making, 160f, 162–164

participation, 262–268
    empirical approaches, 266–268
    theory, 263–266
and perception, 200
see also Group behavior and
            dynamics
Social risk, model of risk taking, 188
Social values, 118, 119f
Social welfare
    ethical judgements, 129, 130
    managerial values, 123t
    managerial values and, 125–126
    values, 116
Society
    constraints on managerial power,
            307
    and ethical judgement, 128
    ethical judgements, 129
    generic nature of decision making,
            8–9
    interdisciplinary framework
        law, anthropology, and political
            science, 164–165
        sociology, 162–164
    maximizing behavior, 85, 87
    metaorganizational decision
            making, 17, 18
    power elites, managerial decision
            makers, 302
    scope of decision making, 11
    strategic decision making
        environmental domain, 325,
            326–327, 333–334
        open environmental system,
            324f
    values, 111, 113, 116–117
    see also Political aspects of decision
            making
Sociology
    groups, see Group behavior and
            dynamics
    interdisciplinary approaches to de-
            cision making, 160f, 162–164
Sociometry, 222
Sociopolitical factors, environmental
            assessment, 333–334
Southwest Airline, 361
Span of decision, 238, 240t
Special interest groups, 307, 326
Spranger, E., 117
Stages of decision making, 38
Stagner, R., 61, 266, 345
Stakeholders
    Chrysler, 416, 422

constraints on managerial power, 305, 306
environmental domain, 325
group decision making, 14
managerial values and, 119
politics in formal organizations, 293–294
scope of decision making, 11
Standards
control system, 64–65
ethical, 128, 130
values as, 111
Stanton, J.L., 184
Stasser, H., 236
State-of-the-art, *see* Technology
Statistics
decision theory, 10
individual decision making, 12
interdisciplinary approaches to decision making, 160f, 166–167
Status
entrepreneurs versus managers, 121
group behavior/dynamics
characteristics of effective groups, 227
communication, 224
conformity, 220
group relationships, 222
and maximizing behavior, 86
participation in decision making, 263
and perception, 195
personality characteristics, 181, 182
social, *see* Social class
Staw, B.M., 61
Steers, R.M., 269
Steinbruner, J.D., 149
Stereotypes, 120, 199
Stereotyping, 196, 197–198, 199, 270
Stimulus, perception process, 194
Stockholders, 164–165
acceptable profit levels, 87
constraints on managerial power, 305
environmental domain, 325
managerial values, 123t
maximizing behavior and, 87
Stogdill, R.M., 266
Strategic alliances, 361
Strategic decision implementation case sets
Challenger disaster, 425–437

Chrysler bailout, 410–425, 430–437
comparison of cases, 402–403
Chrysler bailout-*Challenger* disaster, 430–437
Cuban missile crisis-Iranian hostage crisis, 397–403
Disney Corporation, 484–489
General Motors-Philip Morris, 460–466
Cuban missile crisis, 374–386, 376–377t, 397–403
General Motors, 443–457, 460–466
Iranian hostage crisis, 386–403
Philip Morris, 443–457, 460–466
Walt Disney Company, 469–489
see also specific case sets
Strategic decision making, 319–340
decision making process, 336–338, 337f
environment, 322–327
concept of, 323
domains, 324–325
forces, 325–327
system, 323–324, 324f
evaluation of success, 61–62, 62f
levels of decision making, 7–8
nature of, 321–322
process of, 38
process model, 158
strategic gap concept, 330–334
strategic gap variations, 334–336
uncertainty, 327–330
Strategic decision success, 344–366
composite approach, 362–364
evaluative concepts, 363–364
evaluative frameworks, 362–363
determinants of, 347–354
decision quality, 348–351
implementation, 351–353
studies, 347–348, 349t
study results, 353–354
model, 354–362
applications, 360–362
attitudes toward decision, 357–359
attitudes toward decision making process, 355–357
types of decisions, 359–360
Strategic fit, 336
Strategic gap, 330–334, 363
strategic decision-making case sets
General Motors, 446–450
Philip Morris, 455–457
variations, 334–336

Strategic gap analysis
Chrysler bailout, 415
General Motors, 449–450
Walt Disney in 1990, 474
Walt Disney in 1995, 481
Philip Morris, 457
Strategy
Category I versus Category II decisions, 21, 21t
individual decision making, 13
Structure
Category I versus Category II decisions, 21, 21t
group, 233, 233t
Structure, organizational
implementation of decision, 61
managerial decision making and, 24
restructuring, 261
strategic decision making, 321
Stufflebeam, D., 19
Stumph, S.A., 184
Style, group, 233, 234t, 235
Style of decision making, 61, 184–185
Subconscious influences, 201–204
Subprocesses, 41
and judgement, 135
strategic management, 321
Success
assessment of, objectives and, 43
criteria of, 61
determinants of, 61–62, 62f
factors determining, 40
managerial decision making, 25
see also Aspiration levels;
Outcomes; Strategic decision success
Superego, 178, 201
Superordinate goal, 261
Suppression of conflict, 262
Survival, as organizational value, 116
Sutermeister, R.A., 124
Synergy, 41
System of enterprise, 17
System theory, group behavior, 215

Tagiuri, R., 122
Task, perceptual, 194
Taylor, R.N., 184, 188
Teamwork, 221–222
Technical perspective, decision-making models, 149

Technology
  bounded rationality concept, 97, 97f
  managerial objectives, characteristics of, 44
  strategic decision making, 321
    environmental domain, 325, 327
    open environmental system, 324f
  strategic gap analysis, 331f, 332
    Disney in 1990, 472–473
    General Motors, 447
Technostructure (Galbraith), 288–289
Terminal values, 118, 119f
Testing assumptions, 38
Test of decision, 157
Texas Instrument study, 180
Thematic Apperception Test, 121
Theoret, A., 55, 345
Theoretical persons, 122
Thompson, J.D., 20, 30, 357
Threats
  Disney, 1990, 474
  gap analysis, 331f, 333
  group behavior/dynamics, 215
Three-dimensional perspective, 38
Time and cost constraints, 10, 169
  decision task, 60
  managerial decision making, 25
  rational decision making, 150
    bounded rationality concept, 97, 97f, 98
    satisficing behavior, 96
  strategic decision success, open model, 356
Time frame, 364
  group decision making, 251, 252–253
  individual decision making, 13
  managerial objectives, characteristics of, 44
  models of decision making
    organizational model, 155
    political model, 156
    process model, 158
  personality characteristics, 181
  rational decision making
  satisficing behavior, 100
  speed of decision making, 6
  see also Decision time; Long-term objectives Planning
Time-Warner, 362
Timing
  strategic decision case sets
    Challenger disaster, 431
    Disney, 1995, 485

General Motors and Philip Morris, 461–462
  strategic decision quality, 349–350, 349t
  and strategic decision success, 62, 63f
  Trull study findings, 61
Tobacco litigation, 461
Top management
  locus of decision making, 23–24
  see also Hierarchy, organizational
Toqueville, A. de, 284
Trade-off, individual decision making, 12
Trade-off values, 39–40
Trait theory, 178–179
Transitivity axiom, 54, 150
Trist, E.L., 328
Trull, S., 61, 238, 266, 345, 347, 401
Trull model, 61–62
Trull study, 347, 348, 349, 350–351, 352, 353, 354, 409, 461, 461, 462, 463, 487
Tuden, A., 357
Tuggle, F.D., 235, 236
Turner Broadcasting System, 362
Type A, 359f, 359, 360–361, 365, 402, 403, 404, 466
Type B, 359f, 359, 360, 361, 365, 402, 450
Type C, 359f, 359, 360, 361–362, 365, 402, 488
Type D, 359f, 359, 360, 362, 365, 402, 403, 465
Typology of decisions, 18–22, 20f, 21t

Unanimity, 230
Unattractiveness, 284
Uncertainty, 55
  group decision making, 251
  interdisciplinary framework
    economics and statistics, 166–167
    psychology, 162
  managerial decision making, 25
  models of decision making
    organizational, 154
    rational, 153
  predictability of outcomes, 54
  psychology
    personality characteristics, 182
    risk acceptance/avoidance, 187–188
  strategic decision making, 327–330, 357

Understanding
  strategic decision case set comparisons
    Challenger disaster, 433
    Disney, 1995, 487
    General Motors and Philip Morris, 464
  strategic decision making success, 63, 63f, 365
Undirected viewing, 47
Unions, see Labor unions
Unstructured decision making, 38
Utility, 54
  economic and statistical information, 166
  maximizing behavior, 79, 80, 85
  models of decision making, 160f

Value judgements, 161, 196
Values, 110–136, 114
  classification/typology of, 117–119, 119f
  concept, 110–114
  conflicts of, 131–133
    group decision making, 115–116, 131–133, 261
    with group values, 131–133
    with managerial values, 124, 131–133
    personality characteristics, 183–184
  ethics, 127–131
  gender differences, 270
  group behavior/dynamics, 214, 261
    and conformity, 219
    value conflicts, 115–116, 124, 131–133
  hierarchy of, 114–117
  individual, 126, 126, 127f, 250. See also Values, conflicts of
    conflicts with group and organizational values, 131–133
    conflict with managerial values, 124
  judgments, 133–136
  managerial, see Values, organizational/managerial
  and maximizing behavior, 86
  metaorganizational decision making, 17
  models of decision making
    interdisciplinary framework, 160f
    philosophy, 160, 161

nonrational decision making, 77–78
organizational/managerial, 113,
  116, 119–127, 123t, 127f, 131–133
  and search activity, 47
  strategic gap analysis, 332
and perception, 195
personality characteristics, 183
power, managerial, 301, 302
psychology, 161–162
Values, trade-off, 39–40
Value theory, 255
Van de Ven, 237
van Gigch, J.P., 38
Viewing, structure of search activity,
  47
Vinacke, W.E., 269

Wallach, M.A., 184, 189, 269
Walt Disney Company, 469–490
  comparative case determinants of
    classification of success,
    488–489
  comparative case determinants of
    success, 484–487
  decision-making process
    Capital Cities/ABC, 481–484
    Eurodisney, 474–479
  perspective, 470–471
  strategic gap in 1990, 471–474
    environmental assessment,
      473–474
    gap analysis, 474
    organizational assessment,
      472–473
  strategic gap in 1995, 479–481
    environmental assessment, 481
    gap analysis, 481
    organizational assessment,
      479–481
Warner, W.L., 289
Watergate, 231
Waterman, R.H., 345
Waters, J.W., 119, 130
Wegner, D.M., 232

Wehrung, D.A., 186
Weihrich, H., 64
Weitzel, W., 345
Wells Fargo, 361
Wheel network, 224, 225f
Whyte, G., 345
Williams, J.C., 187–188, 265
Williamson, O.E., 83, 84
Wilson, C.Z., 46, 88, 90
Winter, S.G. Jr., 85–86
Witte, E., 37
Wooldridge, W., 61
Women, *see* Gender

Yeuing, P., 83

Zaleska, M., 254
Zaleznik, A., 292
Zalkind, S.S., 5, 195
Zero strategic gap, 335–336
Zone of cost effectiveness, 49f, 50